Public Speaking

Public Speaking

Challenges and Choices

Dan O'Hair
University of Oklahoma

Rob Stewart
Texas Tech University

with
Hannah Rubenstein

BEDFORD/ST. MARTIN'S   Boston   New York

Senior Developmental Editor: Hannah Rubenstein
Developmental Editor: Michael Gillespie
Senior Production Editor: Shuli Traub
Senior Production Supervisor: Paula Keller
Marketing Manager: Charles Cavaliere
Art Director/Cover Design: Lucy Krikorian
Copyeditor: Alice Vigliani
Text Design: Siren Design, Inc.
Cover Art: Top and bottom right, courtesy of The Stock Illustration Source, Inc. Artist: Jose Ortega; bottom left, courtesy Gerald & Cullen Rapp, Inc., Applied Graphics Technologies, Inc., and the i spot. Artist: Celia Johnson; bottom middle, courtesy The Stock Illustration Source, Inc. Artist: Michael Sheehy.
Composition: EriBen Graphics
Printing and Binding: RR Donnelley & Sons Company

President: Charles H. Christensen
Editorial Director: Joan E. Feinberg
Editor-in-Chief: Nancy Perry
Director of Editing, Design, and Production: Marcia Cohen
Managing Editor: Erica T. Appel

Library of Congress Catalog Card Number: 97–65197

Manufactured in the United States of America.

4   3   2   1   0   9
f   e   d   c   b   a

For information, write:
Bedford/St. Martin's, 75 Arlington Street, Boston, MA 02116 (617-426-7440)

ISBN: 0-312-13722-2

Preface

The ability to speak confidently and convincingly in public is an asset to everyone who wants to take an active role in his or her classroom, workplace, and community. *Public Speaking: Challenges and Choices* guides students in developing the knowledge and skills that will enable them to become effective public speakers. They can apply what they learn from this text to a host of other activities, from reading and writing to alternate forms of interpersonal communication. *Challenges and Choices* builds its practical presentation of the speechmaking process on a strong foundation of communication theory. Informed by a relevant mix of classical and contemporary research, the text has been developed in consultation with public speaking instructors and students across the country. Its flexible chapter structure and integrated components offer instructors the necessary tools to help their students produce outstanding audience-centered speeches.

Challenges and Choices offers a contemporary approach to managing both the *challenges* and the *choices* that have confronted public speakers through time. A central focus is placed on the issues and concerns, both practical and profound, of college students today. Students want to know: What do I need to make it in the job market? What are the necessary skills for success? But they also wonder: Will my voice ever count? Should I care if it does or doesn't? Can I make a difference in the world?

We live today in an era of exploding information. Seemingly endless choices confront us at every turn of the media juggernaut. As we surf the Internet or switch back and forth among 350 cable television stations, how do we evaluate the endless stream of communication? And by what criteria? As citizens of a country that uniquely defends the right to free speech—whether such speech is ethical or not—what standards do we choose for our own speech? Amid the clamor of clashing absolutes, how can we identify our own values and those of our listeners?

While we face such challenges, we also face formidable constraints. For many students, career success is anything but assured, and worries over financial security loom large. It is with some sense of urgency that undergraduates search for a usable set of skills to navigate life. We believe that perhaps more than any other undergraduate offering, the public speaking course both offers extraordinarily useful practical knowledge and skills *and* points to a path of satisfying personal development. In *Challenges and Choices*, students learn not only that public speaking will help them in their professional careers but also that it is a tool uniquely suited to addressing the issues that concern them. Whether as college students facing a university administration or as parents confronting a school board, ordinary citizens can and do accomplish great things through the power of public speaking. We hope students will be encouraged by what Lappe and Du Bois call a "quiet revolution": "Millions are now learning that public life is not just for officials and experts, but part of a rewarding life for each of us.... Across virtually every dimension of our society, from the classroom to the community, from the workplace to city hall—Americans are giving shape to a profound new understanding of the role of everyday people in solving public problems.[1]

HIGHLIGHTS

Emphasis on Critical Thinking Skills

In order to make the best use of the challenges and choices presented to them, students must possess keen critical thinking skills. Defined as the ability to evaluate claims and make judgments on the basis of well-supported reasons, critical thinking is approached in *Challenges and Choices* as both a set of skills (evaluation, analysis, judgment) and the willingness to use these skills in the service of objective judgment.

When students apply solid critical thinking skills to the three fundamental components of speaking—speaker, audience, and message—they maximize their effectiveness and appeal as public speakers. And as they work through the speech process, they are far more likely to become ethical and culturally sensitive speakers. From analyzing assumptions and biases to resisting overgeneralizations and either-or thinking, each phase of the speech preparation process relies on critical thinking as a means of ensuring that students' speeches are effective, appropriate, and ethical.

With this perspective, we introduce critical thinking in Chapter 1 and use it to inform and enliven every applicable topic in the text. For instance, boundless new realms of information may be available to support arguments, but which sources are credible? And how can students avoid plagiarizing when the Internet seems to be a breadbasket of free information? Questions such as these are addressed throughout the text (see Chapters 4 and 7 for plagiarisim and critically evaluating sources, respectively). In addition, brief *Critical Checkpoints* appear several times within each chapter, calling on students to think critically about concepts they have just learned. The specific reasoning skills that comprise critical thinking are explained in-depth in Chapter 3, "Listeners and Speakers," and thereafter integrated into each chapter.

Focus on Technology

Students need specific skills and guidance to make effective use of the new technologies that increasingly permeate the college campus, the workplace, and the community. Now more than ever, they must apply critical thinking skills to chart a course and successfully navigate a technologically sophisticated world. *Challenges and Choices* effectively teaches students to be smart critical users of these powerful new tools. *Focus on Technology* boxes familiarize students with the most current tools and resources. In Chapter 7, "Developing Supporting Material," students learn to search electronic sources when doing secondary research. In Chapter 8, "Organizing and Outlining the Speech," students examine how the computer can help them organize information for more effective presentations. Chapter 12, "Preparing and Using Presentation Aids," provides the latest practical tips to generate visual aids using computers.

---

[1] Frances Moore Lappe and Paul Martin Du Bois, *The Quickening of America* (San Francisco: Jossey-Bass, 1994).

Making a Difference

Public speaking offers a set of tools uniquely suited to solving problems and addressing important issues, whether related to one's profession, personal life, or community. *Making a Difference* profiles highlight everyday people who harness the power of public speaking to make a positive difference in their lives and in the lives of others. In addition to providing inspiration for students, these profiles further illustrate the multitude of ways public speaking skills can improve people's lives.

Focus on Ethics in Public Speaking

Ethics is a concern that is found in every aspect of public speaking. Chapter 4, "Ethical Public Speaking," is devoted entirely to the topic. The chapter considers the dichotomy between legal speech and ethical speech, explores issues such as hate speech, and offers solid guidelines for ethical speaking. Since ethical standards are based on personal values, students are given the opportunity to consider how their own values inform the quality of their speeches.

Because ethical dilemmas can arise at any point during the speechmaking process, *Focus on Ethics* boxes appear in virtually every chapter of the text. Topics include "The Responsibilities of Listening" (Chapter 3); "Hate Speech" (Chapter 4); "Finding Common Ground" (Chapter 5); "Ethical Considerations in Selecting a Topic and Purpose" (Chapter 6); "Ethical Considerations in Research" (Chapter 7); and "Plagiarism Is Plagiarism, No Matter Where It Occurs" (Chapter 9).

Emphasis on Cultural Diversity

Students today are likely to encounter diverse audiences, and they will bring their own unique perspectives to their roles as speakers. *Challenges and Choices* addresses this integral aspect of responsible speechmaking throughout the body of the text and in feature boxes. The example speech excerpts and full-length sample speeches (see Chapters 15, 17, and the appendix) reflect the diverse voices that find expression in the United States. In addition to the standard coverage of demographics, boxed features entitled *Public Speaking in Cultural Perspective* address such topics as "Confidence and Culture—When English Isn't Your First Language" (Chapter 2); "A Cross-Cultural View of Ethics" (Chapter 4); and "African American Oratory—The Call-Reponse" (Chapter 11).

Tools for Building Confidence

Numerous surveys rank public speaking high on the list of things we fear most. Students surveyed for *Challenges and Choices* echoed these sentiments when they told us the key reason they put off taking the public speaking course is their fear of giving speeches in class. In Chapter 2, students will relate to stories from seasoned public speakers who often feel nervous or anxious prior to a speech or presentation, but who have learned how to make anxiety work for rather than against them. The chapter offers specific techniques, including how to interpret anxiety positively, designed to help speakers manage and refocus their tension. The chapter concludes by offering a framework for students giving their first speech, which is often the best way to help them overcome their anxiety.

Since many inexperienced public speakers (and a good number of seasoned ones) need to overcome anxiety at every stage of the process, *Challenges and*

Choices includes confidence-building strategies throughout the text. Practical and innovative tips help students gain confidence while they improve their skills. Additionally, a special section of the *Instructor's Resource Manual* discusses the latest research on speech anxiety.

Providing Real World Perspectives

Foremost in the minds of today's college students are career concerns, and students are eager to learn skills that will help ensure their success in the business world. Public speaking offers numerous opportunities for both personal and professional growth. To reinforce the idea that the skills students learn in this course have real world applicability and are not just for politicians and professional speakers, several chapters feature interviews—called *Real World Perspectives*—with leading business figures who offer practical insights into the value of public speaking from the classroom to the boardroom. Additionally, speech examples used throughout the text from students, professional and political speakers, and businesspeople make students aware of the importance and flexibility of the skills they learn.

Coverage of Business and Professional Presentations

Most students will have the opportunity to apply the public speaking skills they learn in a business context when delivering briefings, reports, and presentations to business and professional colleagues. We believe that a discussion of this important context for prepared, formal speeches warrants a complete, separate chapter, and we explore the topic fully in Chapter 16, "Small Group, Business, and Professional Presentations." We offer unique coverage of the differences between public and presentational speaking and provide guidance on delivering the five most common business presentations, including sales presentations and progress reports.

End-of-Chapter Study Guides

Each chapter ends with a comprehensive, color-tabbed Study Guide so students can locate it easily. Summary questions review important concepts and identify key terms. Thought-provoking activities include Issues for Discussion, Self-Assessment, and Teamwork exercises. These activities encourage students to critically apply the knowledge and skills they have acquired throughout the chapter.

RESOURCES FOR STUDENTS AND INSTRUCTORS

Resources for Students

Untangling the Web

by Deborah Greh, St. John's University

For instructors and students who are inexperienced online, *Untangling the Web* offers practical advice on accessing information through the Internet.

Media Career Guide: Preparing for Jobs in the 21st Century

by James Seguin, Robert Morris College

Designed for students considering a major in communication studies and mass media, this practical, student-friendly guide includes a comprehensive directory of jobs, suggestions for evaluating goals and attitudes, tips for conducting print and electronic job research, and sample cover letters and resumes.

Online! A Reference Guide to Using Internet Sources

by Andrew Harnack and Eugene Kleppinger, Eastern Kentucky University

Online! is a pocket reference guide to using Internet sources, the first book to provide guidelines on choosing, evaluating, citing, and documenting Internet sources using all four styles: MLA, APA, CBE, and *Chicago*.

Research and Documentation in the Electronic Age

by Diana Hacker, Prince George's Community College, and Barbara Fister, Gustavus Adolphus College

This handy booklet covers everything students need for college research assignments at the library and on the Internet, including advice for finding and evaluating Internet sources.

Resources for Instructors

Instructor's Resource Manual

by Theresa Bridges, Tara Crowell, and Juliann Scholl, University of Oklahoma

The *Instructor's Resource Manual* is a valuable resource for new and experienced instructors alike. This comprehensive manual offers extensive advice on many topics, such as: formulating a teaching philosophy; setting and achieving student learning goals; managing the classroom; handling grade complaints and dealing with confrontations; facilitating group discussion; dealing with evaluations, grading speeches, tests, and assignments; teaching strategies; dealing with ethical situations; soliciting student feedback; understanding culture and gender considerations; dealing with ESL students; preparing guidelines for evaluating speeches (for both instructors and students); evaluating Internet resources; and using new technologies in instruction. In addition, each chapter of the main text is broken down into Chapter Challenges; detailed outlines; discussion of *Critical Checkpoints*; suggestions for facilitating class discussion from topics covered in feature boxes; answers to the end-of-chapter Study Guide questions; additional activities and exercises; recommended supplementary resources; and transparency masters. Sample speeches are also available for analysis.

Audio Instructor's Guide

Available on audiocassette, this Instructor's Guide, featuring Dan O'Hair and Rob Stewart, provides additional teaching tips, chapter synopses, lecture ideas, and class discussion starters to help instructors prepare for class wherever they are—at home, in the office, or in the car.

Video Resources

Available exclusively for adopters of *Public Speaking: Challenges and Choices*, Volume XIII of the esteemed *Great Speeches* series offers dynamic contemporary speeches for today's classroom. The most recent in the series, this video features compelling speeches by well-known public figures, such as President Clinton's 1998 State of the Union Address, Madeline Albright's first speech as secretary of state, Christopher Reeve's address to the 1996 Democratic Convention, and a speech on spirituality by the Dalai Lama. Additional videos will be available as part of the Bedford/St. Martin's video Library.

E.S.L Guide for Instructors of Public Speaking

As the United States increasingly becomes a nation of non-native speakers, instructors must find new pedagogical tools to aid students for whom English is a second language. This guide specifically addresses the needs of ESL students in the public speaking course and offers instructors valuable advice for helping their students deal successfully with the challenges they face.

PowerPoint Presentation Software

These PowerPoint slides, which help instructors incorporate technology and visual aids in the classroom, highlight key information and concepts from each chapter. Instructors with PowerPoint software can adapt the slides or make their own. Instructors without PowerPoint can view the slides through the PowerPoint Viewer we provide. Available for Macintosh and Windows.

Public Speaking Resource Center

Visit our Public Speaking Resource Center on the Internet. This site will include valuable links to related Web sites, tips for finding and evaluating resources on the Internet, suggested speech topics, and resources for instructors.

Transparency Masters

Highlighting key information and concepts from each of the chapters in the main text, these transparency masters can be used to create overhead transparencies.

Testing Program

Public Speaking: Challenges and Choices offers a complete testing program, available in print and for Windows and Macintosh environments. Each chapter includes multiple-choice, true-false, and fill-in-the-blank exercises, as well as essay questions. Sample midterm and final examinations are also included in the testing program. Instructors are encouraged to mix and match, add and delete, and experiment with these comprehensive testing materials.

ACKNOWLEDGMENTS

We would like to thank the following reviewers whose advice and feedback were so invaluable throughout the writing of this book: Joyce Allman (Texas Christian University), Richard Armstrong (Wichita State University), Dianne Blomberg (Metropolitan State College of Denver), Doug Brenner (University of South Dakota), Scott Britten (Indiana University–South

Bend), Crystal Rae Coel (Murray State University), Amanda Cooper (Northwestern University), Irene Dugas (McNeese University), Janis L. Edwards (Georgia State University), Darla Germeroth (University of Scranton), Sally Heath (Community College of Aurora), Joseph B. Kauogh, III (North Harris College), Sam Lapin (Northern Kentucky University), Jo Ann Lawlor (West Valley College), Jo Logan (Northwest Missouri Community College), Calvin Logue (University of Georgia), Neil Moura (MiraCosta College), Mike Murray (University of Missouri–St. Louis), Mabry O'Donnell (Marietta College), Jean Perry (Glendale College), Mary Jo Popovici (Monroe Community College), Rena Y. Robinson (James Madison University), Maria Rodriguez (John Jay College), Deanna Sellnow (North Dakota State University), William Sheffield (California State University–Northridge), Roger Soenksen (James Madison University), David Sprague (Liberty University), Aileen Sundstrom (Henry Ford Community College), K. Phillip Taylor (University of Central Florida), Lou Davidson Tillson (Murray State University), James Wolford (Joliet Junior College), Niki Young (Louisiana State University), and George Ziegelmeller (Wayne State University).

We are indebted to the tireless effort of Hannah Rubenstein, whose creativity and remarkable talent for editing and writing helped us craft a more student-friendly book. We are grateful to everyone at Bedford/St. Martin's who has supported this project through its many stages: Steve Debow, Chuck Christensen, Joan Feinberg, Marian Wassner, and Laura Barthule. Special thanks to Lucy Krikorian, Simon Glick, and Alice Lundoff for developing such a beautiful art and photo program. Shuli Traub, project editor, did a wonderful job keeping the book on its production schedule. We are very thankful for the tremendous dedication and effort of our editors: Suzanne Phelps Weir, our acquiring editor, and Michael Gillespie, our development editor.

We are especially appreciative of the conceptual and creative contributions made by Leeza Bearden, Scott Moore, Juliann Scholl, David Worth, Lisa Sparks Bethea, Melinda Morris, Derek Lane, and Charlton McIlwain. A hearty thanks goes to Dr. Karl Krayer who collaborated on Chapter 1. We would also like to recognize the talents of Theresa Bridges, Tara Crowell, and Juliann Scholl, who developed such an outstanding *Instructor's Resource Manual*. Finally, we want to thank our families, who allowed us time to finish this book. Mary John, Darla, Erica, Tyne, Tate, Jonathan, and Tara were extraordinarily supportive and generous with time that was rightfully theirs. This book is dedicated to you.

Contents in Brief

Contents in Detail

2 GETTING STARTED WITH CONFIDENCE 29

4 ETHICAL PUBLIC SPEAKING 75

5 AUDIENCE ANALYSIS 97

6 SELECTING A TOPIC AND PURPOSE *127*

7 DEVELOPING SUPPORTING MATERIAL *149*

8 ORGANIZING AND OUTLINING THE SPEECH 179

USING LANGUAGE: STYLING THE SPEECH 227

11 DELIVERING THE SPEECH 251

12 PREPARING AND USING PRESENTATION AIDS 279

INFORMATIVE SPEECHES *309*

14 THE PERSUASIVE SPEECH 335

15 DEVELOPING ARGUMENTS FOR THE PERSUASIVE SPEECH *367*

16 SMALL GROUP, BUSINESS, AND PROFESSIONAL PRESENTATIONS 393

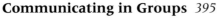

17 SPECIAL OCCASION SPEECHES 419

Appendix A-1

Public Speaking

**Let us say
what we feel,
and feel what
we say; let
speech
harmonize
with life.**

—Seneca

**Speech is civilization itself. The word, even the contradictory
word, preserves contact—it is silence which isolates.**

—Thomas Mann

Challenges and Choices in Public Speaking

Have you ever given a speech? Not necessarily a formal address to a large audience, but a talk to a group of perhaps ten or more people who gave you their undivided attention. **What was the experience like? Were you nervous?** Was it satisfying nonetheless? **Did you want to do it again?**

Nearly everyone who has spoken in public derives great satisfaction from doing so, especially when they've done their best to prepare their remarks. **Most of us take pleasure in being heard and sharing our ideas and experiences with others, even if we struggle with nerves as we do so.** Indeed, few other activities offer quite the same opportunity to make our voices count. **Being heard and making a difference motivates many people to attempt the art of public speaking, even if they never dreamed of doing so in the past.**

Hartford, Connecticut, has seen much better times. Marilyn Rossetti remembers those times. Having spent her entire life within the city limits, her memories include frequent trips to the Mark Twain house, leisurely walks through safe neighborhoods, and the striking architecture of the mammoth insurance buildings. Today, welfare rolls are high and childhood poverty is steep. The public schools struggle to meet the needs of the city's poorest residents. To foot the bill, homeowners are forced to pay higher taxes than their suburban counterparts do.

Marilyn's love of Hartford motivated her to buy a home in her old neighborhood, now saddled with the whole catalog of inner-city ills. Soon thereafter she joined a local neighborhood organization called Hartford Areas Rally Together, or HART. Recognized nationally for its effective tactics, HART's mission is to improve life in Hartford's neighborhoods. It focuses mainly on such down-to-earth issues as taxes, public services, and housing.

A "thirty-something" engineering assistant and parttime undergraduate when she joined HART, Marilyn had neither a college degree nor any specific organizing or public speaking training. All she had was a burning desire to improve her beloved city. After a few months as an interested bystander, she began to get involved. First she chaired a meeting. Although nervous, she felt she did a good job. Eventually she was asked to lead a session that hundreds of people were expected to attend. Marilyn discovered that she actually got more pleasure out of facing a larger group than a smaller one. She found that she liked to make people feel comfortable and seemed to have a knack for moving things along.

Today Marilyn is president of the board of directors of HART, whose membership is some 5,000 strong. "In the past three years I have done things I never thought I could do," Marilyn says. "I've given scores of speeches. I've met with the governor. I've held press conferences. I even attended a meeting at the White House." According to Marilyn, none of this would have been possible if she hadn't returned to school. Currently completing courses for her AA degree, Marilyn thinks she will major in communications, although she's still not sure. "I took a professional communications class in which I learned about making presentations. That, and just being a student and doing well at it, gave me enough confidence to continue to be involved with HART."

One day Marilyn found herself in a plush corporate boardroom, sitting opposite one of the city's most powerful lawyers. As she listened to him explain his position about a city issue to her, she realized with a thrill that she was in a place she never dreamed she would be. Here she was, addressing issues she cared deeply about and being treated as an equal by one of the city's most powerful leaders. To Marilyn, a woman not yet in possession of a college degree, that felt pretty good.

There are many Marilyn Rossettis in the world—ordinary people with a drive to do things. Public speaking is the tool they use to accomplish their goals. In the chapters ahead you'll meet others like Marilyn, people who use public speaking to make a difference in their personal and professional lives.

Chapter Challenges

This public speaking course offers you the opportunity to gain the training you will likely need in the future, both at work and as a member of your community. This first chapter describes how public speaking can benefit you both professionally and personally. You'll discover:

- The similarities and differences between public speaking and other forms of communication.
- The benefits of public speaking for professional and personal development.
- The elements of the public speaking process.
- How diverse voices have shaped, and continue to shape, U.S. society.
- The importance of being a culturally sensitive speaker and listener.
- The broad challenges and choices of public speaking.

WHY PUBLIC SPEAKING?

As you begin this class in an age when electronic communication has taken center stage, you may be wondering if public speaking is still a relevant, let alone important, form of communication. After all, we now have television, radio, email, pagers, personal digital assistants, cellular phones, and electronic bulletin boards. Isn't it rather low-tech to stand "unarmed" in front of an audience and simply talk?

As intriguing and efficient as they are, however, the new technologies cannot substitute for actual public speech. We humans apparently still need to deliver and receive many types of messages the old-fashioned way: live and in person. For example, consider the following scenarios. How important is it that you actually see and hear the person delivering the message? Very important? Moderately important? Not at all important?

- You are asked to vote for a presidential candidate. You've gained information about this individual solely through what the candidate's staff members have written and posted via mass emailings.
- The leader of your church, synagogue, or mosque has decided that because of the Internet, live religious services are no longer necessary. The building has been sold and services are now offered solely through an electronic bulletin board.
- Your company announces a series of drastic layoffs in your division by way of a terse email posting.
- You are nearing the end of your four (or more) years as an undergraduate. You've just been told that the administration has eliminated graduation ceremonies in favor of a "Graduation Web Site." The site will contain graduates' names and grade point averages. It will remain online for two weeks and then be removed.

No doubt for most of you, in these and countless other circumstances public speaking would be the preferred form of communication. Who wants to be laid off via email? Wouldn't a sympathetic address by the head of the company seem more considerate? How spiritually fulfilling would it be to celebrate religious holidays at your desktop computer? And after spending a good many years earning your undergraduate degree, are you really prepared to forgo the time-honored tradition of a commencement ceremony?

Each of us needs to feel recognized and involved in our work, in our communities, and in matters of the spirit. Whether we are listeners or a speaker, public speech addresses these needs. As Don Walker, president of the Harry Walker Agency, notes:

> Public speakers are more in demand than ever before. People want to ask questions eyeball to eyeball and see these people in the flesh. Even in this day of electronic connections, the old-fashioned business of [public] speaking is booming. The number of business and trade conferences is growing, more people are becoming speakers, and fees are rising....The National Speakers Association, a trade group for professional speakers, has grown by 30% in the last five years to 4,000 members.[1]

As you'll discover in the pages ahead, foremost among the public speaker's goals is to demonstrate understanding, respect, and empathy for his or her audience. A well-prepared speech "speaks" to each member of the audience. Whether the occasion is a lecture, commencement address, eulogy, sermon, or campaign speech, we look to public speakers to in some way move, inspire, and motivate us. Together, both speaker and listener feel as if they are forging a meaningful event.

Throughout history, influential men and women have expressed themselves through public speaking. Nelson Mandela, Cesar Chavez, Colin Powell, Martin Luther King Jr., suffragist Elizabeth Cady Stanton, Representative Barbara Jordan—each of these individuals has used the power of speech to influence attitudes and to move nations to action. Successful entrepreneurs such as Bill Gates of Microsoft, Sam Walton of Walmart, and Mary Kay Ashe of Mary Kay Cosmetics also rely on the power of speech to present new ideas to the public, to motivate employees, and to build financial empires. Local business leaders depend on public speaking to sell new ideas and generate profits. Your own community leaders use public speaking to provide information and persuade voters. Members of churches, synagogues, mosques, clubs, and other organizations also depend on public speakers to voice their concerns and promote their causes. Nearly everyone speaks in public at some time or other, and those who perform the task well often become leaders.

An Enduring Legacy

Public speaking is perhaps the single most enduring skill taught in human history. People have studied it, in one form or another, since 476 B.C. At that time a Sicilian teacher named Corax first offered lessons in *rhetoric*, or the art of crafting messages, so that citizens whose property had been seized in battles could argue their claims in court. Even earlier, however, some form of rhetoric was an important part of the traditions of ancient Egypt, Africa, Asia—indeed, worldwide. Surviving texts on oral speech, such as the Egyptian *Maxims of Ptahhotep* (c. 2500 B.C.) and the third century B.C. writings on ethical speech by Confucius, describe principles that remain as relevant and instructive today as they did when first written.

Public speaking was the primary vehicle through which Greeks and Romans expressed their ideas, defended their rights, and otherwise represented themselves in society. They thought that by generating and criticizing new ideas through vigorous public speaking they would make prudent decisions. Public speaking was at the heart of their education, and selected upper-class males attended special "rhetoric schools." (In ancient Greece and Rome, neither women, lower-class males, nor slaves of either sex were allowed to vote or otherwise have a "public" voice.) The Greek philosopher Plato (c. 427–347 B.C.) thought of public speaking, or rhetoric, as a means of seeking the truth—that is, if it wasn't used to mislead people or abused as a form of "flattery." His student, the great philosopher Aristotle (384–322 B.C.), viewed rhetoric as the art of persuasion. He believed that through it, one could obtain, if not the truth, then at least "practical wisdom." Aristotle wrote a three-volume work devoted entirely to the art of persuading others through speech. His *Rhetoric* (330 B.C.) sometimes called the first public speaking textbook, remains the most significant work ever written on the subject. Public speaking continued to be a prominent focus of study for several centuries.

In the eighteenth and nineteenth centuries public speaking was a treasured art, all the more so, perhaps, given the lack of alternative means of communication. Colonists delivered countless speeches in Boston, Philadelphia, and Lexington in the quest to establish their independence

The Lundoff Collection

In the 1858 Lincoln-Douglas debates, the candidates grappled with the issues of slavery and state sovereignty. The debates led Abraham Lincoln to national prominence and eventually to the U.S. presidency.

from England. In the mid-1800s, politicians such as Abraham Lincoln and Stephen Douglas routinely spent five or more hours at a time in heated political discourse. Debates often lasted all day. Audiences were not only accustomed to such performances but relished them. During this time the tradition of the "stump" speaker emerged. Standing by the stump of a felled tree or some equivalent open space, a speaker would gather an audience and, as the saying had it, "take the stump" for two or three hours.[2] Audience participation was high, even boisterous. In the days before electronic media, this was both education and entertainment.

Today's public speakers no longer spend endless hours at the podium. Too many competing media—print, television, radio, the Internet—vie for our time and attention. Yet as we enter the twenty-first century, public speaking remains an indispensable vehicle for expressing ideas. The need to be enlightened and inspired by the insights of others, delivered to us personally, remains as strong today as it did two thousand years ago.

Reasons for Public Speech

There are many reasons for speaking in public. A speaker may hope to teach an audience about new ideas or provide information about some topic. Creating a good feeling or entertaining an audience may be another purpose. Some speakers seek to inspire and uplift their audiences. For many public speakers, the goal is to persuade listeners to modify their attitudes, adopt new opinions, or take certain actions.

For centuries people have used public speaking to inform others, to persuade them to their point of view, and to celebrate with them. These are the three main functions or purposes of public speech: to inform, to persuade, and to celebrate or commemorate special occasions. These functions address important social needs. As social beings we need information to make informed decisions and reasoned arguments to help select a course of action. We also need to learn from others, to share their insights, and to celebrate with them. Public speaking has survived and flourished for so many centuries because it is uniquely suited to fulfilling these needs.

Public Speaking as a Form of Communication

Public speaking has much in common with other kinds of communication, from everyday conversation to speech directed toward large, far-flung audiences. Public speaking also has characteristics that make it unique. Let's look briefly at the various kinds of communication, see how they are similar to public speaking, and then consider what makes public speaking a unique form of communication.

Communication is often described according to the number of people involved. As you know from your own experience, the size of your audience—from one person to many—alters the nature of your communication. Communication scholars generally identify four categories of communication: dyadic, small group, mass, and public speaking.

Dyadic communication is a form of communication between two people, as in a conversation. **Small group communication** involves a small number of people who can see and speak directly with each other. A business meeting is an example of small group communication. **Mass communication** occurs between a speaker and a large audience of unknown people. In this form of communication the receivers of the message are not present with the speaker, or they are part of such an immense crowd that there can be little or no interaction between speaker and listener. Television, radio news broadcasts, and mass rallies are examples of mass communication. In **public speaking** a speaker delivers a message with a specific purpose to an audience of people who are present at the delivery of the speech. Public speaking always includes a speaker who has a reason for speaking, an audience that gives the speaker its attention, and a message meant to accomplish a purpose.[3] Public speakers address audiences largely without interruption and take responsibility for the words and ideas being expressed.

Similarities between Public Speaking and Other Forms of Communication. Public speaking shares many characteristics with other forms of communication. Like small group communication, public speaking requires that you address a group of people who are focused on you and who expect you to clearly discuss issues that are relevant to the topic and occasion. As in mass communication, public speaking requires that you understand and appeal to the audience members' interests, attitudes, and values. And like dyadic communication, or conversation, public speaking requires that you attempt to make yourself understood, involve and respond to your conversational partner, and take responsibility for what you say. A key feature of any type of communication is sensitivity to the listeners. Whether you are talking to one person in a coffee shop or giving a speech to one hundred people, your listeners want to feel as though you care about their interests, desires, and goals. Skilled conversationalists do this, and so do successful public speakers. Similarly, skilled conversationalists are in command of their material and present it in a way that is organized and easy to follow, believable, relevant, and interesting. Public speaking is no different. Moreover, the audience will expect you to be knowledgeable and unbiased about your topic and to express your ideas clearly.

dyadic communication
a form of communication between two people, as in a conversation.

small group communication
a form of communication involving a small number of people who can see and speak directly with each other (as in a business meeting).

mass communication
a form of communication in which the receivers of the message are not present with the speaker, or they are part of such an immense crowd that there can be no interaction between speaker and listener (as in television, radio news broadcasts, and mass rallies).

public speaking
a form of communication in which a speaker delivers a message with a specific purpose to an audience of people who are present at the delivery of the speech; always includes a speaker who has a reason for speaking, an audience that gives the speaker its attention, and a message meant to accomplish a purpose.

	Low		High
Feedback	Mass Communication - - - - Public Speaking - - - - Small Group - - - - - - Dyadic		
Preparation	Dyadic - - - - Small Group - - - Mass Communication - - - - - - - - Public Speaking		
Formality	Dyadic - - - - Small Group - - - Mass Communication - - - - - - - - Public Speaking		

FIGURE 1.1

Distinctions among Dyadic, Small Group, Mass Communication, and Public Speaking

feedback
listener response to a message; can be verbal (e.g., an outburst of applause) or nonverbal (e.g., a nod, an angry stare).

Differences between Public Speaking and Other Forms of Communication. Although public speaking shares many characteristics with other types of communication, several factors distinguish it from these other forms. These include (1) opportunities for feedback, (2) level of preparation, and (3) degree of formality.

Public speaking presents different opportunities for **feedback,** or listener response to a message, than do dyadic, small group, or mass communication. Both dyadic and small group communication offer greater opportunities for feedback than public speaking, whereas mass communication offers fewer such opportunities. Because the receiver of the message in mass communication is physically removed from the messenger, feedback is delayed until after the event, as in TV ratings. Conversely, partners in conversation continually respond to one another in a circular pattern. Feedback is also high in small groups, where interruptions by participants for purposes of clarification or redirection are expected.

Public speaking offers a middle ground between low and high levels of feedback (see Figure 1.1). Public speaking does not permit the constant exchange of information between listener and speaker as happens in conversation, but audiences can and do provide ample verbal and nonverbal cues as to what they are thinking and feeling. Facial expressions, vocalizations (including laughter or disapproving noises), gestures, applause, and a range of body movements all signal the audience's response to the speaker. The perceptive speaker reads these cues and tries to adjust his or her remarks accordingly. On the other hand, a speech would no longer be a speech if the speaker were forced to pause at every sentence to respond to the listeners' concerns.

Because feedback is more restricted in public speaking situations than in dyadic and small group communication, preparation must be more careful and extensive. With less opportunity to know how your listeners feel about what you are saying, you must anticipate how they will react to your remarks. With each audience member focused on you, it is important to be in command of your material. In dyadic and small group communication you can always shift the burden to your conversational partner or to other group members. Public speaking offers no such shelter, and lack of preparation stands out starkly.

Finally, public speaking differs from other forms of communication in terms of its degree of formality. In general, speeches tend to occur in more formal settings than do other forms of communication. The fact that many people gather together for one purpose tends to lend formality to an occasion. Formal gatherings such as graduations, weddings, religious services and the like naturally lend themselves to speeches; they provide a focus and give form—a "voice"—to the event. In contrast, with the exception of formal interviews, dyadic communication (or conversations) is largely informal. Small group communication also tends to be less formal than public speaking, even in business meetings. The issue of formality in mass communication is a moot point, since the message and the receiver are separated. Mass communication can be received within any setting—from the informal living room containing a television, to the more formal theater or auditorium in which a movie is screened.

As you can see, public speaking shares many similarities with dyadic, small group, and mass communication; but there are notable differences as well. Public speaking shares many features of everyday conversation, but because the speaker is the focal point of attention in what is usually a formal setting, listeners expect a more systematic presentation than they do in conversation or small group communication. As such, public speaking requires more preparation and practice than the other forms of communication.

BENEFITS OF PUBLIC SPEAKING

Public speaking is a powerful vehicle for personal and professional growth. The benefits associated with public speaking include:

- Becoming a more knowledgeable person
- Honing critical thinking and listening skills
- Enhancing your career as a student
- Accomplishing professional and personal goals
- Exploring and sharing values

Becoming a More Knowledgeable Person

Like any art, a good speech is a skillful blend of form and content. The speech's basic form, or structure, consists of the *introduction*, *body*, and *conclusion*. Filling out this structure is the individual *topic* of the speech, or the content. By studying public speaking you will learn about the craft of public speaking itself (i.e., how to construct the parts of a speech and how to develop, support, and present it), and you will be exposed to a wide range of topics about which to speak. As you delve into these topics, whether in the library, the field, or on the World Wide Web, you will broaden your horizons and become more educated about the world around you.

Honing Critical Thinking and Listening Skills

Public speaking training sharpens your ability to construct and evaluate claims on the basis of sound evidence—for example, to reason or think critically. As you study public speaking you will learn to make claims and then present evidence and reasoning that logically support them. Critical thinkers look to see whether an argument makes sense and whether the evidence

Ken Kerbs/Monkmeyer

A dynamic speaker conveys important information with style. Here, Harry Belafonte gives a dramatic speech.

supports it. They look for the underlying logic in a speaker's assertions, both their own and others'. They don't just accept information at face value.

Making sound claims depends on the ability to evaluate and analyze a variety of information—from the data you gather about the audience, to the research you collect on the topic. As you practice organizing and outlining speeches, you will learn how to structure your ideas so that they flow logically from one to another. You will be able to identify the weak links in your thinking and work to strengthen them. As you flesh out a theme for your speech, you will learn to carefully substantiate claims with well-supported reasons that achieve your speech goals.

Public speaking training will also help improve your listening abilities. After all, listening and critical thinking go hand in hand. The use of one skill builds the other. As you learn what goes into a good speech, you will become a more critical receiver of speeches. As you learn to listen critically, you'll also find yourself better prepared to make ethical judgments. You will be able to determine if a speaker and his or her message is credible and trustworthy. Knowing how to evaluate the logic and truthfulness of messages is one of the most important skills you can possess. In a world in which misleading information is often disguised as logic for the purposes of selling, deception, or exploitation, the ability to listen critically enables you to separate fact from falsehood. The ability to listen will help you with negotiations at work, with conflict management in relationships, and with problem solving across a wide range of areas.

Enhancing Your Career as a Student

Preparing speeches involves numerous skills that you can use in other courses. Many of the skills that are used in putting together a speech—such as researching a topic, selecting a method for organizing it, and creating effective introductions and conclusions—are also used in many forms of writing, or composition. Moreover, public speaking training will boost your creative thinking. Finding an appropriate topic, for example, often requires you to brainstorm ideas. Your creativity will be further called upon as you develop ways to capture the audience's attention and express your ideas through vivid imagery.

Accomplishing Professional and Personal Goals

Skill in public speaking tops the list of sought-after skills by many organizations. Dozens of surveys of corporate managers and executives reveal that oral communication is the most important skill they look for in a college graduate. As seen in a recent survey of employers (see Table 1.1.), for example, oral communication skills rank even higher than such critical areas as interpersonal, analytical, teamwork, and computer skills.

Whatever career you select, chances are that public speaking will be a valuable, even crucial, skill to have. Public speaking is a key way to get information to employees, supervisors, and colleagues. This may take the form of a report made at a department meeting or a presentation at a professional organization conference. People at work use public speaking to convey information, to persuade and motivate others, and even to celebrate their special skills. Salespeople are often called on to speak to groups

Table 1.1 What Employers Are Looking For in College Graduates

Rank	Type of Preferred Skills
1	Oral Communication
2	Interpersonal
3	Analytical
4	Teamwork
5	Flexibility
6	Computer
7	Proficiency in Field of Study
8	Written Communication
9	Leadership
10	Work Experience

SOURCE: Job Outlook 97, *a survey conducted by the National Association of Colleges and Employers, 1996.*

of people. To sell their products, they make presentations to potential clients and present new sales campaigns to other workers. Many employees are involved in purchasing and deal making. As they advance offers and negotiate purchases, they too rely on public speaking skills.

A recent report entitled "What Students Must Know to Succeed in the 21st Century" stated:

> Clear communication is critical to success. In the marketplace of ideas, the person who communicates clearly is also the person who is seen as thinking clearly. Oral and written communication are not only *job-securing*, but *job-holding* skills.[4]

Training in public speaking also offers the opportunity to accomplish personal goals. Whatever you care deeply about, from the environment to lower taxes, public speaking offers a way to communicate your concerns with others.

Exploring and Sharing Values

A speech is an occasion for speaker and audience to focus on ideas and events about which they feel strongly, even passionately. Thus, public speaking offers a unique opportunity to explore *values*, those deep-seated feelings and ideas about what is important in life. Public speaking enables you to express your values and explore those of others in a civil dialogue,

Speaking in Public: A Real World Perspective

Karl J. Krayer, Ph.D., is a training program manager for Dr. Pepper/Cadbury, North America. He frequently speaks to groups and organizations in a variety of settings. His public speaking background dates back to his days when he was required to deliver memorized speeches in a young men's fraternal organization. He makes over a hundred presentations and speeches per year at work, in social settings, and to professional societies.

Is learning to give speeches all that important for people who do not expect to do much speaking in their personal or professional lives?

Of course, learning to speak opens up many doors for you. No matter what profession you're in, public speaking offers a golden opportunity for career advancement. Just by accepting engagements to speak I've met people and established connections that paid dividends and gave me opportunities for the future. There is no better way to sell yourself to managers or other influential people than through public speaking.

Since you give so many speeches, do you ever get scared?

Some butterflies are good. The worst presentations I've ever given were those where I was completely confident when I walked in. The key is to manage, not eliminate, feelings of anxiety. When I was a youngster, I was shy. Speaking before a group didn't appeal to me. But I joined a Masonic group that required me to memorize lines that were presented in meetings. After a while I got used to speaking in groups. Now I look for opportunities to speak.

What is the key to successful public speaking?

The key is to know your audience and to deliver a focused message that relates to the audience's needs and interests, not yours. There is no magic to giving effective speeches. Once you've prepared properly, everything else falls in place, including the speaking itself.

Are most of the speeches you hear others give effective?

Some speeches are not effective, even those given by experienced speakers. In many cases, ineffective speakers have not had the training in public speaking, even a beginning class in college. In other cases, trained speakers have not taken the time to properly prepare for their speech. All too often, speakers do not carefully analyze what the audience is interested in hearing. Every speaking experience and every audience is unique, and you can't deliver the same speech exactly the same way to every audience.

What other tips would you give to a beginning public speaker?

I have learned a lot from watching other speakers. One of the building blocks of good speaking is good listening. You can pick up a lot of do's and don'ts by watching other speakers. College campuses host a lot of speakers, and observing their strengths and weaknesses gives a beginning speaker a wonderful laboratory from which to learn. The other tip I would offer is to take seriously the training offered through public speaking courses. Giving an effective speech is an exhilarating experience, one that you will want to repeat!

regardless of whether or not the audience shares your viewpoint. Speaking to an audience whose knowledge or opinions differ from your own can be an equally and sometimes even more satisfying experience than addressing a like-minded audience, especially when speaker and listeners end up gaining a fuller appreciation of each other.

As you can see, public speaking can benefit you in a variety of important ways. Perhaps more than any other undergraduate offering, the public speaking course offers both extraordinarily useful practical knowledge and skills *and* points to a path of satisfying personal development.

Critical Checkpoint

....

Benefiting from Public Speaking

Now that you have read about some of the benefits of public speaking, think about what you hope to gain from this class. Which of the benefits mentioned do you think will be most important to you? Do you think the skills you learn in this class will help you in other classes, as well as in accomplishing personal and professional goals? What can you do to make sure you maximize the benefits of learning public speaking?

PUBLIC SPEAKING AND THE COMMUNICATION PROCESS

Communication, whether between two persons or between one person and one thousand, is an interactive process in which people exchange and interpret messages with one another. In any communication event, including public speaking, several elements are present. These include the source, the receiver, the message, and the channel (see Figure 1.2).

Elements of Communication

The Source. The **source**, or sender, is the person who creates a message. The speaker transforms ideas and thoughts into messages and sends them to a receiver, or audience. The speaker decides what messages are to be sent and how they will be sent. Organizing the message, choosing words and sentence structure, and verbalizing the message is called **encoding**. Encoding is the physical process of delivering a message. Encoding also includes the nonverbal methods employed in a message, such as gestures, movement, or vocal variation. A speaker can make a speech positive, negative, boring, interesting, clear, or ambiguous depending on the choices made while encoding.

> **source**
> the person who creates and sends a message.

> **encoding**
> the physical process of delivering a message.

The Receiver. The recipient of the source's message is the **receiver**, or audience. Although the speaker provides meaning for the message, the receiver interprets the message in ways that are unique to himself or herself.

> **receiver**
> the recipient of the source's message; in public speaking, members of an audience.

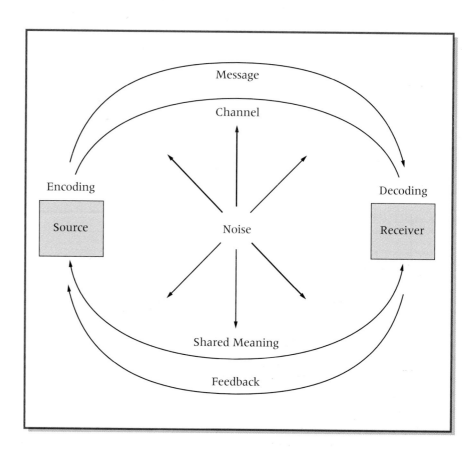

Message

Channel

Encoding

Decoding

Source

Noise

Receiver

Shared Meaning

Feedback

decoding
the process of interpreting the speaker's message.

The process of interpreting the message is called **decoding**: The audience assigns meaning to a message according to previous experience, cultural background, and personal attitudes. Although a speaker may intend a message to carry a specific interpretation, audience members decode the meaning of the message selectively, based on their own experience. The audience response to a message is called feedback, which can be conveyed both verbally and nonverbally. For example, an audience member may blurt out "I don't think so," or might smile and nod. Feedback from the audience often indicates if a speaker's message has been understood.

message
the content of the communication process; the speaker's thoughts and ideas put into meaningful expressions.

The Message. The **message** is the content of the communication process: thoughts and ideas put into meaningful expressions. Content can be expressed verbally and nonverbally. A speaker delivers many messages to an audience; these messages may be conveyed orally (through the sentences and points of a speech) and nonverbally (through eye contact and gestures). Miscommunication can happen when the speaker's intended message is interpreted differently by audience members, or when audience feedback is misinterpreted by the speaker.

channel
the medium through which the speaker sends a message.

The Channel. The medium through which the speaker sends a message is the **channel**. If a speaker is delivering a message in front of a live audience, the channel is the air; sound waves deliver the message by traveling through the air. Other channels include the telephone, television, computers, and written correspondence. If interference, or **noise**, occurs, the message may not be understood. Although noise includes physical sounds such as a slamming door, it can also include psychological, emotional, or environmental interference. For example, if audience members are too hot or too cold, are thinking about their next class, or are feeling ill, they may not accurately interpret the speaker's message. Similarly, if a speaker is extremely nervous, the message may not be clear or may not be sent at all. Anything that interferes with the communication process between a speaker and audience is considered to be noise.

noise
interference that serves as a barrier to communication; can include physical sounds (e.g., a slamming door) as well as psychological, emotional, or environmental interference.

Shared Meaning. When the sender and the receiver interpret the message in the same way, shared meaning occurs. **Shared meaning** is the mutual understanding of a message between speaker and audience. Shared meaning occurs in varying degrees. When a receiver, or audience, is aware that a message is intentionally being sent by the source, or speaker, the lowest level of shared meaning exists; the speaker has caught the attention of an audience. As the message develops, depending on the encoding choices by the source, a higher degree of shared meaning is possible. When the receiver decodes and understands the message in the same way as the source intended the message to be understood, a higher level of shared meaning occurs. Audience feedback indicates to the speaker whether or not shared meaning has occurred; nodding normally indicates shared meaning, whereas blank stares or wrinkled brows indicate that shared meaning has not been achieved.

shared meaning
the mutual understanding of a message between speaker and audience.

Jeff Kaufman/FPG

Many of the skills you use in everyday conversation will also help you deliver speeches and share meaning with an audience.

The primary purpose of public speaking is to convey or share meaning with audience members. Constructing effective speech messages is a complex task involving several processes: selecting an appropriate topic, effectively analyzing the audience, conducting research, developing supporting material, organizing and outlining research materials, using language to achieve maximum power of expression, and using voice and body movements to effectively deliver the speech.

Special Speaker Considerations:
Self, Audience, Context, Goals, and Outcome

By keeping in mind all elements of the communication process, the public speaker ensures that his or her message is effectively delivered. Five other factors are critical to consider when preparing and delivering a speech. These include the speaker's self-concept, the audience, the context, the speech goals, and the outcome.

Self-Concept. As a public speaker you must possess a strong self-concept. When you understand your strengths and limitations, you can take steps to improve your speaking abilities. This course will help identify where your strengths and weaknesses lie and will provide tools that actually improve your self-esteem as a public speaker. When self-concept is strengthened and self-esteem is improved, you will have the confidence to perform the role of speaker in a more positive and assured manner. The goal of Chapter 2 is to build your confidence as a public speaker.

Audience. Have you ever been in a situation in which you said something that embarrassed yourself or another person? Most everyone has said something that he or she regretted because the message was inappropriate. Many times, speakers deliver ineffective or inappropriate messages because they do not know or do not understand their audience (the receivers). Whether you are speaking to an audience of one or one hundred, you should do your best to determine the needs, attitudes, and values of your audience before you begin speaking.

Imagine how your way of speaking would change if you were addressing a class of elementary school children as opposed to a meeting of the American Association of Retired Persons. Consider how your speech would change if you were speaking to a group of right-wing conservatives as opposed to a group of radical liberals, or to a Japanese delegation as opposed to an Arabian delegation. What is deemed appropriate and effective in any given speech occasion depends on a variety of audience characteristics such as age, gender, ethnic or cultural background, political affiliation and a host of linked attitudes and values. *Audience analysis*, the process by which speakers discover what interests and motivates their listeners, allows you to produce appropriate and effective messages before you speak. Beyond the public speaking arena, the ability to analyze an audience is valuable when speaking to small groups and even within one-to-one relationships.

Taking an audience perspective is a critical aspect of public speaking. This textbook ensures that you understand what the audience brings to the speech (attitudes, values, beliefs, interests, biases, etc.), what the audience expects, and how the audience views its relationship with the speaker. It will also guide you to a better understanding of how to manage the speaker-audience relationship.

Critical Checkpoint

. . . .

Considering the Audience

Even if you have never delivered a prepared speech, you have most likely listened to one as an audience member. Recall some speeches you have heard, such as those given by candidates running for office in your high school or by people organizing job or college orientations. Did the speakers do a good job of addressing your concerns or answering your questions? Did they get you interested in what they had to say? Or did it seem to you that the speakers were talking about things that didn't matter to you?

No matter what your topic is, it is crucial to the success of your speech to consider the needs of the audience. As you develop your own speeches, recall your past experiences as an audience member to help shape your message to fit the group you are addressing.

Context. Context influences all aspects of public speaking. Considering the context involves more than just audience analysis. Context includes anything that influences the speaker, the audience, the speech, the occasion, or the situation. In classroom speeches, context would include (among other things) the speech assignment, previous performances, the physical setting, the order in which speeches are given, the quality of other speakers' presentations, and recent events on campus or in the outside world. Context is a way of examining each of the public speaking components in a holistic manner.

Goals. Goal setting is one of the primary tenets of most communication models. A clearly defined goal is a prerequisite for an effective speech. What is it that you want the audience to learn or do or believe? How much ground do you want to cover? What do you want the listeners to take away from the speech? Establishing a set of goals early in the speechmaking process will help you proceed through speech preparation and delivery with a clear focus in mind. All the steps you take will be in concert with the clearly articulated goals that you have set.

Outcome. A speech is not truly complete until its effects have been assessed and you decide whether you have accomplished what you set out to do. Usually this assessment is informal, as in listening to audience reactions. Sometimes it is more formal, as in receiving an evaluation from an instructor. Either form of feedback can help you discover a great deal about how well or poorly you met your goals. Did the audience members learn what you wanted them to learn? Did you affect their attitudes or beliefs in any way? Did they find the speech interesting? Did you speak clearly and maintain eye contact? Answers to questions such as these will alert you to those things you did well and those things you might want to improve on next time. Constructive feedback is an invaluable tool for self-evaluation and improvement. (See Chapter 3 for further discussion and tips on giving and receiving constructive criticism.)

PUBLIC SPEECH AND PLURALISTIC VOICES

> There was a time when our forefathers owned this great island. Their seats extended from the rising to the setting sun. The Great Spirit had made it for the use of the Indians. He had created the buffalo, the deer, and other animals for food. He had made the bear and the beaver. Their skins served us for clothing. He had scattered them over the country and taught us how to take them. He had caused the earth to produce corn for bread. All this he had done for his red children because he loved them. If we had some disputes about our hunting ground, they were generally settled without the shedding of much blood.
>
> But an evil day came upon us. Your forefathers crossed the great water and landed on this island. Their numbers were small. They found friends and not enemies. They told us they had fled from their own country for fear of wicked men and had come here to enjoy their religion. They asked for a small seat. We took pity on them, granted their request, and they sat down among us. We gave them corn and meat; they gave us poison in return.
>
> CHIEF RED JACKET, SPEAKING OUT AGAINST EFFORTS TO
> CONVERT HIS TRIBE TO CHRISTIANITY[5]

These eloquent words of Chief Red Jacket, chief of the Seneca tribe in the 1700s, appear today in various collections of great speeches in history. Yet only a few years ago, rarely if ever were the words of a Native American—or,

Corbis-Bettmann

Cesar Chavez's powerful speeches helped him organize agricultural laborers into the United Farm Workers of America. This group helped raise working standards for thousands of people.

for that matter, a Hispanic American, African American, or Asian American—included in a collection of representative American speeches. Nor were there likely to be many speeches by women, of any color or creed.

Today the tide is starting to turn. With recent publications such as *Voices of Multicultural America*,[6] the gap between the true oratory of the United States and what appears in print is beginning to narrow. Scholars are researching and writing about the oratorical traditions of African Americans, Hispanic Americans, Native Americans, and Asian Americans. What they are finding is that elements of many cultures are woven into the speeches we call our own. Speakers such as Sojourner Truth and the Reverend Martin Luther King Jr., for example, belong to a rich tradition of African American oratory whose roots can be traced to oral African culture. The eloquence and power of Chicano union organizer Cesar Chavez, Native American leader Chief Seattle, and U.S. Senator S. I. Hayakawa also reflect a mix of their ancestors' cultural traditions and their own unique experiences as Americans.

Just as we are now recognizing our rich rhetorical heritage, as a nation we are becoming increasingly sensitive to the diversity of cultural traditions and values that flourish in our midst. Public speaking offers a unique opportunity to recognize and appreciate this diversity in all its forms. Citizens of the United States include persons from every part of the world, including Africa, Asia, Europe, the Middle East, and the Americas. Hispanic Americans have roots in Cuba, Puerto Rico, Portugal, Mexico, Central and South America, and Spain; Asian Americans hail from countries as diverse as China, Korea, India, the Philippines, and Japan. Irish, French, Russian, and German traditions coexist with those of Vietnam, Thailand, and Malaysia. Our pluralistic character is also reflected in our rich religious diversity. Just about one-half of Americans over age 18 identify themselves as Protestant, one-quarter as Roman Catholic, and about 2 percent as Jewish.[7] The balance—about 60 million, or some 30 percent of the population—are followers of Islam, Hinduism, Buddhism, Mormonism, Confucianism, and dozens of other denominations. Various age groups, persons of different sexual orientations, and persons with disabilities and special needs also reflect our true character.

Every audience member wants to feel that the speaker has his or her particular needs and interests at heart, and to feel recognized and included in the speaker's message. To create this sense of inclusion today requires that the public speaker attempt to understand the audience's beliefs and norms and be culturally sensitive. Culturally sensitive speakers assume differences and address them with interest and respect. The flip side of cultural sensitivity is **ethnocentrism**, the belief that the ways of one's own culture are superior to those of other cultures. Ethnocentric speakers presume that listeners share their viewpoints and frames of reference. They don't bother considering other perspectives or ways of behaving. No matter how passionately they believe in an issue, our most admired public speakers always acknowledge and respectfully consider alternative viewpoints.

Whether in the classroom or in the world beyond, as a public speaker you will undoubtedly confront differing values from your own. As you read through this text, you will find numerous discussions about being a culturally sensitive speaker. These discussions range from differing values, stereotypes, and hate speech to the crucial role of language in creating a culturally

ethnocentrism
the belief that the ways of one's own culture are superior to those of other cultures.

sensitive speech. With the classroom as your laboratory, you can investigate others' viewpoints and practice the art of acknowledging and including them even as you express your own, sometimes very different, ideas.

CHALLENGES AND CHOICES OF PUBLIC SPEAKING

Public speaking involves a host of challenges and choices—stimulating tasks or problems (**challenges**) and options or alternatives for solving them (**choices**). If you're like most people, just the act of public speaking itself is a major challenge until you do it once or twice. After that's behind you (momentarily, anyway, for even many seasoned speakers reconquer some nervousness each time they approach the podium), other challenges beckon. Primary among these are mastering your material by learning the skills necessary for preparing and delivering speeches. Each speech that you prepare will present you with a range of choices that you must critically evaluate. Which topic should you select? What should be your goal in addressing an audience? What kind of evidence do you need? How should you organize the speech? How much do you need to know about a topic before you can responsibly explain it to an audience? What can you leave out? What language will best convey your meaning?

The challenges and choices posed by public speaking extend beyond the classroom. As an employee, it's likely that you'll be asked to make sales presentations and participate in small group discussions. As a member of any number of clubs and civic organizations, you might be called on to lead meetings, present findings, and speak out on issues. As a citizen (taxpayer, parent, concerned member of the community), chances are that at some point you will find yourself addressing an audience of neighbors and town officials.

> **challenges**
> stimulating tasks or problems.
>
> **choices**
> options or alternatives for solving tasks or problems.

Challenges and Choices of Speech in a Democracy

Many of the challenges and choices of public speaking are directly linked to living in a democracy. You can vote or remain apathetic in a democracy. You can speak out or remain silent. If you do speak out, you can do so for good or for evil. You can speak irresponsibly and unethically, or morally and with the best interests of the greater good in mind. As a citizen of the most pro–free speech society on earth, you have the right to speak in nearly any situation or context. Even most forms of hate speech are protected (see Chapter 4 for the few exceptions).

Public speaking is one of the primary tools that makes a democracy possible. A democracy is a form of government in which the people rule. Members of an informed citizenry elect their own leaders, who then represent their will. Through its key functions of informing and persuading, public speaking conveys the information people need to make decisions and to convince them to take certain actions. For example, in each presidential election year, volunteer speakers from the League of Women Voters hold public forums in which they describe the issues and profile the candidates. The candidates themselves argue their positions and attempt to persuade voters to adopt one side over another. Various citizens groups join the fray, arguing for or against candidates and issues.

Authors Francis Lappe and Paul DuBois note:

> Democracy is never fully in place. It is always in flux, a work in progress. Democracy is dynamic. It evolves in response to the creative action of citizens. It's what we make of it.[8]

Because you live in a democracy rather than a totalitarian regime, you are more likely to be concerned with your responsibilities (what you should say) than with worrying about your rights (what you are allowed to say). Responsibility lies at the heart of ethics, our moral conduct. The fact that many kinds of speech are legal, for example, does not necessarily mean that they are ethical. In fact, the First Amendment guarantees protection to both the honest and the dishonest speaker.[9]

Consider the debate over a recent ruling by the Supreme Court allowing expanded rights for anti-abortion protesters. It provides a glimpse of the kind of dilemmas posed by the freedom of speech our democracy allows:

> The U.S. Supreme Court bolstered the free-speech rights of protesters at abortion clinics Wednesday, ruling that they can confront patients on public sidewalks as long as they stay at least 15 feet away from clinic entrances....Anti-abortion forces hailed the ruling as a major victory. "There is no longer an exception to...free speech... when the issue deals with abortion," said Jay Sekulow of the American Center for Law and Justice. "The court has sent a resounding message that you cannot silence a message you disagree with."[10]

> But does a listener have rights too? At some point, can the speaker's loud, insistent preaching in your ear go too far and violate your right "to be left alone"? If he follows you and refuses to stop, when does his free speech violate your rights and become illegal harassment, intimidation or even stalking?[11]

As a public speaker, you will continually face the challenge of speaking responsibly in an environment that permits irresponsible speech. Public speakers are in a unique position not only to share their ideas but to influence or persuade others and, at times, to move them to act—for better or for worse. As members of a democratic society, we have the right to speak freely. To ensure the well-being of a free society, we have the equally important responsibility to speak responsibly. (See Chapter 4 for guidelines for responsible speech.)

Making a Difference

Public speaking is a tool uniquely suited to problem solving and to addressing issues that concern you, whether they are related to your professional or personal life. Ordinary citizens—be they students protesting a tuition increase, environmentalists urging legislators to enact a bill, or employees presenting a new business strategy to co-workers—can and do accomplish a great deal through the power of public speaking.

Here are just some of the things everyday people have accomplished—for themselves and for others—through the power of public speaking:

- Wendy Kopp, founder of Teach for America (a volunteer program to get young college graduates to commit to teach for two years in under-resourced public schools), raised the necessary money to implement her program by speaking to countless corporate leaders. Recognized by *Time* magazine as one of America's 50 most promising leaders under age 40, Wendy uses public speaking almost daily to speak to staff, teachers, and the public.

- The Reverend Tom Grey, executive director of the National Coalition Against Legalized Gambling (NCALG), has helped groups in 34 states (and counting) to turn back the tide of gambling expansion and establish legislation that gives citizens a voice in the matter. Grey has spoken passionately against gambling as a predatory enterprise to countless groups, from local community organizations to the U.S. Senate. His powerful speeches have gained him international recognition as the leading opponent of the powerful gaming lobby.

- Craig Kielburger, disturbed by a 1995 newspaper report from Pakistan about the tragic life and death of a young boy sold into slavery to weave carpets, helped form an organization called Free the Children, a children's rights advocacy group. Amazingly, Craig was 12 years old at the time and in the seventh grade. He now gives several hundred speeches a year to audiences ranging from small youth groups to government committees, and he uses public speaking both to inform people about global child labor issues as well as to persuade them to do something about it. He has met with Pope John Paul II and the Dalai Lama to further his cause, and he is recognized as a powerful voice speaking out on behalf of the world's children.

- Charlton McIlwain started giving speeches as a teenager competing in talent contests at family reunions. Today he is a doctoral candidate in communications, and he is the Director of Communications for the democratic nominee for the governor of Oklahoma. Assuming such an important and prominent role in a statewide campaign, Charlton addresses audiences on issues from domestic violence to improving education. When speaking, Charlton seeks not only to inform citizens and to win votes for his candidate, but also to engage people's minds in controversial issues and to foster substantive discussions. Charlton plans to use his public speaking skills throughout his life, speaking out on important issues and speaking up for candidates he believes in.

These people and others are profiled in depth in the Making a Difference boxes that appear throughout this book. These profiles highlight how people use speech to address issues of concern to them. One such person, a high school senior from California named Kristina Wong, claims in the following prize-winning speech (see p. 24) that the United States offers countless opportunities to have a voice.

Kristina Wong and the other "ordinary advocates" featured in this text bring fresh force to the classical belief that public speaking is the glue of a free society, and that by generating and criticizing ideas through public speech we can influence our own fate.

Making a Difference

KRISTINA WONG, VOICE OF DEMOCRACY SCHOLARSHIP WINNER

Note: The following speech was written by Kristina Wong, a high school senior in San Francisco and entered into the 1995–1996 Veterans of Foreign Wars (VFW) Voice of Democracy Scholarship Program. Each year some 100,000 students in tenth through twelfth grade enter this competition; they record their essays on audiocassettes and send them in for judging. For her entry, Kristina won first place at the state level.

"Hello?...Oh, America! How are you!...Great. I'm sure you're still as generous as always....What's that?...Sure...Of course I will. Of course! If you are kind enough to create such opportunities, I should be gracious enough to offer you what I can in return....No, no, no....Don't be silly, we depend on each other. Without you I couldn't be here.... And you couldn't be where you are....Alright, thanks for calling. Bye."

That was America calling. She calls on me as she does all of us to take advantage of her innumerable opportunities. Now, more than ever, the chance for Americans to answer her call is marvelous. These opportunities are practically flung at Americans, so how could anyone resist answering America's call?

...I, too, have answered America's call. I have taken a citizen's role in government through my work canvassing for the Sierra Club on environmental protection issues....This work led me to volunteer at a local recycling center, where I have spoken to the community about keeping open recycling centers which were scheduled to close.

America has kept her promise of life, liberty, and freedom. She gives us the right to voice our opinions on our government. She gives us the freedom to pursue our goals and to reach for excellence. She gives us the opportunities for education and success. She only asks that we answer her call by giving her our time, service, and talents in return. So, the next time America calls, don't hang up.

SOURCE: *http://sacam.oren.ortn.edu/~adpicker/vod/speeches/ca.txt.*

SUMMARY QUESTIONS

What are the similarities and differences between public speaking and other forms of communication?

Public speaking shares many similarities with dyadic, small group, and mass communication; it also has some notable differences. As in dyadic communication, or conversation, public speaking requires that you attempt to make yourself understood and take responsibility for what you say. Like small group communication, public speaking requires that you clearly address issues relevant to the topic and occasion. And as in mass communication, public speaking requires that you understand and appeal to the audience's interests, attitudes, and values. Public speaking differs from other forms of communication in terms of opportunities for feedback (there are fewer than in dyadic and small group, and more than in mass communication); level of preparation (greater than in other forms of communication); and degree of formality (greater than in other forms of communication).

What are some of the benefits of public speaking for personal and professional development?

Public speaking training offers many benefits. These include becoming a more knowledgeable person, developing critical thinking and listening skills, enhancing your abilities as a student, achieving professional success, and exploring and sharing your values and those of others.

What are the elements of the public speaking process?

The source is the sender, or the person who creates a message. The source engages in encoding, which involves organizing one's thoughts, choosing the appropriate words, and verbalizing the message. The receiver is the recipient of the source's message, or the audience. Receivers engage in decoding when they assign meaning to a message based on their own cultural background, experience, and personal attitudes. The message consists of the thoughts, ideas, or nonverbal actions conveyed by the sender. The channel is the medium through which the speaker sends a message to the receiver. Shared meaning is the mutual understanding of a message between a speaker and the audience.

Why is being culturally sensitive so important to success as a public speaker?

Audience members want to feel included and recognized in the speaker's remarks. To foster this sense of inclusion, today's public speaker must attempt to identify and understand the diversity of values and viewpoints held by audience members.

What are some of the challenges and choices of public speaking?

Challenges are the stimulating tasks and problems we face every day (e.g., overcoming nervousness, persuading someone to buy a product). Choices are the options or alternatives we have for solving challenges. Public speaking

presents a host of challenges and choices, ranging from those related to actually putting together an effective speech to the larger issues of deciding if and when to speak out, and how to speak responsibly in a society that permits many forms of irresponsible and unethical speech as a constitutional right.

ISSUES FOR DISCUSSION

1. In what specific ways can effective public speaking benefit both your professional and personal lives?

2. Think of three speakers whom you think are effective. What made them effective as public speakers? In what ways do they influence the people around them?

3. People such as Adolf Hitler and Saddam Hussein would certainly be identified as persuasive speakers. Would you claim they were/are effective? Why or why not? What role do ethics play in judging someone as an effective speaker?

4. The thought of public speaking instills fear in many people. What do you suppose are the sources of these fears? In other words, where do these feelings of anxiety or fear originate?

5. Shared meaning is an important element of the communication process. As a speaker, what criteria would you use to ensure that the meanings within your messages are shared with your audience? More important, is it the speaker's responsibility to ensure that these meanings are conveyed, or do audience members share this responsibility?

SELF-ASSESSMENT

1. Talk to someone who works in a career field that you are interested in. Ask the following questions: What specific communication skills are required by people entering your line of work? How important are public speaking skills to your job? How important to success in your career is effective public speaking?

2. Think back to a conversation in which you tried to achieve a particular result (e.g., giving advice, persuading the listener). What are the similarities between that situation and public speaking?

3. List some examples of feedback conveyed by an audience, and identify each one as "positive" or "negative." When do you think positive feedback is more appropriate than negative feedback? What are some ways speakers can deal with negative feedback they receive while making a speech?

4. Evaluate your own strengths and weaknesses as a speaker. What are three weaknesses that you want to improve during this course?

Key Terms

....

challenges	message
channel	noise
choices	public speaking
decoding	receiver
dyadic communication	shared meaning
encoding	small group
ethnocentrism	communication
feedback	source
mass communication	

TEAMWORK

1. Work in a group of three or four classmates. Individually, divide a sheet of paper into two columns: "Characteristics of an Effective Public Speaker" and "Characteristics of an Ineffective Public Speaker." Fill in these columns, and then compare them with other members of your group. On which characteristics of an effective speaker did your group agree?

2. In a group, formulate a list of objectives or goals you think this public speaking class should accomplish. Compare these with other groups' and, as a class, try to come to a consensus on goals or objectives for the course.

3. In a group, draw a pictorial model or diagram that represents the communication process. Be sure to include all the components of the process (e.g., source, receiver, channel, decoding). How are the relationships among the components illustrated? What are the strengths and weaknesses of your model? Compare it to other groups' models.

You gain strength, courage and confidence by every experience in which you really stop to look fear in the face....You must do the thing you think you cannot do.

—Eleanor Roosevelt

I always tell speakers that their goal is not to get rid of the butterflies, but to get the butterflies to fly in formation.

—Bert Decker

Getting Started with Confidence

Think back to your first date. Were you nervous about it? No doubt you really wanted to go out with the other person, so you managed to find a way to overcome your nervousness. You probably did everything you possibly could to make it all go well. **In fact, the motivation to be your best was stronger than your inhibitions and your nervousness.** You chose confidence over self-doubt.

Well, being confident about giving speeches works in much the same way. Any anxiety you feel about giving speeches can be overcome by being motivated to give the best speeches you possibly can on topics that are important to you and relevant to the audience. **You gain confidence when you expect the best.**

In a speech delivered to the Westchester County Chamber of Commerce in White Plains, New York, John B. Donovan, the president of Donovan Public Affairs, related the following anecdote about people's fear of public speaking.

A few years ago, there was a survey taken to determine which fears were greatest among human beings generally. Now before I tell you which fear came in first, I'll give you a hint by telling you the one that came in second, and that was death. Dying is definitely something that a lot of people are afraid of, and yet it's nothing compared to the thing that came in first in the survey. And what was that? Public speaking.

And what is it they're afraid of? Well, generally, they fear that they're going to forget what they were going to say. Someone has said that the human brain begins working at the moment of birth and never stops until the moment we have to stand up and speak in public. People are afraid to get up in front of other people like this.

And yet opportunities like this can bring results. If you try marketing yourself in an unusual way, bringing yourself to larger and larger groups of people, interesting things can happen.[1]

If you're afraid of public speaking, you're not alone. It turns out that even accomplished speakers often feel jittery before they give a speech. Feeling nervous is normal. In fact, it's desirable. Channeled properly, nervousness boosts performance. When baseball great Lou Gehrig was once asked if he was nervous about coming to bat in the ninth inning, he replied, "Of course I was nervous. If I wasn't, I couldn't have hit that double off the wall."[2] The difference between seasoned public speakers and the rest of us is not that the seasoned speakers don't feel nervous or anxious. It's just that they're more practiced at making those feelings work *for* rather than against them. They've also learned specific techniques to cope with and minimize their tension.

As we saw in Chapter 1, public speaking can open up a rich world of positive experiences and relationships. No one should lose out on its many benefits because of fear. This chapter is based on the principle that gaining confidence to speak in public begins with gaining insight into what makes us lack confidence. This involves knowing why we become anxious about public speaking, what effects it has on us, and, most important, how to manage nervousness so that it works for us rather than against us. This chapter challenges the inexperienced public speaker to:

- Recognize three roots or sources of public speaking anxiety.

- Practice using several strategies for gaining confidence as a speaker.

- Explain how anxiety about public speaking relates to a more general anxiety about communicating.

- Identify points in the speechmaking process where anxiety can occur.

- Anticipate the possible consequences of public speaking anxiety.

- Practice maintaining confidence while delivering a well-planned initial speech.

THE ROOTS OF PUBLIC SPEAKING ANXIETY

What underlies the fear of addressing an audience? Researchers have identified several factors.[3] These include lack of public speaking experience, feeling different from members of the audience, and uneasiness about being the center of attention. Each factor can lead to the onset of **public speaking anxiety (PSA)**, that is, fear or anxiety associated with either actual or anticipated communication as a speaker to an audience.[4]

> **public speaking anxiety**
> fear or anxiety associated with actual or anticipated communication as a speaker to an audience.

Lack of Experience

It can be exciting or frightening to anticipate doing something you've never done before. For example, skydiving might sound thrilling in the abstract, but actually doing it may well bring on considerable anxiety. Anxious anticipation is a natural reaction to new experiences, especially ones that are challenging or complex. And with no experience to fall back on, it's hard to put the anxiety in perspective. It's a bit of a vicious circle. In terms of public speaking, some people react by deciding to avoid making speeches altogether. Even though by doing this they avoid the anxiety of speechmaking, they also lose out on the considerable rewards it brings. The only way to break out of the vicious circle is to give public speaking a try. Your speech class may be the best place to undertake this new experience because it is a controlled environment—the instructor understands and is able to accommodate stage fright, and your classmates may be a better source of confidence than you realize because they will encourage you just as they will want you to encourage them.

Confidence and Culture—When English Isn't Your First Language (Or Even If It Is)

In addition to the nearly universal fear of being at "center stage," some students of public speaking face the burden of worrying about delivering a speech in a non-native language. *If English is your first language*, remind yourself how difficult it would be for you to deliver a speech in another language. As you listen to a non-native speaker, place yourself in his or her shoes. Don't confuse content with delivery. If necessary, politely ask questions for clarification. Native English speakers can also use the following tips.

If English is not your first language, don't despair. After all, you've made it this far! Give yourself a great deal of credit for your accomplishments to this point. Then, regard this class as an opportunity to further develop your language skills in English. In fact, researchers have found that relatively frequent use of a new spoken language is a significant factor in diminishing noticeable accent features.[1] Use this public speaking class to practice your spoken English. You may even wish to ask for constructive feedback related to how well or poorly your speech is understood. It won't always be easy, and in some cases your classmates might have difficulty understanding you. But that's okay. Indeed, your native language and the accent with which you speak are important aspects of what makes you unique as a person—and as a speaker.

Here are some exercises you may wish to try. You can practice some of them when rehearsing your speeches for class. Some can be done alone, and some in conversations with friends.

1. Take your time and speak slowly as you introduce the purpose and main points of your speech. This will give your listeners time to get accustomed to your voice and focused on your message.

2. You may already be aware of certain English words that you have trouble saying. Practice these in repetitive utterances. For example, say "perfunctory" five times. Pause. Then say it again, five times. Progress slowly until the word becomes clearer and easier to pronounce.

3. Avoid using words that you don't really have to, such as some kinds of jargon (and, perhaps, the word *perfunctory*!) Learn to use a thesaurus to find synonyms that are simpler and easier to pronounce.

4. Extend vowel sounds. English uses more vowels than most languages do. Say, "To-o-o-o-ky-y-y-o-o-o is fa-a-a-a-r fro-o-o-m he-e-e-e-re." This gets you used to hearing and feeling the pronunciation of vowels; with practice they'll come more naturally for you.

5. Offer words from your native language as a way of drawing attention to and emphasizing a point you're making. This helps the audience better appreciate your native language and accent. For example, the Spanish word *corazón* has a lyrical quality that makes it sound much better than its English counterpart, *heart.* Capitalize on the beauty of your native tongue.

6. Listen to radio talk shows. Try to repeat statements made by program participants, as though you are speaking the statements originally. See if you can emulate, or model, the person's voice and pronunciation.

Remember, practicing oral English is the surest way to master it.[2]

1. J. E. Flege, M. J. Munro, and I. R. A. MacKay, "Factors Affecting Strength of Perceived Foreign Accent in a Second Language," *Journal of the Acoustical Society of America*, 97 (1995): 3125ff.

2. Some of these ideas are adapted from J. Sprague and D. Stuart, *The Speaker's Handbook*, 2nd ed. (San Diego: Harcourt Brace Jovanovich, 1988).

Feeling Different

It's awkward to feel different from everyone around you. Perhaps you had that feeling early in your first semester as a freshman each time you attended a new social function, orientation session, or class. A common experience among novice speakers is the feeling of being alone—as if no one else has ever been as scared as they are, as if they are the only persons to ever experience the dread of speaking. Moreover, the prospect of getting up in front of an audience makes them extra sensitive to their personal idiosyncrasies, such as a less-than-perfect haircut, a slight lisp in the pronunciation of s-words, being taller or shorter than average, or thinking that no one could possibly be interested in anything they have to say.

These kinds of ideas make us, as novice speakers, anxious because our general assumption is that being different somehow means being inferior. Actually, everyone is different from everyone else in many ways. Just as true, everyone is the same as everyone else in many ways. One of the ways that we're similar (at least in a public speaking class) is that we're all nervous about giving speeches. Ask your instructor whether he or she gets nervous about teaching this class. The answer may surprise you. In terms of the way you look and sound when giving a speech, be assured that you're really no different from anyone else—especially in an introductory public speaking class.

Being the Center of Attention

Feeling conspicuous—that there are many eyes on us—is an uncomfortable sensation. It's especially troubling while we're giving speeches, because that is when all eyes truly are on us! Speakers often comment about how audience members appear to behave toward them during speeches. They may notice some listeners' failure to make eye contact with them, or some listeners conversing with one another during a speech, or a listener pointing at them. When we notice audience members behaving in ways like this, our tendency is to think we must be doing something inappropriate or silly; then we wonder what's wrong and whether the whole audience is noticing it.

This kind of thinking builds rapidly and, if not properly checked, can distract us from our speech, with all our attention now focused on "me." As we focus on "me" we become even more sensitive to things that might be wrong with what we're doing—and that makes us feel even more conspicuous, which increases our anxiety. In actuality (and ironically), an audience notices very little about us that we don't want to reveal, especially if our speeches are well developed and effectively delivered. Consequently, there really is no reason to be anxious about being the center of attention. You see yourself more critically than an audience does, so relax!

Critical Checkpoint

....

Learning from a Lack of Confidence

Recall a recent time when you lacked confidence in doing something. Analyze the reasons for your lack of confidence. Was the activity something you'd never done before? Did the activity make you feel different from others, or make you feel like you were under a lot of scrutiny? Evaluate your feelings about that experience relative to the experience you anticipate with giving speeches in this class. How do they compare? What can you learn from the previous experience that will build your confidence in giving speeches?

PUBLIC SPEAKING ANXIETY: FORMS AND CONSEQUENCES

Communication Apprehension

Communication scholars refer to the general fear or anxiety associated with real or anticipated communication with others as **communication apprehension**.[5] For some people—about 20 percent of the population—anxiety about communicating is chronic, that is, it is felt consistently. Whereas most people do not experience communication apprehension in a chronic sense, many experience it in particular contexts. This gives rise to the term **context-based communication apprehension**. The most common context is public speaking or presentation making; hence, public speaking anxiety is a more specific instance of communication apprehension.

Context-Based Communication Apprehension. This afflicts most people who are anxious about giving speeches. Whereas they generally have moderate to low levels of chronic communication apprehension (i.e., they generally aren't fearful of communicating), their apprehension associated with public speaking is consistently high. What is it about such a context that produces this anxiety in some people? It is most likely a strong sense of impending negative evaluation resulting from a lack of experience, and an anticipation that they will appear different and feel conspicuous while standing before an audience.

Person- or Audience-Specific Communication Apprehension. Sometimes it's not the general context (e.g., whether the communication takes place one-to-one, in a group, or with an audience) that bothers people. Instead, it's a specific person or group of people with whom they must communicate. In this situation the term **audience-specific communication apprehension** applies. For example, you might be perfectly confident and comfortable giving a presentation to a group of co-workers. However, if you are asked to address a group of superiors, you become anxious. Why? Because your superiors are in a position of authority over you. Speaking in front of them showcases your knowledge and abilities as one of their subordinate representatives. They are in a dual position to evaluate you—both as your audience and as your superiors.[6]

Situational Communication Apprehension. This form of anxiety is associated with a particular communication event at a particular time. People who experience **situational communication apprehension** do not necessarily experience it often, or even in the same situation every time. In one instance they might look forward to giving a speech. At another time they might feel anxious. The difference involves how strongly the person experiences the fears of being unfamiliar with, feeling different from, and standing out to an audience. For example, variations in audience size may stimulate anxiety for a speaker. Perhaps he is used to making presentations to small groups of fewer than 10 people. Then comes an occasion when the speaker's boss asks him to make a presentation to an audience consisting of several groups meeting together. Now the audience is 82 instead of 8.

communication apprehension
general fear or anxiety, which may or may not be chronic, associated with real or anticipated communication with one or more people.

context-based communication apprehension
communication apprehension associated with a particular mode or context of communication, such as public speaking.

audience-specific communication apprehension
anxiety about communicating with a particular person or group of people as one's audience.

situational communication apprehension
anxiety about communicating with a particular audience on a particular occasion at a particular time.

Assuming this to be a challenge of proportionally greater magnitude, the speaker experiences increased anxiety. It is due to the particular speaking situation, not to public speaking per se.

Public Speaking Anxiety during the Speechmaking Process

The onset of PSA can occur at different times during the speechmaking process. For certain people it arises as soon as they know that they will give a speech at some point in the future. For others it arises as they approach the podium. Figure 2.1 illustrates the different points during the speechmaking process at which PSA can occur.

Paul Conklin/Monkmeyer

Becoming more comfortable with their audiences helps public speakers manage their audience-specific or situational communication apprehension.

Pre-Preparation Anxiety. Some people feel anxious the minute they know they will be giving a speech. **Pre-preparation anxiety** at this early stage can have several negative consequences. First, depending on its severity, the person may be reluctant to begin planning for the speech. Second, it can preoccupy her to such an extent that she misses vital information required to fulfill the speech assignment.

pre-preparation anxiety
the anxiety experienced once it is realized one will be giving a speech; for example, when a speaking assignment is given.

Preparation Anxiety. For some people, anxiety arises only when they actually begin to prepare for the speech. At that point they might feel overwhelmed at the amount of time and planning required. They might hit a roadblock that puts them behind schedule. They might be unable to locate

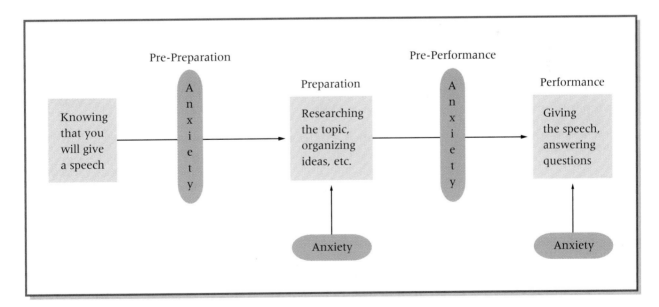

FIGURE 2.1
Anxiety during the Speechmaking Process

Making a Difference

CHARLTON MCILWAIN, DIRECTOR OF COMMUNICATION, LAURA BOYD GUBERNATORIAL CAMPAIGN

Charlton McIlwain, age 26, was born in North Carolina, grew up in San Antonio, Texas, and now resides in Norman, Oklahoma, where he is a doctoral candidate in the Department of Communication at the University of Oklahoma. In addition to his studies,

Charlton is director of communication for the 1998 gubernatorial campaign office of Laura Boyd, the democratic nominee for governor in the state of Oklahoma. An accomplished public speaker, Charlton was selected for one of the most public and prominent roles in a statewide election campaign. After Boyd took note of his political passion and public speaking skills while he was working in a 1996 congressional election, she recruited him to work for her campaign. In his role as director of communication, Charlton delivers speeches to civic organizations, college classes, and political groups on behalf of the Boyd campaign. These speeches address key platform issues such as improving secondary and higher education, and preventing child abuse and domestic violence.

Although giving speeches comes fairly naturally to Charlton these days, this was not always the case. "My first experiences as a speaker were as a teenager during the talent contests held at large family reunions. The audience was large, and there was a lot at stake—ego and pride. I was really nervous getting up in front of people I knew and respected, so I selected topics that I knew something about—the importance of family or the value of a good education. What I found is that once you get started, the nervousness subsides. As people nod and smile, you gain confidence in yourself as a speaker. I also learned that

---

information to adequately support a critical point they wish to make in their speech. These kinds of preparation pressures produce a vicious cycle of more stress, avoidance of the process, and procrastination. All contribute to **preparation anxiety**.

Pre-Performance Anxiety. Some people experience anxiety when they rehearse their speech. At this point the reality of the situation sets in: Soon they will face an audience of people watching and listening *only to them*. As they rehearse, they may also realize that their ideas don't sound as focused or as interesting as they should. Knowing that time is short, they begin to get nervous. If this **pre-performance anxiety** is strong enough, and if they interpret it negatively, they may even decide to stop rehearsing.

Performance Anxiety. Many people who are generally confident about communicating don't experience any high degree of speech anxiety until they begin to deliver the speech. This is true even of well-known celebrities, who report that their worst stage fright occurs just as they walk on stage and begin their performances. **Performance anxiety** in speechmak-

preparation anxiety
the onset of public speaking anxiety once preparation for a speech has gotten under way.

pre-performance anxiety
the onset of anxiety immediately prior to giving a speech.

performance anxiety
the onset and experience of anxiety while giving a speech.

getting applause and compliments about a good speaking job increased my interest in speaking more."

Building on the success of his speeches at family reunions, Charlton began to deliver inspirational devotionals in his church. Despite his past experience speaking in front of his family, he was still nervous each time he spoke in church. "I used that nervous energy to focus on the message I was trying to get across. Even now I am a bit nervous giving speeches, although I use it as a tool for ensuring that my audience gets the message that I came to speak about." Charlton uses his nervousness to his advantage by channeling it into extensive speech preparation and additional practice. In the moments before his speech, he takes several deep breaths to relax his body and clear his mind. Early in the speech Charlton likes to focus his gaze for a few seconds on someone who seems to agree with his message. Finding a "friendly face" in the crowd has a calming effect and also boosts his confidence, allowing him to project his message and make eye contact with the rest of the audience. "I find that the nervousness or apprehension I may have about speaking doesn't last long. It's more of an anticipation thing."

Charlton also suggest that careful selection of a speech topic is important in combating nervousness. "It certainly helps to have a personal involvement with the topic—a connection, so to speak. Having that personal connection and familiarity with the subject helps me handle any distractions that can come up during a speech, and audience members tend to identify more strongly with me and my message when they sense I am speaking from the heart."

Charlton is a big believer in public speaking as a way of reaching out to others and getting information into the hands of people who want and need it. "The more experience in speaking I have gained, the more confident I feel in my abilities. In my early speaking experiences—and I know this to be true for many other speakers—I would mainly look for agreement with audience members. I wanted them to like me. Now I look for opportunities to engage people's minds in controversial issues, hoping that we can discuss these issues after my speech."

Public speaking will continue to play an important role in Charlton's life. He intends to keep speaking out on important causes—such as diversity and race relations—as well as speaking up for candidates he believes in, particularly those who lack the financial resources and large staff of an established incumbent. And each time he rises to address an audience, he will take a deep breath and overcome his apprehension. "Speaking to people is my passion, and I will not let a touch of nervousness get in the way."

ing is probably most pronounced during the introduction phase of the speech. This is when the speaker utters the first words of the speech and is most cognizant of the audience's attention. However, experienced speakers agree that if they control their nervousness during the introduction, the rest of the speech comes relatively easily.

Consequences of Public Speaking Anxiety

Depending on when it strikes, the consequences of public speaking anxiety can include everything from procrastination to poor speech performance. The important thing to remember is to manage your anxiety and not let it manage you—by harming your motivation, or by causing you to avoid investing the time and energy required to prepare and perform a successful speech. The first step in effective management of speech anxiety is to have a clear and thorough plan for each speech. That's really what this textbook is all about—helping you plan successful speeches. Let's continue by considering several strategies to begin the speechmaking process with confidence.

STRATEGIES FOR GETTING STARTED WITH CONFIDENCE

There's nothing magical about gaining confidence in public speaking—except, of course, the glow of accomplishment that sets in after the hard work is done and the speech is over. Confidence comes with knowing what you're doing. And the surest route is through preparation and practice.

Prepare and Practice

Have you ever sat around wishing that you were in better physical shape? Did it work? That's about the size of it in terms of public speaking. Sitting around wishing your speech will be a success isn't a *bad* idea (positive thoughts never are) but it's not a good idea to do it at the expense of actual preparation and practice. After all, preparation and practice build confidence in much the same way that lifting weights builds muscle. There's a direct correlation.

Knowledge is power. If you are confident that you know the material you are to present, and you have adequately rehearsed your delivery of that material, you're far more likely to feel confident at the podium than otherwise. Thus, preparation should begin as soon as possible after a speech is assigned. Once the speech is prepared, it should be rehearsed several times.

Here are some key points to think about as you prepare and practice giving a speech:

- *Manage your time wisely*. Know in advance of doing your work what you need to do and where you need to get it done. When will you need to spend time in the library? When will you need to work on a computer? Consider how you will allocate your time to these different tasks *before* you begin.
- *Don't skimp on the research* required to support your key points (see Chapter 7). Thoroughly knowing your topic is a confidence builder. And try to pick topics you can be enthused about; remember, enthusiasm is catchy.
- *Discover as much about the audience and speaking environment as you can* (see Chapter 5). The more you know about an audience, the more likely you are to tell them something they want to hear—and in the most appropriate way.
- *Rehearse delivering your speech*, beginning two or three days prior to the speech date (see Chapter 11). In this way the actual speech will feel familiar and more natural—and thereby less threatening. Also, check to make sure that any audiovisual equipment you plan to use is in good working order.

Modify Thoughts and Attitudes

As you prepare for and deliver your speech, it's important to regard it as a valuable, worthwhile, and challenging activity. Remind yourself of all the reasons why public speaking is helpful personally, socially, and professionally (see Chapter 1). The point is to think positively about public speaking and remind yourself that it is an *opportunity*, not a threat.

Focus on Technology

Audiocassettes and Confidence

It's the *not knowing* that scares many people: not knowing just how they'll feel, or act, or even sound, once they get up to the podium.

Technology can help—in this case an inexpensive, low-tech piece of machinery called a tape recorder. In fact, many public speaking experts agree that of the vast array of high-tech audiovisual gizmos available, the lowly tape recorder is the only truly indispensable aid to building speech confidence.

Taping the speech while you practice enables you to hear how it will sound to the audience. Taping lets you know if you are speaking clearly and at the right tempo. It helps you decide if your sentences are too long. It helps ferret out tongue-twisters before you stumble on them during the actual speech. It lets you time the speech and may help you decide how to edit it and where to cut. Most important, listening to your speech makes it *real*—and, therefore, less scary.

Ron Hoff, author of a best-selling book on public speaking, *I Can See You Naked*, offers the following advice to people who are scheduled to give a presentation the next day:

> If you have made a cassette tape of your presentation, play it by yourself. Just let the words and thoughts sink in. You're not listening to be critical. You're listening to absorb, to remember.
>
> If you haven't made an audiotape of your presentation, take the time to do it. Just "talk it" into the tape. It doesn't have to be perfect. But once you've got that cassette deck in your hand, you'll feel better. You'll know that the presentation *exists*. That it's tangible, that there's substance to it.[1]

Hoff also suggests practicing positive self-imagery while listening to your voice. Close your eyes and visualize yourself standing in front of the audience and being well received. Let the sound of your voice relax you as you sit back and appreciate all the good work that you've done.

1. Ron Hoff, *I Can See You Naked*, rev. ed. (Kansas City: Andrews and McMeel, 1992) p. 66.

One communication expert has recently shown that altering one's thinking about public speaking from a "performance orientation" to a "communication orientation" can significantly increase confidence in giving speeches.[7] Rather than conceiving of a speech as a formal performance or event in which you will be judged and evaluated, try thinking about it as an extension of ordinary conversation. By regarding an upcoming speech in this manner, you just might feel less threatened and more relaxed about the process. And with each successive speech experience, your mindset about public speaking will grow more positive. You can even find some good in the speeches that do not go as well as you would like. As the saying goes, we learn best from our mistakes.

Visualize Success

Speech communication professors at Washington State University have been working for several years to develop visualization techniques for increasing positive expectations associated with speechmaking.[8] Below is their script for visualizing success on a public speaking occasion. The exercise requires the speaker to close his or her eyes and visualize a series of

visualizing
in the public speaking context,
a process of mentally seeing
oneself give a successful speech.

positive feelings and reactions that will occur on the day of the speech. Studies have shown that such **visualizing** is a highly effective technique for building confidence.

Practicing the mental exercise of seeing yourself give a successful speech will help you prepare with confidence and strengthen your positive attitudes and expectations for speechmaking. Close your eyes and allow your body to get comfortable in the chair in which you are sitting. Move around until you feel that you are in a position that will continue to be relaxing for you for the next ten to fifteen minutes. Take a deep, comfortable breath and hold it...now slowly release it through your nose. Now take another deep breath and make certain that you are breathing from the diaphragm...hold it...now slowly release it and note how you feel while doing this. Now one more deep breath...hold it...and release it slowly...and begin your normal breathing pattern. Shift around if you need to get comfortable again.

Now begin to visualize the beginning of a day in which you are going to give an informative speech. See yourself getting up in the morning, full of energy, full of confidence, looking forward to the day's challenges. You are putting on just the right clothes for the task at hand that day. Dressing well makes you look and feel good about yourself, so you have on just what you want to wear, which clearly expresses your sense of inner well-being. As you are driving, riding, or walking to the speech setting, note how clear and confident you feel, and how others around you, as you arrive, comment positively regarding your fine appearance and general demeanor. You feel thoroughly prepared for the target issue you will be presenting today.

Now you see yourself standing or sitting in the room where you will present your speech, talking very comfortably and confidently with others in the room. The people to whom you will be presenting your speech appear to be quite friendly, and are very cordial in their greetings and conversations prior to the presentation. You feel absolutely sure of your material and of your ability to present the information in a forceful, convincing, positive manner.

Now you see yourself approaching the area from which you will present. You are feeling very good about this presentation and see yourself move eagerly forward. All of your audiovisual materials are well organized, well planned, and clearly aid your presentation.[9]

Use Relaxation Techniques

Relaxation techniques are to public speaking anxiety what warmups are to exercise. Just as you'd warm up before taking a lengthy jog, you should practice relaxation techniques before—and even during—your speech. The goal is to feel a sense of control over the physical reactions you're experiencing, keeping in mind that physical changes are normal. According to public speaking experts Laurie Schloff and Marcia Yudkin,[10] the following techniques will lessen anxiety:

Stress-Control Breathing. When you feel stressed, the center of your breathing tends to move from the abdomen to the upper chest, leaving you with a reduced supply of air. The chest and shoulders rise, and you feel out of breath. With **stress-control breathing**, you will feel more movement on the stomach than on the chest. Try stress-control breathing in two stages:

STAGE ONE. Inhale air and let your abdomen go out. Exhale air and let your abdomen go in. Do this for a while until you get into the rhythm of it.

STAGE TWO. As you inhale, use a soothing word such as *calm* or *relax* or a personal mantra, as follows: "Inhale *calm*, abdomen out, exhale *calm*, abdomen in." Go slowly. Each inhalation and exhalation of stress-control breathing takes about three to five seconds.

Don't wait until the last minute to start practicing stress-control breathing. Start several days before you're scheduled to speak. Then, once the speaking event arrives, begin stress-control breathing while awaiting your turn at the podium (you can even unobtrusively put your hand on your abdomen to check how you're doing). After you've been called to the podium, you can focus on breathing once more while you're arranging your notes and getting ready to begin.

The Wave. Under stress, breathing and voice can get uncoordinated. Unless you coordinate beginning to exhale and beginning to speak, you'll have trouble getting the words out and your nervousness will compound. Fortunately, it's not difficult to get your voice and breathing into harmony. Here's how.

Picture a wave, with the rise from the trough representing inhalation and the fall from the crest representing exhalation (see Figure 2.2). You want to start speaking at the crest of the wave, when the maximum amount of air is in your lungs, so you don't waste breath or run out of air right away. Use the wave technique to begin your speech, and the sound will come out relaxed and rich. Use it in any other tight spots at the beginning of sentences. The beauty of the wave technique is that because you sound relaxed, you'll soon feel calmer mentally as well.

Natural Gestures. Practice some controlled, natural gestures that might be useful in enhancing your speech, such as holding up your index finger when stating your first main point. Think about what you want to say as you do this, instead of thinking about how you look or feel.

Freedom to Walk. You don't have to stand perfectly still behind the podium when you deliver a speech. Walk around as you make some of your points. Movement relieves tension, and it helps to hold the audience's attention.

> **stress-control breathing**
> a form of breathing in which the center of breathing is felt on the stomach rather than on the chest.

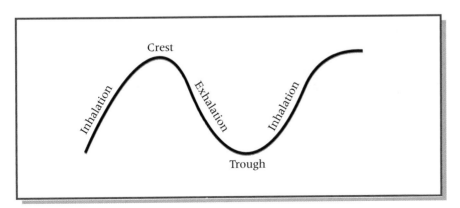

FIGURE 2.2
The Wave Method of Controlled Breathing

Depersonalize the Speech Evaluation

As mentioned, when we sense we are different from others and think we stand out, we feel evaluated. The feeling of evaluation makes us anxious about public speaking. Although no one likes to feel evaluated, it is a necessary part of a speech class; inevitably your speech assignments will be evaluated by the instructors and probably by your classmates as well. Whether the evaluation is formal (i.e., written and graded) or informal, it's easy to take it personally—to feel that whatever is said about your speech performance reflects on the kind of person you are.

But this isn't really the case. First, your instructor and classmates don't know all about *you*; they only know how you've presented a speech. Second, if that speech is planned and delivered well, the listeners will be most aware of your message, not you yourself. That is the way it should be in any good speech. After all, the audience is there to become informed or persuaded or to otherwise learn something new. The audience is there to evaluate the information you've presented. Audience members will be deciding whether the information is "useful" or "not useful," "accurate" or "inaccurate," "persuasive" or "not persuasive," and even "moving" and "powerful" or "flat" and "uninteresting."

Your concern as a speaker should be with the audience's evaluation of your message, not yourself. Thinking in this way helps on two levels. First, it helps lessen your anxiety about presenting the speech. Second, it reminds you of the purpose for making the speech—not you per se, but your message. Remember also to think of your speeches as conversations instead of performances. Seldom do you think of your conversations being evaluated by your conversational partners.

Seek Pleasure in the Occasion

Although no one can be forced to enjoy something, most people ultimately find that giving speeches can indeed be fun. It can also be satisfying

AP/Wide World

With his arms spread wide and his voice rising and falling in rich cadence, Jesse Jackson exudes a sense of empowerment while speaking.

and empowering. After all, it's satisfying and empowering to influence people, and a good speech is a sure way to do that. Imagine how Jesse Jackson feels when he addresses the issue of racism or self-esteem. Imagine his satisfaction in influencing young people to feel good about themselves—and to see it work! Or how baseball great Nolan Ryan must feel when he delivers a motivational talk, and the audience listens raptly as he shares his views. Depending on your goal, public speaking enables you to inform, persuade, entertain, or even console people. In short, it lets you reach out to others.

Preparation and practice, maintaining a positive attitude, managing the inevitable stress of public speaking by making it work for you, and visualizing success—all this makes public speaking both challenging and exciting. Think of it in these terms, and chances are it will come out that way.

Now that you've gained some strategies for building confidence as a speaker, it's time to actually put together and present a speech.

Critical Checkpoint

Gaining Confidence

Consider each strategy for gaining confidence as a speaker:

Prepare and practice

Modify thoughts and attitudes

Visualize success

Use relaxation techniques

Depersonalize speech evaluation

Seek pleasure in the occasion

Evaluate the potential uses of each strategy for yourself. Which ones do you think will be most helpful? Why? Analyze possible barriers that might prohibit you from using these strategies. What can you do to get around those barriers?

GIVING IT A TRY: DOING A FIRST SPEECH IN CLASS

At this point your instructor has probably arranged for you and your classmates to plan and deliver a brief speech, perhaps your first in the class. It should be simple and fun but require you to fulfill each of several steps in speechmaking. It is very important that you try to gauge your anxiety about the speech—from the time the assignment is given, to the few minutes immediately following the speech. Whenever you begin to feel anxious, try some of the strategies for alleviating anxiety that were described previously. Begin by thinking positively!

Critical Checkpoint

Sense Your Level of Confidence

As you read through and implement the steps for developing a first speech, evaluate your level of confidence. If the instructor gives you an actual speech assignment at this time, analyze how it makes you feel. Where do you anticipate having the greatest challenge to your confidence—when the speech is assigned, while you're preparing it, as you are about to give it, or while you are giving it? What can you begin to do now to strengthen your confidence for that most challenging point in the process? Implement that strategy as soon as possible so you'll feel your best about giving the speech.

Select a Topic

The first step in the speechmaking process involves finding something to speak about. Unless the topic is assigned, let your interests—your passions—be your guide. Do you love sports? Is history your hobby? Are there controversies brewing on campus that you might wish to address? Beware, however, that even though personal interest is important (because it ensures that you will bring enthusiasm to the project), it should not be the only criterion for selection. Equally important is to feel confident that your topic will be of interest to the audience. For example, your classmates may be reasonably knowledgeable about football, basketball, and baseball, so it might be more interesting to them if you speak on a less well-known sport in America, such as rugby. Likewise, your classmates might not be terribly excited about yet another talk on American or regional history, but a brief speech on the history of your college or university might enlighten them. Alternatively, most everyone in your class will have an opinion about the most recent campus controversy and will be "all ears" if you can offer a unique solution to the issue. As you can see, selecting a topic involves some knowledge of who the audience is and what their interests are.

Analyze the Audience

Much like the individual people who comprise them, audiences have personalities, interests, and ambitions all their own. These factors affect the audience's receptivity. Thus, it is imperative that you learn as much as you can, given the time and resources available, about the similarities and differences among the members of your audience. Begin with some fairly easily identifiable demographic characteristics—how many are men and how many are women; what racial and ethnic differences are represented in the class; whether there are noticeable age variations within the class; what proportion of the class is from out of state or out of the country. Next, consider how different people (i.e., older and younger, men and women, international and native) might think or feel differently about your topic. For example, if you decide to speak on the controversy of a proposed increase in resident student tuition, your talk will be less interesting to out-of-state and international students than to resident students in the class. Taking these general factors into consideration, how can you know what the audience thinks?

Audience analysis is actually a highly systematic process of getting to know your listeners relative to the topic and the speech occasion. The process involves studying the audience through techniques such as interviews and surveys. Chapter 5 details these and other strategies. However, for this first speech assignment it might suffice to ask three or four classmates a few questions about your topic. For example, what do they already know about it? Does it interest them? What more would they like to know about it? It might surprise you how well a few answers to these questions will help in narrowing your topic and relating it to the audience.

State the Speech Purpose

Once you have a topic in mind, the next step is to decide what you wish to convey about it—and why. As you will learn in Chapter 6, there are three general purposes toward which to direct your speeches—*to inform, to persuade,* or *to entertain.* Regarding the campus controversy topic, for example, you need to decide whether to simply inform your audience about the issue and the positions each side takes, or to persuade the audience to accept one position to the exclusion of other positions, or perhaps even to entertain them by making light of the issue in a creative but judicious way.

Your speech should also have a specific purpose. This is a definite statement of what you expect the speech to accomplish for the audience. For example, if the general purpose of your campus controversy speech is to inform, its specific purpose could be "to identify the three key points on which students and administrators disagree about increasing resident tuition." If the general purpose is to persuade, its specific purpose might be "to convince my listeners that administration has the more sensible position regarding an increase in resident tuition."

Write your specific purpose on a sheet of paper or on a Post-it note placed on the edge of your computer's monitor. It will be an important guide in developing the rest of the speech.

Develop the Main Points

Organize your speech around two to three main points. These are the primary pieces of knowledge (in an informative speech) or the key arguments favoring your position (in a persuasive speech) that you want the audience to understand. If you do a good job of stating the specific purpose of your speech, the main points will be clearly identifiable (if not explicit) in that statement. For example, the statement "to convince my listeners that administration has the more sensible position regarding an increase in resident tuition" points to ideas that can be developed into main points—namely, factors in "the more sensible position." In this hypothetical case, let's say the primary reason for the higher resident tuition is to offset reductions in state appropriations. One main point could be to explain this reason for the proposed plan. Another main point could be to show what students would lose in the way of services or educational quality if the tuition hike were not implemented. As such, your main points build the case for or fulfill your specific purpose.

Think of the main points and specific purpose in this way: The purpose is where you want to go; the main points are "scenic stops" along the way, or "major intersections" that have to be crossed in getting there.

Gather Supporting Materials

Unless your speech is about an extraordinarily compelling personal experience—being held captive by terrorists, for example—plan on researching your topic for supporting materials. For your first, short speech, this research might be as minimal as a few comments other people have made about the topic, editorials in the campus newspaper, statistics gathered from an Internet site, a chalkboard drawing to illustrate what you're saying, a picture or object, or retelling a scene from a movie or novel. As your assignments become more involved, so too will your research. Supporting material is crucial because it lends credibility to your message by signifying that your ideas are consistent with other people's ideas and actual events. Someone once said that everyone has an opinion, but few people have the facts. Those who do are the people we generally want to listen to. Chapter 7 describes the many kinds of supporting material and how to locate them.

Outline the Speech

At first glance, outlining may seem like a tedious exercise. Actually, it is a technique that will make your life easier. Outlining helps you keep track of your thinking and the development of your ideas as the speech takes shape during preparation. In this way it helps you organize the speech—arranging the main ideas and supporting points—in just the sequence and fashion that will make an effective speech presentation. A finished outline is a road map to guide you during the speech—it reminds you where those scenic stops and major intersections are along the journey to fulfilling the speech purpose. Chapter 8 describes outlining in detail.

There are three major parts to every speech: introduction, body, and conclusion. For your first speech, try following the simple outline format below. This format assumes that you have at least two things to say (i.e., two key points) about the topic. You can have more.

Topic:

Introduction. Introductions often set the tone for the entire speech. A good introduction should catch the audience's attention and interest. As described in detail in Chapter 9, some of the many ways speakers do this include making a startling statement, telling a story, or using humor.

Purpose statement. After introducing the topic, tell the audience your specific purpose. This will set them on the journey that is your speech, like the airplane heading from the gate to the runway.

I. *Main point.* A speech's main points are its key ideas. The main points directly support the speech's thesis, or central idea. Chapter 6 describes the thesis in detail. Chapter 8 describes ways of organizing the main points to best support the thesis.

   A. *Supporting material.* Supporting material illustrates the main points by clarifying, elaborating, and verifying the speaker's ideas. Supporting materials include the entire world of information available to you—from stories to statistics. Chapter 7 is devoted exclusively to locating supporting material.

   B. *Supporting material.* Main points are always supported by two or more pieces of supporting material. The second or subsequent piece of support material will extend or complement the support provided by the material preceding it.

II. *Main point*

   A. *Supporting material* (e.g., cite some facts from a recent study)

   B. *Supporting material* (e.g., cite a real-life example to illustrate a fact)

Conclusion. The conclusion restates the purpose and notes how the main points confirm it. Chapter 9 explains how to construct effective conclusions.

Finally, always remember to thank the audience for their attention and wish them well. After all, they have just given you some of their valuable time and focused attention.

Here is a sample outline following the format just described. It is in the form of a *phrase outline* (see Chapter 8 for distinctions among sentence, phrase, and keyword outlines).

Topic: The Evolution of Public Speaking

Introduction
    1. Question: Which is the oldest educational discipline?
    2. Answer: Perhaps public speaking
    3. Four periods of evolution in the discipline
    4. Purpose: To inform audience how the subject of this course has evolved over 2,000 years
    I. The Classical Period
      A. Sophistry emphasized persuasion by any means
      B. Aristotle emphasized sound reasoning
    II. The Christian Period
      A. Augustine applied rhetoric to Christian teaching
      B. Rhetoric became a key feature in education of clergy and aristocracy
    III. The Renaissance
      A. Writing became the focus of rhetoric
      B. Public speaking lost its prominence in education
    IV. The Modern Period
      A. Public speaking regained prominence in the New World
      B. Emerged as its own discipline in the late nineteenth century

Conclusion
    1. Aim has been to show four periods in the evolution of public speaking as a discipline
    2. As possibly the oldest discipline, it is one of most well established
    3. Thank you

Practice Delivering the Speech

The success of even your first speech in class depends on how well prepared and practiced you are. So practice your speech. It has been suggested that a good speech is practiced at least six times. For a two- or three-minute speech, that's only fifteen to twenty minutes (figuring in restarts and pauses) of actual practice time. Make one of them using a tape recorder (see Focus on Technology box in this chapter). After several practice runs, you're ready for the task. Get motivated, be excited about it, and have fun with it. And remember, as longtime women's rights activist Gloria Steinem (who has battled a lifelong fear of audiences) noted in her recently published memoirs, "There is no right way to speak, only your way; you don't die; and it's worth it."[11]

Consider the following speech by Mark Twain. Would you have thought that he frequently experienced stage fright? How does the experience he speaks of compare to your own experience and expectations?

> My heart goes out in sympathy to anyone who is making his first appearance before an audience of human beings....
>   I recall the occasion of my first appearance. San Francisco knew me then only as a reporter, and I was to make my bow to San Francisco as a lecturer. I knew that nothing short of compulsion would

get me to the theater. So I bound myself by a hard-and-fast contract so that I could not escape. I got to the theater 45 minutes before the hour set for the lecture. My knees were shaking so that I didn't know whether I could stand up. If there is an awful, horrible malady in the world, it is stage fright....

It was dark and lonely behind the scenes in that theater, and I peeked through the little peek holes they have in theater curtains and looked into the big auditorium. That was dark and empty, too. By and by it lighted up, and the audience began to arrive.

I had got a number of friends of mine, stalwart men, to sprinkle themselves through the audience armed with big clubs. Every time I said anything they could possibly guess I intended to be funny, they were to pound those clubs on the floor. Then there was a kind lady in a box up there, also a good friend of mine, the wife of the governor. She was to watch me intently, and whenever I glanced toward her she was going to deliver a gubernatorial laugh that would lead the whole audience into applause.

At last I began. I had the manuscript tucked under a United States flag in front of me where I could get at it in case of need. But I managed to get started without it. I walked up and down—I was young in those days and needed the exercise—and talked and talked.

Right in the middle of the speech I placed a gem. I had put in a moving, pathetic part which was to get at the hearts and souls of my hearers. When I delivered it, they did just what I hoped and expected. They sat silent and awed. I had touched them. Then I happened to glance up at the box where the governor's wife was—you know what happened.

Well, after the first agonizing five minutes, my stage fright left me, never to return. I know if I was going to be hanged I could get up and make a good showing, and I intend to. But I shall never forget my feelings before the agony left me.[12]

SUMMARY QUESTIONS

What is public speaking anxiety? What are some of the common fears associated with it?

Public speaking anxiety (PSA) is the fear or dread of giving a speech in front of an audience. Researchers have identified several factors that cause people to feel anxious about public speaking. These include lack of experience, feeling different from members of the audience, and uneasiness about being the center of attention. Understanding these fears is the first step in overcoming them. Public speaking anxiety is experienced by most people in any of three forms. One is context-based anxiety, which is fear of the very act of giving a speech regardless of the audience or occasion. Another is audience-based anxiety, which is felt when a particular group or individual in an audience is perceived to be threatening to the speaker in an evaluative way. The third is situational anxiety, which is associated with the specific features of a particular speech event—the occasion, the topic, the location, and so on.

When can PSA occur in the speechmaking process?

PSA can occur at different times during the speechmaking process. For some people it occurs immediately on learning that they will give a speech sometime in the future (pre-preparation anxiety). For others it sets in as they begin to prepare for the speech (preparation anxiety). Some people become anxious once they start rehearsing the speech (pre-performance anxiety); others only get the jitters once they actually reach the podium (performance anxiety).

What are some consequences of public speaking anxiety?

Public speaking anxiety can affect the speaker in at least three ways: (1) it can inhibit planning and motivation; (2) it can cause the speaker to want to avoid the speechmaking process entirely, including preparation; and (3) it can result in an unsuccessful presentation.

What strategies does this chapter offer for gaining confidence as a public speaker?

Gaining confidence as a public speaker comes about primarily through preparation and practice. Helpful techniques for boosting confidence include: (1) modifying thoughts and attitudes, (2) visualizing success, (3) using relaxation techniques, (4) depersonalizing the speech evaluation, and (5) seeking pleasure in the occasion.

Briefly describe the steps in putting together a speech.

The steps involved in preparing a speech include: (1) analyzing the audience, (2) selecting a topic, (3) stating the speech purpose, (4) developing the main points, (5) gathering supporting materials, (6) outlining the speech, and (7) rehearsing the speech. The rest of this book describes the process in more detail.

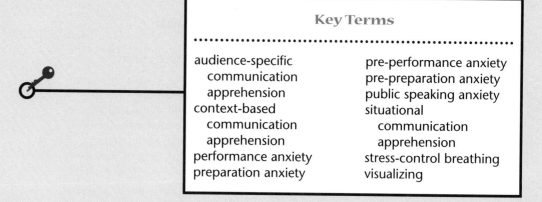

Key Terms

audience-specific communication apprehension

context-based communication apprehension

performance anxiety

preparation anxiety

pre-performance anxiety

pre-preparation anxiety

public speaking anxiety

situational communication apprehension

stress-control breathing

visualizing

ISSUES FOR DISCUSSION

1. Why is public speaking such a source of anxiety for most people?

2. It has been said that practice makes perfect. How can this adage be applied to gaining confidence as a public speaker?

3. In your own experience, which strategies for gaining confidence as a speaker do you find to be the most helpful? Why?

4. Assume one of your friends who has not had a course like this one tells you that she is expected to give a presentation in one of her major classes, and that she's "scared to death" about it. What will you tell her?

5. How can following the general procedures for planning a speech help a speaker to become more confident?

SELF-ASSESSMENT

1. List five experiences that give you the most anxiety. State how your anxiety associated with these experiences compares to your felt level of public speaking anxiety.

2. Describe some occasions when you have felt especially confident. What was it about yourself, the situation, the tasks involved, and other people involved that promoted your confidence?

3. Mark an X on the continuum below to indicate your current level of public speaking anxiety. Next, mark an X in the position on the continuum where you would be satisfied with your level of public speaking anxiety. Circle this second X. Now state some strategies for helping yourself reach the satisfactory point.

virtually no anxiety		high anxiety

TEAMWORK

1. It is common for speakers to feel more nervous than they appear. See if this observation holds true for you and your classmates. Make a pact with two or three classmates to observe apparent indications of nervousness in each of your speeches (jittery movement, shaky voices, blocked thoughts, etc.). After each speech, discuss with each other how nervous you felt in comparison to what was observed. Share stories about each speech experience, starting with how you felt on hearing about the assignment and ending with the feeling you had once it was all over. Talk to each other about which strategies for gaining confidence seemed to work best for you.

It is the
province of
knowledge to
speak, and it is
the privilege
of wisdom to
listen.
—Oliver
Wendell
Holmes

You earn the right to speak by listening.
—Millie Stamm

Listeners and Speakers

3

Think back to the last time you listened to a speech. **Were you able to stay focused on everything the speaker said?** If you're like most people, you are able to pay attention to speeches on interesting topics. Even humorous or inspirational speeches can command attention regardless of the topic. However, many speeches and conversations offer neither of these qualities. **Most of us find it a chore to stay focused on a message that is boring or remain interested in a speaker who is tiresome.** A great deal of information that we need to know is not presented in an entertaining way, so we need to develop listening skills that work in any situation. **The key is to find ways to listen even when our inclination is to focus our attention elsewhere.**

Jerry Mendoza was preoccupied as he walked into his public speaking class. He had a biology project due in two weeks and hadn't started it yet. Today, he needed time to think of a good project, because the instructor would ask for his topic later in the morning during biology lab. Jerry really needed a good grade on the project because he was only pulling a low "C" average in that class. Fortunately, five of his classmates were giving presentations in speech class today. He could spend the entire class period coming up with a biology project.

Later, although he had spent the whole time thinking, he found himself walking out of speech class still without a topic. As he headed into biology lab, Brenda, a classmate of Jerry's in both biology and speech, asked him if he had gotten some good ideas from the speeches today. Although she had been working on a biology topic for two weeks, she thought that three of the public speaking topics from today would be really great for the biology project—environmental ecology, the greenhouse effect, and mutant insects. Jerry was puzzled and annoyed because he couldn't recall anything that had been said in speech class—what a lost opportunity! However, his feelings sank toward nausea as the biology instructor called on him to inform the class about his project topic.

Listening. It seems so, well, lightweight. With all the difficult subjects in the world to master—and only four (expensive) college years in which to do it—why spend precious time on the obvious? After all, isn't listening, at least for people blessed with hearing, second nature?

We wish we could say yes—that everyone who can hear naturally listens well. However, the high human toll exacted by poor listening indicates otherwise. Listening errors cost businesses untold profits in the form of wasted labor, forfeited goodwill, and lost customers.[1] Doctors who are unskilled in listening sometimes misdiagnose patients; patients sometimes fail to follow their doctors' directions. Poor listening habits cost students crucial knowledge, and they cost workers needed promotions. Daydreaming and poor concentration—two key obstacles to effective listening—put people at risk for mishaps and accidents ranging from fires to car crashes.

Consider the fatal mistake made in 1977 that caused a runway collision at Tenerife Airport in the Canary Islands and resulted in deaths of 583 people. Poor listening and misunderstood instructions by pilots and air traffic controllers brought about the tragedy. Consider the example of a large Chicago advertising agency that lost a key client because one of its top executives "dozed off in the front row while colleagues were making a presentation to a prospective client."[2] According to Lyman Steil, president of a

St. Paul, Minnesota, consulting firm that specializes in listening, "If every worker in America makes one $10 mistake a year because of poor listening, 'that adds up to more than a billion dollars a year.'"[3]

These examples indicate why good listening is such a highly valued skill. Top business, academic, and professional people claim that the ability to listen critically is among the most important skills they look for in new hires. Indeed, the art of listening is among the most important of these leaders' own skills and goes a long way toward explaining how they rose to the top in the first place. Even in positions of leadership, listening remains a crucial skill. Effective leaders must coordinate resources, react to changing situations, and respond to the needs of subordinates. Accomplishing this requires effective listening skills.

Chapter Challenges

Competent listeners—people who are conscious of the pitfalls of poor listening as well as the rewards of effective listening—tend to be efficient and successful. Studies indicate that they are perceived as alert, confident, mature, and judicious. They're also some of the most enjoyable people to be around. Competent listeners face numerous challenges, and in this chapter you will learn the most important ones:

- Understanding that listening is a complex behavior that requires a dynamic relationship between speaker and listener.
- Becoming an active listener by overcoming obstacles to effective listening.
- Using critical thinking to listen more competently.
- Learning to critically evaluate speeches in an honest but judicious manner.

LISTENING: A COMPLEX HUMAN BEHAVIOR

Listening is not a passive activity that simply "happens"; rather, it is a complex behavior that can be learned and relearned. In contrast to **hearing**, which is the physiological process of perceiving sound, listening is a selective and discriminating act. Specifically, **listening** is the process of recognizing, understanding, and accurately interpreting the messages communicated by others.

Depending on the circumstance, people vary in the way they listen. In fact, we listen according to our needs. As seen in Table 3.1, in some situations we listen primarily for information and understanding—to learn more about a topic or for instructions and directions (*comprehensive listening*). Sometimes we listen in order to evaluate and judge information (*critical listening*). At other times we listen for emotional reasons—for example, to comfort and support (*empathic listening*). And, of course, there are times when we listen for the sheer pleasure of it—as when we enjoy music, poetry, narration, comedy routines, plays, movies, or TV shows (*appreciative listening*). As a student—and perhaps as an employee or businessperson—much of your time is dedicated to attending lectures or formal presentations. As such, you rely heavily on comprehensive and critical listening skills.

hearing
the physiological process of perceiving sound.

listening
the process of recognizing, understanding, and accurately interpreting the messages communicated by others.

Table 3.1   Functions of Listening

Listening Function	Description of Skills	Strategies for Improvement
Comprehensive	Listening to understand, learn, and recognize.	Listen for main idea; listen for details; listen for organizational pattern; take speaker's perspective; use memory effectively.
Critical	Listening to judge, analyze, and evaluate.	Determine speaker's goal; evaluate source of the message; question logic, reasoning, and evidence of the message.
Empathic	Listening to provide therapy, comfort, and sympathy.	Focus attention on speaker's perspective and goal; give supportive and understanding feedback; show caring; demonstrate patience; avoid judgment.
Appreciative	Listening for pleasure and enjoyment.	Remove physical and time distractions; know more about the source (e.g., artist, composer); explore new appreciative listening opportunities.

SOURCE: *Adapted from Andrew Wolvin and Carol Coakley,* Listening, *4th ed. (Dubuque, IA: W. C. Brown, 1992).*

In one form or another, listening is probably the activity people do the most. For, example, research studies report that high school and college students spend between 42 and 54 percent of their waking hours doing nothing but listening—to teachers, friends, and family members, or to various forms of media such as radio and television.

As a student in a public speaking class, you wear two hats: those of speaker and listener. Listening to your classmates' speeches offers you the opportunity to learn not only about their topics but also about successful and not-so-successful ways of making your own presentations. The more skilled you are at listening to others' speeches, the more you will learn about what will and won't work for your own speech.

In this chapter you'll learn how to build more effective listening skills and to apply them to becoming a better public speaker. It turns out that in addition to being successful in their careers and popular among their friends, many good listeners excel at public speaking.

Listeners and Speakers: A Dynamic Relationship

Listeners and speakers are interdependent: Listeners need someone to whom they will listen, and speakers need someone to whom they will address their remarks. There is a constant interplay. Indeed, a listener who ignores a speaker is by definition no longer a listener. Likewise, a speaker who ignores an audience's reaction cannot be said to be truly communicating.[4]

During a classroom speech on cultural differences in humor, Jesse Ryan noticed that his opening joke—which he thought was hilarious—drew a resounding silence. Expecting hearty laughter, he heard instead a few polite twitters. Jesse quickly acknowledged to his audience that he apparently had a different sense of humor than they did—and that differences in what people find funny was in fact part of the point he would explore in his speech. Noting that Jesse was able to adjust himself to their reaction, the audience breathed a collective sigh of relief. In fact, Jesse had not planned on making that point, but he knew enough about his topic to think quickly on his feet.

Jesse's experience illustrates the constant feedback, or **circular response**, that exists between listeners and speakers. In this process, speakers continually adjust their remarks according to their listeners' reactions, and vice versa. If an audience seems fidgety, for example, a speaker might decide to get to the point more quickly. If, on the other hand, the audience appears relaxed and appreciative, the speaker might decide to expand on that same point.

The circular response points to an important fact about listeners: They have power to help *or* hinder the speaker in delivering his or her message. For instance, what if someone in the audience had heckled Jesse? After all, rudeness on the part of listeners can and does occur. Rather than moving along with his speech, Jesse might have become so upset that he would have lost his train of thought and bungled the rest of his presentation.

Listening Is Selective

Can you recall sharing reactions with a friend about a lecture, movie, or other event and noticing that even though you both attended the same event, you formed quite different impressions? In any given situation, no two listeners process the information in exactly the same way. The explanation lies in **selective perception**; that is, people pay attention selec-

circular response
a process of constant feedback in which speakers continually adjust their remarks based on their listeners' reactions, and vice versa.

selective perception
the process by which people pay attention to certain messages and ignore others.

Focus on Ethics

The Responsibilities of Listening

Beyond short-circuiting communication, rude listening behaviors such as heckling, name calling, and other irritations can sometimes lead to explosive results—for example, from clashes among animal rights activists and their opponents, to eruptions at political rallies.

Controversies over sensitive issues such as school prayer, sex education, and test scores have led to shouting matches and physical altercations at school board meetings across the nation. In Hartford, Connecticut, in 1996 an audience member ran up to the table where the board members sat, grabbed a pitcher of ice water, and threw it in a board member's face. He hadn't liked the board

member's proposal. The police escorted the visibly shaken board member out of the room. The meeting was called off, some board members considered resigning, and many in the audience feared returning to another meeting.

When listeners react rudely to information they don't like—or, worse, when they resort to physical violence—the very foundation of a democratic society is undermined. The rule of law and reason is replaced by threats and intimidation. In such an atmosphere, the back-and-forth of constructive social dialogue becomes impossible to achieve. Clearly, the power to listen can translate into being socially responsible or socially destructive.

tively to certain messages and ignore others. Several factors influence what we listen to and what we ignore.

People Pay Attention to Information They Hold to Be Important. As any successful public speaker knows, people are most motivated to listen if they think that what is being said will be of consequence to them. This is why audience analysis is so crucial to the speechmaking process. (Audience analysis is discussed in Chapter 5.) People look for information that reflects their own interests, needs, values, attitudes, and beliefs. Speakers who don't take these factors into account often find that no one is listening.

David Wells/Image Works

Listeners pay attention when the subject matter is important to them. Capture listeners' interest and their attention will follow.

People Pay Attention to Information That Touches Their Experience and Background. If we listen to something that is totally foreign to us, chances are we'll just "zone out." To catch and sustain listeners' attention, a speaker must in some way touch on their experience and background. This does *not* mean that no one actually listens to new information, of course. People are receptive to new information as long as it appears to have at least some personal relevance to them. Generally speaking, what's relevant to us is a product of our experience and background. For example, if we've never heard of Santeria, we're unlikely to want to hear about it. But if we're told that Santeria is a religion, and that the speaker will address the common links between it and our own religion, we may be more disposed to pay attention.

This brings up a related point about how listening is selective: Unless we can find a connection between new information and what we already know, we aren't likely to listen for long.

People Sort and Filter New Information on the Basis of What They Already Know. According to learning theory, all new concepts are understood as analogies to previous concepts.[5] This means that as listeners we try to understand new information by comparing it to what we already know. An audience who listens to a speech about an exotic destination will "fill in the blanks" of their imaginations with familiar places. An introductory psychology student whose professor lectures on an unfamiliar concept will try to relate that concept to something familiar. Because each person's knowledge base and life experience are unique, no two people interpret a message—or "fill in the blanks"—in exactly the same way. This leaves the door open for misunderstandings, or a **message-perception gap**. One listener may compare a speaker's descriptions of the Bahamas with Florida; another, with Mexico. Unless the speaker "paints" a clearer picture, he or she will fail in the speech goal.

> **message-perception gap**
>
> misunderstandings that arise between a speaker and listener because each person's knowledge base and life experience are unique and no two people interpret a message in exactly the same way.

For a message to be successful, there must be shared understanding. As a speaker, your challenge is to clarify your message through the skillful application of language, audiovisual aids, and other tools of the speechmaking process. Vivid metaphors and similes can create powerful mental images that help listeners "decode" a message (see Chapter 10). Audiovisual aids add images and sound to the mix (see Chapter 12). These tools help speaker and listener move toward a common understanding of the message.

As a listener, your role in bridging the message-perception gap is to actively attend to the speaker's verbal and nonverbal cues, or hints to meaning. It is also important to consciously resist using previous experiences as "filters" with which to block out information that doesn't conform to what you already know or believe. One writer has called this tendency "listening to echoes"[6]—echoes of our own point of view. Open-mindedness is a hallmark of a good listener.

ACTIVE LISTENING: OVERCOMING OBSTACLES

Active listening is focused, purposeful listening. It is a multi-step process of gathering and evaluating information. Before reviewing these steps, however, let's consider the chief barriers to active listening. Active listening isn't possible unless certain poor listening habits are recognized and eliminated.

Barriers to Active Listening

It's not hard to find things that keep us from listening well; just about anything will do the trick. One study of college students' listening habits found that inattentiveness and distractions, script writing and defensive listening, and laziness and overconfidence ranked highest among their poor listening habits.[7] Cultural barriers are other obstacles to active listening.

Inattentiveness and Distractions. A *distraction* is anything that competes for attention that you are trying to give to something else. You may have every intention of listening to a classmate's presentation, but instead you find yourself thinking about an upcoming exam. Or perhaps you're hungry, or tired, or angry at your girlfriend or boyfriend or spousal. Distractions can originate outside of us (in the environment) or within us (in our thoughts and feelings).

EXTERNAL DISTRACTIONS. Virtually anything in the environment—noise, movement, light, darkness, heat, or cold—can distract from listening. Noise can include anything from the din of jackhammers and automobile traffic, to competing conversations and slamming doors. Visual distractions can range from poor lighting to people walking into or out of a meeting room once the session is under way. Poorly ventilated and excessively warm or cold rooms can preoccupy listeners to the extent that they do not listen well.

One way to minimize external distractions is to anticipate and plan for them—even minutes before a presentation is to begin. As you enter the lecture hall or other speech site, consider the listening environment. Classrooms vary in acoustics, and some auditoriums have poor audio systems. How much difficulty will you have in actually hearing the speaker? How can you ensure that you won't miss important nonverbal cues? Gestures, facial expressions, visual aids, or other objects that help comprehension must be readily visible in order for you to take full advantage of the entire message.

active listening
focused, purposeful listening that involves a multi-step process of gathering and evaluating information.

Interview

Listening: A Real World Perspective

Carol Cornwell is a training manager for the Technical Support Center at Software Spectrum, Inc. in Dallas, Texas. She is also a Microsoft Certified Systems Engineer (MCSE) and Microsoft Certified Trainer (MCT)—buzzwords in the computer industry right now. She is putting together the training program for over 300 employees within this department, and is administering a certification program for select individuals who want to become MCSEs and advance in their careers with SSI. She has extensive speaking and presentational experience and has attended numerous workshops and seminars on listening.

How important is listening in the professional world?

Extremely important. It is the one skill that every professional must develop to succeed in his or her career. Listening effectively to customers, co-workers, and other professionals requires that you get a full understanding of their goals and needs as they speak to you.

What kind of listening do you do in your job?

I listen for understanding, and I also listen for feelings. Knowing where a person is coming from emotionally is very revealing. I also listen critically so that I can analyze the motives of speakers.

What are some of the keys for effectively listening to public speeches?

I first listen for the main idea to get an understanding of the purpose of the speech. I also strive to recognize which "filters" I am using to listen to the speech. Filters are those memory devices that cause us to listen with our past. The filters cause us to form expectations, based on past experiences, that may inhibit our listening effectiveness. We have to remove these filters so that we are listening with a fresh slate, giving the speaker a chance to present his or her ideas without our own expectations getting in the way.

What advice do you have for students in public speaking classes?

The most successful way for people to listen more effectively to each other is to "enroll" them. We do this by enhancing our relationships with them by sharing personal characteristics of ourselves. We also enroll them by using audience knowledge to incorporate things into our speeches that they are interested in. If they feel they can personally benefit from what we have to say, they tend to listen more closely. How do we know what interests them? We listen to them—to their conversations, their speeches, their body language. Effective listening is listening with an open mind and looking for information that can be used to benefit both us and those that we want to influence.

To minimize some of the more common external distractions, try following these practical tips:

- If you have trouble seeing or hearing at a distance, go early and sit in the front.
- If you know the room will be cold, dress appropriately.
- If the auditorium will be crowded and you are claustrophobic, go early and sit on the aisle.

- If you are going to a group meeting and you have trouble hearing when others are talking at the same time, sit next to the leader so that most of the messages will be communicated toward your side of the room.

INTERNAL DISTRACTIONS. Whether you suffer from anxiety over deadlines, the urge to daydream, emotional turmoil, or fatigue or illness, it can be difficult to manage the internal distractions of thoughts and feelings.

Daydreaming is a very common internal distraction. Although daydreams have their place (preferably at home in a comfortable chair or in bed), unless you're prepared to miss out on a lot of useful information they are best avoided during presentations. Recognize that those dreams will still be there after you have finished listening. Put them off until an appropriate time, and reward your good listening behavior later with a wonderful daydream.

Alex Quesada/Matrix International

Fidel Castro's yawn is a classic demonstration of how internal distractions affect listeners.

Strong emotions such as anger and joy can all but cripple the ability to listen effectively. Distracting strong emotions are best dealt with before entering the listening environment. If an argument is preoccupying your thoughts, try to settle the issue before attending a presentation or going into an important meeting with other people. Otherwise you will have to redouble your efforts to concentrate on listening. Just as athletes consciously channel their excess emotional energy into focusing on the game, you should channel yours to truly listen. Resolve that you'll come back to your problems after the presentation is over. For now, your task is to concentrate.

Readiness and the ability to listen are affected not just by mental and emotional processes but by physiological ones, as well. Fatigue and illness are powerful barriers to effective listening. Studies confirm that fatigue substantially reduces the ability to accurately perceive information, be it signs on a highway or a speaker's words. Just as speakers are advised to be well rested before they make their presentations, listeners should prepare themselves in a similar way.

Script Writing and Defensive Listening. Rather than focusing on the speaker, people who are "scriptwriters" are usually preoccupied with thinking about what they themselves will say next.[8] Because script writing is often motivated by feelings of defensiveness, it's generally referred to as defensive listening. **Defensive listening** usually occurs when we sense that our attitudes or opinions are being challenged. For example, a speaker might present information that threatens to alter our mindset, and we react by feeling criticized or in some way threatened. In this situation defensive listeners decide either that they won't like what the speaker is going to say, or that they know better. Sometimes defensive listening occurs when we feel passionately about the speaker's topic, and want to show off what we know. In any case, script writing—whether or not it's motivated by defensiveness—precludes you from knowing what's actually been said. As such, you can't even engage in an intelligent debate.

defensive listening
"closed" listening in which the listener blocks out certain messages that may challenge his or her attitudes or opinions.

When you find yourself script writing or listening with a defensive posture, try waiting for the speaker to finish before devising your own arguments. Hear the speaker out. That way, your arguments will be based on the facts as the speaker actually presented them. Focus on the speaker's motives behind the remarks that pique you. You may disagree with the speaker, but you'll do so from a position of actually having heard what he or she has said. Effective listening precedes effective rebuttal.[9]

Laziness and Overconfidence. Sometimes we think we already know, or don't need to know, the speaker's message. Closely related to defensiveness, laziness and overconfidence manifest themselves in several ways: We either expect too little from speakers, ignore important information, or display an arrogant attitude. Later we discover that we missed important information. We might flunk a quiz, miss an important assignment, or fail to register for a course on time.

Several things can help if you're dogged by the poor listening habits of laziness and overconfidence. First, never assume that you already know what a speaker will say. You'll very seldom be right. Second, remind yourself that it's better to be safe than sorry. Third, remember the value of modesty. Rarely do we know as much as we think we do.

Critical Checkpoint

....

Overcoming Obstacles to Active Listening

Which obstacles to effective listening are you most aware of in yourself? The internal distractions of strong emotions? Daydreaming? Script writing, or defensive listening? Laziness and overconfidence? Noise? External distractions? What steps can you take to overcome these poor listening habits?

Cultural Barriers. Cultural barriers include differences in dialects or accents, nonverbal cues, word choice, and physical appearance. Any or all can impede listening—if we permit it. When English is the listener's second language, it takes time to learn the intricacies of both spoken and nonverbal communication. Native language speakers also sometimes have trouble understanding the dialects, accents, or terms unique to certain regions of the United States. For instance, some residents of Charleston, South Carolina, sprinkle their talk with a word that sounds like *Canechew* (pronounced "Cane Shoe"). *Canechew* means "Can't you?" or "Are you not able?" In the southern United States, many people use the term *fixin'* to mean "I am about to…" ("I'm fixin' to work on my speech"). Even U.S. presidents have been known to sling an unintelligible phrase or two. In response to a Republican budget proposal, President Clinton

Public Speaking in Cultural Perspective

Shared Understanding

In any communication encounter, the responsibility for arriving at shared understanding lies with both speaker and listener. Regardless of background, a speaker should learn the most effective ways of communicating with or adapting to the audience. At the same time, listeners should be wary of judging a speaker on the basis of his or her accent, appearance, or demeanor rather than on what is actually being said. This not only confuses *content* with *delivery*, but betrays an *ethnocentric bias*, or the expectation that everyone should look and sound just like oneself. As a listener, be sensitive to cues about a speaker's background. When possible, reveal your needs to the speaker. Gain clarification. Ask questions. Turn confusion into curiosity and an opportunity to learn about other people's experience.

once replied in Arkansas "backwoods-speak." "It is their dog," Clinton said. "And it was a mangy old dog, and that's why I vetoed that dog."[10]

Nonverbal cues such as gestures can also confuse a listener. Most gestures are culture-specific rather than universal. A "thumbs up" gesture in the United States usually means "Good job" or "Things are going fine." In Australia and Nigeria, the same gesture is considered rude and insulting. In the United States, students of public speaking are counseled to maintain eye contact when they speak. In some Eastern cultures, direct eye contact is considered disrespectful or even intolerable. And in Korea, lowering of the eyes signals rejection.

Becoming an Active Listener

Active listeners use their eyes as well as their ears to decode the speaker's nonverbal as well as verbal cues. They listen for the speaker's main points and critically evaluate evidence used to support claims. They know how to use memory effectively. Active listeners:

- *Set listening goals.* They know why they—and the speaker—are there.
- *Focus their listening efforts.* Active listeners concentrate.
- *Listen for the speaker's thesis, or main point.*
- *Watch for the speaker's nonverbal cues.*
- *Evaluate the speaker's evidence.*

Set Listening Goals. Setting listening goals helps you prepare to get the most from a listening situation. Why are you listening? What do you need and expect from the listening situation? Keep these goals in mind as you listen. Before you enter a listening situation, you may wish to write down your goals. Before a classmate's speech, for instance, you might write, "I need to listen for the main points. I must also pay special attention to how Suzanne uses nonverbal gestures so that I can hand in a written evaluation of her efforts on this score."

Try to state your listening goals in a way that encourages action. For example, you might make a goal statement like this: "I will use the steps listed in this chapter to identify Suzanne's main points." Be sure to monitor and evaluate your progress, both while you're listening and after the speech is over. Review your notes before the speaker leaves to ensure that you haven't missed important information. Later, using the active listening steps outlined in the chapter, assess how well you were able to accomplish each step. Table 3.2 illustrates the steps in setting listening goals.

Focus Efforts. Active listening requires physical, mental, and emotional energy. It demands concentration. Being well rested and organized helps you listen more skillfully. Minimizing internal and external distractions helps you concentrate on the message. As you can see, the surest way to focus your efforts is by actively resisting these and other poor listening habits described earlier in this chapter.

Listen for Main Ideas. No one has perfect retention. To ensure that you hear and retain the speakers most important points, it's helpful to specifically listen for the main ideas. Here are some strategies that can help you pull out the main point from a message:

- *Notice the speaker's organizational pattern.* Most speakers use one of three or four organizational patterns (for more details, see Chapter 8).

Table 3.2 Steps in Setting Listening Goals

Identify Need: "I have to know Suzanne's speech thesis, purpose, main points, and type of organization in order to complete and hand in a written evaluation."

Indicate Performance Standard: "I will make a better grade on the evaluation if I am able to identify and evaluate the major components of Suzanne's speech."

Make Action Statement (goal): "I will minimize distractions and practice the active listening steps during Suzanne's speech. I will take careful notes during her speech and ask questions about anything I do not understand."

Assess Goal Achievement: "Before I leave the classroom, I will review my notes carefully and see if I covered everything."

Knowing the sequence and structure of a speech makes it easy for you to understand and remember the content. This helps you to anticipate and then confirm main elements of the speech.

- *Notice introductions, conclusions, and transitions that signal the main points.* Most speakers introduce the main points in their introductory remarks. This gives the listener a chance to identify them and wait for their discussion later ("I have three points I want to make tonight. First,..."). Transitions can also alert the listener that a main point is about to be discussed ("My next major point is,..."). Conclusions are a valuable place to summarize the main points ("Let me recap those three rules for living overseas. One, ...").

- *Listen for verbal identifiers or phrases that give clues to the main points.* This refers to clues beyond those given in introductions, transitions, and conclusions. Speakers often use many of the following verbal identifiers: "One, two, three..."; "First, second, third,..."; "Most important,..."; "Another point (issue) I would raise..."; "Furthermore,..."; "In the next section, I would like to..."; "Next,..." When you hear any of these identifiers, make a mental note that it is likely to preview a main idea.

- *Watch for a more direct eye gaze.* Speakers are more likely to look directly at the audience when they are trying to make an important point. In addition, speakers often shift their gaze to a different part of the audience when moving from one main point to another.

- *Take notes about the speaker's main points.* Making notes of the speaker's main points is an excellent way to retain the gist of the speech. It serves as a memory aid. However, do not write down everything that is said. It is better to pay attention to the speech and note the main points with a few supporting details. Several methods of note taking are possible when listening to speeches. The bullet, column, and outline methods can be very helpful (see Table 3.3).

Watch for Nonverbal Cues. "Listen" with your eyes. You already know that a friend or family member's body language can reveal information that is not verbalized. Likewise, you can learn a lot from a speaker's nonverbal behavior. Because much of a message's meaning is communicated nonverbally, you can use this information as you listen to speeches. *Body language* is an excellent source of information. Watch a speaker's stance and posture. Do they seem rigid and wooden? If so, the speaker may be nervous and may not feel comfortable with the material he or she is presenting. *Facial expressions* also provide cues to help you listen better. Speakers who are committed to their material are more likely to display facial expressions that are consistent with their commitment to the message. Smiling, frowning, raising eyebrows, and other expressions of emotion are useful cues to determine the sincerity and enthusiasm of the speaker toward the message. The same cues can betray the real feelings of the speaker. If verbal and nonverbal messages do not correspond, the nonverbal cues are usually the more honest.

Kathy McLaughlin/Image Works

Body language and physical gestures add emotion and emphasis to a speech: joy, sadness, conviction, or, in this case, stress and agitation.

Gesturing is another type of nonverbal cue that can greatly influence listening. Gesturing can aid the verbal message by providing cues about its meaning. For instance, gesturing is used for *illustrating* (using the hands and arms to show the size of something, or sketching something with the fingers, hands, or arms), for *emphasizing a point* (pointing at the audience, waving the arms), and for *directing the audience's attention toward a person or object*. Of course, the listener must be careful about placing too much importance on nonverbal cues when they have no meaning for the receiver.

Evaluate the Speaker's Evidence. As already noted, a large part of active listening involves learning how to avoid distractions and focus on the speaker's message. But it's not enough to listen intently. Another key part of the active listening process involves questioning the source and distinguishing emotion from logic. An active listener should ask, "What evidence supports and refutes this argument?" and "Are the sources for this argument credible?" In an important sense, evaluating the evidence is what listening—or critical listening—is all about. Because evaluation is also a cornerstone of critical thinking, it is explored further in the chapter.

Table 3.3   Methods of Taking Notes

Method	Description	Example	
Bullet	Notes list the main points and/or supporting material in bullet form.	• Read directions for using insecticide. • Do not pour chemicals when it is windy. • Clean up after use.	
Column	Notes are taken in two columns. One column is used for verbatim notes, and the other is used for interpretations or notes to yourself.	"Make sure your hand is dry."	Grip the ball with the thumb and first two fingers.
Outline	Notes are taken according to the organizational format or outline that the speaker is using.	See Chapter 8.	

ACTIVE LISTENING AND CRITICAL THINKING

Active listening and critical thinking go hand in hand. The use of one skill builds the other. Honing your listening skills is the surest route to improving your learning—and your thinking skills. But what exactly is critical thinking, especially as opposed to just plain thinking?

Critical Thinking

The difference between thinking and critical thinking is like the difference between unfocused and active listening. Whereas thinking is the mental act of producing thoughts (of any kind), **critical thinking** is the ability to evaluate claims on the basis of well-supported reasons. Critical thinking involves both a set of skills and the willingness to use those skills in the service of objective judgment. Critical thinkers are able to look for flaws in arguments and resist claims that have no supporting evidence.[11] They don't take things at face value. Critical thinkers:

- *Evaluate the evidence.* Critical thinkers listen with the following questions in mind: Is the evidence accurate? What evidence supports or refutes the information? What is the source of the evidence? Are the sources credible? Are they reliable?

- *Analyze assumptions and biases.* Part of evaluating the evidence involves looking for the assumptions and biases behind the arguments, claims, and conclusions. "Stiff in opinions, always in the wrong," said the poet John Dryden (1631–1700).[12] What lies behind the speaker's assertions? Does the evidence support or contradict these? Further, what lies behind your own interpretation of or attitude toward the speaker's message? What standards and values do you use to make judgments? Are these interfering with your objective evaluation of the evidence? Are they creating biases?

    Analyzing the speaker's assumptions and biases also includes assessing his or her reasoning for signs of faulty logic. Is evidence presented in the form of *inappropriate causal relationships*, or incorrect conclusions based on cause and effect? Sometimes people assume that because two events occurred in succession or are related, one event must have caused the other. For instance, if all the men in a class receive an "A" for the course, one might conclude that being male "caused" the grade. But other factors—including individual achievement, study habits, related courses, or extra credit assignments—may have influenced the grades. Most events are too complex to be attributed to a single cause-effect relationship. Thinking critically means looking for alternative connections or explanations when a causal connection has been suggested.

- *Resist false dilemmas, overgeneralizations, and either-or thinking.* Critical thinkers are on the lookout for overgeneralizations and either-or thinking. A valid generalization is supported by different types of evidence from different sources and does not make claims beyond a reasonable point. **Overgeneralizations** are unsupported conclusions (e.g., "all

---

critical thinking
the ability to evaluate claims on the basis of well-supported reasons; involves a set of skills and the willingness to use those skills in the service of objective judgment.

---

overgeneralizations
unsupported broad conclusions, such as, "all welfare recipients are lazy."

welfare recipients are lazy"). Critical thinkers test the validity of a generalization by determining if the basis of support is biased in any way. Either-or thinking is dominated by just two choices. Making either-or statements creates **false dilemmas** in which it appears that there are only two mutually exclusive solutions to a problem.

- *Identify contradictions.* Critical thinkers distinguish significant similarities and differences in opposing views, pinpointing specifically where opposing arguments contradict each other. They make decisions about what they hold to be true based on the evidence that best supports a valid conclusion.

- *Consider multiple perspectives.* When listening, critical thinkers remind themselves that there is often more than one way to look at things. Likewise, there are often multiple solutions to problems. Critical thinkers consider different perspectives and realize that both their own perspective and that of the speaker are subject to error. On the other hand, critical thinkers recognize that there are *not* always two sides to every question.

- *Summarize and judge.* Critical thinkers actively summarize for themselves the relevant facts and evidence in clear, understandable statements. If the speaker asks for an action on the part of the listeners (as is often the case in persuasive speeches; see Chapter 14), critical thinkers must decide how they will act on the basis of all the facts and evidence.

Critical Listening:
The Thought/Speech Differential

Did you know that we listen at a much faster rate than we speak? We speak at the rate of between 100 and 180 words per minute; we listen at perhaps as much as 500 to 600 words per minute. The differential between "thought speed" and "speech speed" is one reason why we are so easily distracted. But rather than using the thought-speed differential as an excuse to let your mind wander, turn it into an opportunity to apply your critical thinking skills. The next time you find yourself "thinking ahead" of the speaker (usually by thinking of something unrelated to the speech) use the time instead to listen, with the following questions in mind:

- What's the speaker saying?
- What does it really mean?
- Is he or she leaving anything out?
- Is this an assumption? A generalization? Fact? Opinion?
- Are my biases intruding on my listening?
- How can I use what the speaker is telling me?[13]

EVALUATING SPEECHES

In your public speaking class you will soon be asked to evaluate your classmates' speeches, if you haven't done so already. As you study these speeches, you'll find that you can learn a lot from others' strengths and weaknesses. Consider the fact that one of the ways that coaches train athletes to better understand their sports is to have them critically analyze the athleticism, mental strategies, and confidence levels of other athletes. The same is true of acting coaches and drama coaches. They encourage their students and protégés to study other actors' methods. The same strategies can help the public speaker.

Adjusting to the Speaker's Style

Every individual has a unique communication style, or way of presenting himself or herself through a mix of verbal and nonverbal signals. As listeners, we form impressions of speakers based on this communication style. Depending on our own preferences we may find some speakers dull, others dynamic, others off-putting, and so on. We can't "custom order" people's styles of communication, nor should we want to. Adjusting to the speaker means not judging the content of the message based on the speaker's communication style. Listeners must identify which impressions are the most troublesome and then develop techniques for overcoming any listening problems that arise.

The next time you encounter an irritating communication style, ignore everything about the speaker except the message. You will be surprised at how much you can learn by focusing only on the content of the message. With practice, you will be able not only to listen competently to the verbal message but also to desensitize yourself to the irritations of an aggravating communication style.

Being Honest and Fair in Evaluating

Always keep in mind the need to be honest and fair in your evaluation. Sometimes listeners focus on certain aspects of a speech and, as a result, minimize some of the truly important elements. Focusing on a topic that you really like or dislike, for example, may cause you to place undue importance on that speech element. It is also important to remain open to ideas and beliefs that differ from your own. You can always learn something from differing viewpoints. You should also be fair when critiquing students who present themselves and their material in unusual styles. Accents, awkward grammatical phrases, and word choice are not good reasons to "tune out" a speaker. Maintaining respect for all types of speakers, especially non-native ones, is a sign of good listening.

Being Compassionate in Criticizing

Unless you're supremely confident or a glutton for punishment, you probably aren't too keen on being evaluated in front of a group. And unless you like to hurt people's feelings, you probably don't relish meting out criticism either. Nevertheless, as public speakers we all want and need to know the results of our efforts. Even though the audience's reaction during the speech provides cues to their feelings about it, more specific feedback is needed.

How can you criticize or evaluate a presentation in a way that's constructive rather than cruel? Following the biblical injunction to "do unto others as you would have them do unto you," consider this approach:[14]

1. *Start by saying something positive.* No one's speech is all bad, so why not start by saying something nice? The benefits of this are twofold: You'll

boost the speaker's self-confidence, and he or she will probably be more receptive to any criticism you subsequently offer.

2. *Focus on the speech, not the speaker.* One of the hardest parts about giving a speech is the feeling of being exposed to others. Don't compound the speaker's anxiety by confirming his or her fears of being criticized. Address your remarks to the characteristics of the speech, not the speaker. For example, you might want to say, "Your organization could be tightened up a bit" instead of "You rambled too much."

3. *Target your criticism.* Global statements such as "I just couldn't get into your topic" or "That was a great speech" don't tell the speaker anything useful. If something came up short, be as specific as possible in describing it: "I wanted to hear more about the importance of such-and-such as it related to...."

Critical Checkpoint

Evaluating Speeches

As you listen to speeches, you may wish to use the following guidelines for conducting your evaluations.

Occasion

Did the speaker deliver a speech that was appropriate for the occasion? Were there aspects of the speech that appeared especially sensitive—or insensitive—to the occasion? How comfortable and confident did the speaker appear at this occasion?

Audience

How well did the speaker analyze and prepare for this particular audience? Was the speaker able to adapt to the audience during the speech? How did the audience react to the speech?

Topic and Purpose

Was the topic appropriate for the audience? Were you able to determine the speaker's goal or purpose in giving the speech? Was the main point obvious?

Organization

Was the speech well organized and easy to follow? Did the speaker use appropriate supporting material?

Delivery

How well did the speaker use language and vocal style in delivering the speech? Did the speaker's nonverbal cues seem natural and appropriate for the speech? How well did the speaker use presentational aids during the speech?

Ethics

Did the speaker establish credibility? Did the speaker exhibit ethical behavior in the selection of the topic and the material used? Did the speaker maintain an ethical style in using language and nonverbal cues?

Culture

How well did the speaker conform to the cultural requirements of the speaking situation? What aspects of the speech appeared most sensitive to the culture of the situation?

SUMMARY QUESTIONS

What is listening and why is it important?

Rather than being a reflexive response, listening is a complex, learned behavior. Listening is the process of recognizing, understanding, and accurately interpreting the messages communicated by others.

What is the relationship between listeners and speakers?

Listeners and speakers participate together in co-creating meaning. This is seen in the circular response, or the way that both speakers and listeners adjust their reactions to one another based on each other's cues.

What are the major obstacles to active listening?

Obstacles to active listening include cultural barriers; environmental, emotional, and physiological distractions; daydreaming; script writing and defensive listening; and laziness and overconfidence.

What steps can you take to become a more active listener?

Monitor your listening to avoid the poor listening habits noted above. As you listen, do so consciously and try to apply these steps: Set listening goals; focus listening efforts; concentrate; watch for the speaker's nonverbal cues; listen for the speaker's thesis, or main point; and evaluate the speaker's evidence.

What is critical thinking, and how does it relate to active listening?

Critical thinking is the ability to evaluate claims on the basis of well-supported reasons. It involves both a set of skills and the willingness to use these skills in the service of objective judgment. Critical thinkers evaluate evidence; analyze assumptions and biases; resist false dilemmas, overgeneralizations, and either-or thinking; identify contradictions; consider multiple perspectives; and summarize and judge. Critical thinking goes hand in hand with active listening.

What do you need to consider as an evaluator of speeches, and what are some key points to consider when evaluating speeches?

Try to be honest and fair in your evaluation. Adjust to the speaker's style. When you offer criticism, try to be compassionate and constructive. Say something positive. Focus on the speech, not the speaker. Keep your criticisms specific. Use the guidelines to evaluating speeches on page 69 when considering which key points of a speech to review.

ISSUES FOR DISCUSSION

1. Consider the notion that some people are "natural-born listeners." That is, some people naturally listen well. What qualities make natural-born listeners different from people who must work at being good listeners? Compare these qualities to what you have learned in this chapter.

2. Think about different types of speeches that you have heard in the past year. In each case, what percentage of the audience do you think was listening intently to the speaker? Of those daydreaming, what could the speaker have done to get their attention? What could the listeners have done to maintain more focus on the message?

3. Every time a speech is delivered, audience members have different perspectives on what was actually said. Why do listeners hear things differently? What have you learned from this chapter that could inform your thinking?

Key Terms

active listening
circular response
critical thinking
defensive listening
false dilemmas

hearing
listening
message-perception gap
overgeneralizations
selective perception

SELF-ASSESSMENT

1. Answer the following statements according to whether you Strongly Agree (SA), Agree (A), don't know or have no opinion (?), Disagree (D), or Strongly Disagree (SD). For each statement, place a check mark in the appropriate box.

Statement	SA	A	?	D	SD	SCORE
1. I interrupt others too frequently.						
2. I am not able to respond effectively to others' messages.						
3. I am effective at showing others that I understand what they are saying.						
4. I become apathetic when boring people talk to me.						
5. Sometimes I expect too much of myself when listening to others.						
6. My mind wanders when people talk to me.						
7. I am easily distracted by extraneous sounds when I listen to others.						

Statement	SA	A	?	D	SD	SCORE
8. I am effective at asking questions when I feel I don't understand someone.						
9. I maintain good eye contact when I listen to others.						
10. Sometimes I have to have information repeated to me.						
11. I have been told that I am a good listener.						
12. I am comfortable listening to other people's problems.						
13. I can immediately grasp the main point or idea that a speaker is trying to make.						
14. I have good hearing.						
15. It is sometimes difficult for me to understand someone when other people are talking at the same time.						
16. I am often overconfident of my listening abilities.						
17. I have a good memory for what people have said.						
18. I consider myself to be an effective listener.						
19. I can tell when people are listening carefully to what I am saying.						
20. I am a much better listener in certain situations than in others.						
					Total Score	

Scoring: Place the following scores in the right-hand column labeled "score." For items 1, 2, 4, 5, 6, 7, 10, 15, and 16, give yourself a 1 for SA, 2 for A, 3 for ?, 4 for D, and 5 for SD. For items 3, 8, 9, 11, 12, 13, 14, 17, 18, 19, and 20, give yourself a 5 for SA, 4 for A, 3 for ?, 2 for D, and 1 for SD.

Add up all the scores, and place your total score in the box provided. The higher your score, the higher your listening self-concept. For example, an average score would be 60. If you scored well above this (70–100), you have a favorable listening self-concept. If you scored well below 60 (20–50), you have a low listening self-concept. A low listening self-concept would benefit from work and practice that allows you to identify your true listening skills.

2. To help clarify your attitudes toward your own listening skills and those of others, take this quick test. For each statement, circle the answer that reflects your opinion about yourself.

YES	MAYBE	NO	1. I am a better listener than most people I know.
YES	MAYBE	NO	2. I wish other people would listen to me better.
YES	MAYBE	NO	3. I can tell when I am not listening well to other people.
YES	MAYBE	NO	4. It irritates me to see other people listen so poorly.
YES	MAYBE	NO	5. I get frustrated when I make mistakes because of poor listening.
YES	MAYBE	NO	6. If I could change anything about people, it would be their listening habits.
YES	MAYBE	NO	7. I wish I could be a better listener.

What are your attitudes about listening? If you answered YES to most of these questions, you are a communicator who is concerned about competent listening. If you answered MAYBE or NO to many of these, you probably haven't given listening much attention. Can you form an attitude about listening that will lead you to a commitment to improve? Only through a committed attitude will you become a more competent listener.

TEAMWORK

1. In a small group, brainstorm some songs that have memorable lyrics. Discuss the types of messages in the lyrics that cause listeners to pay more attention and remember better. Bring examples to class to support your ideas. What elements of song lyrics that make them interesting and memorable could be transferred to public speeches?

2. As a team, conduct a search of the Internet and/or World Wide Web using the keyword *listening*. Look for sites that report both problems and solutions associated with listening. Bring back to class the results from your search, and share them with the class.

3. Form a group of between four and six people. Devise a "Listening Challenge" much like games such as Jeopardy, College Bowl, or Twenty-Questions that focuses on listening. Create the rules, procedures, questions, answers, and so on. Have your classmates act as participants. Make it challenging so that the more the participants demonstrate their knowledge of listening, the greater their rewards.

If Thomas Jefferson had heard us, he probably would have said, "We shouldn't have free speech."

—Robin Quivers, co-host of the Howard Stern radio show

You can fool some of the people all the time, and all of the people some of the time, but you cannot fool all of the people all the time.

—Abraham Lincoln

4

Ethical Public Speaking

When was the last time someone questioned your honesty or integrity? Did you feel embarrassed or uncomfortable even though you knew you were sincere and truthful? What led someone to question your ethics? In public speaking situations, the issue of ethical communication looms large because of the formality of the context and the number of people involved. As a speaker in the United States, you are granted great freedom to say nearly anything you want in public. It is up to you to use that freedom responsibly and ethically. **The choices you make while preparing and presenting your speeches will have a great impact on whether or not your audience perceives you as an ethical speaker, and whether or not they find your message credible.**

Tony Baptiste was running for campus president at Simon College. He was preparing for a series of speeches he would deliver during the campaign. He asked his mother about some speeches she had collected from local political campaigns (e.g., county commissioner, city council, and mayoral elections). Tony looked through four or five of these speeches and found them quite effective—very well organized, fairly emotional, and loaded with quotes and phrases that Tony could use in his own speeches. In fact, Tony copied one of the speeches almost verbatim, changing only the issues involved (e.g., substituting campus parking problems for city street parking meter problems, etc.). Just before the election, an editorial in the campus newspaper accused Tony of plagiarism—not in copying the speeches, but in using material from other people without crediting them. Tony learned that much of the material he had borrowed from the politician's speech was taken from people like Thomas Jefferson, Benjamin Disraeli, Karl Marx, and Theodore Roosevelt.

One of the most consistent expectations that audiences have about a speaker is ethical conduct. Why would we spend time listening to a speech unless we felt that the speaker would be sincere, straightforward, and honest? All too often speakers are accused of unethical conduct. Sometimes the accusation is unfounded, but nevertheless it taints the speaker's reputation.

In the story above, Tony's reputation is damaged when he is accused of plagiarism. What did Tony do wrong? First of all, he knowingly adapted a speech by a local politician without citing the source. Secondly, the speech he plagiarized was itself full of plagiarized material, so Tony unknowingly used material from people like Jefferson and Marx. It is unethical to plagiarize—either knowingly or unknowingly—and it gives the audience a reason to question the speaker's integrity. Would you trust Tony to be president of *your* campus?

At each step of the speechmaking process you will be faced with important ethical choices. For instance, when you select a topic, you must consider not only whether it is appropriate for the audience and occasion, but whether it is possible to speak about the subject ethically. For example, would you feel comfortable giving a speech that endorsed stealing from others? Once you select a topic, you also need to think about how you will present information fairly so you don't distort the truth. Will you give a speech that shows a balanced view of a topic? Or will you purposely hide information from your audience? Every choice you make while preparing your speech can ultimately affect whether or not your audience finds you trustworthy. This chapter provides a framework to help you make responsible choices as you prepare and present your speeches.

At the heart of ethical public speaking lies responsibility to self and others. But how does this translate into practical terms? This chapter's challenges include:

- Deciding where to draw the line between your legal right to free speech and your own ethical standards.
- Knowing what makes a speaker credible.
- Recognizing the role that values—both your own and others'—play in ethical speech.
- Incorporating an understanding of and respect for differing values into your speeches.
- Discovering how to bring your own values into sharper focus.
- Infusing trustworthiness, respect, responsibility, and fairness into your speeches.
- Learning how to avoid plagiarism in any form in your speeches.

In 1995 hundreds of thousands of people, mostly black men, traveled from all regions of the country to attend the Million Man March in Washington, D.C. Thousands more people of all colors and creeds watched the event on television. The marchers had come to express unity and send a positive message of change to the black community: Now is the time to build up black families and communities.

The keynote speaker was Reverend Louis Farrakhan, the controversial leader of the Nation of Islam. His many supporters in the audience listened raptly throughout most of his lengthy address. To them, Farrakhan was an admired and revered leader. To his detractors, Farrakhan was a demagogue and an "apostle of hate" who spouted anti-white and anti-Semitic statements such as, "Little Jews were being turned into soap while big Jews washed themselves in it."[1] Repulsed and angered by such rhetoric, his critics denounced the fact that Farrakhan's role of keynote speaker was catapulting him onto the national stage.

AP/Wide World

Reverend Louis Farrakhan, the charismatic and controversial leader of the Nation of Islam, gives the keynote address at the Million Man March in Washington, D.C.

ETHICAL SPEAKING AND RESPONSIBILITY

The controversy over Farrakhan's role as keynote speaker points to several important points about public speaking. First, public speaking is a public act. One definition of *public* is "exposed to general view." Second, when speakers voice their ideas and opinions to a general audience, they subject themselves to the reactions of that audience. More important from an ethical perspective, they subject the audience to *their* views. Public speakers are in a unique position not only to share their ideas but to influence or persuade others and, at times, to move them to act—for better or for worse.

With this unique power to affect the minds and hearts of others comes responsibility—the heart of ethics. One definition of responsibility is "moral, legal, or mental accountability."[2] **Ethics** is the study of moral conduct—how people should act toward one another. In terms of public

ethics
the study of moral conduct, or how people should act toward one another; in public speaking, the responsibilities speakers have toward their audience and themselves.

speaking, *ethics* refers to the responsibilities speakers have toward their audience and themselves. It also encompasses the responsibilities listeners have toward speakers.

Threaded throughout this text is the theme of public speaking as both a right and a responsibility. As members of a democratic society, we have the right to speak freely. To ensure the well-being of a free society, we have the equally important responsibility to speak ethically. Speakers who are ethical demonstrate trustworthiness, responsibility, respect, and fairness.

Free Speech and Responsibility

Perhaps no other nation in the world has as many safeguards for its citizens' rights as the United States. The First Amendment guarantees freedom of speech ("Congress shall make no law...abridging the freedom of speech..."). The Fourteenth Amendment guarantees equal protection under the law, including freedom from discrimination (no state shall "deny to any person within its jurisdiction the equal protection of the laws"). However, finding a satisfactory balance between the right to free expression and the right to freedom from discrimination has proven to be a thorny issue for the judicial system. Supreme Court justices are besieged with cases challenging them to decide whose rights are more important: those of (for example) neo-Nazis, Ku Klux Klansmen, and pornographers to say what they want in public, or those who claim that these groups' speech infringes on others' Fourteenth Amendment right to be free from discrimination (which is what they believe these groups' speech constitutes).[3]

Should the neo-Nazis' right to say that certain groups are racially inferior be upheld over the objection of those groups? As the Constitution currently is interpreted, it would appear so. Free speech is almost always protected, even when the targets of that speech claim that it infringes on their Fourteenth Amendment rights to protection from discrimination. Although the way in which the courts interpret freedom of speech today does not allow limitless freedom, it comes fairly close. Speech that provokes people to violence is not protected, nor is speech that can be proven to be libelous.[4] Certain kinds of "hard core" obscene speech also aren't protected.

The fact that many kinds of speech are legal, however, does not necessarily mean that they are ethical. In fact, the First Amendment guarantees protection to both the honest and the dishonest speaker.[5] Although there are various approaches to evaluating ethical behavior, common to all of them are the fundamental moral precepts of not harming others and telling the truth. From this perspective, many kinds of legally protected speech—be they racist, sexist, homophobic, or just plain mean—are clearly unethical.

The Roots of Ethical Speaking

The question of what constitutes ethical behavior and ethical speech has a long history. Before the third century B.C., Confucius proposed a system

Critical Checkpoint

••••••••••••••••••••••

Ethical Speaking Situations

Consider the following speaking situations that are legally permitted in the United States. Which ones do you find unethical? Which ones violate your values? What are your criteria for deciding whether one situation is ethical and another is not? Discuss your various responses.

The right of anti-abortion activists to direct loud and angry protests toward women entering birth control or abortion clinics.

The right to demonstrate for the homeless by establishing a camp in a public park and daily picketing people who pass by.

The right to sing (or quote) songs in public that contain sexually explicit as well as sexist lyrics.

The right to persuade listeners that the present government should be overthrown.

The right of Ku Klux Klan members to assemble, wear white sheets and hoods, and give speeches describing their beliefs about the inferiority of various groups.

The right to burn a national flag during a speech.

of ethical principles based on the practice of *jen*—sympathy, or "human heartedness." Traditional Chinese ethics and culture still stem from these Confucian teachings.[6] In the West, nearly 2,500 years ago Socrates (470–399 B.C.) sparked debate among his colleagues in Greece about the nature of concepts such as Goodness and Justice. Socrates wanted to discover how one should govern one's conduct in life. His "Socratic method" of questioning endures to this day.[7] The Greek philosopher Aristotle (384–322 B.C.) referred to ethics as "practical wisdom," or "the true and reasoned state of capacity to act with regard to the things that are good or bad for a man."[8] (Note that Aristotle referred only to men. In ancient Greece, neither women nor slaves of either sex were allowed to vote or otherwise have a "public" voice.) Aristotle's texts on the art of persuasion (*The Rhetoric*, sometimes called the first public speaking textbook) and ethics (*Nicomachean Ethics* and *Eudemian Ethics*) continue to be studied today.

Perhaps it was the Roman orator Quintilian (ca A.D. 35–ca 100) who came closest to our present-day conception of the role of ethics in public speaking. Quintilian regarded ethics as a necessary and central component of public speaking. Calling the ideal orator "a good man speaking well," he wrote:

> [H]e who would have all men trust his judgment as to what is expedient and honorable should possess and be regarded as possessing genuine wisdom and excellence of character.[9]

In today's words, Quintilian would say that if you want other people to trust and believe in you, know what you are talking about and be of good character.

Ethics, Ethos, and Speaker Credibility

It is from the Greek word **ethos**, meaning "character," that the modern word *ethics* is derived. According to Aristotle, audiences listen to and trust speakers if they demonstrate positive ethos (positive character). Positive ethos includes *competence* (as demonstrated by the speaker's grasp of the subject matter), *good moral character* (as reflected in the speaker's trustworthiness, straightforwardness, and honest presentation of the message), and *goodwill* (as demonstrated by the speaker's knowledge of and attitude of respect toward the audience and the particular speech occasion).

For Aristotle, speakers were regarded positively if they were well prepared, honest, and respectful toward their audience. Some 2,500 years after Aristotle, surprisingly little has changed. Modern research on **speaker credibility** reveals that people most trust those speakers who

- have a sound grasp of the subject,
- display sound reasoning skills,
- are honest and unmanipulative, and
- are genuinely interested in the welfare of their listeners.[10]

Listeners tend to distrust speakers who deviate even slightly from these qualities. However, merely being an expert is not enough to inspire listeners' trust. Studies reveal that we only trust those speakers whom we believe have our best interests in mind.[11]

ethos
a Greek word, meaning "character," from which the modern word *ethics* is derived.

speaker credibility
the believability of speakers, based on their grasp of the subject, display of sound reasoning skills, degree of honesty, and interest in the welfare of their listeners.

Public Speaking in Cultural Perspective

A Crosscultural View of Ethics

Students of comparative ethics have found that the ethical codes of most societies—from the ancient to the modern period—share certain features.

Most societies have had customs or laws forbidding murder, bodily injury to another person, or attacks on personal honor and reputation. Also, the concept of property rights has existed in some form in almost all societies.

Many societies have rules that define basic duties of doing good and furthering the welfare of the group. Within the family, mothers look after their children, and men support and protect their dependents. In turn, grown-up children are expected to provide care for their aging parents. Helping distant relatives is also considered a duty in some societies, depending on the extent of kinship ties.

In societies where the major religions—Judaism, Christianity, Islam, and Buddhism—are predominant, the duty of helping the needy and the distressed has been acknowledged. These obligations extend beyond family to acquaintances and strangers. Telling the truth and keeping promises (though not always to strangers) are also widely regarded as duties.

Throughout the last 200 years, modern nations have evolved a kind of universal ethic based originally on ideas about human rights to life, liberty, and property that developed during the period of the Enlightenment. Whether universally honored in practice or not, there is an acceptance of the notion that the lives of human beings are meant to be improved by abolishing disease, poverty, and ignorance.

Excerpted from "Ethics and Morality." In Compton's Encyclopedia Online v2.0 © 1997, The Learning Company, Inc. AOL keyword: Compton's.

Our most admired speakers exhibit these qualities of speaker credibility. Consider Bill Cosby, who for years has delighted audiences with his performances about the ups and downs of fatherhood. Having raised five children to whom he is devoted (his only son was murdered in 1997), audiences feel he knows his topic. Although he is usually funny, he is always honest in his insights. And regardless of color or creed, his listeners seem to feel that Cosby has their best interests at heart and that he wants to share his knowledge to help others.

VALUES: THE FOUNDATION OF ETHICAL SPEAKING

values
people's most enduring judgments or standards of what's good and bad, of what's important; they form the basis on which people judge the actions of others.

Our ethical conduct is a reflection of our **values**—the most enduring judgments or standards of what's good and bad in life, of what's important. Values are the prism through which we see the world and the people in it. Values drive our behavior and form the basis on which we judge the actions of others. Our ethical choices—including those we make in our speeches—are our values in action.

In large measure, values are culturally determined and transmitted through key social institutions such as the family, schools, and religious organizations. We learn many of our values fairly early in life and tend to hold on to them for long periods, if not forever. In U.S. culture, researchers have identified such "core" values as achievement and success, equal opportunity, material comfort, hard work, practicality and efficiency, change and progress, science, democracy, and freedom.[12] A survey of several Asian societies reveals such core values as the spirit of harmony, humility toward one's superiors, awe of nature, and a desire for prosperity.[13] In addition to broad societal values, we hold values related to our professions, our relationships, our religion, our sense of the aesthetic, and so forth. The terms *beauty, security, commitment, affiliation, devotion, salvation,* and *wisdom* evoke some of these values.

Value Conflicts and Ethical Dilemmas

However, just like human behavior itself, values are not a tidy affair. Just as feelings can compete with one another, values can conflict or clash. Even a society's core values can and do clash with or contradict each other. As late as the 1970s, for example, one researcher identified equal opportunity on the one hand, and racism and group superiority on the other hand, as core American values.[14] Conflicting values lie at the heart of ethical dilemmas. We value freedom of religion, but does prayer in the schools infringe on the rights of individuals? We value the rights of the individual, but should parents be allowed to withhold their children's medical care on religious grounds? We value free speech, but should pornographers be free to publish anything, no matter how offensive? Should we uphold the rights of the unborn, or the rights of a woman to control her reproductive fate?

Clashes of values—within individuals, between young and old, men and women, parent and child—are a fact of life in all societies. The more diverse the society, the greater these clashes tend to be. In large and multicultural societies such as the United States, many more diverse cultural values coexist with—and sometimes compete with—one another than in more ethnically and religiously homogeneous societies such as Sweden or Japan. For the public speaker in multicultural societies, recognizing audience values becomes especially important. As with feelings, "stepping on" other people's values can cause alienation, pain, and anger.

Robert Brenner/PhotoEdit

Ethical conflicts center on questions of freedom and values. As an ethical speaker, you should stand by your own values but be mindful of the values of others.

Values and the Public Speaker

Successful speeches appeal to listeners' values; speeches that ignore this crucial component of audience analysis often fail miserably. One of your main tasks as a public speaker is to try to identify your listeners' values, attitudes, and beliefs as they relate to the topic, the speaker, and the occasion. Doing so helps you shape the message in ways that will be best received.

But simply knowing the audience's values does not guarantee ethical speaking. In fact, in many instances it can lead to its opposite. By skillfully appealing to our values, unscrupulous salespeople try to sell us things we don't need or want. Cynical politicians get our vote by persuading us that they have our best interests at heart when in fact they may not. Ethical speaking requires not only recognition of but respect for audience values—even when they diverge from our own.

Critical Checkpoint

....

Charting Personal Values

As a way of uncovering where your values lie—both terminal and instrumental—consider Rokeach's list (see Table 4.1) and rank each item from 1 to 10 (from least to most important). Select from these your top five values and write them down in a circle called "Your Values" similar to the one in Figure 4.1. Repeat the exercise, only this time rank each value in terms of how important you think it is to *other* groups of people, such as other students at your college or members of a particular ethnic or political group. Select these top five values and place them in the "Others' Values" circle. Finally, draw arrows to the overlapping circle where your highest values (of those listed) coincide with those you think are most important to others.

An exercise like this can help bring what's important to you into sharper relief. Of course, there are no right or wrong answers. The point is to become more conscious of how your own values may affect your speaking and listening. This helps ensure that what you communicate is valid and important to you. And by identifying other people's values, you can tailor your messages in ways that address them respectfully.

Being alert to differences in values can help speakers deliver their message ethically by:

- being sensitive to the existence of alternative viewpoints,
- reviewing potential topics from a culturally sensitive perspective, and
- being mindful that differences in dialects or accents, nonverbal cues, word choice, and even physical appearance can be barriers to understanding.

How can you identify values, both your own and others'? One way is through interviews or surveys. Another way is to research written and online materials about the group you're going to address (see Chapter 5 for a discussion of methods of audience analysis). For information about trends in U.S. values, the *Gallup Poll Monthly* is helpful. For example, how important is religion in the life of Americans? Fully 96 percent state a belief in God or a universal spirit and say that religion is important in their lives, but only 35 percent (mostly women and the elderly) identify themselves as "religious."[15] How do Americans feel about equal rights for homosexuals? The majority support them. Compared to 1982 (59%) and 1992 (74%), in 1996 fully 80 percent felt that gays should have equal employment opportunity rights. Men and women differ significantly over the issue. Fifty-six percent of women and only 35 percent of men favor extending civil rights protection to homosexuals, and 51 percent of women and 36 percent of men support gays serving in the military.[17]

With data on forty-two nations, the *World Values Survey* offers a fascinating look at how values vary crossculturally. Through this resource you can discover how the peoples of other nations feel about work, family, religion, and even who should do the housework. For example, what percentage of Australians, Icelanders, and Spaniards "believe in God," are "convinced atheists," or consider themselves "religious persons"? The United States tops the list for religious believers. Who approves or disapproves of having a child out of wedlock? In Iceland, 88 percent approve; in Japan, only 13 percent do.[17]

Being an ethical speaker involves being conscious not only of other people's values but of your own as well. Usually, if you find that certain values are important to you and your own life, you will want others to hold the same values important. This is a critical assumption in preparing for and presenting speeches.

If you're like most people, you probably haven't spent much time articulating your values to yourself or identifying those of other people. One way to bring them into focus is to conduct a values assessment. Through extensive research, psychologist Milton Rokeach identified thirty-six values that were very important to a large cross-section of people (see Table 4.1). He distinguished between two kinds of values: "terminal" and "instrumental." Terminal values are desirable ends in themselves; you can think of them as end states or states of being. Instrumental values are valued characteristics that people can possess. Ranking both terminal and instrumental values from least to most important will help you identify what values mean the most to you. You can then compare what you value with what you think others value (see Figure 4.1). When your values overlap those of your audience you should be able to find some common ground from which to approach your topic and present your speech.

Table 4.1. Identifying Values

Terminal Values (states of being you consider important)	Instrumental Values (characteristics you value in yourself and others)
A comfortable life	Ambition
Equality	Broadmindedness
An exciting life	Capability
Family security	Cheerfulness
Freedom	Cleanliness
Happiness	Courage
Inner harmony	Forgiveness
Mature love	Helpfulness
National security	Honesty
Pleasure	Imagination
Salvation	Independence
Self-respect	Intellect
A sense of accomplishment	Logic
Social recognition	Love
True friendship	Obedience
Wisdom	Politeness
A world at peace	Responsibility
A world of beauty	Self-control

SOURCE: *Milton Rokeach,* Value Survey *(Sunnyvale, CA: Halgren Tests, 1967).*

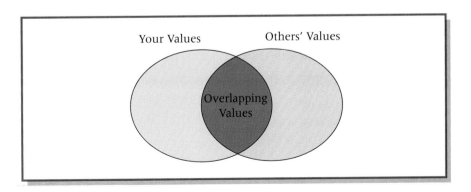

FIGURE 4.1
Comparing Values

Interview

Ethics: A Real World Perspective

Michael Josephson is founder and president of the Joseph and Edna Josephson Institute of Ethics in Marina del Rey, California. The Josephson Institute provides ethics training and education to a broad range of professionals. The Institute also publishes a newsletter entitled *Ethics: Easier Said Than Done.*

Why is ethics an important part of public speaking?

Communicating is the way we relate to one another. There are two dimensions of being an effective speaker, both of which are influenced by ethics. One dimension is at the pragmatic level. That is, in order to effectively achieve your communication goal, whether it be to inform or persuade, you must establish credibility with your listeners. Credibility is based on trust, honesty, and believability. If you lose credibility, your message will be ignored. Look at many of our politicians. Because of misleading or exaggerated claims, many people simply do not believe what politicians are saying. The second dimension is at the moral level. Public speakers have a moral obligation to treat their listeners with respect. We respect our listeners by providing them with information that is truthful and honest so that they can make informed decisions about our messages. It is a moral obligation to our listeners to communicate ethical messages.

Why do some speakers send unethical messages?

Ethics are usually sacrificed because speakers perceive that they can accomplish their goals more effectively by exaggerating, misleading, or lying to their listeners. Talented speakers are faced with

a major moral choice of playing by the rules of ethics. Essentially a speaker must answer this question: Am I willing to sacrifice a level of persuasion in order to be ethical? The answer should always be yes. In the long run, unethical behavior is usually found out; when it is, it leads to a permanent loss of credibility and effectiveness.

How can students in public speaking classes ensure an ethical perspective when preparing for and delivering a speech?

Speakers of all types must be systematic about understanding the ground rules of ethics. These ground rules, or what we call "the pillars of character," include trustworthiness, respect, fairness, and responsibility. *Trustworthiness* involves candor, truth, and being sincere. *Respect* involves being concerned with treating people right. Speakers should focus on the issues rather than personalities when speaking. Above all, avoid rudeness. *Responsibility* involves communicating in ways that are accurate. Speakers should be careful in what they say and how they say it. Speakers must exercise self-restraint in communicating their message so that all sides of the argument are presented—not just the side that helps the speaker. *Fairness* is ensured when the speaker has made a genuine effort to see all sides of an issue and be open-minded. Only using information that helps the speaker's case is unfair to listeners as they attempt to make informed decisions about the content of the message. Speakers should filter their decisions about the message they prepare and deliver through these pillars of character.

GROUND RULES
FOR ETHICAL SPEAKING

Although there is no single agreed-upon code of ethical standards for communication, the qualities of dignity and integrity are universally seen as central to ethical behavior. **Dignity** refers to "feeling worthy, honored, or respected as a person."[18] Each of us wants to be accorded dignity. **Integrity** refers to incorruptibility; being able to avoid compromise for the sake of personal expediency.[19] For example, manipulating data or slanting facts in your favor during a speech to persuade others to take "your side" demonstrates a lack of integrity. Speakers who demonstrate dignity and integrity care about themselves and their listeners. Their own self-interest is secondary. Such speakers exhibit a hallmark of ethical speaking: concern for the greater good. This includes the welfare of the audience as well as society as a whole.

The qualities of dignity and integrity should infuse every aspect of a speech. As Michael Josephson points out in this chapter's interview section, ethical speaking also requires that we be trustworthy, respectful, responsible, and fair in our presentations.

dignity
a feeling of worth, honor, or respect as a person.

integrity
incorruptibility; speakers who demonstrate integrity do not compromise for the sake of personal expediency.

Trustworthiness

As we noted earlier, we find speakers credible when we sense they are honest—both about their intentions and about the information they present. **Trustworthiness** is a combination of honesty and dependability. Just as we look for these qualities in personal relationships, audiences look for them in speakers. Honesty or truth telling is important on many different levels, from the personal to the political. At the broadest level, truth is essential to the democratic process because democracy depends on an informed citizenry.[20]

For the public speaker, trustworthiness includes (but isn't necessarily limited to):

AP/Wide World

Tenzin Gyatos, the fourteenth Dalai Lama of Tibet, won the Nobel Peace Prize in 1989. He is known for his integrity and commitment to human rights worldwide.

- *Revealing your true purpose to your audience—and not sacrificing the truth to it.* Truth telling can be an especially difficult issue in persuasive speeches. When the goal is to try to convince others to accept a certain viewpoint, take a certain action, or change a behavior, the temptation is to fashion the information in a way that fits the goal, even if it means omitting a fact here or there that would convince the audience otherwise. But all kinds of speeches, not just persuasive ones, should be built on the truth. This means acknowledging rather than omitting alternative viewpoints when they are relevant.

trustworthiness
qualities of candor, truth, and sincerity.

- *Not using misleading, deceptive, or false information.* Manipulating information to achieve the speech purpose is unethical, as are any attempts to deceive an audience by misrepresentation, omission, or the manufacture of data. Ethically, you are required to support your points truthfully and accurately.

- *Acknowledging sources.* Acknowledging sources is an essential aspect of ethical speechmaking. Doing otherwise is plagiarism, which is discussed in depth later in this chapter.

Respect

respect
concern for treating people
properly; respectful speakers
focus on issues rather than
personalities.

A shorthand for **respect** is "treating people right." For the ethical speaker, respect ranges from addressing audience members as unique human beings, to refraining from rudeness and other forms of personal attacks.

- *Focus on issues rather than personalities.* Civil disagreement is quite appropriate in a speech. Personal attacks on the character of those with whom you disagree are not. Whether engaged in by the speaker or by members of the audience, behaviors such as heckling, name calling, and other rude outbursts can short-circuit communication and even lead to violence. Unfortunately, this sort of behavior is becoming all too common in many public forums, from local school board meetings to campus demonstrations. Civil discourse forms the basis of democratic society. Its breakdown threatens all of us.

- *Allow the audience the power of rational choice.* Audiences deserve to hear information in a way that permits them the power of rational choice. Sensationalist or lurid appeals rob them of this power. In most cases, it's not necessary to use graphic pictures or upsetting verbal descriptions just to make a point. When and if you feel you need to include something potentially upsetting, give the audience advance warning and allow time for those who wish to leave to do so.

jargon
specialized terminology.

ethnocentrism
the belief that the ways of one's
own culture are superior to
those of other cultures.

- *Avoid in-group and out-group distinctions.* Have you ever experienced the pain of being excluded? Each of us wants to feel included, whether as part of a group of friends or as members of an audience. One of the most unethical things a public speaker can do is make some members of the audience feel excluded or, worse, victimized. Promoting in-group and out-group distinctions goes against the universal rule of avoiding harm to others.

One simple thing speakers can do to make audience members feel included is to maintain eye contact. This indicates acknowledgment and respect for their presence. It lets people know they aren't seen as passive objects but as unique human beings. (However, be aware that preferences for eye contact vary by culture. In many Asian cultures, direct eye contact is perceived as a sign of disrespect. In Japan, looking down is a sign of respect.)

Another relatively simple way to avoid in-group and out-group distinctions is to use language that everyone can understand. Try to prepare remarks in ways that include each audience member. It is fine to use **jargon**, or specialized terminology, when addressing people who are familiar with the terms. Do not use jargon if the terms are unfamiliar to even a small portion of the audience.

Expressions of ethnocentrism, stereotypes, or outright prejudice are far more serious ethical breaches than avoiding eye contact or using jargon. **Ethnocentrism** is the belief that the ways of one's own culture are superior to those of other cultures. Ethnocentric speakers act as though everyone shares their point of view and points of reference, whether or not this is in fact the case. They may tell jokes that require a certain context or refer only to their own customs, even when members of the audience do not share them. Ethical speakers assume differences and address them respectfully.

Critical Checkpoint

....

**Ethical Speaking
and Respect**

Is being sensitive to differences among people really that important, or is it merely "politically correct"? Is it unethical to ignore differences? Consider your own classmates. Does everyone share the same ethnic or cultural heritage? What are the differences? Would assuming that everyone in your class shares the same experiences and views as you set the stage for a successful speech? How can you make certain that these differences do not stand in the way of presenting a successful speech?

Another serious affront to people's dignity occurs when a speaker generalizes about an *apparent* characteristic of a group and applies that generalization to all its members. When such racial or ethnic **stereotypes** roll innocuously off the tongue of the speaker, they pack a wallop of indignation and pain for people to whom the stereotype refers. We'd use an example here, but the point is that a stereotype can be generated about any group—white, black, red, yellow, or green—so why take the chance of hurting someone?

Hate speech is the ultimate vehicle for promoting in-group and out-group distinctions. Hate speech is any offensive communication—verbal or nonverbal—that is directed against people's racial, ethnic, religious, gender, or other characteristics. Racist, sexist, or ageist slurs, gay bashing, and cross burnings are all forms of hate speech. As seen in this chapter's Focus on Ethics box, hate speech is a poisonous mix of stereotypes and prejudice.

stereotypes
generalizations about an *apparent* characteristic of a group that are applied to all its members.

hate speech
any offensive communication, verbal or nonverbal, that is directed against people's racial, ethnic, religious, gender, or other characteristics.

Focus on Ethics

Hate Speech

Hate speech is regarded as a far more serious social problem in the United States than elsewhere in other industrialized nations. It's not that as a group Americans are more bigoted than other people. They are simply freer to express their darker impulses. In virtually every other Western nation, hate speech is illegal.[1] In contrast, the United States' unique tradition of free speech permits the expression of even the most offensive insults, as long as they cannot be proven to "inflict injury or incite an immediate breach of the peace."[2]

The problem of hate speech is particularly acute on U.S. college campuses, where alarm over the rise of bias incidents in the 1980s and early 1990s (including some at the nation's top schools) led to the creation of controversial speech codes. Ultimately, some of the more restrictive of the early campus speech codes were challenged in the courts and found to be unconstitutional. But many remain in place today, and they continue to generate controversy. Critics of speech codes argue that they are not only unconstitutional but counterproductive. Civil libertarians claim that speech codes prevent the discussion of any sensitive issue related to race or gender.[3]

Whether or not this freedom of speech as experienced in the United States is a good thing

has long been the subject of intense debate. In the forefront of those arguing in favor of protecting all forms of speech is the American Civil Liberties Union (ACLU):

> How much we value the right of free speech is put to its severest test when the speaker is someone we disagree with most. Speech that deeply offends our morality or is hostile to our way of life warrants the same constitutional protection as other speech because the right of free speech is indivisible: When one of us is denied this right, all of us are denied.[4]

The ACLU's position on campus speech codes is that they "merely drive biases underground where they can't be addressed." "More speech," says the ACLU, "not less, is the best revenge."[5]

What do you think?

1. Samuel Walker, *Hate Speech: The History of an American Controversy* (Lincoln: University of Nebraska Press, 1994), p. 1.
2. *Hate Speech on Campus*, briefing paper, American Civil Liberties Union.
3. Walker, *Hate Speech*, p.128
4. Ibid.
5. Ibid.

Responsibility

Communication is a strong tool for influencing people. Indeed, even one communication message has the potential to change people's lives. Thus, speaking with **responsibility** includes evaluating the usefulness and appropriateness of your topic and purpose, using sound evidence and reasoning, striving for accuracy, and presenting the speech ethically. When preparing a speech, the responsible public speaker should consider the following:

responsibility
"moral, legal, or mental accountability"; responsible speakers communicate in ways that are accurate, careful, and objective.

- *Topic and Purpose*. Will learning about your topic in some way benefit your listeners? Are your overall speech aims socially constructive? What effect will your speech have on your listeners? Are your topic and purpose appropriate to the audience and the occasion? (See Chapter 6 for additional guidelines for selecting an ethical topic and purpose.)

- *Evidence and Reasoning*. Are your arguments sound? Have you examined them critically? Remember that it is the speaker's responsibility to use sound evidence and reasoning. Failing to do so means you will waste the audience's time. Worse, sloppy evidence and reasoning distort the truth.

- *Accuracy*. Is the content of your message accurate? Are the facts correct? Accuracy is a hallmark of ethical speaking. Remember, there very well may be people in your audience who know the facts of your speech as well as you do. Don't embarrass yourself by inaccurately presenting your case.

- *Presentation*. How often have you been swayed by the emotional appeal of a speech? Is it responsible or ethical to convince an audience of your cause by using a fiery emotional appeal without regard to the factual evidence involved in the issue? Speakers from all walks of life use emotional appeal as a crutch when their side or position is weak on evidence or facts. Such a breach of ethics is unfair to an unsuspecting audience and can damage the credibility of the speaker.

Fairness

As Michael Josephson of the Josephson Institute of Ethics noted in this chapter's interview section, **fairness**

fairness
genuine and open-minded impartiality.

is ensured when the speaker has made a genuine effort to see all sides of an issue and be open-minded. Only using information that helps the speaker's case is unfair to listeners as they attempt to make informed decisions about the content of the message.

Ethically, speakers are obliged to acknowledge alternative and opposing views. Few subjects are black and white; rarely is there only one "right" or "wrong" way to view a topic. Speakers who act as though there were deny their audience the chance to make informed decisions. They also betray a lack of sensitivity to other people's values and moral stances.

PLAGIARISM

To their everlasting regret, more than one otherwise honorable speaker has succumbed to the pressure of creating a moving speech by using someone else's ideas or words as his or her own. For example, as a presidential candidate in 1988, Senator Joseph Biden gave a speech about his background in which the exact structure and phrasing of a speech by the British politician Neil Kinnock were copied. When Biden's opponents got wind of it, they aired a television commercial in which the two speeches played side-by-side. Biden soon dropped out of the race.

Crediting sources is a crucial aspect of any speech. **Plagiarism**—the using of others' information as one's own—is universally regarded as unethical. To plagiarize is to use other people's ideas or words without acknowledging the source. Whether it's done intentionally or not, plagiarism is stealing. Recall the vignette about Tony Baptiste at the beginning of this chapter. Tony was guilty of stealing material that had already been plagiarized by other speakers.

Plagiarism is a serious breach of ethics. Not only is it a form of stealing, but it is also an act of not respecting the sovereignty of someone else's work. Moreover, consider your relationship with your audience. When you present plagiarized material to an audience as your own, you deceive them and take credit for something that is not yours. You violate the trust an audience places in you as a speaker, and therefore you are not respecting the relationship a speaker must have with the audience. It is worth repeating that one of the consequences of plagiarism is a loss of credibility.

In both academic and professional spheres, the consequences of plagiarism are severe. All universities and colleges have strict codes of conduct governing plagiarism. Students who are found to plagiarize generally fail the course in which it occurred. Depending on the severity of the situation, some students are placed on academic probation or expelled. Their academic careers are jeopardized, and many find it difficult to continue their education. Plagiarism poses similar consequences in the business world. Because plagiarism creates suspicion in the minds of others, the offender may no longer be trusted with sensitive information or a promotion. It may well cost the offender his or her job.

The rule for avoiding plagiarism as a public speaker is straightforward: *Any source that requires credit in written form should be acknowledged in oral form.* These include direct quotations, paraphrased information, facts, statistics, and just about any other kind of information gathered and reported by others. Oral presentations need not include the full bibliographic reference (names, dates, titles, volume and page numbers). However, you should include a complete reference on the bibliography page or at the bottom of the speech outline.

plagiarism
the use of other people's ideas or words without acknowledging the source.

Direct Quotations

Direct quotations are statements made verbatim, or word for word, by someone else. Direct quotes should always be acknowledged in a speech. Although it is not a requirement, you can call attention to a source's exact wording with phrases such as "And I quote" or "As (the source) put it" and so forth. For example,

> As my esteemed colleague, Dr. Vance Brown, told an audience of AIDS researchers at the International AIDS Convention last year,

direct quotations
statements made verbatim, or word for word, by someone else.

Focus on Technology

Crediting Online Sources

The explosive growth of the Internet and the availability of electronically stored sources of information such as CD-ROMs have increased the problem of plagiarism. Failing to give proper credit to information found in an electronic source is no less an instance of plagiarism than failing to cite a print source.

After some initial confusion, guidelines are now available for citing data transmitted electronically—either on CD-ROMs or online.[1] Two of the most helpful sources are the *Modern Language Association (MLA) Handbook* and the *Chicago Manual of Style*. Here are some general rules:

- Always indicate the medium in which the source is published—CD-ROM, online database, or computer network (e.g., America Online or the Internet).
- The date provided in electronic information is not necessarily the original date of publication

for the resource. The date may reflect when it was added to the database. Thus, it's important to verify the original publication date.

- The goal of the citation is to allow the information to be retrieved again. Keep this in mind. Check to make sure that the information you provide will allow a subsequent researcher to find the same source.
- Punctuation and capitalization, especially in the electronic address of the resource, should appear just as it is used in the database.[2]
- Always check with your instructor for guidance on online citations. She or he may have special instructions for you to follow.

1. Examples of online citations can be found in Chapter 7.
2. Cited in the *MLA Handbook for Writers of Research Papers,* 4th ed. (New York: Modern Language Association of America, 1995); see also X. Li and N. Crane, *Guide for Citing Electronic Information Based on Electronic Style* (Westport, CT: Meckler, 1993).

---

and I quote, "The cure may be near or may be far, but the human suffering is very much in the present."

As Shakespeare would say, "A rose by any other name would smell as sweet."

Paraphrased Information

paraphrase
a restatement of someone else's statements, ideas, or written work in the speaker's own words.

A **paraphrase** is a restatement of someone else's statements, ideas, or written work in the speaker's own words. Because paraphrases alter the form but not the substance of another's ideas, the speaker must acknowledge the original source. After all, they are not the speaker's ideas. For example:

According to Professor John Slater of the Cranberry Middle School in New York, students' increasing reliance on the Internet as a research tool will only result in more cases of plagiarism. *Slater sees* a trend in which students equate cyberspace with "free." Unless we address the issue at the grade-school level, *Slater says,* we risk raising a generation of plagiarizers.

Facts and Statistics

Any data other than that gathered by you should be cited. The three examples below illustrate how you can incorporate and cite facts and statistics in a speech.

In a lecture on academic honesty, *Grinnell University professor Judy Hunter* described how two-thirds of the cases of plagiarism brought before the university's Committee on Academic Standing resulted not because students deliberately set out to deceive their audience or their professors but from, *and I quote*, "a mistaken notion of the importance of the process of citation."[21]

In the July 1995 issue of *Management Today,* in his article "In Sickness," *journalist Simon Caulkin reports* that Britain's National Health Service is suffering low employee morale.

According to Scott Burns, a columnist featured in the January 14, 1996, edition of the *Dallas Morning News*, saving money in today's economic climate is problematic.

ASSESSING ETHICAL FACTORS AFTER DELIVERING A SPEECH

It is always important to evaluate your speech after you have delivered it in order to improve for your next speech. The following is a checklist to assess ethical factors in your speech.

1. Did the speech respect the values of your audience? Did it reflect your own values in a way that pleases you?
2. Were you honest in your presentation? Did you use accurate information?
3. Did you focus on issues rather than personalities?
4. Was your overall aim socially constructive? Did the audience benefit in some way from your remarks?
5. Did you use sound evidence and reasoning?
6. Was the content of your message accurate? Were your facts correct? Did you disregard any important information?
7. Did you avoid manipulating the emotional sensitivity of your audience?
8. Did you avoid using language (e.g., slang, jargon) that might create in-group and out-group distinctions?
9. Did you avoid all expressions of ethnocentrism, stereotypes, or other kinds of prejudice?
10. If appropriate, did you acknowledge alternative or opposing views?
11. Did you acknowledge your sources of information by citing them appropriately in the speech?
12. Were the citations accurate and complete?

SUMMARY QUESTIONS

What is ethics?

Ethics is the study of moral conduct: how people should act toward one another. In terms of public speaking, ethics implies the responsibilities speakers have toward their audience and themselves. It also encompasses the responsibilities listeners have toward speakers. The word *ethics* derives from the Greek word *ethos*, meaning "character."

What is the relationship between speech that is legal and speech that is ethical?

There isn't necessarily one. The First Amendment ensures protection to both the honest and the dishonest and offensive speaker. Codes of ethical speech are built on moral rather than legal principles.

What is positive ethos?

According to Aristotle, audiences listen to and trust speakers if they demonstrate positive ethos (positive character). Positive ethos includes competence (as demonstrated by the speaker's grasp of the subject matter), good moral character (as reflected in the speaker's trustworthiness, straightforwardness, and honest presentation of the message), and goodwill (as demonstrated by the speaker's knowledge of and attitude of respect toward the audience and the particular speech occasion).

According to modern research on speaker credibility, what speaker characteristics inspire trust?

Modern research on speaker credibility reveals that people most trust those speakers who have a sound grasp of the subject, display sound reasoning skills, are honest and unmanipulative, and are genuinely interested in the welfare of their listeners.

What are values, and what is their relationship to ethics?

Values are our most enduring judgments, or standards, of what's good and bad in life; of what's important to us. Our ethical choices in daily life and in our speeches are our values in action. Ethical speaking requires that we recognize and respect the audience's values, even when they diverge from our own.

Why is an awareness and appreciation of values—both our own and others'—important in ensuring ethical speaking?

Being alert to differences in values can help us speak ethically by sensitizing us to the existence of alternative viewpoints. We can use this awareness to review potential topics from a culturally sensitive perspective. It can also serve as a reminder that differences in dialects or accents, nonverbal cues, word choice, and even physical appearance can be barriers to understanding.

What two characteristics are universally seen as central to ethical behavior?

Although there is no single agreed-on code of ethical standards for communication, the qualities of dignity and integrity are universally seen as central to ethical behavior. Dignity implies the feeling of being worthy, honored, or respected as a person. Integrity implies incorruptibility; being able to avoid compromise for the sake of personal expediency. Speakers who demonstrate dignity and integrity exhibit a hallmark of ethical speaking: concern for the greater good.

In addition to dignity and integrity, what other four qualities do ethical speakers exhibit?

Ethical speaking requires that we be trustworthy, respectful, responsible, and fair in our presentations. Trustworthiness is a combination of honesty and dependability. Respect ranges from addressing audience members as unique human beings to refraining from rudeness and other forms of personal attacks. Responsible speaking includes evaluating your topic and purpose for their usefulness and appropriateness, using sound evidence and reasoning, and being accurate. Fairness is ensured when the speaker has made a genuine effort to be fair and open-minded. Ethically, it is incumbent on the speaker to acknowledge alternative and opposing views.

What is plagiarism, and why is it unethical?

Plagiarism is the passing off of someone else's information as one's own. To plagiarize is to use other people's ideas or words without acknowledging the source. Plagiarism is universally regarded as unethical because it is a form of stealing.

How can you avoid plagiarizing?

The rule for avoiding plagiarism as a public speaker is straightforward: Any source that requires credit in written form should be acknowledged in oral form. These include direct quotations, paraphrased information, facts, statistics, and just about any other kind of information gathered and reported by others.

ISSUES FOR DISCUSSION

1. What advice about ethical public speaking would you give to a political candidate? Why do you think so many people are skeptical of politicians? Can you recall listening to any political speeches that struck you as ethically problematic? In what way?

2. Are profanity and vulgarity always unethical as part of public speeches? Can you think of situations where they would seem appropriate? What types of situations, and why?

3. What do you think the penalties should be for plagiarizing someone else's work? Should the penalty for plagiarizing someone else's work *in entirety* be the same as that for plagiarizing *only parts* of it? Explain your position.

4. What are some ways that a speaker can regain the confidence of those who have accused her or him of unethical communication?

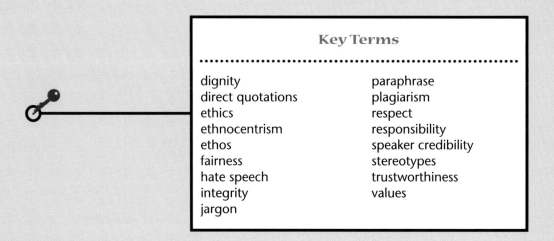

Key Terms

dignity
direct quotations
ethics
ethnocentrism
ethos
fairness
hate speech
integrity
jargon

paraphrase
plagiarism
respect
responsibility
speaker credibility
stereotypes
trustworthiness
values

SELF-ASSESSMENT

1. Listen to a speech on C-Span or check out a speech on videotape from your library. Does the speaker maintain the responsibilities necessary for ethical speaking? Why or why not? What would your responsibilities be as a listener to this speech?

2. Think about the times you have spoken in groups or at meetings. Was there ever an occasion when you could have been more ethical with your messages? Explain.

3. Who are some of the most ethical people you have ever known personally? Have you tried to emulate their behavior? What are some of the qualities that you admired most about these people? On the basis of these qualities, what could you offer to other people as advice about becoming more ethical?

4. Take another look at Table 4.1, Identifying Values. In the Critical Checkpoint exercise on page 82, you were asked to list your five most important values and those of others. This time, list the values from that exercise that are *least important* to you and to others. Now compare the least and most important lists of values. Develop some explanations for why these lists differ. Do you think your own values will change as you become more educated and gain more experience in general?

TEAMWORK

1. Form a team of four or five people. Suppose you have been asked to give a panel presentation at the International Students' Orientation. What are some of the things you should think about to ensure that your speech is ethical?

2. As part of a group project, find a relevant fact or piece of information on the Internet or World Wide Web. Write two ways of conveying this information to your audience; include citations for your source.

3. Working in a small group, find a speech that was given in the last ten years. Examine the speech to detect any problems with ethics. Apply the ground rules from Michael Josephson regarding trustworthiness, respect, responsibility, and fairness. Make a report in class about your results.

Speech belongs
half to the
speaker, half to
the listener.
　　—Montaigne

No man ever looks at the world with pristine eyes. He sees it
edited by a definite set of customs and institutions and ways
of thinking.

　　　　　　　　　　　　　　　　　　　—Ruth Benedict

Audience 5 Analysis

Have you ever seen an advertisement so convincing that you made a mental note to purchase the product it described? Perhaps it advertised a pair of athletic shoes or a particular brand of clothing. **What was it about the ad that made such an impression?** Did the ad suggest that it could fulfill a need you had? Did it suggest an image that you wanted to adopt?

Advertisers are astute analysts when it comes to reading people's needs and wants. The best of them can closely target both our desires and our fears. **In at least one sense, public speakers are like advertisers. To capture an audience's attention, they too must present a topic in ways that will interest their listeners.**

Dan Sanders is director of marketing for United Supermarkets, a regional chain of thirty-eight stores in business since 1916. He delivers approximately twenty speeches a year for school programs and civic groups, most often discussing his experiences in the U.S. Air Force as a U2 pilot during the Gulf War and as a member of the White House Advance Team (responsible for all logistics involved with presidential travel utilizing Air Force One, the president's aircraft). Dan, formerly a communications major and a competitive speaker in college, has nearly twenty years of public speaking experience. Still, he sometimes learns hard lessons about the speechmaking process.

In the spring of 1996 Dan was invited to speak at an assembly of graduating high school seniors. He was barely acquainted with the person who called to extend the invitation—someone who had heard him speak at a civic club luncheon several weeks previously—but accepted it after learning the audience would be high school seniors and their parents and that he could speak on the topic of motivation. When he arrived at the speech site he was surprised to see a large, gymnasium-like room; it seemed to dwarf the audience. The audience was not particularly small, but too small for this room. Also surprising, only because he had not anticipated it, was to find that the audience consisted entirely of Hispanic and African American families. Dan was literally the only Anglo person in the room, and the one to whom all attention was about to be directed. Although the situation struck him as potentially awkward, he maintained his usual confidence because his broad experiences had taught him how to adjust quickly to the unexpected. Then he noticed the unusual arrangement of a speaker's stand. Actually, there was no speaker's stand, or lectern or podium—only a stand-microphone in the middle of the floor, attached to a three-foot cable, approximately fifty feet from the nearest audience members. Dan faced a double bind: He would have to use the microphone to be heard well in the large room, but being tied to the microphone would keep him at an inappropriate distance from the audience.

Dan went ahead with his speech as he had planned it. However, he questioned its effectiveness, partly because he could not tell how relevant and meaningful his material was to the audience, and partly because he felt uncomfortable with the physical facilities.

Dan's experience highlights two critical features of audience analysis in the speech preparation process: learning about the audience, and becoming familiar with the speech setting. Indeed, understanding both the composition of an audience and the setting in which the speech will take place is vital to a successful presentation. Just who are the people in the audience? How much do they have in common? To what extent do they share similar values and beliefs? Do their values and beliefs match those of the speaker? How familiar are they with the speech topic? What concerns them most about the speech topic? Gathering information about the audience takes a great deal of work, but it will ultimately help the speaker to craft the most effective speech possible for the audience.

Chapter Challenges

How does a speaker learn about an audience he or she is going to address, and why is it important to do so? What motivates audiences, and how can a speaker uncover this information? This chapter addresses these and related challenges:

- To understand the role played by audience demographics such as age, gender, cultural background, and religion—and audience psychology, including motivation, values, and personality traits—in audience responsiveness; and to use

this knowledge to plan a more successful speech.

- To become familiar with and use several key tools such as interviews and surveys, and even online sources, for discovering information about an audience.

- To discover how the speech setting—location, time of speech, lighting and sound, and related factors—influences audience receptivity; and to incorporate these factors into planning for the speech.

As illustrated in Figure 5.1, the audience is a key component of the public speaking model. In a crucial sense, the audience is what your speech is all about. A topic may in fact be vital to the national interest and personally fascinating to you, but if it isn't prepared and delivered with the listeners' needs and interests in mind, all your efforts may be in vain. This does not mean that you have to pretend to believe other than you do or in any way betray your own values and beliefs. However, it does require that you prepare your speech so that it stands the best chance of being well received by a given audience.

This chapter will explain just how to accomplish the task of **audience analysis**—the process by which a speaker discovers to the fullest extent possible what the listeners' needs and interests are regarding the topic, and in so doing adjusts the presentation to meet these needs and interests. Audience analysis is the only way to avoid surprises such as the one Dan Sanders received on the day he presented a speech to an unfamiliar group. Let's begin by looking at the kinds of information you can discover about an audience, starting with audience demographics.

audience analysis
the process by which a speaker discovers the needs and interests of a particular audience regarding the speech topic.

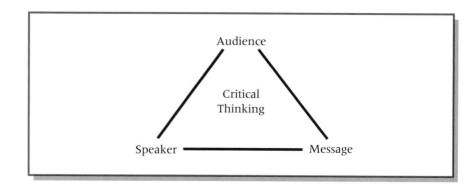

FIGURE 5.1
Public Speaking Model

AUDIENCE DEMOGRAPHICS: BUILDING A PROFILE

demographics
statistical characteristics of a given population or group, including such factors as age, gender, education, and political affiliation.

Speakers use a variety of information to analyze an audience. One important source of such information lies in audience **demographics**. A demographic is a statistical characteristic of a given population. Six such characteristics are typically considered in the analysis of speech audiences: age, gender, ethnic or cultural background, socioeconomic status (including income, occupation, and education) religious and political affiliation, and related values and beliefs.

Advertisers and politicians have long relied on audience demographics to fashion their messages as closely as possible to their target audiences. Likewise, as a public speaker you will win over more of your listeners if you understand who they are. As you read about individual demographics in the discussion that follows, keep in mind that some audiences consist of a large number of people who represent a particular demographic characteristic whereas other audiences are more fragmented. But even in an audience whose members share a given demographic feature— say, all listeners are the same age—a speaker should never assume that this one shared feature is enough to unite the audience. For example, all members of a senior citizen center may be over age 65, but it is a risky proposition to assume they will all vote for candidate X. These senior citizens may be a mix of men and women, more or less religious and of different faiths, and from different ethnic, educational, occupational, and political backgrounds.

Bob Daemmrich/Image Works

Good speakers always consider their audience. Focusing on audience members' beliefs and values will help produce an enthusiastic response.

Age

People who were born in or around the same year often share many common experiences. Certainly they share exposure to the same national leaders, the same national and international calamities, the same popular culture, and so forth. As it happens, most audiences consist of a mix of ages. Even a seemingly homogeneous audience of college students often turns out to consist of students ranging from 17 to 40 years of age or older. Being aware of the audience's age range allows the speaker to develop points, and material to support those points, that are relevant to the experiences and interests of the widest possible portion of the audience. In general, speeches should be applicable across age interests.

Gender

Consideration of gender is important both in developing a topic's key points and in the manner in which you present the speech. Consider the case of Carly below. Had Carly considered gender, she might have realized that in today's world, most single women are more concerned about safety than single men are. (But before making even this blanket assumption, she'd better research her audience!)

Carly thought she had it down pat. She had thoroughly researched her topic—holiday travel in the Caribbean—and felt confident as she addressed a local singles group of people under age 30. She discussed five destinations, including information about hotels, restaurants, and points of interest for each. Her slide show was spectacular. During her presentation, she thought she noticed some of the women in the audience looking anxious. But only when she opened up the presentation for discussion did Carly realize that the concerns of the female half of her audience were markedly different from the male portion—and she wasn't prepared to address them.

It turned out that in the destinations Carly had selected, there had been a run of violent incidents directed toward female tourists. These included several hotel-room break-ins and rapes and a spate of muggings on the beach. The women in the audience were quite concerned about how best to protect themselves, both in their hotel rooms and outside. Carly did not know what to tell them.

Carly could have made a lot of other errors related to gender, but fortunately she didn't. She did not assume, for example, that the women in the audience would be interested in one type of recreation and the men in another. Indeed, her audience analysis surveys had uncovered the fact that more of the women than men were interested in golfing during their vacations. Though Carly failed to uncover her audience's concerns about safety, her presentation avoided **gender stereotypes**—oversimplified and often severely distorted ideas about the innate natures of men or women. Common gender stereotypes in the United States include "the emotional woman" and "the logical man." Another is that boys are naturally independent, whereas

gender stereotypes
oversimplified and often severely distorted ideas about the innate nature of men or women.

girls are dependent. Gender stereotypes emerge from sexism, the unequal valuing of one sex over another.

As a public speaker, it's important to avoid gender stereotypes or any other form of sexism. This includes the use of language. Always avoid the generic use of the pronoun *he*, for example, unless the audience is all men and the topic relates exclusively to men. Also avoid tying one gender to a particular occupational or social category. One student spoke to his class about exploration drilling in the oil fields of Southeast Asia. Early in the speech he apologized for selecting a topic that would be "boring" (excuse the pun) to the women in the class. The apology itself was inappropriate and revealed his lack of preparedness in audience analysis and topic selection. Worse, after the speech a woman classmate declared that both her parents were petroleum engineers who had spent some time working in the oil fields of Southeast Asia. She was very interested in his topic! Needless to say, the speaker was embarrassed by his gender-specific blunder.

Gender sometimes overlaps with age as a determinant of audience interests and experiences. Just a few years ago, for instance, a speech on the care of newborn babies would have been considered appropriate for an audience made up primarily of women in their twenties. Today it would be a mistake not to consider the topic as being of interest to men as well as women, and to parents over age 30 as well. Thus, when analyzing the gender-relevant characteristics of an audience, consider age also.

Ethnic or Cultural Background

Whether it is considered a "melting pot" or, using a newer metaphor, a "salad bowl," the United States is unquestionably a society composed of many different kinds of people. Unlike Japan, for instance, whose population is 99.5 percent of Japanese descent (the remaining 0.5 percent is Korean), the U.S. population includes persons of African, Asian, Hispanic, European, and Native American descent, among others. Increasingly, success in the global economy requires an understanding of diverse cultures. Similarly, the more public speakers are aware of ethnic and cultural variations, the more effective their speeches will be. Just as an astute businessperson would not make a presentation to a group of foreign officials without researching their customs, neither should you ignore this aspect of audience demographics—regardless of where your speech will be given. Even professionals make mistakes, however. In 1997, no one on President Clinton's staff realized that in South Korea wives retain their maiden names. Clinton's staff should have advised him, before he spoke, not to refer to President Kim Yung Sam's wife as "Mrs. Kim." (Another Korean custom is to place the family name before the given name.)

One way to investigate the demographic variable of culture and ethnicity is to look for information about audience members' values. As we saw in Chapter 4, some values—for instance, that of being truthful and of causing no harm to others—apply across many cultures. Other values, or the emphasis placed on them, are more culture-specific. For example, in many Asian societies the value of group harmony is paramount. However, in the United States and many other Western nations the value of individual achievement is more highly prized. Asians place great emphasis on the ceremonial aspects of public speaking, greeting each other by bowing and exchanging gifts before beginning a speech. Some fundamentalist Muslim cultures value the public separation of the sexes as a religious principle and do not permit women to publicly address mixed audiences.

Being alert to differences in values can help speakers deliver their message in any number of ways—from reviewing the topic in a culturally sensitive perspective, to being mindful that differences in dialects or accents, nonverbal cues, word choice, and even physical appearance can be barriers to understanding (see Chapter 3). Keep in mind, however, that although sensitivity to diversity is key, no one can know everything about every group. In one sense, ethnic and cultural demographics—and, for that matter, every demographic characteristic—should be a concern in audience analysis only to the extent that the speaker's message must be relevant and meaningful to the whole audience. Nevertheless, knowing as much as possible about an audience, including its ethnic and cultural composition, can help you craft a well-targeted and respectful message.

Public Speaking in Cultural Perspective

Audience Analysis as Relationship Development

Social scientists who study the development of personal relationships tell us that relationships progress along a continuum of growth stages, from a point of initiation (such as being introduced) to some sort of bonding or public commitment (such as marriage), and, if things don't work out, perhaps to a stage of dissolution or termination of the relationship (such as divorce). In one model of relationship growth, there is an early stage known as *experimenting* in which the participants communicate primarily to exchange basic biographical and demographic information.[1] Here's where they discover each other's fundamental similarities, especially in certain attitudes and beliefs. Communication at this stage is largely an exchange of questions—What kinds of movies do you like? Do you like roller blading? Where did you go on your last vacation?

Analyzing an audience for a speech is much like the experimenting stage of relationship development. It is an opportunity to get to know the audience, just as you might get to know a new acquaintance. The process requires asking questions (in surveys or interviews) to learn how similar the audience's attitudes and beliefs are to your own. This is an especially important perspective when you and the audience are culturally different. Unless there is information to the contrary, our basic tendency is to have expectations about other people that are consistent with our own experiences and knowledge. For example, unless we know that an audience is distinctly different from most other audiences, we expect that audience to be much like the ones we are familiar with already. This is one reason audience analysis is so important: to avoid the trap of assuming that all audiences are alike. Only by asking will we gain an accurate picture of who the audience is and what their likes and dislikes are. After all, any future relationship we hope to have with the audience depends largely on how well we relate to them at the outset.

1. M. Knapp and A. Vangelisti, *Interpersonal Communication and Human Relationships* (Boston: Allyn and Bacon, 1992).

Socioeconomic Status

Socioeconomic status (SES) includes income, occupation, and education. Knowing roughly where an audience falls in terms of these key variables can make the difference between success and failure in delivering a message.

Income. Income determines people's experiences on many levels. It directly affects how they are housed, clothed, and fed and determines what they can afford. Beyond this, income has a ripple effect, influencing many other aspects of life. For example, depending on income, health insurance is either a taken-for-granted budget item or an out-of-reach dream. The same is true for travel and leisure activities. Given how pervasively income affects people's life experiences, speakers should carefully consider this aspect of audience demographics when planning their speech topic.

Occupation. For most people in Western cultures, work is one of the foremost bases of identification. After all, the ability to sustain ourselves derives from the work we do. Moreover, we spend the greater part of our adult lives working, and many of our associations and relationships evolve from work. It's no wonder that work and work-related issues are among the most frequent topics of our daily conversations.

The nature of people's work has a lot to do with what interests them. Occupational interests are tied to several other areas of social concern, such as politics, the economy, education, and social reform. Personal attitudes, beliefs, and goals are also closely tied to occupational standing. People who are unemployed look at many issues differently from people who are working steadily. An audience consisting entirely of nurses and nursing-related specialists has certain unique knowledge, skills, and perspectives that shape the listeners' receptivity to a speech and speaker. The same is true for any audience comprised of a common occupational type (doctors, lawyers, construction contractors, teachers, fashion models, sales representatives, photographers, etc.) or occupational status (professional, skilled, laborer, etc.). Occupation may be a less important factor when the audience spans a wide variety of occupational types. In any situation, occupation is an important and easily identifiable demographic characteristic that successful speakers determine in advance about their audiences.

Education. Level of education strongly influences people's ideas, perspectives, and range of abilities. For example, studies show that people who attain a college education work at higher-status occupations and earn generally higher pay than non-college graduates do. Better-educated members of an audience may respond differently to a subject, or have different ways of understanding it, than those who are less educated. A higher level of education, moreover, appears to be associated with greater fluctuation in personal values, beliefs, and goals. In other words, persons with more education may be more open to changing their minds.

A speaker should review everything from topic selection to use of language in light of the key demographic of education. If the audience is generally better educated than you are, your speech may need to be quite sophisticated. When speaking to a less educated audience, you may choose to clarify your points with more examples and illustrations.

Religion

Religion is another powerful predictor of audience response. Some audience members are deeply devoted to their faiths, and others have few religious convictions. Even those who profess little religious faith, however, likely hold many values that are informed by religious precepts.

Being aware of an audience's general religious orientation can be especially helpful to a speaker when the speech topic is potentially controversial on religious grounds. Topics such as abortion rights, capital punishment, sex education, public school textbook selection, the origins of humankind, school prayer, and gay men and lesbians serving in the military are rife with religious overtones and implications. For some listeners, for example, the question of whether gay men and lesbians should be allowed to be open about their sexual preferences in the military is a religious rather than a political or public policy issue.

Because the speaker's own religious values also play a part in audience reactions, they should be considered as well when planning the speech.

Sam, who attended a public university, selected the topic of sexual abstinence for a presentation in his public speaking class. From interviews, he knew that his audience considered this issue very important and timely, so he was confident they would be interested in what he had to say. However, he did very limited audience analysis and failed to investigate the listeners' values and beliefs. Sam gave a speech in which he tried to convince the audience to accept his view that premarital sexual intercourse was a sin condemned in the Bible. As evidence, he read verses from the Bible. He concluded by asserting that the most obvious reason to practice sexual abstinence is to live a life like Jesus Christ's.

Given the context in which he spoke—a public university—Sam overstepped the bounds of appropriateness by supporting his point with teachings from a particular religious tradition and its central figure and by claiming that the audience should accept and live by those teachings. Although he could have appropriately cited religious faith as a reason why many people abstain from premarital sex, he failed to realize that for many people sexual abstinence may be more an issue of physical, mental, and emotional health than of religious sanctity.

Unless there is evidence to prove it, don't assume that everyone in your audience shares a common Judeo-Christian heritage. As noted in Chapter 1, just about 50 percent of Americans over age 18 identify themselves as Protestant, about 25 percent as Roman Catholic, and about 2 percent as Jewish.[1] This leaves roughly 30 percent of the population—or about 60 million people—of different faiths such as Islam, Buddhism, Confucianism, and Hinduism.[2] Furthermore, don't assume that all members of the same religious tradition agree on all issues. For example, Catholics disagree on birth control and divorce.

Political Affiliation

As with religion, a speaker should never make unwarranted assumptions about an audience's political values and beliefs. Even if they are not directly political, many topics automatically raise political questions—and, if the speaker isn't careful, listeners' hackles. The topic of teenage pregnancy, for example, could easily encompass a discussion of how Republicans as opposed to Democrats in Congress propose to deal with the problem. Unless this was indeed the focus of your speech, you should make a conscious effort to steer clear of the audience's sensitivities on this score.

Some people like nothing better than a lively debate about public policy issues. Others avoid anything that smacks of politics. And many people are very serious, and others are very touchy, about their political views or their views on political issues. Unless you have prior information about the audience's political values and beliefs, you won't know where the listeners stand.

Critical Checkpoint

Your Own Demographic Profile

Build a demographic profile of yourself. Fill in each blank as it applies to you:

Age _____   Gender _____   Ethnic Background _____

Approximate Annual Income _____   Religion _____

Political Affiliation _____

What does this profile say about you? How does it relate to your personal interests and aspirations? How likely is it that other people who have a very similar profile will have interests similar to yours? Why? Change one characteristic in the list (e.g., if for Religion you wrote *Catholic*, change it to *Jewish*). How would this change your profile? Would such a change be reflected in your interests and aspirations? What implications would this have for you as an audience member?

AUDIENCE PSYCHOLOGY

The demographic features of an audience provide many important clues to its profile, but they by no means tell the entire story. Psychological factors also powerfully affect how messages are received and processed.

If you were shopping for a new car, you would consider at least two different sets of features in making your decision (assume money's no object at this point!). One set would be the model, color, accessories, and other features that make the car immediately distinguishable from other cars. But these features don't have a whole lot to do with what makes the car run well. A second set of features does, and it would include the engine components, drive train, electrical system, and fuel system. Audience demographics are like the former set of features—they make one audience clearly distinguishable from another. **Audience psychology**—audience members' attitudes, beliefs, values, and personality traits—is like the second set of features. It alerts the listeners to the ways listeners think and feel about things; it tells the speaker what makes them "tick."

audience psychology
audience members' attitudes, beliefs, values, and personality traits.

Attitudes, Beliefs, and Values

People tend to evaluate messages in terms of their own—rather than the speaker's—attitudes, beliefs, and values. **Attitudes** reflect a predisposition to respond to people, ideas, objects, or events in evaluative ways.[3] To evaluate something is to judge it as relatively good or bad, useful or useless, desirable or undesirable, pretty or ugly, tasteful or tasteless, and so on. People generally act in accordance with their attitudes. If we have a positive attitude toward reading, for example, we're likely to read. And we're likely to want to listen to a speaker discuss books. If we have a negative attitude toward religion, we're likely to avoid attending religious services—as well as speeches praising the value of religion.

Attitudes are based on **beliefs**—the ways people perceive reality to be.[4] They are our feelings about what is true. Whereas attitudes deal with the felt quality of some activity or entity ("Reading is good," or "God is good"), beliefs refer to our level of confidence about the very existence or validity of something ("I believe God exists," or "I'm not so sure that God exists"). The less faith listeners have that something exists—UFOs, for instance—the less open they are to hearing about them.

Both attitudes and beliefs are shaped by **values**—people's most enduring judgments about what's good and bad in life. Values are more general than either attitudes or beliefs. We have fewer of them than the former, but we hold on to them more dearly. They are also more resistant to change. It is important to investigate values because they provide the basis for attitudes and beliefs. For example, if you value a financially comfortable life above all, you will probably form positive attitudes toward steady work. If you treasure freedom from authority, you may form less positive attitudes toward traditional work or, perhaps, toward bosses. Understanding an audience's values points you in the direction of their attitudes and beliefs.

Discovering your listeners' attitudes, beliefs, and values provides crucial clues to how receptive they will be toward your topic and your position on it. Consider the case of Naomi, an outreach health worker who was invited to speak at a local clinic in a small town in the southwestern United States.

Naomi's audience was a group of Mexican Americans, all of whom had been hospitalized for lead poisoning caused by drinking out of cups and bowls made from a certain kind of pottery. The clinic health workers, frustrated at their inability to convince the group to stop using the pottery, turned to Naomi because of her long background in working with this population. Naomi interviewed several of the patients at length and also consulted local healers. She discovered that the patients believed that drinking from the pottery enhanced fertility, a deeply held value. In her speech she acknowledged the group's belief, discussed alternate ways to enhance fertility in keeping with their values, and then argued that using the pottery posed too high a risk to their health.

Had Naomi not uncovered the particular audience belief about fertility, her speech would surely have been ineffective. Regardless of the speech

attitudes
predispositions to respond to people, ideas, objects, or events in evaluative ways.

beliefs
the ways people perceive reality to be; conceptions of what is true and what is false.

values
people's most enduring judgments about what's good and bad in life.

Making a Difference

WENDY KOPP, PRESIDENT AND FOUNDER, TEACH FOR AMERICA

When she was a senior at Princeton University, Wendy Kopp wondered how she could contribute to society once she graduated. What path could she embark on that would really make a difference? The idea she eventually settled on became the subject of her senior thesis. In it Wendy proposed the creation of a national teacher corps, much like a domestic Peace Corps, devoted to improving conditions in education. Wendy's hypothetical organization would be called "Teach For America," and it would attract outstanding recent college graduates willing to commit two years to teach in the many urban and rural public schools that needed them.

The extraordinary thing about Wendy Kopp and her idea is not that she had it, but that she actually implemented it. Within a year of graduating in 1989, Wendy founded Teach For America and placed 500 corps members in various schools across the nation. Writing to 30 corporations, she managed to convince the Mobil Corporation to provide a seed grant. Soon other corporate, individual, and government funding sources followed suit.

Today, less than a decade later, Wendy presides over a staff of 75 fulltime employees in 14 offices nationwide, and a group of 1,000 corps members in the field at any one time. Fanning out from New York to East Los Angeles to Sunflower, Mississippi, recent graduates such as Duke University's Chris Myers, University of California at Berkeley's Eric Ryan, and University of Michigan's Maria Zamora are giving their all to motivate and educate students who have hitherto received little of either.

Wendy's amazing achievement has not gone unnoticed by the country's movers and shakers—from the president on down. She was the youngest

goal, it's important to try to uncover the audiences' attitudes, beliefs, and values—or, for brevity's sake, *feelings*—toward (1) the topic of your speech; (2) you as their speaker; (3) the speech occasion. As in discovering demographic features, you can uncover these through audience analysis by using one or a combination of the methods described later in this chapter.

Feelings toward the Topic. As a general rule, people give more interest and attention to topics for which they have a positive attitude, and which align with their values and beliefs. The less we know, the more indifferent we tend to be. One way to gauge an audience's attitudes toward a topic is by asking: What do they know about the topic? What is their level of interest? How do they feel about it? Once you have this information, adjust the speech accordingly. If an audience knows relatively little, for instance, plan on sticking to the basics and including more background information. Otherwise, listeners might feel lost or alienated. If the topic is new to the audience, you might focus on explaining why it should interest them.

person and first woman to receive the Woodrow Wilson Award, the highest honor Princeton University confers on an outstanding alumnus. In addition, she has received the Jefferson Award for Public Service, Aetna's Voice of Conscience Award, the Citizen Activist Award, and the Kilby Young Innovator Award. *Time* magazine named her one of 40 most promising leaders under age 40, and thus far three universities have awarded her honorary degrees.

As president of Teach For America, Wendy delivers speeches all the time. Her audiences range from staff, corps, and board members to large public audiences of 500 or more. She's spoken at luncheons, receptions, dinners, commencements, and just about everything in between. Wendy sees her public speaking as an essential part of her leadership role, one that allows her to communicate and refine her organization's twofold mission: that of maintaining 1,000 corps members in the field, and that of building an ever-expanding base of corps alumni committed to expanding educational opportunity in this country.

In preparing her speeches, Wendy focuses first and foremost on what she wants to accomplish with a particular audience. Whether addressing potential funders or an entering group of corps members, "Everything—from style to tone to content—flows from this goal. When addressing corps members, for example, my goal is to ensure that they remember the ideals and vision that brought us to this mission in the first place. When addressing potential funders, I'll want to convey that we are an important and powerful investment in our nation's future."

Does she ever use a speechwriter? No. "I find writing speeches so productive," Wendy notes. "It gives me the time to hone my thinking and reflect on our goals. I want to be sure that every single word of my speeches conveys what I mean to communicate."

Some of Wendy's most challenging speaking assignments to date have been her three commencement addresses, at which she received honorary degrees. Though the preparation is arduous and nerve-wracking, the satisfaction of preparing a well-received speech is immense. Most important, however, is that these and other speeches allow her to spread the word about what she believes in most deeply: that one day, all children in this nation will have the opportunity to attain an excellent education.

Note: Students wishing to find out more about Teach For America can call 1-800-TFA-1230, ext 120, or write Teach For America, P.O. Box 5114, New York, NY 10185.

Sometimes you may share the same attitudes as your audience toward the topic. Often, however, your audience analysis will reveal differences.

Andrew, who was an avid deer hunter, decided to use his hobby as a topic for his public speaking presentation. But after analyzing his classmates' attitudes, he discovered that more than half were active in promoting animal rights. This group held negative attitudes toward hunting. On the basis of this information, Andrew decided to change his thesis from "Hunting is a great sport" to "Hunting yields many positive benefits for society." First he acknowledged many of the objections to hunting and offered what he considered to be humane answers to these objections. Next he discussed the current status of the deer population, noting the problem of overpopulation and the related issues of large-scale damage to farmers' crops and traffic accidents. He also described the role deer play in the spread of Lyme disease.

Once Andrew discovered his audience's attitudes toward hunting, he decided that it would be a waste of time to try to convince them that hunting was fun. But rather than abandon the topic, he tried to make it relevant to the audience. He did this by focusing on issues of general social concern and by relating the topic to issues, events, people, and activities that the audience was likely to regard in a positive light.

What if the topic is new to the audience, so they are relatively indifferent to it? You must make it relevant by relating it to issues, events, people, or activities about which they are likely to already have positive attitudes. If the audience has a negative attitude toward the topic, then your work will be a challenge—but you can still give them a speech. It will be necessary both to show your listeners that the reasons for their negative attitudes are unfounded, and to give them good reasons for developing positive attitudes toward the topic. Strategies for doing this are outlined in Chapter 14.

Feelings toward the Speaker. How the audience feels about you will have considerable bearing on their attentiveness and responsiveness to the message. A speaker who is well liked can gain at least an initial hearing by an audience even if the listeners are unsure of what to expect in terms of the substance and quality of the message. After all, we trust people we like. This holds as much for public speakers as it does for anyone. Conversely, even the most important or interesting message will be disregarded by an audience that holds negative attitudes toward the speaker. Our tendency is to put up barriers against people whom we hold in low regard. Generally, you can create positive audience attitudes toward you by displaying the characteristics of a credible speaker described in Chapter 4—knowing the subject, showing goodwill toward the audience, and displaying integrity of character in words and actions.

Feelings toward the Occasion. Depending on the occasion, people bring different sets of expectations and emotions to a speech event. Imagine parents attending a school board meeting on whether to allow sex education in the schools; they may be anxious or poised for attack. In contrast, when these same parents attend their child's high school graduation ceremonies they are likely to feel joy and goodwill. Imagine a businessperson, her third night away from home, tired from long hours of meetings, who now must attend the closing session of a conference and listen to company officers give their routine charges for breaking new production records in the coming fiscal year; she may have a less than stellar attitude about this speech occasion.

In each event, the audience's attitudes toward the occasion should be one of the speaker's key considerations in planning and delivering the speech. Failure to consider audience expectations risks alienating them, either by saying something inappropriate or by failing to state certain things. For instance, if you suspect that an audience may be anxious or hostile, you might consider ways of introducing the topic that defuse rather than inflame the situation. When speaking at a graduation, wedding, or other celebratory occasion, you might decide to incorporate into your speech acknowledgments and congratulations of achievements. Whatever the occasion, plan on investigating the audience's attitudes toward it.

Personality Traits

Another area to consider in analyzing audience psychology is that of personality traits. Communication research has uncovered numerous traits that affect the way people react to messages and message sources.[5] It can be very helpful for a public speaker to be aware of how some of these traits might characterize and determine the receptivity of the audience. Two traits are particularly important: receiver apprehension and argumentativeness.

Receiver Apprehension. Receiver apprehension is the relative degree of fear or anxiety that people experience when listening to messages that are too complex, are contrary to their traditional beliefs, or in some way represent potential harm.[6] For example, assume you are going to give a speech on a controversial issue such as legalizing late-term abortions. Any members of your audience who are receiver apprehensive will find it difficult to attend to and process your message because of the controversial nature of the topic. Controversy makes them uneasy and blocks their thinking about this subject. In a similar way, if you are going to present a speech on a complex subject—say, economic forecasting, nutritional chemistry, or the electoral college—the receiver apprehensive members of your audience will likely become inattentive because of the difficulty of the material.

If you can determine in advance your listeners' degree of receiver apprehension, you will be better able to present your points and arguments to them. For instance, if the audience contains numerous people who appear to be receiver apprehensive, you should temper the controversial nature of your points or make the information suitable for a lay (i.e., nonexpert) audience.

Argumentativeness. Argumentativeness is another communication-based personality trait that can affect the way individual audience members react to a speaker's messages. Some people enjoy arguing about controversial issues, and some people do not.[7] An argumentative person considers arguing to be a productive form of communication that promotes critical thinking and idea development. Speeches that present controversial ideas and challenge existing ways of thinking will be welcomed by argumentative people but may threaten those who are nonargumentative.

Imagine your instructor telling the class that she has decided to double the grade value of the last speech assignment. Many of your classmates may find this a rather unappealing plan. Those who are argumentative will be compelled to refute the instructor's plan, not by personally attacking her but by arguing how the plan might be unfair and should not be

> **receiver apprehension**
> the relative degree of fear or anxiety experienced by people when listening to messages that are too complex, are contrary to their traditional beliefs, or in some way represent potential harm.

> **argumentativeness**
> a personality trait that distinguishes people who consider arguing to be a form of communication that promotes critical thinking and idea development.

AP/Wide World

Flag burning is a highly charged political issue. Understanding audience psychology can be especially useful when giving a speech on a controversial topic.

implemented. Nonargumentative members of the class, even those who disagree with the instructor's plan, will likely say nothing and assume the instructor will make the best decision, whether it seems fair or not.

This is not to suggest that argumentative audience members will jump up and challenge you in the midst of a speech. Rather, the point is this: Knowing the relative level of argumentativeness of an audience can help you plan how to best present a speech. If a majority of the audience is more rather than less argumentative, you know you will be able to present hard evidence—even controversial evidence—in a direct and definite manner. However, if the majority is nonargumentative, you should be more tentative with your arguments, showing consideration for their views. Being too direct or assertive will turn them off because they will feel threatened.

Measuring Personality Traits. How can personality traits such as receiver apprehension and argumentativeness be measured in an audience? Full assessment of these characteristics requires specialized personality measures. However, by carefully phrasing a few general questions you can approximate audience members' feelings about arguing and hearing complex or potentially threatening information. Consider the following sample set of questions for these purposes. The wording borrows heavily from personality measures used by researchers to study argumentativeness and receiver apprehension.[8]

1. Do you find it enjoyable to defend your position and refute opposing views on controversial issues?	Yes	No	
2. Would you consider yourself to be someone who likes to argue about important issues?	Yes	No	
3. Is _____ a subject you would enjoy debating with someone?	Yes	No	
4. Do you find it difficult to listen to new information that is complex and hard to understand?	Yes	No	
5. Does it bother you to hear new information that puts a totally different perspective on something you believe or thought you knew?	Yes	No	
6. Are there some subjects or categories of information that frighten you or otherwise make you feel uneasy?	Yes	No	
7. How does talk about the topic of _____ make you feel?	Good	Bad	Indifferent

If the majority of respondents answers "Yes" to questions 1, 2 and 3, the audience will likely be receptive to a speech on a controversial topic. And you can be confident to address the issues head on. If, on the other hand, a majority of respondents answers "Yes" to questions 4, 5, and 6, you should consider introducing the key speech points gradually. Rather than bombarding the audience with information, try presenting smaller chunks of information that can be processed more easily. If you will be presenting information that is new or is likely to counter existing audience beliefs, frame the message in terms the audience can easily understand and apply.

METHODS OF AUDIENCE ANALYSIS

There are a variety of tools you can use to analyze an audience. Four helpful methods include interviews, surveys, reviewing written sources, and sharing information with other speakers. The selection of methods depends on the speaker's personal resources—time and access being chief among them—as well as those of the audience. Within the bounds of what's possible, a speaker should strive to discover as much as possible about how a topic will likely affect an audience.

The Interview

An **interview** is a person-to-person communication with a basic information-gathering purpose.[9] Interviews can be conducted one-on-one or in a group, depending on the amount of time available to both the interviewer and respondents and on the feasibility of getting together singly or in a group. In any case, interviews are a rich source of information about the speech audience.

> **interview**
> a form of person-to-person communication with a basic information-gathering purpose that can occur one-on-one or in a group.

Sarah has just been invited by one of her former high school teachers to speak to the school's senior-level history class. The teacher is concerned about the students' mounting anxiety as the year ends, and she wants Sarah to make a presentation to them about the transition from high school to college. Although the prospect of speaking in front of any group is nerve-wracking, Sarah accepts the invitation (with curiosity and nostalgia, if not sheer enthusiasm!). She finds some comfort in the fact that since she recently made the transition herself, she feels qualified to address the topic. She's pleased, too, that apparently she has some credibility with the teacher; otherwise she would not have been invited. After thinking it over, Sarah decides to develop three or four key points for high school seniors to think about in making the transition to college. She's uncertain, however, about what to do next.

Sarah needs to find out just what it is about making the transition from high school to college that most concerns the class. She can do this in a number of ways. She could ask the teacher about the students' concerns. She could ask her teenage neighbor, who is in her senior year at a different school. Better still, she could interview the students themselves to learn about their needs and interests regarding the transition. Are their concerns largely social? Are they afraid of academic failure? Are they concerned about being lonely? What worries them the most? The least?

🖊 open-ended questions

questions that seek no particular response and allow respondents to elaborate as much as they wish.

🖊 closed-ended questions

questions that elicit a small range of specific answers supplied by the interviewer or surveyer.

To assess the concerns of her audience, Sarah asks the teacher to recommend three or four students whom the teacher believes are representative of the class as a whole. Next, she devises a set of questions to guide her interviews. Some are **open-ended questions** that seek no particular response and allow the respondents to elaborate as much as they wish. For example, Sarah might ask several students, "How do you feel about going to college right out of high school?" The open-ended nature of the question leaves open the possibility that each response will be different. Sarah can also create some **closed-ended questions**, which are designed to elicit a small range of specific answers supplied by the interviewer. For example, she might ask the students, "Do you feel confident about going to college next year?" Their answers will most likely be "Yes," "No," or the occasional "I'm not sure."

Most interviews contain a mix of question types. Closed-ended questions are especially helpful in uncovering shared attitudes, experience, and knowledge of audience members. Open-ended questions are particularly useful for probing beliefs and opinions. They elicit more individual or personal information about the audience members' thoughts and feelings. They are also more time-intensive than closed-ended questions.

Regardless of the type of question selected, each one should be designed to uncover the audience's knowledge about and interest in the key ideas and principles associated with the speech topic. In the case of Sarah's speech, her key ideas may be academic requirements, social life, and independence away from home. Her questions, then, should uncover the audience members' attitudes toward each of these ideas. As Sarah gathers the responses, she will gain considerable insight into her audience's feelings and knowledge about the topic. The information may confirm that she should keep key ideas as main points; alternatively, it may point to the need to modify them or develop another set entirely.

The Survey

The written survey method of audience analysis is in many ways similar to interviews, with some key differences. Both formats allow a mix of open- and closed-ended questions, so you can use many of the same questions for both surveys and interviews. The major differences are the number of people you can get to answer surveys, as well as the number and types of questions you can include in them. Surveys are designed to gather information from a large pool of respondents. Thus, they yield a wider representation of the potential audience. Another key difference is time: Surveys take less time to implement than do interviews.

🖊 questionnaires

series of questions that elicit information from respondents.

🖊 fixed alternative questions

questions that offer respondents a limited choice of answers.

🖊 scale questions

questions that measure the respondent's level of agreement or disagreement with particular issues.

Surveys generally take the form of **questionnaires**, a series of questions designed to elicit information. Generally speaking, more questions can be included in a survey than in an interview, especially closed-ended ones. Closed-ended questions may be either fixed alternative or scale questions. In **fixed alternative questions** the respondent is presented with a limited choice of answers, such as "Yes," "No," or "Sometimes." **Scale questions**—also called attitude scales—measure the respondent's level of agreement or disagreement with specific issues.

The following sample questionnaire might be constructed by a speaker to survey an audience's feelings about flag burning, a highly charged political issue. It contains a variety of open- and closed-ended questions.

1. What is your age?   _____ years

2. What is your sex?   _____ Male   _____ Female

3. Please indicate your primary heritage:

   _____ American Indian   _____ African American   _____ Asian American

   _____ European   _____ Latino   _____ Middle Eastern

4. Please indicate your level of formal education:

   _____ high school   _____ some college   _____ college degree

   _____ other (please specify:_____)

5. If employed, where are you employed?_____

   What type of job do you have?_____

   How long have you done this sort of work?_____

6. What is the approximate annual income range of your parents (or your-self if you are no longer dependent on your parents)?

   _____ less than $10,000   _____ $10,000–$20,000

   _____ $20,000–$30,000   _____ $30,000–$40,000

   _____ $40,000–$50,000   _____ over $50,000

7. With which political party are your views most closely aligned?

   _____ Democratic   _____ Republican   _____ Neither (Independent)

8. What do you view as the most significant problem facing the United States today?_____

9. Please check the box below that most closely matches your religious affiliation:

   _____ Buddhist   _____ Christian   _____ Hindu

   _____ Jewish   _____ Muslim   _____ Not religious

   _____ Other (please specify: _____)

10. What are your views on flag burning?_____

11. Indicate whether you agree (a), disagree (d), or are undecided (u) with each statement:

    Anyone has the right to burn a flag.   a   d   u

    The flag is just a symbol.   a   d   u

    The flag should be revered and protected   a   d   u

12. Flag burning should be outlawed.   a   d   u

13. People who burn flags should be imprisoned.   a   d   u

Let's look at the questionnaire in some detail. Items 1–7, and 9 investigate each of the demographic factors described earlier. Questions 1–4, 6, 7, 9, and 11 are closed-ended. Each is worded in such a way that the respondent can quickly and easily mark a response from among a few options. Notice that item 6 provides ranges for response options. Most people are more willing to mark an income range than to reveal the exact amount they earn annually. Questions 5, 8, and 10 are open-ended. Item 5 asks about work experience. An open-ended response is appropriate here because the speaker does not know what occupations are represented in the audience. Item 8 is a follow-up question to the political affiliation question that precedes it. It allows the respondents to voice their opinions, and it may give the speaker additional information about the audience members and their political concerns. Perhaps some will list freedom of expression as a concern, which would be directly relevant to the topic of flag burning. Item 9 on religion, as well as item 5 on employment and item 6 on income, may have no direct bearing on the speech topic but are easy to include in the survey or interview and may provide useful information that was not anticipated. Items 10 and 11 deal specifically with the speech topic. Item 10 is an open-ended question seeking respondents' direct views on flag burning. From this the speaker can determine who in the audience is for, against, or uncertain about the issue—and, more important, perhaps why they feel the way they do. Item 11 includes three attitude scales. Agreement on the first and second scales might indicate a "pro" attitude toward flag burning; agreement on the third scale could indicate a "con" attitude. Moreover, the speaker might expect that people who agree with the two "pro" statements will disagree with the "con" statement, and vice versa. In this way the attitude scales clarify what the respondents write in answer to item 10, giving a clearer picture of audience attitude about the topic. Items 12 and 13 are scale questions that measure the respondents' level of agreement with two statements about the issue.

As you can see, it takes just a few questions to get some idea about where audience members stand on each of the demographic factors. A questionnaire like this can help the speaker draw a fairly clear picture of audience background and attitude. With knowledge of each factor, the speaker is more capable of planning a speech that hits home with the audience, meets their needs, and is relevant to them.

Written Sources

Yet another way to uncover information about an audience is to read about it. Written sources include brochures, newspaper articles, organizational bylaws and charters, annual reports, and reference books such as industry guides and agency abstracts. Often, the group sponsoring the speech is able to provide some of these sources. Other places include local libraries, college or university libraries, company libraries, and online in cyberspace.

What can you expect to find by reading these materials? The information can be categorized into at least three areas: missions and goals, operations, and achievements.

Missions and Goals. Many groups have written statements of their missions and goals. An organization's mission statement conveys its self-determined purpose for existing and functioning. For example, Women in Communications, Inc. (WICI), has as its stated mission:

(1) To unite women engaged in all fields of communications; (2) to work for a free and responsible press; (3) to recognize the distinguished achievements of women in communications; (4) to maintain high professional standards; (5) to encourage members to greater individual effort.[10]

A mission statement reveals the goals a group seeks to accomplish for itself and its constituents and points to the valued outcomes shared by the group's members. Knowing the mission gives the speaker insight into the group's core values, that is, what its members collectively consider to be most important in their work or activity. A speaker addressing a chapter of Women in Communications, for example, would know from its mission statement that the audience values the encouragement of women in their pursuit of excellence in careers in communications.

Operations. Written sources may also provide information about a group's standard method of operating and conducting its affairs—namely, governing structure, how it conducts meetings, how it determines projects and tasks, how it adapts to new ideas, and how it secures funding and prioritizes expenditures. By understanding these details the speaker can tailor the speech topic even more closely to the experience of the audience. Suppose, for example, that you were invited to speak to a company's managing directors about how your own company implements principles of teamwork in solving problems and making decisions. Your knowledge of the other company's policies can help you focus the presentation to fit with their needs and experiences.

Achievements. Most groups keep records of their achievements. The group's contact person is usually pleased and proud to make them available; he or she might even provide clippings from newspapers or trade magazines featuring particularly noteworthy accomplishments. One of the authors of this book recently made a presentation to a professional group. Shortly after issuing the invitation to speak, the contact person sent him an inch-thick set of materials. Included were brief biographies of everyone who planned to attend the presentation, along with notes about his or her role in the organization's most recent significant achievements. The materials also included an organization chart indicating each audience member's position within the overall structure of the organization. Little of this material was directly relevant to the presentation, but it provided many ideas for examples, illustrations, and personal anecdotes to capture and hold the audience's attention and make the presentation topic all the more meaningful.

What advantages do written sources have over interviews and surveys? Although the best route to analyzing an audience often involves a combination of methods, written sources do have some distinct benefits. First, through written sources the speaker can process in-depth information without the

Mission Statements and More—Searching the Net

Everyone's doing it, or so it seems. Just a few years ago, companies scrambled to install fax machines and then posted the numbers prominently on their company stationery and business cards. Having a fax number showed they were serious about doing business. Today a Web site on the Internet suggests a similar degree of seriousness. Web site addresses have been appearing on everything from stationery to television advertisements.

From large corporations such as General Motors to nonprofit groups such as Toastmasters (an organization dedicated to helping people learn the art of public speaking), Web sites have become the latest method of communicating a group's message. As a result, the Internet now provides excellent written resources for public speakers.

If you have access to a computer, try a search using the name of a company, organization, or special activity that interests you. Chances are good that you will find a relevant Web site. Just about any company's Web pages have links to different kinds of information about the company, such as its mission statement and goals, quarterly or annual reports, product developments, marketing plans, employment opportunities, and even photographs of its employees.

Recently a librarian was asked to address the organization REFORMA, a national association devoted to promoting library services among the Spanish-speaking population. She quickly found REFORMA's Web site, which contained information that was extremely useful in preparing her speech.

REFORMA

THE NATIONAL ASSOCIATION TO PROMOTE LIBRARY SERVICES TO THE SPANISH SPEAKING

REFORMA is committed to the improvement of the full spectrum of library and information services for the approximately 22 million Spanish-speaking and Hispanic people in the United States.

[Note the mission statement and goals here and below:]

Established in 1971, REFORMA has actively sought to promote the development of library collections to include Spanish-language and Hispanic oriented materials; the recruitment of more bilingual and bicultural library professionals and support staff; the development of library services and programs which meet the needs of the Hispanic community; the establishment of a national information and support network among individuals who share our goals; the education of the U.S. Hispanic population in regards to the availability and types of library services; and lobbying efforts to preserve existing library resource centers serving the interests of Hispanics.

[Note the discussion of the group's structure and operating methods:]

The organization is governed by an Executive Board which includes the officers, committee chairs, and the Presidents chapters and our one affiliate.

Nationally there are eleven REFORMA chapters, including local Chicago Area Chapter and one affiliate. These groups function autonomously, working through their local library systems and state library associations to achieve local objectives.

[Note below the discussion of accomplishments:]

One of REFORMA's most noteworthy activities is the annual scholarship drive. The association awards a number of scholarships to library school students that may express interest in working with Hispanics. Other activities that benefit the members include the publication of a quarterly newsletter which keeps members abreast of the latest developments in the organization and in library services to Hispanics; publication of an annual Membership Directory which has, in effect, established a national network of librarians, library trustees, community and library school students with mutual concerns; and programs and workshops which focus on serving Hispanics.

We warmly invite all interested persons to join us in our efforts.

HOMEPAGE	RNC PAGE	ADDRESSES

Comments and/or changes to Francisco Garcia fgarcia@atm-info.com

Page last updated on: Apr 9 20:29:10 1997.

distractions and time constraints of preparing, conducting, and processing responses from interviews and surveys. Second, organizational missions, policies, and achievements are usually more clearly and systematically stated in written form than are expressed in interview and survey responses.

The real trick to success in using written sources for audience analysis is simply finding them. Often a few well-targeted phone calls are all that's needed. And with the rapid growth of the Internet and other computer network systems, many speakers find all the information they need online.

Other Speakers as Resources

Yet another way to analyze an audience is to learn about it from speakers who have gone before you. There are certain kinds of information that only someone who has already addressed an audience can offer. These speakers are in a unique position to describe how the audience reacted to humor, to the length of the speech, and to stories and examples that were particularly effective. They might also be able to note the audience's "touchy spots," whether listeners responded favorably or unfavorably to controversial ideas,

Focus on Ethics

Finding Common Ground

Suppose the listeners' analysis reveals that an audience's opinions on issues related to your topic are strikingly different from your own. However, you've already put in hours of work on your presentation and are loathe to abandon it now. Furthermore, you're downright passionate about the issues on which you and the audience differ. What should you do? Should you pretend to share their opinions in the hope of making a successful speech? Should you confront the audience with your beliefs and challenge the listeners to accept them?

Ethical speakers resolve the dilemma of divergent viewpoints by working to find common ground between the audience's interests and their own. Once they find common ground, they use it as the basis for pursuing their own interest in the speech—while at the same time making it interesting and relevant to the listeners.

For example, a librarian was invited to address a chapter of REFORMA, a group dedicated to promoting library services to the Spanish-speaking population. Although she was firm in her conviction that all U.S. citizens should learn English as quickly as possible, she did not favor bilingual education. However, through her audience analysis, she learned that the members of REFORMA are fervent bilingualists. She also believed, nonetheless, that it is crucial that libraries serve the needs of all U.S. citizens, including the newest Americans. The librarian therefore decided to focus her presentation on the growing number of libraries whose staffs include bilingual librarians and whose collections include books in both Spanish and English. In this way she focused on her own convictions about the importance of the library as a key community resource while at the same time appealing to the audience's concerns. As for her opinion that bilingual education is not the best route to educating the nation's children, as an ethical speaker she did not pretend to believe otherwise. She simply found a way to address other issues in which both she and her audience believed.

and so forth. Human nature being what it is, our perceptions of ourselves are often at odds with how others see us. Consequently, these sorts of insights rarely emerge from questionnaires and interviews.

At first, this method of audience analysis might seem to be beyond the scope of many novice speakers. Professional public speakers may seem better positioned to do this sort of "networking," since they often belong to speaker's bureaus and go on speaking circuits. But, in fact, many people address groups to which they also belong. And other members may have already addressed the group. Consider the classroom, one group to which you currently belong. You've probably shared notes with at least one of your classmates about how he or she feels about speaking to the class. In the course of your conversation, you might have learned things about the audience (i.e., the class) that you didn't know. It's natural to seek the opinion of others whose experiences precede or coincide with our own. Doing so can make the difference between a speech that hits the mark and one that misses it altogether.

AUDIENCE ANALYSIS AND THE SPEECH SETTING

Another important aspect of preparing for the speech involves learning about the speech setting or context—size of audience, time of speech, and physical speech setting. No good sports team would plan for an "away" game without learning about the opponent's home field or court. Visiting teams know that familiarity with the physical space gives the other team a distinct "home court advantage." And so it is with public speakers. Speaking in an auditorium is an entirely different experience from addressing a small group in a classroom. Addressing one thousand people in an outdoor amphitheater raises very different planning issues than speaking indoors to twenty-five members of a local civic group. You should consider at least four characteristics of a speech setting that will affect how you interact with the audience and how they will physically receive your message: location, time, seating, and lighting and sound.

Location

When former presidential candidate Bob Dole ran for office in 1996, his wife, Elizabeth Dole, spoke on his behalf to a packed audience at the Republican National Convention. Rather than standing behind the podium, Mrs. Dole made the unconventional (pardon the pun) decision to walk among the audience as she spoke. By physically joining her listeners, Mrs. Dole created a sense of intimacy with the audience.

As Mrs. Dole clearly understood, the physical setting in which a speech occurs can have a significant effect on the speech outcome. The atmosphere of a classroom is different from that of a banquet room, outdoor amphitheater, or large auditorium. Each venue requires different preparations on the speaker's part, affecting how loudly he or she must speak (and whether or not acoustical equipment is needed), how to dress, and where to position oneself in relation to the audience. To combat the impersonality of the cavernous national convention space, Mrs. Dole created a "space within a space" among the front rows of the center.

AP/Wide World

During her speech at the 1996 Republican National Convention, Elizabeth Dole strode into the front rows of the auditorium, heightening the sense of intimacy between speaker and audience.

Time

Few matters of speech etiquette are as annoying to an audience as a speaker's apparent disregard for time. A few years ago one of the authors of this book attended a large religious rally at which some 3,000 people were in attendance. Thirty-five minutes passed beyond the scheduled starting time for the keynote speech. Finally the speaker arrived, harried and hurried. His first words were to explain his tardiness: His plane had been delayed by stormy weather. Fair enough—weather and airline delays were beyond his control. And he did give a moving speech. Nonetheless, the audience was very annoyed. As is often the case with such occurrences, the delay is the first item mentioned when people talk about that evening. The moral of the story is obvious: Do everything you can to be on time with your speech. Start on time and end well within the time allotted to you.

Another aspect of time to consider is when the speech will be presented. Will it be in the morning, afternoon, or evening? Will it be a luncheon or dinner speech? These factors can help you prepare for the audience's mood and energy level, as well as your own.

Seating Capacity and Arrangement

When you are invited to give a speech, you should expect that someone else will be in charge of seeing to the details of the setting, but never take this for granted. You should always be prepared to ask how many people are expected to attend and whether there will be enough seating to accommodate them. It is useful to know how the audience seating will be arranged. Will it be the traditional lecture or auditorium style, or will audience members be seated at round tables in a dining room format? You may also want to ask about seating for yourself, for example, if you will be seated at a head table or speaking from the floor or from a stage. Knowledge of the seating arrangement can help you determine how much space will be available to you for moving around the room as you speak or having audience members actively participate in some part of the speech.

Lighting and Sound

Dim lighting can lull an audience to sleep, even in the most intriguing speech situations. Poor sound quality is not only a distraction but an outright annoyance to audience members. Although someone else will likely be in charge of these facilities, it is always wise to follow up on them yourself. Lighting should be bright enough for people to easily see the speaker from a distance and take notes. There should be no shadows cast on the speaker or on visual devices used for the speech. Sound should be loud but not shocking, and clear and crisp. People in the back of the room should be able to hear the speaker as clearly as those in the front, but the sound should not be so loud that those in front feel as if they are sitting too close.

All the work you put into getting to know your audience well will be insufficient unless you also get to know the speech setting. When preparing speeches, remember to think like a coach preparing a game plan—you need the most accurate and complete information available about the field of play.

SUMMARY QUESTIONS

What are audience demographics, and what can they reveal about an audience?

A demographic is a statistical characteristic of a given population. Audience demographics focus on roughly six such characteristics: age, gender, ethnic or cultural background, socioeconomic status (including income, occupation, and education), religious and political affiliation, and related values and beliefs. Audience demographics provide important information about audience members' interests and concerns. Armed with this knowledge, a speaker can better plan a speech that hits home with the audience, meets their needs, and is relevant to them.

What psychological factors are important to know about an audience?

Audience psychology alerts the speaker to the ways people (i.e., listeners) think and feel about things. It focuses on what motivates people—their attitudes, beliefs, values, and certain personality traits that predispose them toward or away from certain kinds of experiences and information. Attitudes are predispositions to respond to people, ideas, objects, or events in evaluative ways. Beliefs are conceptions of what is true and what is false. Values are people's enduring judgments about what is good and bad in life. A speaker should try to identify how an audience feels—what their attitudes, beliefs, and values are—in relation to the topic, occasion, and speaker. Knowledge of these factors will provide the speaker with greater insight for shaping his or her specific purpose, researching the topic, crafting key points and arguments, and establishing credibility with the audience.

What are four methods of audience analysis?

This chapter describes four methods by which a speaker can analyze an audience: interviews, surveys, written sources, and sharing information with other speakers. Interviews and surveys are most useful when it is possible for representative members of the audience to answer questions reflecting their attitudes and beliefs about the speech topic. Written sources of information are useful when the audience represents a particular group or organization for which written documents exist, such as those stating the group's mission, operations, and achievements. Finally, other speakers who have addressed the same group are good sources of information about audience reactions.

Which features of the speech setting should be assessed as part of audience analysis?

At least four features of a speech setting should be considered: location, time, seating, and lighting and sound. Being familiar with the physical setting enables a speaker to anticipate and plan for its impact on the speech delivery.

ISSUES FOR DISCUSSION

1. Why is it important to always conduct a thorough audience analysis, even when a speaker will be giving a speech he has given several times before?

2. Which would likely be most advantageous to conducting an audience analysis of classmates—interviews, surveys, printed material about them, or talks with others who have given speeches to them? Why?

3. Why would it matter that an audience may be comprised of more women than men, or more Asian Americans than Hispanics, or more argumentative people than nonargumentative people? How would this information affect the way you choose to prepare for and deliver a speech?

4. As far as you are concerned, what are the most essential features of a speech setting to consider in preparing to give a speech? Why?

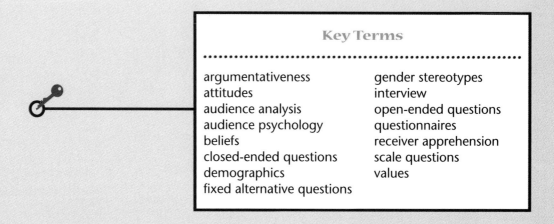

Key Terms

argumentativeness

attitudes

audience analysis

audience psychology

beliefs

closed-ended questions

demographics

fixed alternative questions

gender stereotypes

interview

open-ended questions

questionnaires

receiver apprehension

scale questions

values

SELF-ASSESSMENT

1. Prepare a survey to conduct an audience analysis of your class. Include both closed-ended and open-ended questions to determine audience age, gender, socioeconomic status, ethnic or cultural background, and religious and political affiliations. Also include some questions that will give an impression of where the audience stands in terms of argumentativeness and receiver apprehension.

2. Consider the topic you plan to pursue for your next speech. Decide which of the factors included in your audience analysis survey are the most pertinent to the development of your speech. Write a rationale for why these factors should be considered in planning the speech.

3. Construct a set of interview questions based on your speech topic and purpose. Select a sample of five members of the class who represent the demographic and dispositional qualities obtained in your survey analysis. Interview these individuals. Make notes about which aspects of your topic seem most relevant and interesting to these people.

4. Consider the features of your classroom and the kinds of presentation equipment available. Write a brief proposal to the instructor suggesting improvements in facilities and equipment that would benefit audience receptivity to speeches in your classroom.

TEAMWORK

1. The classroom provides an excellent laboratory for practicing audience analysis. Like the larger world, the classroom contains people from a variety of socioeconomic, ethnic and cultural, and religious backgrounds. It most likely contains both men and women representing different age groups. Values, beliefs, and political opinions may also diverge widely. How well do you think you know the audience demographics of the classroom? To find out, try to answer the following questions. Next, compare your answers with those of your classmates.

1. What is the age range of your class? _____

   What is the average age? _____

2. What are most of your classmates?

   _____ freshmen   _____ sophomores   _____ juniors   _____ seniors

3. What is the ratio of men to women?

   _____ 1:1   _____ 1:2   _____ 1:3   _____ 1:4   _____ 1:5   _____ other

4. What percentage of your classmates anticipates pursuing a graduate degree?

   _____ 10% or less   _____ 10–30%   _____ 30–50%

   _____ 50–75%   _____ more than 75%

5. What percentage of your class holds a part- or full-time job?

   _____ 10% or less   _____ 10–30%   _____ 30–50%

   _____ 50–75%   _____ more than 75%

6. Which religious category do you think most of your classmates would identify as their own?

   _____ Christianity   _____ Judaism   _____ Islam
   _____ Buddhism   _____ Other   _____ None

7. Which political party do you think is most heavily represented in your class?

   _____ Republican   _____ Democrat
   _____ Independent   _____ Other

8. List three issues that you consider to be of great importance to your

   classmates: _____

   _____

How did your answers compare with those of your classmates? In what ways can this profile of your class be useful in preparing your next speech assignment? How likely are you to get an accurate profile of an audience without conducting a well-planned audience analysis?

Ideas are like rabbits. You get a couple and learn how to handle them, and pretty soon you have a dozen.

—John Steinbeck

The secret of success is constancy to purpose.

—Benjamin Disraeli

Selecting a Topic and Purpose

Have you ever tried to strike up a conversation with someone, only to find yourself awkwardly struggling to engage his or her attention? **Choosing a speech topic is much like striking up a conversation: You look for something that will hold the attention of the listener.** Sometimes the process occurs effortlessly, and sometimes it's a struggle. However, once you establish common ground with your listener it's usually smooth sailing.

Selecting a topic for a speech is also very similar to selecting a topic for a research paper. How did you choose an appropriate subject for a world history course term paper or an English essay? **Skills you have often used to develop topics for your writing assignments will be invaluable as you develop topics for your speeches.**

Liesel Reinhart has been assigned to present an informative speech to her public speaking class. What can she talk about that will make her assignment interesting to her and to the class? While wondering what to speak about, she scans the campus newspaper. On the editorial page, she notices a story about a controversial book that was recently banned from the school library. Suddenly Liesel finds herself free associating concepts—vulgarity, obscenity, free speech, censorship....She then hits on the idea of book burning. Realizing that she's always been fascinated by such incidents in history, Liesel decides to go to the library and research book burning in the twentieth century. Perhaps there are some lessons to be learned that she can share with her class.

As you read these words, people throughout the world are listening to speakers. Journalists are recording the comments of heads of states, customers are listening to sales pitches, and worshippers are congregating to hear their spiritual leaders. Some audiences are gathering for weekly or monthly meetings of clubs or organizations. Others are coming together more spontaneously, as in the crowds that form around a street performer.

Why do people assemble to listen to a speaker? One reason is credibility. Some audiences want to hear a speaker because of who that person is. Indeed, a speaker's title, position, experience, or reputation motivates many people to gather as an audience.

Sometimes the occasion itself prompts audiences to listen to speakers. Formal gatherings such as graduations, weddings, and religious services naturally lend themselves to speeches; they provide focus and give form—a "voice"—to the event.

Another key reason we listen to speakers is the topic. Something may interest us and we want to learn more. Thus constructing a speech begins with selecting a topic and purpose that are appropriate to the audience and the occasion. All else flows from here. In choosing a topic and purpose, a speaker must keep in mind three important questions: "What do I want to tell the audience? What is the general purpose or goal of my speech? What specifically do I want—or need—to convey?"

Whether speaking to two, ten, or one hundred people, formulating an effective and appropriate topic is a crucial part of the speechmaking process. In this chapter you'll discover a number of challenges posed by choosing a topic. These include:

- Becoming familiar with the various sources that can be used to select a topic, from personal interests and experiences to current events.

- Discovering how to brainstorm ideas.
- Recognizing the different types of general speech purposes.
- Understanding how to narrow a topic and state a specific speech purpose.
- Composing effective thesis statements in support of your topic.

What Do I Speak About?

Public speakers are either provided with a topic or asked to choose one of their own. In either case, the challenge of adapting the topic to the audience and the occasion remains the same.

When Topics Are Assigned

Many speakers who are known for their expertise in a given area repeatedly receive requests to address the same topic. Each year, for example, gun control activists James and Sarah Brady field many invitations to speak on this topic. As a speaker, you may encounter a variety of situations in which the topic has already been selected:

- An instructor may ask you to prepare a five-minute speech on the university's proposals to eliminate the current grading system.
- A sales manager may ask you to present a business review at an upcoming regional sales meeting.
- A local high school may invite you to address an all-school assembly on "voting responsibly."
- The local Lions Club may ask you to speak at its weekly noon luncheon because its president knows that you recently developed a 25-minute speech on "popular science fiction" that you successfully delivered on several other occasions to organizations and groups.

AP/Wide World

After James Brady was seriously wounded during an assassination attempt on President Reagan in 1981, he and his wife Sarah lobbied for a bill setting new restrictions on the sale of handguns.

- An instructor may require you to participate in an impromptu speaking assignment in which each student draws a topic out of a grab bag and speaks on that subject to the class for five minutes.

Even when the topic is assigned, your job has just begun. You still must refine and adapt the topic in accordance with a host of factors ranging from those associated with the audience and occasion, to time and research constraints. You also must decide on a purpose or goal for the talk. For example, will you take a position on whether the university should change its grading policy, or will you simply inform the listeners of the situation?

When Topics Are Self-Selected

Many students report that selecting a topic is the most difficult part of classroom training in public speaking. For them, having a pre-assigned topic is a great relief. But you shouldn't want to avoid selecting a topic. After all, a good part of the pleasure of speechmaking is discovering a topic that appeals to you and that also is appropriate for the audience and speech occasion. Selecting a topic is like putting together a puzzle, and it offers a similar sense of fun and satisfaction when all the pieces fit together.

Often you will be asked to select your own speech topic. Rarely, however, will you be asked to speak without some direction. For example:

- You may be given a *purpose*. The advisor to the youth group you volunteer for may ask you to speak at the next meeting to "boost morale." You can select the topic.
- You may be given *time constraints*. Your boss may inform you that a group of grade-schoolers will be visiting next Monday, and you are on the agenda to talk to them for three to five minutes. How you fill this time is up to you.
- You may be given a *challenge*. The master of ceremonies for a roast to honor a retiring local newspaper writer may ask you to "make the audience laugh."

Seldom does anyone mean it when they say, "Whatever you talk about is fine." The choice of topic may be fine, but in most cases the person inviting you to speak has in mind a specific outcome or end result. In the list of examples above, none specifies a topic, but two include intended results in the form of a purpose or challenge. Even in the example that involves time constraints, implicit in the boss's directions is the objective of keeping the grade-schoolers occupied. In other words, when you select a topic for a speech, you are also held accountable for accomplishing a certain purpose.

THE GENERAL SPEECH PURPOSE

general speech purposes
three general goals of speeches— to inform, to persuade, or to celebrate or commemorate a special occasion.

Public speeches can be classified as addressing one of three **general speech purposes**: to inform, to persuade, or to celebrate or commemorate a special occasion. The general purpose for any speech answers the question, Why am I speaking on this topic *for this particular audience and occasion*?

Consider the different kinds of speeches you've heard: commencement addresses, lectures, keynote speeches, awards presentations, sales talks, eulogies, campaign speeches, sermons, and so forth. In each instance the audience assembled for a reason. The student attends a lecture to learn, a campaign speech to decide how to cast his or her vote, and a commencement address to celebrate the occasion of graduation.

The general speech purpose is sometimes defined or at least suggested by the occasion. For example, at special occasions such as awards ceremonies and funerals the speaker's task is to adapt the topic to the occasion at hand. Oftentimes, however, rather than specifically dictating a speech purpose, the occasion only suggests parameters of appropriateness. For example, one commencement speaker may decide to prepare a persuasive speech that exhorts the graduates to contribute time after graduation to public service, whereas another speaker might decide to entertain the audience with a light-hearted look at what the students' degrees will, or perhaps will not, do for them in the future. Although the two speakers select different general speech purposes (one to persuade, and the other to entertain), both select and adapt their topics to ensure appropriateness to the occasion.

Speaking to Inform

When you deliver an informative speech, you share your knowledge about a subject with others. To do so, you define, describe, explain, and/or demonstrate this knowledge. Thus the general purpose of an informative speech is to increase the audience's understanding and awareness of a topic. You want the audience to learn something.

When selecting an informative purpose, try to gauge how much the audience already knows about the topic. There's no surer way to lose audience members' attention than to speak over—or under—their heads. If the speech topic assumes a lot of background knowledge, make certain that the audience has it. Generally, unless you are an expert addressing an audience of your peers, this is unlikely to be the case. Likewise, if the audience is familiar with the topic, it's important to present it in a way that is new and interesting. Everyone knows about taxes, for instance, but we're always eager to hear about new ways to avoid paying them!

Just about any topic is appropriate for an informative speech, as long as you present it with the goal of enlarging the audience's understanding and awareness of that given topic. Topics may include *objects* (their construction, function, symbolic or concrete meaning); *people* (their history, accomplishments, anecdotes about); *events* (noteworthy occurrences, both past and present); *concepts* (abstract and difficult ideas or theories); *processes* (a series of steps leading to an end result); and *issues* (problems or matters of dispute that people seek to bring to a conclusion). These topic categories are explored at length in Chapter 13.

Speaking to Persuade

As with informative speeches, persuasive speeches also increase listeners' knowledge of a topic. They too enlighten or extend an audience's awareness of a subject. But rather than primarily seeking to increase listeners' knowledge of a topic, the general purpose of a persuasive speech is to effect some degree of change in the audience—one that convinces listeners to accept the alternative offered by the speaker. The change may be directed at certain attitudes, beliefs, or even their basic values (the latter being the hardest to change). Or the purpose may be to change specific behaviors (e.g., "Don't practice unsafe sex") or reinforce existing behaviors (e.g., "Keep practicing safe sex").

Topics or issues on which there are competing perspectives are particularly suitable for persuasive speeches. Controversial issues such as abortion and gun control naturally lend themselves to a persuasive purpose because people hold strongly contrasting opinions about them. But other topics can be suitable as well. The only requirement is that the topic allows the speaker to fashion a message that is intended to effect some kind of a degree of change in the audience.

Consider cigarette smoking. A persuasive purpose (e.g., "Stop smoking cigarettes now") would be appropriate if:

- the audience feels considerably different about the topic than the speaker does (e.g., the audience consists of members of a right-to-smoke group called "Butt Out of Our Lives");
- the audience holds similar attitudes and beliefs about the topic as the speaker does, but needs direction to take action (e.g., the audience consists of patients at a stop-smoking clinic; they want to quit but so far have been unsuccessful);
- the audience agrees with the speaker's position but is likely to encounter opposing information in the near future (e.g., a major cigarette producer will soon publicize a report purporting to show that cigarette smoking is no longer dangerous; the audience will likely hear about that information).

The Special Occasion Speech

Special occasion speeches are prepared for a special occasion and for a purpose dictated by that occasion. Special occasion speeches include speeches of introduction, speeches of acceptance, speeches of presentation, roasts and toasts, eulogies, and after-dinner speeches. Depending on the specific event, the general purpose of a special occasion speech will be variously to entertain, celebrate, commemorate, inspire, or set a social agenda (see Chapter 17).

The connection between the speech topic and the occasion is especially intimate for special occasion speeches. As such, it is crucial to sensitively align the topic with the speech purpose. Can you imagine planning an awards speech and never mentioning the recipients or the nature of their accomplishments? Or giving a eulogy and ignoring the deceased?

One instance in which the "topic" failed to match the occasion occurred in 1996 when Don Imus, a well-known radio personality with a scathing wit, was invited to participate in an annual roast of the president at the White House. Although listeners at roasts expect biting wit, they also expect that the roasters' underlying intentions will be good-natured. Imus's "jokes," however, were aimed at such controversial topics and were so pointed and mean-spirited that their effect was to humiliate rather than to entertain. The audience winced in pained silence. The lesson should be clear: When giving a special occasion speech, be sure to match the topic to the appropriate general speech purpose.

SELECTING A TOPIC

Along with choosing a general speech purpose, the speaker must select a topic that is appropriate for the audience. If you already have a topic, you can proceed to adapt it to the audience and occasion. If you don't yet have a topic, there are a wealth to choose from. A speaker can either delve into his or her personal library of interests and experiences, or select from the vast body of general knowledge.

Personal Interests: Let Passion Be Your Guide

Beginning novelists are often counseled to write about what they know. The rationale is that by doing so, they will bring a greater sense of authenticity to the story. Rather than adding the burden of mastering foreign material to the already difficult task of creating an interesting story, writers begin by honing their writing skills in more familiar territory. Later, when they are more comfortable with their craft, they can venture further from home.

Of course, many now-famous writers ignored this advice, immediately tackling foreign material. And not all seasoned public speakers have started out in

Making a Difference

**CRAIG KIELBURGER,
FOUNDER, FREE THE CHILDREN**

One spring day in 1995, a 12-year-old seventh grader named Craig Kielburger read an article in the *Toronto Star* that changed his young life. The article described the short life and death of a Pakistani boy named Iqbal Masih. Iqbal was 4 years old when he was sold into slavery for less than $15. Until his escape at the age of 10, he was shackled to a carpet loom, tying thousands of tiny knots, for up to 12 hours each day, six days a week. Once free, Iqbal joined forces with other activists and began speaking out against child labor. His many efforts brought him worldwide attention, and in 1995 he was awarded the Reebok Human Rights Award. Tragically, after just two years of freedom, at the age of 12 this young advocate for change was murdered, presumably by members or associates of the carpet industry.

According to the Human Rights Commission, Pakistan has an estimated 6 million child workers age 14 or younger. They can be found in the carpet factories, in brick-making plants, on farms, and as household servants. Worldwide, officials of the International Labor Organization estimate that some 250 million children are in some form of bondage.

Craig was the same age as Iqbal when Iqbal was killed, and his death affected Craig enormously.

> I asked myself what I could do to help Iqbal's cause. With my friends I started researching the issue of child labor around the world, and what we learned shocked us. In India, children are employed in workshops, garages, and small factories making matches, fire-

works, and glass. They often work up to 15 hours each day in hazardous conditions. In Thailand and the Philippines, a virtual industry has grown up around the girls and boys who are used in the sex trade....Poor children in many countries are employed in the textile, sporting goods, and toy industries, making products that may eventually end up on the shelves of North American stores. We decided to form an organization made up of school-age children around the world who want to end the exploitation of kids our age.

The organization they formed is called Free the Children, a children's rights advocacy organization. Today, scores of Free the Children (FTC) affiliates dot the U.S. and Canadian landscape; the group is also represented globally, from Germany to Sweden. FTC's mandate is to combat child labor and all other forms of abuse and oppression of children. The group's philosophy is that young people can be effective agents of change. FTC has rallied around the cause of Rugmark, a system of labeling that carpet manufacturers can adopt to certify that their rugs are not produced by child labor. (Those who join Rugmark agree to unannounced inspections of their looms by child advocacy groups.) The group has also established a rehabilitation/education center in Alwar, India, for freed bonded child laborers; in yet another project, the group is providing cows and sewing machines to families in India so that they can sustain themselves and send their children to school.

Craig's father, Fred Kielburger, notes:

> Free the Children fosters public speaking as a means to accomplish its mandates. Kids must be taught public speaking skills; they soon learn that if they want to get the respect of adults, they must prove they know their material very well. Toward this end, the group's leadership conferences feature representatives from Toastmasters, an organization dedicated to helping your people improve their public speaking skills, as well as professional speakers who donate their expertise.

Craig, now age 14, gives several hundred speeches each year, to audiences ranging from small youth groups to huge convention gatherings of 5,000. Craig has met many world leaders, including Pope John Paul II and the Dalai Lama. He has addressed business groups, labor conventions, teachers conferences, and government committees around the world. (One address, to the U.S. congressional subcommittee on International Relations and Human Rights, is reprinted in Chapter 15 of this book; see p. 387.)

To prepare for his speeches, Craig studies his topic well. He uses some notes but speaks largely from memory. He is clearly driven by passion to help the children he has met. One journalist who profiled Craig noted that, "He is startlingly poised and articulate, and speaks without notes with terrific clarity and force."[1]

Craig's public speaking skills did not appear out of thin air. As he relates:

My brother Marc, six years older that me, became involved in environmental issues when he was 13. He used to give speeches to students and to other groups. I used to tag along and watch him in action. I can remember trying to mimic his speeches. But I used to have an articulation problem because of ear infections and would slur my words or drop letters. I would say to my mother, "Someday, I will give speeches." My mother, who was just concerned with me speaking properly, would answer, "You don't have to give speeches. You will be good at something else." It wasn't until I was 10 that all of my speech problems cleared up.

At 11, I heard about a public speaking competition in Toronto. I found out only one day before the competition. My mother said I should only do my best and not expect to win. "Being a winner," she said, "is trying." So that is what I wrote my speech about—"What it means to be a winner." The day of the speech I was very nervous. I became even more nervous when I discovered that last year's winner was in the room....

When my number was called I began to speak but was so nervous that I forgot everything my mother and I had written. So I spoke from the heart. Being a kid, this was a subject I knew a lot about. I spoke about how coaches and adults scream at kids at games and competitions when they make a mistake, how children tear up their work and feel like failures when they don't win at science fairs....When I returned to my seat I could hardly hear the

applause....The previous year's winner spoke after me. She was confident. Articulate. Flawless in her delivery. I could tell she had a lot of experience. I declared her the winner....

The judges gave second place to the girl. They gave first place to me....

I learned a very valuable lesson that day. There was no doubt in my mind that the girl had given a better speech. Why was I given the gold medal? Because I spoke from the heart, with passion. They were not just words on a piece of paper. It came from my soul. It meant something to me and people got that message. That was a lesson I never forgot....

Today, when I speak about working children and child workers I don't only speak about facts and statistics, or theory. I speak about children whom I have met....I find that I grow every day as I accumulate knowledge and experiences.... Every day I go through the newspaper and cut out articles relevant to my topic. I search the Internet and am on a mailing list with groups from around the world working on the issue of child labor and children's rights.

People can make a difference. As Robert Kennedy taught us, "History is shaped by individual acts of courage and belief." American adults and children have the power to change the world—if they choose to get involved. I challenge the girls and boys across America to turn off their televisions, to get out their pens and turn on their computers, and continue the campaign that was started by a poor boy in Pakistan who had no possessions to his name. Remember we are young, but we are many!

1. Michele Landsberg, "Boy, 12, Takes OFL by Storm with Child Labor Plea," *Sunday Star* (Toronto), November 26, 1995.

SOURCES: *Interviews and correspondence with Craig and Fred Kielburger, December 10–31, 1997; Margaret Deschamps; "Speaking Out for the Children of the World"; "Conference Inspires Action" (no author cited); Craig Kielburger, "Stop Child Exploitation by Shopping with a Conscience!" Maclean's, December 23, 1996. (All articles retrieved from Free the Children Web site at http://www.freethechildren.org.)*

For more information on Free the Children, visit its Web site at http://www.freethechildren.org.; you can also write to: 16 Thornbank Rd., Thornhill, Ontario, Canada L4J 2A2, or call 905-881-0863.

this way. Nevertheless, selecting a topic with which you are familiar—and, most important, enthusiastic about—offers many advantages. Because you are interested in the topic, researching it will be enjoyable. You'll look forward to learning more about it and probably will pay more attention to what you discover. You'll bring a sense of genuine enthusiasm to your presentation. Depending on the depth of your background knowledge, you may convey great competence and the audience may perceive you as a highly credible speaker.

Personal interests range from *favorite activities and hobbies* (e.g., sports, reading, home repair, sewing, woodworking, collecting, travel, playing music) to *specific subject areas* (e.g., local history or politics, ancient history, warfare, feminism, diet and nutrition, foreign languages) to, well, the list truly is endless. Perhaps your greatest passion is skiing. Or cooking. Or fixing up your home (If so, join the crowd: Home improvement is the fastest growing industry in the United States.)

Sometimes personal experiences provide powerful topics, especially if by sharing them the audience in some way benefits from your experience. For example, when former first lady Betty Ford decided to reveal her breast cancer, few women before her had done so. As a result of Ford's disclosure, breast cancer moved "out of the closet" and onto podiums across the country. Beyond health crises, personal experiences can range from firsthand accounts of exciting travel adventures to brushes with danger or disaster. "What it's like" stories also yield interesting topics. Best-selling author Scott Turow, for example, started his writing career with a true-life account of his first year as a law student. Others have written and spoken about their trials as medical interns.

Although selecting a topic from among your personal interests will likely raise your own interest level, it's not a guarantee of success. You still must decide whether the topic is appropriate for the audience and the occasion. You should also consider whether it will arouse enthusiasm and interest among the audience members. Also, avoid making assumptions about what the audience knows about the topic. What is obvious and second-nature to you may not be clear at all to the audience. As we saw in the previous chapter, a thorough analysis of the audience is the soundest foundation on which to base your topic selection.

Audience Concerns and Interests

As you consider your topic, review it in light of the audience's demographic and psychological profile. How does it fit with the audience's age, gender, ethnic or cultural background, socioeconomic status (including income, education, and occupation), and religious and political status? How can you present the topic in a way that appeals to the audience's attitudes, beliefs, and values. The more you gear a topic to the interest and needs of the audience, the greater the acceptance your speech will have.

Current Events and Controversial Issues

Current events—as gleaned from daily and weekly newspapers, magazines, and online publications—offer another rich source of public speaking topics. People are constantly barraged with newsworthy topics but few of us have the time to delve into them. What was actually behind the hostage-taking situation in Peru? Where is the country called Belize? Who were the rebels there? Alternatively, perhaps you'd like to speak about some aspect of the conflict in the Middle East. You might focus on one crucial year that illustrates some of the roots of the conflict there.

Controversial issues of the day—assisted suicide, abortion, surrogacy, welfare, gun control, drug abuse—usually earn their place in the limelight because they reflect our deepest concerns and profoundly affect us as individuals and as members of society. Many of us appreciate and even hunger for information that broadens our understanding of these topics. Keep this in mind, whether you are informing the audience of facts and details or persuading the audience to accept a particular point of view.

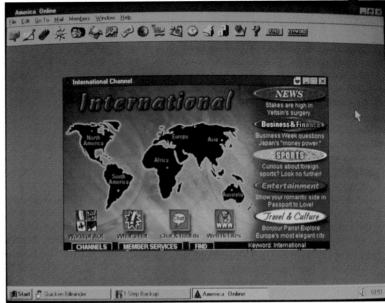

Robert Ullmann/Monkmeyer

Online sources bring you the whole world in a few mouse clicks. You can use the Internet to explore newspapers, magazines, and databases from all across the globe.

Local Issues

In addition to national and international events and issues, consider those specifically connected to school, community, and state. The majority of people react with interest to issues that affect them directly, and (barring war and federal tax hikes) these tend to be of a local nature. Parents of young children want to know the status of the school system. Town residents are interested in new service programs. Virtually all homeowners are eager to find out how revised property tax guidelines will affect them.

Are there plans for a new park in your town? Is there a referendum pending on whether or not to fund a new sports arena? The audience may be quite interested in such details. People are also interested in what other people in their communities are doing. Are you involved in a club on campus, or do you volunteer for a local charity? Consider giving a speech about the organization's mission, membership, or upcoming event.

Little-Known or Unusual Information

Another source for topics is new or unusual information about a well-known or even shopworn subject. Some topics captivate audiences beyond any reasonable timetable. For example, the O. J. Simpson case, the John F. Kennedy assassination, and certain religious groups' mass suicides continue to appeal to many people. What keeps these topics alive is the steady outpouring of "new" or uncovered evidence that catches audiences' attention.

You might consider topics for your speech that:

- have recently been reinvestigated, resulting in new conclusions or results;
- involve an influential person who has reversed his or her opinion about the topic;
- have recently been uncovered or discovered, ending years of speculation.

Focus on Technology

Finding Topics Online

The Internet, the World Wide Web, and online companies such as America Online and CompuServe offer potentially good sources of information for topic ideas. You can surf the Web for home pages that offer lots of ideas. You can click on the menu items What's New or What's Hot on the first Web page of most browsers for events, issues, or people that are innovative or novel. To learn more about a potential topic, you can conduct global searches by submitting a general, one-item keyword to a comprehensive search engine. If you find something of interest, you can narrow the search by following the hyperlinks.

Lest you think that cyberspace is heaven-sent for the topic searcher, however, think again. Without discipline and planning, searching in cyberspace can be a tremendous waste of time. You can easily spend endless hours surfing for a topic, only to find yourself bleary-eyed and empty-handed as the clock strikes midnight. How can you avoid this? Here are a few suggestions:

- Before you plunge in, familiarize yourself with how best to use the various search engines and research tools. Consider reading a book on sources on the Internet first so that you can target the search more effectively.

- If you're searching cyberspace for a general topic, limit yourself to one hour. This way, you'll avoid being side-tracked by miscellany such as dog catching in India and the price of varsity jackets in Las Vegas. If you do find a general topic, brainstorm about it off-line for a while before proceeding.

- If you're trying to narrow the topic, limit yourself to one hour *unless you hit the jackpot*. If you do find yourself on a fruitful path, by all means keep going. Otherwise, early to bed and early to the library.

Brainstorming

brainstorming
an individual or group problem-solving technique that involves the spontaneous generation of ideas.

One of the most popular ways to select a topic involves **brainstorming**—an individual or group problem-solving technique entailing the spontaneous generation of ideas. You can brainstorm (alone or in groups) by making lists and by using word association. If you are more visually or artistically inclined, you can also brainstorm by drawing a concept map (see Figure 6.1).

Lists. One way to brainstorm is to simply list all the subjects that you can comfortably prepare to speak about and that your audience may be interested in hearing about. Begin by making a list. Don't attempt to rank the topics or test them against any criteria. Just be as open-minded and creative as possible. You can include any subject that you are somewhat knowledgeable about, or that you'd like to investigate in more depth. The list might include such things as your hobbies, a subject you are studying in school, an adventure you've had recently, or a famous personality that you admire.

After creating the initial list, narrow the possible topics to two or three. Before making a final selection from these few potential topics, consider your expertise on the subject and the audience's interest or motivation for listening to each topic. Then select a topic from the narrowed list.

Several computer software programs enable students to creatively brainstorm speech topics. One of the most popular is IdeaFisher.

Word Association. Another way to brainstorm is by word association. Begin by writing down one single topic in which you are interested and that you think will interest the audience. If you have trouble getting started, write down a favorite movie, song title, or place. Once you have done that, write down the first thing that comes to mind when you read the word or words you have just written. It doesn't have to be related to the first topic. As soon as your words remind you of something, write it down. Now read the second item on the list, and write down your next thought. If a word or words remind you of more than one thing, write down all of them. Try writing your thoughts as quickly as you can, without analyzing them as topics. Repeat the process until you have a list of fifteen or twenty items.

Once you have generated a list, review each item as a potential topic. Narrow the list to two or three, and then select a final topic. The following list is an example of the word association brainstorming technique:

- health ⟶ alternative medicine ⟶ naturopathy ⟶ fraud
- children ⟶ parenting ⟶ working ⟶ daycare ⟶ living expenses
- diving ⟶ snorkeling ⟶ Bahamas ⟶ conch shells ⟶ deep-sea fishing
- Internet ⟶ searching ⟶ search engines ⟶ wasting time
- exercise ⟶ Stairmasters ⟶ weight lifting ⟶ swimming

REFINING THE TOPIC AND PURPOSE

Once you've selected a topic and general speech purpose, they must be refined or narrowed. This process provides the opportunity to develop a topic and purpose that will appeal to the greatest number of people in the audience.

Narrowing the Topic

A topic is necessarily just a general idea. When you narrow a topic, you focus on specific aspects of it to the exclusion of others. Naturally, you focus on those aspects of the topic that interest you the most. You also carefully evaluate them in light of audience interests, knowledge, and needs. If you already know the general speech purpose, you incorporate this knowledge into the process.

Two additional considerations are time and research constraints. How long is the speech to be? How much research do you have access to? Is it too expensive to pursue the research? How much of it can you responsibly review so that you avoid distorting or falsifying the material?

Imagine, for example, how your approach to the topic of The Flat Income Tax may change as you take the following factors into account:

- the time limit is five to seven minutes;
- the speech is for an informative speaking assignment;
- the library does not have a copy of a recent speech by an influential member of Congress, and the computer is down.

Brainstorming. Just as brainstorming can be used to discover a general topic, it can also be helpful in narrowing one. One way is to brainstorm by

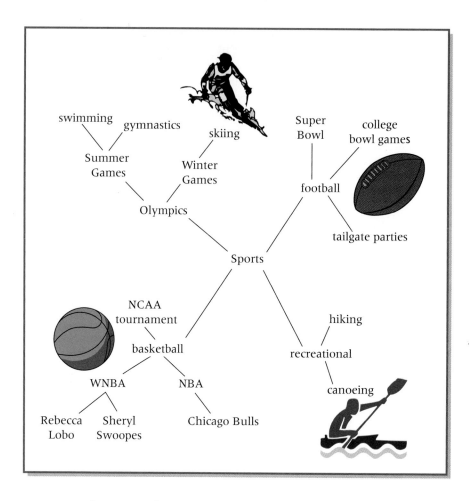

FIGURE 6.1
Concept Map

category. What sorts of categories can you break your general topic into? Say your general topic is Cars. One related category is Models; another, Manufacturers; a third, Foreign and Domestic. As you brainstorm by category, ask yourself: What questions do I have about the topic? Am I more interested in how cars work or how much they cost? What kinds of cars interest me? What aspects of cars would the audience most likely want to hear about?

Some people who are visually or artistically inclined find it helpful to draw concept maps. A *concept map* is a visual representation of brainstorming, as seen in Figure 6.1.

Forming a Specific Speech Purpose

specific speech purpose
expresses both the topic and general purpose in action form and in terms of the speaker's objectives; focuses more closely than the general speech purpose on the goal of the speech.

The **specific speech purpose** focuses even more closely than the general speech purpose on the goal of the speech. It expresses both topic and general purpose in action form and in terms of the speaker's specific objectives. The specific purpose statement answers the question, What is it about my topic that I want the audience to learn/do/reconsider/agree with?

Consider the topic of World War II. You've narrowed the topic to The Effects of Food Rationing on Families in Mississippi during World War II and selected an informative speech purpose. Now decide what you want to accomplish in your speech. Perhaps you want the audience to more fully appreciate the hardships people faced as a result of food rationing. Or perhaps you want them to understand that food rationing was more widespread in Mississippi than in other states. Whatever your primary objective is becomes your specific speech purpose:

GENERAL TOPIC: World War II

NARROWED TOPIC: The Effects of Food Rationing on Families in Mississippi during World War II

GENERAL PURPOSE: To inform

SPECIFIC PURPOSE: To inform my audience about what it was like to live with food rationing for several years in Mississippi during World War II

Focus on Ethics

Ethical Considerations in Selecting a Topic and Purpose

The First Amendment guarantees the right to free and unrestricted public expression. But it does not tell us how to ethically exercise this right. In fact, the Amendment ensures protection to both the honest and the dishonest speaker.[1] What guidelines, then, should be used when considering the ethical implications of a speaker's topic and purpose?

Ethical speechmaking goes beyond a consideration of whether language, visual aids, or examples may offend listeners. What makes a speech ethical or not depends on how the speech empowers listeners to think or act as a result of listening to the speaker. In other words, ethical considerations begin with the speaker's intent or purpose. Is the speaker deliberately distorting information to achieve a desired result? Is his or her intent to deceive? Is the speaker trying to coerce the audience into thinking or acting in a certain way? Is he or she knowingly trying to appeal to harmful biases? Speakers who select persuasive purposes should be particularly careful to evaluate their speech from an ethical perspective. Under pressure to sway an audience, speakers may be tempted to tamper with the truth.

Respect for the audience and adaptation to its needs and interests should always guide your speech choices. Among the many considerations you must make is whether a topic is, on an ethical level, "right" for an audience. All groups have needs and sensitivities; ethically it is the speaker's responsibility to address these respectfully. If the audience consists of school-age children, for example, one aspect of reviewing your topic should include its appropriateness for this age group. Does the speech contain material that will disturb or exploit the children? Is your purpose responsible; for example, will it in some way benefit the audience?

Although there are few hard and fast rules when it comes to ethical guidelines for selecting topics, some areas are clearly off limits—at least in U.S. culture. When selecting a topic, consider whether it involves any of the following:

- The topic shows an audience how to perform actions that are prohibited by law.
- The topic provides audience members with methods or steps that may result in their physical or psychological harm. For example, in May 1995 radio talk show host G. Gordon Liddy advised listeners on how to shoot at federal agents in the event that they illegally stormed the listeners' homes. "Aim for the head," Liddy first advised. Later he amended that to "the groin."
- The topic humiliates or degrades the fundamental values of an audience's culture, religion, or political system.

If the topic falls into any of the categories above, consider it an unethical choice and select another.

1. Andrew D. Wolvin and Carolyn Gwynn Coakley, *Listening* (Dubuque, IA: Wm. C. Brown, 1982) p. 125.

Mario Savio was an eloquent speaker and a leader of the Free Speech movement at the University of California at Berkeley in the 1960s. He gave moving extemporaneous speeches supporting his claims.

UPI/Corbis-Bettmann

Consider another example:

GENERAL TOPIC: Giving Blood

NARROWED TOPIC: The American Red Cross System of Collecting, Storing, and Distributing Blood

GENERAL PURPOSE: To persuade

SPECIFIC PURPOSE: To move the audience to raise money on behalf of the American Red Cross

FROM TOPIC AND PURPOSE TO THESIS

At this stage you know your topic and have formulated your general and specific purposes. The next step is to formulate a thesis statement. The **thesis statement** is the theme or central idea of the speech. It is a single line that serves to connect all the parts of the speech. The main points, the supporting material, and the conclusion all relate back to the thesis. Think of the thesis as an "umbrella" or "canopy" for the speech.

> **thesis statement**
> a single statement that expresses the theme or central idea of the speech and serves to connect all the parts of the speech.

The thesis statement and specific purpose are closely linked. Both state the speech topic, but in different forms. The specific purpose describes what you want to achieve with the speech; the thesis statement concisely identifies what the speech is about.

Making a Claim

The thesis statement makes a statement, claim, or assumption about the topic. Whether the speech is informative or persuasive, the thesis statement proposes that the statement made is true or is believed. For instance, the thesis statement "Five major events caused the United States to go to war in 1941" makes the claim that the statement is true. The speech is then developed from this claim; it presents facts and evidence to support the claim as true. Similarly, the statement "Abstinence is the best personal policy for alcohol" indicates that you have adopted that belief. As such, you must develop the speech through rational arguments in order to persuade others to adopt this belief.

The thesis statement makes your claim. The organization and the body of the speech are structured to lend support for your claim. Thus, the thesis statement aids you in developing a coherent, understandable speech. It also aids your listeners in that they expect you to provide support for the claim. Without the thesis statement, or claim, the audience cannot easily follow the ideas that make up the body of the speech.

The nature of the thesis statement varies according to the speech purpose. In a persuasive speech, the thesis statement represents what you are going to prove in the address. All the main points in the speech are arguments that develop the thesis. Consider the following examples:

GENERAL PURPOSE: To persuade

SPECIFIC PURPOSE: To move the audience to raise money on behalf of the American Cancer Society.

THESIS: A donation to the American Cancer Society is the best charitable gift you can give.

SPECIFIC PURPOSE: To elect a political candidate

THESIS: A vote for Politician "X" is a vote for progress for this city.

SPECIFIC PURPOSE: To convince the audience that abstinence is the way to avoid the harm alcohol can cause

THESIS: Abstinence is the best way to avoid the harm alcohol can cause.

Notice that in each case, after you read the thesis you find yourself asking "Why?" or saying "Prove it!" This will be accomplished by the main points (see Chapter 8).

In *informative speaking*, the thesis describes the scope of the speech. It describes what the audience will learn. Consider the following examples:

GENERAL PURPOSE: To inform

SPECIFIC PURPOSE: To educate the audience about how the U.S. government is structured

THESIS: There are three branches of the U.S. government.

SPECIFIC PURPOSE: To enable audience members to invest their money properly.

THESIS: There are six steps to investing in the stock market.

SPECIFIC PURPOSE: To "set the record straight" on the chronology of an event

THESIS: Five major events caused the United States to go to war in 1941.

Notice the link between purpose and thesis in each example. You should always postpone the development of main points or the consideration of supporting material until you have correctly formulated the purpose and thesis (see Chapter 8).

Making It Relevant

Once you have defined the specific speech purpose and identified the claim, you need to express the thesis statement in a way that will motivate the audience to listen. This can often be accomplished by pointing out the relevance of the topic. Making topic and thesis statement relevant to audience members helps maintain their interest and enthusiasm.

Creating relevant statements can be accomplished rather easily by adding a few key words or phrases to the claim. For example, you can preface an informative thesis statement with a phrase such as "Few of us know" or "Contrary to popular belief" or "Have you ever." Thesis statements for persuasive claims can also be adapted to establish relevance for the audience. Phrases such as "As most of you know" or "As informed members of the community" or "As concerned adults" can help gain the audience's attention and interest and make listeners see the topic's relevance.

The exact phrasing or rewording of your thesis statement depends on the type of audience to which you are speaking. Once you gain some information about the audience members, you won't have any trouble in making the topic relevant for them. Consider how the previous thesis statements have been adapted to show relevance for a working-class audience:

SPECIFIC PURPOSE:	To enable audience members to invest their money properly
THESIS:	There are six steps to investing in the stock market.
THESIS WITH RELEVANCE:	If you want to make money work for you instead of the reverse, then you should know the six steps to investing in the stock market.
SPECIFIC PURPOSE:	To persuade the audience to elect a political candidate
THESIS:	A vote for Politician "X" is a vote for progress for this city.
THESIS WITH RELEVANCE:	Because the time has come for us to prosper in this community, a vote for Politician "X" is a vote for progress for this city.

With a well-worded phrase, the thesis statement gains enthusiasm from the audience members because the topic's relevance for them has been established.

SUMMARY QUESTIONS

What are the various sources a speaker can use to select a topic?

In most cases, it may be best to start with what you already know or are most familiar with—such as personal interests. This will give your speech a sense of authenticity and enthusiasm. Other sources for topics may be found in current events or controversial issues. Whether the speech is informative or persuasive, controversial topics can generate audience interest simply because most people have very strong opinions on those issues. Take advantage of certain issues that reflect your own concerns and those of the audience. It may also be helpful to think of the local or regional community. Finally, little-known or unusual information and facts provide an excellent source for topics.

What is brainstorming, and how is it used to generate ideas for topics?

Brainstorming can be done individually or in a group. Write down anything that you know something about or that may capture your interest—the key here is quantity. Then narrow the list to two or three topics that can be researched. You also can try word association, in which you first write down a single word that interests you. Then, write down the next thing that comes to mind. Repeat this process until you have a satisfactory topic.

What are the various kinds of general speech purposes?

The purpose of an informative speech is to define, describe, explain, or demonstrate knowledge. When you deliver an informative speech, you share your knowledge about a subject with the audience. Persuasive speeches go beyond simply conveying information; they offer arguments that promote one alternative over others. Moreover, persuasive speeches attempt to change others' beliefs, attitudes, or behavior. Special occasion speeches entertain, inspire, and commemorate; they may include awards presentations, acceptance speeches, dedication speeches, roasts, and eulogies.

What kind of techniques can be used to narrow the topic?

A topic is just a general idea. When you narrow a topic, you focus on specific aspects of it that you want the audience to remember. You need to reduce the topic to include those aspects you believe are relevant and also to fit time and research constraints. You can do this by brainstorming the various categories that represent the topic. Then, from this list, choose the categories you are most interested in or feel you can adequately research.

How can a speaker clearly state a specific speech purpose?

A specific speech purpose expresses both the topic and the general purpose in action form and in terms of the speaker's specific objectives (main points). The specific purpose answers the question, What is it about my topic that I want my audience to know?

What are some ways of composing effective thesis statements in support of the topic?

The thesis statement is even more narrow than the specific speech purpose, in that the thesis statement conveys the theme or central idea of the speech. The thesis is a single line that connects all parts of the speech. Remember that the thesis statement is a claim you are making to the audience, and it represents the arguments or main points you are going to develop.

ISSUES FOR DISCUSSION

1. How might a different general purpose (e.g., to inform versus to persuade) change the way you would present a topic?

2. How would you describe the difference between the specific purpose statement and the thesis statement?

3. What ethical considerations figure into selecting a topic and speech purpose?

SELF-ASSESSMENT

1. By using the word association brainstorming technique, generate a list of fifteen to twenty speech topics suitable for an informative speech. Start with some of the following general topics and see where they lead you: Hobbies, Passions, Campus Issues, Personal Weaknesses.

2. For the speech topics generated from the brainstorming activity in Exercise 1, write five different thesis statements for five different topics. Be ready to report your work to the class.

3. Describe those elements of an audience's characteristics that affect topic selection (e.g., age, gender, etc.). How do these elements affect audience outcomes?

4. Connect online with some bulletin boards and listservs on the Internet, or browse some home pages on the World Wide Web. Start searching or browsing with general keywords or topics, then narrow your search to more specific topics. Make notes of how these topics lead to others. Bring to class some printed copies of what you found through these sources about topics that interest you. Share them with your classmates during class discussion.

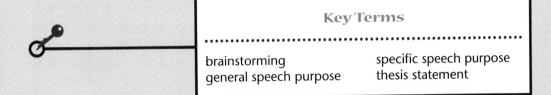

Key Terms

brainstorming   specific speech purpose
general speech purpose   thesis statement

TEAMWORK

1. In a group of four to five people, list ten current events or local issues that would make interesting speech topics for your class. Identify topics that could be used to inform, to persuade, and to celebrate or commemorate a special occasion. Identify at least one topic for each speech purpose.

2. Try brainstorming a topic in a group of three to four people. One person should write down the first word or phrase that comes to mind. That person then passes the paper to someone else, who, through word association, writes down the next word or phrase that comes to mind. The paper should be passed around so that everyone has a chance to write something down. This method of brainstorming allows members in a group to provide each other with ideas and feedback.

3. In a group of three to four people, formulate a questionnaire to be circulated throughout the class asking for demographic information (e.g., sex, academic major, ethnic or racial background, age, hobbies) about the audience. The questionnaire can be altered by each group member in order to obtain specific information that may relate to each person's speech topic.

The essence of knowledge is, having it, to apply it; not having it, to confess your ignorance.
—Confucius

The hyper-speed of change today means that given "facts" become obsolete faster—knowledge built on them becomes less durable.

—Alvin Toffler

Developing Supporting Material

Recall the last time that you had a friendly (or maybe not-so-friendly) argument with someone. As you were thinking of ways of driving home your argument, you probably searched your memory for things to say that would support your position. **What type of support did you use? Facts? Figures? Examples? Experiences from your past? Quotes or stories from other people?** As reasoning beings, it is natural that we rely on supporting evidence or material to prove our points. Even our courts of law are based on the issues of "burden of proof" and "beyond reasonable doubt." Enlisting the appropriate evidence for your argument will help you establish credibility. This chapter will show you how to locate and use supporting material to strengthen your speeches.

Archana Pachanck and Brenda Terry were neighbors in Wallston, Wisconsin. One day, Archana got a call from Brenda about a newspaper article that reported on Archana's hobby—growing herbs. Brenda, who was chair of special events for the town's Gourmet Club, thought Archana would make an interesting speaker for one of the club's meetings. Archana was flattered and agreed to speak. Then Brenda cautioned Archana, "Our members are really serious about learning to grow herbs. They use them all the time in their cooking and they're anxious to get practical advice."

After the call, Archana thought about her knowledge of herb growing. She decided she could use additional supporting material beyond her own experiences and the books she had on her shelf. She developed a plan for getting information from the local college library, searching the Internet, and interviewing other gardeners she knew in town, as well as some she regularly interacted with in cyberspace. After collecting this information, Archana felt more confident in facing the "experts" at the Gourmet Club.

Almost everyone experiences the need to acquire information at some point. Within the legal profession, the process of collecting evidence is called "discovery." For the public speaker, such discovery involves finding the information or evidence that gives substance to the speech. Because at this stage you can indulge your interests, developing supporting materials can be one of the most enjoyable aspects of the speechmaking process. Now is the time to delve into the topic, sift through sources, and select materials that best convey and support your message. As Archana realized in the preceding vignette, there will always be "experts" in your audience and you should be prepared by having appropriate supporting material.

Often, the most important element in a good speech is not the topic itself but how it is developed and supported. Good speeches contain accurate, relevant, and interesting supporting material in the form of memorable examples, stories, opinions, and facts. These "flesh out" the speech—they give substance to the speech's thesis, or central idea.

Supporting material performs three functions: (1) it illustrates or clarifies a point in a speech, (2) it often elaborates on an idea, and (3) it substantiates or proves that a statement is correct. Speeches often combine all three functions through the use of a variety of supporting materials.

Usually, there's no shortage of information to choose from when selecting information to support a speech. Newspapers, books, journals, magazines, television, radio, cyberspace, and other people all represent potential sources. Rather than finding *enough* materials, in today's information age the challenge is to learn how to locate, critically evaluate, and select from among so many of them. Other challenges involved in developing supporting material include:

- Deciding which types of supporting materials—examples, narratives, testimony, or facts and statistics—are most appropriate for your speech.
- Locating supporting materials that sustain and uphold your thesis and main points.
- Organizing and documenting the material you use in your speech so that audience members can be convinced of its worth and authenticity.
- Critically evaluating your supporting material so that it satisfactorily provides the type of assistance your speech requires.

TYPES OF SUPPORTING MATERIAL

Supporting materials include examples, narratives, testimony, and facts and statistics. They all serve different purposes.

Examples

Examples illustrate, describe, or represent things. Their purpose is to aid understanding by making ideas, items, or events more concrete, and by clarifying and amplifying meaning. Good examples are interesting and colorful; the best are memorable. "We learn by example" became a popular saying because it is indeed true. (Actually, *Bartlett's Familiar Quotations* indicates that this idea was originally expressed in the eighteenth century by the English essayist and poet Samuel Johnson. His exact words were, "Example is more efficacious than precept."[1] In today's language, this means that example is more effective than principles or rules.)

Successful speeches are liberally sprinkled with good examples that clarify and enliven the speaker's points. These examples may be brief or extended, and they may be factual or hypothetical (actual or imaginary).

A **brief example** offers a single illustration of a point. Dr. Robert E. McAfee, president-elect of the American Medical Association for 1994–1995, used a brief example to illustrate the rewards of medicine:

> [A]n ophthalmologist [came] up to me in Portland to tell me that he got a hug from a grandmother after he had done her cataract surgery. She said, "My grandson is one year old today. I have held him, and I have kissed him, and I have talked to him, but before today, I had never seen him. And you know—he is really beautiful." Then she gave my ophthalmologist friend a hug.[2]

One of the authors of this book delivered a commencement address at a graduate campus in the Washington, D.C., area. The theme of the speech was celebrating the rewards and challenges of getting a master's degree while working fulltime. At one point, the speaker used the following

examples
illustrations, descriptions, or representations.

brief example
a single illustration of a speaker's point.

humorous example to sympathize with the graduates about how expensive a college education can be:

> I guess you read about the couple who won 20 million dollars in the Texas lottery, but they had to keep working. They had three kids in college.

In concluding, the speaker used a personal example to emphasize the intrinsic value of education:

> Let me leave you with a personal thought. My wife's grandmother during the Depression had to leave school at age 14. This was one of the personal tragedies of her life—she loved to learn, she loved school. After the graduation ceremonies when I received my doctorate she hugged me, and with tears in her eyes said, "In this hard world, people may be able to take away your job, or take away your home, but there's one thing you can count on: No one can *ever* take away your education."

extended example
multifaceted illustrations of an idea, item, or event being described.

Sometimes it requires more than a brief example to effectively illustrate a point. An **extended example** offers multifaceted illustrations of the idea, item, or event being described. Consider how David Scott, chancellor of the University of Massachusetts, used an extended example to illustrate how difficult it is to change people's minds:

hypothetical example
an illustration of a point made by describing something that could happen in the future.

> Take a lesson from history. In 1589 Galileo summoned a collection of the world's most learned professors to the Leaning Tower of Pisa for a demonstration which would disprove a 2,000-year-old physics principle of Aristotle's—that the heavier an object is, the faster it will fall to earth. From the top of the tower, Galileo simultaneously dropped a ten-pound and a one-pound weight, which both landed at the same time. The result? Conventional wisdom was so powerful and change so threatening that the professors all denied the truth as seen by their own eyes.[3]

Critical Checkpoint

· ·

Selecting the Right Example

Examples bring your speech to life. They also help prove your point. However, selecting the right example requires critical thinking. In considering the use of examples for a speech, evaluate each one in light of the following questions: Does the example truly illustrate or prove the point? Is it credible? Is it suitable for the audience's background and experiences, or would another illustration be more appropriate?

All the foregoing examples are based on actual events. Sometimes, however, you may need to make a point about something that might happen in the future. This is where a **hypothetical example** becomes useful. In 1997, Republican representative Vernon Ehlers of Michigan spoke at a Congressional hearing in support of a bill to ban human cloning. Representative Ehlers, who is also a research physicist, claimed that human cloning should be banned because it will create moral dilemmas that humanity is not prepared to handle. To illustrate one such moral dilemma, Ehlers offered the following hypothetical example:

> What if in the cloning process you produce someone with two heads and three arms? Are you simply going to euthanize and dispose of that person? The answer is no. We're talking about human life.[4]

narrative
a story or tale, either real or imaginary.

Narratives

One of the most powerful means of communicating messages is through the use of narratives. A **narrative** is simply a story. Narratives tell tales, both real and imaginary. Scholars of narratives have commented that all of human history consists of stories. They can take the form of fairy tales, legends, religious narratives, or myths. They can take the form of Horatio Alger–type success stories and Charles Dickens–type hard-luck tales. Many narratives, such as those told by Native American storytellers, are passed down orally from one generation to the next. Survivors of wars, crimes, and natural disasters have their own powerful tales. Common to all narratives are the essential storytelling elements of plot, characters, setting, and some sort of timeline.

Jose Galvez/PhotoEdit

As supporting material, narratives may be brief and simple descriptions of short incidents worked into the body of the speech, or relatively drawn-out accounts that constitute most of the presentation. In the following example, Bonnie Campbell, director of the Violence Against Women Office of the U.S. Department of Justice, used a brief real-life story to introduce her speech entitled "Breaking the Silence on Domestic Violence":

Native American storytellers use narratives that have been passed down orally from one generation to the next.

> Last November 26, Christopher Bailey of St. Albans, West Virginia, finished the argument by beating his wife, Sonya, until she collapsed. Then he put her in the trunk of their compact car and drove for five days through West Virginia and Kentucky before taking her to an emergency room. Sonya Bailey suffered irreversible brain damage and remains in a permanent vegetative state—becoming another domestic violence statistic.[5]

Sometimes speakers incorporate a story from a novel, film, or play to artfully illustrate an important theme. In a convocation speech to the class of 1999 entitled "Idealism for Your Sake and That of Society," James O. Freedman, president of Dartmouth College, referred to a novel by Paul Theroux to convey his theme that a fulfilling life requires hard work and dedication[6]:

> Take, for example, the protagonist of another novel, and one of my favorites, *Saint Jack* (1973) by Paul Theroux. Jack Flowers is a middle-aged American expatriate who languishes as a pimp in Singapore, longing for an affirmation of his moral innocence and for the achievement of goals he cannot summon the self-discipline to pursue. "For as long as I could remember," he writes, "I had wanted to be rich, and famous if possible."
>
> Unable to achieve wealth or fame by his own efforts, he lived, as Theroux writes, "in expectation of an angel." He daydreams about receiving letters that bestow great wealth upon him and confirm the esteem in which he wishes he were held.

After relating more of Theroux's story, Freedman explicitly tied the narrative to his own theme that a fulfilling life requires hard work and dedication:

> Such, then, are the very human yearnings for protection against the contingencies of life and the indifference of the universe, for achievement of success and riches and recognition—all made more clear and dramatic by artistic hyperbole....But such fantasies are not the stuff of which full and satisfying lives are created. Waiting passively "in expectation of an angel" is no substitute for grappling with the dilemmas of being human.

Personal experiences can be the basis for powerful narratives. In a keynote address delivered to the annual convention of the Asian American Journalists Association (AAJA), Helen Zia, a Chinese-American writer and activist, revealed a personal experience that shed light on growing up an Asian American in the 1950s and 1960s:

> I, like most of you, remember what it was like never to see people who looked like me in the world beyond my immediate circle. When I was growing up in the 1950s, Asians were nowhere to be found in the media, except occasionally in the movies. There at the Saturday matinee, my brothers and I would sit with all the other kids in town watching old World War II movies—you know, where the evil zero pilots would be heading for their unsuspecting prey, only to be thwarted by the all-American heroes, who were, of course, always white. These movies would have their defining moment, that crescendo of emotion when the entire theater would rise up, screaming "Kill them! Kill them! Kill them!" ("Them" being the Japanese.) When the movie was over and the lights came on, I wanted to be invisible so that my neighbors wouldn't direct their red-*white*-and blue fervor toward me.[7]

anecdote
a short story of an interesting, humorous, and/or real-life incident.

One popular type of brief narrative or story is the **anecdote**—a short story of an interesting, humorous, and/or real-life incident. Many speakers at award banquets, as well as ministers at Sunday morning pulpits, use anecdotes. The most effective anecdotes are those that the audience hasn't heard before and that can be artfully linked to the speaker's theme. In the following example, notice how Ron Glover of Dun & Bradstreet Information Services, North America, was able to link an anecdote with the theme of his speech, "Establishing a Presence around the Globe":

> Sending messages across borders can sometimes cause translation problems even when there are no language differences. For example, a few years ago the British division of McDonald's Hamburgers was damaged by a persistent rumor that the company supported the Irish Republican Army. They spent a lot of time and money tracing that rumor to its source. They found that the rumor began when a CNN program seen in England reported that McDonald's senior management encouraged its employees to invest in IRA's. Of course, IRA in the U.S. means "Individual Retirement Accounts," while in Britain it means "Irish Republican Army."

That incident is a handy reminder of George Bernard Shaw's observation that "England and America are two countries divided by a common language."[8]

Testimony

The Latin root of *testimony* is *testis*, meaning "witness." **Testimony** encompasses firsthand findings, eyewitness accounts, and opinions by people, both lay (non-expert) and expert. As you may recall from the O. J. Simpson trials, expert and lay testimony are an important part of proving cases in a court of law. Experts are called in to report their findings about the crime scene or to explain the nature of certain types of evidence; lay witnesses report on what they saw, heard, and felt.

Expert testimony includes any findings, eyewitness accounts, or opinions by professionals who are trained to evaluate or report on a given topic. A medical doctor may provide highly technical information about the threat of cholesterol to the body. A championship football coach may offer firsthand information about training and conditioning habits. A nuclear engineer may shed valuable information on radiation hazards.

At the Annual Speech Writers Conference in Chicago on November 11, 1993, Dr. Alan M. Perlman offered his opinion about why many business executives rely on speech writers. Because he himself is a business executive with many years of experience, his opinion could be considered a form of expert testimony. Perlman's audience was speech writers:

> My experience, for what it's worth, is that where rhetoric is concerned, executives' abilities are not generative, but reactive: they may not be able to produce what they want to say, but they sure can recognize it when the writer produces it. So it's up to the speech writer to present possibilities, either by generating ideas him- or herself, or by collecting them from knowledgeable people in the organization or elsewhere.[9]

Lay testimony, or testimony by non-experts who have witnessed or experienced events related to the subject, can also serve as strong supporting material. Eyewitnesses, for example, can reveal information that is unavailable to others—often in powerful fashion. The survivors of the 1995 Oklahoma City bombing provided audiences riveting firsthand accounts of the tragedy.

As a speaker, you can also offer your own testimony. After all, you may be able to provide the best eyewitness account or evaluation. For example,

testimony
firsthand findings, eyewitness accounts, and opinions that directly support a fact or an assertion.

expert testimony
findings, eyewitness accounts, or opinions by professionals who have been trained to evaluate or report on a given topic.

lay testimony
testimony by non-experts who have witnessed or experienced events related to the subject under consideration.

people who have witnessed a space shuttle launch, met an important political leader, or traveled to a foreign country can give firsthand accounts of events that interest audiences. When providing personal opinions, however, be sure to identify them as such. Because audiences frequently misinterpret opinion as fact, the speaker is ethically bound to alert them to the distinction. Moreover, don't overuse this type of support. Unless audiences are convinced of a speaker's qualifications, they soon become wary of one who continually says, "My opinion is…" or "I think…" or "In my view…."

Credibility Is Key. Whether the source is the speaker, an expert, or a lay person, credibility plays a key role in enhancing the effectiveness of this type of support. Audiences who assign a source little credibility usually will reject the speaker's message. In the O. J. Simpson murder case, one supposed eyewitness to Simpson's whereabouts on the night of the murders was found to have a long criminal record. Once the prosecution revealed this to the jury, they discounted that eyewitness's testimony. Further, expert testimony is not exempt from attack. By demonstrating errors in methods and procedures, O. J. Simpson's defense team successfully challenged the credibility of police detectives, medical pathologists, and laboratory technicians who had been called in by the prosecution. Of course, in public speaking it won't be the speaker who attacks the source's credibility; depending on the source's reputation, some members of the audience may do so.

The Speaker Must Establish Credibility. It is the speaker's responsibility to establish the reputation of the source—and to do so in as compelling and accurate a manner as possible. When using testimony in a speech, always cite the source's name, title, and relevance to the topic. Because testimony is often expressed in speeches through the use of quotations, and sometimes through paraphrases, proper citation is also essential. (Refer to Chapter 4, Plagiarism section, for a review of how to do this.)

In the following examples from real-life speeches, note how the speakers briefly but accurately establish their sources' credibility:

> According to John Miller, one of the three founders of the community's rapid transit committee,…

> Teresa Allen, fund-raising chairperson from the Chicago Society of the Performing Arts, gave some insight into the proper way to obtain donations when she said…

> I spoke with Martha Peters, a registered nurse from Detroit's Halliet West Hospital, who was present for the first liver transplant. She said…

Critical Checkpoint

• •

Selecting the Right Testimony

Regardless of which type of testimony you consider, determine first whether it meets these essential criteria[1]:

· Are the experts I'm considering citing proven in their fields? Are they respected?

· Do they have any obvious biases?

· Will their views effectively support my thesis?

· Will their views add weight to my assertions or arguments?

Testimony that does not meet these standards is likely to do more harm than good.

1. The idea for these questions was spurred by Otis M. Walter and Robert L. Scott, *Thinking and Speaking: A Guide to Intelligent Oral Communication*, 3rd ed. (New York: Macmillan, 1973), p. 52.

Facts and Statistics

Facts include actual events, dates, times, people involved, and places. Facts represent documented occurrences; that is, it is assumed that they can be backed up with supporting evidence. Research has demonstrated that

facts
documented occurrences that include events, dates, times, people involved, and places.

most people require some type of evidence, usually in the form of facts and statistics, before accepting someone else's claims or position.[10] Most people think that facts are not open to interpretation. However, facts are only truly considered facts when they have been independently verified by people other than the source. For example, we accept as true the fact that Abraham Lincoln was the sixteenth president of the United States because it has been independently verified by eyewitnesses, journalists, historians, and so forth. Listeners are not likely to accept a speaker's statements as factual unless he or she backs them up with credible support. For example, in a speech about global foods John Ruff, of Kraft Foods International, used a fact generated from a study that proved his point:

Alex Quesada/Matrix International

Conduct research to find facts, statistics, and details that will make your speech more concrete, authoritative, and interesting.

> The truth is that there are very few truly global food or beverage brands, such that the product is named the same, and tastes exactly the same, all around the world. An exhaustive study by Young and Rubicam concluded that of 6,200 brands from all over the world, only *one* maintained an identical product and image—and that was, if you haven't already guessed, Coca-Cola.[11]

In a speech that was intended to convince an audience of his company's commitment to saving energy and controlling emissions, in 1996 Alex Trotman of Ford Motor Company used facts from his own corporation's research and production areas to demonstrate a trend:

> In 1965, U.S. cars on average used 200 grams of fuel per mile. Enough to almost fill an average water glass. About this much. Today, our cars use 100 grams of fuel per mile. In other words, we've cut average fuel consumption in half.[12]

In the following example the speaker, H. L. Fuller, chairman and chief executive officer of Amoco Corporation, used factual information from a well-known source to prove his point about global competition:

> Almost every country on the planet has a market-oriented economic system, and is attempting to be a player in the global marketplace for goods and capital....
>
> Just before the fall of the Berlin Wall, according to the Hoover [Institute] analysis, "almost 70 percent of mankind was living under Marxist and Socialist economic systems, which greatly inhibited trade and investment." But then came the great upheavals of the last half decade, and suddenly, "there are now three billion players in the capitalist system."[13]

Statistics are used to express data in numerical form. In the preceding illustration, statistics were used to emphasize the speaker's point. Usually statistics are cited to prove the existence of a trend or relationship. There are two classes of statistics that may be included in your presentation: descriptive and

statistics
data expressed in numerical form.

descriptive statistics
data or information that characterize a group or classification.

inferential. **Descriptive statistics** provide information to characterize a group or classification, as in the following:

- the percentage of African Americans currently residing in Delaware who are under 40 years of age
- the number of registered voters who are currently enrolled in a university
- the number of liver transplants performed in public hospitals in the past year
- the amount of money all Fortune 500 corporations spent on travel in the past year

Descriptive statistics represent only the people, places, or things they reference. They cannot be extended to any other person, place, or thing. However, some conclusions can usually be drawn from descriptive statistics. This is borne out by the following excerpt from a speech by Peter G. Peterson, chairman of the Blackstone Group:

> The problem, it seems to me, is that we have special interest constituencies that can exercise raw terror in our political structure. Let's just take the American Association of Retired Persons (AARP) for a moment. It has 28 million members and more than 5,000 state and local chapters. It includes one in every four registered voters. It is larger than any organization in the United States other than the Catholic Church. It is twice the size of the AFL-CIO. If it were a private company, its annual cash flow would put it near the top of the Fortune 500. When AARP speaks, and it speaks loud and clear on the question of entitlement, you can bet the Congress listens.[14]

inferential statistics
data collected from a sample or representative group and generalized to a larger population.

Inferential statistics are data collected from a sample or representative group and then generalized to a larger population. For example, years ago your parents or neighbors may have completed forms for Nielsen television ratings. For many years, a survey of fewer than 1 percent of all viewers was considered sufficient to generalize about the television-viewing habits of many millions of Americans. Likewise, if you wanted to determine how prevalent cheating on exams is among students at your college or university, you could either survey every student or poll a sample of representative students. Time and money would likely prevent you from studying everyone. However, inferential statistics would allow you to generalize the results from a small survey to the larger population of students at your school. But using this type of statistic requires that the data or information come from a representative sample. This means that your data must come from the same sample source (people, raw numbers) as what you are inferring or comparing.

Statistics are an excellent type of supporting material; but, like facts, they should be approached critically and used with care. Statistics are not truth. They are merely reports of data. Peter Francese, founder and president of *American Demographics*, a magazine that reports all kinds of statistics about U.S. life, offers a caution:

> No number can represent the truth perfectly. Every survey has some error or bias. Data from public records, such as crime reports, can be underreported or mis-classified. And even perfectly collected data are open to different interpretations.[15]

Selecting the Right Facts and Statistics

Because people are exposed to so many facts and statistics, it is natural that a healthy level of skepticism exists about this type of supporting material. To ensure that you are using the best available facts and statistics, put this type of support to several "critical" tests:

How was the information collected? Are you ready to defend the way in which the facts or statistics were derived?

Is it primary data—that is, data from the person or group who collected and analyzed it? Or is it secondary data—that is, a second-hand report of the original data? Does the secondary source validly represent the original data?

Can you be certain that the facts and statistics give the whole story, or have selected facts and statistics been provided that prove a biased point of view?

If the data come from polls or surveys, is the source organization likely to be partisan (e.g., National Rifle Association, GreenPeace, Libertarian Party) or one that is considered more objective (e.g., CNN, Gallup, Neilsen)?

Is the source credible? Will the audience think so?

Now that you know about the various kinds of supporting materials used in speeches, how do you find them? This chapter's interview gives a good introduction.

LOCATING SUPPORTING MATERIAL

The purpose of finding supporting materials is to substantiate the speech thesis, and to do so in a way that achieves your specific speech purpose. Thus, you need enough information to clarify, elaborate, or prove your major points in a form that successfully communicates them to your audience.

You can find supporting materials by conducting primary or secondary research, or by using a combination of both. **Primary research** is original, or firsthand, research such as interviews and surveys conducted by you, the speaker. **Secondary research** is the vast body of information gathered by others.

▬ **primary research**
original, or firsthand, research conducted by the speaker.

▬ **secondary research**
the vast body of information gathered by others.

Getting Started

Regardless of the method, or combination of methods, you select, before rushing out with your tape recorder or hunkering down in the library, take a few minutes to focus on the purpose of your search. Think about who your audience is and what type of research, data, or proof will most influence them. That was one of the key points made by Van May in his interview with the authors of this book (see p. 160).

A common pitfall of research is getting sidetracked. Especially in reviewing secondary research, the biggest pitfall is wasting time in the wrong places. Hours after reviewing reams of documents, many a researcher has

Supporting the Speech: A Real World Perspective

Van May is president and CEO of Plains Cotton Cooperative Association, a parent company for various cotton businesses located throughout the world. In his job as president, May is required to deliver dozens of speeches each year to diverse groups of people. Some of the audiences are composed of professionals like himself, whereas others are cotton farmers, gin operators, and textile workers. The use of supporting materials in his speeches is essential for forming the right impression with audiences who are concerned about their economic welfare.

Do you find it difficult to locate supporting material for many of the speeches you give each year?

Many of the speeches I deliver are on topics for which the audience expects certain types of facts and figures. For instance, stockholder meetings require that I present data about the earnings of the company. That type of information is easy for me to obtain and assimilate. The key is presenting the supporting material in a manner that is understandable by the audience. In other instances, I am required to give speeches on topics for which I have to look for information.

What kind of speeches are those, and what kind of supporting material do you use?

Often, I need to give speeches that talk about the cotton industry and other markets, or speeches on where the future of agribusiness is going. Information supporting those topics usually is not at my fingertips. I search through magazines and journals related to the topic, and more currently, I will surf the Internet to look for current information on a particular topic.

Have you found the Internet to be a useful tool for locating supporting material for speeches?

The Internet and the Web can be very helpful. You have to be careful, however, about getting caught up in a maze of interesting information that's unrelated to your search. You have to remain focused on your task to avoid wasting time when surfing the Net.

Do you have a preference for one or two types of supporting material?

I really enjoy using humor in my speeches to keep the audience interested. That requires using lighthearted examples and illustrations. Telling stories is another way of using supporting material that keeps the speech moving. Obviously, many of my topics also require the use of facts, data, and statistics. I try to weave the use of hard facts into all parts of the speech so that I don't overwhelm the audience. Also, when very many statistics are involved, I favor the use of visual aids. Slides, transparencies, and Microsoft PowerPoint are the tools I have found most helpful in this regard.

Do you ever do any of your own research as a way of developing supporting material?

Yes. I talk to staff and occasionally to our stockholders or vendors to help develop arguments for my speeches that are timely and relevant. I also conduct interviews to get information that I need. Conducting research like that can be a lot of fun and I always learn something.

What cautions or advice would you give to students of public speaking about using supporting material in their speeches?

Every speech is different and requires a careful look at what you intend to present to the audience. Think about who your audience is and what they will expect in the way of support. Try to match their expectations with your material. Most audiences prefer a variety of supporting material. One thing for sure—if you are boring, you lose them in a hurry.

discovered that he or she has failed to find the material necessary to support the speech. In the case of primary research, the problem tends to be poorly constructed interview and survey questions—with the same outcome.

By keeping the reason for your search—to substantiate the speech thesis—clearly in mind, you can avoid the trap of getting sidelined. Take a few moments to review your thesis statement. Consider what you need to support it. Here are some examples:

THESIS STATEMENT:	"Several American cities have large numbers of citizens living in poverty."
ELABORATE:	Which cities? How many citizens? How much below the poverty line?
THESIS STATEMENT:	"Unions have been very good for U.S. businesses."
PROVE:	Why? In which ways? What are some examples?
THESIS STATEMENT:	"The community should establish free public Internet access centers."
DEMONSTRATE:	Why is there a need for free public access? How could the centers be set up? How would such centers be advantageous?
THESIS STATEMENT:	"Education should be given higher priority in the allocation of state funding."
EXPLAIN:	What is the current level of priority? Why is that inadequate?
THESIS STATEMENT:	"Fraternities and sororities give college students an edge after graduation."
SUBSTANTIATE:	What kind of edge? How many college graduates attribute their success in part to membership in these organizations?
THESIS STATEMENT:	"The plan to improve facilities for the College of Business is too expensive."
CLARIFY:	How much is too expensive? Why?

Evaluate Resources. What resources are at your disposal, and what constraints might affect the research process? If your next speech assignment is due in a few days, you probably won't have time to wait for pamphlets or brochures to arrive by mail. Nor can you wait three weeks for a book to arrive from interlibrary loan. Before committing time and energy, consider your ability to carry a project through. For example, some research is costly to conduct. Mail surveys involve printing costs and postage. Telephone interviews may involve long-distance rates, and additional time and expense to transcribe the conversation.

Decide on Research Methods. Different topics suggest different research methods, so spend a few moments to consider what might work best for your particular situation. A topic such as drinking habits on campus requires primary research in the form of interviews, surveys, and/or personal observations. Other topics can be supported only through secondary research (such as fertility drugs). Many topics benefit from a mix of both.

For example, although a fine speech about black pilots in World War II could be constructed entirely from secondary research, personal interviews with a few surviving pilots would add considerable weight to the presentation. Consider the experience of one particular student. In the course of conducting library research, he happened on an Air Force pamphlet containing the names of several living World War II fliers. The student was able to contact them and conduct telephone interviews. His speech, which relied on both interviews and articles and books, was so well received that he was later invited by a classmate to deliver the speech to a local church group.

Primary Research: Interviews and Surveys

Supporting material drawn from primary research may include any source developed directly by the participants in that research. The Declaration of Independence is a primary document created by the founding fathers of the United States. Firsthand oral or written histories, diaries, and recordings of meetings and other events are also primary sources. All can provide valuable information to support and enliven a speech.

You can also create your own primary sources by conducting interviews and surveys.

Interviews. Interviews are a key tool in gathering information about an audience. This method of collecting data can also be used to gather information for your speech, often to great effect. People are fascinated by information "from the horse's mouth." Firsthand information from local experts in their field can readily capture an audience's attention. Such accounts also build speaker credibility. When thinking about "experts" to interview, don't aim too low. You might be surprised by the type of people who are willing to participate in an interview that is used in a college speech assignment (e.g., city or county officials, local heroes or sporting figures, prominent members of the community).

Bonnie Kamin/PhotoEdit

An interview is an excellent way to gather primary source material from an expert. Be sure to prepare your questions ahead of time and conduct yourself professionally.

PLANNING THE QUESTIONS. Many topics lend themselves to interviews. If your topic is about human cloning, for example, you may be able to find a researcher working on campus who will agree to talk about his or her work. In a world full of specialists, there is no shortage of people with the knowledge you need. These same people are often very busy, however. Don't waste the interviewee's time asking questions unrelated to his or her area of expertise. And whether the interview will be conducted in person or over the telephone, plan on constructing your questions well in advance of the actual interview date. To ensure that they address the information you need, review each question in the light of your thesis statement.

PHRASING THE QUESTIONS. The wording of a question is almost as critical as the information it seeks to uncover. Poorly phrased questions can be vague, leading, or hostile. *Vague questions* don't give the person being interviewed enough to go on. He or she must either guess at what you mean, or spend time interviewing *you* for clarification. Vague questions are a waste of the interviewee's time and reflect a lack of preparation on the part of the interviewer. *Leading questions* encourage, if not force, a certain response. For example, "Like most intelligent people, are you going to support candidate X?" Likewise, *hostile questions* are phrased to reinforce the interviewer's agenda. They may also have a hostile intent. "You've always been prejudiced, haven't you?" is an example of a hostile question.

Interviewers who use leading and hostile questions try to foist their own agenda on those whom they are interviewing. Rather than eliciting information about the person being interviewed, they tend to generate one of two responses. First, the respondent might be intimidated into agreeing with the interviewer but not be forthcoming in response to further questioning. Second, the respondent might strenuously object to the interviewer's line of questions and react angrily and/or stalk off. Whether they are leading or hostile, poorly worded questions color the respondent's answers and defeat the purpose of the interview. Because they do not respect the integrity of the respondent, they are unethical as well.

RECORDING THE INTERVIEW. More than one interview has gone splendidly—and entirely unrecorded. You can avoid this pitfall by taking detailed notes, tape-recording the interview, or using a combination of note taking and recording. As long as you ask your subject's permission, you have the option of audiotaping or videotaping. To establish an air of authenticity, you might even decide to replay short excerpts during your speech—again, with your subject's permission.

CONDUCTING THE INTERVIEW PROFESSIONALLY. Conducting yourself professionally is a requirement throughout the interviewing process. The interviewees are helping you out by giving you something that you can use, and in return you should treat them in a professional manner. When requesting an interview, arrange the time and place at their convenience, not yours. During the interview, allow them to set the pace, and always allow them to ask you questions or make comments that are not part of your questionnaire. Offer them a copy of your results when your research is complete. And always send a written note of thanks to each interviewee.

Surveys. Like interviews, a survey is useful both as a tool to investigate audience attitudes (see Chapter 5) and as supporting material. Surveys are an especially effective source of support for topics related to the attitudes, values, and beliefs of people in your immediate environment. Perhaps, for example, your topic is the drinking habits of the sophomore class at your university. Unless someone else has already conducted that research, you'll need to do your own. Or perhaps your thesis is that "College students in the United States who regularly attend religious services have a greater sense of well-being than those who don't." Although secondary research would be necessary to prove your claim, a survey of students at your own college could serve as an excellent source of additional support with direct relevance to your audience. (For information on creating surveys, refer to Chapter 5.) Just remember, although surveys are an excellent way of generating data, effective surveying is no simple matter. You have to be very careful in planning, conducting, and analyzing data for your survey.

Secondary Resources:
Print, Electronically Stored, and Online Sources

Secondary research includes all information recorded by persons other than actual participants in an event or study. Of course, it is always preferable to obtain the original source of research whenever possible, rather than relying on someone else's report (e.g., it is better to get the actual text of a speech than to rely on a newspaper article about the speech). However, secondary resources can be quite useful in many cases. The most likely sources of secondary research include books, newspapers, periodicals, encyclopedias, almanacs, government publications, biographical reference works, books of quotations, and atlases. In the past, these sources appeared only in print. Increasingly, however, the information they contain is being stored simultaneously on CD-ROMs or in online databases. A **database** is simply a place, or "base," in which information is stored. Books are databases that store information on paper; online databases store information electronically.

database
a "base," or place, in which information is stored, such as books or computers.

The Reference Desk. Every library contains a unique mix of print and electronic reference works, as well as several online search and retrieval systems. At the reference desk you can find out what this mix is and, with the help of a reference librarian, learn how to use these works to research your topic.

The Card or Online Catalog. You can find out what the library owns by consulting its card or online catalog. The former is an older, manual system; the latter is computerized. Both are organized by author, title, and subject. Libraries organize books and other holdings according to the Library of Congress call number or a Dewey Decimal number. Once you've located an entry in the catalog, jot down this number so that you can locate it on the shelves.

Books. Books explore topics in depth. A well-written book provides detail and perspective and can serve as an excellent source of supporting examples, stories, facts, and statistics. Depending on your need for current information, you may have to supplement the material you find in books with more recent sources of information, such as newspapers and periodicals.

To search the titles of all books currently in print in the United States, refer to *Books in Print* (in print form) or, if your library has it, *Books in Print Plus* (on CD-ROM). To locate a book in your library's holdings, refer to the library's card or online catalog or other system of retrieval.

Newspapers. Newspapers are a rich source of support material. In addition to reports on the major issues and events of the day, many newspaper stories—especially feature articles—also include detailed background or historical information. The single most comprehensive source for searching newspapers is *Newspaper Abstracts on Disc* (CD-ROM). This reference indexes ten of the largest and most widely read newspapers in the country: *New York Times, Washington Post, Christian Science Monitor, Boston Globe, Los Angeles Times, Chicago Tribune, Atlanta Constitution, Atlanta Journal, Wall Street Journal,* and *USA Today*. In addition to providing a comprehensive subject heading index, *Newspaper Abstracts on Disc* offers short summaries, or abstracts, of the articles. Researchers can access this resource online through *Newspaper and Periodical Abstracts*. Both forms of the index are updated monthly.

Periodicals. A periodical is a regularly published magazine or journal. Periodicals are an excellent source because they usually include all types of supporting material discussed in this chapter (examples, narratives, facts and statistics, and testimony). Periodicals include general interest magazines such as *Time* and *Newsweek* as well as the thousands of specialized academic, business, and technical magazines, newsletters, and journals in circulation. Most popular magazines are indexed in the *Reader's Guide to Periodical Literature* (available in print, online, and on CD-ROM). Many libraries offer access to the online database *UnCover*, which indexes over 12,000 magazine and journal articles. Another popular online database is EBSCO's *Magazine Index*, which covers 400 magazines. If you find an article that interests you in either of these databases, in many instances you can retrieve the full text.

There are also many periodical databases devoted to special topics. For business-related topics, consider using the *Business Periodicals Index*. If you plan to talk about a health or science topic, examine *Index Medicus*. The *Public Affairs Information Service* (PAIS) selectively indexes a wide range of publications on business, economics and social conditions, public policy and administration, and international relations. Other specialized databases are listed in Table 7.1.

Table 7.1 Specialized Databases

Online Database	Description
ABI/INORM	Index and abstracts of business articles, 1987–present.
America: History and Life	Index and abstracts on the history and culture of the United States, 1982–present.
Contents1st	Tables of contents of journals, 1990–present.
Dissertation Abstracts	Index and abstracts of dissertations and theses in all subject areas, 1861–present.
ERIC	Index of reports and journal articles in education, 1966–present.
FastDoc	Index of articles with text online or by email; subset of Article1st.
Medline	Index of journal articles in medicine and related fields, 1985–present.
PapersFirst	Index of papers presented at conferences, 1993–present.
Proceedings	Index of conference proceedings, 1993–present.
PSYCHLIT	Index and abstracts in psychology and related disciplines in the behavioral sciences, 1974–present.
SOCIOFILE	Index and abstracts in sociology and related disciplines, 1974–present.

Encyclopedias. Encyclopedias summarize knowledge that is found in original form elsewhere. Their usefulness lies in providing an overview of subjects. Because they provide broad overviews of so many topics, encyclopedias are a good place to start your research. *General encyclopedias* are truly "encyclopedic": They attempt to cover all important subject areas of knowledge. *Specialized encyclopedias* delve deeply into one subject area such as religion, science, art, sports, or engineering.

The most comprehensive of the general encyclopedias is the *New Encyclopedia Britannica*, available both in print form and on CD-ROM. Published continuously since the 1700s, the *Britannica* is revered by scholars worldwide as the most authoritative compendium of information in encyclopedia form. Almost one-third of the encyclopedia is devoted to biographies, making it an ideal reference if your topic is about a person.

The *Academic American Encyclopedia*, although not as comprehensive as some other encyclopedias, provides useful summaries of many recent topics. Other easy-to-use encyclopedias include the *Collier's*, *Grolier's*, *Compton's*, and *Columbia* encyclopedias. All are helpful in gaining a general overview of a given subject. For a more in-depth look at a topic, there are specialized encyclopedias of all types, ranging from the *McGraw-Hill Encyclopedia of Science and Technology* to the *Encyclopedia of Religion* to the *Encyclopedia of Physical Education, Fitness, and Sports*.

ELECTRONIC ENCYCLOPEDIAS. Various online and CD-ROM versions of encyclopedias are likely to be available at your library. Part of the appeal of electronic encyclopedias is the ability to cross-reference topics via **hyperlinks**, or highlighted words that link to related topics. Another attractive feature is the search function, which allows you to quickly search your topic by keywords as well as by author or topic.

The following encyclopedias can be found on CD-ROM or online, or both[16]:

Britannica CD 98 (CD-ROM). With 67,000 articles, this CD-ROM contains nearly twice as many entries as any other CD-ROM. Like its print counterpart, this reference work contains far fewer illustrations and multimedia links than other encyclopedias, concentrating instead on rigorous academic content.

Compton's Interactive Encyclopedia 1998 (CD-ROM and online versions available). This resource contains 37,000 articles, most of which are fairly brief. Its multimedia format includes icons next to lists of topics that indicate whether an entry includes text, photos, sound, video, map, or online connection.[17]

Grolier Multimedia Encyclopedia (CD-ROM and online versions available). This resource contains 35,000 articles, video and animation clips, sound, and 1,200 maps. It includes all the printed articles that appear in the *Academic American Encyclopedia*, plus articles that were written just for the electronic version.

Infopedia (CD-ROM). This resource combines eight different reference works in one useable source, making it one of the most comprehensive electronic encyclopedias available.

Microsoft Encarta Multimedia Encyclopedia (CD-ROM). Containing 30,000 articles, this encyclopedia is distinguished by its superior

hyperlinks
in electronic encyclopedias, highlighted words that link to related topics.

Elizabeth Simpson/FPG

CD-ROMs hold vast amounts of information in a small space. Hyperlinks and search functions make them useful research tools.

multimedia features, including a 360-degree feature that lets viewers travel great distances with their eyes.

World Book Information Finder (CD-ROM). Although this resource is not multimedia (no sound or video), it does include the complete text of the *World Book Encyclopedia* and all the entries in the *World Book Dictionary*. Many articles are covered in a comprehensive manner.

Almanacs. To find facts and statistics that support your topic, almanacs and fact books are a good choice. (See also U.S. government publications listed below.) As with encyclopedias, there are both general and specialized almanacs. In the general category, one of the most comprehensive sources is the *World Almanac and Book of Facts*. This reference's well-organized alphabetical index allows readers easy access to subjects. It contains facts and statistics in many categories, including those related to historical, social, political, and religious subjects. The *World Almanac* also includes the top ten news stories of the year, notable Supreme Court decisions, notable quotes of the year, and a complete listing of vital statistics for all nations of the world. Other helpful almanacs include the *Information Please Almanac*; *Famous First Facts: A Record of First Happenings, Discoveries, and Inventions in American History*; and the *People's Almanac*. The well-known *Guinness Book of Records* provides facts on world records of all kinds—from A to Z.

Information from almanacs can supplement other research for your speech. As with encyclopedias, however, don't rely on them as your only means of support.

Government Publications. Part of every tax dollar goes to support the constant production of publications by the U.S. Government Printing Office (GPO). The GPO is responsible for publishing and distributing all information collected and produced by federal agencies, from the U.S. Census Bureau to the Environmental Protection Agency. GPO publications also include all congressional reports and hearings.

One of the most helpful of all government publications is the *Statistical Abstract of the United States*. Published annually in a paperback, this volume provides a staggering array of statistics on the social, political, and economic organization of the United States. It offers such information as how long it takes undergraduates to earn bachelor's degrees by sex, ethnicity, and academic major (at last count, most undergraduates took six years or less).

Finding and using government documents can be daunting, but given the fact that nearly all the information comes from primary sources, it's usually well worth the effort. The *Guide to U.S. Government Publications*, which is available in print and microfiche formats, offers a step-by-step guide to researching government publications. The guide describes both what is available from the GPO and how to use the indexes it publishes.

The easiest way to search government documents is via the *GPO on Silver Platter*. Updated monthly, this CD-ROM database contains most documents published by the federal government. Subjects or title headings are searched by keywords. Note, however, that not all libraries carry the documents found on the index. Ask your librarian for the nearest library designated as a federal government depository. If it is too far to travel there, you may request an interlibrary loan.

Multicultural Reference Works—Filling the Gap

Until recently, standard reference works such as encyclopedias and almanacs claimed to be comprehensive but, in fact, generally paid little attention to the culture and accomplishments of the many minority groups that make up the United States. Today, publishers are addressing the long-standing need for detailed information on these groups' experience. *Discovering Multicultural America*, for example, is a multimedia CD-ROM examining the significant people, issues, events, organizations, and documents in the history of African, Asian, Hispanic, and Native Americans. Included are some 2,100 biographical profiles, essays, timelines, and video and audio clips.

Among biographical resources, Gale Research publishes *African American Biography*, *Hispanic American Biography*, *Asian American Biography*, and *Native American Biography*. All are multi-volume sets containing portraits, quotes, interviews, and articles about prominent men and women.

Among specialized almanacs, available now are the *Asian American Almanac*; the *Native North American Almanac,* the *African American Almanac*, and the *Hispanic American Almanac* (all published by Gale Research). Each reference work contains essays focusing on all major aspects of group life and culture.

Many other reference works—from poetry anthologies to genealogical sourcebooks—are also available, and more are being published each year. One way to see what's available is to consult a book that lists all known reference materials: the *Guide to Reference Books*. It is considered the reference librarian's "bible," and your reference librarian will be glad to help you use it.

Biographical Resources. For information about famous or noteworthy people, the *Biography Index* is an excellent starting point. Available in both print and CD-ROM versions, this comprehensive resource indexes biographical material from periodicals, books, and even obituaries from the *New York Times*. Published quarterly, it is quite up-to-date. For analyses and criticism of the published works of persons you may be speaking about, see the *Essay and General Literature Index*, *Dictionary of American Biography*, *Dictionary of World Biography*, and *Current Biography*.

Books of Quotations. For many public speakers, books of quotations are an indispensable tool. As we'll see in Chapter 9, quotations are often used in the introductions and conclusions of speeches; they are also liberally sprinkled within examples, narratives, and, of course, testimony. First published in 1855, *Bartlett's Familiar Quotations* contains a collection of passages, phrases, and proverbs traced to their sources in ancient and modern literature. The *Columbia Worldbook of Quotations* contains 65,000 quotations by some 5,000 authors. It is also available on CD-ROM. Also useful are collections targeted directly to public speakers, including *And I Quote: The*

Definitive Collection of Quotes, Sayings, and Jokes for the Contemporary Speechmaker.

Poetry Collections. Lines of poetry, if not whole poems, are often used by speakers both to introduce and conclude speeches and to illustrate points in the speech body. Every library has a collection of poetry anthologies as well as the collected works of individual poets. Updated yearly, the *Granger's Index to Poetry* indexes poems by author, title, and first line. All libraries carry print versions of this index; some may also have it on CD-ROM.

Atlases. An atlas is a collection of maps, text, and accompanying charts and tables. An atlas can be a handy reference tool if your topic involves a geographic location. Atlases provide information about where a particular country, state, or city is located; its terrain and demographic information; and its proximity to other places. Also, the atlas itself or the pictures and graphics from it can be used as a visual aid in support of your speech. Two excellent atlases are the *National Geographic Atlas of the World* and the *Rand McNally Commercial Atlas and Guide.*

Organizing and Documenting Source Material

Just as you'll need to avoid the pitfall of getting sidetracked in reviewing source material, you'll need to avoid the mistake of failing to properly document the sources you've found. When you copy quotations, statistics, or other information from a source, make sure to record them accurately (see Chapter 4, Plagiarism section). If you expect to rely on several parts of a particular source, copy the material (within the confines of copyright regulations) and then underline, highlight, or otherwise mark the passages that are most useful for the purpose of your speech.

Your bibliography should identify all of the sources cited in your speech. Each source should contain the following elements:

Names of author(s) or editor(s) as cited

Title of publication

Volume or edition number, if applicable

Name of publisher

Place of publication (city and state); if only published online, give Internet address

Date and year of publication

Page numbers on which material appears

The most commonly used systems of reference are the *APA method* (American Psychological Association), the *MLA method* (Modern Language Association), and the *Chicago Style method* (University of Chicago Press). You can follow any style guide you choose to record your sources, as long as you obtain complete information such as author, title, publication, date, page numbers, and so forth. Here are some examples:

APA method

BOOK

Brooks, B., Pinson, J. L., & Wilson, J. G. (1997). *Working with words.* New York: St. Martin's Press.

JOURNAL ARTICLE

Pellegrew, R. (1998). Satisfying employees. *Journal of Employee Development, 34,* 67–90.

NEWSPAPER

Unemployment rate still low. (1999, January 7). *USA Today,* p. 1A.

WEB/ONLINE

Lynch, C. (1997). Searching the Internet. *Scientific American. [Online].* Date Accessed: March 10, 1997. Available: http://www.sciam .com/0397lynch.html.

MLA method

BOOK

Brooks, Brian, James L. Pinson, and Jean Gaddy Wilson. *Working with Words.* New York: St. Martin's Press, 1997.

JOURNAL ARTICLE

Pellegrew, Refugio. "Satisfying Employees." *Journal of Employee Development* 34 (1998): 67–90.

NEWSPAPER

"Unemployment Rate Still Low." *USA Today* 7 January 1999: 1A.

WEB/ONLINE

Lynch, Clifford. "Searching the Internet." *Scientific American. online.* Date Accessed: March 10, 1997. Available: http://www.sciam.com/ 0397lynch.html.

Chicago Style method

BOOK

B. Brooks, J. L. Pinson, and J. G. Wilson. *Working with Words.* (New York: St. Martin's Press, 1997).

JOURNAL ARTICLE

R. Pellegrew, "Satisfying Employees," *Journal of Employee Development* 34 (1998): 67–90.

NEWSPAPER

"Unemployment Rate Still Low." *USA Today,* 7 January 1999, p. 1A.

WEB/ONLINE

C. Lynch. "Searching the Internet." *Scientific American (online).* Date Accessed: March 10, 1997. Available: http://www.sciam.com /0397lynch.html.

Focus on Technology

Managing Online Resources

Throughout this book you are encouraged to use online resources as part of your research. When doing so, keep two important issues in mind. First, be sure that you have the URL (Universal Resource Locator) for each of the Web pages that you copy. This is the "address" of where you obtained the Web material. Without the URL, you will have difficulty retrieving that site on the Internet again. URLs are the actual "source" for Web material and are used just as a journal title or publishing company name.

Each part of a URL is important. Therefore, if you want someone to be able to find it again, or if you yourself will need to find it again, make sure to reproduce the URL exactly as it appears on the site where you got the information. Web browsers and Web servers use the information in a URL to locate specific places on the Web and specific files at those places. A URL looks like this:

http://www.slamonline.com

This is a URL for *Slam* magazine. The first part of the URL, "http," stands for HyperText Transport Protocol, the format that the World Wide Web follows for transferring information. This part is always followed by a colon and two front slashes. The "www" stands for World Wide Web. The next element of the URL designates the actual Web site, in this case "slamonline." The fourth element designates the domain in which the site resides.

This will be ".gov," ".com," ".org," or ".edu," depending on whether the site is a government, commercial, organizational, or educational site. Any elements after this part of the URL designate the directory path, within the Web site, in which a particular file is stored. Directory paths are always set within slashes. This is often the part of the URL that looks the most unusual, such as the title in this example.

Documenting the full citation of an online source is not much different from the citation patterns listed on page 170. Depending on which style you choose, you should format the author, title, publication, dates, and volume numbers in a similar manner. Be sure to include the date you accessed the site and the URL address. Here is an example:

The New York Times on the Web. Date Accessed: March 16, 1999. Available: http://www.nytimes.com/

The second issue to remember about using online sources such as the Web and the Internet is that they have limits. In fact, many sites on the Internet are quite useless. Information at some Web sites is inaccurate, biased, and misleading. When gathering supporting material for your speech, consider a wide range of sources so that you will have a variety of accurate supporting material.

When recording references, try to develop a system in which you can organize them by major ideas or main points. Using separate notecards for each reference often works well. Placing related material together gives a sense of how the supporting material will eventually fit into your speech outline (see Chapter 8). Using separate file folders is an ideal way of organizing the material you have collected.

CRITICALLY EVALUATING SOURCES

Respect for the written word is deeply ingrained in many of us, and for good reason. Yet not all words are created equal. Some are written by people who distort the facts, either knowingly or unknowingly. In an age of exploding information, it is now easier than ever for both the honest and the dishonest to get into print—or its electronic equivalent in cyberspace. Thus, it is vital to critically evaluate sources before using them. Whether you are reviewing a book, a newspaper article, a Web site, or any other source, keep in mind the following:

- What is the author's background—for example, his or her experience, training, and reputation—in the field of study?
- How credible is the publication or Web site? Who is the publisher or site operator? Is the person or organization reputable?
- How reliable are the data, especially the statistical information? Generally, statistics drawn from government documents and scientific and academic journals are more reliable than those reported in the popular press (e.g., general interest magazines). This is because the former kinds of publications print primary data officially collected by the government or by researchers who are subject to peer review.
- How recent is the reference? As a rule, it is best to use the most recent source you can find, even when the topic is historical. Scholars are continually uncovering new information and offering new perspectives on past events.

Critical Checkpoint

Critically Evaluating Internet and Web Sites

Here are some questions and pointers to help guide you in determining the credibility of a particular Web site:

Is there information on the Web page that will allow you to contact the author of the page? Look for email addresses or email links, phone numbers, and physical mail addresses. Chances are that an author who doesn't want to be found might not be a good source to cite.

Can you tell anything from the URL? Is there anything unusual about the origin of the Web page? Does it contain overly cryptic or strange elements? The URL can also tell you where the site is. Country codes usually follow the domain designation, if the site is outside the United States.

Does the Web document thoroughly credit the sources it uses? How credible or trustworthy are those sources?

Examine any other links you find on the page. These can tell a lot about the people who designed the page—what they like, and what they think is important.

Is there a mission statement for the Web site? Many sites have sections that explain the purpose of the site. These can tell a great deal about the nature of the content of the site.

Finally, follow your instincts. If something about the site makes you uncertain, don't include that information in your research. Be suspicious of unusual language use, writing quality, overall tone, or anything else that seems out of place.

As you evaluate supporting materials for your speeches, strive to use original sources as much as possible. Much of what you read in the popular

Focus on Ethics

Ethical Considerations in Research

Central to conducting ethical research is properly citing sources. As described in Chapter 4, using other people's ideas or words without acknowledging their source is plagiarism—a serious breach of ethics. Any source that requires credit in written form should be acknowledged orally when you give your speech. Such sources include quotations, paraphrased information, facts, statistics, and just about any other kind of information gathered and reported by others.

Other kinds of unethical research conduct include fabricating information, deceiving research subjects about your real purposes, and breaching confidentiality.

Fabrication of any kind distorts the truth, whether you make up information, a source, or both. (Perhaps the most publicized case of fabrication in recent times was that of *Washington Post* journalist Janet Cooke, who won a Pulitzer Prize in 1981 for what turned out to be a fabricated story about an 8-year-old drug addict. When the fraud was discovered, the *Post* returned the prize and fired Cooke.) In addition to making up whole stories, fabrication can include altering quotes to "fit" a point; claiming credentials or expertise for yourself that you don't possess, in an effort to boost your credibility; inflating figures to boost your point; and so forth. Each of these examples represents an act of deception. Recall from Chapter 4 that trustworthiness, which includes truth telling, is one of the four pillars of character exhibited by ethical speakers.

Another area of concern involves treating research subjects fairly. Years ago, universities banned the practice of involving individuals in studies who did not know they were subjects, who were not aware of risks, and who did not formally consent to participate. Although the old "candid camera" approach to research may amuse you, these methods humiliate unsuspecting participants. The consensus today is that researchers are ethically bound to reveal their purposes to their subjects.

When conducting primary research such as interviews and surveys, respecting the rights of participants should be paramount. Remember that the people you interview or survey are volunteering their time, attitudes, knowledge, and—sometimes—their honor. In some cases, people will not talk with you or provide information unless you agree to maintain their anonymity. Ethically, it is the speaker's responsibility to protect the subjects' confidentiality when requested. This is true whether the source is a respondent to a questionnaire to whom you have promised anonymity or an expert in a field who gives you an inside "tip."

Greater Good

Ethical conduct in public speaking goes beyond doing no harm. The goal of any speech should be to in some way serve the audience well. For example, by investigating that a certain food ingredient can harm the body, a speaker may help audience members live healthier and longer lives. By conducting research into the pros and cons of different savings options, a speaker may assist audience members in better preparing for retirement. Use your research to advance the knowledge of other people or to show them a new way of viewing a problem or issue.

press, and even in some research and trade journals, is a citation of someone else's reporting. If at all possible, track down the original source so that you can make your own judgment about the quality of the material or research. In addition to boosting your confidence in the material, quoting or reporting from the original source enhances your credibility as a speaker.

Developing Conclusions

One of the problems in investigating any topic for support material is "seeing what you want to see." In your quest to find material that supports your thesis or premise, you may be tempted to ignore evidence that "doesn't fit." As discussed in Chapter 4, part of being an ethical speaker includes acknowledging rather than omitting alternative viewpoints when they are relevant.

Before you arrive at a conclusion and present it to the audience, ask yourself whether you have included sufficient quantity and quality of evidence to substantiate your claim. How many examples of American cities do you need to cite in order to suggest that "the crime rate has dropped significantly"? How many and what kind of experts do you need in order to state that "Americans are taking better care of their personal health today than at any time in our history"? Usually, two or three examples that support your claim are sufficient for convincing your audience. Just be sure that your examples are relevant to one another and to the argument you are making.

Beware of Errors in Data Interpretation

Does the supporting material actually say what you think it says? The prospect of having an audience member correct your conclusions or question your evidence and data is not pleasant. One speaker recently defended the results of a fund-raising campaign by stating that "a high percentage, specifically 11 percent, of all persons invited to participate, attended the banquet." The audience did not think that "11 percent" was a "high" percentage, and it labeled this effort a failure. Was the speaker incompetent or misleading?

SUMMARY QUESTIONS

What are the best types of supporting material for speeches?

Supporting material includes examples, narratives, testimony, facts, and statistics. Examples illustrate or describe things. Their purpose is both to aid understanding by making ideas, items, or events more concrete, and to clarify and amplify meaning. A narrative is a story. Narratives tell tales, both real and imaginary. As supporting material, narratives can be brief and simple descriptions of short incidents worked into the body of the speech, or relatively drawn-out accounts that constitute most of the presentation. Testimony is firsthand findings, eyewitness accounts, and opinions by people, both lay (non-expert) and expert. Facts include actual events, dates, times, people involved, and places. Facts represent documented occurrences; that is, it is assumed that they can be backed up with supporting evidence. Statistics express data in numerical form. Usually statistics prove the existence of a trend or relationship.

Where can you find good supporting material?

You can find supporting material by conducting primary or secondary research, or by using a combination of both. Primary research is original or firsthand research such as interviews and surveys conducted by you, the speaker. Interviews and surveys are the most common ways of gathering primary data for a speech. Secondary research is the vast body of information gathered by others. The most likely sources of secondary research are books, newspapers, periodicals, encyclopedias, almanacs, government publications, biographical reference works, books of quotations, and atlases. In the past, these sources appeared only in print. Increasingly, however, the information they contain is stored simultaneously on CD-ROMs or in online databases, as well as in print.

What are the best methods for documenting supporting material?

The most commonly used systems of reference are the APA method (American Psychological Association), the MLA (Modern Language Association), and the Chicago Style method. You can follow any style guide you choose to record your sources, as long as you obtain complete information such as author, title, publication date, page numbers, and so forth.

How is supporting material critically evaluated?

You can evaluate supporting material by reviewing it in light of the following questions: What is the author's background—his or her experience, training, and reputation—in the field of study? How credible is the publication? Who is the publisher? Is the person or organization reputable? How reliable are the data, especially the statistical information? How recent is the reference?

Key Terms

anecdote
brief example
database
descriptive statistics
examples
expert testimony
extended example
facts
hyperlinks

hypothetical example
inferential statistics
lay testimony
narrative
primary research
secondary research
statistics
testimony

ISSUES FOR DISCUSSION

1. What are the most important features of a source that contribute to its credibility? When people are used as sources, would being famous be the only requirement? Consider talk-show hosts. Would they be considered credible experts on the topics discussed on their shows? What about their guests?

2. How much time should you spend locating, analyzing, and organizing supporting material for a 5- to 7-minute speech? What factors would affect this time frame?

3. When you listen to speeches, how much supporting material do you expect to hear? What type of speeches require the most supporting material? Are some topics more dependent on support than others? Give some examples. Can a speech ever have too much supporting material? If so, when?

SELF-ASSESSMENT

1. Develop a list of data sources with which you are currently familiar. Include as many print and electronic sources as possible (including those found on the Internet or World Wide Web).

2. Make a list of sources that you think are not credible and/or unethical. Explain why each one falls into this category.

3. Write a one-page summary of unethical practices you have witnessed by a speaker (in person, in print, or on the radio or television), or in another form of communication such as a magazine article, advertisement, or radio or television commercial.

4. Find two examples of errors in data interpretation. Alternatively, draw conclusions or interpretations from one data source from each of the following: the Internet, a national newspaper, and a research journal.

TEAMWORK

1. In a group of four or five people, critically analyze and evaluate the supporting material found in a few speeches delivered by members of Congress. Use C-SPAN or the local Democratic and Republican headquarters as sources for these speeches. As a group, be prepared to give a short oral report to the class explaining your analysis.

2. In a small task force of four or five class members, make decisions about which forms of support (e.g., examples, narratives, testimony, facts, or statistics) would be best for the following speech topics. Do this exercise for two different types of audiences. Your task force can either select its own audiences, or choose from the options given with each topic below. Be prepared to justify your decisions.

   - *Helping the Homeless* (Audiences: local Rotary club; Student Government Association for your college)

   - *The Joy of NASCAR Racing* (Audiences: Horseback Riding Club; Boy Scout troop)

   - *Selecting an Academic Major* (Audiences: students right out of high school; nontraditional, returning students)

   - *Corrective Surgery for Near-Sightedness* (Audiences: American Association of Retired Persons meeting; Student Pharmacy Club meeting)

   - *Reasons for Becoming Bilingual* (Audiences: church/synagogue group; training class for obtaining U.S. citizenship)

   - *Developing a Career before Marriage* (Audiences: League of Women Voters meeting; local college fraternity)

   - *Starting Your Own Business* (Audiences: your speech class; vocational counseling class)

3. Working with a small group of four to five people in your class, develop a short survey that can be conducted among the other members of the class. Choose a topic, develop a goal, construct some questions, and distribute your survey. Tally and analyze the results. Discuss the results of the survey in class, and recommend methods of how your survey could be enhanced. From your own experience as a respondent to other class groups' surveys, suggest ways that their surveys could be improved.

A place for
everything,
everything in
its place.
—Benjamin
Franklin

Order of one kind or other is, indeed, essential to every good discourse; that is, every thing should be so arranged as that what goes before may give light and force to what follows.

—Hugh Blair

8

Organizing and Outlining the Speech

Imagine taking a road trip to a place you've never **gone before. How important would it be to have a well-organized set of directions from your starting place to your destination?** You would want to know where to make the proper turns, where the scenic spots and other high points are, and maybe most important, how far you have to go. **Having a clear plan to get to your destination is just as important as knowing the destination itself. Organizing a speech is much like mapping out a road trip.** Laying out where you want to go with the speech, and pinpointing each key thought along the way, helps you plan more precisely how to deliver the speech and, when you actually give it, help the listeners follow along with less effort.

Four years after joining Literacy Volunteers of America as a reading tutor, Aaron Weinberg was notified by the director of the local chapter that he was to receive the organization's Tutor of the Year award at the chapter's annual banquet. The director asked Aaron if he would like to address an audience of about one hundred people, including board members, fellow volunteers, and members of the press. Aaron enthusiastically agreed to prepare a 20-minute speech in which he would describe the process of tutoring and relate some of the highlights of his volunteer experience.

A week before the banquet, Aaron began to think about what he would say. He recalled the 70-year-old janitor who struggled for two years before he was finally able to read the words on maps and menus; the 32-year-old Russian immigrant, trained as a physician, who needed to learn English quickly so he could take the medical boards....As he thought, Aaron jotted down some notes. He didn't put them in any particular order. Since he was so familiar with his topic, he didn't think he needed to worry about being systematic. After all, he would be addressing his own experience.

Unfortunately, Aaron's speech went poorly. He felt some stage fright, which clouded his memory, and his skimpy notes did little to help. Rather than briefly describing three or four of his students, as he had planned, he spent all his time on one. And although the director, at the request of the board members, had specifically asked Aaron to describe his tutoring methods, he ran out of time before he could do so. The audience applauded politely, but Aaron knew they were disappointed—as he was with himself. Next time, he promised himself, he'd do a far better job of organizing a speech.

Are there really significant consequences if a speech is poorly organized? Research shows that audience understanding of a speech is directly linked to how well it is organized.[1] Apparently a little bit of disorganization won't ruin a speech if the speaker is otherwise engaging, but audience attitudes take a decidedly negative turn when the speech is very disorganized.[2] Studies have also shown that speech organization affects audience perceptions of speaker credibility. Speakers with well-organized speeches are perceived to be more credible than are those with poorly organized speeches.[3]

Together with psychological studies of memory, the research on speech organization suggests four important points about how audiences process speech information:

1. A poorly organized speech will fail to convey the speaker's intended message, but the audience will nonetheless attempt to make sense out of the information.

2. In attempting to make sense out of the information, the listeners will organize it in unique ways that are relevant and meaningful to them. Their patterns of organization may differ from the pattern the speaker would have followed in a well-organized speech.

3. When audience members organize speech information on their own because the speech itself is poorly organized, some key points will likely be lost or confused. This can lead to misinformation and misunderstanding.

4. If audience members spend their energy trying to make sense of the speech, their attention will soon drift away. Even if they continue to pay attention, their rate of retention and recall will be poor. The result is a speech that fails to reach its audience.

Chapter Challenges

Clearly, it does matter how well your speeches are organized. Aaron learned this fact the hard way. The better your speeches are organized, the more positive the attitudes your audience will have toward your speeches, the better they will understand your messages, and the more the audience will consider you a credible speaker.

This chapter focuses on organizing the body of speeches. It challenges novice speakers to:

- Use the specific speech purpose and thesis statements as guideposts for organizing a speech.
- Arrange main points in support of the thesis, and subordinate points in support of the main points.
- Select an appropriate organizational pattern for arranging the body of the speech.
- Become familiar with three methods of outlining, and understand the benefits and drawbacks of each.

MAIN POINTS, SUPPORTING POINTS, AND TRANSITIONS

Riding past a steel-frame building under construction, the six-year-old son of one of the authors of this book exclaimed to his dad, "Look! Building bones!" He had made an analogy between the basic structure of buildings and the dinosaur skeletons displayed in his picture books. Like dinosaurs and buildings, speeches also have a structure or "skeleton." And like dinosaurs and buildings, speeches that lack a firm structure tend to fall apart. A speech structure is simple, composed of just three general parts: an introduction, a body, and a conclusion. The *introduction* establishes the purpose of the speech and shows its relevance to the audience. It lets listeners know where the speaker is taking them. The *body* of the speech presents main points that are intended to fulfill the speech purpose. Main points are developed with various kinds of supporting material to fulfill this purpose.

The *conclusion* ties the purpose and main points together. It brings closure to the speech by restating the purpose and by reiterating why it is relevant to the audience, and by summarizing the main points in support of the purpose. In essence, the introduction of a speech tells listeners where they are going, the body takes them there, and the conclusion lets them know they have arrived.

In Chapter 9 we'll look more closely at introductions and conclusions. Here, though, we explore the body of the speech. It consists of three elements: main points, supporting points, and transitions. The main points represent each of the main elements or claims being made in support of the speech topic. Supporting points do just as their name suggests: They support the information or arguments put forth in the main points. Transitions serve as links for the audience, alerting them to the speaker's direction as he or she moves through the speech.

Main Points: Making the Claim

main points
express the key ideas and major themes of a speech; used to make statements or claims in support of the thesis.

Main points express the key ideas and major themes of the speech. Their function is to make statements or claims in support of the thesis. The first step in creating main points is to identify the central ideas and themes of the speech. What are the most important ideas you seek to convey? As you review your research, what important ideas emerge? What ideas can you substantiate with supporting material? Each of these ideas and themes should be expressed as a main point.

Using the Purpose and Thesis Statements as Guideposts. You can use the specific purpose and thesis statements as guideposts to help generate main points. As discussed in Chapter 6, the *specific purpose statement* expresses the goal of the speech. Formulating it lets you know precisely what you want the speech to accomplish. The *thesis statement* expresses the theme or central idea of the speech. It concisely lays out what the speech is about. The main points should flow directly from these two statements expressing the speech goal and central idea, as seen in the following examples:

SPECIFIC PURPOSE STATEMENT:	To inform my audience of young adults about the steps they will need to take to ensure financial security in retirement, including setting investment goals, investing early, and committing to the long haul.
THESIS STATEMENT:	To ensure financial security in retirement, young adults need to set investment goals, invest early, and commit to the long haul.
MAIN POINTS:	I. Setting investment goals is the first step. II. Invest as early and as much as possible. III. Invest for the long haul.
SPECIFIC PURPOSE STATEMENT:	To persuade my audience that in order to protect children, programs containing explicit sex and nudity should be banned from all television channels rather than just prime time programming.
THESIS STATEMENT:	To protect children, programs containing explicit sex and nudity should be banned from all television channels rather than just prime time programming.

MAIN POINTS:
    I. Exposure to explicit sex and nudity on television is harmful to children.

    II. Parents cannot always adequately monitor their children's viewing habits.

Number of Main Points. As we've seen, how the speech is organized has a lot to do with how the listeners will receive it. In fact, research has shown that audiences can only comfortably take in from two to seven main points.[4] Moreover, listeners have a better recall of the main points made at the beginning and end of a speech than of those made in between. Thus, if you want the audience to remember your words, stick to as few main points as possible. Depending on the topic, the amount of material to be covered, and the length of the speech, approximately three main points should be sufficient for almost any speech.

Form of Main Points. A main point should not introduce more than one idea. If it does, it should be split into two (or more) main points:

Incorrect: I. West Texas has its own Grand Canyon and South Texas has its own desert.

Correct: I. West Texas boasts its own Grand Canyon.
    II. South Texas boasts its own desert.

Main points should also be stated in **parallel form**. That is, they should be stated in similar grammatical form and style. This helps listeners understand and retain the points and lends power and elegance to your words:

> **parallel form**
> involves stating main points in similar grammatical form and style.

THESIS STATEMENT: The Red Cross accomplished three major goals this year.

Incorrect: I. The organization met its annual giving objective.
    II. Blood donations rose.
    III. They implemented an ad campaign.

Correct: I. The organization met its annual giving objective.
    II. The organization increased the number of blood donations it received.
    III. The organization implemented a widespread ad campaign.

Supporting Points: Supplying the Evidence

It is not enough simply to state the main points and expect the audience to understand and accept them. Instead, you have to support them. **Supporting points** represent the supporting material or evidence you have gathered to justify the main points and lead the audience to accept the purpose you have for the speech (see Chapter 7).

> **supporting points**
> represent the material or evidence gathered to justify the main points.

In an outline, supporting points appear in a subordinate position to main points. This is indicated by indentation. As with main points, supporting points should be ordered in a logical fashion. That is, they should be arranged in order of their importance or relevance to the main point. The most common format is the Roman numeral outline (used thus far in this chapter). Main points are enumerated with upper-case *Roman numerals*, supporting points are enumerated with *capital letters*, and third-level points are enumerated with *Arabic numerals*, as seen on the following page.

I. Top management should sponsor sales contests to halt the decline in sales over the past two years.
   A. Sales have fallen from $600,000 in 1994 to $525,000 at the end of 1995.
   B. The decline is due to poor sales presentations.
      1. Sales staff has lost motivation and enthusiasm.
      2. Commissions are believed by many to be too low.
II. Sales contests will lead to better sales presentations.
   A. Sales personnel will be motivated by competition.
   B. Contests are relatively inexpensive.
      1. Contests cost less than losses in sales revenues.
      2. Contests cost less than training new sales staff.[5]

Note that different levels of points are also distinguished by different levels of indentation. These differences clearly indicate the direction of your speech. They also help your recollection of points and make it easy for you to follow the outline as you speak.

Transitions: Giving Direction

transitions
words, phrases, or sentences that tie the speech ideas together and enable the speaker to move smoothly from one point to the next.

Transitions are words, phrases, or sentences that tie the speech ideas together and enable the speaker to move smoothly from one point to the next. Transitions can be considered the "neurosystem" of speeches: They provide consistency of movement from one point to the next. They make the speech active, keeping the audience attentive.

Speakers use transitions to move the listener from one main point to the next, from main points to supporting points, and from one supporting point to another supporting point. For example, to move from Main Point I (*Top management should sponsor sales contests to halt the decline in sales over the past two years*) to Main Point II (*Sales contests will lead to better sales presentations*), the speaker might use the following transition:

Now that we've established a need for sales contests, let's look at what sales contests can do for us.

Transitions among supporting points can be handled in a similar manner. For example, the transition from Supporting Point A (*Sales personnel will be motivated by competition*) to Supporting Point B (*Contests are relatively inexpensive*) could be made by the following transition:

Another way sales competitions will benefit us is by their relative cost effectiveness.

Likewise, the transition from Supporting Point B1 (*Contests cost less than losses in sales revenues*) to Supporting Point B2 (*Contests cost less than training new sales staff*) could be stated as:

In addition to costing less than a loss in revenues, sales competitions are less expensive than training new people.

Transition statements are often posed in "restate-forecast" form, as in the preceding examples. That is, the transition restates the point just covered and previews the point to be covered next:

Now that we've established a need for sales contests (*restatement*), let's look at what sales contests can do for us (*forecast*).

Transitions can also be stated as rhetorical questions:

Will contests be too expensive? Well, actually…

How do the costs of contests stack up against the expense of training new people?

Using rhetorical questions as transitions stimulates the audience to anticipate probable answers, making them alert to the forthcoming point.

Note that even though all the examples provided thus far are in the form of full sentences, transitions don't have to be stated as such. Full-sentence transitions are especially effective when moving from one main point to another. When moving between supporting points, however, words or phrases such as the following can be just as effective:

Next…

First… (second, third, and so forth)

We now turn…

Finally, let's consider…

If you think that's shocking…

Critical Checkpoint

···

Identifying and Organizing Main and Supporting Points

The body of the speech serves to provide a solid and firm structure to the speech. Main points represent the primary elements of the thesis or specific purpose statement. Supporting points (and their subpoints) substantiate the main points. Transitions allow listeners to follow smoothly from one point to the next.

Organizing points and making transitions require critical thinking. You must *analyze* your thesis or purpose statements for the key elements that can serve as main points. You must *assess* the appropriateness of your supporting material for each main point and the thesis. You must *plan* transitions to adequately connect one point to the next.

Principles of Organizing Main and Supporting Points

Whether one is creating a painting, an essay, a musical composition, or a speech, certain principles of good form apply. A well-organized speech is characterized by unity, coherence, and balance. As you arrange main and supporting points, try to keep these principles in mind.

Unity. There is a type of skilled speaker—usually a preacher—who routinely seems to meander off point, only to surprise the audience at the end by artfully tying each idea to the speech theme. Such speeches retain the quality of unity, if only at the last minute. A speech exhibits **unity** when it contains only those points that are implied by the purpose and thesis statements. Nothing is extraneous or tangential. Each main point supports the thesis, and each supporting point provides evidence for the main points. Each subpoint supports each supporting point. Moreover, as noted previously, unity also means that each point focuses on a single idea.

Coherence. Coherence refers to clarity and logical consistency. A coherent speech is one that is logically organized. The speech body should follow

unity
characteristic of a speech that contains only those points that are implied by the purpose and thesis statements.

coherence
clarity and logical consistency; a coherent speech is logically organized.

logically from the introduction, and the conclusion should follow logically from the body. Within the body of the speech itself, the main points should follow logically from the thesis statement, and the supporting points should follow logically from the main points. The transitions serve as logical bridges that help establish coherence.[6]

You can ensure coherence by adhering to the principle of **subordination and coordination**—the logical placement of ideas relative to their importance to one another. An idea that is subordinate to another is given relatively less weight. Ideas that are coordinate are given equal weight. Outlines are based on the principle of subordination and coordination. Subordinate points are indicated by their indentation below the more important points. Coordinate points are indicated by their parallel alignment:

I. The electronic media have profoundly altered the form and substance of political campaigns.
   A. Today's campaigns rely largely on television's fast-paced visual images and sound bites.
      1. Politicians must manage themselves "telegenically."
      2. Politicians must compress issues into phrases that can fit into 2-minute reports on the evening news and 30-second commercials.
   B. Politicians and their pollsters now use computers, sophisticated telephone link-ups, faxes, and online services to take the pulse of the public.
II. The altered form of political campaigns threatens the health of our democracy.
   A. Politicians use the new technology to constantly take the public's "temperature."
   B. Politicians now spend more time reacting to minute shifts in public opinion polls than governing.

AP/Wide World

When you are speaking, you want to be the only thing in audience members' "viewfinders." A speech outline will make your speech unified and coherent and will keep attention on you.

As you can see, subordinate points are indented below the points that they substantiate. Coordinate points are aligned with one another. Thus, Subpoint A is subordinate to Main Point I. Subpoint B is coordinate with Subpoint A. Main Point II is coordinate with Main Point I, and so forth.

Balance. A common mistake on the part of many students is to give overly lengthy coverage to one point and insufficient mention to others. Another common mistake is to give meager evidence in the body of the speech after presenting an impressive introduction. The principle of **balance** suggests that appropriate emphasis or weight be given to each part of the speech relative to the other parts and to the theme. Stating the main points in parallel form is one aspect of balance. Assigning each main point at least two supporting points is another. Think of a main point as a table top and supporting points as table legs; without at least two legs, the table cannot stand.

Types of Organizational Arrangements

Once a speaker has determined what the main and supporting points will be, she can proceed to organize them according to one or a combination of patterns. Often the nature of the speech topic will determine the type of organization selected: topical, chronological, spatial or geographical, causal, or problem-solution.

Topical Arrangements

When each of the main points of a topic is of relatively equal importance, and when these points can be presented in any order relative to the other main points without changing the message, a **topical pattern of arrangement** may be most appropriate. Consider an informative speech about choosing Chicago as a place to establish a career. The speaker plans to emphasize three reasons for choosing Chicago: the strong economic climate of the city, its cultural variety, and its accessible transportation. These three points can be arranged in any order and not affect each other or the speech purpose negatively. For example:

> **topical pattern of arrangement**
> used when each of the main points of a topic is of relatively equal importance, and when these points can be presented in any order relative to the other main points without changing the message.

I. Accessible transportation
II. Cultural variety
III. Economic stability

This is not to say that the speaker should arrange the main points without careful consideration. Sometimes it is possible to arrange the main points in ascending or descending order according to the relative importance, size, familiarity, or complexity of the topics. Perhaps the speaker has determined that the listeners' main concern is economic, but that they have a significant interest in leisure and entertainment. The speaker may then decide that the following arrangement is best in order to address the audience's most immediate needs and interests first:

I. Economic stability
II. Cultural variety
III. Accessible transportation

Topical arrangements give the speaker the greatest freedom to structure main points according to the circumstances of the occasion and audience. The other four organizational patterns are more restrictive.

Chronological Arrangements

Many speech topics lend themselves well to the arrangement of main points according to their occurrence in time relative to each other. A **chronological pattern of arrangement** follows the natural sequential order of the main points. To switch points around would make the arrangement appear unnatural and might confuse the audience. Topics that describe a series of events in time or that develop in line with a set pattern of actions or tasks should be organized according to a chronological pattern of arrangement. For example, a speech describing the development of automobile technology calls for a chronological or time-ordered sequence of main points, possibly around four general periods:

> **chronological pattern of arrangement**
> used to reflect the natural sequential order of the main points.

THESIS STATEMENT: Advances in automobile technology correspond to four periods of development in our nation's commerce.

Public Speaking in Cultural Perspective

Arrangement Formats and Audience Diversity

The cultural diversity of the audience may require a speaker to carefully think through the organizing plan and select an appropriate structure. Consider the chronological arrangement format. It assumes a largely North American and Western European orientation to time, because these cultures view time as a linear (or chronological) progression in which one event follows another along a continuum. In contrast, some Asian, African, and Latin American cultures view time holistically; in this orientation, events are seen as discrete points that are distinct from one another.[1] Thus, when a speaker follows a chronological arrangement of the typical linear fashion, audience members from cultures with different time orientations may have trouble following the speaker's thinking and understand the message differently.

For example, the chronological listing of main points below for a speech on the development of the automobile is arranged in a linear fashion. Audience members who conceive of time as a linear progression would follow the pattern of that speech easily. But audience members who conceive of time in a more holistic fashion might have difficulty making the connection between horses, the Depression, World War II, and changes in automobile technology.

1. J. K. Burgoon, D. B. Buller, and W. G. Woodall, *Nonverbal Communication: The Unspoken Dialogue* (New York: Harper & Row, 1989).

MAIN POINTS:
 I. The transition from horses to engines
 II. Advances during the Depression and after World War II
 III. Automobiles designed for superhighways
 IV. Meeting the demands of fuel shortages

Any topic that involves a series of sequential steps also calls for a chronological arrangement. One example might be that of changing a flat tire. Another might be a cooking topic, where the gathering of ingredients and utensils, the steps of the recipe, and the cooking task represent distinct procedural points.

Spatial or Geographical Arrangements

When the purpose of a speech is to describe or explain a place, scene, or object, logic suggests that the main points be arranged in order of their physical proximity or direction relative to each other. This calls for a **spatial or geographical pattern of arrangement**.

For example, a speech describing a computer company's market growth across regions of the country might use the following geographical arrangement:

spatial or geographical pattern of arrangement
used when the main points are arranged in order of their physical proximity or direction relative to each other.

THESIS STATEMENT: Sales of Digi-Tel Computers have grown in every region of the country.

 I. Sales are strongest in the Eastern Zone.
 II. Sales are growing at a rate of 10 percent quarterly in the Central Zone.

III. Sales are up slightly in the Mountain Zone.

IV. Sales in the Western Zone are lagging behind the other regions.

A geographical arrangement is also useful when describing the features of a particular place:

THESIS STATEMENT: El Morro National Monument in New Mexico is captivating for its variety of natural and historical landmarks.

I. Visitors first encounter an abundant variety of plant life native to the high-country desert.

II. Soon visitors come upon an ages-old watering hole that has receded beneath the 200-foot cliffs.

III. Beyond are the famous cliff carvings made by hundreds of travelers over several centuries of exploration in the Southwest.

IV. At the farthest reaches of the magnificent park are the ancient ruins of a pueblo dwelling secured high atop "The Rock."

Causal (Cause-Effect) Arrangements

Some speech topics represent cause-effect relationships. Examples might include (1) Events Leading to Higher Interest Rates, (2) Reasons Students Drop Out of College, and (3) Causes of Spousal Abuse. In cases like this, a **causal (cause-effect) pattern of arrangement** is used to relate something known to be a "cause" to its "effects." The points in such speeches are usually of the following form:

I. Cause

II. Effect

Sometimes a topic can be discussed in terms of multiple causes for a single effect, taking the following form:

I. Cause 1

II. Cause 2

III. Cause 3

IV. Effect

In these two examples, the speaker first presents information about the causes, then develops the point concerning the effect. On the topic of teen pregnancy, for example, the following sequence of points might be determined:

THESIS STATEMENT: Dysfunctional family relationships, poor social relationships, and early sexual activity are three chief causes of teen pregnancy.

I. (Cause) Dysfunctional family structure

II. (Cause) Dysfunctional social relationships

III. (Cause) Early sexual activity

IV. (Effect) Early unwed pregnancy

The purpose of this speech is to inform the audience of possible causes of teen pregnancy, so the audience knows from the thesis statement what the point of concern is (i.e., the effect) before the main points are detailed. The

causal (cause-effect) pattern of arrangement used when the main points of a speech compare something known to be a "cause" to its "effects."

first three main points are developed in turn as independent but related factors that contribute to the effect.

Occasionally it is appropriate to present the effect first and the cause or causes subsequently. For example, a speech on tornadoes might be arranged in the following way:

THESIS STATEMENT: Tornadoes are a unique kind of cloud formation that results when a mass of cold air collides with a mass of warm air.

I. (Effect) Funnel clouds
II. (Cause) Cold air mass
III. (Cause) Warm air mass

In this case, the speaker would present information about funnel clouds as the first main point. He would then make a statement or ask a question about how funnel clouds are produced, leading to the second main point on cold air masses. He would then note that something in addition to cold air is involved in the formation of funnel clouds—a mass of warm air, the third main point.

Speakers usually select a causal arrangement when the cause-effect relationship is well established and the general speech purpose is to inform. When a topic is of a causal nature but the cause-effect relationship is not widely established or proven, a problem-solution arrangement may be required.

Problem-Solution Arrangements

In a **problem-solution pattern of arrangement**, the main points are organized to demonstrate the nature and significance of a problem and then to provide justification for a proposed solution. This type of arrangement can be as general as two main points:

I. Problem (define what it is)
II. Solution (offer a way to overcome the problem)

But many problem-solution speeches require more than two points to adequately explain the problem and to substantiate the recommended solution:

I. The nature of the problem (identify its causes, incidence, etc.)
II. Effects of the problem (explain why it's a problem, for whom, etc.)
III. Unsatisfactory solutions (discuss those that have not worked)
IV. Proposed solution (explain why it's expected to work)

In the previous section the example of teen pregnancy was used as a cause-effect speech topic. However, information for the same topic can be arranged in a problem-solution format:

THESIS STATEMENT: Once you realize the nature and probable causes of the problem of teen pregnancy, it should be clear that current solutions remain unsuccessful and an alternative solution should be considered.

I. Early unwed pregnancies
  A. Average age of teen mothers
  B. National and local incidence

problem-solution pattern of arrangement
used when the main points are organized to demonstrate the nature and significance of a problem and then to provide justification for a proposed solution.

II. Probable causes of teen pregnancy
   A. Dysfunctional family structure
   B. Dysfunctional social relationships
   C. Early sexual activity
III. Unsuccessful solutions
   A. School-based sex education
   B. Mass media campaigns
IV. Peer counseling as a possible solution
   A. How peer counseling works
   B. Coupled with school-based sexuality curriculum

OUTLINING SPEECH MATERIAL

Outlines are critical to planning and presenting a speech. **Outlines** are a visual representation of the basic structure of the speech, revealing any weaknesses in the logical ordering of points. The actual outline layout—in which supporting points are indented (i.e., subordinated) below the main points and subpoints are indented below the supporting points—makes it difficult to ignore such lapses.

While developing a speech, you will actually create two outlines: a working outline and a speech, or delivery, outline. **Working outlines** (also called preparation or rough outlines) are an essential tool in planning the speech. Here, you refine and finalize the specific purpose statement, brainstorm main points, and develop supporting points to substantiate them. Working outlines may change as you investigate the topic and gather new materials. You may find it necessary to rearrange the main points, or to omit and add different kinds of supporting materials several times before deciding on precisely the arrangement you want to use.

Once you've completed the working outline, you must transfer its ideas to a **speaking outline** (also called a delivery outline)—the one you will use when practicing and actually presenting the speech. As a rule, speaking outlines are much briefer than working outlines, containing the ideas in condensed form.

The following section describes the three main types of outline formats: sentence, phrase, and keyword. The sentence outline format is generally reserved for use in working outlines. Speaking outlines are usually prepared by using either the phrase or keyword outline format.

Sentence Outlines

In **sentence outlines** each main and supporting point is stated in sentence form, as a full declarative sentence. (A declarative sentence makes a statement or assertion about a subject.) So too are the introduction, conclusion, and transition statements. Usually these sentences are stated in precisely the way the speaker wants to express the idea.

outlines
a visual representation of the basic structure of a speech.

working outlines
rough outlines that help refine and finalize the specific purpose statement, brainstorm many points, and develop supporting points.

speaking outline
an outline used when practicing and actually presenting a speech.

sentence outlines
state each main and supporting point as a full declarative sentence.

Focus on Technology

Software for Outlining Speeches

Many versions of speech outlining software are available today. In fact, such software is often available to instructors of public speaking classes for use by their students. Outlining software is sometimes found as one of several utilities in a large word processing package. For example, in Claris Corporation's ClarisWorks the pull-down menu in the word processing component contains an Outline category. Within this category the user can select to view a piece of text in any of several outline formats, including Legal, Bulleted, and Check List. Automated outlining functions such as these allow the user to write each line without having to individually key one or more tab stops for each level of the outline. Once you have gotten familiar with such a program, you can prepare a printed copy of the outline in many formats—from index cards to legal size paper—and in significantly less time than a conventional word processing program would require.

Sentence outlines represent the full "script," or text of the speech. Generally they are used for working outlines, although they may be recommended for use in delivery under the following conditions:

1. When the speaker is inexperienced and wants to rely on full sentences to avoid misstating a point or losing a thought.
2. When the point is highly controversial or emotion-laden for listeners, and precise wording is needed to make the point as clear as possible.
3. When the material is highly technical, and exact sentence structure is critical to accurate representation of the material.
4. When a main point or supporting point takes the form of a quotation from another source.

Preparing a working outline in sentence format is important for several reasons. First, full sentences force you to pay attention to the underlying logic of each idea and its relationship to the other ideas in the speech. Second, because main points should always be stated as full sentences during delivery of the speech, you should write them out in the working outline to know exactly how you will phrase them during delivery.

In the introduction of a speech about the trucking industry, Thomas Donahue posed some questions as a preview to his main points.[7] The first question was, "What are the fundamental factors that play a role in highway safety?" The second was, "Which of these factors can trucking influence to improve safety?" Each question introduced a different main point in the body of Donahue's speech. A sentence outline would depict each of these points in the words he actually spoke. Consider the second point as an example:

II. Let's look at each of the elements and touch briefly on areas where trucking has made a difference and where we've prepared to do more.
A. The trucking industry supported and helped build the Interstate Highway System.

B. We have done a great deal for truck safety, and the results speak for themselves.

C. Truck drivers are at the heart of our industry, and they are obviously central to the safety equation.

Phrase Outlines

Phrase outlines use a partial construction of the sentence form of each point, instead of using complete sentences that present precise wording for each point. The idea is that the speaker is so familiar with the points of the speech that a glance at a few words associated with each point will serve as a reminder of exactly what to say. Thomas Donahue's sentence outline would appear as follows in phrase outline form:

phrase outlines express each main and supporting point with a partial construction of the sentence form.

II. Elements where trucking has made a difference
  A. Industry helped build Interstate Highway System
  B. Truck safety results speak for themselves
  C. Drivers are heart of industry and central to safety

Keyword Outlines

The briefest of the three forms of outlines, **keyword outlines** use the smallest possible units of understanding associated with a specific point to outline the main and supporting points. Thomas Donahue's outline would appear as follows in keyword outline form:

keyword outlines convey each main and supporting point with the smallest possible units of understanding, such as a single word or very brief phrase.

II. Elements
  A. Interstate Highway System
  B. Safety
  C. Drivers

Benefits and Drawbacks of Each Outline Format

Of the three types of outline formats (sentence, phrase, and keyword), sentence outlines permit the least amount of eye contact with listeners. However, eye contact is essential to successful delivery of a speech. The less you rely on your outline notes, the more eye contact you can have with the audience. For this reason, phrase outlines or keyword outlines are recommended over sentence outlines in delivering most speeches. In most cases, the main benefit of sentence outlines is in drafting a working outline.

An important benefit of the phrase outline is that it allows greater eye contact than do full sentence outlines. However, it offers less than full security to the speaker who might experience a failure of nerves or memory, or both. Phrase outlines work best when you have thoroughly rehearsed the speech—something that should be done regardless of the type of outline

Spencer Grant/Monkmeyer

Maximize your eye contact. Well-practiced, confident speakers are familiar with their speech outlines and can focus their attention on connecting with the audience.

selected. They are a direct reminder of how to state the main and supporting points. If you're well rehearsed, you need only take a brief look at these points to know what to say for each one. But if it is important to you to deliver statements in the exact form as you've prepared them, phrase outlines may not adequately jog your memory. You either must practice the speech often enough to feel confident you can remember the main and supporting points, or use a full sentence outline.

Keyword outlines are easier to handle and follow than are sentence or phrase outlines. They are also less conspicuous to the audience. Keyword outlines are the better alternative for presenting the main points to an audience via slides or overhead projection, where they can also serve as your speaking notes and free you from having to hold paper notes. However, if at any time during the speech you experience stage fright or lack of memory, a keyword outline may not be of much help. This is why preparation is essential when using one. The speaker must be confident in knowing the topic and speech arrangement well enough to deliver the speech extemporaneously. In this scenario, the keyword outline serves more as a safety net than as a device on which to rely.

Critical Checkpoint

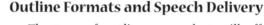

Selecting an Outline

Speeches can be outlined in complete sentences, phrases, or keywords. When deciding which approach to take with your next speech, evaluate its benefits and drawbacks relative to the other approaches:

- How will it impact your eye contact with the audience?
- Is it conducive to being projected overhead for the audience to see?
- Is it appropriate for the venue in which you will be speaking?
- Will it require more or less thorough rehearsal than the other approaches?

Selecting an appropriate outline format will boost your confidence and increase the odds for a successful speech delivery.

Zigy Kaluzny/Gamma Liaison

The student who wrote the outline on the facing page was fascinated by beer brewing. When you are interested in your topic, you may have an easier time using a phrase or keyword outline.

Outline Formats and Speech Delivery

The type of outline you select will affect how well you deliver the speech. As mentioned previously, sentence outlines restrict eye contact whereas keyword outlines promote it. Sentence outlines offer the most protection against memory lapses, but they may prompt you to look too much at the outline rather than at the audience. Keyword outlines permit more eye contact, greater freedom of movement, and better control of your thoughts and actions than any of the other outline formats.

Keyword outlines are the format of choice for use in extemporaneous speeches. Most of the speech assignments you do in class will be delivered extemporaneously. Extemporaneous speeches are carefully planned and practiced in advance and then are delivered from a keyword or phrase outline. The surest way to give a successful extemporaneous speech is to practice. (See Chapter 11 for a discussion of this and other types of speech delivery.)

Regardless of the type of outlining method you select, when you actually deliver the speech you should always express each of the main points as declarative sentences. Presenting each main point as a declarative statement emphasizes the point and makes it stand out from the others. For example, if one of your main points is that poor children are suffering because of changes in welfare laws, you should clearly state, "Today, poor children are suffering because of changes in the welfare laws." Main points reflect back to the purpose statement, and this connection between purpose statement and main points keeps the audience on track and properly oriented to listen effectively to your speech.

Sample Speech Outlines

The following outlines are from a speech delivered by Chris Cotty at Texas Tech University in the spring of 1997.

SENTENCE OUTLINE

TOPIC:	Brewing beer
GENERAL PURPOSE:	To explain
SPECIFIC PURPOSE:	To overview the malting, mashing, brewing, and fermenting processes involved in cultivating a beer.
THESIS:	Brewing beer is a process involving a series of complex steps, each modified to give the beer its individual flavor.

Your speaking outline should state the topic, general and specific purposes, and thesis at the beginning. This provides both a reminder and a record of these features.
Label the parts of your speech outline so you know exactly where you are.

Introduction
1. Have you ever wondered how this (*show a vial of grains*) turns into this (*show a bottle of beer*)?
2. It's amazing how much goes into crafting a beer. It's a process not many of us have thought about as we chug down a Miller Lite.
3. (Thesis) Brewing beer is a process involving a series of complex steps, each modified to give the beer its individual flavor.
4. (Preview) By providing an overview of the malting, mashing, brewing, and fermenting processes involved in cultivating a beer, I hope to give you a better understanding of the brewing process.

Note that the Thesis and Preview are clearly marked for easy identification.

Body
I. The first step in the brewing process is called malting.
  A. Barley is placed in a maltster.
    1. The grains are steeped for a couple of days.
    2. The grains are then dried.
    3. The grains are roasted.
      a. This step gives flavor to the barley.
      b. We now have malted barley.
II. The second step in brewing is called mashing.
  A. The barley is sent to the mill, where it is cracked.
  B. The cracked grain is sent from the mill to the mash tunnel, where the mashing process begins.
  C. The mash is filtered.
  D. Think of this process like that of brewing coffee.

When your main points are enumerated, as these are, state their number as you bring them up—first step, second step, etc.

III. The third step in brewing beer is actually brewing the liquid.
    A. Think of this step like brewing a stew—heating and seasoning.
    B. The liquid is heated to sterilize and coagulate proteins.
    C. Hops are added near the beginning of the boil.
       1. Hops are a flower that is picked off a vine and pelletized for brewing purposes.
       2. They can be thought of like roses or grapes.
       3. Hops add a bitter flavor and aroma to the beer.
IV. The fourth major step is fermentation.
    A. Liquid is strained and cooled.
    B. This is the step where the liquid actually turns to beer.
    C. The yeast begins to consume the sugars, producing equal parts alcohol and carbon dioxide.
    D. This process goes on anywhere from four to seven days.
V. After the brewer decides the process is complete, the beer is piped into the serving vessel as any additional yeast and hop particles are filtered so that the beer is as crisp and as clear as possible.
VI. The final step is to keg and bottle the beer, and then you get this (*hold up unopened bottle of beer*).

Conclusion
1. So you're fascinated, right? Or maybe you're just content to enjoy your beer and not care where it came from. Or maybe you don't even like beer.
2. Whatever your stance, I hope you leave today with a better understanding of the brewing process—and maybe a little trivia.

Phrase Outline

Introduction
1. Ask how grains (*show vial*) turn into this (*show bottle of beer*).
2. Amazing how much goes into crafting a beer
3. (Thesis) Brewing—a process of complex steps to give beer its flavor
4. (Preview) Overview of malting, mashing, brewing, and fermenting processes

Body
I. First step is called malting
    A. Barley placed in maltster
       1. Grains steeped for couple days
       2. Grains are dried
       3. Grains are roasted
II. Second step is mashing
    A. Barley sent to be cracked
    B. Cracked grain sent to mash tunnel
    C. Mash is filtered
    D. This process like brewing coffee
III. Third step is actually brewing the liquid
    A. This step like brewing a stew
    B. Liquid heated to sterilize, coagulate proteins
    C. Hops added near beginning of boil
       1. Hops a flower that is picked off a vine
       2. Thought of like roses or grapes
       3. Add bitter flavor and aroma

When this speech was actually given, the speaker had samples of hops for audience members to smell and taste, making the point about bitterness very real.

You can see how lengthy points can become in a sentence outline. This can be a limitation to effective eye contact with the audience.

A phrase outline is much like a sentence outline, but it is economized by omitting words such as articles and verbs.

Compare these phrases to the corresponding sentences in the previous outline. Notice the greater economy of the phrase outline. Note also how much more the speaker will need to know the content in order to speak from the briefer phrase outline.

IV. Fourth major step is fermentation
   A. Liquid strained and cooled
   B. Where liquid turns to beer
   C. Yeast consumes sugars, producing alcohol and carbon dioxide
   D. Process continues four to seven days
V. After brewer decides process complete, beer piped to serving vessel
VI. Final step to keg and bottle beer, getting this (*hold up unopened bottle of beer*)

Conclusion
1. Fascinated?
2. Hope you leave with better understanding of brewing process

It can be helpful to include notes on actions to take, as done in this outline for reminding the speaker to hold up the bottle of beer.

KEYWORD OUTLINE

Introduction
1. Ever wondered (*show grains and bottle of beer*)
2. Amazing
3. (Thesis) Brewing beer is a process involving a series of complex steps, each modified to give the beer its individual flavor.
4. (Preview) By providing an overview of the malting, mashing, brewing, and fermenting processes involved in cultivating a beer, I hope that you will gain a better understanding of the brewing process.

Even in a keyword outline you want to put your thesis and preview statements in complete sentences, because you want to say them exactly as you planned them.

Body
I. Step One—Malting
   A. Barley in maltster
      1. Steep grains
      2. Dry grains
      3. Roast grains, give flavor
II. Step Two—Mashing
   A. Barley cracked in mill
   B. Cracked grain to masher
   C. Filter mash
   D. Like brewing coffee
III. Step Three—Brewing
   A. Like brewing stew
   B. Heat liquid
   C. Add hops
      1. A pelletized flower
      2. Like roses or grapes
      3. Give flavor, aroma
IV. Step Four—Fermentation
   A. Strain and cool liquid
   B. Liquid becomes beer
   C. Yeast consumes sugars
   D. Four- to seven-day process
V. Beer to serving vessel
VI. Step Five—Containment

Consider the brevity of the keyword outline as compared to the other two formats. You will need to know your content very well to speak from this outline, but it will promote strong eye contact with the audience.

Remember, the keyword outline is used not as a source of your speech but as a road map in case you forget where you're going. Just a quick glance is all that should be needed when looking at this outline during the speech.

Conclusion
1. Fascinated?
2. Better understanding

Economize the conclusion section of your outline by simply listing a word or two that cues you to exactly what to say in closing.

SUMMARY QUESTIONS

How critical is organization to the overall success of a speech?

Research shows that audience understanding of a speech is directly linked to how well the speech is organized. Very disorganized speeches turn audiences off. Poor organization also affects speaker credibility; speakers who deliver organized speeches are seen as more credible than are speakers with poorly organized speeches.

What is the function of main points? How are they generated?

Main points express the key ideas and major themes of a speech. Their function is to make statements or claims in support of the thesis. The first step in creating main points is to identify the central ideas and themes of the speech. What are the most important ideas you seek to convey? As you review your research, what major ideas emerge? What ideas can you substantiate with supporting material? Each of these ideas and themes should be expressed as a main point.

How can the specific purpose and thesis statements help generate main points?

Because the specific purpose statement expresses the goal of the speech, and the thesis statement expresses the theme or central idea of the speech, the main points should flow directly from them. These two statements can therefore serve as guideposts in generating main points.

What is the function of supporting points?

Supporting points represent the supporting material or evidence gathered to justify the main points. In an outline, supporting points appear in a subordinate (i.e., indented) position to main points. Main points are enumerated with upper-case Roman numerals, supporting points are enumerated with capital letters, and third-level points are enumerated with Arabic numerals.

What are transitions, and how are they used in speeches?

Transitions are words, phrases, or sentences that tie together the speech ideas and enable the speaker to move smoothly from one point to the next. Speakers use transitions to move the listeners from one main point to the next, from main points to supporting points, and from one supporting point to another supporting point. (As seen in Chapter 9, transitions also alert listeners to the beginning and conclusion of a speech.)

How do the principles of unity, coherence, and balance apply to the organization of a speech?

A well-organized speech is characterized by unity, coherence, and balance. A speech exhibits unity when it contains only those points that are implied by the purpose and thesis statements. Each main point supports the thesis, and each supporting point provides evidence for the main points. A coherent speech is one that is logically organized. The body should follow logically from the introduction, and the conclusion should follow logically from the body of the speech. Within the body itself, the main points should follow logically from the thesis statement, and the supporting points should follow logically from the main points. The principle of balance suggests that appropriate emphasis or weight be given to each part of the speech relative to the other parts, and to the theme.

What are the main types of organizational patterns described in this chapter?

This chapter describes five main types of organizational arrangements: topical, chronological, spatial or geographical, causal, and problem-solution. Selection of a certain pattern of arrangement depends largely on inherent characteristics of the topic and main points.

What are the three types of outlines?

The three types of outlines are sentence, phrase, and keyword. Sentence outlines make declarative statements of the main points. Phrase outlines present each point as a partial construction of the sentence form, using only the most meaningful words. Keyword outlines reduce the wording of each main point to the one or two most meaningful words representing the point. Each approach has benefits and drawbacks, but the keyword outline is the most conducive to extemporaneous speaking and therefore allows more versatile speaking opportunities.

Key Terms

balance
causal (cause-effect)
   pattern of arrangement
chronological pattern
   of arrangement
coherence
keyword outlines
main points
outlines
parallel form
phrase outlines
problem-solution pattern
   of arrangement

sentence outlines
spatial or geographical
   pattern of arrangement
speaking outline
subordination and
   coordination
supporting points
topical pattern
   of arrangement
transitions
unity
working outline

ISSUES FOR DISCUSSION

1. Why is it important to organize speeches in a coherent and meaningful way?

2. If a speaker will follow the procedures recommended here and write out a speech before converting it to keyword phrases, why not speak from the manuscript to begin with? Alternatively, why write out the speech at all? Why not just start and end with a keyword outline? Why are outlines useful?

3. Why is it important to use transition statements in the body of speeches?

SELF-ASSESSMENT

1. Assume that you have been asked to deliver a speech to incoming freshmen on the topic of social life at your college. Write a specific purpose statement for this speech that reveals three main points.

2. Give an example of a topic that can be presented according to each of the following types of arrangements:
   a. topical
   b. chronological or procedural
   c. geographical or spatial
   d. causal
   e. problem-solution

3. From among sentence, phrase, and keyword outlines, which is generally the most conducive to effective speech delivery? Why?

4. Assuming that most of your speech assignments will be extemporaneous, the following procedure is recommended for planning your speech arrangement once all your material has been collected and organized. This exercise will help you see the strengths and weaknesses in your material and its pattern of organization. Go through the steps now to see how well you can complete them. Use them more formally for your next speech assignment, or as your instructor directs.

   Steps 1–5 help create a working outline. The remaining steps help create a speaking outline.

   1. Prepare a rough keyword outline of the main and supporting points.

   2. Referring closely to your supporting material notes, write the main and supporting points in sentence form.

   3. Using the principles of unity, coherence, and balance, revise the wording and arrangement of the sentence outline for logical consistency and clarity.

   4. Using the sentence outline format, write out the entire speech as you would want to say it.

   5. Read over the manuscript several times, becoming familiar with the structure of your ideas and how the points work together. Revise the arrangement as needed to strengthen the impact you hope the speech will have.

   6. Now discard the original keyword and sentence outlines. Working from the manuscript, write a sentence outline of the speech. Read over this outline several times to make sure the arrangement works as you planned it in the manuscript form.

   7. You are now ready to generate a speaking outline. Read through each point of the sentence outline again. Delete any unnecessary words, leaving only phrases—or perhaps just keywords—for the main and supporting points.

8. Prepare a final draft of the keyword outline. This will be your official practice outline. With additional notes about your introduction, conclusion, and transitions, it will become your actual speaking outline.

TEAMWORK

1. Together with four or five of your classmates, view a speech broadcast on television or borrowed from your library. Working individually, try to outline the speech, beginning with elements of the introduction. Note the main points and the type of arrangement used to structure them. Compare your findings with those of your classmates. What similarities and differences are evident in your observations? How clear was the organization of the speaker's message? How would you rate the quality of the speech in terms of its organization?

2. Working with three classmates, identify a current issue on campus or in town that each of you has followed and is interested in. Individually, brainstorm a brief outline as though you were going to give an informative talk on the issue's development. When everyone has finished, compare your outlines. What main points do the outlines have in common? In what ways do the outlines differ? Why? Despite the differences in outlines, would essentially the same speech be given from each one, or would there be entirely different speeches?

Begin at the beginning and go on til you come to the end; then stop.
—The King, in Lewis Carroll's *Alice's Adventures in Wonderland*

In everything one must consider the end.

—Jean de La Fontaine

Developing Introductions and Conclusions

Y ou have probably noticed that magazines like *Time*, *Sports Illustrated*, *Cosmopolitan*, *People*, and *Newsweek* preview the stories or features that will appear in the next issue. The purpose is to get readers interested so they will buy and read the next issue. **This is essentially no different from a speaker using a speech introduction to pique the listeners' interest about his or her following remarks.** Think about the last time you or a family member or friend bought a new car. When the car was ready to be driven home, the salesperson likely went over the various options of the car, reviewing many of the same points covered earlier during the sales pitch. This conclusion to the sale is no different from the conclusion to a speech. **A lasting impression is sought to be made in both cases.** **Introductions and conclusions are important devices for just about any message. In public speaking they act as the "bookends" of a speech.**

It was Jackie Wey's turn to give a monthly progress report on her department's performance. She worked at a small advertising agency, and the monthly meetings consisted of information exchange among the various departments. Jackie had some very important information to convey, but she knew that most people attending the meeting would sleep through the presentations because they were uninterested in anything that didn't pertain to them. This time she had to make sure they listened because she needed their input on some new advertising accounts she was hoping to obtain. Jackie had noticed at her Toastmasters meetings (a professional group dedicated to developing communications skills) that the speakers who garnered the most attention were those who opened with a snappy introduction and finished with a strong conclusion. In light of this, she decided to cut short her progress report so that she could build in both of these elements. She focused on three of her department's most promising accounts and gave each one a nickname—"Bashful," "Sleepy," and "Grumpy." She introduced the nicknames in a humorous introduction and concluded by asking audience members to give her suggestions about handling these challenging accounts.

When we recall speeches that were particularly memorable, we usually do so because of the way they were introduced and concluded. Introductions prepare the audience to hear the speech. A good opening previews what's to come in a way that invites listeners to stay the course. Speakers who fail at this goal might as well stop speaking. Conclusions ensure that the audience remembers the speech and reacts in a way that the speaker intends. The conclusion offers the last chance to make the kind of impression that will accomplish the goals of the speech.

Many novice speakers think that if the body of their speech is well developed, they can "wing" the introduction and conclusion. Leaving these elements to chance, however, is a formula for failure. While introductions and conclusions are not more important than the body of the speech, they are critical to its overall success. Engaging the audience with a compelling introduction and a memorable conclusion can ultimately make the difference between a great speech and one that is merely satisfactory.

This chapter presents a number of strategies for developing effective introductions and conclusions. In it, you will discover how to:

- Win the audience's attention through the use of quotations, stories, humor, and other kinds of supporting materials.

- Convey the speech purpose and topic and preview the main points.
- Set the stage for audience receptivity.
- Develop a speech conclusion that succinctly summarizes the speech points.
- Produce a conclusion that is motivating and memorable.

THE INTRODUCTION: ENLISTING THE AUDIENCE

The choices you make about the introduction can affect the outcome of the entire speech. In the first several minutes (one speaker pegs it at 90 seconds[1]) audience members will decide whether they are interested in the topic of your speech, whether they will believe what you say, and whether they will give you their full attention. Even the most well-disposed listeners want assurance that they won't be wasting their time. Will the speaker address the topic they are interested in? Will he or she do so in a compelling fashion? Is the speaker someone they find credible? A good introduction addresses each of these concerns.

Introductions have four functions. They serve to:

- arouse the audience's attention,
- introduce the topic and purpose,
- motivate the audience to accept the speaker's goals, and
- preview the main points.

In general, any kind of supporting material—examples, stories, testimony, facts, or statistics—can be used to open (and conclude) a speech, as long as it accomplishes these purposes. Here we review some of the more effective ways to do this.

Gaining Attention: The First Step

The first challenge faced by any speaker is to win the audience's attention. Some of the more time-honored techniques for doing this include: using quotations, posing questions, saying something startling, bringing in humor, telling a story, using imagery, referring to recent events, and expressing interest in the audience.

Use a Quotation. A good quotation, one that elegantly and succinctly expresses an idea, is a very effective way to draw the audience's attention. Quotations can be culled from literature, poetry, film, or the statements of

AP/Wide World

Marian Wright Edelman, founding president of the Children's Defense Fund, uses quotations and repetition to create riveting introductions to her speeches.

notable people. If the ideas are relevant and truly interesting, you can even quote your grandmother (whether famous or not). What counts is the power of the quotation itself. Of course, quotations are also used to build credibility. Audiences instinctively confer status on speakers who adroitly weave statements by people of renown into their remarks. In a sense, the speaker "borrows" the source's status.

For example, in a keynote speech at the Tenth International Conference on the Freshman Year Experience, Dr. Joseph Hankin, president of Westchester Community College, effectively used a quote by Mark Twain. Dr. Hankin opened his remarks by acknowledging the man who had just introduced him as keynote speaker:

Thank you, John, for that all too generous introduction. If, as Mark Twain said, a man can live a month on one compliment, you have just assured me of immortality, and you will go to heaven for your charity—unless you go somewhere else for your exaggerations.[2]

Marian Wright Edelman, founding president of the Children's Defense Fund, uses two quotations—one from a novel by Charles Dickens, and one from the writer Frederick Douglass—to introduce her speech on "Educating the Black Child":

It was the best of times, it was the worst of times, it was the age of wisdom, it was the age of foolishness, it was the epoch of belief, it was the epoch of incredulity, it was the season of light, it was the season of darkness, it was the spring of hope, it was the winter of despair.

—*A Tale of Two Cities*, Book 1, Chapter 1

You have no right to enjoy a child's share in the labors of your fathers unless your children are to be blest by your labors.

—*Frederick Douglass*

For many of you sitting in this room, it is the best of times. Black per capita income is at an all-time high, and many of you have moved up the corporate ladder even if the ladders you are on frequently don't reach towards the pinnacle of corporate power....

But there is another black community that is not riding high tonight and that is going down and under....

It is the worst of times for poor black babies born within a mile of this hotel....

It is the worst of times for black youth and young adults trying to form families without decent skills or jobs and without a strong value base.[3]

Notice that Edelman combined the use of quotations with another tool for focusing audience attention—that of *repetition*. Repeating a key word or phrase places emphasis on a key idea or theme of the speech; it also lends the speech cadence or rhythm. Repetition and other ways of using language to add power to a speech are the subject of Chapter 10.

Pose Questions. Can you recall a speech that began with a question? As the following examples indicate, posing questions is an effective opening technique. Doing so draws the audience's attention to what you are about to say. Questions can be real or rhetorical. **Rhetorical questions** (like the one that opens this paragraph) do not invite actual responses. Instead, they make the audience think.

When using a rhetorical question in your introduction, always let the audience know that your speech will attempt to answer it:

> Do you feel overwhelmed by the information revolution? Are you intimidated by your computer? Do you feel as though you are missing out? Well, you are not alone. Many people today feel intimidated by the frighteningly rapid changes in information technology. In the next few minutes, I will be talking about how you can overcome those fears and use personal computers to be more productive and get more out of life.

Posing questions that seek an actual response, either in a show of hands or by verbal reply, also sparks interest. Here is an example of how the speech on computers might be introduced by using real, or "polling," questions:

> How many of you have a personal computer? (*Speaker waits for a show of hands.*) How many of you feel that you are actually getting as much use out of your computer as you thought you would before you bought it? (*Speaker waits for a show of hands.*) How many of you are intimidated by your computer? (*Speaker waits for a show of hands.*) As you can see by looking around this room, you are not alone. Most people are prevented from getting the most out of their computers by their own fear—fear of looking or feeling stupid. Today I'll show you how to get more out of your computer by overcoming that fear. The first step is to realize that you are not alone—and, as you just saw, you are not.

Polling the audience members is an effective way to gain their attention, but there are several potential drawbacks. One is the possibility that no one will respond, or that the responses will be unexpected. Another is that the speaker will be called on to answer in unanticipated ways. Incorporating questions into your introduction is fine as long as you feel comfortable improvising if things don't go according to plan.

Say Something Startling. Did you know that the average student in Fictionland takes sixteen years to graduate? Surprising the audience members with unusual information is one of the surest ways to get their attention. Startling statements—in the following example, one phrased as a rhetorical statement—offer yet another way to do this. Such statements stimulate the audience's curiosity and make them want to hear more:

> The trouble with many men is that they have got just enough religion to make them miserable.[4]

So began a famous sermon about religion by evangelist William Sunday. You can be sure this statement made his listeners want to hear what he would say next.

Startling statements are especially effective when they are placed within a series of statements. In the following example from a student's speech,

rhetorical question
a question that is posed to make listeners think about something rather than offer an answer verbally.

the audience's attention is directed toward something quite different from what was expected:

> It grows on your face. It grows on your chest. It may even grow on your back. You cannot shave it. It's acne!

Frequently, speakers base their startling statements on statistics. Statistics are a powerful means of illustrating consequences and relationships, of how one thing affects another. They tend to quickly bring things into focus. In the following example, a student addressing the issue of minimum wages uses statistics to drive home the difficulty of "making it" in a low-wage job:

> Imagine going to work for nine hours a day, five days a week, fifty-two weeks a year, and having only about $8,600 to show for it (before taxes). Now imagine having to support not only yourself, but your spouse and kids as well. The next step to imagine is you standing in welfare lines. All of us want to be able to support ourselves and our families without outside help, but working at a minimum wage job makes this impossible. A full year's salary at minimum wage is $2,000 below the poverty level for a family of four. The minimum wage has not increased since 1989.

Use Humor. Few things get people interested and put them at ease as effectively as humor. Because well-handled humor and confidence generally go hand in hand, introducing a speech on a humorous note can also boost credibility. Caution is in order, however. Simply telling a series of unrelated jokes might initially get the audience's attention, but unless it makes a relevant point it will likely do more harm than good. Moreover, few things turn an audience off more quickly than tasteless or inappropriate humor. Speech humor should always match the topic and occasion. This doesn't mean, however, that serious topics leave no room for humor. Sometimes a lighthearted introduction offers just the needed touch. Note how Henry C. Cisneros, a former Cabinet secretary in the Clinton administration, uses humor to introduce a speech about a very serious issue—the problems facing America's urban poor:

> Gil, thank you very much and thank you, everyone, for the wonderful opportunity, the invitation to be with you today. It is a treat, an honor to be in this distinguished institution, and I can't tell you what a treat it is to be introduced by someone who can get through the introduction and actually pronounce my name correctly. This is a treat for me because it isn't always so. On one occasion in Washington I was introduced as "Henry Cisnerosis."
>
> On another—and I'll admit I wasn't in Washington—I was introduced in a way that was so off the mark that I really couldn't understand how it might have occurred until a week or so later. I was reading the style section of the local newspaper and came across an article that described a memory-jogging technique for remembering people's names. It said, try to focus on a prominent feature on a person's face and associate it with their name and it will bring you somewhere. And then it dawned on me why I had been introduced as "Henry Cisnernose."[5]

Self-deprecating humor such as this often gets a chuckle. In the following example, Vice President Al Gore also uses this sort of humor to gain the attention of a group of television executives:

> It's great to be here at the Television Academy today. I feel I have a lot in common with those of you who are members of the Academy. I was on Letterman. I wrote my own lines. I'm still waiting for residuals.
>
> At first, I thought this could lead to a whole new image. And maybe a new career. No more Leno jokes about being stiffer than the Secret Service. Maybe an opportunity to do other shows. I was elated when *Star Trek: The Next Generation* wanted me to do a guest shot—until I learned they wanted me to replace Lieutenant Commander Data.[6]

Gore's use of humor succeeded in gaining the audience's attention and putting them at ease. His remarks were clearly on target in terms of both his topic (telecommunications) and his audience (television executives).

Tell a Story. In the words of William Safire, one of America's most respected speech writers, stories are "surefire attention getters."[7] Speakers like to use stories to illustrate points, and audiences like to hear them, because they make ideas concrete and colorful. Stories personalize issues, encouraging identification and making things relevant. Most important, they entertain.

The key to successfully introducing a speech with a story is choosing one that strikes a chord with the audience. In a speech to her class on community service as an alternative to spring break vacation, Karen begins with a story:

Molly Washington is an eighty-seven-year-old great-grandmother whose sole income is a monthly Social Security check and a small pension her husband earned as a custodian. She lives alone in a two-room house near downtown Houston. Her yard is barren and unkempt because she fears being out long in the open of the dangerous neighborhood. The house is in disrepair, sorely in need of

Mark Richards/PhotoEdit

patching and painting. One spring day, seventeen youths from a city upstate arrive at Molly's door. They are cheerful and energetic. They carry buckets, brooms, brushes, and cans. The group of teens has come to patch and paint the exterior of Molly's house. They leave late that evening feeling victorious, tired but exhilarated, like champion athletes.

An inspiring story, such as the description of youths cleaning up Molly Washington's Houston home, is a great way to win over an audience.

Focus on Ethics

Plagiarism Is Plagiarism, No Matter Where It Occurs

It's sometimes tempting in the opening remarks to "adopt" material as one's own. A story found in a magazine or a joke reprinted in a book somehow becomes something you thought up. You may fear that crediting the source will interrupt the flow of your remarks. Or you might think that your listeners will find you more clever if they believe you thought of something yourself. But giving credit where credit is due is as important in introductions and conclusions as it is in the body of the speech. And plagiarism is plagiarism, no matter where it occurs. In fact, audiences react favorably to the speaker who acknowledges the source of his or her material. In general, they assign speakers who credit their sources *more* rather than less credibility.

What a way to start a spring break. And the best part is, there are four more days ahead just like this one.

Karen's story presents characters and circumstances that are real, making her topic—community service—all the more relevant to her listeners.

In the following example, *New York Times* editor A. M. Rosenthal introduces a speech on freedom of the press with a personal story about his days as a reporter in Communist Poland:

Let me tell you a true little story about how a reporter I knew operated. Every day he would go out and cover his beat the best way he knew and the only way he knows: by talking to people in the town about what concerned them....Every night the reporter went home, wrote a story, and then carefully burned his notes or flushed them down the toilet....Now it is twenty years later, and I am the editor of the same newspaper for which I was a reporter in Poland.[Here Rosenthal asserts that freedom of the press is under assault in the United States].

Like a joke, stories should be able to stand on their own. People want to be entertained. They don't want to listen to the speaker's explanation of what the story means. Of course, not all stories have to be real. Hypothetical stories can serve the same purpose as real ones. Just remember that the hypothetical story must be plausible.

Illuminate with Images. The effectiveness of using stories in introductions comes from the power of imagery to make a speech more vivid.[9] Images, or vivid descriptions, paint mental pictures. They help listeners visualize and relate to the content of the speech. Imagery can be very useful for gaining audience attention even when it is not used specifically in a story. Images also bring ideas and arguments to life.

In a 1995 address to the United Nations Fourth World Conference on Women, First Lady Hillary Rodham Clinton used imagery to gain the attention of the thousands of delegates in attendance:

> This is truly a celebration—a celebration of the contributions women make in every aspect of life: in the home, on the job, in their communities, as mothers, wives, sisters, daughters, learners, workers, citizens and leaders. It is also a coming together, much the way women come together every day in every country.
>
> We come together in fields and in factories. In village markets and supermarkets. In living rooms and board rooms. Whether it is while playing with our children in the park, or washing clothes in a river, or taking a break at the office water cooler, we come together and talk about our aspirations and concerns. And time and again, our talk turns to our children and our families.[10]

Rodham Clinton's introduction used images of children playing and women working to depict the many kinds of lives women lead. This helped to highlight the nature of the conference, which brought together women from all over the world. The use of such imagery in the introduction probably helped every woman there relate to the speech because her kind of life was most likely mentioned in the introduction.

Refer to a Recent Event or Person in the Public Eye. Introductions that include references to recent events or people in the news tend to capture attention for several reasons. First, such references make audiences feel involved. Second, people are generally curious about other people's perspectives on a given issue. They also want to discover how the speaker will ultimately link the event or person to the speech topic.

In some instances, *failure* to acknowledge events that have affected or will soon affect the audience can work against the speaker. Audiences may well perceive a speaker who ignores a riot, for example, or a natural disaster that just demolished half the audience members' homes, as out of touch, uncaring, or both.

But such references need not relate solely to negative occurrences. In a speech on information management delivered in Boston, James A. Unruh, former chief executive officer of Unisys Corporation, began his remarks by acknowledging both the city's unseasonably cold weather and its participation in the Super Bowl:

> Thanks, John, for that introduction and for inviting me to speak to you. Even considering the weather, it's good to be in Boston.
>
> Braving the cold is nothing new to me. I grew up in North Dakota, where anything above freezing is considered summertime.
>
> And it's always good being in a town that has something to cheer about on Super Bowl Sunday....Good luck.[11]

Express Interest in the Audience. In the same way that friends are made by showing interest in others, audiences are won over when speakers express interest in them. As discussed in Chapter 4, audiences only trust or find credible those speakers whom they believe have their best interests in mind. Focusing on the audience demonstrates interest and respect, and thereby builds speaker credibility.

When Nelson Mandela, an anti-apartheid leader in South Africa, was first released from prison after 27 years of incarceration, he addressed a huge crowd of supporters. He began this way:

> Friends, comrades, and fellow South Africans. I greet you all in the name of peace, democracy, and freedom for all. I stand here before you not as a prophet but as a humble servant of you, the people. Your tireless and heroic sacrifices have made it possible for me to be here today. I therefore place the remaining years of my life in your hands.[12]

Although Mandela had tasted his first hours of freedom after more than two decades in prison, he chose to focus on the audience rather than himself, expressing respect and admiration for *them*. In response, his listeners could not help but hold Mandela in even higher esteem.

Introducing the Purpose and Topic

Another function of introductions is to identify the speech topic and purpose. In the attention-getting phase you may have already alluded to your topic, sometimes very clearly. If not, however, you now need to actually declare what your speech is about and what you hope to accomplish.

In the next example, Dr. William J. Madia, senior vice president of Battelle Corporation, begins with a direct reference to his purpose and topic:

> My talk tonight is about choices—choices we make every day as a society in the actions we take or in how we spend our limited resources. I hope to demonstrate this evening that we need to do a much better job of solving the right environmental problems in this country, not the ones that are politically popular or media favorites. And I hope to show that a technique called risk assessment can be a powerful tool to help us make some ethically difficult, environmental tradeoffs.[13]

Topic and purpose are also clearly explained in this introduction to a speech by Marvin Runyon, postmaster general of the United States:

> This afternoon, I want to examine the truth of that statement— "Nothing moves people like the mail, and no one moves the mail like the U.S. Postal Service." I want to look at where we are today as a communications industry, and where we intend to be in the days and years ahead.[14]

Previewing the Main Points

Introductions should also preview the main points. **Previewing** the main points helps the audience mentally organize the speech and also helps you, the speaker, keep their attention. Introductory previews are straightforward. You simply tell the audience what the main points will be and in what order you will address them.

In a speech about information management, James A. Unruh previews his main points in this way:

> This afternoon I want to talk to you about three essential requirements for capitalizing on this remarkable information asset:
>
> First, senior management recognition of the critical role that Information Management plays in creating value for the customer;

Second, the importance of an organizational culture that fosters knowledge; and

Third, the importance of using best-in-class technology infrastructure as the enabler of the creation of value.[15]

In a speech entitled "U.S. Roads and Bridges: Highway Funding at a Crossroads," the president of the American Automobile Association, Robert L. Darbelnet, effectively introduces his topic, purpose, and main points:

Good morning. When I received this invitation, I didn't hesitate to accept. I realized that in this room I would find a powerful coalition: the American Automobile Association; the National Asphalt Pavement Association. Where our two groups come together, no pun intended, is where the rubber meets the road.

Unfortunately, the road needs repair.

My remarks today are intended to give you a sense of AAA's ongoing efforts to improve America's roads. Our hope is that you will join your voices to ours as we call on the federal government to do three things:

Number one: Perhaps the most important, provide adequate funding for highway maintenance and improvements.

Number two: Play a strong, responsible yet flexible role in transportation programs.

and Number three: Invest in highway safety.

Let's see what our strengths are, what the issues are, and what we can do about them.[16]

Motivating the Audience to Accept Your Goals

Most people do not blindly accept everything that someone says. This is particularly true in today's world where people are bombarded daily with countless messages. To make your message stand out, you must convince the audience members why they should care about your topic and why they should believe what you have to say about it.

Make the Topic Relevant. As mentioned earlier, people are selective about what they listen to. People look for information that connects with their background and experiences. And they are most motivated to listen when they think that what is being said will be of consequence to them.

A good introduction demonstrates why the audience members should care about your topic. One way to do this is to describe the topic's practical implications for them. Another is to specify what they stand to gain by listening to you. A student speech about groundwater shows how this can be accomplished:

Anytime we are thirsty, water is available through a tap or drinking fountain. None of us ever stops to think about where water comes from or how it's processed. It may surprise you to learn that frequently in the United States simple tap water has been found to contain dozens of pollutants and impurities. Fertilizers from irrigation fields, petroleum products from leaking underground storage facilities, and even the motor oil your neighbor dumped in the alley may end up in your drinking water.

Establish Credibility as a Speaker. During the introduction, the audience members make a decision about whether they are interested not just in the topic, but also in you. They want to know why they should believe you. To build your credibility, make a simple statement of your qualifications for speaking on the topic at the particular occasion and to the specific audience. Briefly emphasize some experience, knowledge, or perspective you have that is different from or more extensive than that of your audience.

The student giving the groundwater speech quoted above might establish credibility by stating, "I've been active in groundwater issues for five years. I have worked for governmental water conservation agencies and have been an advocate for clean water outside of my job during this time."

In the following example, a student speaker proposes that students do community service during spring break:

> My first two college spring breaks were spent swimming at South Padre Island and skiing at Taos. I spent several hundred dollars on each of those vacations. I returned to school tired and feeling a little guilty about the money I'd spent. Last year I did something different that changed my whole outlook on taking a break. I accompanied a church youth group to Houston to paint run-down houses in inner-city neighborhoods. I spent less money that week than I do in a typical week here at school. I came back completely refreshed, with a strong sense of proud accomplishment, and ready to tackle the end of the semester.

The speaker establishes her credibility by revealing that she personally committed her time to community service. Her references to money and feeling refreshed appealed to her listeners' practical concerns. The speaker has given them reason to listen to her further.

Critical Checkpoint

Motivating the Audience to Accept Your Goals

Previewing the main points and motivating the audience to accept your goals is a logical "one-two punch" for ending an introduction. The first step is fairly easy to accomplish, as the previous examples illustrate. Simply state what the key points are going to be and then move into the last segment of the introduction—motivating the audience to accept your goals. Critical thinking skills can help you with the following:

1. Making the topic relevant for the audience:
   - Determine what the audience wants and expects.
   - Stress things that are applicable to their varied interests.
   - Convince the audience that your purpose is consistent with their motives and values.

2. Establishing your credibility as a speaker:
   - Evaluate and assess how much the audience knows about you before the speech.
   - Provide the audience with reasons for listening to you.
   - Demonstrate that you have a sincere interest in having the audience join you as a partner in the speaker-audience relationship.

THE CONCLUSION: MAKING IT MOTIVATING AND MEMORABLE

The conclusion provides the final opportunity for the speech to leave the right impression. Conclusions give you the opportunity to drive home your purpose, and they offer you a final chance to reinforce your main points. A well-constructed conclusion ensures that you go out with a bang and not a whimper.

Similar to introductions, conclusions consist of several elements that work together to make the end of a speech as memorable as the beginning. Conclusions have three functions. They serve to:

- alert the audience that the speech is coming to an end,
- summarize the key points, and
- leave the audience with something to think about.

Alerting the Audience

Audience members like to know which part of the speech they are listening to at any particular time. Knowing this helps them mentally follow along the "road map" the speaker gave them in the introduction. Part of your job as a speaker is to tell the audience where you are in the speech. You do this with transitions, as described in Chapter 8. Similarly, speakers alert audiences that a speech is about to be over with a transition statement or phrase. **Signpost words and phrases** such as *Finally, Looking back, In conclusion, In summary, As I bring this to a close,* and *Let me close by saying* all signal closure.

> ◗ **signpost words and phrases**
> cues that alert the audience where the speaker is, and where he or she is going, in a speech.

Summarizing the Main Points and Goals

Repetition is one of the most effective ways for listeners to remember the key elements of oral communication. One of this chapter's opening epigraphs relates the age-old advice for giving a speech: "Tell them what you are going to tell them, tell them, and tell them what you told them." The idea is that emphasizing the main points three times will help the audience to remember them. In the introduction, you tell them what you are going to tell them. In the body of the speech, you tell them. In the conclusion, you tell them what you've told them.

Summarizing the main points in the conclusion accomplishes the last step of "telling them what you've told them." However, the summary or review should be more than a rote recounting. Let's return to the student speaker who was discussing groundwater. In addition to mentioning each main point, in this conclusion the speaker comments on their significance:

> In the last few minutes, we have covered the major sources of groundwater contamination and some solutions to this problem. First, we explored the major causes of contamination and found that lack of knowledge about the effects of underground storage, agricultural chemicals, and consumer practices have led to a very real and dangerous problem. We then discovered that inadequate legislation and lack of public awareness campaigns has allowed this problem to persist. Finally, we explored some specific solutions, such as stricter

Introductions and Conclusions—A Real World Perspective

Robert O. Skovgard is editor and publisher of the *Executive Speaker*, a monthly newsletter devoted to speech writing and public speaking. Each issue features excerpts of speeches by leading executives in business, industry, and government. One of the regular features of the publication is "Openings," which focuses on how speakers have crafted effective introductions in their presentations. Another feature presents examples of conclusions used in speeches.

What are the purposes of introductions and conclusions?

Beyond introducing the topic, the opening of the speech is like a handshake. Most audiences are already favorably disposed toward the speaker and are willing to grant their goodwill. It is the speaker's task, in the manner of a firm, vigorous, sincere handshake, to reciprocate and tell the listeners, as clearly and quickly as possible, what the speech is about—usually what the topic is and what the speaker's point of view on the subject is.

For a writer or speaker, conclusions are probably the most interesting part of a speech because it's where you try to create some fireworks, something memorable or emphatic that will make the point you want your listeners to remember or act on. Here's where it's appropriate to put that special anecdote or example or the rhythmical device that signals the listener that *this* is something important.

How can introductions and conclusions be developed effectively?

Successful openings and closings, like other parts of the speech, depend first of all on a careful analysis and understanding of the audience. It's like an anvil in the old blacksmith's shop against which he could test and bend and shape the metal. The more you know about your audience and the occasion, the easier and more natural it is for you to decide what type of supporting material is appropriate: self-directed humor, examples, an inspirational call for action, personal anecdotes, a family-related story, a sports analogy, a Vince Lombardi quotation versus a Bill Gates quotation. The more you know about your audience the easier it is to zero in on the most appropriate means of persuasion. As a rule of thumb, every minute you spend on careful audience analysis early in the process can be worth an hour later in the writing process because it saves you from false starts and chasing down some dead-end trail.

What are some of the best introductions and conclusions you have either used or heard?

One of my all-time favorite, general purpose introductions is a line by the late comedian Groucho

regulation of industry practices and introduction of campaigns to alert the public to the problem, and how these solutions might benefit everyone.

As the speaker reiterates each point, the audience is able to mentally check off what they've heard during the speech. Did they get all the main points? A restatement of points like the ones above brings the speech full circle.

Marx, who prefaced something he said with, "Before I speak I have something important to tell you." I think it came from on old Irish line about the grandfather who said, "I'll be taking a nap now, before I go to sleep." In general, good openings and closings, after they've met the test of appropriateness in terms of content, will also make use of a *variety* of techniques and devices—perhaps a reference to the location or audience, combined with an example or personal anecdote, phrased in conversational language. A "layering" of these interest-arousing devices tends to firmly establish the subject and point of view in the minds of listeners.

How much of the speech should be devoted to the introduction and conclusion?

As a general rule, about one-sixth of the speech can be spent on the introduction, one-sixth on the conclusion, and the remaining four-sixths devoted to the body of the speech. However, each speech is going to be different. You may want to start the conclusion earlier if you need time to drive home an especially important point. I have found that speeches are getting shorter, especially in the business arena, and this often affects how much time is spent on the beginning and end. Remember, all parts of the speech have to fit together. Plato thought of speeches as an organic whole. He used the human body as a metaphor—the head is the introduction, the feet are the conclusion, and the body represents the body of the speech. Like a human body, all the individual parts of a speech must be in place and working properly in order to be effective.

Will introductions and conclusions be developed differently depending on the type of speech?

Yes, but the type of speech is not the only criterion. Introductions and conclusions must also be sensitive to the speaker, the occasion, and the audience. You have a wide range of tools at your disposal for developing effective introductions and conclusions. If the speaker is well known to the audience, the speaker can use her or his reputation in a conclusion, let's say, to emphasize an important point. She could say, "It is *this* final point that is important to me." In this way, the power of the speaker's reputation can be used to make a strong conclusion.

Anything else?

Although this applies to the entire speech, it is absolutely necessary to introductions and conclusions (and it also reflects my bias as a speech writer): Regardless of how you eventually deliver the speech, write it down first. Writing it helps to clarify your thinking and economize your listeners' time. And when you're editing, take it to the point that the script starts looking a little too simple and repetitious. If you look at great speeches or speeches that go over well, they are usually expressed in simple, conversational language.

Similarly, Holger Kluge, president of CIBC, in a speech entitled "Reflections on Diversity," summarizes his main points in this way:

I have covered a lot of ground here today. But as I draw to a close, I'd like to stress four things.

First, diversity is more than equity....

Second, weaving diversity into the very fabric of your organization takes time....

Third, diversity will deliver bottom line results to your businesses and those results will be substantial, if you make the commitment....

Fourth, and above all, remember this. Diversity means recognizing the uniqueness of another person whether they are a customer, an employee, or ourselves. It means acknowledging the right to be who they are.[17]

Reiterating the Topic and Purpose. Sometimes speakers alert audiences of the impending conclusion by reminding them of the topic or the purpose of the speech. Gerald A. Johnston of McDonnell Douglas Corporation uses this strategy in a speech about defense spending:

> In summing up, I would like to return to the thought that we still live in a dangerous world—a world of great instability. Moderate governments in every region of this world are depending on continued U.S. military leadership to safeguard their security.[18]

The student who was cited earlier in discussing spring breaks alerted her audience that she was concluding and, at the same time, reiterated her purpose:

> I wish to close by reminding you of my purpose for speaking today. Each of us needs to reconsider how best to spend our spring vacation, and to consider spending a few days in community service as an alternative to expensive resort vacations.

Leaving the Audience with Something to Think About

Beyond summarizing and providing closure, conclusions also function to make the speech memorable. According to a communication theory called "the recency effect," many people remember best what they've heard

Focus on Technology

Software Tips

Using many of the special features of computer word processing programs can make it easy to develop effective introductions and conclusions. Since you will outline and write the body of your speech before writing the introduction and conclusion, you can use the Outline and Split Screen functions on the word processing program to see at a glance the important points in your speech that you want to highlight in the introduction and conclusion. For example, when you convert written text to outline form, you can see several pages at once. This gives a better sense of how the main points "hang together" and what type of examples and illustrations would be most effective. By using the Split Screen function, you can work on the introduction in one window and scroll through the body of the speech in the second window appearing on the screen.

Your word processor can also help you identify key words in the body of your speech that you may want to emphasize in your introduction and conclusion. Simply use the Search function to identify and count key words or phrases, take notice of their frequency, and use them in your introductions and conclusions.

most recently. A good conclusion increases the odds that the speaker's message will linger after the speech is over. A speech that makes a lasting impression is one that listeners are most likely to remember and act on.

Effective conclusions employ many of the same attention-getting techniques described above for introductions: quotations, stories, imagery, humor, and questions. One technique that is unique to conclusions is the *challenge*, or **call to action**.

Challenge the Audience to Respond. A strong conclusion challenges the audience members to put to use what the speaker has taught them. This applies to both informative and persuasive speeches. In informative speeches, the speaker challenges the audience to use what they've learned in a way that benefits them. In a persuasive speech, the challenge usually comes in the form of a call to action. Here the speaker challenges the audience to act in response to the speech, see the problem in a new way, change their beliefs about the problem, or change both actions and beliefs about the problem.

A concluding challenge is important because it shows the audience members that the problem or issue addressed is real and personally relevant to them. In the introduction, part of the goal is to show the relevance of the topic to the audience; the call to action is a necessary part of completing that goal in the conclusion.

Note how Hillary Rodham Clinton makes a specific call to action in her conclusion to the 1995 address to the United Nations Fourth World Conference on Women:

> We have seen peace prevail in most places for a half century. We have avoided another world war. But we have not solved older, deeply rooted problems that continue to diminish the potential of half the world's population. *Now it is time to act on behalf of women everywhere. If we take bold steps to better the lives of women, we will be taking bold steps to better the lives of children and families too.* Families rely on mothers and wives for emotional support and care; families rely on women for labor in the home; and increasingly, families rely on women for income needed to raise healthy children and care for other relatives.
>
> As long as discrimination and inequities remain so commonplace around the world—as long as girls and women are valued less, fed less, fed last, overworked, underpaid, not schooled and subjected to violence in and out of their homes—the potential of the human family to create a peaceful, prosperous world will not be realized. Let this conference be our—and the world's—call to action.[19]
>
> And let us heed the call so that we can create a world in which every woman is treated with respect and dignity, every boy and girl is loved and cared for equally, and every family has the hope of a strong and stable future.

In this very direct call to action, Rodham Clinton appeals to her audience to act to better the lives of women around the world. Moreover, she

call to action
a concluding challenge by a speaker to an audience to act in response to the speech.

John Ficara/Sygma

At the 1995 U.N. World Conference on Women, Hillary Rodham Clinton used the conclusion to her address as a call to action. Follow her lead and make your conclusion reinforce your message.

specifically calls the conference a "call to action" to highlight that she wants audience members to personally take steps to fulfill this goal.

The student cited earlier who discussed spring break challenged her audience to respond by asking them to visualize how they would feel if they took up her challenge of community service:

> Think about sitting in class early that Monday after spring break. Which will feel better—reminiscing about a week of serving yourself or a week of serving others?

Use Quotations. As with introductions, using a quotation that captures the essence of the speech can be a very effective way to close a speech. Note how Edwin Dorn, undersecretary of defense for personnel and readiness, concludes a speech:

> I think we need to ask ourselves: Do I believe in this country's greatness? Do I support leaders who bring us together—and reject those who spread bitterness and spite? Can I embrace change? Am I willing to join hands with my fellow Americans and walk toward tomorrow's light? Bobby Kennedy once said, "Some people see things as they are, and ask, why? I dream things that never were and ask, why not?" In that spirit, I say, my friends, it's time to dream again.[20]

Dorn uses the quote from Robert Kennedy to convey the importance of dreams, which was an important theme of his speech. The closing quote helps to reinforce this theme.

Robert G. McVicker, vice president of worldwide technology, quality assurance, and scientific relations for Philip Morris Management Corporation, concludes a speech with a quotation from a current sports hero:

> But let me close on a motivational note, with a quote from a man who is a recognized innovator in his field...who has spent his life turning challenges into opportunities...and who is something of an artist and craftsman himself. He's Michael Jordan, who, even as we speak is going for the brass ring again—and, as a Bulls fan, I promise you he will succeed. Michael once said, "If you put your mind to it, you can do anything you want." That's as true of business as it is of basketball. Let us all put our minds to the task of creativity and innovation. And I assure you...that we will be absolutely astounded by what we can accomplish—together.[21]

Relate a Story. A short concluding story can bring the entire speech into focus very effectively. It helps the audience visualize the speech. For example, in a speech before the Malt Beverage Distributors Association of Pennsylvania, Thomas Koehler of Miller Brewing Company uses a story to focus the audience on his central theme of taking an active role in promoting the industry:

> I would conclude with a story that applies to all of us in this industry. In ancient times there was a philosopher who had many disciples. One day a cynical young man decided to humiliate him by asking him a question he couldn't possibly answer correctly. The cynic put a recently hatched chick in the palm of his hand and asked the

Critically Evaluating Introductions and Conclusions

Every person wants to be seen as a unique human being rather than merely a faceless member of a group. At the same time, everyone has sensitivities. The best way to avoid stepping on those of your audience is to assume differences. This is just as true in introductions and conclusions as it is in the body of a speech. One way to evaluate the introduction and conclusion for potentially offensive material is to review the content in light of the four pillars of character described in Chapter 4: trustworthiness, respect, responsibility, and fairness.

What kind of things might potentially offend people? That depends on several factors: the source of the material, the material itself, and even your goal in using it. Depending on whom you quote, for example, some groups may respond favorably whereas others may be unimpressed or turned off. The more controversial the source, the greater are the odds of this happening. The same thing applies to humor, stories, and other kinds of supporting material. The key is to review the material with an eye toward others' sensitivities. Although you don't want to censor yourself, neither do you want to communicate in ways that alienate or cause others distress.

philosopher, in front of a large audience, whether what he had in his hand was dead or alive. His intention, if the philosopher said "alive," was to crush the chick to death and prove the master to be wrong. If the philosopher said "dead," then he planned to let the chick live—to prove the great man wrong. The philosopher looked the cynic in the eye, smiled, and calmly replied: "The answer, my son, lies in your hands." Well, like that young man, the future of our industry lies in our hands. Our actions over the next few years will determine whether the brewing industry—as we know it—will be alive...and will thrive...or only a memory.[22]

Another technique is to pick up on a story that you left off in the introduction:

Remember the story of Timmy I told in the beginning, the young hero who gave up everything he ever wanted to help his family? Well, I am happy to tell you that Timmy, or I should say Tim, is today one of the most successful entrepreneurs in the state of Florida. He went to college and graduated, he started many successful businesses, and all along the way, and even today, he continues to help those who are less fortunate than himself.

Here the speaker has brought the speech full circle.

Ask a Rhetorical Question. Yet another effective way to make a speech linger is to leave the audience with a rhetorical question. Just as such questions focus attention in the introduction, they can drive home the speech theme in the conclusion. The speech on groundwater contamination, for example, might end with a rhetorical question:

> Water has been cheap and plentiful, for most of us, for our entire lives. Easy access to our most necessary resource is now greatly threatened. Given this danger, we need to ask ourselves, "How long can we ignore the dangers of groundwater contamination?"

In a speech before independent insurance agents in Colorado, Edward J. Hoha, chairman of CNA Insurance Companies, uses a quotation from Benjamin Franklin and then repeats a rhetorical question in the conclusion in order to drive home his point:

> Long ago, just after our nation's founders drew up the Constitution, someone asked Benjamin Franklin: "What do we have now, Mr. Franklin?" He said: "You have a republic—if you can keep it." If you can keep it. It hasn't been that easy, but for more than two centuries we've kept this republic. We've kept its tradition of political freedom. And we've kept its tradition of economic freedom, of private enterprise....But this heritage is more than a gift from the proud past. It carries with it a solemn obligation. This is a precious heritage we've been handed—but a fragile heritage. *Can we keep it?* Only if we realize that today it's not just in peril in a few states—but in every state. *Can we keep it?* Only if we realize that preserving it calls not on some of us—but all of us. *Can we keep it?* Only if we're willing, each of us, to fight for it, now.[23]

Critical Checkpoint

Leave the Audience with Something to Think About

How can you use critical thinking skills to build a solid conclusion with all the trimmings? Of the three parts to a conclusion, the first two are pretty simple—alerting the audience that the speech is about to close, and summarizing the main points. The tricky part is leaving the audience with something to think about. To accomplish this you can:

challenge the audience to respond

use quotations

tell stories

pose rhetorical questions.

Selecting one or more of these strategies involves assessing the occasion, the audience, the topic, the type of speech, and your role as speaker. If your goal is persuasive, you will want to use challenges and dramatic stories or quotes in a climactic way. If your goal is to entertain, use humorous stories or quotes. If you are informing an audience, stories or quotations can reinforce your purpose. Take some time to consider the type of response you are seeking.

SUMMARY QUESTIONS

What are the functions of introductions?

Introductions serve four functions: They arouse the audience's attention, introduce the topic and purpose, motivate the audience to accept the speaker's goals, and preview the main points.

What are some of the more effective ways to capture an audience's attention?

Introductions must first gain the attention of the audience. Introductions may include virtually any of the types of supporting material described in Chapter 7, but some of the most effective ways to capture attention include using quotations, telling a story, using imagery, bringing in humor, posing questions, expressing interest in the audience, referring to recent events, or saying something startling.

What can you do to motivate an audience to accept your goals?

Audiences must be convinced both that the topic is relevant to them and that you are qualified to address it. One way to demonstrate the topic's relevance is to stress its practical implications and/or the benefit the audience will reap by listening. You can establish credibility by briefly noting your qualifications for speaking on the topic, citing professional or personal experience or knowledge—and by doing a good job!

What are the functions of conclusions?

Conclusions serve three functions: They alert the audience that the speech is coming to an end, summarize the key points, and leave the audience with something to think about.

How does a speaker alert an audience that the speech is about to end?

Audiences like to know whether the speaker is at the beginning, middle, or end of the presentation. Just as you use transition words, phrases, and statements to cue in the audience to shifts within the body of the speech, you can use them to conclude the speech. Signpost words and phrases such as *Finally, Looking back, In conclusion, In summary, As I bring this to a close*, and *Let me close by saying* all signal closure.

Why is it important to challenge the audience to respond to the speech?

A concluding challenge is important because it shows the audience that the problem or issue that has been addressed is real and personally relevant to them. In the introduction, part of the goal is to show the relevance of the topic to the audience; the call to action is a necessary part of completing that goal in the conclusion.

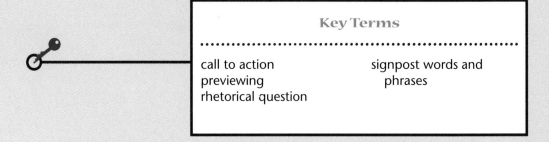

ISSUES FOR DISCUSSION

1. How often do you think people only listen to the introduction and/or conclusion of a speech and tune out the rest? If they tune out the body of the speech, shouldn't the introduction and the conclusion of a speech have to be especially effective?

2. How can speakers develop introductions that interest listeners enough to listen all the way through a speech? What clever strategies can you think of?

3. Think about the best introductions to television shows or movies that you have ever seen. What made these introductions so effective? Discuss as many features as you can think of. How could these techniques be applied to a speech introduction?

4. How much does a speaker's personal style affect the type of conclusion he or she selects? Should a serious person try a humorous conclusion or stick with a quotation or rhetorical question instead? Should a person with a keen sense of humor take advantage of it, or try something like a somber story or anecdote instead?

SELF-ASSESSMENT

1. Practice writing introductions and conclusions based on narratives or stories for each of the following speech topics:

   • Drunk Driving
   • Illegal Immigration
   • Health Care in the United States
   • Financial Aid for College Students
   • Your Favorite Vacation Spot

   (This could be repeated or changed for each of the kinds of introduction/conclusion devices in the chapter.)

2. Think of two of your personal hobbies or interests. If you were to write a speech about them, how would you build your credibility in the introduction? List statements you might make to support your credibility for each.

3. Think of two of your personal hobbies or interests. Brainstorm three main points for a speech about each hobby or interest. How would you build previews containing the topic, purpose, and main points for each speech?

TEAMWORK

1. In a group of three or four people, find copies of three or four speeches from a speech archive such as *Vital Speeches of the Day* or by searching the Internet using the World Wide Web, Gopher, or File Transfer Protocol. Isolate the introductions and conclusions for each speech. In a paragraph, describe the type of supporting material each speaker selected—a story? quotations? humor? Did the speaker select appropriate opening and closing material for the occasion and audience? Be prepared to discuss your findings with the class.

2. As part of a small group exercise, watch a few Senate or House of Representatives speeches on C-Span. Make a list of the most common ways you see of introducing a speech in Congress. Do these speakers use effective introductions and conclusions? Why or why not? In a short report, give examples supporting your conclusions.

3. Form a small group and have each member separately observe a speaker on campus, at a community center, or at a religious gathering. Have the group meet and discuss how each speaker uses introductions to gain attention. How do the speakers use conclusions to reinforce the message? Collaboratively write your answers in a short essay.

4. Working individually, write a paragraph describing a funny incident that has happened to you. Next, divide into groups of four or five students and take turns telling your stories to the group. Were you comfortable using humor? Why or why not? Were the audience members comfortable with your use of humor? Why or why not?

It is
my ambition
to say in ten
sentences
what others
say in a whole
book.
  —Friedrich
    Nietzsche

Music is your own experience, your own thoughts, your wisdom. If you don't live it, it won't come out of your horn.
  —Charlie Parker

10 Using Language: Styling the Speech

Can you recall listening to someone relate something so vividly that you felt you could really "see" what he or she described? Conversely, have you ever asked a friend to describe something or someone to you only to find that you could not form a mental picture from his or her recounting? **What is it about language that lets us visualize an image and even get a sense of sound or smell?** Poets and novelists use descriptive language to breathe life into that someone or something and to make their words leap off the page into the reader's mind. **In public speaking, you too can use the evocative power of language to captivate your audience.**

Diana was deeply disappointed that a sudden bout with the flu caused her to miss a lecture by a famous Chinese poet whom she greatly admired. As soon as she recovered, she phoned a classmate for details. "What did she look like?" Diana asked her friend Meg. "What did she say?"

"Oh," Meg replied, "she was just an old woman who wore weird clothes and jewelry." With that, Diana knew she wasn't going to learn much from this source of information.

Fortunately, Diana soon received a call from another classmate, Lynne, who had also attended the lecture. Just as excited as Diana about the writer's work, Lynne painted a vivid picture of the poet. "The woman's face," she began, "was brown and withered like a ginger root; she wore dark blue clothes, a necklace of turquoises and sharp little silver knives, and her hair in pigtails like two grey wires."[1]

style
the specific language and techniques used to express a speaker's thoughts.

A speech is a mixture of substance and style. The substance comprises the ideas as embodied in the topic and purpose, and the types of supporting materials used to illustrate them. Equally important to the success of a speech is its **style**, or choice of words and sentence structure. Style is the specific language you select and the techniques you use to express it. Varying the way you use language and taking advantage of its richness are two primary ways you can encourage the audience to identify with your topic and thereby achieve your goal of communicating.

In addition to using style to help craft a message with heightened impact, you can also use style to express your individuality as a speaker. Consider known orators like Jesse Jackson and Mario Cuomo, stylish speakers who have used language to communicate ideas but also to build a strong public image. From their examples you can learn that in public speaking the messenger is often as important as the message; the way you style a speech will affect how the audience *perceives* you and *receives* your message. The words you choose, the metaphors you employ, the images you create—all of these style choices are crucial to connecting with your audience and successfully communicating your message.

Language is an essential tool in creating any speech. This chapter will help you use language to achieve three critical objectives in public speeches:

- Share meaning with the audience.
- Build trust and credibility with the audience.
- Create a lasting impression with the audience.

WRITING FOR THE EAR

One of the most important things to remember when developing a speech is that written language and oral language are different. Using language for a reader is distinct from using language for a listener. As most professional speech writers know, speeches should be *written for the ear*. Whereas readers can take their time and re-read text if they wish, listeners have only one chance to get the message. If the language in a speech is unclear, complex, inaccurate, or inappropriate, listeners will have a tough time getting the meaning.

More so than writers, successful speakers use familiar words, easy-to-follow sentences, and straightforward syntax (subject-verb-object agreement). They avoid complicated words and long sentences in favor of shorter words and sentences. They steer clear of obscure terms whose meaning many people might not know. Repetition also figures more prominently in oral than in written language. Many successful speakers repeat key words and phrases to reiterate major points and to weave them into a central theme. Oral language is often more interactive and inclusive of the audience than is written language. The personal pronouns *I* and *you* occur more frequently in spoken than in written text. Audiences want to know what the speaker thinks and feels, and that he or she recognizes them and relates them to the message. Speakers accomplish this by making specific references to themselves and to the audience.

Another difference between oral and written language is the frequent use of transitions to tie ideas together and enable listeners to follow the speaker's direction (see Chapter 8). Speakers use transitional words, phrases, and sentences such as "next," "first (second, third, and so forth)," and "we now turn" to move the listener from one main point to the next, from main points to supporting points, and from one supporting point to another. Written language also uses transitions, but in less pronounced form. Transitions in written text, for example, often are indicated solely by paragraph breaks and topic headings.

In general, oral or spoken language is more conversational than written language. Yet because public speaking usually occurs in more formal settings than everyday conversation, listeners expect a somewhat more formal style of communication from the speaker. When you hold the floor of communication for an extended period of time, as in a speech, listeners expect you to speak in a clear, recognizable, and organized fashion. Thus, in contrast to conversation, in order to develop an effective oral style you must practice the words you will say and the way you will say them. This is especially important for extemporaneous delivery, which is the mainstay of classroom speech assignments.

Critical Checkpoint

Identifying Differences in Spoken and Written Language

One good way to recognize differences between spoken and written language is to record a speaker for ten or fifteen minutes, perhaps by watching a videotape of a speech or by tuning in to C-Span. Listen to the tape and then transcribe a five-minute segment word for word, including such "vocal fillers" as "um" and "ahh." Then choose a well-crafted writing sample—perhaps a newspaper or magazine article—that is on the same topic as the speech. As you compare the transcription of the speech with the article, what differences do you note in language usage? How do the two compare in terms of simplicity of language, transitions, sentence structure, length and completeness of sentences, and use of personal pronouns?[1]

1. Adapted from Andrea Lunsford and Robert Connors, *The St. Martin's Handbook*, 3rd ed. (New York: St. Martin's Press), 1995, p. 14.

We now turn to some of the specific techniques of oral language you can use to share meaning, build trust and credibility, create a lasting impression, and motivate and persuade.

USING LANGUAGE TO SHARE MEANING

Your choice of language should create shared meaning between you, the speaker, and your audience members. To accomplish this, speech language should be culturally sensitive, unbiased, simple, concise, concrete, and vivid.

Culturally Sensitive and Unbiased Language

Perhaps more than any other component of human society, language defines and creates culture. It is through language that people are able to communicate with one another—to share meaning. Language is universal in the sense that all human groups possess it. But every language is particular in terms of the meanings it assigns to various sounds. It is the distinctive words, phrases, and *colloquialisms* (i.e., regional variations in expressions) that pass from one generation to the next that define and perpetuate a culture, and that make it distinct from other cultures.

Many audiences today are culturally diverse, and rarely will you speak to an audience solely comprised of members of your own culture or subculture. Thus, as a public speaker it's important to be sensitive to cultural variations in language, whether you are addressing people of another nationality or audiences for whom local variations in language are significant.

Cultural sensitivity is a conscious attempt to be considerate of cultural beliefs, norms, or traditions that are different from your own. It means being aware of and adapting language for a diverse audience.

Cultural sensitivity is exemplified by speech that conforms to the four pillars of character introduced in Chapter 4: trustworthiness, responsibility, respect, and fairness. Recall the discussion of *ethnocentrism*, the belief that the ways of one's own culture are superior to those of other cultures. Ethnocentric speakers act as though everyone shares their own point of view and points of reference, whether or not this is in fact the case. They may tell jokes that require a certain context or refer only to their own customs, even when members of the audience do not share them. In contrast, speakers who are culturally sensitive assume differences and address them respectfully. They steer clear of words that may be construed as derogatory to any specific racial or ethnic group, and they avoid jargon unknown to the audience.

Being culturally sensitive, as well as being an ethical speaker, involves using language that is free of bias. Nothing offends an audience more than **biased language**; that is, any language that relies on unfounded assumptions, negative descriptions, or stereotypes of a given group's age, class, gender, and geographical, ethnic, racial, or religious characteristics. When you offend an audience member, you cannot achieve your objective. Listeners will focus on their reactions to your language and stop listening to the content of your speech.

Biased language also includes any terminology that is sexist, ageist, or homophobic. In one recent incident a speaker referred to women as *girls*. Although there is nothing wrong with saying *girls* in speaking about females under the age of 18, this particular speaker was talking about professional accountants who worked in his firm. Although his remarks actually complimented the workers' expertise and work ethic, he failed to win his point because his use of sexist language offended the audience.

An audience can be likewise offended by the use of **sexist pronouns** that unnecessarily restrict the gender of the person or persons in question. For example, a speaker who continually refers to one category of professionals, such as engineers, as "he," and another category, such as interior designers, as "she" is guilty of using sexist language.

You can root out biased or sexist language by being sensitive to its presence as you put together your speech:

- Are the pronouns and nouns inclusive of both sexes (*he* and *she*, *his* and *her*, *salesperson* instead of *salesman*)?
- Does the language include any unintentional assumptions about a given group, such as assigning all members a general characteristic?
- Does the language reflect any disparagement toward a person's or group's nationality, geographic origin, or religion?

Simplicity

Language is endlessly complex. Look up a word in a dictionary or thesaurus, and there is likely a host of synonyms. Of these, which one should you select? Successful speakers strive for simplicity. They say what they mean in short, clear sentences. When selecting between two synonyms, they choose the simpler term. Unless the audience consists of specialized professionals, they translate **jargon**—or the specialized language of a given

cultural sensitivity
a conscious attempt to be considerate of cultural beliefs, norms, or traditions that are different from one's own.

biased language
any language that relies on unfounded assumptions, negative descriptions, or stereotypes of a given group's age, class, gender, or geographical, ethnic, racial, or religious characteristics; also includes language that is sexist, ageist, or homophobic.

sexist pronouns
the exclusive use of *he, she, him, her,* and so on when referring to both men and women.

jargon
the specialized language of a given profession.

profession—into commonly understood terms. William Safire, a speech writer and newspaper columnist, once commented:

> Great speeches steer clear of forty-dollar words. Big words, or terms chosen for their strangeness—I almost said "unfamiliarity"—are a sign of pretension. What do you do when you have a delicious word, one with a little poetry in it, that is just the right word for the meaning—but you know it will sail over the head of your audience? You can use it, just as FDR used "infamy," and thereby stretch the vocabulary of your listeners. But it is best if you subtly define it in passing, as if you were adding emphasis."[2]

Safire's advice is worth taking. After crafting the language of your speech, look back over it for any instances of jargon or specialized language. If it is necessary for the speech, be sure to define it for your audience (e.g., "When you fly into DFW, the Dallas–Ft. Worth airport, be prepared to wait on the runway for a while.").

Conciseness

A common tendency among novice speakers is to "overload" listeners with unnecessary words and long sentences. As the audience waits for you to finish a complete thought or take a breath, many listeners will become distracted. As a rule, strive to use as few words as possible to express your thoughts. The use of shorter sentences aids listening comprehension. Consider the following examples. Which would you rather hear?

> It is difficult to believe that the United States government is attempting to tax us at every level of our personal and professional lives, whether it be capital gains taxes, value-added taxes, or of course, your favorite and mine, income taxes.

> It's hard to believe, but true. The U.S. government is taxing us to death. They've got their hands into every conceivable pocket. Capital gains taxes. Value-added taxes. And, of course, your favorite and mine: income taxes.

The second example conveys the same points as the first, but in a more concise manner.

In addition to short sentences, concise language includes the use of contractions, phrases, and sentence fragments. In the second example above, notice how the use of a contraction ("It's" instead of "It is") makes speaking more conversational. The same is true of phrases and sentence fragments. Although they are often avoided in written language, phrases and sentence fragments can effectively help communicate an oral message. The following examples demonstrate how they can add punch to a speech:

> *Intrapreneurialism. One minute management. Strategic alliances. Leveraged recapitalizations. Right-brain thinking.* These are some of the exotic plants that grow in management's magic garden. This garden has rich soil, the kind of loam that has generated fads—and confusion—throughout history.[3]

> *Wisdom from the mouth of babes.* The older I get, the more impressed I am with the ability of small children to cut to the heart of complex

Public Speaking in Cultural Perspective

Defining Terms

During her first public speaking assignment in class, Sarah decided to give a light-hearted speech about "pet peeves." Assuming that most everyone has at least one pet peeve, she felt certain that her audience members would be interested and that they would identify with the subject. However, in the class there were several international students from such diverse places as Malaysia, Iran, China, Nigeria, Pakistan, and Germany.

Sarah began her speech by introducing her own pet peeves. She talked about the lack of parking on campus, the poor service in fast-food restaurants, and pesky younger brothers. Sarah noticed that a few audience members were pay-

ing close attention, but others seemed to look at her with blank stares. Soon her confidence was wavering, as she wasn't sure why she had not connected with all the audience members. At the end of the speech, Kai, a student from Malaysia, raised her hand and asked what a pet peeve was. Sarah had assumed that *pet peeve* was common terminology; instead, it was an unfamiliar term to many in the audience.

How could Sarah have reworded the phrase to make it understandable for listeners from all cultures? How do you think Sarah could have realized there would be a problem with this term before she gave her speech?

issues. They have a way of getting to the un-adult-erated truth. Take the issue of leadership...[4]

Being concise also means eliminating unnecessary conjunctions between sentences, as well as ridding remarks of "vocal fillers." **Conjunctions** show relations between sentences. They include words such as *and, but, for, although, because, since,* and *as soon as.* Excessive use of conjunctions can distract and annoy listeners. Imagine how difficult it would be to concentrate on content if you heard the following:

> Going on a camping trip for the first time is like visiting another planet. And it's a planet I don't want to revisit. And you don't have all the conveniences of home. And my first camping trip was a disaster.

Unnecessary words and sounds, or so-called vocal fillers, within or between sentences also distract listeners from the speech content:

> It was like, ahh, visiting, um, another planet. And it's a planet I don't, like, want to revisit.

Vocal fillers such as "um," "ahh," and so forth alienate listeners because they distract from the point. Keeping the audience interested means using concise language.

> **conjunctions**
> words that show relations between sentences; for example, *and, but, for, although, because, since, as soon as,* and *and so forth.*

Concreteness

Speeches that contain a majority of concrete words and phrases have a better chance of succeeding in getting a message across than speeches that rely solely on abstract language. **Concrete language** is specific, tangible,

> **concrete language**
> words that are specific, tangible, and definite.

and definite. The flip side of concreteness or concrete language is abstraction or **abstract language**, language that is general or nonspecific. Abstract words such as *power, spirit*, or *peace* do not have a specific reference and could mean many things to a listener. You may know exactly what you mean when you use abstract words but every audience member may have slightly different, individualized meanings for those words. In contrast, concrete words such as *penny* and *wristwatch* call up more specific images for the listener.

Studies show that listeners retain concrete nouns and verbs more easily than abstractions. In fact, each time listeners hear an abstract word they try to locate a concrete reference for it, and if you haven't given it they will search their own experience for it. The meaning they ultimately attach to the word may not match your own, and further, if they are sufficiently puzzled they will be distracted from focusing on the remainder of your message. If you were to say in a speech that the federal deficit is *huge*, what would it mean to the audience? Wouldn't the audience get a better sense of your meaning if you were to say that the federal deficit itself is the size of "most national economies in the world"?

Examine the following ten words. Which ones do you think are abstract?

old	big
thing	a lot
bad	long
short	good
new	late

Actually, all these words are abstract, and they are some of the most overused abstractions in student speeches.[5] Look at the following examples to see how you can turn abstraction into concrete meaning:

ABSTRACT: The big policeman was mean to us.

CONCRETE: The policeman, who must have weighed 350 pounds, screamed obscenities at us.

ABSTRACT: That computer system has a lot of accessories.

CONCRETE: Her personal computer system has a printer, modem, and CD-ROM.

Notice in the last example that not only are the accessories more concrete, but the computer system itself is personalized ("personal") and given possession by someone the speaker knows ("her").

As you construct your speech, consider which words and phrases may be abstract. Consult a dictionary or thesaurus to find more concrete words that would strengthen your message. For example, consider the following levels of concreteness:

ABSTRACT	LESS ABSTRACT	CONCRETE
summer	hot weather	sweltering heat
congestion	traffic jam	gridlock

It is well worth the effort to substitute concrete words that help listeners easily grasp your intended meaning.

Vivid Imagery

Another way to use language to share meaning is through vivid imagery, which makes stories come alive for listeners. By painting a mental picture for them, you invite listeners to use their imaginations and thus become involved in your message. Vivid imagery enhances meaning by making ideas concrete and by evoking feelings and associations.

You can create vivid imagery by selecting concrete and colorful words, by appealing to the senses, and by using figures of speech such as metaphors, similes, analogies, and hyperbole.

Mike Maziarz/Uniphoto

Icy winds whistle all around as you leap across the snow! Don't settle for boring language; use vivid imagery to evoke exciting mental pictures.

Select Words That Are Colorful and Concrete.

Describing objects and activities with colorful and concrete language helps create an image for the audience. Fortunately, countless adjectives and adverbs are at your command. For example, think of all the ways you can describe the sky: Rather than characterizing it merely as "blue," you can specify it as "faint blue," "sea blue," "blue with feathers of white," or "blue with pillows of dark gray." Similarly, you can use adverbs to add color and detail to descriptions. For example, rather than saying "He was unhappy," you can say "He was utterly and miserably unhappy."

Appeal to the Senses. Another way to create vivid imagery is to appeal to the listeners' senses of smell, taste, sight, hearing, and touch. Table 10.1 illustrates how an abstract word or idea can be translated into a vivid image that appeals to one of these senses.

Table 10.1 Vivid Imagery	
Abstract Idea	**Imagery That Appeals to Listeners' Senses**
War	1. The smell of victory was in their nostrils.
	2. The roar of battle was deafening to the ears.
	3. The flash of the rockets was blinding.
	4. His dead skin was icy cold to the touch.
College Life	1. Fridays are a sight for sore eyes.
	2. You can almost taste the end of final exams.
	3. The sweet aroma of springtime makes it hard to attend class.
	4. Just walking across the graduation stage gave me goose bumps.

figures of speech

forms of expression that create striking comparisons to help the listener visualize, identify with, and understand the speaker's ideas.

simile

an explicit comparison of one thing to another, using *like* or *as*.

metaphor

a direct comparison of two things in which one thing is described as actually being the other.

analogy

an extended metaphor or simile that compares an unfamiliar concept or process to a more familiar one to help the listener understand the unfamiliar one.

Use Figures of Speech. Vivid imagery is often composed of figures of speech such as similes, metaphors, and analogies. **Figures of speech** make striking comparisons that help the listener visualize, identify with, and understand the speaker's ideas.

A **simile** explicitly compares one thing to another, using *like* or *as* to do so. Examples of similes include "He works like a dog" and "The old woman's hands were soft as a baby's." A **metaphor** also compares two things but does so by describing one thing as actually being the other. Metaphors do not use *like* or *as*. Examples of metaphors are "Love is a rose," "Education is an uphill climb," and "Life is a parade." An **analogy** is simply an extended metaphor or simile that compares an unfamiliar concept or process to a more familiar one to help the listener understand the unfamiliar one.[6] An example of an analogy would be: "If you really want to know what it's like to be catapulted off the deck of a ship on a navy jet, think about the scariest part of your last roller coaster ride."

When Dr. Martin Luther King Jr. delivered his now-famous "I Have a Dream" speech on the steps of the Lincoln Memorial in 1963, he began with a financial metaphor of a bad check. As he spoke, he extended the metaphor to include the "bank of justice" and the "vaults of opportunity":

> In a sense we have come to our nation's capital to *write a check*. When the architects of our republic wrote the magnificent words of the Constitution and the Declaration of Independence, they were signing a *promissory note* to which every American has fallen heir. This note was a promise that all men would be guaranteed the unalienable rights of life, liberty, and the pursuit of happiness.
>
> It is obvious today that America has defaulted on this *promissory note* insofar as her citizens of color are concerned. Instead of honoring this sacred obligation, America has given the Negro a *bad check*; a check which has come back marked "insufficient funds." But we refuse to believe that the *bank of justice* is bankrupt. We refuse to believe that there are insufficient funds in the great *vaults of opportunity* of this nation.[7]

Similes, metaphors, and analogies can help a speech come alive for the audience, help maintain the audience's interest in the speaker's subject, and help generate a theme. When used effectively, they can make a speech powerful. However, it is important to draw these and other figures of speech very clearly in order to avoid confusion and misunderstandings. For example, it is often useful to extend a metaphor (as did Dr. King) to help the audience understand its relation to the topic. If you are discussing love and decide to say "Love is a rose," you might make reference to the first date as the "first bloom" and the first heartache as "thorns of the rose." If you say "Life is a parade," you might make reference to friends as "cheering crowds" and college years as "brief and colorful." Always include detailed descriptions that explain to the audience what the parts of the metaphor represent.

In a speech delivered at the Harvard Business School, Alan Born of AMAX, Inc., includes an effective level of detail to clarify his metaphors. Notice how he uses three metaphors, each with enough detail to make the speech memorable. The metaphors (surgeon, chef, orchestra conductor) refer to the roles played by a chief executive in the recovery of a failed business:

The initial diagnosis is simple. The patient is dying, quite rapidly. It's time to be a *surgeon* and for surgery to begin at once. That means *cutting* manpower but keeping quality.

At this point you become the new *chef*—and there's room for only one chef in any company. The chef's job is to find the right *ingredients* and the proper people to *cook up* a strategy that will make things happen....

Still in the first 100 days, you change roles and become the *orchestra conductor*—now you *bring all the people together*, give them your understanding of what must be done, and then you *orchestrate* their efforts to get it done....

Happy second anniversary. Surgical duties are at a minimum and the chef is in charge, with the conductor doing some orchestration and waiting for the time to become a full-time performer.[8]

When including a well-known metaphor in a speech, make sure that you have it right. If you're unsure, ask someone or consult a source such as *Bartlett's Familiar Quotations*. Look at some of the mistakes made by the famous movie maker Samuel Goldwyn.[9]

- "You've got to take the bull by the teeth." (take the bull by the horns)
- "I love the ground I walk on." (I worship the ground you walk on)
- "I'm going out for some tea and trumpets." (tea and crumpets)

As illustrated in Table 10.2, other figures of speech that contribute to more vivid imagery include personification, understatement, irony, allusion, and hyperbole.

Table 10.2 Figures of Speech

Figure of Speech	Description	Example
Personification	Endowing abstract ideas or inanimate objects with human qualities.	"Computers have become important members of our family."
Understatement	Drawing attention to an idea by minimizing or lowering its importance.	"Flunking out of college might be a problem."
Irony	Using humor, satire, or sarcasm to suggest a different meaning than what is actually said.	"Our football players are great. They may not be big, but they sure are slow."
Allusion	Making vague or indirect reference to people, historical events, or concepts to give deeper meaning to the message.	"His meteoric rise to the top is an example for all of us."
Hyperbole	Obvious exaggeration to drive home a point.	"Have you seen those students carrying backpacks the size of minivans filled with five-course dinners, cell phones, and an occasional textbook or two?"

SOURCE: *Andrea Lunsford and Robert Connors,* The St. Martin's Handbook, *3rd ed. (New York: St. Martin's Press, 1995) pp. 428–429.*

Using Language to Build Credibility

Your use or misuse of language has a significant effect on the level of credibility you establish with your audience. When you mishandle language, either by using words inappropriately, inaccurately, or ungrammatically, or by lacking confidence and conviction, listeners become skeptical and cynical. When you cannot handle language properly, why should your audience trust what you have to say? If your language lacks confidence and conviction, why should they put any stock in your message?

Conversely, proper language usage builds trust and credibility. When you wield words correctly—in the right way and in the proper context—you demonstrate competence, an important aspect of credibility. By being appropriate, being accurate, and showing conviction for your topic, you demonstrate trustworthiness.

Appropriateness

Just as in any form of behavior, language that is appropriate in one context or for one audience may be inappropriate in another. Effective speakers are careful to use language that is appropriate to the audience, occasion, and subject matter.

As a rule, the public speaker should strive to uphold the conventional rules of grammar and usage associated with Standard English. The more diverse the audience, as well as the more formal the occasion, the closer you will want to remain within these bounds. Sometimes, however, especially when the audience is more homogeneous, it may be appropriate to mix casual language, regional dialects, or even slang in your speech. For instance, a rap music expert, speaking to an audience of other experts, might use such slang terms as *jaw-jacking* and *dissing* to communicate a point and to build identification between speaker and audience. Similarly, a computer hacker speaking to other hackers might well catch the audience's attention with such computer slang as *flame, core-dump,* and *cruftly.*

As long as the meaning is clear, interposing slang, regional, or ethnic terms into an otherwise more formal speech can simultaneously reveal who you are and add vivid imagery to your speech. Consider the following excerpt:

> On the gulf where I was raised, *en el valle del Rio Grande* in South Texas—that triangular piece of land wedged between the river *y el golfo* which serves as the Texas–U.S./Mexican border—is a Mexican *pueblito* called Hargill.[10]

Avoid Inflammatory and Libelous Speech. Using language appropriately also means avoiding inflammatory and libelous language. Neither type is ever appropriate in a speech. **Inflammatory language** is language that incites others to anger and that creates disorder or tumult. Throughout your career you will likely speak to audiences rather than actual crowds, and the chances of one of your speeches inciting a riot or disturbance are minimal. Yet you do need to be careful when your purpose is to stir up

inflammatory language
language that incites others to anger and that creates disorder or tumult.

Focus on Ethics

Is the Use of Vivid Language Ever a Bad Idea?

To help pay for his college tuition, David worked as a part-time cameraman for a local television station. As part of the job David had videotaped numerous auto accidents, some of which involved fatalities. Many of the wrecks that David witnessed were caused by drunk drivers. Because he had seen the damage that drinking and driving caused, David decided to deliver a speech about drinking and driving. Although his instructor warned him that graphic photographs might have negative effects on his audience, David wanted to make his speech memorable. He decided not to bring any photographs, because he thought the instructor might lower his grade. However, he was determined to make the violence memorable.

During his speech, David graphically described the accident victims—their bloody appearance, the torn body parts, the fluids that drained from their bodies. David's descriptions were so vivid that audience members began to grimace, and a few held their stomachs in nausea. One student ran out of the room crying; her fiancé had been killed by a drunk driver two weeks earlier. David was pleased because he knew his speech had made an impact.

Do you think David's use of language in this situation was ethical? Did the ends justify the means? Would you have developed the speech differently? Why or why not?

---

emotions, especially anger. Recently there have been instances of parents who, when speaking before their local school boards, used language that created such a stir among audience members that the officials had to end the meetings. (Note that a call to action, or challenge issued to the audience [see Chapter 9] is not necessarily an example of inflammatory language. Many violent social protests in our country's history started with "call to action" speeches designed to incite insurrection or resistance against authority. One of these preceded the Boston Tea Party.)

Slanderous or libelous language, or false and malicious statements that defame the reputation of others, is never appropriate in a speech. There is simply no time or place where saying ugly and untrue words about another person is proper. Indeed, you should always verify the accuracy of any information about someone else that you decide to "spread" through one of your speeches. Recent court rulings have applied guilty verdicts, resulting in large fines, to individuals who have violated this principle.

Accuracy

To build trust and credibility, language must be accurate. You must use the correct labels and terminology that accurately reflect the person or topic you are discussing. If you fail to do so, the audience will likely disregard

Bob Daemmrich/Image Works

People have strong reactions when they care about the issues at hand or when the issues affect them personally. Make sure to gauge your audience and choose your words carefully.

slanderous or libelous language
false and malicious statements that defame the reputation of others.

Using Language to Build Credibility • 239

Focus on Technology

Using the Word Processor to Help Craft a Speech

As every writer knows, the process of writing is really the process of rewriting, or revising. Writing a speech is no different. Indeed, it can take many drafts to get a speech the way you want it.

Three tools common to nearly all word processing programs that you can—and should—make use of as you write speeches are the spelling checker, the thesaurus, and the grammar checker. Most high school and college students today know how useful the Spell Check function is for verifying and correcting the spelling of words. In addition, the Thesaurus function is invaluable in searching for synonyms that most closely match your meaning. Also, since you'll want to use shorter words wherever possible in your speech, you can also use the Thesaurus to replace long words with shorter ones. The Grammar Check function identifies grammatical and stylistic errors and offers suggestions for improvement. It counts sentences per paragraph, words per sentence, and characters per word. Importantly, the grammar function also flags passive sentence constructions. Most Grammar Check functions provide three rule groups—Formal, Business, and Casual—that you can apply to your speech. Finally, after checking grammar, the Grammar Check function displays "readability statistics"; that is, it assigns a grade level of reading difficulty to what you've written. All these functions are extremely useful, even indispensable, in improving the language of your speech.

In addition to these built-in features of word processing programs, there are a wealth of stand-alone software programs for sale to help improve your speech's language. To find the latest programs, call a computer software store or get on a Web-based search engine such as Yahoo and type in: language+software.

---

your message. People trust and believe speakers more when they perceive them as truthful and honest. If you are not completely sure that you are using a word correctly, check its definition or use another term that is more familiar to you and the audience.

denotative meaning
the literal, or dictionary, definition of a word.

connotative meanings
the special associations that different people bring to bear upon a word.

Consider Connotative Meanings. When considering the accuracy of your language, remember that many words have both a denotative meaning and a connotative meaning. The **denotative meaning** of a word is its literal, or dictionary definition. Although some concrete words have mainly denotative meanings—*surgery* and *saline*, for example—through long use most words have acquired special associations that go beyond their dictionary definitions. The **connotative meanings** of a word are the special associations that different people bring to bear on it. For example, you may like to be called *slender* but not *skinny*, or *thrifty* but not *cheap*.

Words can evoke powerful responses in listeners. As a speaker, be sure to choose words that are both denotatively and connotatively appropriate for the audience. Try to be aware of the audience members' values. After all, people's values influence the meanings they attach to certain words. Ask yourself whether the words you have chosen carry connotative meanings to which the audience might react negatively. For example, members of a mainstream church or synagogue may associate the word *cult* with an off-center or even bizarre religious group. But to people who belong to an emerging religious group (which according to sociologists of realism is the denotative meaning of *cult*), being described as a cult may be offensive. Similarly, to a staunch Republican, the words *bureaucrat, welfare,* and *poverty* are likely to have quite different connotations than they would to a liberal democrat.

Report Information Correctly. Along with being sensitive to the appropriate connotative meaning of words, being accurate also involves reporting correct information. As described in Chapter 4, exaggerating facts and inflating or deflating figures to impress an audience is unethical. For example, if you are reporting a statistic of 95 percent, it is inaccurate to substitute the word *all*. A general rule to follow is this: *Eliminate all absolute terms from your speech.* Such terms include *all, every, none, only, always,* and *never.* These terms are rarely accurate (and they are certainly not concrete), and such obvious exaggerations damage your credibility as a speaker.

Confidence and Conviction

Yet another way to enhance credibility is to use language that expresses confidence and conviction. You can convey these qualities by using the active voice and personal pronouns.

Use the Active Voice. *Voice* is the feature of verbs that indicates the subject's relationship to the action. A verb is in the active voice when the subject performs the action. A verb is in the passive voice when the subject is acted upon or is the receiver of the action.[11] Just as in writing, speaking in the active rather than the passive voice will make your statements clear and assertive instead of indirect and weak:

PASSIVE: A test was announced by Ms. Carlos for Tuesday.

A president was elected by the voters every four years.

ACTIVE: Ms. Carlos announced a test for Tuesday.

The voters elect a president every four years.

Use Personal Pronouns. Personal pronouns such as *I, me,* and *my* also create an impression of conviction. Instead of saying, "This is a good idea for our university," you sound more convincing when you say, "I personally support this idea." If audience members are expected to accept your ideas and arguments, you must indicate convincingly that you accept them as well. Personal pronouns help you do that. In the statements listed below, notice how the use of personal pronouns improves the level of conviction:

Giving blood can save many lives.

I am convinced that giving blood can save many lives.

The speakers that come with this stereo system are the best value.

I know that the speakers that come with this stereo system are the best value.

The car has a great ride.

I test-drove the car myself and I know it has a great ride.

USING LANGUAGE TO CREATE
A LASTING IMPRESSION

Much of what makes a speech memorable is not just the specific words a speaker selects but the way these words are arranged. Just as certain lyrics and bits of music replay themselves in our minds, oral language that is artfully arranged and infused with rhythm leaves a lasting impression on listeners.

Speakers can create the cadenced arrangement of language through rhetorical devices such as repetition, alliteration, and parallelism.

Repetition

repetition
involves repeating key words or phrases at various intervals to create a distinctive rhythm.

One of the most effective strategies for using language in a speech is **repetition**. Repeating key words or phrases at various intervals creates a distinctive rhythm and thereby implants important ideas in listeners' minds. Repetition works extremely well when delivered with the appropriate voice inflections and pauses. One of the most famous examples of this was Dr. Martin Luther King Jr.'s speech in Washington, D.C., in 1963 when he repeated the phrase "I have a dream" numerous times, each with an upward inflection and followed by a pause.

Repetition is often used to create a thematic focus as well. A speaker may repeat key phrases that emphasize a central or recurring idea of the speech. Repeating a key word, phrase, or sentence throughout the duration of the speech stimulates and captures the audience's attention and brings the speaker closer to the listeners. Repeating a theme also reinforces your imagery, thereby increasing the odds that listeners will remember the speech.

The theme words normally first appear in the introduction, then the idea is repeated in the body, and the words or phrases are repeated in the conclusion. Thus, when you create a theme you need to identify words or phrases that help convey meaning to the audience. For example, if you are giving a speech about sky-diving, you might add the phrase "the thrill of danger" to the speech and repeat the phrase at appropriate times. You might begin the introduction with "I love the thrill of danger." Then, in the body of the speech, you might repeat the phrase, such as "The thrill of danger intensifies when you step out of the plane," or "As you feel your feet touch the earth beneath you, you know the thrill of danger has ended." To make the theme complete, consider adding the phrase in the conclusion, as in "Sky-diving isn't for everyone, but as for me, I'll continue in my quest for the thrill of danger." In this way, you have used language to create a theme that helps your speech become organized, cohesive, and interesting to the audience.

The Reverend Jesse Jackson has delivered many memorable speeches characterized by the repetition of key phrases, which he often encourages the audience to repeat along with him. In a speech delivered to a conference of teenagers in Atlanta, Georgia, for example, Jackson repeats the theme that the teenagers "are somebody":

> This morning I want to speak on the subject, "It's Up to You," for it is important for you to get involved and be part of what's happening.

AP/Wide World

Pop singers, poets, and public speakers use repetition to reinforce their points. Martin Luther King Jr. used this strategy to great effect in his famous "I Have a Dream" speech.

You must feel that you count in order to appreciate yourself and develop yourself in relation to other people.

People to my right, I am
[Audience answers] "I am"
Now don't sound all scared and timid. I know better. I am
[Audience answers] "I am"
Somebody.
[Audience answers] "Somebody."

Jackson continues in this vein, repeating the phrase "I am somebody" at various points throughout the speech. He concludes by saying:

My mind is a pearl. I can learn anything in the world.
I am somebody.
Nobody will save us but us.
Right on![12]

Alliteration

Alliteration is the repetition of the same sounds, usually initial consonants, in two or more neighboring words or syllables. Political campaign slogans often use alliteration to catch the attention of voters: "Love that Lyndon" (Lyndon Johnson); "Tippecanoe and Tyler Too" (William Henry Harrison); "Wilson's Wisdom Wins Without War" (Woodrow Wilson). Phrases such as "nattering nabobs of negativism," former U.S. vice president Spiro Agnew's disdainful reference to the U.S. press, and Jesse Jackson's "Down with Dope, Up with Hope" are examples of alliteration in speeches.

Alliteration lends speech a poetic, musical rhythm. When used well, it drives home themes and leaves listeners with a lasting impression. Alliteration is a great device for the ear. On the other hand, if poorly crafted or hackneyed, alliteration can distract from, rather than enhance, a message. The trick is to use alliteration prudently. Use only those alliterative phrases that convey your point more concisely and colorfully than can be conveyed otherwise.

 **alliteration**
the repetition of the same sounds, usually initial consonants, in two or more neighboring words or syllables.

> ### Critical Checkpoint
> ....
> **Carefully Choosing the Right Language**
> While preparing and practicing your speech, be sure to leave yourself enough time to shape and refine the language you will use. Pay particular attention to how the speech sounds as you practice it aloud. Words, images, metaphors, or rhetorical devices that seemed to work well when you were drafting the speech may sound awkward or strange once you speak them out loud. And if they sound awkward to you while practicing, they will surely sound that way to the audience.

Parallelism

Another device that is characteristic of memorable speeches is **parallelism**—the arrangement of words, phrases, or sentences in a similar form.

parallelism
the arrangement of words, phrases, or sentences in a similar form.

Parallel structure can help the speaker emphasize important ideas in the speech. Like repetition, it also creates a sense of steady or building rhythm.[13]

Orally numbering your points—for example, "first, second, and third"—is one use of parallel language. Another method, which works well when your speech contains chronological material, is to state the different years, months, or days to introduce an idea or evidence. For example, a speaker recently recapped the major events of World War II by beginning each main point with a phrase such as "December 1942," or "March 1943," followed by a pause.

Parallelism within individual sentences creates a powerful effect. Two of the most common types of parallel language are *pairs* and *triads*. Pairs take two ideas, phrases, or words to create a powerful idea; triads, three. Pairs are easily constructed by using conventional devices such as "either...or," "if...then," and "why...because."

> If we are well-educated, then we can educate well.

> Ask not what your country can do for you, ask what you can do for your country.

> Apathetic people create pathetic societies.

In the following example, the speaker added drama and humor by concluding an anecdote with pairs:

> Many years ago, a large American shoe manufacturer sent two sales reps out to different parts of the Australian outback to see if they could drum up some business among the aborigines. Some time later, the company received telegrams from both agents.
>
> The first one said, "No business here. *Natives don't wear shoes.*"
>
> The second one said, "Great opportunity here—*natives don't wear shoes.*"[14]

Triads make use of threes. A combination of three elements may be natural to a speech. In other cases, a speech may be manipulated to accommodate the use of triads. In fact, many speeches are carefully confined to three main points in order to take advantage of triads. There is something powerful about grouping concepts or ideas into threes. Consider the following examples:

> ...of the people, by the people, and for the people.
>
> —Abraham Lincoln

> Duty, honor, country. Those three hallowed words reverently dictate what you ought to be, what you can be, what you will be.
>
> —General Douglas MacArthur, farewell address at West Point

In the following two examples, the speakers make use of a pair of triads by asking a question, issuing a challenge, or stating a claim, and then answering with a triad. The first example is from a speech by Lloyd E. Reuss of General Motors Corporation, addressing the Grand Rapids, Michigan, Chamber of Commerce:

> *Others may wonder whether* General Motors knows where it's going. *I know that* it does. *Others may wonder whether* our products can grab and excite and satisfy our customers. *I know that* they can—and do. *Others may wonder whether* GM is doing what's best for it's own long-

term growth and for the economic health of our country. *I know that it is.*[15]

Robert Kilpatrick effectively uses paired triads in a speech to the American Chamber of Commerce Executives Management Conference:

For five decades now, business has told "big government" that there are better ways of doing things than proliferating the bureaucracy and throwing money at problems.
We have said, *"Give us a chance to prove what we can do."*
For five decades now, the states and communities of America have said to Washington, "We know better than you how to solve the social and economic problems on our own doorsteps. *Give us a chance to prove what we can do."*
For five decades now, business has said to the people of America, "We care about the quality of life in this country. We want a bigger share in improving the process of education, of training, of transportation, and of getting essential services to the public. *Give us a chance to prove what we can do."*[16]

These examples indicate that when used appropriately, parallelism creates a powerful, poetic effect for the audience.

SUMMARY QUESTIONS

Why is "writing for the ear" important, and what are some ways to accomplish this?

"Writing for the ear" involves using language in ways that will best be received by listeners rather than readers. In general, oral language is simpler and contains shorter and less complex sentences than written language. Repetition of key words and phrases, as well as the use of personal pronouns and transitions, occur more frequently in spoken than in written text. In general, oral language more closely resembles conversation than written language. However, because listeners expect public speakers to be clear and organized in their language presentation, practicing the speech is critical.

How can you ensure that your language is culturally sensitive and unbiased?

Speakers can be culturally sensitive—considerate of cultural beliefs, norms, or traditions different from their own—by adapting their language for a diverse audience. Speakers who are culturally sensitive steer clear of biased language; that is, any language that relies on unfounded assumptions, negative descriptions, or stereotypes of a given group's age, class, gender, and geographical, ethnic, racial, or religious characteristics.

Why is it important that speech language be simple and concise?

Successful speakers strive for simplicity and conciseness. To ensure that they get their message across, they avoid complex words and jargon that may not be shared by everyone. They also pay attention to sentence length. Striving toward more concise language also includes the use of contractions, phrases, and sentence fragments, all of which make speaking more conversational.

What is concrete language?

Concrete language is specific, tangible, and definite. In contrast, abstract language is general and nonspecific. Abstract words such as *power* and *peace* do not have a specific reference and could mean many things to a listener. However, concrete words such as *statistic* and *dollar* call up specific images for the listener. Concrete language is most effective in describing real objects and real experiences. Abstract language is often the most effective way to communicate the broad characteristics and values of an issue.

How can you create vivid imagery in your speeches?

Vivid imagery can be created through concrete and colorful words and through figures of speech such as similes, metaphors, and analogies. A simile explicitly compares one thing to another, using *like* or *as* to do so. A metaphor also compares two things but does so by describing one thing as actually being the other. An analogy is an extended metaphor or simile that compares an unfamiliar concept or process to a more familiar one to help the listener understand the unfamiliar one. Similes, metaphors, and analogies help a speech come alive for the audience, help maintain the audience's interest in the subject, and help generate a theme.

How can you use language to build credibility?

Speakers can build credibility with their audiences by using words appropriately, accurately, grammatically, and with confidence and conviction. Being appropriate means using language appropriate to the audience, occasion, and topic; and refraining from using inflammatory and libelous language.

How can you use language to create a lasting impression?

Three effective strategies for using language to make speeches memorable are the rhetorical devices of repetition, alliteration, and parallelism. Repetition is repeating key words or phrases at various intervals to create a distinctive rhythm and thereby implant important ideas in listeners' minds. Repetition is often used to create a thematic focus. Alliteration is the repetition of the same sounds, usually initial consonants, in two or more neighboring words or syllables. When done well, alliteration lends speech a poetic, musical rhythm or cadence. Parallelism is the arrangement of words, phrases, or sentences in similar form. Parallel structure can help the speaker emphasize important ideas in the speech. Like repetition, it creates a sense of steady or building rhythm. Two of the most common types of parallel language are pairs and triads. Pairs take two ideas or phrases to create a powerful idea; triads, three.

Key Terms

abstract language	inflammatory language
alliteration	jargon
analogy	metaphor
biased language	parallelism
concrete language	repetition
conjunctions	sexist pronouns
connotative meanings	simile
cultural sensitivity	slanderous or libelous
denotative meaning	language
figures of speech	style

ISSUES FOR DISCUSSION

1. Why is it so important to consider the connotative meanings of words in appealing to the audience? How can an analysis of audience attitudes, values, and beliefs be used to evaluate the connotative implications of certain words?

2. Think of three or four instances in which you could incorporate slang, regional, or ethnic terms into a speech in a way that would be appropriate to the audience, occasion, and topic. Be ready to discuss these in class.

3. How skillful are you in selecting words that have just the meaning you seek? Many people use a printed thesaurus or one that is part of their word processing package. For one of the most complete online thesauruses and dictionaries we have found, go to the following URL:

   http://humanities.uchicago.edu/forms_unrest/ROGET.html

   Type in a keyword and notice the comprehensive listing of alternate words. Be ready to discuss your results with the class.

SELF-ASSESSMENT

1. Choose an ordinary object in the room around you. Without explicitly naming the object, write a paragraph describing it in detail. Read your description to a classmate and see if your peer can guess what the object is.

2. Review the paragraph from the assessment in Exercise 1, above, looking for metaphors, similes, and analogies. Have you created any? If not, try to describe the object in these terms.

3. Select a piece of recent writing you have done—a speech, a term paper, or other work—and edit it for conciseness. Can certain words and sentences be deleted to make the message clearer and more concise? Try using a thesaurus to substitute brief words for unwieldy ones.

TEAMWORK

1. As part of a class activity, work in groups of five to generate between five and ten sensitive words that could be substituted by more appropriate forms. Each group should report its results to the class. To spur your thinking, consider the following substitutions:

INSTEAD OF SAYING...	CONSIDER...
janitor	maintenance worker
repairman	repairperson
congressman	senator or representative
handicap	disability

2. In groups of three to five classmates, read aloud from one classmate's speech. Evaluate how he or she has handled language in terms of the following: simplicity and conciseness of language; vividness of imagery; accuracy of word usage, including connotative meanings; transitions; sentence structure; length and completeness of sentences; and use of personal pronouns.

3. In a team of four or five people, locate a selection of newspaper or magazine articles and select some text that could be appropriately used as spoken language in a speech. Next, find some text that would be ill-suited for use as spoken language. Report your results to the class.

> Speak clearly, if you speak at all; carve every word before you let it fall.
>
> —Oliver Wendell Holmes

> Talking and eloquence are not the same: to speak, and to speak well, are two things.
>
> —Ben Jonson

Delivering the Speech

11

Recall the last time you saw an excellent production of a play. What was it about the actors' performance that made it so memorable? **Did the actors look natural and confident on stage? Did they moderate their voices to reflect different emotions or moods? What did the actors' body language convey?** Skilled actors artfully combine both verbal and nonverbal behavior to captivate an audience.

In some ways, delivering a speech is like giving a performance. Each component of your speech "performance," from the tone and volume of your voice to your facial expressions and hand gestures, affects how your isteners respond to you. **You will need to call on body language as well as vocal skills to deliver an effective and engaging speech.**

Here comes a man who has seen a great race, or has been in a great battle, or is on fire with enthusiasm for a cause. He begins to talk with a friend he meets on the street; others gather, twenty, fifty, a hundred. Interest grows intense; he lifts his voice that all may hear. But the crowd wishes to hear and see the speaker better. "Get upon this cart!" they cry; and he mounts the cart and goes on with his story or his plea.

A private conversation has become a public speech; but under the circumstances imagined it is thought of only as a conversation, as an enlarged conversation. It does not seem abnormal, but quite the natural thing....

I wish you to see that public speaking is a perfectly normal act, which calls for no strange, artificial methods, but only for an extension and development of that most familiar act, conversation.

—James Albert Winans, *Public Speaking*[1]

For most of us, topic selection, research and development of supporting material, arranging and outlining the points, and practice may be challenging and even difficult, but what often creates the most anxiety is contemplating or actually getting up in front of an audience and speaking. Delivery makes us feel anxious or awkward because it is now that all the eyes are upon us—making us feel conspicuous and somehow different. Added to this uneasiness is the unfounded idea that speech delivery should be formulaic, mechanical, and highly exaggerated; that it is, in a way, unnatural or artificial.

But as the late public speaking scholar James Albert Winans noted, a speech is really just an enlarged conversation, "quite the natural thing." Indeed, **effective delivery** in a speech or presentation is the skillful application of natural conversational behavior in a way that is relaxed, enthusiastic, and direct. As Winans put it, "a style at once simple and effective."[2]

In the previous chapter you learned the importance of using oral rather than written language when constructing your speech. Oral language is more conversational and therefore easier for an audience to follow. Similarly, it is important to incorporate elements of conversational delivery style in your speech. Just as gestures, facial expressions, and variations in voice and tone can help you convey information in an interpersonal conversation, so too can they help you deliver your message and engage the interest of the audience during a speech. The delivery of a speech should enhance the content, emphasize the message, and capture the attention of your audience members so they will be actively engaged listeners. This chapter will show you how to maximize the impact of your message by synthesizing the content and delivery of your speech.

effective delivery
in a speech or presentation, the skillful application of natural conversational behavior in a way that is relaxed, enthusiastic, and direct.

Delivering the speech is one of the most challenging parts of public speaking. It's also one of the most rewarding. This chapter will challenge you to:

- Work on achieving the qualities of naturalness, enthusiasm, confidence, and directness as you practice and deliver your speeches.

- Understand how nonverbal speech behavior can clarify the meaning of verbal messages, facilitate feedback, create identification and build rapport, and help establish credibility.

- Learn how to use your voice to achieve an effective delivery by varying your volume, pitch, rate, and pauses.

- Be conscious of how you pronounce and articulate words.

- Gain familiarity with the four methods of delivering a speech.

- Describe the impact of effective delivery on audience attitudes, comprehension, and perception of speaker ethos.

QUALITIES OF EFFECTIVE DELIVERY

Researchers who have studied speech delivery have identified four general qualities of effective delivery. They have found that effective delivery is natural, enthusiastic, confident, and direct. These qualities characterize the conversational, communicative nature of giving a speech.

Effective Delivery Is Natural

What is an effective style of delivery? Is it dramatic? Humorous? Emotional? Must you use certain gestures? Tone of voice? Facial expressions? Many students become anxious when they think about delivery because they assume that it will require them to behave in ways that are unnatural. Had you been born in the 1900s during the heyday of the elocutionary movement, such fears would have been justified. The elocutionists regarded speechmaking as a type of performance, much like acting.[3] Students were given a rigid set of rules on how to use their eyes, faces, gestures, and voices to drive home certain points in the speech and to manipulate audience members' moods. More than ever in the history of speechmaking, delivery was emphasized to such an extent that it often assumed more importance than the actual content of the speech.

Today, the extremes of elocutionism no longer hold sway. Rather than delivery, the content or message itself is seen as most important. Nevertheless, delivery remains a critical part of successful speechmaking. Rather than stressing the theatrical elements, contemporary delivery emphasizes naturalness. As communications scholar James McCroskey noted, effective delivery rests on the same natural foundation as everyday conversation. It doesn't call attention to itself.[4]

Planning and executing the delivery of a speech, according to contemporary scholars, is much the same as engaging in a particularly important conversation. In most conversations you don't have to give a lot of thought to what you're going to say and how you're going to say it; you just say it. Sometimes, however, you approach a conversation with a bit more forethought. Perhaps you're going to propose marriage or break off a relationship. Perhaps you're about to interview for a new job or resign from your present one. In such situations you may even practice what you will say, going over it once or twice ahead of time. Even so, there's no formula to follow, no mechanized procedure to enact.

Delivering a speech may be a relatively new experience for you, but the behavior required is very similar to that of a "serious" conversation. Although it requires more thinking and effort than ordinary conversation, it rests on the same basic principles. Of course, the fact that delivery is natural doesn't mean doing what you do out of habit, for even bad habits are natural.

Effective Delivery Is Enthusiastic

No one wants to listen to someone who is bored. After all, if speakers aren't interested in what they have to say, why should listeners be? Enthusiasm, on the other hand, is contagious. When you talk about something that excites you, you are naturally enthusiastic. You talk more rapidly, use more gestures, look more at your listeners, use more pronounced facial expressions, and probably stand closer to your listeners and may even touch them more. Your enthusiasm shows in the way you act, and such excitement spills over to listeners. Enthusiasm makes audience members feel more involved. As their own enthusiasm grows, they listen more attentively because they want to know more about the thing that excites you. In turn, you sense their interest and responsiveness and realize that you are truly connecting with them. The value of enthusiastic delivery is thus accomplished—it focuses your audience's attention on the message.

Of course, it's possible to be overly enthusiastic. When you appear to act in an unnatural way (i.e., artificial, strange, or weird), audience members are drawn away from the message because they are more intrigued with your unusual behavior, or they are turned off by it altogether and try to ignore you as well as the speech. At the opposite extreme, a lack of enthusiasm also results in a loss of audience attention because they are lulled to sleep, or they focus instead on some nearby attraction other than your message. The rule for enthusiastic delivery is far from either extreme, somewhere slightly above moderation. James Winans suggested that delivery should display a "lively sense of communication." He meant enthusiasm.

Effective Delivery Is Confident

It's obvious when someone in a conversation is nervous about something. It shows in their behavior. The same is true of anxious public speakers. They speak too rapidly, too softly, with a quivering, monotone voice; they stammer and hunt for words; they avoid eye contact, grimace, or have blank facial expressions; their posture is rigid and tense, or they fidget, sway, and shuffle their feet.[5] Lack of confidence stifles their delivery, and their speeches fail. Effective delivery, by contrast, is confident and composed. It conveys certainty and comfort. When you're speaking about something that excites you and you're telling it enthusiastically, confidence follows almost naturally. Your focus is on the ideas you want to convey, not on memorized words and sentences. Instead of thinking about how you look and sound, you're thinking about what you're trying to say and how well your listeners are grasping it. Confident delivery directs audience attention to the message and away from the speaker's behavior itself.

Effective Delivery Is Direct

Communication with an audience requires connecting personally with the listeners. This is done by building rapport with the audience, showing that you care about them and their understanding of the message. You can build this rapport in two general ways: by the things you say that make the message relevant to the interests and attitudes of the audience, and by your delivery—the way you act to demonstrate your interest and concern for them. The best way to do this is by being direct.

There are several ways to establish a direct connection with listeners. One is to maintain eye contact. Another is to use a friendly tone of voice. Yet another is to animate your facial expressions, especially positive ones

Focus on Ethics

A Tool for Good and Evil

The philosopher Plato believed that the art of public speaking—or rhetoric, as it was then known—was corrupt.[1] He considered it a form of flattery, much as cosmetics flatter the wearer's face and as cooking "flatters" food. Plato's cynicism about public speaking was the result of unethical practices he witnessed among his peers in ancient Greece. From his perspective, rhetoric (at least as practiced) too often distorted the truth.

Today, few people condemn public speaking per se as a dishonest form of communication. But many are aware of the power of delivery to corrupt. If history is any guide, these fears are well founded. One only has to think of Adolf Hitler. His forceful delivery—his scorching stare, gestures, and staccato voice—so mesmerized his listeners that millions accepted the horrific idea that an entire people should be annihilated.

In the 1980s and 1990s, powerful televangelists such as Jim Bakker and Jimmy Swaggart amassed extensive television audiences with their artful delivery styles. These men were masters at

appearing to be loving, compassionate ministers. All the while, they were engaged in false representations and unlawful money handling. Ultimately their credibility was destroyed, along with the savings of thousands of people who had been fooled into believing them.

Like any tool, delivery can be used for both ethical and unethical purposes. Countless speakers, from Abraham Lincoln to Martin Luther King Jr., have used their flair for delivery to uplift and inspire people. Yet there will always be those who try to camouflage weak or false arguments with an overpowering delivery. You can ensure that your own delivery is ethical by reminding yourself of the four pillars of character described in Chapter 4: trustworthiness, responsibility, respect, and fairness. Always reveal your true purpose to the audience. Review your evidence and reasoning for soundness. And always allow the audience the power of rational choice.

1. T. M. Conley, *Rhetoric in the European Tradition* (New York: Longman, 1990).

such as smiling. Positioning yourself so that you are physically close to the audience also creates a more direct connection. Of course, you don't want to go overboard, becoming annoying or overly familiar with the audience. But neither do you want to appear distant, aloof, and uncaring. Both extremes draw audience attention away from the message. Who wants to listen to a speaker who doesn't care? Give your audiences a speaker who cares, whose delivery is direct.

James Winans likened a speech to an "enlarged conversation." Thus, effective delivery involves *communication with* an audience, rather than merely *talking to* the audience. In other words, effective delivery is a function of what the speaker *does* rather than what the speaker *says*. Your delivery has a natural quality when your behavior does not call undue attention to itself. Your delivery has a relaxed quality when you present your message with confidence and poise. An enthusiastic quality of delivery is evident when your presentation is lively and animated, energetic and expressive. And you create a direct quality of delivery when you display such interest in the audience that every individual listener feels connected with you.

THE FUNCTIONS OF NONVERBAL COMMUNICATION IN DELIVERY

Beyond the actual words that are spoken, audiences receive information from a speech through two nonverbal channels: the aural and the visual. The **aural channel** is made up of the speaker's vocalizations that form and accompany spoken words. These vocalizations, or "paralanguage," include volume, pitch, rate, pauses, vocal variety, and pronunciation and articulation. The **visual channel** is made up of the speaker's physical actions and appearance—facial behavior and eye contact, gestures and body movement, physical appearance, dress, and objects held.

Aural and visual nonverbal elements are critical to an audience's full understanding of a speech. They directly influence how an audience attends to, processes, and retains speech content. Through these elements the speaker communicates nuances of meaning. And listeners use these same signals to clarify their understanding of the speaker's message.

Researchers have identified several ways in which nonverbal behavior works together with the verbal component of a speech[6]:

- Nonverbal behavior clarifies the meaning of verbal messages;
- Nonverbal behavior facilitates feedback, creating a loop of communication between speaker and audience;
- Nonverbal behavior helps establish a relationship between speaker and audience; and
- Nonverbal behavior helps establish speaker credibility.

Nonverbal Behavior Clarifies Verbal Messages

In normal conversation, you naturally change facial expressions, make different gestures, and vary your speaking voice. These nonverbal accompani-

---

aural channel
the speaker's vocalizations that form and accompany spoken words.

visual channel
the speaker's physical actions and appearance—facial behavior and eye contact, gestures and body movement, physical appearance, dress, and objects held.

Public Speaking in Cultural Perspective

African American Oratory—The Call-Response

The *call-response* is a spontaneous verbal and nonverbal exchange that takes place between speaker and audience. It is part of a rich tradition in African American oratory whose roots extend to Africa. Eloquent and persuasive speakers such as Sojourner Truth and Frederick Douglass, and more recent speakers such as the Reverends Martin Luther King Jr. and Jesse Jackson, have all made use of the call-response.

The call-response is a way of uniting the speaker and audience, making the communication between them circular rather than one-way. Many early black orators were preachers, and their congregations continued the African tradition of providing an immediate response to the spoken messages. These responses were both verbal and nonverbal, such as saying "Amen!" "Hallelujah!" or "Thank you Lord!" as well as waving one's hands or standing and pointing toward the preacher. In call-response, the speaker does not consider the verbal and nonverbal feedback from the audience as an interruption. In fact, many African American speakers solicit this kind of feedback to determine whether they are reaching their audience, asking questions such as "Is anyone with me?" or "Can I get a witness?" The audience gives an immediate response ("Right on!" "Make it plain," "Go 'head," "Take your time"). This in turn affirms the speaker and urges him or her to greater oratorical heights.[1]

1. Adapted from Dorothy L. Pennington, "Traditions in African American Oratory," Deborah Gillan Straub, ed., in *Voices of Multicultural America: Notable Speeches Delivered by African, Asian, Hispanic, and Native Americans, 1790–1995* (New York: Gale Research, 1996), pp. xi–xv.

ments to the words you speak help listeners get the full impact of your message. They serve an identical function in public speaking. The impact of the verbal component of your speech—what you say—depends largely on what you are doing vocally and bodily while saying it. The same words spoken with different body movements or different vocal emphasis convey different meanings. To see how this works, try placing emphasis on just the italicized word as you say each sentence aloud:

"I have a *dream*."

"*I* have a dream."

"I *have* a dream."

What different meanings are conveyed by each sentence as you stress a different word? The first one suggests a grand vision or image. The second stresses the speaker as the possessor of the dream. The third indicates that the dream is present and ongoing. The words are the same, but variations in vocal emphasis—a kind of nonverbal behavior—change the meaning.

Similar shifts in meaning occur with gestures. For example, if you were to say "*I* have a dream" while clenching your fist tightly against your chest and leaning forward toward the audience, you would convey an even greater sense of possessing the dream. Or, if you want to convey that you believe an idea is absurd, you might shrug your shoulders and roll your eyes in an "I just don't know" or "Who could believe it?" gesture.

Nonverbal Behavior Facilitates Feedback

Much of the interaction between speaker and audience occurs through the exchange of nonverbal behavior. Through the use of nonverbal behaviors such as facial expressions and voice adjustments, speaker and listener ensure that communication can occur. For example, as seen in Chapter 3 there is a constant interplay, or *circular response*, between speakers and listeners. In the circular response, speakers continually adjust their remarks according to their listeners' reactions, and vice versa. Audiences signal their degree of involvement in what the speaker is saying by facial expressions and body movements. Experienced speakers are alert to such cues and adjust their own verbal and nonverbal responses accordingly. If they notice that members of the audience to their left are losing interest, for instance, they look in this direction more frequently and for longer periods to keep them involved. When someone in the audience begins to cough, they increase their speaking volume.

As seen in the Public Speaking in Cultural Perspective box, on page 257, an African American oratorical tradition known as the "call-response" exemplifies how both nonverbal and verbal responses from the audience facilitate feedback.

Nonverbal Behavior Helps Establish a Relationship between Speaker and Audience

Jon Levy/Sygma

Phil Donahue: talk show pioneer and master of informal speaking. Donahue had a knack for making his audience members feel comfortable and at ease.

Nonverbal behavior allows speakers to modify feelings of closeness and familiarity with an audience, thereby establishing an appropriate relationship based on topic, purpose, and occasion. For example, to stimulate a sense of informality and closeness the speaker can move out from behind the podium and walk or stand among the audience. Former television talk show host Phil Donahue was a master at this. By taking off his suit coat, loosening his tie, speaking at a moderate rate, and showing more spontaneous movement he established a casual speech atmosphere.

Conversely, remaining behind the speaker's stand, using a more formal vocal quality, and speaking at a somewhat slower and consistent rate establish a more formal relationship with listeners. Thus, nonverbal behavior can help build rapport and create identification. It can also establish more formal boundaries between speaker and audience.

Nonverbal Behavior Helps Establish Speaker Credibility

Nonverbal speech behavior affects speaker credibility—the audience's perception of the speaker's competence, trustworthiness, and character. From the sound of your voice to how you choose to dress, nonverbal cues play a key part in the influence you will have on your audiences.[7] For example, audiences respond more positively to speakers whom they perceive as well dressed and attractive. They are apt to take them more seriously and are more objective in their responses than they are to speakers whom they do not find attractive. Audiences are also more readily persuaded by speakers who emphasize vocal variety, eye contact, nodding at an audience, and standing with an open body position than by those who minimize these nonverbal cues.[8]

We now turn to the specific kinds of nonverbal behavior speakers use: vocal characteristics and qualities, facial and eye behavior, gestures and body movement, and personal appearance. As you review these, keep in mind that rather than any single behavior in isolation (e.g., rate of speech or eye contact), it is the effect of these various nonverbal behaviors *working together* that determines how well or poorly the audience will react to your speech.

THE VOICE IN DELIVERY

Audiences are highly sensitive to a speaker's voice. Regardless of the quality and importance of your message, if you have inadequate control of your voice, you may lose the attention of your audience and may not gain a successful speech outcome. Fortunately, as you practice your speech, you can learn to control each of the elements of vocal delivery discussed in this section. These include volume, pitch, rate, pauses, vocal variety, and pronunciation and articulation.

Volume

Volume, the relative loudness of a speaker's voice while giving a speech, is usually the most obvious and frequently cited vocal element in speechmaking. If you do not speak loud enough for the entire audience to hear you, your speech is essentially a failure. The proper volume for delivering a speech is somewhat louder than that of normal conversation. Just how much louder depends on three factors: (1) the size of the room and number of persons in the audience, (2) whether or not you use a microphone, and (3) level of background noise.

- *Size of room/number of persons.* Naturally, the bigger the room and the more people in the audience, the louder you need to speak. At the same time, it is important not to be so loud that audience members in the front of the room feel like covering their ears.
- *Availability of a microphone.* A microphone is a must for large rooms and audiences. One advantage of a microphone is that it allows you to speak at a fairly normal, conversational volume. A disadvantage is that it can cause potential disturbances such as reverberation or static, and it is vulnerable to power outages. Nevertheless, in many speaking situations you will have available and should use a microphone.
- *Background noise.* Most speakers compete with some level of background noise when they give a speech. The source might be hallway traffic, air conditioning, thunderstorms, or people talking in the back of the room. One of your tasks as a speaker is to be alert to the noise level and adjust your volume accordingly.

volume
the relative loudness of a speaker's voice while giving a speech.

Kevin Rose/Image Bank

If you gave an unamplified speech in Atlanta's beautiful Fox Theater, you would have to project your voice if you wanted to reach audience members at the back of the hall.

Critical Checkpoint

Using Proper Volume

You can achieve proper volume by practicing some exercises. Try counting from one to twelve in a normal to loud voice. If you can hear a slight echo from the back wall of the room, you are using adequate volume.[1] Another exercise is to ask a friend to act as your coach. Engage in a five-minute conversation across a medium-sized table. As you speak, ask the friend to indicate the need for greater or lesser volume by gesturing "up" or "down" with hand signals.

One more exercise is to place a tape recorder at the back of a room. Speak a few sentences from the front of the room. If your voice is audible on the tape, you are speaking loudly enough. Remember, though, that doing these exercises in an empty room will produce slightly different results than when speaking in a room full of people. You will need even somewhat more volume in a full room than in an empty room. But these exercises will give you some indication of the need to raise your volume to project from the front or the back of a room.

1. Otis M. Walter and Robert L. Scott, *Thinking and Speaking: A Guide to Intelligent Oral Communication*, 3rd ed. (New York: Macmillan, 1973), p. 108.

Pitch

pitch
the range of sounds from high to low (or vice versa).

Imagine the variation in sound between the left end and the right end of a piano or harmonica. This variation represents the instrument's **pitch**, or range of sounds from high to low (or vice versa). The classic warm-up exercise "Do re mi fa so la ti do" is an exercise in pitch. Vocal pitch is important in speechmaking—indeed, in talk of any kind—because it powerfully affects meaning associated with spoken words. For example, say "stop." Now, say "Stop!" Hear the difference? The difference in pitch, termed *inflection*, conveys two very distinct meanings. Inflection or pitch is what distinguishes a question from a statement:

"It's time to study already."

"It's time to study already?"

What differences in meaning do you get from these two expressions?

As you speak, pitch conveys your mood, reveals your level of enthusiasm, expresses your concern for the audience, and signals your overall commitment to the occasion. When there is no variety in pitch, speaking becomes monotone. A monotone voice is the death knell to any speech. Speakers who are consistently monotone rapidly lose the audience's attention, along with its goodwill. If you tend toward using a monotone voice, practice your speeches with a tape recorder and then listen to them. You will readily identify instances requiring better inflection.

Rate

Some speakers bore audiences with their slow, plodding rate of speech. Others irritate with their rapid-fire rate, making it difficult to listen to them and follow their intended messages. The most effective way to hold an audience's attention, as well as to accurately convey the meaning of your speech, is to vary your **speaking rate**. A slow rate at the right time indicates thoughtfulness, seriousness, solemnity, and the like. A lively pace indicates excitement, adventure, happiness, and so on.

The normal rate of speech for adults is estimated to be between 120 and 150 words per minute. The typical public speech occurs at a rate slightly below 120 words per minute, but there is no standard, "ideal," or most effective rate. Being alert to the audience's reactions is the best way to know whether your rate of speech is too fast or too slow. An audience will get fidgety, bored, listless, perhaps even sleepy if you speak too slowly. If you speak too rapidly, listeners will appear irritated and confused as though they can't catch what you're saying. Again, listening to yourself speak on audiotape is an effective way to gauge and correct your speech rate.

 speaking rate
the speed with which a speaker talks; it should vary during a speech depending on the mood or emotion the speaker wants to convey.

Critical Checkpoint

Speaking at the Right Speed

How rapidly do you normally talk? Do you know people who talk at extreme rates of speed, say, very slow or very fast?

From your experience watching television, compare the variation in speech rate between a sports commentator calling a game and a newscaster giving a daily news report. What differences in rate do you notice? How do these differences affect the meaning of what is said?

---

pauses
strategic elements of a speech that enhance meaning by providing a type of punctuation, emphasizing a point, drawing attention to a key thought, or just allowing listeners a moment to contemplate what is being said.

Pauses

Many student speakers are uncomfortable with pauses. It's as if there is a social stigma attached to any silence in a speech. We often react the same way in conversation, covering pauses with vocal fillers such as "uh," "hmmm," "you know," "I mean," and "It's like." Similar to pitch, however, pauses are important strategic elements of a speech. **Pauses** enhance meaning by providing a type of punctuation, emphasizing a point, drawing attention to a key thought, or just allowing listeners a moment to contemplate what is being said.

In his famous "I Have a Dream" speech, the Reverend Martin Luther King Jr. exhibited masterful use of strategic pauses. In what are now the most memorable segments of the speech, King paused, just momentarily, to let the audience anticipate the words about to be spoken:

"I have a dream [pause] that one day on the red hills of Georgia…"

"I have a dream [pause] that one day even the great state of Mississippi…"

Imagine the impact of this speech if Dr. King had uttered "uh" or "ya know" at each of these pauses!

Critical Checkpoint

Identifying Vocal Filler

The first step in changing a pattern is noticing it. Take a few days to consciously observe your vocal filler pattern. How often do you fill pauses with "um" and "er"?

As you speak, deliberately insert silent one- or two-second pauses into your speech. The goal is to replace vocal fillers with slight pauses.[1]

1. Laurie Schloff and Marcia Yudkin, *Smart Speaking* (New York: Plume, 1992), p. 7.

Vocal Variety

vocal variety
the varied use of multiple vocal cues to achieve effective delivery.

Rather than operating separately, all the vocal elements described so far—volume, pitch, rate, and pauses—work together to create an effective delivery. Indeed, the real key to effective vocal delivery is to vary all these elements, thereby demonstrating **vocal variety**. For example, as Dr. King spoke the words "I have a dream," the pauses were immediately preceded by a combination of reduced speech rate and increased volume and pitch—sort of a crescendo. The impact of this variety is vivid in the memory of anyone who has ever heard the speech.

One key to achieving effective vocal variety is enthusiasm. Vocal variety comes quite naturally when you are excited about what you are saying to an audience, when you feel it is important and want to share it with them. Strive for these kinds of feelings when planning and practicing your speeches, and vocal variety should follow. On the other hand, be careful not to let your enthusiasm overwhelm your ability to control your vocal behavior. Talking too rapidly can lead to more filled pauses because you forget what you want to say. Overexcitement can lead to a consistently high pitch that becomes monotone. Hence, it is essential that you practice vocal delivery even if you are already enthusiastic about your speech.

Pronunciation and Articulation

pronunciation
the correct formation of word sounds.

articulation
clarity or forcefulness in saying words so they are individually audible and discernible.

Another important element of vocal delivery involves correctly saying the words you speak. Few things distract an audience more than improper pronunciation or unclear articulation of words. **Pronunciation** is the correct formation of word sounds. **Articulation** is the clarity or forcefulness with which the sounds are made, regardless of whether they are pronounced correctly. In other words, you can be articulating clearly but pronouncing incorrectly. In this way, good articulation may betray poor pronunciation. It is important to pay attention to and work on both areas.

Consider these words that are routinely mispronounced:

- oil (*oyel*) is often stated as *o-ell* or *oy-yel*.
- effect (*ee-fect*) is stated as *uh-fect*.
- going (*go-ing*) is said as *go-in*.
- mobile (*mo-bel*) is said as *mo-bull* or *mo-bill*.
- leaves (*leevz*) is stated as *leephs*.

Incorrect pronunciations are a matter of habit. Normally you may not know that you are mispronouncing a word, probably because most people you talk with say the word in much the same way you do. This habit may be associated with a regional accent or dialect. In that case, speaking to an audience of local origin may pose few problems if you pronounce words in regionally customary ways. But if you speak to an audience for whom your accent and pronunciation patterns are not the norm, it becomes especially important to have practiced and to use correct pronunciations to the fullest extent possible. In fact, the better your pronunciation all around, the more enhanced the audience's perceptions will be of your competence, and the greater the potential impact of your speech.

Articulation problems also are a matter of habit. (Exceptions are problems associated with oral, periodontal, or other conditions that impede articulate speech, such as wearing orthodontics, having a cleft palate or tongue thrust, or having injuries to teeth or gums.) A very common pattern of poor articulation is mumbling—slurring words together at a very low level of volume and pitch such that they are barely audible to listeners. Sometimes the problem is lazy speech. Common examples are saying "fer" instead of "far," "wanna" instead of "want to," "gonna" instead of "going to," "theez' er" instead of "these are," and so on. Such poor articulation in a speech indicates—or at least suggests—lack of preparedness, simplicity of thinking, or insincerity or inconsiderateness toward the audience.

Like any habit, poor articulation can be overcome by unlearning the problem behavior. If you mumble, practice speaking more loudly with emphatic pronunciation. If you tend toward lazy speech, put more effort into your articulation. Consciously try to say each word clearly and correctly. Practice clear and precise enunciation of proper word sounds. Say "articulation" several times until it seems to roll off your tongue naturally. Do the same for these simpler instances: "want to," "going to," "Atlanta," "chocolate," "sophomore," "California." As you practice giving a speech, consider words that might pose articulation and pronunciation problems for you. Practice saying them over and over until doing so feels as natural as saying your name. A co-worker of one of the authors of this volume terribly mispronounces his last name. She says "Stir-rut" instead of "Stewart." Each time he hears her say it, it gives him occasion to practice its correct pronunciation himself. Every little bit helps!

Vocal Delivery and Culture. Every culture has subcultural variations on the preferred pronunciation and articulation of its languages. These variations represent different dialects of the language. In the United States, for example, there is so-called standard English, Black English(or, more recently, Ebonics), and Tex-Mex (a combination of Spanish and English spoken with the distinct Texas drawl or accent), and regional variations as in the South, New England, and along the border with Canada. In parts of Texas, for example, a common usage is to say "fixin' to" in place of "about to," as in, "We're fixin' to go to a movie." Your own dialect may be a factor in the effectiveness of your delivery when speaking to an audience of people whose dialect is different. At the least, your different dialect might call attention to itself and be a distraction to the audience. One strategy you can use is to determine which words in your usual vocabulary are spoken dialectically, then practice articulating them in standard English pronunciation.

FACE, EYES, AND BODY IN DELIVERY

Beyond vocal delivery, the way in which a speaker uses body language—facial expressions, eye behavior, and body movements—also affects how well or poorly audiences react to a speech. And just as the speaker's body language sends certain cues to the audience, audience members' body language sends signals back to the speaker.

Facial and Eye Behavior

Facial expressions convey emotion: sadness, happiness, surprise, boredom, fear, contempt, compassion, anger, interest, surprise. By our facial expressions, audiences can gauge whether we are excited, disenchanted, or indifferent about our speech—and about the audience to whom we are presenting it.

Smile, and the World Smiles with You. Few behaviors are more effective for building rapport with an audience than smiling. A smile is a sign of mutual welcome at the start of a speech, of mutual comfort and interest during the speech, and of mutual goodwill at the close of a speech. Smiling when you feel nervous or otherwise uncomfortable can help you relax and gain heightened composure. Of course, facial expressions need to correspond to the tenor of the speech. Reporting to a board of directors that profits are on a seven-month downward trend is no time to express glee! Again, doing what is natural—simple and effective, normal for the occasion—should be the rule.

The Eyes Have It. Have you ever spoken to someone who kept glancing around the room? If so, you probably felt uncomfortable. If you were meeting the person for the first time, you probably did not see much chance for building a friendship. Poor eye contact is alienating, whether it occurs in everyday conversation or between speaker and audience. If smiling is an effective way to build rapport, maintaining eye contact is mandatory. Public speaking professional Roger Axtell notes that "the single most important physical action in public speaking is to have eye contact with the audience."[9] Even in audiences as large as 75 to 100 people, individuals will comment about whether or not the speaker made eye contact with them. Eye contact maintains the quality of directness in speech delivery. It lets people know they are recognized, indicates acknowledgment and respect, and signals to audience members that the speaker sees them as unique human beings.

With an audience of several hundred to over a thousand, it's impossible to look at every listener. But in most speaking situations you are likely to experience, you should be able to look at every person in the audience by using a technique called **scanning**. When you scan an audience, you move your gaze from one listener to another and from one section to another, pausing as you do to gaze briefly at each individual. One speaking pro suggests following the "rule of three": Pick three audience members to focus on—one in the middle, one on the right, and one on the left of the room; these audience members will be your anchors as you scan the room.[10] Initially this may be difficult. But with just a little bit of experience you will find yourself doing it naturally.

scanning
moving your gaze from one listener to another, pausing briefly to make direct eye contact.

Gestures and Body Movement

Friend 1 to Friend 2: "How was the fishing trip?"

Friend 2: "Great! The best I've had in years."

Friend 1: "Caught a monster, eh? How big was it?"

Friend 2 [extending two hands, palms facing each other]: "About this big!"

Words alone seldom suffice to convey what we want to express. Head, arm, hand, and even leg gestures are often critical in helping to clarify the meanings we try to convey in words. Physical gestures fill in the gaps, as in illustrating the size or shape of an object (e.g., by showing the size of a fish by extending two hands, palms facing each other), expressing the depth of an emotion, (e.g., by pounding a fist on a podium), or emphasizing a certain word (e.g., by using one's index finger to "write" the word in the air while speaking it).

Where to Put 'Em? Beginning speakers often have difficulty knowing what to do with their arms and hands during a speech. Many speakers are tempted to jam their hands in their pockets, clutch an object in one or both hands, or repeatedly fuss with their hair or clothing. Some speakers rigidly fold their arms across their chest and keep them there for the duration of the speech. This awkwardness may arise from the assumption that gestures should be scripted into a speech, with notes indicating when to raise your hand, point your finger, step back, straighten up, and so on. But this would be an artificial, unnatural way to work appropriate gestures into a speech, and it would be distracting and unproductive for effective delivery. To achieve a natural, relaxed quality in delivery, use gestures to fill in meaning gaps in the same manner as you would in everyday conversation.

Bonnie Kamin/PhotoEdit

You don't need to script all the body language in a speech. As in conversation, body language during a speech helps speakers convey information in a natural and personalized way.

General body movement is also important to maintaining audience attention and processing of your message. Audience members soon tire of listening to a "talking head" that remains steadily positioned in one place behind a microphone or podium. When this position is unavoidable, either because there is a fixed microphone at the podium or too little room to move from behind it, gestures and facial expressiveness become all the more important. But as space and time allow, try to get out from behind the podium and stand with the audience. As you do, move around at a comfortable, natural pace.

Body Movement and Presentation Aids. Just as you would feel uncomfortable conversing with someone who is facing away from you, perhaps with their shoulder in your face, audiences react poorly to speakers who don't face them. Positioning your body so that it is oriented toward the audience is critical. This is especially important to remember when using visual aids such as posters or flip charts. Facing the audience lets you maintain eye contact and in general signals a posture of respect to the audience. Speakers who face their visual aids rather than the audience end up talking to their displays.

You can arrange visual displays in a variety of ways so that you continue to directly face the audience. Always avoid putting the visual aid directly behind you. Place it to one side so that the whole audience can see it *and* you can back away from it and still face the audience. Doing so will help you resist the tendency to "talk" to it rather than to your listeners.

Listeners' Body Language. Just as the speaker's body language sends cues to the audience, audience members' body language sends signals back to the speaker. Perhaps the most blatant negative signal a listener can send to a speaker is closing his or her eyes, as if asleep. Other negative cues include frowning, facing away from the speaker, and sitting with arms rigidly folded across the chest. Conversely, positive cues include returning the speaker's gaze, smiling, and sitting directly facing the speaker in a relaxed but alert fashion.

What can you do in response to listeners' cues? If their cues are positive—that is, if your listeners return your gaze, smile and nod in agreement, and generally look as if they are comfortably paying attention—you needn't do anything but continue on as you are. On the other hand, if you do receive negative cues such as frowns, rigid and facing-away posture, head shaking in disagreement, and so forth, you will feel compelled to respond in some way. If the audience appears puzzled, try clarifying your point. If the audience appears to disagree with you, try presenting additional evidence.

Dress and Objects

"She wears her clothes, as if they were thrown on her with a pitchfork."
—Jonathan Swift, *Polite Conversation*

Clothes are part of your identity to others. The first thing an audience is likely to notice as you approach the speaker's position is your clothing. Clothing that is appropriate for the occasion does not draw attention to itself. If you dress with the intention of having your attire noticed, you are dressing inappropriately. The natural quality of delivery is thus diminished. The critical criteria in determining appropriate dress for a speech are audience expectations and the nature of the speech occasion.

An extension of dress is the possession of various objects on or around your person while giving a speech—pencil and pen, briefcase, glass of water, or papers with notes on them. Always ask yourself if these objects are really necessary. A sure way to distract an audience from what you're saying is to drag a briefcase or backpack to the speaker's stand and open it while speaking. If it's your habit to hold a pen while conversing with others, you need to break or halt the habit while giving a speech. Fumbling around with a pen can be a distraction to the audience. Similarly, fumbling around with a pointer, albeit useful for referring to certain visual displays, can be distracting. Put down a pointer when you're not using it. Perhaps you will be speaking long enough to need a sip of water during your speech, but be careful to do so without causing a distraction (e.g., taking a sip in the middle of a point or sentence). Finally, if you prefer to speak from prepared notes, do your best to keep them out of sight and quiet—loose paper notes have a tendency to rattle when held during a speech (it's probably nervous trembling!).

METHODS OF DELIVERY

The methods of delivery include speaking from manuscript, speaking from memory, extemporaneous speaking, and impromptu speaking. Each method is distinguished by the nonverbal behavior it uses or restricts, and by the qualities of delivery it promotes or impedes.

Speaking from Manuscript

Speaking from manuscript involves reading the speech from prepared written text that contains the entire speech, word for word. The speaker reads it to the audience, either from paper or off a TelePrompTer. This method is popular among politicians, corporate officers, and other public figures. You'll notice the use of a TelePrompTer if you watch the president give a formal address.

Unless the speaker practices adequately or uses appropriate visual aids, speaking from manuscript can be quite monotonous and boring. Manuscript delivery restricts the speaker's use of eye contact and body movement, and it may limit expressiveness in vocal variety and quality. The natural, relaxed, enthusiastic, and direct qualities of delivery are all limited by this method.

Manuscript delivery is most useful when very precise messages are required. When a disaster or tragedy strikes, for example, a public official or corporate executive may present a prepared statement offering an account of the incident and plans for dealing with it. Other circumstances in which manuscript delivery is appropriate include (1) when some portion of your speech is likely to be quoted and you must be precise in what you say, (2) when precise words are needed to cue changes in slides or other visual accompaniment, and (3) when tradition demands that your remarks be read from a manuscript, as when presenting an award.

> **speaking from manuscript**
> reading the speech from a prepared text.

Speaking from Memory

Instances of **speaking from memory** occur rarely. The formal name for this type of speaking is *oratory*. The term is reminiscent of ancient public speakers whose speeches (some of them extremely long) were fully committed to memory. If you were to use the oratorical style, you would put the entire speech, word for word, into writing and then commit it to memory. No wonder that speaking from memory is the most time-consuming method of delivery.

Memorization is not a natural way to present a message. It stifles authentic and sincere enthusiasm, and it poses a considerable threat to maintaining a relaxed delivery. Since the speaker is required to recall exact words from memory, true eye contact with the audience is unlikely (try maintaining eye contact with someone while you recall something from memory; you'll notice a loss of directness if you can manage to maintain eye contact at all). Moreover, memorization invites potential disaster during a speech because there is always the possibility of a mental lapse or block. When a mental block occurs, the speaker is left optionless and directionless, in silence, having focused practice on nothing else but the exact wording of the speech.

Some kinds of brief speeches, however, such as toasts and introductions, can be well served by memorization. Sometimes it's helpful to memorize a part of the speech, especially when you must present the same information many times in the same words, or when you use direct quotations as a

> **speaking from memory**
> delivering a speech after memorizing it word for word.

form of support. By and large, though, there will seldom be a need for you to memorize an entire speech of any kind. If you do find an occasion to use the memorization strategy, be sure to learn your speech so completely that in actual delivery you can focus on conveying enthusiasm and directness.

Speaking Impromptu

The word *impromptu* means unpracticed, spontaneous, or improvised. **Speaking impromptu** involves speaking without prior preparation. It's not advisable to speak impromptu when you've been given adequate time to prepare and practice a speech (that's called procrastination), but there may be occasions when you will be asked or compelled to make some remarks on the spur of the moment. In a church service you might be asked to offer a public prayer. In a meeting you might feel compelled to state your opposition to a proposal that someone has made. In class your instructor might invite you to summarize key points from the weekend reading assignment.

The greatest threat of impromptu speaking is to the qualities of directness and composure. How can you effectively deliver a speech that you don't plan and practice? One of the authors' friends, upon being introduced to speak impromptu at a banquet, stood and said:

> When people are called on to speak without any prior notice, one of two things will happen: Either they will say something significant or they will be brief. I will be brief.

Brevity is good, but so is significance. These four tactics are useful:

- Be familiar with and anticipate contexts in which impromptu speaking is possible, such as those mentioned in the previous paragraph.
- If you are faced with an impromptu situation, assess the needs of the audience. Consider factors such as the nature of the issue, the people who are present and their views on the issue, and whether there is a question-and-answer period.
- As you are listening to what others around you are saying, take notes in a key-word format and arrange them into main points from which you can speak.
- Finally, when you do speak, give a brief statement summarizing what you've heard others say, state your own position, make your points, and restate your position, referring as needed to the notes you made.

Taking steps like these will enhance your effectiveness because you will maintain qualities of natural, enthusiastic, and direct delivery. And having even a hastily prepared plan can give you greater confidence than having no plan at all.

Speaking Extemporaneously

Speaking extemporaneously falls somewhere between impromptu and written or memorized deliveries. When you give an extemporaneous speech, you prepare well and practice in advance, giving full attention to all facets of the speech—content, arrangement, and delivery alike. Instead of memorizing or writing the speech word for word, you speak from an outline of key words and phrases, having concentrated throughout your preparation and practice on the ideas you want to communicate.

<!-- margin notes -->
speaking impromptu
delivering a speech without prior preparation.

speaking extemporaneously
delivering a prepared and practiced speech without memorizing it or reading it from a text.

Most of the speech assignments you do in class will be delivered extemporaneously. In fact, probably more public speeches—from business presentations to formal public addresses—are delivered in this method than any other. It is interesting to note that in a thesaurus the word *extemporaneous* is interchangeable with the word *impromptu*. That is misleading, because extemporaneous delivery is quite different from impromptu. As Winans put it, "By the term *extemporaneous* we have come to describe, not a speech without preparation (that we call *impromptu*), but a speech which is not written out in full. Its peculiar merit is its greater adaptability to a situation."[11]

Knowing your idea well enough to present it without memorization or manuscript gives you greater flexibility to adapt to the specific speaking situation. You can modify wording, rearrange your points, change examples, or omit information as appropriate to the audience and setting. You can have more eye contact, more direct body orientation, greater freedom of movement, and generally better control of your thoughts and actions than in any of the other delivery methods. Because extemporaneous speaking is the most conducive method for achieving natural, conversational qualities of delivery, many public speaking practitioners and communication scholars consider it to be the preferred method of the four types of delivery.

Using a Delivery Outline

A well-prepared delivery outline is your best friend when delivering a speech extemporaneously. Professor James McCroskey states five rules for using an outline in extemporaneous delivery.[12]

1. *The outline should include only key words.* The more dense your outline, the greater the likelihood you'll be reading from it. The more time you spend looking at the outline, the less time you spend in direct contact with the audience. As described in Chapter 8, key words should be selected on the basis of the main ideas you want to communicate. That way, when you do look at your outline, your thinking will be stimulated by the association of the key words and ideas.

2. *The outline should be kept to a minimum.* Look back at Chapter 8, Organizing and Outlining the Speech. Remember to prepare an outline that covers all your main and supporting points, but no more.

3. *The outline should be prepared on small note cards.* Sheets of paper are cumbersome and noisy to handle. Note cards are firm and small enough to handle stealthily, but spacious enough to contain your key words (assuming about one main point and supporting points per card). You can use different colored cards for each main point or section of your speech.

4. *The outline should not be used in hand gestures.* Don't let your note cards become pointers or flags. This distracts an audience. It can make you look like you're swatting at flies or fanning yourself!

5. *Attempts to conceal your notes should not become a distraction.* It's all right to prevent your notes from being a main visual feature of your speech delivery, but don't get so intent on hiding them that you appear obvious. Keep them in a position on the podium or in one hand that is easy to glance at

Critical Checkpoint

· ·

Making Decisions about Methods of Delivery

Consider each type of situation listed below. Which of the four methods of delivery would you choose for giving a speech in each situation? Why?

An announcement to an assembly of employees that there will be large-scale termination of jobs over the next few months.

A speech on the 4th of July about the history of your community.

A presentation to a group of prospective students touring your campus.

A presentation to the city council seeking approval for your service group to plant trees in a city park.

A toast at a wedding banquet.

Focus on Technology

Delivery on Camera

It is becoming increasingly common for ordinary people to make public appearances on television. Whether in the role of business executive, professional expert, political advocate, or citizen on the street, it is not unreasonable to expect that someday you yourself could make an appearance as a speaker on television. As you might guess, speaking on television presents a different challenge from speaking to a live audience.

One consideration is appearance. This includes not only the clothes you wear, but also makeup. Generally, the same rules that apply for dress in giving speeches apply to giving speeches on television. Dress for the occasion. Plan to wear medium or neutral colors, such as blues, grays, and browns. Avoid bright colors and multiple pieces of jewelry. Television professionals advise that both men and women use a light covering of a medium makeup

to cut the glare of natural skin oils and to lighten shadows under the eyes or around cheekbones.

Another consideration is movement. If there is not a live audience in the room with you, look directly at the camera throughout the speech as you would an audience in the room. If there is both an audience and a camera, treat the camera as just another member of the audience, glancing at it only as often as you would at any other individual as you scan the entire audience during your speech. Stand erect as you speak, and exaggerate your gestures slightly more than you normally would so that every move is captured on camera. Still, the key to effective delivery on television is to be natural.[1]

1. Adapted from J. Vesper and V. R. Ruggiero, *Contemporary Business Communication* (New York: HarperCollins, 1993).

and move back out of the way. And again, when you get to a point of frequent or intense gesturing, put the cards back on the podium or table.

Finally, it is necessary to mention a couple of possible drawbacks to extemporaneous delivery. Because of its flexibility, it is easy to get off track when speaking in this method. Because you are not speaking from specifically written or memorized text, you may become repetitive and wordy. Fresh examples or points may come to mind that you want to share, so the speech may take longer than you anticipated. Occasionally, even a glance at key words will fail to jog your memory about a point you wanted to cover, and you momentarily find yourself searching for what to say next. But these simple and common blemishes are insignificant in comparison to the overall greater quality of delivery the method provides when you are well prepared.

PRACTICING THE DELIVERY

Practice is vital to effective delivery. The more you practice, the greater your comfort level will be when you actually deliver the speech. More than anything, it is uncertainty that breeds anxiety. By practicing your speech, you will know what to expect when you actually stand in front of an audience.

You will be comfortable with the sound of your own voice and gestures. You will be confident that you can correctly pronounce difficult words. You will have a good sense of how your volume, pitch, rate, and pauses will vary from one section of the speech to another. In other words, you will know what you are getting into.

Focus on the Message

The purpose of your speech is to get a message across, not to display your talent as a speaker. Therefore, clarity of your message should be the primary concern in your planning of a speech. But clarity is affected by delivery, so once you have the content down the way you want to present it, you'll need to concentrate on delivery—how you present the message.

Some practitioners and speech teachers recommend practicing speeches in front of a mirror. This is not a good idea. Looking at yourself in the mirror as you try to speak presents a considerable distraction. Rather than worrying about how you look, concentrate on getting your words out as you speak. Imagine there are audience members far across the room, as well as those in the immediate front, who need to hear you. Project your voice and gestures to "reach" them. This may feel awkward at first, but after a few run-throughs of the speech it will become quite natural.

Before you actually practice a stand-up delivery of your speech, talk it out into a tape recorder. This is an effective way to know how the quality of your voice is affecting the clarity of your message. At a later stage in the practice process, you can place the tape recorder across the room from you and practice projecting your voice to the back row of the audience.

Focus on Technology

Videotaping the Delivery

As with audiotaping, videotaping your speech can help you pinpoint problems and practice solutions. If your instructor cannot provide a video camera, you may be able to rent one. Many video stores now rent camcorders. Video playback equipment is easy to operate and allows you to observe any one sequence over and over again in just a few minutes.

Videotape is an excellent way to isolate specific movements that might hinder effective delivery. You can see, for example, whether you spend too much time looking down at your notes rather than at the audience; whether you have your hands in your pockets instead of using them for appropriate gestures; or whether you're standing too long to one side of the speaker's stand, appearing to favor that side of the audience. You can also note your vocal characteristics and pronunciation and articulation.

Before scrutinizing your delivery on camera, wait until you've given at least one, and preferably two, speeches. Why? Seeing yourself on tape focuses your critical attention on how you look instead of on what you're saying. Before you do this, you should gain the experience of speaking in front of the class and presenting a well-planned set of points.

Practice under Realistic Conditions

As closely as possible, try to simulate the actual speech setting as you practice. Ideally, you should practice in an empty classroom. At home, think of your bedroom or living area as a classroom. Standing at one side of the room, picture the audience sitting in front of you. Pick out some objects around the room to look at, just as you'll look at members of your audience. Use a podium of some kind. Stack some boxes to form a makeshift podium if you have to. Practice working with your delivery outline until you are confident that

Making a Difference

BEVERLY DeSMITH, VOLUNTEER AND TELEVISION HOST, SIMSBURY COMMUNITY TELEVISION (SCTV)

When the last of her five boys turned 13, Beverly De-Smith found she finally had some time on her hands. Married when she was just out of college in the 1950s, in the ensuing decades she raised one feisty toddler after another in a whirlwind of laughter, laundry, and skinned limbs. Finally all but the youngest was out of the house, and Beverly decided to embark on yet another career.

Committed to helping her local community of Simsbury, Connecticut, which she had come to treasure over the years, Beverly decided to volunteer with a fledgling community television station called Simsbury Community Television (SCTV). SCTV is one of thousands of public access cable stations nationwide. Its mission, shared by all pubic access stations, is to

serve the community with productions of general interest and to provide information and programming that gives a voice to town residents. Legally, public access stations cannot refuse any resident who wants to voice an opinion on any issues, especially town-related ones. Anyone who takes the trouble to prepare a statement may appear on a public service announcement, or PSA. (PSAs generally run between two and five minutes and often feature opposing viewpoints.) Most public access stations also broadcast town meetings in their entirety, with no editing. The balance of the programming includes talk shows, school events, sports, financial programs, travel tours, and the like.

In the 12 years since Beverly began volunteering for SCTV, she has served as the station's publicist, board member, vice president, and president. She has sat on virtually all the station's committees, from volunteer recruitment to program development. Currently she produces and hosts her own television series called *Take Care*. The programs feature health experts in fields ranging from Lyme disease and diabetes to allergies and alternative medicine.

Volunteering for SCTV has brought Beverly deep satisfaction and taught her many things. Producing *Take Care* has led her to discover many fascinating topics and people, and positive comments from viewers confirm that her efforts are indeed making a difference in the lives of her neighbors. But Beverly's beginnings as a talk show host were shaky. "I shuddered when I watched that first interview," she recalls. "I realized I did not photograph well. My voice level was much too low. I spoke in a monotone. I was so mortified I nearly gave up on the series."

Realizing that there was more to on-camera delivery than just looking at the lens when the red light came on, she conferred with colleagues and studied their delivery. She watched the pros. She borrowed li-you can refer to it without overly relying on it. The point is to have a way to practice placing your outline on a podium and moving around the podium for effective delivery.

At some point you need to practice your speech in front of a live audience. Use your roommates or parents as audience members. Ask them to identify the purpose and key points of your speech. Question them about what they did or did not understand. Question them about the quality of your delivery, and what in particular may have been distracting in the way you presented the message.

---

brary books and even dug out her old college public speaking text. And she learned from hard experience.

On Interviewing

"The cardinal rule in interviewing," Beverly claims, "is to appear interested. Show some interest and, when appropriate, get excited. Have moments where you display animation. If I'm discussing a disease and there is a possible cure on the market, for example, I might say, 'Is it *true* that there is a possible cure on the market?' By adding a lilt to my voice, I generate enthusiasm for my viewers."

Another way to generate interest is to listen intently. "In an interview situation," Beverly notes, "it's sometimes hard to simultaneously listen to the guest, plan what to say next, and not look distracted. The tendency is to think about what you will say next rather than to appear interested in the speaker. But this has a negative effect on both your guest and your audience. The best way to avoid this is to be aware of your facial expressions while listening. I make a conscious effort to smile, for instance. Smiling conveys interest. Of course, you don't want to keep a smile plastered on your face all the time. But an unrelieved serious expression can sometimes make you look like a deadbeat."

On Vocal Delivery

"Over the years I've seen many people appear on camera. Virtually everyone has some problem with their voice. Some guests speak too fast, while others talk very hesitatingly. Some slur their words."

Beverly's own problem is speaking too softly and sometimes veering into a monotone. "I've had to learn to project my voice. I consciously try to be more forceful. Sitting up helps because it raises the diaphragm and lets you bring more air into your lungs.

I also know that I have a tendency to speak in a monotone. This usually occurs about two-thirds of the way through a show."

On Appearing Confident

"You appear confident by knowing your subject. Lack of preparation really comes across. Each program should be pre-planned—from letting your guest know what to expect, to practicing his or her name and title so that you get it right in the introduction. Also remember to practice any strange-sounding medical terms or other jargon that you don't normally pronounce."

On Eye Contact

Just as in speaking in front of a live audience, maintaining eye contact with the camera lens is critical in on-camera delivery. "By looking directly into the camera," Beverly notes, "you are in effect looking directly into the eyes of your unseen viewers. Of course, it is also important to look directly at your guest, especially when asking questions and when listening to replies.

"Try not to read from notes, since doing so kills eye contact. Stick to as brief an outline as you can. Of course, it is perfectly acceptable to read technical information and quotes from notes, as long as you don't overdo it."

"I'm continuously learning and trying out new roles," Beverly concludes. "With each new task I undertake, I become a little bit more adept at presenting myself. It's an ongoing, very satisfying process."

This article does not necessarily represent the views or opinions of Simsbury Community Television, its staff, Board of Directors, or volunteers.

Just how often should you practice? Many expert speakers recommend practicing your speech about six times in its final form. Although this may sound like a lot, six practices of a 5-minute speech—the length of many class speeches—will take only about 30 minutes. Add several more minutes to account for stops, and you're still looking at far less than an hour of practice time. So really, practice of your speech is not the most time-consuming part of the process, but it could well be the most important part.

DOES DELIVERY REALLY MAKE A DIFFERENCE?

Joel Gordon

Practice, practice, practice. Becoming comfortable with your speech helps you work the kinks out of your content and delivery.

The question of whether delivery makes a difference is at least as old as Aristotle. He stressed that speechmaking should concern itself solely with the presentation of facts and the development of arguments, and that the true test of speaking effectiveness would be in the acceptance of the message by its audience. Reluctantly, however, Aristotle recognized that on many occasions the speaker's delivery would make the difference in the effect of a speech. He attributed this reality to "the sorry nature of an audience."[13] Aristotle meant that many audiences would be moved more by the appearance or actions of the person speaking than by the quality of the speech itself.

Minus the negative spin, modern communication research supports Aristotle's belief that appearances matter to audiences—sometimes as much as or more than the speaker's message, at least to a degree.[14] First, delivery does affect attitude change in persuasive speeches. Studies show that better delivery produces more audience attitude change in response to a well-developed message, whereas poor delivery interferes with the outcomes of a strong message. Second, delivery does affect audience comprehension of speeches. Research indicates that better delivery is associated with clearer messages, and poorer delivery with less clear messages. In turn, clearer messages are associated with better comprehension. Hence, better delivery leads to better comprehension of speech content by audiences. Finally, delivery does affect audience perception of speaker ethos (i.e., trustworthiness and character). Studies show that poor delivery leads audiences to discredit the trustworthiness of the speaker, even when the speech is relatively strong.

Yes, delivery does make a difference in speech outcomes. Even if you have very well developed speech content, it is essential that you practice and hone the qualities of effective delivery in order to achieve your intended outcomes of speaking. And remember how Professor Winans put it: "It is quite the natural thing."

Summary Questions

What are the four general qualities of effective delivery?

Today's scholars of public speaking agree that a natural style of delivery is most effective. Effective delivery is natural, enthusiastic, confident, and direct.

What role does nonverbal behavior play in speech delivery?

Speech delivery is the process of conveying through nonverbal behavior and paralanguage the meaning of the spoken message. Through nonverbal behavior the speaker communicates necessary nuances of meaning. And listeners use these same nonverbal signals to clarify their understanding of the speaker's message.

What are the functions of nonverbal behavior in delivery?

Nonverbal behavior (1) clarifies the meaning of verbal messages; (2) facilitates feedback, creating a loop of communication between speaker and audience; (3) helps the speaker establish a relationship with the audience; and (4) helps establish speaker credibility.

What are the elements of vocal delivery?

The elements of vocal delivery include volume, pitch, rate, pauses, and pronunciation and articulation. Volume is the loudness or softness of the speaker's voice. The proper volume for delivering a speech is somewhat louder than that of normal conversation. Just how much louder depends on three factors: (1) size of the room and number of persons in the audience, (2) whether or not you will use a microphone, and (3) level of background noise.

Pitch is the range of sounds from high to low (or vice versa) made by the speaker's voice. Differences in pitch are inflections. Varying your pitch, or using inflections to convey meaning, is a crucial part of effective vocal delivery.

The most effective way to hold an audience's attention, as well as to accurately convey the meaning of your speech, is to vary your speaking rate—how rapidly or slowly you talk. Pauses are important strategic elements of a speech. They enhance meaning by providing a type of punctuation, emphasizing a point, drawing attention to a key thought, or just allowing listeners a moment to contemplate what is being said. Vocal variety involves simply making use of each of these elements so that they work together to create an effective delivery.

The other element of vocal delivery involves correctly saying the words you speak. Few things distract an audience as much as improper pronunciation or unclear articulation of words. Pronunciation is the correct formation of word sounds. Articulation is the clarity or forcefulness with which the sounds are made, regardless of whether they are pronounced correctly.

How does the speaker's body language—face, eye, and body movements—affect the way audiences receive the spoken message?

By our facial expressions, audiences can gauge whether we are excited, disenchanted, or indifferent about our speech, and about the audience to whom we are presenting it. Head, arm, hand, and even leg gestures are often critical in helping to clarify the meanings we try to convey in words.

What are the four methods of delivery described in this chapter?

The four methods of delivering a speech are (1) speaking from manuscript, (2) speaking from memory, (3) speaking impromptu, and (4) speaking extemporaneously. Speakers who deliver a speech from manuscript read the entire speech word for word from a prepared manuscript. Speakers who deliver a speech from memory put the entire speech, word for word, into writing and then memorize it. An impromptu speech is one delivered without prior preparation. Finally, speakers who deliver a speech extemporaneously speak from an outline of key words and phrases. They have prepared well and practiced in advance, giving full attention to all facets of the speech—content, arrangement, and delivery alike.

Why is practicing the delivery so important, and what are some key points to remember when practicing the speech?

Practicing the speech is critical to effective delivery. Practice decreases anxiety and lets you become comfortable with your material. Practice is most effective if you focus on the message, tape-record your speech, and practice under realistic conditions. Practice your speech about six times for maximum effectiveness.

ISSUES FOR DISCUSSION

1. In what ways is a speech like a conversation? What are some differences between conversations and speeches? What implications do these differences have for understanding speaker delivery?

2. Why is enthusiasm important to effective delivery? How can too much enthusiasm be a detriment to a speech?

3. Can you think of other people besides Adolf Hitler and the televangelists mentioned in the Focus on Ethics box (page 255) who were powerful but unethical speakers? What was it about their delivery that was so persuasive to listeners?

4. Can you think of some speakers you've heard whose vocal delivery particularly impressed you? What did you find particularly appealing about the vocal quality? Consider pitch, rate, pauses, articulation, and pronunciation in your answer.

5. Why is eye contact so critical in effective delivery?

6. Because we tend to excuse people's articulation and pronunciation errors in conversations, why should we expect them to be more accurate in public speaking?

7. When selecting clothes to wear for your next speech, should comfort or appropriateness be your first consideration? Why?

SELF-ASSESSMENT

1. Select a favorite passage from a novel, play, poem, or other piece of writing. Read the passage silently to yourself several times, trying to get a sense of what it means. Next, read the passage aloud into an audiocassette recorder. Then listen to yourself reading the passage. Does your voice convey the meaning you think the writer intended? How accurate are your pronunciation and articulation? How would you assess your pitch, rate,

and volume? Is every word clearly audible? Record another reading of the passage, this time trying to improve the way you convey the meaning. Listen again. Now identify your strengths and weaknesses in vocal delivery. How might these help or hinder your delivery of a speech?

2. Try to videotape yourself giving a speech. Perhaps your instructor videotapes class speeches, or perhaps you can have a friend or relative videotape your practice of an upcoming speech assignment. Evaluate your physical delivery in terms of how natural, relaxed, enthusiastic, and direct your nonverbal behavior is. Pay particular attention to your facial behavior and eye contact, gestures and body movement, and your attire and use of objects. Which elements are used effectively, and how? Which elements are potentially distracting, and why? Specify what you could do to overcome the distracting behaviors.

3. Observe yourself in a conversation with one or more friends. Recall how James Albert Winans likened a speech to a conversation. Note the ways in which your part in the conversation sounds and looks like giving a speech. How would you rate the quality of your composure, enthusiasm, and directness in the conversation? In what ways does the conversation feel "natural"? What similarities and differences do you see between your behavior in the conversation and your behavior in giving a speech?

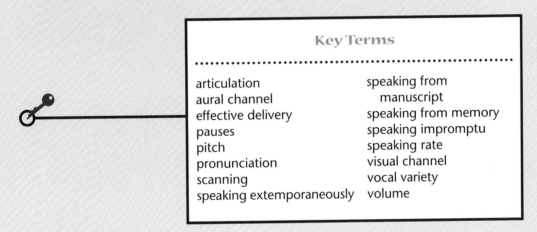

Key Terms

articulation
aural channel
effective delivery
pauses
pitch
pronunciation
scanning
speaking extemporaneously

speaking from manuscript
speaking from memory
speaking impromptu
speaking rate
visual channel
vocal variety
volume

TEAMWORK

1. If you have access to an Internet service, go to a chat room where participants discuss the U.S. president and other national and international leaders. Initiate a discussion of what people like or dislike about the way a selected leader presents him- or herself to the media and the public. Among these likes and dislikes, what might be attributed to the person's delivery? Discuss your findings with a small group of classmates.

2. Discuss the attire worn by your instructors. Is it suitable for the tasks they perform in your classes? Have there been any occasions when you caught yourself thinking about your instructors' clothes instead of attending to their instructions or message? Share the best and worst examples. What implications do differences in clothing have for what you remember about these instructors' communication?

We don't see things as they are, we see them as *we* are.

—Anais Nin

Men are born with two eyes, but only one tongue, in order that they should see twice as much as they say.

—Charles Caleb Colton

12

Preparing and Using Presentation Aids

During the 1992 and 1996 presidential campaigns, did you watch any of Ross Perot's televised "infomercials"? **If so, how did you react to his use of charts and graphs?** If you can't remember watching Perot, can you recall other instances in which speakers effectively used graphics to illustrate their points? **What struck you about the way they used graphics?** What was so helpful about the graphic? Conversely, have you ever sat through a confusing presentation that would have benefited from an effective visual aid? **While preparing your speech you should consider ways to incorporate visual elements that heighten the effectiveness of your message.**

Of all public figures in recent history, it is probably fair to say that former presidential candidate and "United We Stand" Party founder Ross Perot is the undisputed master of the graph and chart. While other candidates spoke only in sound bites, Perot nearly always combined memorable one-liners ("It's time to pick up a shovel and clean out the barn") with striking visual aids. On the campaign trail and in televised appearances, a graph or chart was never far from his side. With pointer firmly in hand and a stack of boldly colored charts at his side, he would expound on the state of the economy, health care, and other weighty issues of the day. "It's just that simple," he would claim as he demonstrated with this red line how the deficit actually worked or with that blue bar why the federal budget was faulty.

Perot's charts and graphs were as crisp and clear and professionally produced as one would expect to see in a top Fortune 500 annual report. Viewers who spent years trying to understand the deficit could now see it explained in a series of simple poster-sized graphics. According to Perot, it was "just that simple."

His critics, of course, countered that things were definitely not as simple as Perot's visuals suggested. They charged that Perot presented information selectively, slanting figures to make his point and leaving out data that did not support his views. But even they had to concede the power of the visual aid as a tool of explanation. People wanted clear explanations, and visual aids were obviously a potent tool for helping to deliver them. In the future, more than a few politicians would remember the lesson—albeit with less zealousness.

For many speakers, putting together presentation aids is one of the more enjoyable challenges of the public speaking process. Here's the chance to unleash your hidden, or not-so-hidden, artistic talents. Drawing, painting, lettering, and reproducing objects to scale are just some of the ways you can use your creativity. If you like working with computers, you can try your hand at computer-generated graphics, or even producing a full-fledged multimedia production. It is important to think about how you can clarify or emphasize your message with effective visual aids.

This chapter explores how presentation aids can enhance a speech. It begins with a discussion of the importance of presentation aids in speaking. Next, it explores numerous presentation aid options that are available to the speaker and how to prepare them. It concludes with a discussion of rehearsing with the aids. Along the way, you'll be challenged to:

- Become familiar with various types of presentation aids and the usefulness of each in conveying specific kinds of information.

- Learn about the different options for displaying presentation aids, from the low-tech chalkboard to the high-tech LCD (liquid crystal diode) display technology.
- Review key guidelines for creating effective presentation aids, such as use of color and typeface.
- Learn how to effectively incorporate the aids into the delivery of your speech.
- Understand the role of rehearsal in successfully using presentation aids in a speech.

UNDERSTANDING THE ROLE OF PRESENTATION AIDS

An old cliché states, "A picture is worth a thousand words." To modernize the cliché we should say: "A picture *plus sound plus motion and other special effects* is worth a thousand words"—that is, of course, when they are used in a context appropriate to the topic, audience, and occasion.

Presentation aids include objects, models, pictures, graphs, charts, video, audio, and multimedia. Each of these elements, used alone and in combination, helps listeners to see relationships among concepts and elements, to store and remember material, and to critically examine key ideas. Just as vivid language adds concreteness to meaning, so do actual visual images and sound. Visual representations reinforce the speaker's message, help listeners process and retain information, add concreteness to ideas and events, organize information clearly and concisely, appeal to listeners' imaginations, enhance an image of professionalism, and reduce speech anxiety. They also save time.

If presentation aids do all this, you may be thinking, why even bother to spend much time on the speech itself? Why not just concentrate on the aids, throwing in a little content here and there? The answer is that the strength of a presentation aid lies in the context in which it is used. No matter how powerful a photograph or chart or video may be, the audience will be less interested in merely gazing at it than in discovering how you will relate it to a specific point. If even superior-quality aids are poorly related to a speech, listeners will be turned off. Thus, presentation aids should be used to *supplement* rather than serve as your ideas. The primary function of a presentation aid is to act as a supplementary source to meaning, and often as a more concrete referent to meaning than the spoken word. In a speech presentation, aids are considered clues to meaning rather than the meaning, or message, itself.

presentation aids
visual or auditory elements, used alone and in combination, that help listeners see relationships among concepts and elements, remember material, and critically examine key ideas.

Presentation Aids Help Listeners Process and Retain Information

Most people process and retain information best when information is presented in more than one format. Research findings indicate that we remember only about 20 percent of what we hear, but over 50 percent of what we see *and* hear.[1] As the old saying goes, "Seeing is believing." Further, we remember about 70 percent of what we see, hear, and actually *do*. Messages that are visually and otherwise reinforced are often more believable than those that are simply verbalized.

Presentation Aids Promote Interest and Motivation

Effective presentation aids draw audiences into a speech and provide stimulation that keeps them interested. They allow listeners to engage the right side of their brains—the hemisphere that plays an important role in such nonverbal tasks as visualization, music, and drawing. As audience members listen to you, they can simultaneously participate in evaluating the information in the aid, thereby becoming actively engaged.

Presentation Aids Save Time

By expressing difficult thoughts and ideas without lengthy explanations, presentation aids save speakers time. This time can be used to communicate other information. For example, a 15- to 30-second video clip can say as much as 10 minutes of verbal explanation.[2] Pictures can vividly describe an object, scene, or event instantaneously. Statistical relationships can be communicated much more efficiently and effectively through graphs and charts than through verbal description. Audience members can quickly see and understand the difference between two elements of a bar graph or the dips and rises on a line graph.

Critical Checkpoint

....

Thinking Visually

Try this experiment. Picture a person, place, or thing with which you are familiar. Think of as many words and phrases that describe it as you can. Next, look at a picture of it. Was your description adequate? How many more ways to describe it occur to you as soon as you see the picture? Chances are that many more will occur because the picture "describes" it much more fully.

Presentation Aids Inform and Persuade

Regardless of your general speech purpose—to inform, persuade, or celebrate a special occasion—some combination of presentation aids can help you accomplish it. This is particularly so with informative and persuasive speeches. As described in Chapters 13 and 14, the general goal of informative speeches is to increase understanding and awareness. This is done through a combination of description, explanation, demonstration, and comparison. Presentation aids can help you in each of these functions. To help explain complex processes, for example, you might break down a procedure into a series of easily followed steps, which you can present in diagram form. Or you may create a flowchart showing product movement through a manufacturing plant from beginning to completion. Any number of pictures, charts, graphs, videos, and so forth will help audience members visualize the process and gain increased understanding and awareness.

Persuasive speakers try to influence the audience's choices through well-reasoned argument. Literally seeing the facts of an argument laid out in front of you can make a significant difference in how you respond to an appeal. When appealing for donations for the homeless, for instance, a photograph that graphically portrays homeless conditions, or a chart that starkly illustrates high rates of homelessness, often speaks more directly to listeners than any verbal pleading a speaker can summon.

Presentation Aids Reduce Speaker Anxiety

As explained in Chapter 2, speaker anxiety most often results from (1) feeling uncomfortable about being the focus of attention, and (2) worrying that you will forget what you are going to say. Presentation aids can help in both areas.

First, presentation aids take the attention off the speaker. As you explain the aid, the audience will focus on it rather than on you, giving you a bit of breathing space. Second, the aid can serve to spark your memory and serve as a form of notes. Third, you can actually use presentation aids to help organize a speech for yourself as well as for the audience. In addition to your speaker's notes, for example, you can create an organizing visual (e.g., an outline of your main points) to help stay on track. Knowing that you have information you need will boost your confidence. If you

Focus on Ethics

Credibility and Presentation Aids

Is it ever possible to look too polished, too slick? Apparently it is. According to noted public speaking expert Ron Hoff, credibility often declines as reliance on audiovisual aids goes up—especially on devices like TelePrompTers, which make viewers wonder if the speaker actually wrote the speech. But even the speaker who doesn't use a TelePrompTer can fall prey to too much of a good thing. This is particularly the case today, when there are so many electronic "toys" to choose from in producing presentation aids. Computer buffs, for example, may become so enamored of generating graphics or creating a jazzy multimedia program that they forget their primary mission is to communicate through the spoken word, and through their physical persons. As Hoff notes, "It's OK to be partially electronic—everybody can use a bit of glitz—but when all votes are counted and all scores are in, the presenter who is most *alive* will carry the day."[1]

Beyond using too many aids, credibility is affected by the appropriateness of the aid to the audience, setting, and occasion. For example, a flip chart is fine as long as everyone in the audience can see it, but not when half the viewers must either strain to see it or give up. Similarly damaging to speaker credibility are poor audio quality; illegible text on charts, graphs, or other exhibits; missing information; and false and misleading information, the use of which is unethical. Cultural considerations are also important. Everything from pictorial symbols to the meaning of different colors may vary crossculturally. To be seen as credible by an international audience, your first task is to ensure that the presentation aid is understood.

Thus, although presentation aids can go far in enhancing your professional image, too much glitz, too little consideration of the appropriateness of the aid, and unclear, incorrect, or misleading information contained within it can do just the opposite.[2]

1. Ron Hoff, *I Can See You Naked*, rev. ed. (Kansas City: Andrews and McMeel, 1992), p. 143.

2. Cheryl Currid, *Make Your Point: The Complete Guide to Successful Business Presentations Using Today's Technology* (Rocklin, CA: Prima Publishing, 1995).

have organized your presentation electronically, you can actually purchase "delivery software" such as Harvard Spotlight. Such software lets you visualize the overall flow of the presentation and time and pace the different parts of your speech.

Presentation Aids Create a Professional Image

Quality visual aids give your presentation a professional feel. They demonstrate that work has gone into the presentation. By giving your listeners the impression that you approach the presentation professionally, you motivate them to approach it in the same way. This increases your credibility, which in turn helps get your message across. Of course, a bad presentation aid can have just the opposite effect, marring an image of professionalism (see the discussion under Types of Presentation Aids for tips on creating effective aids). And as seen in the Focus on Ethics box on page 283, a presentation that is too "slick" can also backfire, damaging credibility.

TYPES OF PRESENTATION AIDS

A number of presentation aids are at your disposal. Some are more complicated to design and use than others. The selection and use of particular types of presentation aids should be based on the speech content, the audience, and the occasion.

Objects

Objects add substance and authenticity to a speaker's descriptions. An **object** can be live or inanimate—a snake or a stone, for instance. Showing the actual subject of your speech (or one of your main points) can solidify your description in the listeners' minds and help them more fully understand your explanations. Seeing an item up close, handling it, and perhaps even smelling it reveal a lot about an object while also saving the speaker's time. And as noted earlier, people remember best that which they see, hear, and do. By actually touching an object, the audience is actively engaged in learning about it.

Models

Sometimes it is impractical to bring objects into the presentation. The object may be too large, too small, too dangerous, or too delicate to be handled and examined. In these cases, a model can be a good substitute. A **model** is a three-dimensional, scale-sized representation of an object.

As with objects, models offer opportunities for tactile learning. They offer a sense of depth, thickness, height, and width that makes it possible to understand concepts and relationships in more concrete ways than any other media format except the actual object itself. Models offer the benefits of actual objects without introducing unnecessary complexity. Suppose, for example, that you were to give a speech on a new kind of car engine and how it compared with a regular engine. Not only would the actual engines be too heavy to haul in, but displaying them might provide your listeners

Dennis Paquin/AP-Wide World

Imagine what that looked like with a face! Some objects really help a speaker get attention.

object
a live or inanimate thing, such as a snake or stone, that illustrates the actual subject of a speech or one of its main points; adds substance and authenticity to descriptions.

model
a three-dimensional, scale-sized representation of an object.

with too much detail to inspect. Rather than listening to what you say, they would spend time gazing at both machines. A model lets you show in detail only the areas you want to talk about, thereby solving this problem.

There are a few drawbacks to models. They can be expensive and time consuming to build or have built. A speaker may also need to plan well in advance for the use of a model in order to have enough time to complete it and integrate it into the presentation. Also, size may limit the use of models in large groups.

Pictures

Can you recall the image of the lone protester standing in the way of a tank during the 1989 protests at Tiananmen Square in China? If so, you probably agree that few verbal descriptions could create as powerful an impact as simply displaying that photographic image. Photographs, drawings, paintings, and other illustrations are all forms of pictures. A **picture** is a two-dimensional representation of persons, places, ideas, or objects produced on an opaque backing. Pictures add detail and shades of meaning that verbal description cannot. They help explain things, events, and processes and help make abstract ideas concrete.

Among the types of pictures commonly used by speakers are photographs, line drawings, diagrams, maps, and posters. A **diagram** (also called a "schematic drawing") explains how something works or how it is constructed or operated. Diagrams are best used to simplify and clarify complicated procedures, explanations, and operations. They are the aid of choice when you need to explain how to construct and/or use something. Figure 12.1 is a diagram showing how to assemble monitor stand cables for a computer.

A **map** is a representation on a flat surface of a whole or a part of an area.[3] Maps help audience members visualize geographic areas and illustrate various relationships between them. At the simplest level, maps illustrate the layout of a geographic region. Thus, if your speech is about becoming familiar with college, you could incorporate a map of a college campus into your talk (see Figure 12.2).

Maps are also an excellent way to illustrate the proportion of one thing to something else in different areas of a region. You could create a map to illustrate the proportion of manufacturing plants to distribution centers, for example, or distribution centers to retailers, and so forth. If your speech is about the disappearance of forests in the United States, you could create a map indicating how many forests are left in each state. Similarly, as seen in Figure 12.3, for a speech on finding a suitable Ph.D. program in communications in a certain region of the country, you could create a map illustrating the number of Ph.D.-granting institutions in that region.

A **poster** is a large, bold, two-dimensional design incorporating words, shapes, and color placed on an opaque backing. Posters are used to convey a brief message or point forcefully and attractively. They make good choices for introducing topics or concepts early in the introductory part of a presentation, or later when simple concepts need to be introduced. Posters are economical and easy to use; they are good choices for speakers who give the same presentation many times. Posters of good quality can be produced inexpensively on poster board. They require little in the way of equipment beyond a ruler and colored markers. They convey simple information and

picture
a two-dimensional representation, such as a photograph or drawing, of persons, places, ideas, or objects.

diagram
a picture, or schematic drawing, that explains how something works, is constructed, or is operated.

map
a representation on a flat surface of a whole or a part of an area.

poster
a large, bold, two-dimensional design incorporating words, shapes, and color placed on an opaque backing.

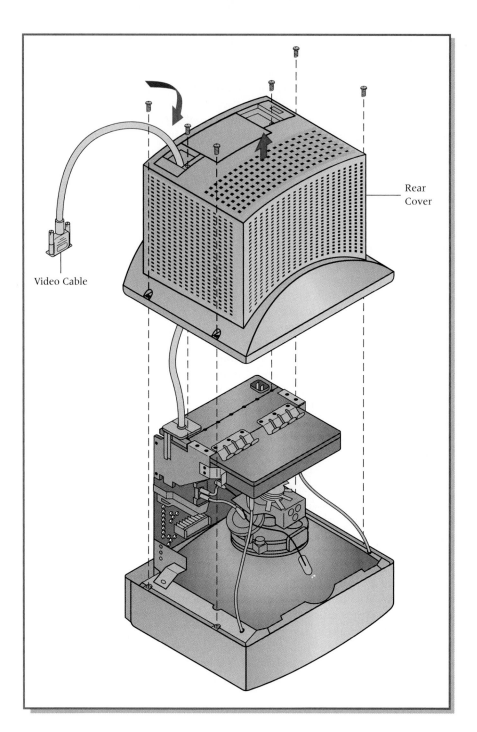

Rear
Cover

Video Cable

FIGURE 12.1
Diagram or Schematic Drawing of
Monitor Stand Cables

concepts succinctly and efficiently. They are also easily portable and can be used repeatedly. They do not require any equipment to use, so they can be used in a variety of settings. Easels are useful if you have several posters to show one at a time, and chalkboard railings can hold posters as well.

As a two-dimensional medium, posters have many of the same inherent limitations as other kinds of pictures. That is, they lack depth and motion, and they cannot communicate complicated aspects of a concept. In addition,

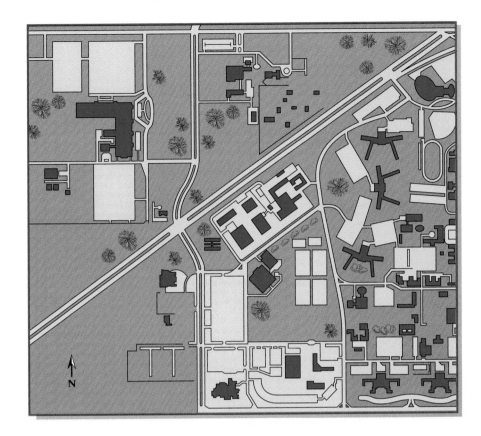

FIGURE 12.2
Map of College Campus

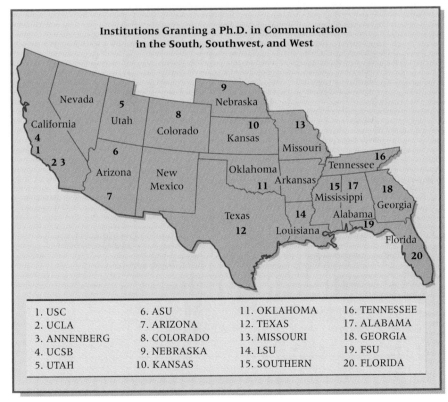

FIGURE 12.3

Map Illustrating Number of
Universities in the South,
Southwest, and West Granting a
Ph.D in Communications

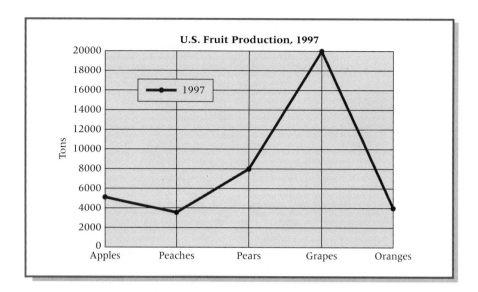

FIGURE 12.4
Line Graph of U.S. Fruit Production, 1997

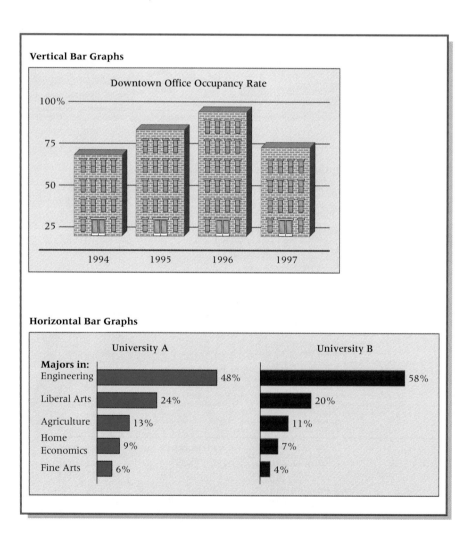

FIGURE 12.5
Bar Graphs of Quantities and Magnitudes

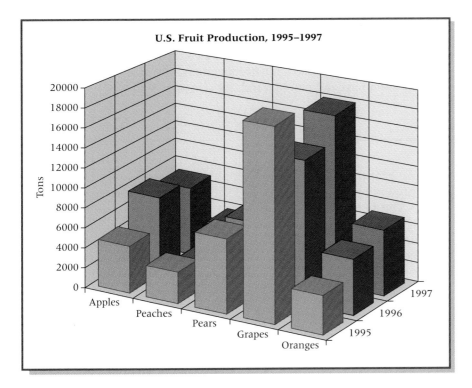

U.S. Fruit Production, 1995–1997

FIGURE 12.6
Multidimensional Bar Graphs of U.S. Fruit Production, 1995–1997

because they should not look overcrowded, posters can convey only very limited information. Overall, posters are a simple medium that should be used for simple concepts.

Graphs

A **graph** represents numerical data in visual form. Graphs are useful tools in a speech because they neatly illustrate relationships among components or units and demonstrate trends. Four major types of graphs are: line graphs, bar graphs, pie graphs, and pictograms.

A **line graph** displays one measurement, usually plotted on the horizontal axis, and units of measurement or values, plotted on the vertical axis. Each value or point is connected with a line. Line graphs are especially useful in representing information that changes over time, such as trends. For example, Figure 12.4, represents fluctuations in fruit production for a one-year period. Line graphs remain a favorite among most presenters and listeners because they simplify complex information and are easier to read than more complicated tables and charts of data.

A **bar graph** shows bars of varying lengths to compare quantities or magnitudes. The main parts of a bar graph are the bars and the grid on which the bars are placed. As seen in Figure 12.5, bars may be arranged either vertically or horizontally.

Speakers sometimes use *multidimensional bar graphs,* or bar graphs distinguished by differing colors or markings, when they need to compare two or more different kinds of information or quantities in one chart. Although multidimensional bar graphs are visually appealing, they are somewhat

graph
a representation of numerical data in visual form.

line graph
contains one factor, usually plotted on the horizontal axis, and units of measurement or values, plotted on the vertical axis.

bar graph
shows bars of varying lengths to compare quantities or magnitudes.

more difficult to read than vertical or horizontal bar graphs. When using a multidimensional bar graph, do not compare more than three kinds of information or the audience is likely to become confused. Multidimensional bar graphs are best presented to audience members who thoroughly understand your topic and have monitored trends for several years.

A **pie graph** depicts the division of a whole. In this type of graph, the pie, representing 100 percent, is divided into portions or segments called "slices." The slices are sized according to their relationship with the whole pie and other slices. As illustrated in Figure 12.7, each slice constitutes a percentage of the whole.

Select a pie graph when you want to highlight how much of the whole each portion represents. When creating the graph, restrict the number of pie slices to seven; begin slicing the pie at the 12 o'clock position and then move clockwise. This results in an organized-looking graph. You should also identify the values or percentages of each slice. In addition, consider using color or background markings to distinguish the different slices of the pie.

A **pictogram** shows comparisons in picture form. The pictures represent numerical units and are drawn to relate to the items being compared. Figure 12.8 is a pictogram that demonstrates an increase in college students. When you construct a pictogram, make sure that you follow these three rules: (1) select only pictures that clearly relate to the topic; (2) make sure that all pictures are of equal size; and (3) make certain that your pictorial representation will be understood by a broad spectrum of viewers, including those from other cultures. In Figure 12.8, a pictogram, the pictures are drawn to resemble students. The meaning of the pictogram is immediately clear to the audience members because it clearly shows the increase in students over time. Furthermore, if you look closely at the drawings you will note that each student is identical in size and shape to all other students in the graph. Picture equality is extremely important

pie graph
depicts the division of a whole.

pictogram
shows comparisons in picture form.

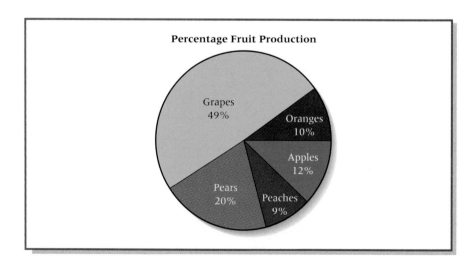

FIGURE 12.7

Pie Graph Showing Percentage Fruit Production

New College Freshmen				
🚶🚶 = 1 million	1970	1980	1990	2000 (projected)
Private Universities	🚶🚶🚶🚶🚶	🚶🚶🚶🚶🚶	🚶🚶🚶🚶🚶	🚶🚶🚶🚶🚶
Public Universities	🚶🚶🚶🚶🚶🚶🚶🚶🚶🚶🚶🚶🚶🚶	🚶🚶🚶🚶🚶🚶🚶🚶🚶🚶🚶	🚶🚶🚶🚶🚶🚶🚶🚶🚶🚶🚶🚶🚶	🚶🚶🚶🚶🚶🚶🚶🚶🚶🚶🚶🚶🚶🚶🚶🚶🚶🚶🚶🚶🚶🚶🚶🚶🚶🚶

FIGURE 12.8
Pictogram Showing Increase in College Students

because the human eye does not function well when comparing numerous pictures that differ in more than one dimension.

Charts

A **chart** visually organizes complex information into compact form. Several different types of charts are helpful for speakers: flowcharts; organization charts; and tabular charts, or tables.

A **flowchart** is a diagram that shows step-by-step progression through a procedure, relationship, or process. Usually the flow of a procedure or process is drawn horizontally or vertically and describes how key components fit into a whole. To show the sequence of activities or the directional flow in a process, the flowchart is the visual aid of choice (see Figure 12.9).

chart
visually organizes complex information into compact form.

flowchart
shows step-by-step progression through a procedure, relationship, or process.

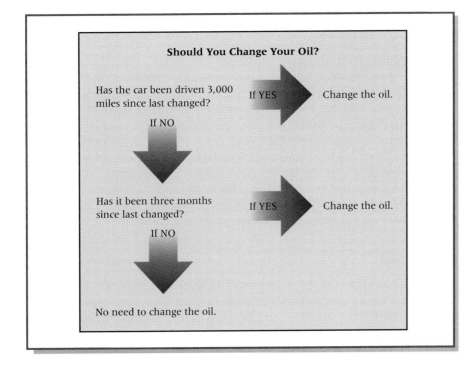

FIGURE 12.9
Flowchart Showing Oil-Changing Decision Process

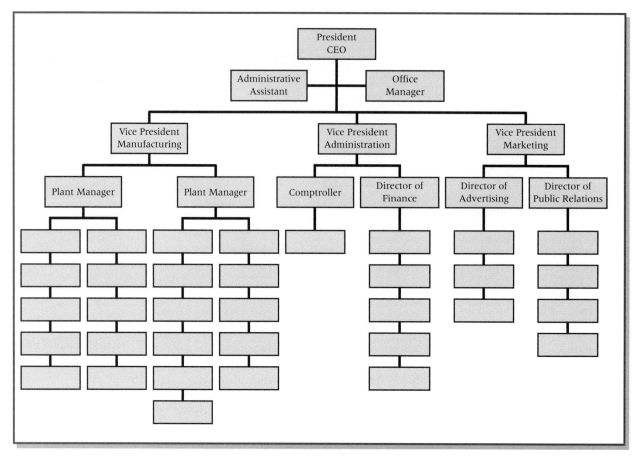

FIGURE 12.10
Organizational Chart Showing Personnel Hierarchy

 organizational chart
illustrates the organizational structure or chain of command in an organization.

 table
a systematic grouping of data or numerical information in column form.

An **organizational chart** illustrates the organizational structure or chain of command in an organization. It shows the interrelationship of the different positions, divisions, departments, and personnel. Figure 12.10 shows an organizational chart for a hypothetical organization.

A tabular chart, or **table**, is a systematic grouping of data or numerical information in column form. Tables are not truly graphic, because they are not really pictures. However, even if they lack visual appeal, they often present valuable data that the viewer can examine quickly and make comparisons about easily. For example, the table in Figure 12.11 allows the viewer to compare fruit production over a three-year period. Table 12.1 summarizes the best uses of different types of graphs and charts.

Audio Aids

 audio clip
a short recording of sounds, music, and/or speech.

An **audio clip** is a short recording of sounds, music, and/or speech. Introducing sound into a speech can add interest, illustrate ideas, and even bring humor to the mix. The authors of this text recently heard a public radio essay in which the speaker, whose subject was infertility, used a short audio clip from a *Jerry Seinfeld* segment to illustrate the lengths to which

U.S. Fruit Production in Tons, 1995–1997

Type of Fruit	Year 1995	1996	1997
Apples	5000	8000	7000
Peaches	3450	2000	3800
Pears	8000	7600	6500
Grapes	20,000	15,000	18,000
Oranges	4125	6000	7000

FIGURE 12.11

Table Showing U.S. Fruit Production in Tons, 1995–1997

Table 12.1 Best Use of Different Types of Graphs and Charts

Type of Graph or Chart	Best Use
Line graph	To represent trends or information that changes over time
Bar and column graph	To compare individual points of information, magnitudes
Pie graph	To show proportions such as sales by region, shares
Pictogram	To show comparisons in picture form
Flowchart	To diagram processes
Organizational chart	To show reporting relationships in a hierarchy
Table	To show large amounts of information in easily viewable form

people go to become fertile. In the clip, one of the characters tells Jerry that his doctor advised him to wear boxers instead of jockey shorts to keep the genitals from getting too warm. The interchange was brief but hilarious, and it reinforced an important point in the oral essay.

Many topics can benefit from audio clips. For a speech on different styles of speech delivery, you might use short audio clips of various speakers. If your theme is different styles of musical composition, you might include several representative clips. One important note: Always check to see whether the material you are using is copyrighted. If it is, make sure that your use is acceptable according to copyright laws and the specific dictates of copyrighted material.

Audio is an easy-to-use and inexpensive medium. Audio playback equipment is compact, portable, and accessible, and tape recorders are simple to operate. When using audio clips, make sure to cue the tape before your presentation. This way, you can segue smoothly into the clip without wasting valuable time trying to find where it begins. Remember, too, to tell the audience what they should listen for (so that no one misses the point of the clip) and to discuss its significance afterwards.

Video

video
visual and audio medium that combines sight, sound, and movement to illustrate speech concepts.

Video—including movie, television, and other recording segments—can be a powerful presentation aid that combines sight, sound, and movement to illustrate key speech concepts. As mentioned previously, a 15- to 30-second video clip can say as much as 10 minutes of verbal explanation.[4] Short videos that are whole may also be used, as in the case of training videos shown in many professional settings. Because most facilities that regularly host presentations own video equipment as part of their in-house supplies, and because the equipment is relatively simple to operate, video is generally a safe choice as a presentation aid. Tapes are reusable, making the medium durable and cost effective.

As with audiotapes, be sure to cue the tape to the appropriate segment *before the presentation*. Fumbling for the right spot during your speech is a sure way to lose credibility and attention. And as with other visual aids, alert the audience members to what they will be viewing before you show the tape, and reiterate its main points once it is over. As with audio material, always check to see whether the video material you are using is copyrighted and that you are using it in a manner consistent with copyright laws.

Multimedia

multimedia
combines several media (voice, video, text, and data) into a single production.

Multimedia combines several media (voice, video, text, and data) into a single production. Today multimedia is the presentation aid of choice in the business world. At the forefront of innovation are such companies as Microsoft and Apple Computer, which routinely announce new product lines with extravagant multimedia productions.

The idea behind multimedia is that the more senses you evoke, the more memorable the event will be. Studies confirm that the visual and auditory reinforcement of multimedia helps people learn and master information more quickly than by conventional means.[5] But even though it's an increasingly popular option, multimedia does require more planning than other forms of presentation aids. It is also more time consuming. Piecing together video, sound, and still images can take hours of work. To produce multimedia, you must have a high-powered computer capable of handling sound and video. You will also need to become familiar with *presentation graphics programs* such as PowerPoint, Persuasion, Freelance Graphics, Charisma, or Compel. With these programs you can create graphs and charts, import still and moving pictures, and dub in sound. Other programs you might add to the mix include high-powered drawing and paint programs, clip art programs, and video and sound-mixing programs.

Some students even use the Internet and the World Wide Web during their presentations if the classroom is appropriately connected. Although accessing the Internet can be visually powerful, there are some potential pitfalls. Considering how quickly Web pages become outdated or even

Presentation Software

Today's presentation software programs come equipped with everything you need to create a professional-looking presentation: outlining, drawing, graphing, the ability to import text, clip art, and so on. The most important feature of a presentation program is the *template*. This feature is a guideline with fonts, colors, and backgrounds already set up. If you want to produce a slide or overhead transparency, for example, but aren't particularly confident about your abilities as a designer, you can simply choose from among the many pre-designed templates included in the program.

Presentation software programs such as Microsoft's PowerPoint allow you to create graphs and charts, slides, overhead transparencies, hand-

outs, and speaker's notes. You can delve into the ClipArt Gallery, find an image that you like, and import it into anything you generate. The Slide Master function allows you to insert text and visuals of all sorts into slide form and then present them in an electronic slide show. Each slide in a presentation has an accompanying note page in which you can jot down ideas about the slide to discuss with the audience. At the same time, you can create speaker's notes and handouts.

Most presentation software programs are easy to learn and are available from the campus computer center. Each has advantages and disadvantages that you can learn about from friends, magazines, and computer specialists.

disappear overnight, you need to make sure that the page will exist when you want to access it during your presentation. Also remember that at times access to the Internet is very slow or a particular site may be too busy for you to connect. This may disrupt your presentation and leave you with a lot of time to fill. One way to avoid both problems is to download Web pages onto your own computer before the presentation so you can access them without actually being live on the Internet.

As seen in the Focus on Technology box above, presentation software is useful not only for multimedia but for preparing handouts, creating slides and overhead transparencies, and organizing speaker's notes.

Handouts

No discussion of presentation aids would be complete without a discussion of the **handout**—page-size items that convey information that is either (1) impractical to give to the audience in another manner, or (2) intended to be kept by audience members after the presentation. Handouts can effectively and cost-efficiently convey large amounts of information to an audience, because elements may be included that are not covered in depth during the actual presentation. Handouts may include other information that audience members examine and use after the presentation. It is important to remember, however, when using handouts with extra information to briefly describe to the audience what it encompasses. Otherwise, listeners will wonder what is in the handout. With this precaution, a handout can be a good way to get information to the audience that can be

handout
page-size items conveying information that is impractical to give in another manner or is kept by listeners after the presentation.

addressed individually by listeners after the presentation. Handouts can also be used when it is best to have audience members follow along with you while going over information. This ensures that all listeners will be able to see the information.

In general, handouts should be used only in the cases described above, because they may be sources of distraction to an audience. After all, audience members will naturally want to look at any item you pass out, and you may end up competing with your own handout for their attention. Don't pass out something that will not be covered in the presentation; stick to handouts that primarily contain information you will be addressing. Also, pass them out only when you are ready to talk about them. This keeps the audience from becoming distracted by the handout and helps you focus their attention on the concept the handout covers. However, be aware that when the audience is large, passing things out during the presentation may take away valuable presentation time. Finally, remember that having too many handouts may undercut their effectiveness. Sifting through pages and pages of information may become tiresome for audience members, who may decide it is not worth the trouble and lose interest.

OPTIONS FOR DISPLAYING THE PRESENTATION AID

Now that you've learned about the different kinds of presentation aids, or ways of presenting information, consider the various ways you can display them. The varieties of presentation media include chalkboards, flip charts, overhead projection, slides, and computer projection and display technology.

Chalkboards

chalkboard
a board on which to write with chalk or another type of marker.

A **chalkboard** is just what it sounds like—a black (or white or blue or green) board upon which you can write with chalk, or with a marker if the board is the chalkless type. If you present your speech in a classroom, auditorium, or other type of hall, chalkboards are usually part of the backdrop. Just as teachers use chalkboards to illustrate points, so can you, the speaker.

In general, try to reserve the chalkboard for simple explanations. You might, for example, use a chalkboard to demonstrate the spelling of words or to draw a simple map. Chalkboards are also helpful in presenting processes that are done in steps, as long as they are simple processes. These may be sketched on the board step by step, keeping the audience's attention focused on each step as it unfolds. Chalkboards are also excellent for impromptu explanations, as when someone asks a question for which you do not have a visual aid but feel you can clarify with words or drawings.

Try to keep it simple. Elaborate presentation aids should be prepared before the presentation. Because everything must be drawn or written by hand, complicated designs may be difficult or impossible to render on the chalkboard. Handwriting may be sloppy or otherwise hard to read. Moreover, the processes of writing or drawing reduce contact between the presenter and the audience, since the presenter's back is turned to the audience while working on the board. If a great deal of writing or drawing is done, audience members may become distracted or bored as they wait for the visual aid to be completed. Finally, chalkboard presentation aids are single-use items. Material on a chalkboard cannot be saved and used again in other presentations.

Flip Charts

A **flip chart** is simply a large (27″ × 34″) pad of paper on which to draw visual aids. Many such aids are prepared in advance, although you can also write and draw on the paper as you speak. As you progress through the speech, you simply flip through the pad to the next exhibit. The flip chart is one of the most inexpensive ways of creating aids. In terms of equipment, a ruler and colored markers are all that are required. To compete with other kinds of aids, however, you do need some artistic skill so that your images aren't sloppy and awkward.

flip chart
a large pad of paper on which to draw visual aids.

Slides

A **slide** is an image that has been photographed, drawn, or otherwise reproduced on a transparent film mounted in a frame and projected onto a screen or wall for viewing. Slides offer clear, precise images in vivid color. This can be useful for presentations that require precise, detailed two-dimensional images. Slides are either inserted into a carousel projector and shown one at a time (or two or three at a time if you use multiple projectors), or transmitted by a computer via a cable onto a screening device (see subsequent discussion on Computer Projection and Display Technology). Slides may be ordered in any way the speaker desires and shown for as long as the speaker wants. They can also be accompanied by audio or other media.

On the downside, slides must be shown in a darkened room, which prevents eye contact between speaker and audience. They also entail some time and expense. Unless you buy film specifically to create the slides, they are usually made from film negatives. In either event, unless you create the slides by computer, the images must be shot and developed. If a carousel projector is used, they must be arranged in the proper order and placed in the carousel. Computer-based slide sorters, now a feature of most presentation graphics packages, allow you to produce slides in your computer, view them side by side, and rearrange them simply by pointing and clicking on a mouse. (If you are arranging slides the old-fashioned way, remember to project them in advance to make sure they project well and are placed right side up. Slides that are upside down can be an embarrassment and interrupt the pace of a presentation.)

slide
an image reproduced on transparent film mounted in a frame and projected onto a screen or wall for viewing.

Overhead Transparencies

An **overhead transparency** is an image on a transparent background that can be viewed by transmitted light, either directly or through projection onto a screen or wall. The images may be written or printed directly onto the transparency. If it is handwritten during the presentation, the transparency can be used much like a chalkboard. Parts of the transparency

overhead transparency
an image on a transparent background that can be viewed by transmitted light.

may be covered with opaque paper and revealed progressively during the presentation. Alternatively, transparencies may be overlaid on each other so that successive details can be added. Objects may also be placed on the stage of the projector to project silhouettes.

Because they have several distinct advantages, transparencies are one of the most common presentation media. First, most facilities that host presentations have overhead projectors. Second, transparencies are inexpensive and overhead projectors are portable and simple to operate. Third, overhead projection is flexible. Material may be added to or taken away from the projector during the presentation, making the overhead a good choice for presentations that need many visual aids. Fourth, projection allows you to interact with the audience easily. Unlike writing on a chalkboard or handing out other visual aids, overhead projection allows you to face the audience while using it. You can check the visibility of a transparency by placing it on the floor. If you can clearly see the image, it is very likely that it will illuminate well. The room does not have to be completely dark, as in showing a video. When you point out an item on the transparency, the image of the pointer will be projected onto the screen, enabling the audience to follow along as you explain.

Transparencies that are poorly produced may appear sloppy and distract the audience. A print of a quarter-inch or more is usually required. Moreover, the widespread use of transparencies may lead to overreliance on the overhead. Be careful not to use the overhead when a more appropriate medium is available. Not everything fits within the limitations of a transparency.

Computer Projection and Display Technology

Even though slides, overhead projectors, and big-screen televisions have advantages, none lets you customize your presentations the way that LCD panels/projectors and video projectors do. With each of these projection and display devices, a computer serves as the source of the information or image (e.g., tables, charts, graphs, figures, photos,) and the projection technology enlarges and displays the image on a large screen that everyone in the room can easily see.

Joel Gordon

Video projectors, LCD panels, and LCD projectors help bring speeches to life for large audiences and can be used to create memorable multimedia presentations.

LCD panel
a device connected to a computer and placed on top of an overhead projector that allows a speaker to project what is on the computer screen.

LCD projector
a device with its own light source that allows a speaker to project what is on a computer screen.

LCD Panel/Projector. LCD stands for liquid crystal diode. LCD display technology is now widespread and can be found in laptop computer screens, digital watches, and countless other digitized products. Projection devices that use LCD technology for displaying information come in two forms. The **LCD panel**, which connects to a computer, is a square, thin box that sits on top of an overhead projector. In the middle of the box is a screen on which images appear. The computer sends what is on its screen to the LCD panel, and the image appears on its screen. The overhead projector provides the illumination necessary to project the image to a wall or projection screen. An **LCD projector** carries an illumination or light source in its own case, eliminating the need for an overhead projector. LCD panels are less expensive and more portable than LCD projectors, and as such they remain the more popular projection device. However, if you take your presentation on the road, you can never be sure of the quality of the overhead projector that will be provided for you. LCD panels require over-head projectors with a very bright projection light; if the meeting room in which you will be presenting has a poor-quality projector, the projected image may be compromised. LCD projectors are favored when the speaker wants a stand-alone device without the worry of hassling with an overhead projector.

Video Projector. When your presentation requires high resolution, crisp color, and a large projected image, the **video projector** offers an attractive alternative. Used most often in large meeting rooms or auditoriums, video projectors, like LCD panels/projectors, connect to a computer and project an image as large as 25 feet long. Video projectors display a sharp, large image through three lenses (red, green, blue). The downside of video pro-jectors is their expense—two to three times more costly than LCD technol-ogy—and their size and weight. Video projectors weigh from 80 to 100 pounds, rendering them a very limited portable device. Video projectors usually remain at a fixed site.

> **video projector**
> a device connected to a com-puter that displays large, sharp images through three lenses.

PREPARING PRESENTATION AIDS

Once you have selected the types of presentation aid you will use and decided on the method of displaying it, you can begin design and construc-tion. Many options are available, ranging from pen and paper to the com-puter. Today the computer is by far the most popular choice for generating drawings, charts, graphs, maps, and other graphics. Presentation software programs such as PowerPoint, Aldus Persuasion, and Harvard Graphics allow you to import data from other programs. Some programs attempt to make the computer resemble a drawing studio. They contain a number of different drawing and painting options as well as millions of colors to choose from. All that's needed is a laser or color printer to print out the graphic.

The first step in creating a presentation aid is to establish the need for one. Once your speech is complete, carefully read through it to identify places where an aid would help clarify your ideas. Look for relationships, processes, key points, and conclusions that call out for an aid. The following sections present general principles to keep in mind once you're ready to actually construct the aid.

Simplicity and Continuity

Presentation aids should be as simple and uncomplicated as possible. Less is best. Concentrate on presenting one major idea per aid. To help maintain continuity, carry through any key design elements—colors, fonts, upper- and lower-case letters, styling (boldface, underlines, italics)—throughout each aid. Follow the same general page layout throughout, placing repeating elements such as titles in the same place and in the same typeface. If you select a certain color background for one aid, use that same background for all the aids. Remember to carry through the same symbols as well, be they colors or pictograms or logos of one sort or another. For example, if you prepare an aid comparing the computer buying habits of men and women, and you've illustrated the purchase habits of men in red and those of women in green, follow through with these colors in subsequent aids.

Color

Color stimulates. It helps listeners see comparisons, contrasts, and emphases. Color can draw attention to key points and set a mood. But although it has many useful properties, color must be used wisely. Colors evoke distinct associations in people, so care must be taken not to summon a meaning, or even a mood, you don't intend. In the United States, for example, we associate certain colors with particular holidays: orange and black with Halloween, and red and green with Christmas, for instance. Unless you specifically want to remind your audience of these holidays, it's best to steer clear of these combinations. Color associations also vary cross-culturally. In China the color of mourning is white, not black.[6] Universally, red evokes associations with blood and fire. In some cultures it also indicates debt.

The following brief guidelines can help you effectively incorporate color into your presentation aids:

- Use bold, bright colors to emphasize important points. For instance, speakers often use bright yellow to draw attention to important points. Warm colors such as yellow, red, and orange move to the foreground of a field. Thus, they are good colors to use when you want to highlight something.
- Use softer, lighter colors to de-emphasize less important areas of a presentation.
- Keep the background color of your aid constant, whether you are using one or a series of aids. As a general rule, the best background colors are lighter, more neutral colors such as tan, blue, green, or white. For typeface and graphics, use colors that contrast rather than clash with the background color.
- Limit the number of colors you use. Two or three are sufficient for simple presentation aids; more color choices can be used in complex and detailed aids.
- Be aware that many presentation software packages provide templates in which the color is preselected.

Integrating Text and Graphics

typeface
a specific style of lettering.

fonts
different sizes of typefaces.

As one professional presenter notes, "for the painter, there is the paintbrush; for the presenter, there is typeface."[7] A **typeface** is a specific style of lettering, such as Palatino, Times Roman, or Courier. As you probably know from using word processing programs, typefaces come in a variety of **fonts**, or sets of sizes (called the "point size") and upper and lower cases. In Microsoft Word, for example, you can select from about 27 typefaces and 16 font sizes—from 8 to 72.

- Here is Palatino typeface in size 8 font.

- Here is Palatino in size 12 font.
- Here is Courier typeface in size 14 font.

There are thousands of typefaces beyond those found in word processing programs, many of which you can purchase in separate software packages. Designers keep creating them because type is so expressive. For example, some typefaces, such as **Helvetica**, suggest "plain and unadorned." Others, such as **Cheltenham**, carry more mysterious overtones. You probably know this aspect of type intuitively from years of selecting typefaces to write school papers.

Although it is beyond the scope of this text to explore the intricacies of type, following are a few key points when using type in your presentations:

- Most text for on-screen projection should be a minimum of 24 points or larger. Titles should be 36 points or larger.
- As a rule, the further away your audience sits from your aid, the larger the point size should be. Table 12.2 offers some useful guidelines.
- Don't overuse boldface, italics, and underlining. Use them sparingly to call attention to important items.
- Minimize the amount of words you use on each presentation aid. A maximum of six words per line and six lines per presentation aid is sufficient.
- Spacing between lines should be 1½ times the word height.
- When constructing titles, use concise words, preferably ones that promote the key terms found in your spoken text. Your heading should always tell viewers what to look for in a chart.

Proofreading for Errors and Design Flaws

It is essential to proofread presentation aids to correct errors or design flaws. Incorrect spellings, errors in computations, and missing letters will be quickly spotted by your listeners, and your credibility will suffer. Make sure that the aids are not inaccurately plotted or labeled, and that you have not miscopied information onto them. Proof all your figures.

Additionally, check to see that you have designed your aid effectively. Are the proportions correct? For example, varying width in bar graphs,

Table 12.2 Room Sizes and Corresponding Font Sizes for Presentation Aids		
Room Size	Text Font Size	Title Font Size
Small conference room for 8 to 12 people	24 point	36 point
Mid-sized conference room for 12 to 40 people	28 point	40 point
Large room for over 40 people	34 point	44 point

Source: Cheryl Currid, Make Your Point: The Complete Guide to Successful Business Presentations Using Today's Technology *(Rocklin, CA: Prima Publishing, 1995), p. 68.*

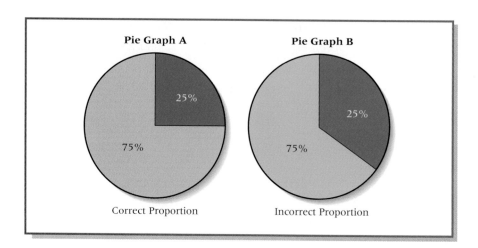

FIGURE 12.12
Proportions and Percentages

incorrectly drawn pie graphs, or uneven sizes of images in a pictogram can be misleading to readers. Beginning the reference point of a line graph or bar graph at a point other than zero, or using inconsistent values between grids or lines, will also distort the information. As seen in Figure 12.12, if you aren't careful to draw pie pieces in correct proportion to the whole pie, misrepresentation can occur. The proportion in Pie Graph B looks larger than the proportion in Pie Graph A. In actuality, the proportion in Pie Graph B consumes more than 25 percent of the whole pie.

Critical Checkpoint

....

Keeping an Eye on Design

Now that you're thinking about design, as you walk around campus, drive around town, or read and watch television, look at billboards, ads, and other designs. Notice foreground and background colors, types of fonts, and general design layout. What catches your eye? What do you particularly like? Jot down some of the things that appeal to you most so that you can make use of them when you put together your next presentation. As always, be sure that the style of the layout you select is consistent with the topic and purpose of your speech, as well as with the occasion for which you are speaking.

USING PRESENTATION AIDS IN YOUR SPEECH

Selecting the appropriate kind of aid and properly preparing it are extremely important to its overall effectiveness. Even more critical is how you actually integrate the aid into your speech. Even a well-designed visual aid can fall flat or undercut the effectiveness of a presentation if it is used improperly. Several factors are particularly important to consider when using presentation aids. These include placement, interpretation, and timing and sequence.

Placement

Placement involves making certain that the audience can see and hear your aids, and that you can access them easily without interrupting the flow of your speech. Obviously, presentation aids are most effective when placed where all audience members can get a full view of them. They should be positioned to maximize the viewing potential. Similarly, if you are using an audio aid, place the playback equipment where everyone can hear it.

Situate all aids so that they do not interrupt the rhythm of your presentation. Make sure that you can easily access the equipment you need—projectors, screens, electrical outlets, and so on. If your aid is two-dimensional, set it up before starting. Cover it to avoid distracting the audience before you are ready to display it. If the aid requires equipment, place it within reach and turn it off, to avoid distraction. This way, you will avoid creating "dead time" as you walk to the equipment or set something up, and in the process lose the audience's attention.

Interpretation

As you display the presentation aid, remember to interpret and explain it to the audience members rather than simply letting them stare at it and figure it out for themselves. Clearly state the point of the aid and provide a brief summary. Ask if everyone can see it clearly and if there are any questions. Consider using the **Point-Pause-Present method (P-P-P)**, a technique that has been shown to help listeners focus their attention: Display and gesture (*point*) to the aid, *pause* briefly to let the audience examine it, and then interpret and explain (*present*) it, always relating it to the ideas in your speech.

Point-Pause-Present method (P-P-P)
a technique used by the speaker to help listeners focus their attention on the visual aid as well as on how it relates to the speech.

Timing and Sequence

Display your aid only when you are about to discuss it. Otherwise, audiences will become distracted if they see something they don't understand. Rather than listening to you, they will try to figure out what the aid is. This makes planning the use of presentation aids very important. You must know exactly at what point in the presentation you will be discussing each item. As seen in Figure 12.13, one sure way to remind yourself of where in your speech an aid will occur is to write annotations in your speaker's outline indicating which portions of the speech are accompanied by aids.

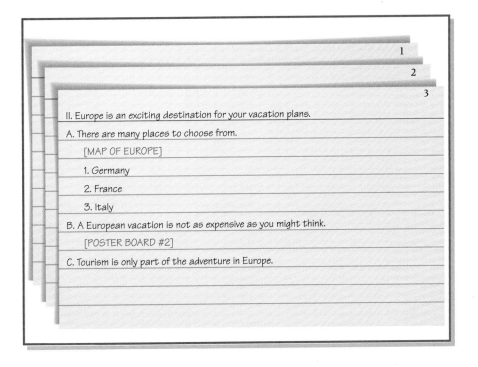

II. Europe is an exciting destination for your vacation plans.

A. There are many places to choose from.

[MAP OF EUROPE]

1. Germany

2. France

3. Italy

B. A European vacation is not as expensive as you might think.

[POSTER BOARD #2]

C. Tourism is only part of the adventure in Europe.

FIGURE 12.13
Speaker's Outline with Annotations

Using Presentation Aids in Your Speech ● 303

PRACTICING WITH THE PRESENTATION AID

Even the best-laid plans can meet with disaster. Unanticipated difficulties with an aid can ruin an otherwise well-thought-out presentation. The safest course is to head off these problems with practice. Whenever possible, investigate the room size, lighting, and seating arrangement in advance of giving the speech. Run through the presentation as it will actually be performed, using the aids exactly as you will in the actual presentation. Decide in advance on the best arrangement for equipment, best sequence for slides, and so forth. Plan on what to say during unavoidable "dead time," such as time spent walking over to an overhead projector.

Anticipate the Unexpected

Have a backup strategy in the event that equipment fails or is suddenly unavailable. Be prepared for malfunctions. VCRs break, projector bulbs burn out, and computers are subject to a host of glitches. Be ready to discuss your information without the aid in the event that you cannot display it.

Don't Overdo It

Presentation aids can do a great deal for a speech, yet there *can* be too much of a good thing. Once you get into the swing of creating aids, a common temptation is to keep on making them. Caution is in order, however. Always remember that a speech is foremost an activity in which the speaker communicates with words. Having too many aids distracts an audience. After all, listeners have come to listen to a speaker, not to stare at a screen or a flip chart. Use aids in key places, and let verbal explanation be the mainstay of the presentation.

SUMMARY QUESTIONS

What are presentation aids? What role do they play in a speech?

Presentation aids include objects, models, pictures, graphs, charts, hand-outs, video, audio, and multimedia. Each of these elements, used alone and in combination, helps listeners to see relationships among concepts and elements, to store and remember material, and to critically examine key ideas. Presentation aids help listeners process and retain information, increase interest and motivation, help speakers inform and persuade, create a professional image, reduce speech anxiety, and save time.

What are some of the ways to present or display a presentation aid to the audience?

Options include chalkboards, slides and transparencies, overhead projection, and computer projection and display technology.

What are some of the factors to consider when preparing the aid?

Many considerations are important in constructing an effective visual aid. Size, shape, color, proper labeling, simplicity, and continuity are all important. Preparation of the aid as a part of, instead of as an addition to, the presentation helps maintain a close fit between the presentation and the aid. Presentation aids should be as simple and uncomplicated as possible. The use of color in a presentation helps audience members see comparisons, contrasts, and emphasis. Use bright, strong colors to emphasize important points and softer, lighter colors for less important ones. Minimize the amount of words used on each aid. A maximum of six words per line and six lines per aid is sufficient.

What are some of the things to consider when actually using the aid in a speech?

Pay particular attention to placement, interpretation, and timing and sequence. Make sure the audience can see and make sense of the aid. Use your speaker notes as a reminder of when to use the aid.

Why is practice so important?

Many things can go wrong when you incorporate presentation aids into a speech. Equipment may fail, or you may be tempted to speak to your aid rather than to the audience. Practicing with the aid can forestall many problems that may otherwise arise during the speech, thus giving you the confidence you need to approach the task.

ISSUES FOR DISCUSSION

1. Discuss the best way to use objects in presentations for large audiences of one hundred or more. Make recommendations for small, medium, and large objects.

2. What type of speeches do not really require presentation aids?

3. What are your own personal challenges for preparing and using presentation aids?

4. Discuss several ways that visual aids can reduce speaker anxiety.

SELF-ASSESSMENT

1. Think back to the last presentation you attended. Write a brief description of the aids used in the presentation, and evaluate the speaker's choice of aids. Do you think these were good choices for the topic? What aids would you use for the same topic?

2. Suppose you were asked to give a 20-minute presentation on differences in crime rates among major cities. Make a list of the kinds of presentation aids you would probably use. Next to each item, write a few words explaining why the item is on the list. Would your choice of presentation aids vary in relation to your audience (i.e., presenting to a national meeting of law enforcement agencies versus presenting to your classmates)?

3. What kind of presentation topics are likely to be appropriate for the following kinds of aids? Generate a short list of presentation topics that would be likely to include the use of each.

- objects
- graphs
- diagrams
- computer projection and display technology
- slides
- models

TEAMWORK

1. Suppose your presentation on tourist attractions in the Southwest requires the use of many slides. You do not have your own equipment and have been told that the equipment in the facility where you are to speak is unreliable. The presentation is taking place tomorrow. In a small group, discuss possible backup strategies to save your presentation in the event that the equipment fails either before or during your presentation.

2. Obtain some examples of actual presentation aids that have been used in past presentations. Critique them working in groups of three to four people. If you know the topic for which they were used, evaluate the appropriateness of each aid for the topic. If you do not know what the topic was, make a guess based on the clarity of the aid itself.

3. Obtain some examples of actual visual aids that have been used in past presentations. Divide the visuals between groups. Each group should try to generate a short presentation of two or three minutes based around a single visual or a small set of presentation aids.

The strongest
human
instinct is
to impart
information,
the second
strongest is
to resist it.
—Kenneth
Grahame

Enlighten the people generally, and tyranny and oppressions
of body and mind will vanish like evil spirits at the dawn of
day.

—Thomas Jefferson

Informative

Speeches

13

When was the last time you attended an interesting and useful informative speech? **What made it stand out? What was it about the speaker and his or her method of presentation that made the experience enlightening?** How did you use the information you learned?

Perhaps you remember a time when you were drawn in by a television documentary about an unfamiliar subject. **What made you stop and watch it?** Was it the subject matter itself? The way the documentary presented information? **As you think about your informative speeches, it's a good idea to reflect on situations in which you were absorbed by material being presented to you.**

Ever wondered how to prune a tree so that it will flower profusely the following year? Or which careers will be most financially rewarding in the next decade? Interested in learning about the best cities for recent college graduates—for example, the ones with the most job opportunities, hottest night life, and premium recreation spots? Why is vegetarianism good for you—or is it? Are you curious about how the Dutch approach euthanasia (assisted suicide)? What about the difference between a stock and a bond? What was it like to intern at Death Row Records in Los Angeles while rap singer Tupac Shakur was alive? What about new sources of scholarship money? How does a car engine work? What is a nebula and how is one formed?...

Chances are, at least one or two of these topics would be of interest to you, especially if you could hear about them from a dynamic and knowledgeable speaker. Informative speaking about these and countless other topics is one of the primary ways we transmit and share knowledge. In the guise of the classroom lecture, you've been exposed to informative speaking since grade school. Beyond the classroom, communicating information is a mainstay of the business, professional, and personal-interest spheres. Every day, managers gather employees to explain new procedures and describe company developments. Officers of local clubs and civic organizations keep members abreast of recent events and outline plans for new projects. Researchers report and explain their findings to their colleagues and to the press, and authorities on everything from banking to breast cancer share their expertise from the podium.

Applying the knowledge you have gained in previous chapters will help you craft an effective informative speech that successfully transmits knowledge to your audience. Once you have selected an appropriate topic, you will need to carefully analyze your audience to determine the level of detail the group will need to understand your subject matter. After researching your topic and gathering support materials, you will need to strategize the best structural organization for your speech. While the content matter of an informative speech often gets the most attention from both the speaker and the audience, it is also important to spend time thinking about the language you will use and the delivery style you will employ. In addition, be sure to consider ways you can enhance your speech with visual aids. Ultimately, the reward for developing and delivering an effective informative speech is the satisfaction of imparting knowledge to audience members who can use it in their lives.

Of all the skills in the public speaking course, research suggests that both former public speaking students and their instructors prize most highly the ability to speak informatively.[1] In this chapter you'll find a number of challenges posed by learning how to create an informative speech. These include:

- Recognizing the underlying goal of informative speaking.
- Discovering how to present information through definition, description, explanation, and demonstration.
- Becoming familiar with the techniques that foster audience understanding and awareness, and learning how to incorporate them into the informative speech.
- Reviewing the categories of subject matter you can address in an informative speech.
- Effectively organizing your informative speech according to an appropriate pattern.
- Discovering pointers that will help you create a more effective informative speech.

INFORMATIVE SPEAKING GOALS AND STRATEGIES

To inform is to communicate knowledge. The goal of informative speaking is to increase the audience's understanding or awareness through imparting knowledge. Informative speeches provide an audience with new information, new insights, or new ways of thinking about a topic. As an informative speaker, you might introduce listeners to new ideas, events, people, places, or processes. You might explain information with which listeners have some familiarity but little real understanding. Your speech might be an in-depth analysis of a complex subject, a simple description of an event, or a physical demonstration of how something works. As long as your audience learns something, the options are nearly limitless.

Building Understanding and Awareness

As mentioned, the goal of informative speaking is to increase audience understanding and awareness. But how can you ensure that you achieve this goal? After all, people are not simply empty vessels into which you can pour facts and figures and expect them to recognize and remember all that information. Before we can retain information, we must be able to recognize and understand it.[2]

A variety of public speaking techniques and principles exist to help audiences understand information. Many have been the subjects of preceding chapters. For example, in Chapter 7 we saw that illustrating and substantiating the speech with effective supporting materials such as examples is a primary way of aiding comprehension. We also saw the importance of defining terms and of relating the unknown to the known. Both techniques are proven to help listeners understand material.[3] Research confirms that comprehension is also aided by:

- Selecting an appropriate organizational pattern. Studies suggest, for example, that audience understanding of a speech is directly linked to how well it is organized[4] (see Chapter 8);
- Providing effective preview statements and transitions, in addition to well-organized introductions and conclusions (see Chapter 9);
- Using language that best conveys meaning and that emphasizes and reiterates key points. Sentence length, appropriateness of vocabulary, and concrete words affect the audience's ability to recall information. Further, one of the most effective ways to reinforce new information is through repetition[5] (see Chapter 10);
- Skillfully delivering the speech. Speakers who effectively make use of repetition, pauses, speech rate, and other features of delivery produce clearer messages, and clearer messages are associated with better comprehension[6] (see Chapter 11);
- Using effective presentation aids (see Chapter 12).

As you can see, virtually everything you have learned in previous chapters directly applies to effectively presenting information in a speech. One final element that is vital to ensuring understanding of your message is audience analysis (see Chapter 5).

Audience Analysis

As in all types of speeches, understanding of the audience and the factors affecting it is critical to delivering an effective informative speech. Consideration of the audience and the context, or the situation surrounding the speech, can make the difference between a successful informative speech in which the audience learns something new, and a lackluster event in which you lose the listeners' attention or never capture it in the first place. The audience must be able to identify with the topic, see its relevance to their lives, and logically follow it to its conclusion. To ensure that this occurs, you will need to gauge what your listeners already know about a topic, as well as what they *want* and *need* to know about it.

What Do Your Listeners Want to Know? Have you ever sat through a lecture in which you already knew most of what the speaker had to say? It's annoying to have to listen as someone tells us what we already know. Likewise, most people don't want to be forced to learn *more* than they want to know. Using the tools described in Chapter 5—including surveys, interviews, written sources, and other speakers—try to discover how familiar your listeners are with the speech topic. What are the audience's demographics—age, gender, ethnic or cultural background, socioeconomic status, religious and political affiliation, and related values and beliefs? What is it about the speech topic that most concerns them? What might they most want to know? What are they least likely to be interested in? Answering questions such as these will help you shape your message in ways that will most motivate the audience to listen.

What Does the Context Require? The context of a speech (e.g., its setting, the occasion, and the nature of the speech) also affects how you shape

Interview

Informative Speeches: A Real World Perspective

Monica Flores-Mason is an instructor of speech communication at West Valley College in Saratoga, California. She teaches public speaking and communication courses. She has assigned and graded hundreds of informative speeches in the past several years.

Why are informative speeches one of the most popular types in beginning speech classes?

Informative speeches serve as a building block for other types of speeches. Many persuasive speeches and special occasion speeches have to use elements of informative speeches in order to be effective.

Are informative speeches the easiest type to prepare and deliver?

On the contrary. Informative speeches can be some of the most difficult to deliver. It is quite a task to inform an audience about a topic in only six to eight minutes. The speaker has to know how much knowledge the audience already has and build upon that. Also, many students are afraid that their speech will be boring since it is only to inform. What they sometimes don't

understand is that informative speeches can be funny and quite entertaining.

What makes a good informative speech?

It is essential that an informative speech topic be relevant to the audience members. They should learn something new by listening to the speech. A good informative speech must also be well organized. This involves not only constructing a solid outline for the speech, but also making sure that the topic is limited enough to do it justice in a short speech. Visual aids are also important, especially if the topic is complicated or unknown to the audience.

What advice do you have for students who are thinking about giving an informative speech?

Selecting a good topic is the first big step. Make sure you like the subject matter of the speech topic. Then do your homework. Find out as much as you can about the topic so that you are an expert in the area. Above all, plan ahead. Too many students wait until the last minute to work on their speech, and this usually shows during the presentation.

your information. For example, the protocols for a business meeting and a neighborhood safety gathering may differ substantially. The former is likely to be more formal in tone and structure than the latter. Audiences also bring different expectations depending on the nature of the presentation. Violating audience expectations may result in wandering attention and disregard for your message. Will your speech be brief, covering only highlights; in-depth, covering deeper aspects; or even longer, as in a seminar that lasts for several hours? In a brief presentation, listeners expect a bare-bones synopsis delivered in a short period. In a lecture, they expect the talk to last about an hour. In a seminar, they expect detailed information as well as practical aspects like short breaks. Listeners expect a spokesperson at a press conference who is describing efforts under way to rescue stranded mountain climbers to relate events surrounding the stranding of the climbers and the response of the rescuers. They do not expect the spokesperson to discuss contemporary mountain-rescue techniques. On the other hand, a safety professional attending a seminar on recent advances in rescue technology would expect a discussion with more depth, describing and discussing the new technology and techniques.

Strategies for Presenting Information

To achieve the goal of increasing understanding and awareness, informative speakers rely on one or more of the following approaches to presenting information: definition, description, explanation, and demonstration. Some informative speeches rely almost exclusively on a single approach. Many speeches employ a combination of strategies in a single speech.

Steve Lehman/SABA

It is especially important to define your terms carefully when speaking on a controversial topic such as affirmative action.

operational definition
describes something by explaining what it does: *A computer is something that processes information.*

definition by negation
describes something by explaining what it is not: *A computer is not something to be afraid of; it isn't an unconquerable enemy to be struggled with and beaten by.*

definition by example
provides examples of the subject under discussion: *Victims include persons subjected to childhood sexual abuse and those who have been abandoned by their parents.*

Defining Information. In an age of information overload, even the most educated people cannot keep up with all the new information generated each day. Thus, one important function of the informative speech is definition. When you define information, you identify the essential qualities and meaning of something. What is a black hole? What is the computer programming language JAVA? What is herpes? What is affirmative action?

Many speeches center on questions such as these, addressing the meaning of a new and/or complex concept. For example, a speaker might choose to define the Internet or the World Wide Web to a group of colleagues. A corporate spokesperson might define the Americans with Disabilities Act to the heads of various divisions within the company.

An informative speaker might also select definition when clarifying a complex or controversial idea or issue. For example, many people are vaguely aware of affirmative action and the controversy surrounding it, but precisely how does the law define it? And what exactly is it about the plan to which opponents object?

Although defining information may sound straightforward, there are in fact a number of ways to define something. Consider the following:

- **Operational definition**—When something is defined operationally, it is defined by what it does. For example:

  A computer is something that processes information.

- **Definition by negation**—Definition by negation describes something by explaining what it is not. For example:

  A computer is not something to be afraid of; it isn't an unconquerable enemy to be struggled with and beaten by.

- **Definition by example**—Definition by example provides examples of the subject under discussion. For example:

  Victims include persons subjected to childhood sexual abuse and persons who have been abandoned by their parents.

- **Definition by synonym**—Speakers often define something by comparing it to another term that has an equivalent meaning. For example:

  A friend is a comrade or a buddy.

- **Definition by etymology (word origin)**—Etymology is the account of a word's history. When you define by etymology, you illustrate the roots of the term in question. A speaker might use etymology to define the word *rival* in this manner:

  Our word *rival* derives from the French word, which in turn derives from the Latin word *rivalis*. The original meaning of *rivalis* was "one living near or using the same stream." This word derives from the Latin word *rivus* (brook), which comes from the Indo-European verb meaning "to flow."[7]

In this excerpt the speaker is quite thorough in his review of the origins of the word *rival*. But a speaker may not always be quite this systematic. He might simply touch on the roots of a word, as in the following speech excerpt from "Children, Culture, and Crisis" by UNICEF volunteer John B. Donovan. (Note that following his discussion of the origin of the word *culture*, Donovan also defines it by negation):

It's wonderful to be at the culture festival. In fact, *culture* in its original sense is something that has been quite vividly on my mind since yesterday, when my daughter came in with seven magnificent roses that she had just picked. She had been working in the garden with a master gardener who knows everything there is to know about preparing the soil.

It was all such hard work that she was covered with dirt, but it is preparation of the ground that is properly called "culture." So often we use the word to refer to art and music, as if they were the full flower of culture, but they're not. They and other influences are part of the preparation of the ground in which the human spirit can grow. Then, when the human spirit is in full flower, it shows itself in situations like this, where people are showing appreciation for one another and admiration for what they can offer. That's the full flower of culture and the sign of cultured people in the truest sense.

The opposite of culture, therefore, is the complete breakdown of that sense of mutual high regard, which is what happens in times of conflict, and that is what I want to talk to you about for a few minutes today, even in the midst of this celebration, about war and in particular about children and war and the role of UNICEF, for which I am a volunteer.[8]

Describing Information. When you describe information, you provide an array of details that paint a mental picture of your topic. You may be describing a place, an event, a person, object, or process. Regardless, the point is to offer a vivid portrayal of the subject under discussion. You might describe an uprising on the West Bank of the Jordan River, trends in fashion or art, or how a dress is woven.

definition by synonym
describes something by comparing it to another term that has an equivalent meaning: *A friend is a comrade or a buddy.*

definition by etymology (word origin)
describes something by illustrating the roots of the term in question.

Critical Checkpoint

....

Determining Meaning
Researchers who have studied people's understanding of the meaning of a term have found that the greatest difficulty they face is distinguishing a term's *essential meaning* from its many *associated meanings*. One way to help listeners do this is to:

- provide a typical example of the term, one that illustrates its essential meaning;

- provide an operational definition listing the term's essential features;

- provide several examples of the common use of the term;

- provide one or more negative examples, or definitions by negation.[1]

1. Katherine E. Rowan, "A New Pedagogy for Explanatory Public Speaking: Why Arrangement Should Not Substitute for Invention," *Communication Education* 44 (July 1995): 236–250.

In a speech about architecture, Prince Charles of Great Britain described pre-war London:

> It is hard to imagine that London before the last war must have had one of the most beautiful skylines of any great city, if those who recall it are to be believed. Those who do, say that the affinity between buildings and earth, in spite of the city's immense size, was so close and organic that the houses looked almost as though they had grown out of the earth and had not been imposed upon it— grown, moreover, in such a way that as few trees as possible were thrust out of the way.[9]

Critical Checkpoint

....

Describing Information Visually

When describing information, consider it visually. Ask yourself questions such as: How big is it? What shape (color, height, length, weight) is it? What is it similar to? If you're describing a person, think about distinct characteristics, both physical and psychological. What is her temperament? How does he hold his body? What about voice and gesture? The more vividly you describe, the more readily your listeners will understand.

Explaining Information. Explanation goes beyond simple clarification of terms or concepts or a description of them. When you explain information, you provide reasons or causes and demonstrate relationships. Often you will rely on interpretation and analysis to make your points.

The classic example of explaining information is the classroom lecture. But many kinds of speeches rely on explanation, from those that address difficult or confusing scientific theories to those that explain the meaning of a painting. Why are some people vegetarians? What is the difference between a 401K Keogh retirement plan and a SEP IRA? Why does arranged marriage flourish in India but not in the United States? What did the artist Picasso mean to express when he created *Guernica*, his famous painting about war?

Demonstrating Information. Yet another approach to presenting information is to explain how something works or to actually demonstrate it. The many "how to" shows on television, ranging from cooking to carpentry, rely on demonstration. Speech topics such as Asking for a Raise, or Childproofing Your Home, or Pruning a Fruit Tree may not include an actual physical demonstration, but the speaker will nevertheless verbally demonstrate the steps involved. Speeches that rely on demonstration work with either the actual object, representations or models of it, and/or visual aids that diagram it.

Critical Checkpoint

....

Choosing an Approach

Many speeches contain a mix of some or all elements of definition, description, explanation, and demonstration. Others focus primarily on one or two of these elements. The particular method of presenting information you select will depend on the unique mix of topic, audience, and occasion for your speech. How little or much does the audience know about the topic? If listeners know little or nothing, your goal might be to define and describe the topic to them. If they have some knowledge, you might wish to explain a subject in some detail. Does your topic beg for description or demonstration? As you ask yourself questions such as these, you will comfortably be able to decide on an appropriate approach—one that will best help your audience gain understanding and awareness.

TYPES OF INFORMATIVE SPEECHES

Informative speeches can be classified in a variety of ways. In this section they are categorized according to the subject matter they address. Thus, an informative speech may be about objects, people, events, processes, concepts, or issues.

Speeches about Objects

An object is just about anything that isn't human. It can be animate, as in the animal kingdom, or inanimate, as in skis or skates. **Speeches about objects** run the gamut from ribbons used to commemorate AIDS and other diseases, to the musical score for *Les Misérables*, to seeing-eye dogs.

Objects that many of us take for granted often make excellent speech topics, as long as they are relevant to the audience. Water, for example, may seem boring or mundane at first glance. But if it is cast as a necessary but endangered substance, many people will no doubt pay attention.

The following are topics on objects that may interest you or may trigger other topics for speeches:

expensive lingerie	home exercise equipment
the brain	rollerblades
cartoons	Impressionist art
bumper stickers	the moons of Saturn
fire	cutting-edge digital watches
high-definition television sets	computerized toys
UFOs	

Each of the four informative speaking strategies described previously may be appropriate when speaking about an object. You can define an object, describe it, explain it, or demonstrate it. Of foremost importance in speeches about objects is that you adequately define and describe it. Depending on the specific speech purpose, the speech could conclude at that point or continue as you explain the object in depth and even demonstrate how it works.

Speeches about People

Speeches about people inform audiences about historically significant individuals and groups, those who have made contributions to society (both positive and negative), or those who for one reason or another we simply find compelling. You might want to speak about Jeanne Calment, who at age 122 was the oldest known living person until her recent death. Great sports figures such as Tiger Woods and Arthur Ashe, novelists such as John Grisham, or musicians such as Elvis Presley represent other possibilities. One student was interested in speaking about the founders of the White Rose, a student group in Munich, Germany, who were anti-Nazi activists during World War II. This student was interested in the history of Nazi Germany but wasn't sure her audience would share this interest. Once she realized that the White Rose founders were college students, she felt

> **speeches about objects** discuss anything that isn't human, including both animate and inanimate objects.

> **speeches about people** discuss historically significant individuals and groups, those who have made contributions to society (both positive and negative), or those who for one reason or another we simply find compelling.

confident that she could use this fact to make the topic interesting and relevant to her audience.

The following are examples of topics about people:

skinheads	Otoe Indians
the Grateful Dead	the Mayans
Amelia Earhart	twins
the homeless	Michael Jordan
Mother Teresa	supermodels
talk show hosts	blues musicians
Diana, the Princess of Wales	Pope John Paul II

When speaking about a person or group, consider using description to paint a picture of your subject for the audience. To address the person's or group's significance, most likely you will rely on explanation.

Speeches about Events

speeches about events
discuss noteworthy occurrences, past and present.

Speeches about events focus on noteworthy occurrences, past and present. What was it like to attend an opening of the Olympics? What about covering the war in Bosnia? What occurred during the strike by United Parcel Service union members in 1997? Beyond these high-profile events, a speech about an event can encompass just about anything that happened that might be of interest to your audience. An event can include noteworthy advances or breakthroughs in science or art, for example, as well as "my summer vacation."

Because it's usually not possible to describe the entirety of an event in a four- to six-minute speech, most speeches about events focus on one aspect of it, preferably one that has significance for the audience. Mardi Gras, for instance, is too broad to cover in one speech. However, you could devote your attention to one aspect of Mardi Gras, such as the history of Mardi Gras or its traditions.

Andrew J. Cohoon/AP-Wide World

Wild, colorful, festive Mardi Gras. It's not possible to describe every detail of such a sprawling and chaotic event. Instead, focus your speech on a specific aspect.

Here are more examples of topics about events:

Tiananmen Square uprising	Woodstock
the funeral of Diana, the Princess of Wales	Special Olympics
history of the Pony Express	Oklahoma City bombing
professional baseball strike of 1995	Cuban missile crisis
Hong Kong's return to Chinese rule	Monica Lewinsky affair

Speeches about events can have any number of specific purposes. One speaker may wish to paint a vivid picture or description of what it was like to be among the throngs who lined the streets of London to watch Princess Diana's coffin being borne by horses to Westminster Abbey. Another speech on the same topic might focus more on explaining or analyzing the meaning of the event. A speech about trends on the Internet may be largely descriptive. Yet a speech about Operation Desert Storm may focus on defining what the Operation was about.

Speeches about Processes

Speeches about processes refer to a series of steps that lead to a finished product or end result. In this type of speech you can talk about how something is done, how it is made, or how it works. Some topics about processes are similar to topics about events. That is, some events consist of a sequence of happenings that lead to an end result or finished product. For example, the building of the Union Pacific Railroad can be referred to as both an event (a particular occurrence that has historical significance) and a process (a series of steps that yields an end product).

> **speeches about processes**
> discuss a series of steps that lead to a finished product or end result; how something is done, how it is made, or how it works.

When discussing a process, you will most likely have one of two purposes. One is to explain how something works or develops. How do fetuses develop? How are automobiles manufactured? Another is to actually teach audience members to perform the process. Such topics might include how to change a tire, make salsa at home, or interview for a job.

When describing how to do something, speakers often perform the actual task during the speech, doing each step as they describe it. When it is not possible to perform the task, visual or audio aids may be used to illustrate the steps. Clearly, this kind of speech requires demonstration as the primary means of presenting information. Visual aids are also essential in explaining processes. To illustrate the growth of a fetus, for example, a speaker might use drawings or photographs of fetuses at various stages of development.

Here are some examples of topics about processes:

manufacture of automobiles	obtaining a pilot's license
applying for U.S. citizenship	surfing the Internet
development of tornadoes	nuclear meltdown
writing a comic strip	micro-brewing
planning for retirement	improving memory
performing CPR (cardiopulmonary resuscitation)	voter registration

Speeches about Concepts

Speeches about concepts focus on abstract or complex ideas or theories and attempt to make them concrete and understandable to an audience. What is chaos theory? What is art? Is it a child's drawing, a master's painting, or both? We've heard the term *hate speech* but are confused because it seems to encompass everything from racist expressions to racist actions. What does it really mean?

> **speeches about concepts**
> discuss abstract or complex ideas or theories and attempt to make them concrete and understandable.

Definition is critical to speeches about concepts. As noted previously, the more difficult a concept is, the more ways you will want to define it for the audience. Description can also be useful when informing audiences about

Focus on Ethics

Responsibility, Opportunity, and the Right to Inform

Beyond the classroom, you are likely to give informative speeches under three broad conditions. One, you have a professional responsibility to do so. Two, you've been given an opportunity to do so. Three, you decide to exercise your constitutional right to do so. Whichever reason underlies your informative speech, you have an obligation to present information truthfully and accurately— to be trustworthy, responsible, respectful, and fair.

Responsibility

Many of us are obligated to inform as part of our professional responsibilities. In fact, many job positions are built around informative speaking. Teachers give informative presentations on a daily basis. Public relations and public affairs professionals relay information to the press and public. Job trainers and employee benefits personnel demonstrate new methods to workers, apprise employees of their benefits, and keep them informed of relevant regulations. As part of their job responsibilities, business and professional persons routinely deliver sales, productivity, and other informative reports to co-workers, management, and the public.

In each of these cases, the speaker informs because it is his or her professional responsibility to do so. With this responsibility comes an ethical obligation not to mislead or misinform listeners. Informative speakers can mislead audiences inadvertently, by unknowingly relying on incorrect sources, or deliberately, by engaging in the willful dissemination of misinformation. In the business world, some people deliberately distort information to benefit themselves and/or their companies. Although this strategy may work in the short term, ultimately it almost always backfires as the truth filters out.

Opportunity

On many occasions you may wish to give an informative presentation even though you are not required to do so. You might be invited to speak on a subject you know well; for example, as an accountant who advises the officers of a homeless shelter on how to make better use of their funding and improve their financial practices. Various hobby, charity, or volunteer groups may ask you to share your knowledge in a short presentation at one of their meetings. A group might ask you to give a short demonstration speech and answer questions; for example, as a computer expert who gives a short training session at a local library.

Some speakers think that because they are donating their time, they can "slack off" on the details. But whether or not you are paid for sharing your knowledge, you are ethically obligated to present it to the best of your abilities. Every audience relies on its speaker to be accurate and honest.

The Right to Inform

Because you live in a democratic society that closely guards your right of free speech, many situations may present themselves in which you opt to exercise your right to speak out. Perhaps you find that people are misinformed about an issue you know well, and you decide to set the record straight. You may want to alert people to the existence of a health hazard or other form of danger. You might serve as a witness at a hearing or supply key information at an important meeting. By speaking out, you call attention to an issue and inform others about what you know.

Ethically, the right to speak out informatively carries clear responsibilities. These include acting with the audience's best interests at heart, striving for accurate and bias-free reporting, and responding to alternative viewpoints with respect.

concepts. Listeners may not be able to *see* a concept, but a deft speaker can evoke its meaning by associating it with certain actions or behaviors. In describing anxiety, for example, the speaker might illustrate it by noting the increased heart rate and distressed facial expressions that accompany the condition. Clearly, you will also use explanation to explain the significance of the idea or theory.

Here are examples of concepts that can be interesting topics for speeches:

The American Dream	chaos theory
family values	honesty
Yankee imperialism	birth order theory
supply-side economics	vegetarianism
radical feminism	natural medicine
schizophrenia	infidelity

Critical Checkpoint

Starting with What the Listeners Know

Educational researchers have found that in explaining concepts or theories, especially those that are difficult, it is helpful to start with what the listeners already know. In other words, build from the known to the unknown. If the concept under discussion is often misinterpreted or misunderstood, begin by acknowledging the common perception of it. Then illustrate why this perception is faulty.[1] For example, many people believe that because herbs are "natural" they can be taken in any quantity without adverse effects. After first acknowledging this perception, the speaker might explain that herbs contain powerful natural chemicals and that they are in fact potent substances that must be handled with just as much care as synthetic medicines.

1. Katherine E. Rowan, "A New Pedagogy for Explanatory Public Speaking: Why Arrangement Should Not Substitute for Invention," *Communication Education* 44 (July 1995): 236–250.

Speeches about Issues

An issue is a problem or a matter in dispute, one that people seek to bring to a conclusion. Teenage pregnancy, welfare reform, gun control, and sex education in the schools are examples of topics about issues. Informative **speeches about issues** provide an overview or report of problems in order to increase understanding and awareness. This goal stands in contrast to that of the persuasive speech, which attempts to influence audience attitudes, values, beliefs, or behavior about an issue. Whereas a persuasive speech would seek to modify attitudes or ask the audience to adopt a specific position (such as "for" or "against" the issue in question), the goal of an informative speech stops at providing the audience with knowledge about it. In other words, the informative speech seeks to educate whereas the persuasive speech advocates. An informative speech about teenage pregnancy might define the nature of the problem and describe the various positions people take with respect to it. Such a speech might also offer explanations of why teenage pregnancy occurs. A persuasive speech on the same topic might claim that teenage pregnancy results from unprotected teenage sex and that, consequently, people should not engage in this activity.

Of all the types of informative speeches discussed here, speeches about issues have the greatest potential of "crossing the line" into the persuasive realm. Most public speaking scholars acknowledge that there is no such

speeches about issues provide a report or overview of problems or issues in dispute in order to increase understanding and awareness.

thing as a purely informative or persuasive speech. That is, there are always elements of persuasion in an informative speech, and vice versa. Rarely are speakers entirely dispassionate about a subject, especially one that tends to elicit strong reactions. For this reason, many speeches about issues are persuasive. Nevertheless, if the informative speaker keeps in mind the general informative speaking goal, he or she will be able to deliver a speech about an issue whose primary function is to educate rather than advocate.

Here are some potential topics for speeches focusing on issues:

cloning	pornography on the Internet
tax reform	gay men and lesbians in the military
instant replay for television sports	Cuban cigars
music CD warning labels	sterilization
sexual harassment	parking on campus
global warming	swimsuit competition in beauty/scholarship contests
fertility drugs	

ORGANIZING THE INFORMATIVE SPEECH

Although organization is important to all speeches, it is especially important to informative speeches. Clearly organized speeches are easier to understand than those that are poorly organized. A clear organizational pattern helps the audience follow and remember new information. It also helps the speaker keep the speech clear and concise.

Depending on your topic, any of the organizational patterns described in Chapter 8 may be appropriate. The following discussion recaps these patterns and suggests ways they can be applied to the informative speech.

Chronological and Spatial Patterns

In the *chronological pattern*, the arrangement of main points illustrates a sequence of time. The chronological pattern is the logical choice for speeches about processes, in which each step is described in sequence. This pattern is also useful for speeches that describe events and the sequence of happenings that constitute them. Using the chronological pattern, for example, a police chief may give a short informative speech in a press conference describing the events of a criminal investigation. A speaker might also use this pattern to illustrate the current or historical developments or trends associated with a topic.

The chronological pattern is often the logical choice for speeches about people, especially if the presentation follows the sequence of events in someone's life. A self-proclaimed chocolate lover, for instance, recently gave a speech about Milton S. Hershey, the founder of Hershey Foods Corporation. The speech began with Hershey's childhood, progressed to his young adult life and work, culminated with his founding of the Hershey Foods Corporation, and concluded with a word about his death and contributions to society. The chronological pattern might even be an appropriate choice for certain issues that follow a series of events in time, such as social movements.

Making a Difference

PEDRO ZAMORA, AIDS ACTIVIST

Pedro Zamora (1972–1994) was a feisty and passionate AIDS educator and television celebrity who was famed for his participation in the MTV documentary series *The Real World*. By the time of his death from AIDS in 1994, this inspirational 22-year-old Cuban American had already spent some five years, or almost one-quarter of his life, using his voice to make a difference for others.

In 1989, while a junior at Miami's Hialeah High School, Pedro found out that he was HIV positive. By this time he had already experienced more than his share of misfortune, including his family's traumatic escape from Cuba when he was 8 years old and the death of his beloved mother from cancer when he was 13. An honors student, star athlete, and winner of Hialeah High School's "Best-All-Around Person" award, Pedro at first reacted to the devastating news of his illness with withdrawal and silence. Soon, however, he decided to speak out. He began by volunteering to give an oral report on AIDS to his schoolmates. Impressed by Pedro's presentation, his teacher encouraged him to give more talks.

Speaking about the disease gave Pedro a sense of purpose and served as an outlet for his emo-tions. He passed around condoms in the classroom, and he openly told students that he had gotten HIV because he had had unprotected sex. He stressed that he would probably not live to the age of 30, and that if they were not careful, any student in the room could get the virus. Soon requests for him to speak began to multiply. By mid-1993 he was traveling across the country talking about AIDS, addressing Congress, and serving on dozens of task forces and panels. Pedro had become a national spokesperson, informing and educating young people about how AIDS is transmitted and how to avoid it. All the while Pedro maintained that, "What I was always talking about, I know, was my own death."

In January 1994, about five years after he first learned he was HIV positive, MTV selected Pedro as one of seven young cast members who were to live together in one house and be filmed some 20 hours a day. MTV's unique show endeared Pedro to millions and allowed him to continue educating and teaching others about the disease. The program also chronicled his budding relationship with Sean Sasser, a fellow HIV-positive AIDS educator, with whom Pedro shared a ring ceremony on the show. Pedro continued to appear on *The Real World* until the following summer, when he fell ill with a brain infection. He died on November 11, 1994.

For many people, Pedro was the first person to bring a human face to AIDS. When he died, millions mourned the loss of a brave crusader for AIDS education. At the funeral President Bill Clinton eulogized Pedro via satellite, saying that, "In his short life, Pedro educated and enlightened our nation. He taught people living with AIDS how to fight for their rights and live with dignity."

"All I want is to make people think, and make them care," Pedro often noted. "I can't stop, because AIDS doesn't stop."

SOURCE: The Pedro Zamora Center Web Page, a Davis S. Haueter project since February 1996. Date accessed: December 3, 1997. Address: http://www.geocities.com/WestHollywood/1635/pz4.html.

In the *spatial pattern*, the arrangement of main points illustrates physical direction relative to one another. When your speech describes a location or otherwise focuses on the natural attributes of something, the spatial pattern will best illustrate your points. Spatial patterns are appropriate for speeches about processes (e.g., restoring a home), objects (e.g., placement of ancient

James Pickerell/Image Works

As this aerial view displays the national mall in Washington, D.C., spatial patterns in your speech give a "tour" of a place or event.

pyramids), and certain places or events (e.g., giving listeners a "tour" of a place or the "layout" of an event). A speech that gives a "virtual tour" of a college campus, for instance, calls for a spatial pattern of organization.

Some speeches combine elements of the spatial and chronological patterns. For example, a speech about the national mall in Washington, D.C., may combine a spatial description of landmarks, such as the Lincoln Memorial, with a chronological description of when each landmark was built.

Recall from Chapter 6 that the best method for beginning a speech design is to state a general purpose, followed by a specific purpose and thesis statement.

Chronological Pattern

SPECIFIC PURPOSE: To inform the audience how to prepare for graduate school.

THESIS STATEMENT: Getting accepted and succeeding in graduate school requires careful preparation.

ORGANIZATIONAL PATTERN

I. Many jobs and careers require a graduate degree.
II. The beginning of the junior year of college is a critical time to start specific preparation.
III. Preparation for the admission tests should begin no later than the summer before the senior year.
IV. Securing strong letters of recommendation must commence in the senior year.

Spatial Pattern

SPECIFIC PURPOSE: To inform the audience how to read a food label.

THESIS STATEMENT: Food labels contain several pieces of information that are necessary for safety and nutritional health.

ORGANIZATIONAL PATTERN

I. The first area of a food label is the Principle Display Panel (PDP), located on the front of the food item.
II. Located to the right of the PDP is the information panel.
III. Directly underneath the information panel is the name and address of the producer.

Topical Pattern

This is the most commonly used of all patterns. Speakers select the *topical pattern* when all the main points of a topic are of relatively equal importance and can be presented in any order relative to the other main points without changing the message. Any informative speech topic that falls within these parameters is a candidate for the topical pattern, including speeches about concepts, issues, events, and people. For example, in a speech about the athletic program at your school you might use the different sports as your main points, and you might arrange the speech by topic, such as football, basketball, baseball, and tennis. The main points would be connected through the use of effective transitions.

Topical Pattern

SPECIFIC PURPOSE: To inform the audience of four basic personality types and to describe the communication style of each.

THESIS STATEMENT: Each person displays characteristics of one of the four basic personality types, which may explain why people communicate differently.

ORGANIZATIONAL PATTERN

I. The sanguine personality is outgoing and popular.
II. The choleric personality is very strong willed and tends toward leadership.
III. The melancholy personality tends to be a perfectionist.
IV. The phlegmatic personality tends to be a peacemaker.

Cause-Effect Pattern

In a *cause-effect pattern* of arrangement, the main points are arranged to reflect a cause-effect (or effect-cause) relationship. Cause-effect patterns are generally used with speeches about issues (e.g., lack of voter participation), processes (e.g., cooking, chess moves), and events (e.g., buying from ticket scalpers). A speech on the relationship between residential water use and the depletion of aquifers, for example, could easily fit into a cause-effect organizational pattern. One main point could discuss the cause (water use) and a second main point could discuss the effects (aquifer depletion). A third main point could explore the relationship between the two and discuss projected water loss in the near future. Likewise, a speech about a widespread power loss affecting several states would benefit from a cause-effect pattern. One student who majored in atmospheric science gave a speech on weather patterns in the United States resulting from El Niño. First she explained the technical aspects of the weather, specifically the high and low pressure systems that moved across the nation in 1996. Then she explained the outcome of those movements—the massive flooding in the Midwest, the blizzards in the Northeast, and the record snowstorms in the Northwest. By doing this she used a cause-effect pattern, first explaining the cause of the weather and then explaining the effects and outcomes.

Cause-Effect Pattern

SPECIFIC PURPOSE: To inform the audience of the benefits of regular exercise.

THESIS STATEMENT: A regular exercise program can lead to better health and a more satisfying life.

ORGANIZATIONAL PATTERN

I. Most people do not exercise enough.
II. A lack of exercise can lead to physical, psychological, and emotional problems.
III. Regular exercise results in improved appearance, health, and attitude.
IV. Certain types of exercise are best for your particular lifestyle.

Problem-Solution Pattern

In a *problem-solution pattern* of organization, the main points are arranged to demonstrate the nature and significance of a problem and then to provide justification for a proposed solution to the problem. Problem-solution patterns are ideal for speeches about processes (e.g., fixing a broken toaster), concepts (e.g., dishonesty), and issues (e.g., littering).

Problem-Solution Pattern

SPECIFIC PURPOSE: To inform the audience members how to manage their hectic lives through time management.

THESIS STATEMENT: Using effective time management techniques can reduce the stress in your life and make you more productive.

ORGANIZATIONAL PATTERN

I. Managing time is one of the biggest problems reported by most people.
II. Effective time management can help you keep your commitments, improve your grade point average, and reduce your stress.
III. Today there exist many time management techniques that can work for you.

TIPS FOR EFFECTIVE INFORMATIVE SPEECHES

In addition to principles and strategies already discussed, paying attention to several other strategies will help you create an effective informative speech. These include striving for balance, defining your terms, emphasizing the topic's relevance to the audience, reinforcing your message through repetition, relating new ideas to old ones, presenting new and interesting information, striving for clarity, using visualization, and incorporating presentation aids into the speech.

Strive for Balance: Neither Too Much Nor Too Little

Knowing what to say and what not to say is a skill that begins with the art of conversation and extends to public speaking. In the informative speech, finding the right balance between saying too much and offering too little is especially important.

In general, informative speakers tend to err on the side of including too much rather than too little information. This tendency is particularly

Focus on Technology

Surfing, Swimming, or Drowning on the Internet

As you search for information to support your speeches, you will most likely spend some time online. Chapter 6 of this text discussed finding topics online, noted the potential to waste time aimlessly searching in cyberspace, and offered suggestions for minimizing this problem. These included familiarizing yourself with the various search engines and research tools available, and limiting the amount of time you spend surfing for a general topic once it becomes apparent that your "yield" is poor.

Beyond these suggestions, what else can you do to cope with the vast amount of electronic information? Two writers who have considered the problem make a distinction between *surfing*, *swimming*, and *drowning* in this unparalleled sea of information. According to Walt Crawford and Michael Gorman,[1] surfing is "skimming over the Sea of information; maneuvering without getting in too deeply." Swimming is exploring topics in detail; it involves reading whole articles and even whole books online. Drowning is simply information overload; the searcher becomes so overwhelmed by disjointed bits of information that nothing is gained.

Crawford and Gorman contend that to be properly informed in the electronic age, today's online user must strike a fine balance between surfing and swimming. Surfing is important to get an overview of what is happening in a field, of what's being published. But as its name implies, surfing is a surface activity. To delve into a topic and analyze and synthesize it requires swimming. When you swim, you spend time on a topic and investigate it in depth.

The metaphors of surfing, swimming, and drowning apply to both traditional avenues of library research and electronic searches. In either approach, finding the right balance between skimming the surface of available resources and delving into selected ones is key in ending up with a sufficient knowledge base. The Internet does pose additional hazards, however. In a library, sources have been evaluated by trained information specialists. On the Internet, anyone who can type and log on can "publish"—and can do so without subjecting the work to any kind of review. Thus, an integral part of surfing and swimming online involves critically evaluating the credibility of your sources with even more scrutiny than you use when reviewing library sources.

1. Walt Crawford and Michael Gorman, "Coping with Electronic Information," in Julie Bates Dock, ed., *The Press of Ideas: Readings for Writers on Print Culture and the Information Age* (Boston: Bedford Books of St. Martin's Press, 1996), pp. 588–598.

pronounced when the topic is one in which you, as the speaker, are very interested. It is sometimes easy to view a great deal of material as "essential" when you are very involved with the topic. Because of this tendency, it is important during the planning stages of a speech to critically evaluate the amount of content you will include with other important speech elements, such as a solid introduction and conclusion and effective transitions.

Define Your Terms

When planning a speech, a good practice is to ask yourself whether any terms will sound foreign to the audience. You might also think back to the time when you were unfamiliar, or only slightly familiar, with the topic. What were the terms and concepts *you* needed to understand before moving on to more complicated topics? Because you are already making predictions about the level of knowledge the audience has about the topic, these questions should be relatively simple to answer.

When deciding which terms to define, it is better to err on the side of caution. If you are at all unsure whether audience members will know the meaning of a term, plan to define it in the speech.

Emphasize the Topic's Relevance to Your Audience

To remain interested throughout the speech, audience members must see the topic's relevance to themselves. You must demonstrate to your listeners how they can use the information you are giving and how the knowledge will be beneficial to them. For example, if you are demonstrating to a group of young entrepreneurs how to set up a Web page, you would want to demonstrate the business advantages of having one (e.g., networking or gaining job connections). Regardless of the topic, emphasizing its relevance to the audience in strategic places makes your speech interesting to them and keeps their attention.

Reinforce Your Message through Repetition

One of the simplest and most effective ways to reinforce new information is through repetition. Repeating key words or phrases at various intervals creates a distinctive rhythm and thereby implants important ideas in listeners' minds. As noted in Chapter 10, speakers often use repetition to create a thematic focus. The speaker may repeat key phrases that emphasize a central idea or recurring theme of the speech. Repeating a theme also reinforces imagery, thereby increasing the odds that the audience will remember your speech.

Repetition can be as simple as emphasizing a word several times or as sophisticated as continually relating main ideas back to the theme of the speech. In the former instance, suppose one of the main points of a speech on giving informative presentations addresses rehearsal techniques. If the speaker wants to emphasize the importance of this point, he or she might start by saying, "There is no substitute for practice, practice, practice." This very simple repetition highlights the upcoming section of the speech. In the following example, notice how the speaker uses repetition in the introduction to preview main points:

> Using the World Wide Web as a research tool is fast, effective, and convenient. *It is fast* because results from a search service are usually returned in a matter of seconds. *It is effective* because many avenues of information, such as video and audio archives, are only available to most people on the Web. *It is convenient* because most colleges have many ways to access the Web. From personal accounts to free terminals in the library, getting access is rarely a problem.

Relate Old Ideas to New Ones

New information can be hard to grasp. One proven way to help listeners understand new concepts is to relate them to something already known. Draw comparisons to concepts with which audience members are familiar. Try to relate your information to their everyday lives. By relating old ideas to new ones, you enable listeners to better understand the information you are giving. Once you have established a common ground of understanding, the audience will have an easier time venturing into new territory, especially if the information you present contradicts misconceptions they might have.

Present New and Interesting Information

Even though it is easier to understand something new by linking it to something already known, audiences do seek knowledge, which means learning something new. As you research your informative speech, try to uncover information that is fresh and compelling. Seek out unusual sources (but make certain they are credible). Look for startling facts and novel (but sound) interpretations. Tell your listeners something they haven't heard but will appreciate knowing once they hear it.

Strive for Clarity

Because the goal of informative speaking is to get the information out to the audience in an understandable fashion, you want to do everything you can to make the message as clear as possible. One way to do this is to clarify the goal of the speech early in the preview statement (see Chapter 9). Tell the audience exactly what you want them to get out of the speech. A statement like, "By the end of this presentation, I hope that you will not only be more familiar with cars, but will have gained enough knowledge to know when you are being deceived at the repair shop" can go a long way in helping the listeners remember why they are listening to you in the first place. In addition, strive to make explanations and examples as clear as possible. Try to select examples that minimize the possibility of misunderstanding. Finally, remember that simplicity is always a safe bet. Find the simplest way of informing that still allows you to communicate everything you need to, and use it. This applies to all aspects of the speech, from choosing an organizational pattern to picking out examples that illustrate your points.

Use Visualization

Informative speeches often require a lot of description. Speakers need to ensure that audiences have a solid grasp of what they are talking about before moving on to the next point. Visualization is an effective way of doing this. As mentioned in Chapter 10, you can help audiences visualize your message by using language that is concise, concrete, and vivid. Such language helps turn abstract concepts into concrete examples and builds interest. Consider the following example:

Can you imagine this? You are driving along through a small town. You pull up to a stoplight. You glance into the next lane and notice a horse-drawn carriage. It doesn't look like an antique carriage—like a covered wagon or a colonial carriage. It appears to be made of modern materials and has reflectors and a slow-moving-vehicle symbol on it. "Interesting," you think and drive on. Outside the town, you drive past farmland. Nothing out of the ordinary—until you start noticing that the fields are being worked by men on horse-drawn plows. Continuing down the highway, you pass several more horse-drawn carriages. At this point, you might begin to ask yourself, "Have I been transported back in time?" The answer is—probably not. Most likely, you're driving through Pennsylvania Dutch Country and the people you have been seeing are members of the Amish culture, a culture that chooses to live at a different level of technology than other parts of the United States.

In this example, visualization is used to create interest about the subject of the speech, the Amish people. Visualization is also used to give the audience a mental picture of Amish country; it helps make the concept of the Amish more concrete.

Incorporate Presentation Aids

A speech in which the speaker stands stiffly behind a podium, moving little and offering no relief from his or her words, *can* be mesmerizing. The authors of this text once attended a reading by a famous author in which he stood perfectly still and simply read from his latest book for 90 minutes. The audience was so enthralled that hardly a sound could be heard during the entire reading.

Unfortunately, few of us can match the power of a best-selling writer. But generally the informative speaker can capture an audience's attention by adding some (non-gimmicky) activity and movement to the presentation. Usually this takes the form of presentation aids. As described in Chapter 12, people process and retain information best when information is presented in more than one format. Informative messages that are visually and otherwise reinforced with objects, models, pictures, graphs, charts, video, audio, and multimedia are often more understandable and believable than those that are simply verbalized.

SUMMARY QUESTIONS

What is the general goal of informative speaking?

The goal of informative speaking is to increase the audience's understanding or awareness through imparting knowledge.

What four strategies or approaches for presenting information are available to the informative speaker?

To achieve the informative speaking goal of increasing understanding and awareness, informative speakers rely on definition, description, explanation, and demonstration. When you define information, you identify the essential qualities and meaning of something. You can define information (1) operationally, or by what it does; (2) by negation, or by what it is not; (3) by example; (4) by synonym, or by comparison with something that has an equivalent meaning; (5) and by etymology, or word origin. When you describe information, you provide an array of details that paints a mental picture of your topic. When you explain information, you provide reasons or causes and demonstrate relationships. When you demonstrate information, you actually show how something works or what it does.

How can a speaker help the audience comprehend the message?

Before we can retain information, we must be able to recognize and understand it. Adopting the principles and practices described in preceding chapters can help make your informative message understandable to an audience. These include: (1) illustrating and substantiating the speech with effective supporting materials, defining terms, and relating the unknown to the known; (2) selecting an appropriate organizational pattern; (3) providing effective preview statements and transitions, in addition to well-organized introductions and conclusions; (4) using shared vocabulary, concrete words, and repetition; (5) focusing on the delivery features of repetition, pauses, and rate; (6) incorporating effective presentation aids; and (7) conducting a thorough audience analysis.

What kinds of subject matter can be addressed in an informative speech?

An informative speech may be about objects, people, events, processes, concepts, and/or issues. Speeches about objects discuss just about anything that isn't human, from ribbons used to commemorate AIDS and other diseases, to the musical score for *Les Misérables*, to seeing-eye dogs. Speeches about people inform audiences about historically significant individuals and groups, those who have made contributions to society (both positive and negative), or those who for one reason or another we simply find compelling. Speeches about events focus on noteworthy occurrences, past and present. A speech about an event can encompass just about any happening that might be of interest to the audience. Speeches about processes refer to a series of steps that lead to finished products or end results. This type of speech can talk about how something is done, how it is made, or how it works. Speeches about processes usually have one of two purposes: to explain how something works or develops, or to actually teach audience members to perform the process. Speeches about concepts focus on abstract or difficult ideas or theories and attempt to make them concrete and understandable to the audience. A final category of informative speech topics is issues. An issue is a problem or a matter in dispute, one that people seek to bring to a conclusion. Informative speeches about issues provide an overview of the problem in order to increase understanding and awareness.

How can a speaker effectively organize an informative speech?

Several organizational patterns can be used to arrange the information in a logical progression through the speech. These patterns include the chronological, spatial, topical, cause-effect, and problem-solution patterns of organization.

What are some key points to keep in mind while creating an informative speech?

Paying attention to informational strategies will help you create an effective informative speech. These include striving for balance, defining your terms, emphasizing your topic's relevance to the audience, reinforcing your message through repetition, relating old ideas to new ones, presenting new and interesting information, striving for clarity, using visualization, and incorporating presentation aids into the speech.

ISSUES FOR DISCUSSION

1. What is the general purpose of informative speaking? Is it difficult to present a "purely" informative speech, for example, one that does not reflect the biases of the speaker?

2. Do you think informative speaking lies in your future? If you have selected an academic major, relate it to possible situations in which you might give an informative speech. In what areas of your personal life might you be called on to give an informative speech?

3. What are some of the things you can do in an informative speech to help listeners understand and process your message?

SELF-ASSESSMENT

1. Imagine that you have been asked to give a short informative presentation about the Internet to a group of fourth graders. Write a few paragraphs on message requirements for this presentation. What kind of organizational pattern will you use? How much technical information will you include? (Remember, children often know as much or more about computing than many adults do.) What can you do to be direct and to maintain clarity in your explanation?

2. Practice using visualization and descriptive language. Think of an everyday object such as a chair or kind of food, and describe it in as many ways as you can.

3. Using the speech topic of welfare reform (an issue), how would you present the information to your classmates? What combination of definition, description, explanation, or demonstration would you select? What organizational pattern would you use?

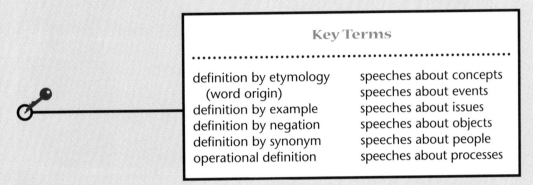

Key Terms

definition by etymology (word origin)
definition by example
definition by negation
definition by synonym
operational definition

speeches about concepts
speeches about events
speeches about issues
speeches about objects
speeches about people
speeches about processes

TEAMWORK

1. In a group of three to four people, make a list of speech topics (at least five) for each of the informative speech types (objects, people, events, processes, concepts, issues) that would be interesting for classroom speeches. Don't use speech topics already mentioned in this chapter. Be prepared to discuss your topics in class.

2. As a small group of three to four people, listen to a speech on campus or in your community that you feel would be primarily informative in nature. Conduct a meeting of your group after the speech to determine the type of informative speech you heard and its organizational pattern. What were the strongest features of the speech? The weakest? Report your findings to the class.

3. In a group of four to five classmates, compare the various sources you use for information (television, radio, newspaper, magazines, Internet, etc.). Brainstorm about different situations, topics, and audiences where giving an informative speech (compared to the sources above) is the best way to provide information. Report your findings to the class.

Reason
is God's
crowning
gift to man.
— Sophocles

Speech is power; speech is to persuade, to convert, to compel. It is to bring another out of his bad sense into your good sense.

— Ralph Waldo Emerson

14 The Persuasive Speech

Recall a persuasive speech you have heard that made you change your opinion about an issue or that convinced you to support a particular person or idea. **What made the speech so effective? Did the speaker appeal to your sense of logic? To your emotions?** Did the speaker seem to know how to address your needs and concerns and answer them within the speech? Did the speaker seem trustworthy? When developing a persuasive argument, you need to think about what kind of information your particular audience will need to agree with your point of view. **Ultimately, delivering a persuasive speech is one of the most powerful means available to you to enlist support for your ideas, beliefs, and attitudes**.

Well, children, where there is so much racket there must be something out of kilter. I think that 'twixt the Negroes of the South and the women at the North, all talking about rights, the white men will be in a fix pretty soon.

But what's all this here talking about? That man over there says that women need to be helped into carriages, and lifted over ditches, and to have the best place everywhere. Nobody ever helps me into carriages, or over mud-puddles, or gives me any best place. And ain't I a woman? Look at me! Look at my arm. I have plowed and planted and gathered into barns, and no man could head me. And ain't I a woman? I could work as much and eat as much as a man—when I could get it—and bear the lash as well. And ain't I a woman? I have borne thirteen children, and seen them most all sold off into slavery, and when I cried out with a mother's grief, none but Jesus heard me! And ain't I a woman?

Then they talk about this thing in the head; what's this they call it? [Someone nearby whispered, "Intellect."] That's it, honey. What's that got to do with women's rights or Negroes' rights? If my cup won't hold a pint and yours holds a quart, wouldn't you be mean not to let me have my little half-measure full?

Then that little man in black there, he says women can't have as much rights as men, 'cause Christ wasn't a woman. Where did your Christ come from? Where did your Christ come from? *Where did your Christ come from?* From God and a woman! Man had nothing to do with Him.

If the first woman God ever made was strong enough to turn the world upside down all alone, these together ought to be able to turn it back and get it right side up again. And now they is asking to do it, the men better let them.

Obliged to you for hearing on me, and now old Sojourner hasn't got nothing more to say.

—"Men Better Let Them," a speech by Sojourner Truth

Sojourner Truth, a former slave emancipated in 1828, was an abolitionist famed for her fiery oratory. She frequently gave public speeches throughout the North, preaching religion, promoting abolition, and espousing women's rights. Truth delivered the speech reprinted here at the Ohio Women's Rights Convention in 1851.[1] Persuasive speeches such as Sojourner Truth's are created to evoke reactions in listeners. They are meant to appeal to the audience's attitudes and beliefs about the issue in question and to sway listeners to the speaker's point of view. How do you react to Truth's speech? How does it make you feel about the rights of women and of African Americans? Does it move you in any way? What thoughts does it leave you with? The strength of your response offers a good indication of the persuasiveness of Truth's message.

Chapter Challenges

Persuasive speaking may be the type of public speaking you will practice most frequently throughout your professional and personal life. This form of speaking involves informing your audience, presenting well-supported arguments, contrasting a better alternative with competing ones, and leading the audience to a reasoned choice. Whether you are reasoning with a child, bargaining for a raise, convincing an employer of your talents, or giving a formal speech, success or failure rests on how well or poorly you practice the art of persuasion.

This chapter will challenge you to understand and apply several classical and contemporary principles of persuasion to your persuasive speeches. You will learn to:

- Recognize the similarities and differences between informative and persuasive speeches.

- Identify the four general conditions that suggest a persuasive purpose.
- Understand the factors that increase the odds that persuasion will succeed.
- Discover Aristotle's three modes of persuasion, or forms of rhetorical proof, and see their relevance to modern-day methods of persuasion.
- Become familiar with contemporary approaches to persuasive speaking, including appeals to audience needs, attitudes, values, behavior, and ways of processing messages, and the speaker-audience relationship.
- Review a technique of organizing persuasive speeches called the motivated sequence.

WHAT IS A PERSUASIVE SPEECH?

In ancient Greece the art of persuasion, or *rhetoric*, was a vital tool for self-defense. In an era predating lawyers, citizens (free white males) served as their own advocates in the courts. Depending on their rhetorical skill (defined by Aristotle as "the available means of persuasion") they either kept their land or lost it; held their taxes steady or paid more; and otherwise retained their rights or saw them forfeited.

Although most people now depend on lawyers to represent them in the tangled web of the legal system, the ability to persuade remains a critical skill in the modern world. Derived from the Greek verb meaning "to believe,"[2] **persuasion** is the process of influencing attitudes, beliefs, values, and behavior. **Persuasive speaking** is speech that is intended to influence the beliefs, attitudes, values, and acts of others.

persuasion
the process of influencing attitudes, beliefs, values, and behavior.

persuasive speaking
speech that is intended to influence the beliefs, attitudes, values, and acts of others.

Persuasive versus Informative Speaking

One way to understand persuasive speaking is to compare it to informative speaking. In Chapter 13 we saw that the general goal of informative speeches is to increase understanding and awareness. Persuasive speeches also function to increase understanding and awareness. They present an audience with new information, new insights, and new ways of thinking about an issue. And as with informative speeches, persuasive speeches enlighten or extend an audience's awareness of a subject by using description, explanation, and demonstration. For instance, the persuasive speech by Sojourner Truth at the beginning of this chapter contains several examples that inform her audience of the similarities between her own experiences and those of men.

Persuasive speeches, in fact, do all the things informative speeches do. But rather than seeking to increase understanding and awareness, the goal of the persuasive speech is to *influence audience choices*.[3] The persuasive speaker tries to somehow influence the opinions or actions of his or her audience. These choices may range from slight shifts in opinion to wholesale changes in behavior. For example, depending on a combination of oratorical skill and degree of change sought, a speaker who wants to persuade listeners to attend college may bring about anything from a slight modification in thinking (e.g., "I could never decide about going to college, but now I'm giving it some consideration"), to a complete reversal in thinking (e.g., "I don't need to go to college" to "I think the best thing for my future will be to go to college"), to an entirely new way of behaving (e.g., "I never had any plans to go to college, but now I'm going to apply for admission to Southeastern Technical University").

In line with the goal of influencing choices, two other characteristics distinguish persuasive speeches from informative speeches: Persuasive speeches present listeners with a limited number of alternatives to consider, and persuasive speeches seek a response. As with informative speeches, however, persuasive speeches respect audience choices.

Persuasive Speeches Limit Alternatives. Any issue that would constitute the topic of a persuasive speech represents at least two viewpoints. For example, there are "pro-choice" advocates and "right-to-life" advocates; supporters of candidate Brezinski and supporters of candidate Morales; those who oppose a new holiday bonus plan and those who advocate it; and those who prefer Brand X vacuum cleaners over Brand Y. With any such issue, it is the objective of a persuasive speaker to limit the audience's alternatives to the side the speaker represents. This is done not by ignoring the unfavorable alternatives altogether, but by contrasting them with the favorable alternative, and showing it to be of greater value or usefulness to the audience than the other alternatives.

Persuasive Speeches Seek a Response. By showing an audience the best of several alternatives, the persuasive speaker asks listeners—sometimes explicitly and sometimes implicitly—to make a choice. If the speech has worked well, the choice will be limited for the audience. That is, listeners will understand that the alternative presented by the speaker is the "right" choice.

It is important to note that by no means do all persuasive speeches *explicitly* seek a response. Many persuasive speeches focus on "perspective taking"—

leading the audience to a perspective that is the speaker's. Sojourner Truth's "Men Better Let Them" speech is of such a variety. The speech did not expressly ask listeners to make a specific choice, such as "Vote tomorrow to free the slaves." Yet it did appeal to them to share her attitudes and beliefs about the roles of women and African Americans in her day.

Persuasive Speeches Respect Audience Choices. Even though persuasive speeches present audiences with a choice, the successful and ethical persuasive speaker recognizes that the choice is ultimately the audience's to make—and he or she respects their right to make it. People take time to consider what they've heard and how it affects them. People make their own choices in light of or despite the best evidence. Your role as a persuasive speaker is not to force the audience to accept your viewpoint, but to present as convincing a case as possible so that they might willingly do so. For instance, you might want to persuade members of your audience to become vegetarians, but you must respect their choice not to as well.

Persuasive Purposes

How can you determine whether your topic and goals are persuasive? The persuasive purpose is appropriate under four general conditions:

1. When you seek to influence an audience's *attitudes* about an issue—by making listeners more accepting (or nonaccepting) of a new set of procedures or new policy.
2. When you seek to influence an audience's *beliefs* or understanding about something—by getting listeners to accept your own beliefs about it.
3. When you seek to influence an audience's *behavior*—by convincing listeners to undertake a particular set of actions.
4. When you seek to *reinforce* an audience's existing attitudes, beliefs, or behavior so listeners will continue to possess or practice them. Antismoking advocates, for example, often address groups of nonsmoking teenagers with the goal of reinforcing their nonsmoking behavior. Fund-raisers often address groups of loyal givers in order to reinforce the likelihood of receiving donations in the future.

Another way to consider persuasive purposes is to decide whether you want to "stimulate," "convince," or "actuate" your audience. When you speak to stimulate, you assume that the audience shares your attitudes. Your goal is to bring these attitudes into sharper relief. When you speak to convince, you assume that your attitudes and those of the audience differ to some degree. Your goal is to modify the audience members' attitudes to bring them more in line with your own. When you speak to actuate, your goal is to get the audience to actually take some action.[4]

Critical Checkpoint

Persuading with Different Purposes

Consider the following persuasive speech topics:

Does legalized gambling help or harm citizens?

Should you vote for gun control?

Are gay parents a good influence for children?

Think about how you would approach these topics differently depending on whether you want to stimulate, convince, or actuate your audience.

The Process of Persuasion

Persuasion is a complex psychological process of reasoning and emotion. When you speak persuasively, you try to guide the audience to adopt a particular attitude, belief, or behavior that you favor. But getting people to change their minds, even a little, is difficult and requires considerable skill. Just because you think something is reasonable or right does not guarantee that someone else will think so too. Each of us has a unique way of looking at the world based on our own particular blend of attitudes, beliefs, and values.

Recall from Chapter 5 that **attitudes** are predispositions to respond to people, ideas, objects, or events in evaluative ways.[5] To evaluate something is to judge it as relatively good or bad, useful or useless, desirable or undesirable, and so on. We generally act in accordance with our attitudes. If we have a positive attitude toward reading, we're likely to read. If we have a negative attitude toward religion, we're likely to avoid attending religious services. Attitudes are based on **beliefs**—the ways we perceive reality to be[6] or our feelings about what is true. Beliefs reflect our level of confidence about the very existence or validity of something (e.g., "I believe God exists" or "I'm not so sure that God exists"). The less faith listeners have that something exists—UFOs, for instance—the less open they are to hearing about them. **Values** are our most enduring judgments about what's good and bad in life. Values are more general than either attitudes or beliefs. They are also more resistant to change. Both attitudes and beliefs are shaped by values.

As described in Chapter 5, discovering your listeners' attitudes, beliefs, and values provides crucial clues as to how receptive they will be toward your topic and your position on it. Thus, as in informative speeches, audience analysis is extremely important in persuasive speeches. To influence your audience, you must understand how their attitudes, beliefs, and values might affect the way they view your position. Once you know this information, you can adapt your appeals in ways that might best reach them. As one scholar of persuasion notes, "Persuasion requires curiosity. It demands a willingness to explore the mind-set of others…a Sherlock Holmes mentality."[7]

Be aware, however, that regardless of how thoroughly you have conducted audience analysis, or how skillfully you present your point of view, audiences seldom respond immediately or completely to a persuasive appeal. Persuasion does not occur with a single dose. An audience can be immediately "stirred," as the Roman orator Cicero put it, with relative ease. However, producing a lasting impact on their attitudes, beliefs, and behavior is a more difficult matter. Changes tend to be small, even imperceptible, especially at first.

Several factors increase the odds that your efforts at persuasion will succeed:

- To be most persuasive, a message should meet the psychological needs of the audience. Barring coercion, people are unlikely to change unless they think that it will benefit them.[8] Further, people are more likely to act on strong attitudes than on weak ones.[9]
- The persuader who seeks only minor changes is more successful than the speaker who seeks major ones.
- Speakers who establish a common ground between themselves and the audience are more likely to persuade than those who fail to establish such identification. The listeners' feelings toward the speaker strongly influence how receptive they will be toward his or her message.

attitudes
predispositions to respond to people, ideas, objects, or events in evaluative ways.

beliefs
the ways people perceive reality to be; our conceptions about what is true and what is false.

values
people's most enduring judgments about what's good and bad in life.

- People want to feel satisfied and competent. If you can show that an attitude or behavior might keep them from this state, they are more likely to be receptive to change. For example, some people might believe that because they don't know how to dance, they must be uncoordinated. If you can convince them that learning to dance is easy and will promote better coordination, they might change their attitude toward dancing *and* toward their self-concept as uncoordinated. Note that in this example the behavior (not knowing how to dance) affects the attitude ("I'm uncoordinated"). Just as changes in attitudes can influence behavior, changes in behavior can influence attitudes.[10]
- You are more likely to persuade audience members if their position differs only moderately from yours. For example, if you are trying to convince an audience to support a bill that protects the environment, you are more likely to convince those who in general, or at least in some instances, are favorably disposed toward environmentalism than those who have a consistently strong track record of opposing such legislation.
- For change to endure, people must be convinced that they will be rewarded in some way. For example, to convince people to lose weight and keep it off, you must make them believe that they will be healthier if they do so. Persuaders who achieve this are skilled at motivating their listeners to help themselves.[11]

Now that we've seen some of the factors that influence persuasion, let's look at how the ancient scholars of rhetoric, and Aristotle in particular, viewed this process. Following this, we will see how contemporary social scientists approach persuasion. Both perspectives provide useful tools for creating successful persuasive speeches.

CLASSICAL PERSUASIVE APPEALS

In his classical treatise on rhetoric, Aristotle explained that persuasion could be brought about by the speaker's use of three modes of persuasion, or forms of **rhetorical proof**. The first concerns the nature of the message in a speech; the second, the nature of the audience's feelings; the third, the qualifications and personality of the speaker. According to Aristotle, and generations of theorists and practitioners who followed him, any one or a combination of these factors is useful as a means of persuasion.

rhetorical proof
as explained by Aristotle, the speaker's use of three modes of persuasion: the nature of the message, the audience's feelings, and the personality of the speaker.

Logos: Appeals to Audience Reason

Many persuasive speeches focus on serious issues requiring considerable thought. Should we enact gun control legislation? Should we require pregnant teenagers to seek their parents' permission to have an abortion? Is a certain television program too violent for children? When an audience needs to make an important decision or reach a conclusion regarding a complicated issue, appeals to reason and logic are necessary. Aristotle used the term **logos** to refer to persuasive appeals directed at the audience's reasoning on a topic. Such appeals make considerable use of arguments—that is, stated positions, with support, for or against an idea or issue. (See Chapter 15 for an in-depth discussion of argument.)

logos
used by Aristotle to refer to persuasive appeals directed at the audience's reasoning on a topic.

Aristotle differentiated between two forms of rational appeal and offered the second as especially useful for persuasive speaking. The first is the **syllogism**, a three-part argument consisting of a major premise or general case, a minor premise or specific case, and a conclusion. The classic example is this:

MAJOR PREMISE: All men are mortal.

MINOR PREMISE: Socrates is a man.

CONCLUSION: Therefore, Socrates is a mortal.

Syllogisms are frequently used in persuasive appeals today. Some are positive and constructive, leading to clearer understanding of an issue; others are inappropriate and poorly applied, leading to unfounded conclusions. Here is an example of a contemporary syllogism with positive implications:

MAJOR PREMISE: Regular exercise enhances your abilities to study productively.

MINOR PREMISE: Swimming is good exercise.

CONCLUSION: Swimming regularly will enhance your abilities to study productively.

And here is one with negative implications:

MAJOR PREMISE: College athletes get unfair breaks for missing classes and assignments.

MINOR PREMISE: Rosslyn is on the softball team.

CONCLUSION: Rosslyn won't have to make up the work she misses.

The preceding example shows how erroneous conclusions can be reached if you begin with a major premise that is unfounded. In this case, the major premise is an *overgeneralization*, or an attempt to support a claim by asserting that a particular piece of evidence is true for all persons concerned. Although the minor premise may be true, the conclusion is based on the overgeneralization. In contrast, the previous example is an effective syllogism. It reaches a sound conclusion from an accurate major premise applied to a minor premise. Thus, appeals to reason using syllogism require accurate knowledge of the information that forms your major and minor premises.

The second form of rational appeal is the enthymeme. An **enthymeme** is a syllogism stated as a probability instead of an absolute, and it states either a major or minor premise but not both. The premise not stated is left to be implied. The syllogism about Socrates leads to the absolute conclusion that Socrates is a mortal if both of the stated premises are accurate and true. The syllogism about swimming can be restated as an enthymeme so that the conclusion is *probably* true but not necessarily always true:

FROM MAJOR PREMISE TO CONCLUSION: Regular exercise enhances your abilities to study productively, so swimming regularly should enhance your studying.

Implied in this example is that swimming is a good form of exercise. Implied in the next example is that exercise will enhance your ability to study well:

FROM MINOR PREMISE TO CONCLUSION: Swimming is good exercise and should enhance your studying.

The use of "should" in each case makes the conclusion tentative instead of absolute. Why would you want to offer probable conclusions instead of certain conclusions? Because most arguments are not based on absolutes. It is not absolutely certain, for example, that swimming regularly will enhance your studying because many other factors are involved in studying. The point is, the conclusion has to be certain enough (but not necessarily absolute) for the audience to accept the premise in order for your argument to hold. The key for both syllogisms and enthymemes is for your premises to be acceptable according to sound reason or logic. Chapter 15 describes reasoning and argument in depth.

Pathos: Appeals to Audience Emotion

Pathos involves the appeal to audience emotion. It requires, according to Aristotle, "creating a certain disposition in the audience."[12] Aristotle taught that successful public speakers should be able to identify and appeal to four sets of emotions in their listeners.[13] He presented these sets in opposing pairs: anger and meekness, love and hatred, fear and boldness, shame and shamelessness. There are two means of invoking these emotions in a speech: through *vivid description* and *emotionally charged words*. Consider the following example of vivid description from Mario Cuomo, former governor of New York, who delivered the keynote speech at the Democratic National Convention on July 16, 1984. The speech praises the values of America's working class and the freedom given them by a democratic government to pursue their work and their dreams. Cuomo uses his father as an example:

> I watched a small man with thick calluses on both hands work fifteen and sixteen hours a day. I saw him once literally bleed from the bottoms of his feet, a man who came here uneducated, alone, unable to speak the language, who taught me all I needed to know about faith and hard work by the simple eloquence of his example. I learned about our kind of democracy from my father. I learned about our obligation to each other from him and from my mother. They asked only for a chance to work and to make the world better for their children and to be protected in those moments when they would not be able to protect themselves. This nation and its government did that for them.[14]

The vivid description of what Cuomo learned from observing his immigrant father evokes emotions of boldness and pride in his democratic heritage, and perhaps anger toward those who would oppose that heritage.

The use of particularly emotional words also helps a speaker attempt persuasion through pathos. In 1967, as the Vietnam War escalated and public disapproval of the war became increasingly vocal, Senator Eugene

pathos
as used by Aristotle in terms of persuasive appeals, the audience's feelings.

AP/Wide World

Mario Cuomo's pathos: Cuomo appeals to the emotions of the audience with an uplifting gesture.

McCarthy of Minnesota announced his intentions to run for the Democratic Party's nomination for president. McCarthy was a staunch opponent of the Johnson administration's policy on the war. On December 2, 1967, he gave a moving antiwar speech in Chicago:

> John Kennedy set free the spirit of America....All the world looked to the United States with new hope, for here was youth and confidence and an openness to the future. Here was a country not being held by the dead hand of the past, nor frightened by the violent hand of the future which was grasping at the world.
>
> This was the spirit of 1963.
> What is the spirit of 1967?...
> It is a joyless spirit—a mood of frustration, of anxiety, of uncertainty.
> In place of the enthusiasm of the Peace Corps among the young people of America, we have protests and demonstrations.
> In place of the enthusiasm of the Alliance for Progress, we have distrust and disappointment.
> Instead of the language of promise and hope, we have in politics today a new vocabulary in which the critical word is war.[15]

McCarthy uses a string of emotionally charged phrases in just these few lines: "dead hand of the past...violent hand of the future...grasping at the world." The wording connotes hopelessness for most of the world except the United States under John Kennedy. Then, after Kennedy, the United States faced "a joyless spirit—a mood of frustration" and became a country consumed by "distrust...disappointment...war."

Although emotion is a powerful means of moving an audience, relying solely on naked emotion to persuade will likely fail. As Aristotle stressed, pathos functions as a means to persuasion not by any persuasive power inherent in emotions per se, but by the interplay of emotions—or desire—and sound reasoning. Emotion gets the audience's attention and stimulates a desire to act on the emotion; reason is then presented as justification for the action. For example, a popular television advertisement in the 1980s depicted a grandfatherly man in a series of activities with family members. An announcer made the logical appeal that persons with high blood pressure should maintain their prescribed regimen of medication; this was followed with the emotional appeal, "If not for yourself, do it for them." The message invoked the desire to stay healthy as long as possible for the benefit of loved ones. The reason was sound enough—blood pressure is controllable with medication, but one must take the medicine in order for it to work. In this case, as in many, emotion helped communicate the idea.

Appealing to an audience's emotions on the basis of sound reasoning ensures that your speech is ethical. However, as seen in the Focus on Ethics box on page 345, there are a host of ways emotions can be used unethically.

Ethos: Appeals to Speaker Character

No matter how well reasoned a message is, no matter which strong emotions its words target, if the audience members have little or no regard for the speaker they will not respond positively to his or her persuasive appeals. Aristotle believed that speechmaking should emphasize the quality

Focus on Ethics

Using Emotions Ethically

The most successful persuaders are those who are able to understand the mindset of others. With such insight comes the responsibility to use emotional appeals in speeches for ethical purposes only. As history attests only too amply, not all speakers follow an ethical path in this regard.

Demagogues, for example, clutter the historical landscape. A demagogue relies heavily on irrelevant emotional appeals to short-circuit the listeners' rational decision-making process.[1] Senator Joseph McCarthy, who conducted "witch hunts" against alleged Communists in the 1950s, was one such speaker. McCarthy was noted for his ability to manipulate the reactions of others, to play on their fears and anxieties. He willingly sacrificed reason and truth to pursue his goal of "rooting out" Communists from within American society. Many cult leaders are also masters of manipulating their followers' emotions toward unscrupulous ends. Adolf Hitler, possibly the most masterful emotional manipulator in history, played on the fears and dreams of German citizens to urge them toward despicable ends.

Persuasive speakers can manipulate their listeners' emotions in a variety of ways: by arousing fear and anxiety, and by using propaganda.

- *Fear and anxiety.* Some speakers deliberately arouse fear and anxiety in listeners so that the listeners will follow their recommendations. Sometimes this is done by offering a graphic description of what will happen if the audience doesn't comply (e.g., people will get hurt, children will starve). Although the fear appeal has a legitimate place in persuasion—as in demonstrating to children the harm caused by smoking, or showing a group of drunk drivers graphic pictures of the results of their actions—it must be used carefully and fairly. For example, to convince a group of children to refrain from drinking alcohol, it is acceptable to describe the medical effects of excessive drinking. It is unethical, however, to embellish these facts or paint a bleaker picture than actually exists. Nor should the argument be "packaged" in ways that upset listeners unduly. Never try to intimidate listeners or present them with information that they are not psychologically prepared to handle.

- *Propaganda.* Speakers who employ propaganda aim to manipulate an audience's emotions for the purpose of promoting a belief system or dogma. Propagandists tell audiences only what they want the listeners to know, deliberately hiding or distorting opposing viewpoints. They engage in name calling and stereotyping to arouse their listeners' emotions.

Unlike the ethical persuader, the propagandist does not respect the audience's right to choose. Nor does the speaker who unwisely uses fear appeals. Ethically, appeals to emotion in the persuasive speech should always be supported by sound reasoning.

1. Charles U. Larson, *Persuasion: Reception and Responsibilty*, 6th ed. (Belmont, CA: Wadsworth, 1992), p. 37.

---

and impact of ideas, but he recognized that the nature of the speaker's character and personality also plays an important role in how well the audience listens to and accepts the message. This effect of the speaker he referred to as **ethos**, or moral character. Several centuries after Aristotle, the Roman orator Cicero emphasized even more strongly than Aristotle the importance of the speaker's character in realizing the full achievement of a speech's purpose. He asserted that the ideal orator would be characterized as "a good man speaking well."[16] At issue is the consistency between a speaker's wanting an audience to accept his or her message as valid and

> **ethos**
> as used by Aristotle in terms of persuasive appeals, based on the nature of the speaker's moral character and personality.

relevant, and the speaker's being qualified and reliable to speak on the subject of the message. As the Roman orator Quintilian put it, "For he who would have all men trust his judgment as to what is expedient and honorable, should possess and be regarded as possessing genuine wisdom and excellence of character."[17]

Just what are the elements of an appeal based on ethos? Let's briefly consider each element in turn, and how you as the speaker can manifest them.

First is *good sense*. Another term for this element of ethos is *competence*, or the speaker's knowledge and experience with the subject matter. Ethos-based appeals emphasize the speaker's grasp of the subject matter. Skillfully preparing the speech at all stages, from research to delivery, as well as emphasizing your own expertise, evoke this quality.

The second element of an ethos-based appeal is the speaker's *moral character*. This is reflected in the speaker's straightforward and honest presentation of the message. The speaker's own ethical standards are central to this element. Current research suggests, for example, that a brief disclosure of personal moral standards relevant to the speech or occasion made in the introduction of a speech will boost audience regard for the speaker.[18] Indeed, you should prepare and present every aspect of your speeches with the utmost integrity so that your audiences regard you as *trustworthy*. The fact that you are an honest person will not be the most memorable aspect of your speeches because no one expects you to do any part of the job dishonestly; but by the very fact that dishonesty is not expected of you, it is easily identified in the content or in the delivery of your message.

The third element of an ethos-based appeal is *good will* toward the audience. Everything this text has discussed regarding audience analysis and knowledge of the speech occasion applies to this element. A strong ethos-based appeal demonstrates an interest in and concern for the welfare of your audiences. Speakers who understand the concerns of their listeners and who address their needs and expectations relative to the speech exhibit this aspect of the ethos-based appeal. Ethos is strengthened even further when you display high regard for the occasion of the speech, even if it is unfamiliar to you or outside your primary areas of interest. Ethos is even expressed in how well you work with the physical setting and accommodations available to you at the speech site. Audiences generally respond negatively to speakers who complain about the speaking environment, whether in reference to room temperature, lack of a microphone, or quality of the refreshments. Such comments suggest the speaker's mind is elsewhere, not with the audience and the speech.

Critical Checkpoint

Logos, Pathos, and Ethos

Classical rhetoricians taught that to persuade an audience, the speaker must use three different kinds of appeals. *Logos* is the appeal to an audience's reasoning and analysis of a topic. *Pathos* is the appeal to audience emotion. *Ethos* is the speaker's appeal to his or her own character as a basis for audience acceptance of the speaker's propositions. Consider the speech by Sojourner Truth at the beginning of this chapter. Where in her speech do you see the use of each kind of appeal?

CONTEMPORARY PERSUASIVE APPEALS

The classical modes of persuasion are as useful today as they were some two thousand years ago. However, with advancements in behavioral sciences and the application of scientific methods to the study of communication, the approaches taught by Aristotle have been significantly refined and expanded.[19] The discussion turns next to a consideration of several current models of persuasion that can be applied to planning and delivering persuasive speeches. These approaches include appealing to audience needs; audience attitudes, values, and behavior; the audience's ways of processing messages; and the speaker-audience relationship.

Motivating the Audience: Appeals to Audience Needs

Have you ever wondered why there are so many fast-food commercials during and after the evening news? Advertisers know that by this time of night many viewers are experiencing a strong need—to eat! Appealing to audience needs is one of the most commonly used strategies for motivating people, whether in advertising or in public speaking.

Perhaps the best-known model of human needs is that formulated by Abraham Maslow in the 1950s.[20] Maslow maintained that each person has a set of basic needs ranging from the essential, life-sustaining ones to the less critical, self-improvement ones. This set includes five categories arranged hierarchically. According to Maslow, an individual's needs at the lower, essential levels must be fulfilled before the higher levels become important and motivating. **Maslow's hierarchy of needs** has long been a basis for motivation-oriented persuasive speeches. The principle behind the model is that people are motivated to act on the basis of their needs; thus for a speaker to best persuade listeners to adopt suggested changes in attitudes, beliefs, or behavior, he or she should point to some need they want fulfilled and then give them a way to fulfill it. Let's look at Maslow's five categories of needs, beginning with the most essential one.

Physiological Needs. Physiological needs manifest our very sense of survival and require regular, if not daily, fulfillment. These include needs for water, air, and food. Most likely your audiences won't be starving for food or water, but you might be speaking to an audience just before mealtime or on a hot day in a park. When your listeners are hungry or thirsty or in need of cool air and a shady seat, they won't be attentive to messages having to do with any higher-level needs. Remember that part of your planning for a speech is to know the physical surroundings where the speech will take place. You should make sure that adequate accommodations are provided for your audience and yourself well in advance of the speech date.

Safety Needs. Safety needs relate to feelings of protection and security. We have immediate needs for shelter and comfort, and long-term needs for continued safety. Home security agencies make their pitches to sell monitored alarm systems by playing on the potential buyer's perceived need for protection. Safety needs are also the appeal of television's McGruff the Crime Dog,® whose famous line, "Take A Bite Out Of Crime,"® has convinced thousands of individuals and groups to take proactive stances against community-based crime.[21]

> **Maslow's hierarchy of needs**
> a set of five basic needs ranging from the essential life-sustaining ones to the less critical self-improvement ones.

McGruff the Crime Dog® and Take A Bite Out Of Crime® are registered marks of the National Crime Prevention Council.

TAKE A BITE OUT OF CRIME

McGruff the Crime Dog® provides helpful crime prevention advice and motivates people by appealing to their safety needs.

Most of your audiences will be unable to relate to the daily experiences of people who are homeless, but if you can get your listeners to imagine living without the daily comforts they are used to, you may be able to get them to empathize with the homeless (and, thus, perhaps support a policy intended to help them). Whenever you can stress to your listeners a safety benefit associated with your topic, you make your message more attractive.

Social Needs. Each of us has powerful social needs to establish and maintain lasting, meaningful relationships with other people. Perhaps you belong to a fraternity or sorority, a service or honors organization, a college chapter of a professional association, an athletic club, or a study group. Your membership in such groups reflects your social needs. In fact, social needs are the basis of many persuasive appeals. A common theme in televised cigarette commercials, for example (before they were banned in the late 1960s), was group activity—people sailing together, playing cards, sitting after a meal, and so on. Today an interesting reverse theme is in effect, one in which anti-smoking campaigns focus on the social harm of cigarette smoking. This harm takes the form of secondhand smoke and the generally negative stigma that is now attached to smoking. In the same vein, appealing to teenagers' desire to appear attractive and physically fit for their peers may be a more effective way of persuading an audience of teens to quit smoking than referring to the long-term consequences of the habit. The point is, if you can relate your persuasive message to the significant social relationships of your audience members, you will have struck a chord that will hold their attention and secure their careful consideration of your propositions.

Self-Esteem Needs. Self-esteem needs reflect our desires to feel good about ourselves. These needs compel us to exercise regularly, eat wholesome foods, get proper amounts of sleep, and use particular personal hygiene products. We purchase certain brands of cars and clothing, travel on certain airlines and cruise lines, hope to attend the most prestigious and tradition-rich colleges or universities, and aspire to success in just the right profession—all to feel good about ourselves. The self-esteem needs of an audience make the "good will" element of speaker ethos so important—audience members want to have the sense that the speaker cares about them, that they are worth the speaker's best effort.

As noted earlier, people are more likely to change if they believe that it will make them feel satisfied and competent. Thus, to appeal to your audience's self-esteem needs, concentrate on topics and purposes that make your listeners feel good about themselves. Show them how they will benefit by adopting your position.

Self-Actualization Needs. The highest level in Maslow's hierarchy is self-actualization needs. To be self-actualized is to reach your highest potential. Slogans that aim at this need include "Soar like an eagle," "Do your best, and then some," and "When the going gets tough, the tough get going." Appeals to self-actualization are highly suited to persuasive speeches that move the audience toward a group goal. Thus, when a coach charges his or her team at half-time to get back out on the court and play like they've never played, he or she is appealing to the team members' need to achieve their best.

Targeting Behavior:
Appeals to Audience Attitudes and Beliefs

The audience is not merely a collection of empty vessels waiting to be filled with whatever wisdom and knowledge the speaker has to offer. Members of an audience are rational, thinking, choice-making individuals. Their day-to-day behavior is directed mainly by their own volition, or will. If you want your listeners to adopt a course of action, then you should address the factors that affect the choices they make about their behavior. **Expectancy-Outcome Values Theory** is helpful in this regard.[22] The theory maintains that people consciously evaluate the potential costs and benefits, or value, associated with taking a particular action. As they weigh these costs and benefits, people consider their own attitudes about the behavior in question (e.g., "Is this a good or bad behavior?") as well as what other people who are important to them think about the behavior (e.g., "My friend would approve of me taking this action"). On the basis of these assessments, they develop expectations about what will happen if they do or do not take a certain action (e.g., "My friend will think more highly of me if I do this"). These expected outcomes become their rationale for acting in a certain way.

The Expectancy-Outcome Values Theory model has four components: attitudes about the behavior in question, subjective norms (what other people think), intentions, and behavior. The theory is graphically represented in Figure 14.1; recycling is used as the behavior in question. Let's examine each component and its implications for persuasive speaking.

Attitudes. Attitudes consist of feelings about the behavior in question, and feelings about the consequences associated with the behavior. If your goal is to convince the audience to practice recycling, you could determine through audience analysis their feelings about recycling and their feelings about the consequences of recycling or not recycling. Assume you find that most audience members consider it a good practice to recycle, and most agree that not recycling has potentially serious negative risks for the community and environment. Knowing these attitudes, you have a good foundation for presenting the audience with evidence that will support their attitudes and strengthen your argument that they should recycle.

Expectancy-Outcome Values Theory
a theory of persuasion; maintains that people consciously evaluate the potential costs and benefits, or value, associated with taking a particular action.

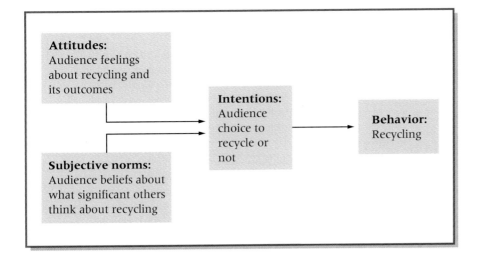

FIGURE 14.1
Expectancy-Outcome Values Theory Model of Attitude Change

Subjective Norms. Subjective norms are what audience members believe other people feel about the behavior in question, and the audience members' willingness to comply with those beliefs. You could find out through audience analysis the extent to which the listeners think their family members, close friends, and neighbors think about recycling, and whether the listeners would be more or less willing to comply with these other people's presumed preferences. Assume you find that most audience members believe their partners would approve of recycling, and that most would go along with their partners' preferences. You now have a basis for appealing to your audience's concern for their partners' preferences regarding the practice of recycling.

Intentions. Intentions relate to audience members' conscious choices to do or not do the behavior in question. According to Expectancy-Outcome Values Theory, attitudes and subjective norms determine people's intentions to do or not do something. Intentions directly determine whether or not the audience will actually take the action suggested by the speaker. Will members of the audience smoke or not smoke? Use condoms or not? Vote or not vote? The greater the audience's intentions, the more likely they will act on them.

Behavior. Behavior is the action taken by the audience any time after the speech. To change or affirm listeners' behavior, the persuasive speaker should direct the listeners' intentions by focusing on their attitudes and beliefs about the behavior. For example, if you want the audience to actually practice recycling, you should focus the speech on their attitudes and beliefs about recycling. If you can strengthen these attitudes and beliefs in a positive way, it is likely that their intentions to recycle will strengthen and they will therefore be more likely to practice the behavior in question—recycling.

The principles of Expectancy-Outcome Values Theory can help you plan a persuasive speech in which the specific purpose is to target behavior. A thorough audience analysis is critical to this approach, however.

> ## Critical Checkpoint
>
> **Appealing to the Audience**
>
> Maslow's hierarchy identifies five successively higher-order needs that can be the basis of persuasive appeals, especially those that seek to motivate audiences by demonstrating that the speaker's "solution" will address their needs. The five categories are physiological needs, safety needs, social needs, self-esteem needs, and self-actualization needs. What are some specific needs of your classmates that could be targeted to help you develop a persuasive speech?
>
> Another way to appeal to audiences is through their attitudes and subjective beliefs associated with a specific behavior or set of actions proposed by the speaker. This is referred to as the Expectancy-Outcome Values Theory of persuasion. See if you can identify some attitudes and subjective beliefs associated with a persuasive appeal to get teenage smokers to stop their habit.

Making the Message Relevant: Appeals to Audience Understanding

Sometimes the specific purpose of a persuasive speech is to convince the audience to accept a new way of looking at a problem or issue. For example, one specific purpose may be "To persuade my audience that contrary to popular belief, the federal government is really not threatened by the budget deficit." Another might be "To persuade my audience that their mental health would improve if they took a two-week 'holiday' from television."

How can you convince listeners to accept your ideas or adopt your proposal? One theory of persuasion, called the **Elaboration Likelihood Model** (ELM), suggests that people process persuasive messages by one of two routes, depending on their degree of involvement in the message. According to this theory, when people have the motivation and ability to think critically about the contents of a message, they engage in **central processing** of the message. People who process messages "centrally" are influenced primarily by the strength and quality of the speaker's arguments. They seriously consider what the speaker's message means to them and are the ones most likely to act on it. These are the listeners who are most likely to experience a relatively enduring change in thinking favorable to the speaker's position.

Not everyone listens critically, however. When people lack the motivation or ability to pay close attention to the issues, they engage in **peripheral processing**. For these listeners, the message is seen either as irrelevant, or too complex to follow, or just plain unimportant. Listeners who process messages peripherally are far more likely to be influenced by such non-content issues as the speaker's appearance or reputation, certain slogans or one-liners, and obvious attempts to manipulate emotions. Even though such listeners may "buy into" the speaker's message, they do so not on the strength of the arguments but on such factors as reputation or personal style. In this case the listener "goes with whatever the speaker says" because of who the speaker is, not because of the quality and substance of the message. Although this may seem like a positive speech outcome, the problem is that such shallow acceptance of a speaker's message has very limited impact on the listener's enduring thoughts and feelings about the matter. Listeners who use peripheral processing are unlikely to experience any enduring changes in attitudes or behavior. Central processing produces the more long-lasting changes in audience perspective.

How can you use the Elaboration Likelihood Model of persuasion to plan a speech? Imagine you are asked to address an audience of workers in the data processing division of a large insurance company. Each worker is responsible for processing dozens of claims daily. The company has decided to replace the data processing equipment and software, upgrading it to a new system that will enable each worker to increase productivity by two or three dozen more claims each day. Unfortunately, the workers are very unhappy with the impending change. They're convinced that the changeover will take weeks, their productivity will decrease during and after the changeover, and they'll be held accountable for the lower rate of productivity.

Your goal is to change the workers' perceptions of the new system and its implications for their work, convincing them to accept the system with optimism. What can you do to make it more likely that they will process

Elaboration Likelihood Model
a theory of persuasion; suggests that people process persuasive messages by one of two mental routes (central processing or peripheral processing), depending on their degree of involvement in the message.

central processing
occurs when listeners are influenced primarily by the strength and quality of the speaker's arguments and seriously consider what the speaker's message means to them.

peripheral processing
occurs when listeners lack the motivation or ability to pay close attention to the speaker's issues and become influenced by such non-content issues as the speaker's appearance or reputation.

your message via the central processing route? According to the ELM, people pay less attention to messages they perceive as irrelevant, uninteresting, or too complex. *Thus, your first step is to make the message relevant to the workers' concerns.* Avoid directly promoting the new system too much; rather, concentrate on the workers' productivity. Note how good it has been, and how, with the right tools, it can get even better with little additional effort. Second, present the message at an appropriate level of understanding. Perhaps part of the workers' uneasiness stems from learning about the new system solely through brief bursts of technical jargon. What they need is someone to explain it to them in terms they understand so they can see how it will benefit their daily tasks. Third, consider yourself, the speaker. Ideally you should speak, not as an expert on the system per se, but as someone experienced in using the system for the same application the workers will be using. This would show your commonality with them, keeping them attentive and open to your message.

The lesson behind the Elaboration Likelihood Model of persuasion is to focus on the needs and interests of your listeners. Making the message relevant to them increases the odds that your persuasive appeals will produce lasting, rather than fleeting, changes in their attitudes and behavior.

Public Speaking in Cultural Perspective

Native American Oratory

The modes of persuasion attributed to Aristotle and other classical thinkers represent well the primary means to persuasion used throughout the great speeches of Western history. But other cultures have relied throughout their own histories on different forms of rhetorical proof. Native American oratory provides one example. Whereas Western tradition relies on external sources, such as historical figures, as a form of proof (e.g., a political speaker might quote Abraham Lincoln), existing speeches of Native American speakers show few if any instances of such proof. The high value placed by Native American culture on self-reliance precludes the use of rhetorical appeals from authorities of the past.[1] Whereas Western culture places great value on the words and wisdom of figures from the past, Native Americans find such sources less relevant than those of a living authority.

An example is seen in the 1854 speech of Chief Seattle. The speech was made on his tribe's acceptance of the establishment by the U.S. government of a reservation for them. Note the chief's use of present and future tense and his use of references to nature to support his point that it doesn't matter whether his people live on a reservation or not, for their days as a sovereign people will not be long.

> It matters little where we pass the remnant of our days. They will not be many. The Indians' night promises to be dark. Not a single star of hope hovers above his horizon. Sad-voiced winds moan in the distance. Grim fate seems to be on the red man's trail, and wherever he goes he will hear the approaching footsteps of his fell destroyer and prepare stolidly to meet his doom, as does the wounded doe that hears the approaching footsteps of the hunter.[2]

1. G. Kennedy, *Comparative Rhetoric: An Historical and Cross-Cultural Introduction* (New York: Oxford University Press, 1998).
2. Gregory R. Suriano, *Great American Speeches* (New York: Gramercy Books, 1993), pp. 64–65.

Establishing Credibility:
Appeals to the Audience's Relationship with the Speaker

The relationship between speaker and audience is a crucial element in planning and delivering persuasive speeches. It's what Aristotle, Cicero, Quintilian, and their students dealt with long ago through the persuasive appeal of ethos. Beyond the qualities of speaker knowledge, moral character, and good will toward the audience that these ancient scholars described, modern behavioral science has identified other speaker-based factors that affect the outcomes of persuasive messages. Taken as a set, these factors are referred to as the speaker's credibility.

Credibility includes some of the elements of ethos, but it is different. Whereas ethos is invoked in the speaker's message, **credibility** is a matter of audience perceptions of and attitudes toward the speaker.[23] In a sense, ethos makes a message more appealing to an audience, and credibility makes the speaker more appealing.

Studies have shown that perceptions of a speaker's expertise and trustworthiness—reflective of ethos—are important contributors to persuasiveness.[24] *Speaker expertise* contributes to the persuasive outcomes of a speech under two conditions. First, when an audience is relatively unmotivated or unable to fully grasp a message, their responses to the speech will likely be in the speaker's favor if the speaker is perceived as an expert on the subject. You may recognize from the earlier discussion of the ELM that this involves peripheral processing of the message. The audience will support the speaker because "experts know what they're talking about." Second, when the audience itself is well informed about the message and perceives the speaker to have expertise, he or she will be more apt to persuade them. Perceiving that an expert speaker is presenting a subject of considerable interest, the listeners are especially tuned in to the speaker's points and evidence, comparing their own understanding to what they are now hearing, and assessing any need for modification in their own understanding. Note that "expert" doesn't mean you're a world authority on the topic or issue of your speech. It does mean that you have enough knowledge and experience on the subject that you can help the audience to better understand and accept it.

If there is one speaker attribute that is more important than others, it is probably *trustworthiness*.[25] Audiences often question speakers' sincerity, not because audiences are naturally skeptical but because it is natural to wonder what a person's motives and intentions are when they are speaking on a complex or controversial issue. (Don't you sometimes wonder why your instructors say those quirky things they do?) It's a matter of the "good will" that Aristotle taught—audiences want more than information and arguments; they want what's relevant to them from someone who cares. Indeed, the most successful persuasive speakers are those who are perceived by their audiences as sincere and forthright. Never do anything deceptive or demoralizing in speaking to an audience. Any loss in perceived trustworthiness is a significant loss in credibility. Which salesperson do you like better—the one who beats around the bush, seeming to hide some facts about the product and dodging your tough questions; or the one who cuts right to the chase, asking you directly what you want, is honest with you about the features of each option, and helps you decide on the option that is best for you? Which salesperson will you buy from and return to the

credibility
audience perceptions of and attitudes toward the speaker's perceived expertise, trustworthiness, similarity to audience members, and attractiveness.

next time you need the same product? Audiences have the same responses to speakers whom they perceive to be trustworthy.

Two additional critical elements in the speaker-audience relationship that influence the outcome of a persuasive message are speaker similarity and physical attractiveness. *Speaker similarity* involves listeners' perceptions of how similar the speaker is to themselves, especially in terms of attitudes and moral character. Generally, audience members are more likely to respond favorably to the persuasive appeals of a speaker whom they perceive to be a lot like them. This is not always the case, however. In certain situations we attach more credibility to people who are actually dissimilar to us. For example, we are more likely to be persuaded by a dissimilar speaker, especially one viewed as an "expert," when the topic or issue emphasizes facts and analysis. This is why lawyers seek the expert testimony of psychiatrists or other specialists to provide insight into the personality of a suspect, the features of a crime scene, and the like. On the other hand, an audience is more likely to be persuaded by a similar speaker when the subject is more personal or relational. For example, we prefer to watch the "Oprah Winfrey Show" instead of "60 Minutes" when the subject is fathers and daughters, or bosses and secretaries. We tend to perceive Oprah Winfrey to be more similar to us in relational concerns than we do Mike Wallace. But if the issue involves new details in a political scandal or a foreign agreement, we would likely turn to Mike Wallace as our preferred source.

AP/Wide World

Oprah Winfrey holds a warm place in the hearts of many Americans, who trust the way she handles interpersonal issues. Here she appears with golf champion Tiger Woods.

These facts point to an important lesson for the persuasive speaker: For speeches that involve a lot of facts and analysis, play on whatever amount of expertise you can summon. For speeches that concern matters of a more personal nature, however, it's best to emphasize your commonality with the audience.

Finally, *physical attractiveness* of the speaker affects persuasive outcomes. A quick look at the physical features of any of a dozen television news anchors and talk show hosts suggests that physical attractiveness is a significant benefit to speakers. By and large, looking good does pay off for a speaker in terms of persuasive outcomes. In our culture, attractive people are perceived to be competent, in control of themselves, well organized, and confident. We tend to generalize these perceptions to public speakers as well. But there are limitations, even drawbacks, to physical attractiveness as a factor in persuasive speaking.

First, highly attractive speakers can be a distraction to an audience, drawing their attention away from the message. Isn't it more pleasant to daydream about being in the poolside company of an attractive speaker than to listen to him or her speak about some new amortization formula? Second, physical attractiveness can interfere with persuasive appeals when the speaker's appearance violates expectations for the occasion or the topic. It would be distracting for a speaker to wear a tuxedo to a high school basketball team's end-of-season banquet. Even a coat and tie might be pushing it. Likewise, the speaker who appears at a Rotary luncheon in faded jeans and a pullover shirt will not have many attentive listeners. Third, any positive outcomes of a persuasive speech that can be attributed to the speaker's attractiveness will probably be short-term gains at best. Our tendency is to respond positively to attractive speakers because we want to be like them or associated with them. But responding primarily on that basis leads only to superficial understanding of the message and fleeting attention to it. So what advice should you take with respect to physical attractiveness? Be yourself, be neat and professional, dress for the occasion, and concentrate on your message.

Critical Checkpoint

Maintaining Credibility

It's vital to successful persuasive speaking that you be perceived as a credible source of information. You must be seen by the audience members as somewhat more knowledgeable or experienced on the topic than they are, trustworthy to present accurate information in a caring way, similar to them in some ways, and reasonably attractive in your appearance and attire. Yet according to the Elaboration Likelihood Model of persuasion, sometimes an audience's high regard for a speaker can result in a superficial understanding of the speech message. The following tips will enable you to maintain audience perceptions of your credibility while simultaneously keeping the audience focused on understanding your message. Noted in parentheses are the elements of credibility that are strengthened by each strategy.

- Whenever appropriate, cite proper authorities who both support your perspective and help refute the alternatives. (*expertise, trustworthiness*)
- Refer to your own experiences with the topic. Be careful not to overstate your knowledge—don't be self-promoting. (*expertise, trustworthiness*)
- Express specific beliefs and values that you share with the audience. Let them know your personal viewpoint. These expressions must be consistent with and relevant to the topic. (*similarity, trustworthiness*)
- Dress appropriately for the speech occasion. Dress on the same level or slightly better than your audience is expected to dress. (*attractiveness, similarity*)
- Use some appropriate humor, but don't force it. It's better not to use any than to fail at getting laughs and appear unable to relate to the audience. (*similarity*)
- Express gratitude for the opportunity to speak to the audience. Recognize by name—humorously, if possible—any person you know who is held in high regard by the audience. (*trustworthiness, similarity*)
- Be physically active during the speech delivery. Use vocal variety. Maintain direct eye contact. Show with your delivery that you care about the topic and the audience. (*attractiveness, trustworthiness, expertise*)

A PLAN FOR ORGANIZING PERSUASIVE SPEECHES

To this point, both classical and contemporary principles of persuasive speaking have been examined. A basic understanding of these principles should enable you to select strategies that are applicable to any persuasive speech you might give. However, application of any of the principles alone does not make a speech persuasive nor does it guarantee that you will achieve persuasive outcomes. Achieving persuasive effects involves a process—a chain of occurrences, if you will. In the mid-1930s, public speaking professor and scholar Alan Monroe developed the **motivated sequence**, an organizational pattern for planning and for presenting persuasive speeches.[26] The motivated sequence provides a time-tested model of the chain of occurrences that leads to success in persuasive speeches. The discussion that follows explores each step of the motivated sequence and shows how some of the principles of persuasive speaking are used in it.

📢 **motivated sequence**
an organizational pattern for planning and presenting persuasive speeches that involves five steps: attention, need, satisfaction, visualization, action.

Step 1: Attention

As with any speech, a persuasive speech should begin by getting the audience's attention. This does not mean simply getting the audience to look at and listen to the speaker, but getting them oriented to the speech itself. The *attention step* addresses core concerns of the audience, making the speech highly relevant to them. Here is one example:

> Ladies and gentlemen, because of trafficking in illegal drugs, the health and well-being of our children are at risk. Our democratic systems are under assault. And the very sovereignty of our countries is threatened. Allow me to describe the magnitude of the common danger we face.[27]

In this example, the speaker immediately draws attention to the theme of the speech with a startling statement about the risk to children of illegal drug trafficking. To stress its relevance to listeners, the speaker uses the phrases "our children," "our democratic systems," and "our countries." In addition to addressing core concerns of the audience members and enticing them to wonder what's coming next, this passage engages the audience in central processing of the message. And by striking at emotionally sensitive entities, especially children, the speaker also invokes the classical principle of pathos.

Many speeches make use of the attention step to create a positive speaker-audience relationship. Here is such an example:

> Thank you, Don, and thanks to all of you for having me back again. The Economic Club of Detroit is one of those rare institutions whose reputation does, indeed, speak for itself, and speak well.
>
> So, you can understand if my ego was engaged just a little when the club extended me its third invitation. One of my colleagues suggested that this is kind of an encore performance.
>
> But Don clarified that. He said: "In Detroit, we think of it as a re-call."
>
> But, under any circumstances, I'm delighted to be here.
>
> Business and government have worked hard to diversify Michigan's economy. But to most people in the world, the name "Detroit" still means automobiles. And so, as I thought about joining you here today, I began to think back to the first car I ever owned.[28]

This speaker rekindles an already established relationship with the audience (he notes that this is his third time to speak to this group). He maintains a positive rapport by mentioning one of the audience members by name ("Don"), retelling a joke on himself that the named person had told, and giving praise to the quality of the organization and expressing how privileged he feels to speak to its members again (his ego is "engaged" by their invitation to speak). The story he goes on to tell about his first car further reinforces the speaker-audience relationship and is used to make a transition into the topic and purpose of the speech. Such a transition opens the way for Step 2 of the motivated sequence.

Step 2: Need

Sometimes called the problem step, the *need step* isolates and describes the issue to be addressed in the persuasive speech. Referring to it as a "need" reminds us of the need-based principles of persuasive speaking described earlier. If you can show an audience that they have an important need that must be satisfied or a problem that must be solved, they have a reason to listen to your propositions. Consider this example from Roy Romer, governor of Colorado:

> Today we come together in an extraordinary session to take the first step in solving an extraordinary problem.
> Let's define the problem. The problem is violence.
> The problem is kids killing kids.
> The problem is gangs in our neighborhoods.
> The problem is guns in the hands of children....
> This is not just a Denver problem. It's a problem throughout the state....
> And this is not just a Colorado problem. It's a national problem.[29]

In these few brief sentences, the speaker establishes a significant need—to do something about the problem of youth violence. Romer's use of the plural possessive "our" makes the problem the audience's problem. The need to do something about the problem is their need. The speaker also uses emotionally charged phrases—"kids killing kids," "guns in the hands of children." A few lines later he extends the depth of the problem by using recent statistics:

> On your desks is a copy of a survey of over 2,500 kids from around the country, grades 6 through 12, conducted this summer by Lou Harris.
> Do you know what it says?
> It reports that 15 percent of the kids surveyed said they carried a handgun on their person at some point during the previous 30 days.
> Nine percent said they'd shot a gun at someone else.
> Eleven percent said they'd been shot at by someone else during the past year.[30]

According to ELM theory, these tactics of personalizing the problem and providing fear-inducing statistics should lead the audience to attend closely to the message.

Step 3: Satisfaction

Once you have gotten the audience's attention and have established a need or problem that is personally important to them, you are ready to introduce your proposed solution to the problem. The *satisfaction step* identifies the solution. This step begins the crux of the speech, offering the audience a proposal to reinforce or change their attitudes, beliefs, and values regarding the need at hand. Here is an example from the speech on youth violence by Roy Romer:

> This special session is only a first step. Our first responsibility is to get the bullets off the streets and the guns out of the hands of our kids. There will be many steps that must follow concerning prevention, but for the next few days we need to focus on four simple but critical tasks.
>
> One, we must ban the possession of handguns by kids under 18.
>
> Two, we must make the consequences of violating this law immediate and serious.
>
> Three, we must provide more detention space and programs so that those who do violate the law spend time in the strict discipline of detention or a boot camp—instead of immediately being turned back on the streets.
>
> And four, we must provide a special sentencing program for the most hardened and violent young offenders. We call this the Youth Offender Program.[31]

The satisfaction step continues by providing more detail about the solution. In this case, the speaker goes on to provide support for each of the four strategies specified for dealing with the problem. The support includes statistics, testimony, and even stories that illustrate or demonstrate the feasibility of the proposed solution and its superiority over other alternatives and the status quo. Some of the support is rational (logos), some is more emotional (pathos). The process followed by the speaker in this step is the development of arguments in favor of his proposal.

Step 4: Visualization

After presenting arguments that support the feasibility of your proposed solution to the problem, you provide the audience with a vision of anticipated outcomes associated with the solution. This is the *visualization step*. Its purpose is to carry the audience beyond accepting the feasibility of your proposal to seeing how it will actually benefit them. In the following example, the speaker sums up the solution and then presents a vision of the way things can be:

> A new political vision requires people to engage each other, endure the pain of candor, learn from each other's history, absorb each other's humanity and move on to higher ground. Such is the task of those who care about racial healing. It won't happen overnight nor will one person bring it, however illustrative his career, nor will one person destroy it, however heinous his crime or poisonous his

rhetoric. It can never be just about numbers. What will be built has its foundation in the individual interactions of individual Americans of different races who dialogue and then act together to do something so that like a team, a platoon, a group building a home or cleaning up a park, something is transformed because of the common effort. Slowly, with acts of brotherhood transforming physical circumstances even as they bind the ties among the participants, we can say that racial progress has ceased retreating and is once again on the advance.[32]

The speaker's appeal is to a change in understanding and beliefs about the nature of race relations in America. His next proposition is the visualization of what race relations can become if his perspective on renewing interracial dialogue is accepted. Throughout this speech (beyond what is excerpted here) the speaker refers to various racial communities and the attitudes they have toward other groups, reflecting the attitude and subjective norm components of the Expectancy-Outcome Values Model of persuasive speaking. The visualization step invokes needs of self-esteem and self-actualization, such that Americans of all races can feel better about themselves and each other through renewed dialogue.

Step 5: Action

The final element of a persuasive speech following the motivated sequence involves making a direct request of the audience. The request is for the audience members to act according to their acceptance of the message. This may involve reconsidering their present way of thinking about something, continuing to believe as they do but with renewed vigor, or implementing a new set of behaviors or plan of action. The speaker seeks an implicit or explicit response of: "I agree with you all the way. I am going to do it." The following speech samples are *action step* excerpts.

The first excerpt is an implicit suggestion to build a competitive local telephone market.

> The technology available today raises the possibility that local telephone service *could be converted into a competitive market*, with all the benefits that competition brings.

The second example is an explicit call to include objective measures of competition.

> The time has come for government and the telecommunications industry to see if we can make that happen. And *any plan to do that has to include objective measurements* to determine when market competition is a reality.[33]

The third example makes the explicit call to action to begin the plan now.

> This is a troubling issue, but there is good news in Colorado. We have the strongest economy in the nation. This remains one of the best places to live and work and raise a family. We are here today

Making a Difference

REVEREND TOM GREY, EXECUTIVE DIRECTOR, NATIONAL COALITION AGAINST LEGALIZED GAMBLING (NCALG)

The Reverend Tom Grey is determined to stop the spread of legalized gambling in the United States. An ordained Methodist Minister who spent a quarter-century at the pulpit and a former infantry officer who served in Vietnam, Grey has been battling the issue since 1992. At that time the county officials in his hometown of Galena, Illinois, wrangled approval for a riverboat casino despite a referendum in which 80 percent of the town's citizens voted it down. Grey subsequently organized the town's citizens, with the result that the casino was not able to establish itself and eventually went out of business.

Although he was pleased with his victory, Grey knew that just down the river in Alton, Illinois, riverboat gambling was taking off like wildfire. Moreover, casino builders were having similar successes all across the country. In fact, legalized gambling is now one of the most rapidly growing enterprises in the United States, with casinos in 23 states and counting; many are owned by corporate giants like International Telephone and Telegraph (ITT) and Hilton Hotels Corporation. Total profits from casinos alone exceed $17 billion annually. In one form or another, eight out of ten Americans gamble.

Believing that organized gambling is an opportunity for "millionaires to become billionaires" at the expense of the ordinary citizen, Grey and other activists revitalized a little-known group called the National Coalition Against Legalized Gambling (NCALG) and turned it into an effective fighting force. Grey's goal is not to eliminate gambling altogether but to stop its rapid spread, to study the enterprises that do exist, and to see if legalized gambling is indeed good public policy. He has had con-

because we want to keep it that way, because we want to keep control of our own destiny. It is not too late to do that, if *we begin now*.[34]

The final example is an implicit statement that following the plan now will result in a better future.

Only together can *we chart a brighter future*.[34]

The motivated sequence is not a secret formula for persuasive speaking. It does provide a general framework to give you direction as you work to put together the pieces of a persuasive speech. And each speech you give may call for a different implementation of the motivated sequence. If you're presenting a highly complex problem, you may need to spend much of the speech detailing the characteristics and effects of the problem. If you're talking to an audience that is familiar with the problem, you'll only need to highlight the problem and spend most of the speech on satisfaction siderable success. Since 1994, 35 states have said no to gambling expansion. Grey personally strategized 19 of these victories.

Grey has spoken passionately against gambling to countless groups, ranging from local community organizations to the U.S. Senate. As executive director of NCALG he spends 280 days a year on the road, warning communities that legalized gambling is not the cure-all it claims to be. In the short term it may create jobs and add to the states' coffers, but, Grey argues, the new result is a social deficit, not a plus. "It's as simple as the ABCs," Grey says: "Gambling brings addiction, bankruptcies, crime, and corruption to the communities that invite it in. The fact that many casinos are opening up all-night child-care centers shows the length to which they will go to separate people—in this case, families—from their money."

Like all great persuaders, Grey understands that he has to appeal to his audiences' attitudes, beliefs, and ways of understanding messages rather than simply preaching what be believes. "Americans don't like to be told what they can and cannot do," he says. "Rather than attacking the morality of gambling, I take on gambling as a predatory enterprise. The issue is not whether people should gamble, but whether gambling should be taking place on Main Street. I try to work on people's perceptions and then allow them to make their own choices." Grey

also notes that it's impossible to convince all of the people all of the time. "In Vietnam, one out of four soldiers fired their rifles. If I get one out of ten in my speeches, I'm doing well."

Through his long years as a minister, Grey was accustomed to speaking in front of people. But even more important for his current mission, this background taught him how to deal with a variety of people in a variety of circumstances. "I don't see what I do now as preaching," Grey says, "but hollering fire where no one smells smoke." A passionate speaker, he never gives the same speech twice. He always personalizes the speech by incorporating information from the community. For him, the key to a successful speech is information. "I call it ammunition," Grey says. "I then find out how I can help the people who invite me to achieve their objectives. The pro-gambling public relations people have a standard line. I think I have the truth. I try to push everything to a ballot. Then we can have an honest debate instead of having decisions made in back rooms."

"There is a burden when you get up in a public arena to say we shouldn't have public gambling," Grey notes. "I feel a tremendous responsibility to back up my arguments with sound evidence and reasons. All I have is my credibility."

and visualization. The extent of material required for the attention step and the nature of the specific statement of action will depend on your own relationship with the audience—how well they know you, your experience with the problem, and so on. Finally, as described in Chapter 8, the way you pattern any speech, persuasive ones included, ultimately will depend on your topic and your specific speech goal.

SUMMARY QUESTIONS

What is a persuasive speech, and how does it differ from an informative speech?

Persuasive speaking is speech intended to influence the beliefs, attitudes, values, and acts of others. Like informative speeches, persuasive speeches also increase understanding and awareness and present audiences with new information. But rather than seeking to increase understanding and awareness, the goal of persuasive speeches is to influence audience choices. Persuasive speeches present listeners with a limited number of alternatives to consider and ask for a response. As with informative speeches, persuasive speeches respect audience choices.

Under what four conditions should a speaker choose a persuasive purpose?

You should select a persuasive purpose if your goal is to: (1) influence an audience's attitudes about an issue; (2) influence an audience's beliefs or understanding about something; (3) influence an audience's behavior; or (4) reinforce audience members' existing attitudes, beliefs, or behavior so they will continue to possess or practice them.

What are some key factors or principles that, when heeded, will increase the odds that efforts at persuasion will succeed?

Paying attention to the following principles will increase the odds that your efforts at persuasion will succeed. (1) A message should meet the psychological needs of the audience. People are unlikely to change unless they see that it will benefit them and people are more likely to act on strong attitudes than on weak ones; (2) the persuader who seeks only minor changes is more successful than the persuader who seeks major ones; (3) speakers who establish a common ground between themselves and the audience are more likely to persuade than those who fail to establish such identification; (4) if the speaker can show that an attitude or behavior will satisfy people and make them feel competent, they are more likely to be receptive to change; (5) the speaker is more likely to persuade audience members if their position differs only moderately from the speaker's; and (6) for change to endure, people must be convinced that they will be rewarded by making the change.

By what three means did classical rhetoricians such as Aristotle teach that a speaker could persuade an audience?

In his classical treatise on rhetoric, Aristotle explained that persuasion could be brought about by the speaker's use of three forms of rhetorical proof: appeals to the audience's reasoning on the topic (logos), the audience's emotions (pathos), and the audience's regard for the speaker's character (ethos).

How can Abraham Maslow's five-level hierarchy of needs be used to appeal to an audience's needs and interests?

Maslow's model of needs has long been a basis for motivation-oriented persuasive speeches. Maslow maintained that each person has a set of basic needs ranging from the essential, life-sustaining ones to the less critical, self-improvement ones. Needs at the lower, essential levels must be fulfilled before the higher levels become important and motivating. The principle behind the model is that people are motivated to act on the basis of their needs; thus, to best persuade listeners to adopt your suggested changes in attitudes, beliefs, or behavior, you should point to a need they want fulfilled and then give them a way to fulfill it.

Physiological needs manifest our very sense of survival and require regular, if not daily, fulfillment. Part of your planning for a speech is to know the physical surroundings where the speech will take place. Make sure that adequate accommodations will be provided for your audience and yourself well in advance of the speech date. Safety needs are often used to convince people to take action against situations described by the speaker as dangerous. If you can relate your persuasive message to the significant social needs of the audience, you will have struck a central chord that will hold their attention and secure their careful consideration of your propositions. To appeal to the audience's self-esteem needs, concentrate on topics and purposes that make the listeners feel good about themselves. Show them how they will benefit by adopting your position. Finally, to appeal to listeners' self-actualization needs, stress how achieving various goals can make them feel fulfilled.

How can the principles of the Expectancy-Outcome Values Theory model be used to seek a change in an audience's behavior?

Members of an audience are rational, thinking, choice-making individuals. Thus, to convince them to adopt a course of action you should appeal to factors that influence the choices they make about their behavior. Expectancy-Outcome Values Theory maintains that people consciously evaluate the potential costs and benefits, or value, associated with taking a particular action. As they weigh these costs and benefits, people consider their own attitudes about the behavior in question as well as what other people who are important to them think about the behavior (i.e., subjective norms). On the basis of these assessments, they develop expectations about what will happen if they do or do not take a certain action. These expected outcomes become their rationale for acting in a certain way. Therefore, if your goal is to convince the audience to change a certain behavior, you could determine through audience analysis their feelings about that behavior, as well as their perceptions of the attitudes of others who are important to them. With this information, you have a good foundation for presenting the audience with evidence that will support their attitudes and strengthen your case that they should adopt the behavior in question.

How can the principles of the Elaboration Likelihood Model of persuasion be used to increase the likelihood that audience members will understand the speaker's message and modify their beliefs on an issue?

The ELM offers a theory of how listeners receive and interpret persuasive messages. The model suggests that people "hear" messages by one of two routes (central and peripheral processing) depending on their degree of involvement in the message. People who process messages "centrally" seriously consider what the speaker's message means to them and are the most likely to act on it. Those who engage in peripheral processing are more likely to be influenced by such non-content issues as the speaker's appearance or reputation, certain slogans or one-liners, and obvious attempts to manipulate emotions. Unlike listeners who use central processing, those who use peripheral processing are unlikely to experience enduring changes in attitudes or behavior. The lesson behind this model of persuasion is to focus on the needs and interests of your listeners. Making the message relevant to them increases the odds that your persuasive appeals will produce lasting, rather than fleeting, changes in their attitudes and behavior.

How can the principles of speaker credibility be used to increase the persuasive appeal of a message?

The speaker-audience relationship provides another area of appeal on which persuasive speakers can rely. Persuasive outcomes are especially influenced by audience perceptions of speaker expertise, trustworthiness, similarity to audience members themselves, and attractiveness.

ISSUES FOR DISCUSSION

1. How can you tell the difference between a persuasive speech and an informative speech?

2. Which do you think is most important to achieving persuasive outcomes in a speech—logos, pathos, or ethos? Why?

3. Name someone you consider to be a credible speaker. How much does the person's credibility depend on his or her message as compared to who he or she is as a person (e.g., character and trustworthiness, similarity to you, etc.)?

4. List some needs that are common and salient to people your age. Where do these needs fall among the categories on Maslow's hierarchy?

5. Describe a behavior common to your peers that could be the focus of change based on the Expectancy-Outcome Values model of persuasion. How can you apply the model to the behavior?

6. Using the Elaboration Likelihood Model as a framework, what suggestions can you give your instructor that would help him or her enhance the class's understanding of persuasive speaking?

7. Why do you think Monroe's organizational plan is called the motivated sequence? List some occasions when this pattern might be useful for giving persuasive speeches.

SELF-ASSESSMENT

1. Select one of the sample speeches in the Appendix. Analyze the speech for its use of logos, pathos, and ethos. Identify examples where the speech makes appeals to audience needs and attitudes, and state what behavior or set of actions (if any) the speaker wants the audience to engage in. Estimate the extent to which you could attend fully to this speech without being distracted by characteristics or qualities of the

speaker. Note anything the speaker says that works to enhance the speaker-audience relationship, and state whether it promotes perceptions of the speaker's expertise, trustworthiness, similarity, or attractiveness.

2. Referring to the same speech, analyze its use of the motivated sequence. Identify where the attention, need, satisfaction, visualization, and action steps occur in the speech.

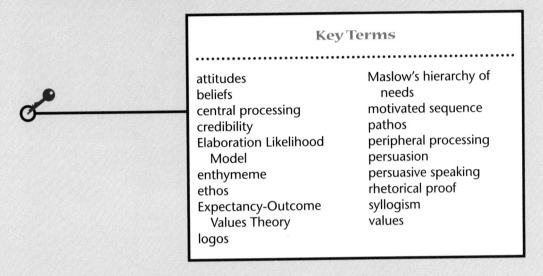

Key Terms

attitudes
beliefs
central processing
credibility
Elaboration Likelihood
   Model
enthymeme
ethos
Expectancy-Outcome
   Values Theory
logos

Maslow's hierarchy of
   needs
motivated sequence
pathos
peripheral processing
persuasion
persuasive speaking
rhetorical proof
syllogism
values

TEAMWORK

1. In a group of four or five classmates, take turns stating needs that each of you has that are especially sensitive to persuasive appeals. Consider television commercials or a recent election campaign as possible sources of persuasive appeals that have affected you.

2. Discuss with classmates the aspects of persuasive messages that draw your attention away from the message itself, leading you to peripheral processing. On the basis of your discussion, choose some strategies you could use to maintain your classmates' central processing of a persuasive message.

The truth is
always the
strongest
argument.
—Sophocles

Nothing can be lasting when reason does not rule.

—A Latin proverb

Developing Arguments for the Persuasive Speech

Think about the last time you had a discussion about a controversial issue. If some people's opinions were different from yours, how did you go about formulating arguments to support your views? **What kind of evidence did you cite to validate your claims?** In other situations when people have tried to change your opinion, what kinds of arguments and evidence did they need to provide before you would change your view? **What kind of evidence are you most likely to believe? Whether you are listening to a persuasive speech or delivering one, you will need to call on your critical thinking skills to determine what kinds of arguments you or your audience will find most convincing.**

Maria Morales, an early childhood major and public speaking student, needed to prepare a persuasive speech for her class. She selected as her topic "Should Children Be Allowed to Divorce Their Parents?" A recent case in the news, in which an 11-year-old boy actually sued for the right to divorce his mother and be legally adopted by his foster parents, had moved Maria deeply. In addition, her state's legislature was considering passing a bill that would permit such divorces under certain conditions. Herself a product of foster homes, she knew only too well the destructive effects of endlessly waiting and hoping for biological parents to claim a child. She fervently hoped the bill would pass.

To prepare for her speech, Maria researched the current laws on children's rights. She read reviews of the divorce case in the legal and popular press, interviewed a child rights advocate, and even planned on using her own experience as evidence. With all this data in hand, Maria considered her specific purpose. Should it be to move the audience closer to her own attitudes, or to persuade them to support the pending legislation by getting them to sign a petition that she could take to the state capitol? Having learned the difficulty of getting people to act, she decided to concentrate on constructing an argument that would move the audience's attitudes in the direction of her own. As she had learned in class, to accomplish this she would need persuasive evidence and sound reasons to support her claim.

The ability to reason, it is often said, is what separates humans from all the other animals. Ancient scholars of rhetoric, such as Aristotle, believed public speaking was one of the greatest applications and tests of reasoning. Aristotle also recognized that Greece's fledgling democracy rested on the rule of reason over force. Reason is the tool that free citizens everywhere use to decide public policy and respond to the many complex issues that shape their daily lives. As one writer notes, "democracy depends on a citizenry that can reason for themselves, on men [and women] who know whether a case has been proved, or at least made probable."[1]

One definition of reasoning is "the power of comprehending, inferring, or thinking, especially in orderly rational ways."[2] Reasoning in this sense is the process of critical thinking that we try to engage in throughout our everyday lives and in our roles as public speakers and active listeners. It is the kind of reasoning we use when we gather and arrange supporting materials for an informative speech, as well as when we critically evaluate such a speech. Another definition of **reasoning**, one that applies directly to creating a persuasive speech, is "the process of proving inferences or conclusions from evidence."[3] Reasoning in this sense is synonymous with argument. Reasoning through a persuasive speech is a process of building one or more arguments. Indeed, arguments are created to change people's opinions, influence behavior, or justify the arguer's beliefs or actions.[4]

Chapter 14 explored classical and contemporary approaches to appealing to an audience's needs, attitudes, beliefs, and values. This chapter describes how to use argument as a method for making appeals in persuasive speeches. In fact, persuasive speeches use arguments to present one alternative as superior to other alternatives that are available to an audience. Most persuasive speeches consist of several arguments.

reasoning
in persuasive speeches, the process of building one or more arguments by proving inferences or conclusions from evidence.

Chapter Challenges

One of your greatest public speaking challenges lies in learning how to reason through the speech in order to prove or argue a major proposition or claim. Beyond its application to public speaking, the ability to reason is important in any situation where you are required to defend your ideas. Reasoning skills will enable you to articulate your views clearly and forcefully in academic, business, and personal settings. In your role as a citizen, the ability to reason will help you make a convincing case for or against issues such as new taxes or school funding. The same skills will also help you separate fact from fallacy in the arguments of others, whether they be salespeople urging you to undertake an expensive purchase or politicians seeking your vote.

In this chapter you will learn how to build or structure an argument in a speech. In the process, you'll discover how to:

- Develop original arguments by stating claims, giving evidence, and providing warrants.
- Use different types of claims depending on the topics and purposes of your speeches.
- Select the appropriate type of evidence for specific claims.
- Apply tests of evidence to the supporting material you select for your speeches.
- Distinguish the kinds of warrants that are operating for your claims.
- Identify and avoid certain kinds of fallacies that can weaken your claims and thwart the purpose of your speeches.

WHAT IS AN ARGUMENT?

An **argument** is a stated position, with support, for or against an idea or issue. Speakers who present arguments ask listeners to accept a conclusion about some state of affairs by providing evidence and reasons why that evidence logically supports the claim. An argument consists of a claim, evidence, and warrants:[5]

argument
a stated position, with support, for or against an idea or issue.

1. The claim states the speaker's conclusion, based on evidence, about some state of affairs.
2. The evidence substantiates the claim.
3. The warrants provide reasons why the evidence supports the claim.

Stating a Claim

claim
also called a proposition; declares
some state of affairs, often stated
as a thesis statement.

To state a **claim** (also called a proposition) is to declare a state of affairs. Claims are often, but not always, stated as thesis statements. Claims answer the question, What are you trying to prove?[6] If you want to convince the audience members that they need to be more careful consumers of blue jeans, your claim might be this: "The cost of blue jeans will increase steadily over the next two years." This claim asserts the state of affairs regarding the cost of blue jeans. But unless the audience already agrees with the claim, it's unlikely that they'll accept it at face value. To make the claim believable, the speaker must provide proof, or evidence in support of the claim.

Providing Evidence

evidence
material that provides grounds
for belief in a claim.

Every claim you make in a speech must be supported with **evidence**, or material that provides grounds for belief. You've already reviewed several forms of evidence in Chapter 7 on supporting materials: examples, narratives, testimony, facts, and statistics. In a speech about the price of blue jeans, for example, to support the claim that their cost will increase steadily over the next two years you might provide *statistics* showing the price trends for textile cotton over a five-year period. Perhaps the data would show a steady increase in the wholesale price of textile cotton from year to year over the next five years. You might then couple this data with *testimony* from textile industry analysts and mercantile exchange brokers who predict continued price increases for textile cotton.

The goal in using evidence is to make a claim more acceptable, or believable, to the audience. If the evidence itself is believable, then the claim is more likely to be found acceptable by the audience. If, however, audiences question the evidence, then it too must be treated as a claim and some other evidence provided to substantiate it.

Warrants, the third component of arguments, help to both support a claim and substantiate the link between the claim and the evidence.

Giving Warrants

warrant
a statement that provides the
logical connection between some
evidence and a claim.

Although a piece of evidence may provide strong support for a claim, in order for the audience to accept the argument, the connection between the claim and the evidence must be made clear. A reason, or **warrant**, serves as a bridge between a claim and evidence. In the example of cotton prices, it may not be clear to listeners how the price of blue jeans is directly related to the price of textile cotton. Some good warrants can make the link clearer. The argument developed so far is that:

> The price of blue jeans will increase over the next two years [CLAIM] because the price of textile cotton continues to increase [EVIDENCE].

The argument can be further developed by showing that as cotton prices increase, so does the cost to consumers of blue jeans. This could be done, for instance, by plotting trend data on the price of textile cotton against trend data on the price of blue jeans for a five-year period. This provides a sound reason for accepting the link between the evidence and the claim:

The consumer price of blue jeans is directly correlated with the market price of textile cotton, and because the price of textile cotton is forecast to continue increasing, the cost of blue jeans can be expected to increase.

The claim is supported.

Diagramming the argument lets you visualize how the evidence and warrants can be presented in support of your claim. Figure 15.1 illustrates the three components of the preceding argument about the price of cotton casual wear. As you consider formulating an argument, try to diagram it in similar fashion:

1. Write down the claim.
2. List each possible piece of evidence you have in support of the claim.
3. Write down the corresponding warrants that link the evidence to the claim.

The following speech excerpts contain various elements of effective arguments. In the first excerpt, from a 1997 commencement address at the University of California at San Diego, President Clinton speaks about the social importance of maintaining affirmative action programs. Speaking against a voter-approved initiative that repealed affirmative action laws in California, Clinton claims that the U.S. military exemplifies how affirmative action effectively equalizes opportunity and fosters racial cooperation without sacrificing performance levels.

> The best example of successful affirmative action is our military [CLAIM]. Our armed forces are diverse from top to bottom—perhaps the most integrated institution in our society and certainly the most integrated military in the world [EVIDENCE]. And, more important, no one questions that they are the best in the world. So much for the argument that excellence and diversity do not go hand in hand [WARRANT].[7]

A commencement address by the columnist William Safire offers another example of an effective argument. In his address, Safire speaks about our society's growing dependence on the telephone. He claims that few people

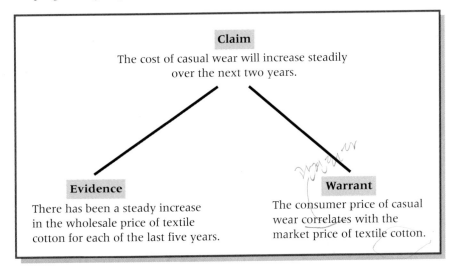

FIGURE 15.1
A Model of Argument

write personal letters because they would rather use the telephone. As evidence in support of his claim, Safire provides some interesting statistics:

> Most people are not writing personal letters anymore [CLAIM]. Oh, the volume of first-class mail has doubled since 1950, but here's the way the mail breaks down. Over 80 percent is business related; over 10 percent is greeting card and Christmas card; and only 3 percent is from one person to another to chew the fat [EVIDENCE].
>
> More and more we're relying on commercial poets and cartoonists to express our thoughts for us. Tomorrow is Mother's Day, how many of us are relying on canned sentiments?...
>
> When was the last time you wrote, or received, a long, thoughtful letter? When was the last time you wrote a passionate love letter? No, that takes time, effort, thought—there's a much easier way, the telephone [WARRANT].[8]

Safire supports his claim by using comparative statistics on types of mail that are processed. His warrant in support of his claim is that letters have been replaced by telephone calls. With the growing popularity of email, it would be interesting to hear Safire's thoughts today.

In a 1991 convocation to incoming students at Elizabethtown College in Pennsylvania, Professor Jacob Neusner—a scholar of Judaica and a popular speaker on college teaching and college life—speaks of the relationship between teacher and student. His claim is that instead of "teaching," good teachers help students "learn." To support his claim, he offers the example of three great teachers:

> Great teachers don't teach. They help students learn. Students teach themselves [CLAIM]. Three of the all-time great teachers—Socrates, Jesus, and his Jewish contemporary, the sage Hillel—shared a dislike of heavyweight speeches. They spoke briefly, painting pictures and telling tales ("parables"), and always raised more questions than they settled [EVIDENCE].
>
> Socrates was the greatest philosopher of all time, and all he did was walk around the streets and ask people irritating questions. Jesus was certainly the most influential teacher in history, and his longest "lecture"—for instance, the Sermon on the Mount—cannot have filled up an hour of classroom time or a page in a notebook. And Hillel's greatest lesson, in answer to someone who told him to teach the entire Torah while standing on one foot—"What is hateful to yourself, don't do to someone else. That's the whole Torah, all the rest is commentary. Now go study"—directed people to go off and learn on their own [EVIDENCE BY EXAMPLES].[9]

Professor Neusner's claim is that great teachers are those who help students learn; he substantiates this claim by reminding his audience of how three of the greatest teachers in history operated. Here, the warrants are implied rather than stated outright: These three men are examples of great teachers because they engaged the learners in thinking on their own instead of telling the learners what they needed to know. Neusner's points about brevity are relevant to this text's concern with public speaking.

In summary, making an argument is the process of substantiating a claim with reliable evidence and logical reasons. Reading published speeches is a good way to learn various uses and constructions of arguments, such as identifying claims, evidence, and warrants. But these elements of arguments are multifaceted, so it's important to spend some time distinguishing types of claims, evidence, and warrants.

VARIATIONS IN ARGUMENT: TYPES OF CLAIMS, EVIDENCE, AND WARRANTS

There are a variety of claims, evidence, and warrants at your disposal for making an argument. The ones you select will depend on the nature of your topic and the specific purpose of your persuasive speech.

Types of Claims

Depending on the nature of the issue being addressed in the persuasive speech, claims can be classified as claims of fact, claims of value, or claims of policy. Different types of claims require different kinds of supporting evidence.

Claims of Fact. Arguments based on **claims of fact** focus on conditions that actually exist, existed, or will exist in the future.[10] Claims of fact usually address one of two kinds of questions: those for which two or more controversial, competing answers exist; or those for which an answer does not yet exist. In the former case, the answer already exists. The question is, which is the best or right answer? In the latter case, the answer does not yet exist.

> **claims of fact**
> focus on conditions that actually exist, existed, or will exist in the future.

Questions for which two or more controversial, competing answers exist might include:

- Did Lee Harvey Oswald kill President Kennedy, and if he did, did he do it alone?
- Did O. J. Simpson kill his former wife and her friend despite a jury's determination otherwise?
- Does affirmative action discriminate against non-minority job applicants?
- Is homosexuality a genetically determined orientation, an outcome of environmental influences, or the result of a combination of factors?

An argument based on any of these questions will need to give evidence in support of one answer as superior to an alternative answer.

The other kind of question of fact addresses questions for which, as of yet, there are no answers. Probable answers to such questions are called **speculative claims**. Such questions might include:

> **speculative claims**
> provide probable answers to questions for which no known, verifiable answers exist yet.

- Will there be a woman president of the United States within your parents' lifetime?
- Will the telephone be replaced by multimedia computer technology?
- Will the North American Free Trade Agreement (NAFTA) be abolished for failure to produce its intended outcomes?
- Will gasoline be unnecessary for automobiles within 20 years?

At present, the only answers to such questions are speculative. In the future, however, the answers will be able to be verified. As such, they are also claims of fact (in this case, future facts).

To make a claim of fact argument in answer to the foregoing questions requires evidence convincing enough for the audience to believe. It's the same form of question meteorologists answer every day. For example, the temperature for next Saturday is not yet a recorded fact, but given ample evidence from existing weather patterns, meteorologists forecast next Saturday's temperature. Only when Saturday actually arrives can the fact (i.e., the forecast) be verified.

Notice how one student uses present facts to support a speculative claim:

Marci is a student in mechanical engineering. She has prepared a speech in which she claims that within 15 years most cars will be entirely battery-powered. As evidence, she cites her own department's rapid progress in developing electric power sources for cars. She also notes that work in materials science is making possible the production of ever-smaller batteries with larger power capacities, as well as lighter vehicle frames and bodies requiring less energy to propel them at reasonable speeds. Based on the progress made in each of these areas, she believes that the goal will be reached in 15 years.

Claims of Value. Known in much of the media as "Dr. Death" and "The Suicide Doctor," Dr. Jack Kevorkian is often in the headlines because of his practice of helping terminally ill patients commit suicide. Kevorkian has been brought to trial several times in his home state of Michigan for violating various suicide laws. With each trial new questions arise about the morality of assisted suicide, suicide in general, and the role of medical practitioners in aiding death as they aid life.

> **claims of value** address issues of judgment, showing why something is right or wrong, good or bad, worthy or unworthy.

Cases such as Kevorkian's lie in the realm of claims of value. **Claims of value** address issues of judgment. Is assisted suicide ethical? Should doctors be in the business of helping patients to die as well as to live? When does suicide make sense, if ever? Rather than attempting to prove the truth of something, as in claims of fact, a speaker arguing a claim of value tries to show that something is right or wrong, good or bad, worthy or unworthy.

Craig had prepared a speech about the merits of having an official college day of prayer. His claim is that an official prayer day would unite students and others in the surrounding community, all of whom represent many faiths, in a joint effort to express their shared needs and thanksgivings. He also contends that such a recognition would foster greater understanding and cooperation among various student groups.

Craig's claim, concerning the usefulness of prayer and its place in college life, is one of value. As in claims of fact, claims of value require evidence. However, the evidence in support of a value claim tends to be more subjective than factual. For instance, Craig must be able to show that a prayer day can bring better understanding among different student groups and unite students with members of the general community. He might do so by sharing stories of how prayer days at other schools and in other communities have been associated with positive changes.

Claims of Policy. Another type of claim is the claim of policy. Speakers use **claims of policy** when recommending a specific course of action to be taken, or approved of, by an audience. Legislators regularly construct arguments based on claims of policy: Should we pass a law restricting the use of handguns/abortion/firecrackers and so forth? Politician or no, anyone can argue for a claim of policy as long as he or she advocates for or against a given plan. Such claims might include:

claims of policy recommend a specific course of action to be taken, or approved of, by an audience.

- The city should provide walking paths in all municipal parks.
- Fulltime students who commute to campus should be granted reduced parking fees.
- Students who earn an A average on all speech assignments should be exempt from the final exam.
- Property taxes should be increased to fund classroom expansions at the city's elementary schools.
- You and your friends should go to Branson, Missouri, for spring break.

Rudi Van Briel/PhotoEdit

Notice that in each claim the word *should* appears. A claim of policy speaks to an "ought" condition, proposing that certain better outcomes would be realized if the proposed condition were met.

How would you support a claim of policy that the city should provide walking paths in all municipal parks? You might emphasize the needs of walkers, offer the paths as a solution, and cite evidence of the low cost of building paths to establish feasibility.

To build a strong case for a claim of policy, you must provide the audience with a three-part justification consisting of (1) a need or problem; (2) a solution; and (3) evidence of the solution's feasibility.

First comes a *need* or *problem*. The policy must speak to a real issue that the audience would like to have resolved. This assumes the audience will benefit if the proposal is adopted. Using the walking path example, the need is for park facilities that better accommodate recreational and fitness walkers. Second, the justification for a policy must provide a *solution* to the problem, a specific way to fulfill the need. The policy claim for a walking path states its own solution: the walking path. Even though in this instance the solution is self-evident, the speaker's argument would be strengthened by providing some design detail about the proposed walking path (e.g., materials and length) and perhaps by providing some examples from paths in comparable cities and parks. Third, the justification for the policy claim should offer evidence of the solution's *feasibility*. In this case, the speaker could provide cost estimates as well as other data to show the costs of building walking paths relative to the costs of maintaining existing greenscape. The speaker also might provide a priority list of parks to be equipped, based on park size and pedestrian numbers, to justify equipping one or two parks at a time as revenues allow.

By nature, claims of policy involve claims of fact and often involve claims of value as well. Consider the example of the walking path:

POLICY CLAIM: The city should provide walking paths in all municipal parks.

FACT: Most every park in the city is busy several times each day with recreational walkers. The activity is noticeably greater on weekends.

VALUE: Walking on properly maintained paths is healthier for both walkers and the park landscape.

The fact and value claims become, essentially, pieces of evidence in support of the policy claim. The fact statement provides objective evidence, and the value statement offers a more subjective justification of the policy. This suggests that successful speakers need to be quite familiar with all three kinds of argument.

Critical Checkpoint

· ·

Identifying Claims Used in Argument

Arguments can consist of three types of claims: claims of fact, claims of value, and claims of policy. Read the editorial and letters page of today's local or campus newspaper. See if you can identify examples of the three types of claims among the opinions expressed. Perhaps you'll be able to find multiple claims in the same message.

Thus far we have seen that an argument can consist of three different kinds of claims: of fact, of value, and of policy. Regardless of the type of claim you make, if you fail to provide convincing evidence in support of it, the audience will not accept it. The following section reviews the different types of evidence used to support a claim.

Types of Evidence

In addition to the kinds of evidence described in Chapter 7 (examples, narratives, testimony, facts, and statistics), all of which can be considered external evidence, there are several other kinds, or "orders," of evidence that speakers can use to persuade audiences to believe their claims. They might, for example, rely on the audience's existing knowledge and opinions—on what the audience already thinks and believes—as evidence for their claims. Or they might use their own knowledge and expertise as evidence. Finally, they might use the kind of "external" evidence with which you are already familiar—that of narratives, testimony, facts, and statistics. Let's start with the less familiar kinds of evidence, then consider external evidence.

Audience Knowledge and Opinions. One way to support a claim is to use the audience's existing knowledge or opinions as evidence. Research suggests that what your audience already knows or thinks about your topic ultimately determines their acceptance or rejection of claims you make about it. If they are aware of a given issue and the evidence used to support it, they are more likely to accept your claim than if you were to introduce unfamiliar evidence about an unfamiliar topic. Further, nothing is more persuasive to listeners than a reaffirmation of their own attitudes, beliefs, and values, especially when making claims of value and policy. For this reason, audience knowledge and opinions are sometimes referred to as the highest, or "first order," of evidence.

Using the audience's existing knowledge and beliefs as evidence for a claim works something like this:

CLAIM:	Natural life-support for human activity on the moon may come sooner than we think.
AUDIENCE KNOWLEDGE AS EVIDENCE:	You've no doubt read in the papers and seen on the news that scientists recently discovered sources of water on the moon.
WARRANT:	Water found on the moon can be used to produce oxygen for human life-support.

Here the speaker uses the audience's knowledge of the discovery of water on the moon to support the claim that natural life-support will eventually be possible there. The warrant that water on the moon could be converted to oxygen makes the bridge between the evidence and the claim.

How can you use an audience's knowledge and opinions to support your claim? The key is audience analysis. Through audience analysis, you can uncover what your listeners know about your topic and elicit their opinions on it. For example, if your topic is gun control and you plan to address your classmates, you could conduct interviews or distribute surveys that elicit their opinions and gauge what they know about recent gun laws or other pertinent information. On the basis of their responses, you could select that evidence with which they most likely will have some familiarity. For instance, if your local community has recently passed an ordinance outlawing hunting rifles, you could refer to that article as evidence.

Of course, if an audience lacks knowledge on the subject of your claims, you cannot use this first order of evidence. One of the other orders of evidence is required.

Speaker Knowledge and Opinions. Arguments can sometimes be built on the basis of the speaker's own knowledge and opinions, or expertise. Doing so will only work if the audience believes the speaker has the authority or credibility to speak on the matter. This credibility may derive from the speaker's personal experience or from his or her original contribution to the topic.

As support for a claim, speaker expertise might work like this:

CLAIM:	Natural life-support for human activity on the moon may come sooner than we think.
SPEAKER ASSERTION AS EVIDENCE:	My colleagues and I recently found signs of the existence of water on the moon.
WARRANT:	Water found on the moon can be used to produce oxygen for human life-support.

In this case the speaker is one of a group of scientists who discovered reserves of water existing on the moon. The audience accepts the speaker's professional assertion as evidence.

Speaker knowledge and opinion are sometimes referred to as "second-order" evidence because no matter how credible, the speaker's knowledge and expertise are still "once removed" from the audience. And, as noted, nothing is more persuasive to listeners than a reaffirmation of their own attitudes, beliefs, and values. Nevertheless, if an audience finds a speaker credible, they will generally accept his or her knowledge and opinions.

Before deciding to use your own expertise as evidence, a word of caution is in order. Unless you are truly an expert on a topic, be aware that very few speeches can be convincingly built on speaker experience and knowledge alone. Some points in a speech might be substantiated by your own credentials, but not most. For that reason, it is important that you do your research.

If the audience lacks sufficient knowledge to use as evidence and you are not a known expert on the subject, you will need to use yet another, "third-order," type of evidence to support your claims. This is the kind of evidence with which you are already familiar.

External Evidence. External evidence is any information in support of a claim that originates with sources other than the audience or the speaker. External evidence consists of the sorts of evidence presented in Chapter 7 as varieties of supporting material—examples, narratives, testimony, facts, and statistics. External evidence is sometimes called "third-order" evidence because it is borrowed from somewhere else by the speaker. It is "twice removed" from the audience. Unlike evidence based on audience knowledge and beliefs, external evidence is most powerful when you cite information that the audience has not previously used in forming an opinion.[11]

For a claim to be successfully supported with external evidence, the audience must believe that the speaker has selected credible information. It works something like this:

CLAIM: Natural life-support for human activity on the moon may come sooner than we think.

EXTERNAL EVIDENCE: According to an article in last week's issue of *Science* magazine, scientists recently discovered sources of water on the moon.

WARRANT: Apparently, water found on the moon can be used to produce oxygen for human life-support.

In this case the speaker gets evidence for the claim from outside reading material. The strength of the evidence for the audience's acceptance of the claim depends on the level of credibility the audience assigns to the outside source—in this case, *Science* magazine.

Tests of Evidence. In countless television sitcom dramas, as well as in real-life televised trials on channels such as Court TV, you may have noticed that lawyers for the prosecution and lawyers for the defense often approach the same piece of evidence in markedly different ways. What sways the jury to accept one party's interpretation of the evidence over the others? And if each party presents different evidence, what sways the jury to favor one piece of evidence over another? Three factors, or "tests" of evidence, are particularly influential. These include relevance, timeliness, and source credibility.

RELEVANCE. The evidence you select to support a claim must be directly relevant to the claim. One student gave a speech on the attractions of his hometown. A key point he raised was the town's growing economy. He attempted to support the point with evidence regarding (1) the recent arrival of two new industries, and (2) the falling unemployment rate of the state. The unemployment rate was not directly relevant to his point about the town's growing economy. It could have been relevant if he had been able to show that the town, like the state, had a falling unemployment rate, but he didn't. He simply offered the state's unemployment rate as evidence of the town's economic strength. The problem is, a state's unemployment rate reflects both those cities and towns with rates that are falling and those with rates that are rising. The state rate does not necessarily constitute relevant data regarding a particular town's rate. Astute members of an audience notice such subtleties in a speaker's arguments. Be careful not to lose your own credibility with an audience by providing them with irrelevant information.

AP/Wide World

TIMELINESS. Good evidence is recent and represents the current or projected state of affairs addressed by your claim. One student, Margarite, spoke to her class about purchasing portable compact-disc (CD) players. To support her claim that Brand X was the best buy, she cited a 1989 article from *Consumer Reports* magazine. Her speech was given in 1995. Even if the 1989 article was the only one published on audio CD equipment in the six-year span, it was too far removed from the current market for CD equipment to be of any real benefit to the audience's purchasing decisions. Many developments may have occurred and many different brands may have emerged in that time, making the original information obsolete to the interests of Margarite's audience.

When attorneys present evidence they face a tough audience: the jury. Make sure your evidence stands up to the audience's tests of relevance, timeliness, and source credibility.

SOURCE CREDIBILITY. As a final test of external evidence, consider the actual source of the evidence. Is the source one with which the audience is familiar, by reputation if not by firsthand experience? In the example of Margarite's speech, she cited *Consumer Reports* magazine. Most people have heard of this source and would consider its information as reliable. On the other hand, if she had cited the *Trotterville Retail Gazette* as her source, the reliability of the evidence might have been suspect to her audience, regardless of how timely it might be. Moreover, she could have cited an industry magazine, such as *Stereo Review*, to lend even greater credibility to her claim of which CD player is the best buy.

A good practice to keep in mind to ensure relevance, timeliness, and source credibility of external evidence is to rely on multiple sources of information regarding the same point. Let's again use Margarite as an example. She might have been able to find a relatively recent article in *Stereo Review* to corroborate the older information she obtained from *Consumer Reports*. In this way she would have greatly strengthened her claim about which product would be the best buy for her audience.

Critical Checkpoint

....

Orders of Evidence

The highest order of evidence is the audience's knowledge and opinions about the topic of a claim. Your own assertions, based on your personal experience and knowledge, are the second order of evidence. Information from external sources—such as statistics and testimony—is the third order of evidence. You can assess the quality of external evidence for your claims by applying three tests: Is the evidence directly relevant to the claim? Is the evidence the most recent available on the subject? Is the evidence from a credible, reputable source?

Even evidence that is relevant, timely, and credible is useful only to the extent that it can give the audience good reasons to accept the claim. Such is the purpose of warrants in argument. Warrants provide the link between the claim and evidence with reasoning.

Types of Warrants

As with claims and evidence, there are different kinds of warrants, or reasoning, that can be used in your argument. These include motivational, authoritative, and substantive warrants.

Motivational Warrants: Appeals to Emotion. No doubt most readers have seen television and magazine advertisements asking viewers to give just pennies a day to sponsor a starving child in a distant land. The claim may say, "You can easily afford to join this organization dedicated to ending the hunger of thousands of children." The evidence may be stated as, "For the price of one soft drink you can feed one child for a week." What's the warrant? "You don't want any child to starve or go without proper medical care." The warrant is intended to motivate listeners by arousing their value for basic human necessities, even life itself.

Motivational warrants use the needs, desires, emotions, and values of audience members as the basis for accepting some evidence as support for a claim, and thus accepting the claim itself. More often than not, motivational warrants are implied rather than stated outright. In terms of the ad to support a starving child, we don't have to be told that we don't want children to starve; if the value or desire is meaningful to us, we realize it while attending to other parts of the message. Here are some other needs and values that can operate as motivational warrants in arguments:

career success	strong marriages	happy families
quality leisure time	meaningful friendships	health and wellness
financial security	good taste	quality education
physical attractiveness	fine material possessions	

Authoritative Warrants: Appeals to Credibility. Sometimes warrants rely on an audience's beliefs about the credibility or acceptability of a source of evidence. Such is the case with **authoritative warrants**. For example, in terms of sponsoring a hungry child, the speaker might make the claim that we should contribute financially to an agency that feeds hungry children. The speaker's evidence is that whatever little bit of money we give will go far in meeting the agency's objectives. As a warrant, the speaker notes that a certain celebrity or popular politician works with the agency and its recipients; perhaps that individual is even offering the message.

The success or failure of authoritative warrants rests on how highly the audience regards the authority figure. If listeners hold the person in high esteem, they are more likely to find the evidence and claim acceptable. Thus, authoritative warrants make the credibility of sources of evidence all the more important. In other words, it's possible that naming the source of evidence can also provide the authoritative warrant. For example, in support of the claim that "McDonald's Big Mac sandwiches are among the most popular fast food sand-

---

motivational warrants
use the needs, desires, emotions, and values of audience members as the basis for their accepting some evidence as support for a claim.

authoritative warrants
rely on an audience's beliefs about the credibility or acceptability of a source of evidence.

wiches enjoyed by famous persons," you could offer the evidence that "President Clinton has said that Big Macs are his favorite fast food"; this gives both the evidence (a famous person who eats Big Macs) and the warrant (the specific famous person is our nation's president) in the same sentence.

If you happen to be highly experienced and knowledgeable on the subject of a claim you make in a speech, an authoritative warrant can be made by reference to yourself. In this case, the warrant provides second-order evidence. For example, in a speech on diet plans that work, you might claim that "Diet Plan B is more effective than Plan A or Plan C for many people" and use yourself as both a source of evidence and basis for the warrant: "I have used all three plans and have had the most success with Plan B." Your experience (described as speaker assertion above, or second-order evidence) offers evidence for the claim, and you, having had the experience, give warrant to the evidence.

Substantive Warrants: Appeals to Reasoning. Motivational warrants operate on the basis of audience needs and emotions. Authoritative warrants operate on the basis of credibility attributed to the source of evidence. Finally, substantive warrants assume that some functional relationship exists between two or more phenomena of concern in the subject of an argument. More precisely, **substantive warrants** operate on the basis of the audience's beliefs about the reliability of factual evidence. If you claim that your fellow college students should concern themselves more with learning from courses than with the grades they receive, you might offer as evidence the point that what is learned in a course is more applicable to future job responsibilities than is the grade received in the course, and you might provide as the warrant a statement that whereas better grades may lead to more job opportunities, better learning leads to better grades. The relationship between the claim and the evidence is that students will increase their chances for job opportunities if they concentrate on learning instead of on grades. The warrant substantiates the relationship—better grades follow from better learning.

> **substantive warrants** operate on the basis of an audience's beliefs about the reliability of factual evidence.

There are several types of substantive warrants. Three that occur most commonly in speeches are causation, sign, and analogy.

Warrants by cause offer a cause and effect relationship as proof for the claim. For example, welfare critics often reason by cause when they suggest that providing funds to people without making them work causes them to be lazy. Their opponents also reason by cause when they rebut this argument. Rather than suggesting a cause-to-effect, however, they might suggest an effect-to-cause, as in: "Welfare mothers don't work outside the home [EFFECT] because the welfare system does not help them with day care [CAUSE]." Similarly, a speaker might argue that:

> **warrants by cause** offer a cause and effect relationship as proof for a claim.

CLAIM: Senator Bob Dole lost the 1996 race for the presidency largely because of his age.

EVIDENCE: Many available media reports refer to the age issue with which Senator Dole had to contend.

WARRANT: In our society, less competency is attributed to older age than to younger age.

Older age is assumed to be a cause of Mr. Dole's loss in the presidential campaign. The warrant substantiates the relationship of cause (age) to effect (loss of race) on the basis of our society's negative stereotypes of older age.

When using warrants by cause, it is essential to make relevant and accurate assertions about cause and effect. Avoid making hasty assertions of cause or effect, many of which are based on stereotypes, hearsay, tradition, and the like. Also, be certain that you don't offer a single cause or effect as the only possibility when others are known to exist. When multiple causes or effects can be given, be sure to note their relative importance to one another.

Warrants by sign infer that such a close relationship exists between two variables that the presence or absence of one may be taken as an indication of the presence or absence of the other.[12] For example, smoke is a sign of fire. Coughing and sneezing are signs of a cold. A claim and evidence are often associated by sign:

warrants by sign
infer that such a close relationship exists between two variables that the presence or absence of one may be taken as an indication of the presence or absence of the other.

> CLAIM: Summer employment opportunities for college students will probably decline at resort locations in the southern Rocky Mountains.
>
> EVIDENCE: There were record numbers of forest fires throughout the southern Rockies in the late winter and early spring that destroyed many resorts.
>
> WARRANT: Widescale natural disasters curtail employment in the affected areas.

In this example, negative effects on employment are an economic sign of natural disasters. The claim is supported by the evidence if the audience accepts the warrant that employment becomes unstable in the aftermath of natural disasters.

Finally, **warrants by analogy** compare two similar cases and infer that what is true in one is true in the other. The assumption is that the characteristics of Case A and Case B are so much alike, if not the same, that what is true for B must also be true for A. Warrant by analogy or comparison occurs frequently in speeches. Consider this example:

warrants by analogy
compare two similar cases and infer that what is true in one is true in the other.

> CLAIM: Students will have a better feeling about Mr. Honnacker's speech class if he drops the absence policy.
>
> EVIDENCE: Student satisfaction increased substantially in Ms. Orlander's math class when she dropped the absence policy.
>
> WARRANT: Mr. Honnacker's speech class and Ms. Orlander's math class are equivalent with respect to other factors that satisfy students.

Here the speaker compares the speech class to the math class, assuming that both have in common students who are equally satisfied or dissatisfied depending on the nature of the absence policy. The analogy links the evidence from the math class example to the claim about the speech class.

In summary, an argument consists of claims, evidence, and warrants. Moreover, there are varieties of claims, evidence, and warrants. If you are like most students, you may feel a little overwhelmed with all this variety. Take it less as representing the complexity of arguments and more as indicating the array of resources available to build constructive arguments and better speeches.

Focus on Technology

Technology and Argument

If you have access to an online service, enter a chat room and initiate a debate on some controversial topic of interest to the users. You might even log on to an ongoing debate. Just observe the users' comments for several minutes. See if you can identify varieties of claims, evidence, and warrants in the discourse you read. Are there any arguments that you find particularly convincing? Do people seem to use support material to back their points or do they tend to offer personal opinions?

Come back to this activity after reading the rest of the chapter. It will be especially interesting to identify and count occurrences of argument fallacies in the chat sessions you observe. What do your observations tell you about the quality of reasoning that goes into people's online discussions?

REFINING THE ARGUMENT

Jaman plans to give a speech on recent findings from research investigating the genetic determinants of homosexuality. He believes the evidence is compelling. In order to get his audience to accept it, as open-minded as they may be, he knows he will have to show how the genetic evidence outweighs evidence to the contrary. He decides to present all sides of the issue, comparing the genetics evidence to other evidence point-by-point to substantiate his claim.

As Jaman knows, there are at least two sides to every argument. Thus, all attempts at persuasion are subject to counter-persuasion. Your listeners may be persuaded to accept your claims, but once they are exposed to counter-claims, they may change their minds. According to a theory called the **inoculation effect**, by anticipating counter-arguments and then addressing or rebutting them, you can "inoculate" your listeners against the "virus" of these other viewpoints. The theory rests on the biological principle of inducing resistance through exposure to small quantities of a harmful substance. Just as you can induce resistance to disease in this manner, inoculation theory posits that you can induce resistance to counter-claims by acknowledging them.

As noted, if your listeners are unaware of any counter-claims, they may be persuaded by your arguments for a time. However, once they hear other viewpoints, they may change their minds. If listeners *are* aware of counter-claims and you ignore them, you risk the loss of credibility.[13] This does not mean, however, that you need to painstakingly acknowledge and refute all opposing claims. It isn't always necessary to deal directly with competing claims. Here are some more specific suggestions.[14]

inoculation effect
a theory that resistance to counter-arguments can be induced in an audience by "inoculating" listeners with small "doses" of the counter-arguments, acknowledging the counter-arguments in such a way as to weaken their impact.

Esbin & Anderson/Image Works

When making a claim, be mindful of both sides of the argument. Reinforce your argument by addressing the major counter-claims opposing your position.

1. If the audience knows of claims and evidence that oppose yours, and those claims and evidence can be refuted, raise them in your speech and refute them.
2. If you don't have time to refute counter-claims that are known to your audience, mention the counter-claims and concede them if your evidence can withstand it. In other words, simply note that there are claims to the contrary, specify the claims, reiterate your own claim, then move on.
3. If there are counter-claims that your audience may be unaware of, ignore them if there is not time to refute them. Otherwise, if time permits, state the counter-claims and refute them.

From an ethical perspective, you may ignore competing claims only when they do not severely weaken your own claims and when you have no time to address them adequately. "Be on your toes" and "Look both ways" are useful sayings to remember when preparing your arguments.

FALLACIES IN REASONING: THE PITFALLS OF ARGUING

It is one thing to know the variety of types of claims, evidence, and warrants that can be used to build arguments in your speeches. It is something else to use them skillfully, appropriately, and effectively. Sound reasoning through argument requires objectivity in the sense of remaining focused on the topic or issue, and avoiding subjectivity in the sense of letting what is said about the topic or issue become personal. Rather than attacking the people who hold opposing views, appropriately stated claims are restricted to targeting their issue-relevant claims and evidence.

Of course, it is natural for some degree of subjectivity to play a part in any speech. After all, the topic is no doubt compelling to you and, one hopes, to members of the audience. But no matter how passionately you feel about a subject, it's critical not to get caught up in the emotion of the argument at the expense of sound reasoning. Doing so weakens your claims and lessens the chance that the audience will act on your message. This section describes several faults, or fallacies, in reasoning that harm the quality of a speech. A **fallacy** is either a false or erroneous statement, or an invalid or deceptive line of reasoning.[15] In either case you need to be aware of fallacies, both in order to avoid making them in your own speeches and to identify them in speeches of others.

fallacy
either a false or erroneous statement, or an invalid or deceptive line of reasoning.

Focus on Ethics

Presenting Ethical Arguments

Unscrupulous persuasive speakers may attempt to use fallacious reasoning to their advantage. They may attempt to win over audiences with forms of reasoning that present no real substantive arguments at all, but instead deceive and mislead unwary listeners. It is a danger for novice speakers in using argument to become defensive about claims and evidence. After all, defensiveness can lead to fallacious argument as a means of self-protection. Argumentation scholar James Herrick advises that in order to present ethical arguments you need to:

- accurately represent your own views,
- give the greatest consideration possible to your audience, including your opponents, and
- accurately represent the best understanding of the topic.[1]

Herrick further encourages honesty in arguing. He notes that honesty may be the most important virtue in communicating with others.

1. J. A. Herrick, *Argumentation: Understanding and Shaping Arguments* (Scottsdale, AZ: Gorsuch Scarisbrick, 1995).

Begging the Question

A bumper sticker that was often seen during the Vietnam War declared, "War kills!" On reading such a slogan today, students might be heard to say, "Duh!" This is because the slogan does something called **begging the question**. The claim may sound impressive, but it has no substantive meaning. There is no way to argue against it, so there really is no claim at all. In begging the question, the subject of a claim is defined in such a way that it cannot help but support the claim, thereby revealing a circular pattern of thought. The answer to the question raised by the claim simply restates the claim.

begging the question
stating in an impressive-sounding way a claim that really has no substance at all.

Bandwagoning

Perhaps your parents are reluctant to permit you to travel to the crowded Florida beaches for spring break. Your reply might be, "Everyone else is going! I'll be a dweeb if I'm the only one who doesn't go." The "everyone else" in your reply makes it a case of **bandwagoning**—the practice of assigning a claim greater substance by making it appear more popular than it really is. If it's all that popular, then you're more likely to want to "join in" too. Indeed, there are cases when a large majority of people do endorse a particular claim, but widespread endorsement does not make a claim factual, only popular. The claim that "In Las Vegas, everyone can have their best vacation ever" cannot be supported—even by evidence indicating that the majority of vacationers interviewed said their favorite vacation was in Las Vegas—because a majority is not "everyone."

bandwagoning
assigning a claim greater substance by making it appear more popular than it really is.

Overgeneralization

overgeneralization
attempts to support a claim by asserting that a particular piece of evidence is true for all persons concerned.

Whereas bandwagoning attempts to support a claim by asserting that all persons accept the claim, **overgeneralization** attempts to support a claim by asserting that a particular piece of evidence is true for all persons concerned. The claim that "Dentists recommend Nuko-Plak for daily plaque control" represents a common instance of overgeneralization. It asserts that all dentists recommend Nuko-Plak, when in fact it is likely that the claim is based on a selective survey of a fraction of the whole population of dentists. The claim is fallacious because it is based on insufficient evidence. It would be fallacious, for example, to claim a recall of all 1996 models of a certain all-wheel-drive vehicle because three of them experienced braking problems in harsh weather. The question is, Are three occurrences sufficient for concluding that all 1996 models of this vehicle will likely experience brake problems in harsh weather? The answer is probably "no."

Ad Hominem Argument

ad hominem arguments
attack an opponent instead of the opponent's arguments.

One form of fallacious argument that targets people instead of issues is the ad hominem argument. **Ad hominem arguments** attack an opponent instead of the opponent's arguments; they attempt to incite an audience's dislike for an opponent. Consider this claim: "Governor Wilson supports the dissolution of affirmative action laws because he wants to see white males retain control of the state's leading economic and social institutions." This ad hominem attack labels the governor as a racist. In the winter of 1996, presidential candidate Pat Buchanan reputedly remarked that, "Feminists are a bunch of man-hating, lesbian, baby-killing witches."[16] His alleged statement is also an example of arguing ad hominem—attacking the personal character of an opponent by name-calling. Note also that this particular example includes overgeneralizations. Some feminists hate men; some are lesbians, but not all; some have had abortions, but not all; and some may practice Wicca, but not all. The fallacy of this claim is that it has nothing to do with whatever issue Buchanan was trying to promote because it is not an issue-based claim. Sound argument focuses on issues, not people or their characteristics.

The fallacies presented here are just a few of the variety that exist, but they are the most common in student speeches.[17] Becoming familiar with these types of fallacies is critical to building a sound argument based on objective evidence. Understanding fallacies is also critical to you as a listener. Armed with this knowledge, you will be better able to critically evaluate and judge other speakers' claims.

Sample Persuasive Speech

Craig Kielburger was profiled in the Making a Difference box in Chapter 6 (p. 134). His work as an advocate for Free the Children has offered him the opportunity to deliver hundreds of persuasive speeches to enlist the support of individuals, organizations, and governments to protect children from exploitation. In the following speech, Kielburger faces a formidable challenge as a 13-year-old addressing the U.S. Congressional Sub Committee on International Relations and Human Rights. He proves his competence and eloquence early on, earning his audience's attention while using both his youthful perspective and his expertise to great effect throughout the speech. As you read Kielburger's words, keep in mind what you have learned about developing persuasive arguments in the past two chapters.

June 11, 1996

Mr. Chairman, Members of the Committee, Ladies and Gentlemen:

I am pleased to be here today to represent children—Child labor affects children—children are being exploited and denied their basic rights, children are being abused. I believe that children must be heard when speaking about child labor—I believe that we must be part of the solution.

I recently spent seven and a half weeks traveling through South Asia to meet with working and street children. I wanted to better understand their reality—to ask them what they wanted so that we would not be imposing our western culture on them.

I can tell you stories of what I saw—stories which would shock you. I met children as young as four years old, working in brick kilns making bricks seven days a week from dawn to dusk, children working 14 hours a day loading dangerous chemicals into firecracker tubes, children working in metal and glass factories, children physically and verbally abused. Some children I'll never forget—like Nagashar, who worked as a bonded laborer in a carpet factory. He had scars all over his body including his voice box where he had been branded with red hot irons for trying to escape. Or the nine-year-old boy with a deep scar that ran across the top of his head where he was had [sic] been hit with a metal bar for making a mistake on the job. Then there was Munianal, the eight-year-old girl who worked in a recycling plant taking apart used syringes and needles gathered from hospitals and the streets. She wore no shoes and no protective gear. No one had ever told her about AIDS. These are the working children.

Not just facts and statistics but real children.

Some of you may say, "Well these children are poor. Don't they have to work to help their families survive? Studies by UNICEF, the ILO and other nongovernmental organizations have shown that child labor is actually keeping Third World countries poor, because a child at work means an adult out of work. Factory owners prefer to hire children because they are cheaper labor, easily intimidated and won't organize trade unions. Kailash Satyarthi, who last year won the Robert Kennedy International Award for Human Rights, heads 150 nongovernmental organizations working with child laborers in South Asia. He stresses that India has 50 million child workers, but 55 million adults unemployed. And because these children are not able to go to school they remain illiterate, and the cycle of poverty continues. Child labor keeps people poor.

As consumers, we bear part of the responsibility. Is it fair for children to be sitting on the ground for 12 hours a day, for pennies a day sewing famous brand name soccer balls—which they will never get to play with—soccer balls shipped to countries like ours for your children, your grandchildren, or for me?

It is simply a question of greed and exploitation—exploitation of the most weak and vulnerable. These greedy people include companies going into the Third World countries contracting out work to the cheapest factories which will produce goods up to standard. This only encourages factory owners to seek out the cheapest labor—underpaid workers and children. Poverty is no excuse for exploitation. Poverty is no excuse for child abuse.

In the introduction, Kielburger establishes his credibility in two ways: he asserts his seriousness (1) by stating that children (like himself) should be involved in discussing child labor and developing solutions to the problem; and (2) by offering his first-hand knowledge of the tragic results of child labor. His descriptive accounts are meant to put a human face to the suffering and to gain audience sympathy.

Kielburger then offers external evidence from respected organizations to help support his claims. By linking child labor to a cycle of illiteracy, poverty, and adult unemployment, he also shows the far-reaching ramifications of child labor.

By implicating consumers, including audience members and himself, as part of the problem, Kielburger brings the issue home and shows how audience members share culpability in the problem. He attempts to enlist audience involvement by making an ethical appeal to the audience's sense of responsibility.

We, the children of North America have formed an organization called Free the Children. Free the Children is a youth movement dedicated to the elimination of child labor and the exploitation of children. Most of our members are between 10 and 15 years old. We now have groups in provinces across Canada and chapters quickly spreading throughout the United States—in Washington, San Francisco, Maryland, Idaho, Iowa. Calls are coming in from all over the world—from young people, from children, who want to help. You don't need a lot of committee meetings to understand that exploiting children in child labor is wrong. We may be young, but it is very clear to us that this child abuse must stop.

We believe that children must be removed from factories and jobs given to adult members of the family—adults who can negotiate for better rights and working conditions.

We believe that companies which go into Third World countries for cheap labor must pay their workers a just wage so that children will not have to work to supplement their parents' income. These same companies should also be willing to put money back into the country to help in the education and the protection of children.

We have consumers calling our Free the Children office from all over North America telling us that they don't want to buy products made from the suffering children.

That is why a labeling system, with independent monitoring, which clearly identifies items not made by child labor is necessary. Another solution is to hold importers responsible for making sure that the products they are importing into North America have not been made from the exploitation of children. Consumers have a right to know who made the products they are buying.

In May 1995, UNICEF set an example with a no child labor clause in its buying policy based on the United Nations Convention on the Rights of the Child.

I have been told that the United States already has a Tariff Act passed in 1930. Section 3:07 prohibits products being made from prison or unindentured labor from coming into the United States. If this is true than why are carpets, soccer balls, brick work and other items made by children in bonded and slave labor not banned from coming into the United States under this law?

Child labor should not be used, however, as an excuse to stop trade with a developing country. We are advocating selective buying, not a boycott of all products which could harm children even more.

I don't know why anyone would oppose laws which protect the children of the world. Maybe companies, sports and TV personalities, maybe consumers, might have said until recently, that they didn't know about child labor and the exploitation of workers in Third World countries but now they do. There is no excuse anymore. We have all been educated. Knowledge implies responsibility. You and I, all of us, are now responsible to help these children.

Eliminating child labor comes down to a question of political will. Why are countries with a high incidence of child labor spending on average 30 times more on the military than on primary education? How serious are world leaders about helping these children? Where is the social conscience of multinational corporations?

I have hundreds of pictures of children which I could have shown you today. I have brought only one. When I was in Calcutta, I participated in a rally with 250 children who marched through the street with banners chanting, "We want freedom. We want an education." Children should not work in hazardous industries—Never Again. Today I am here to speak for these children, to be their voice. You are an influential nation. You have the power in your words, in your actions and in your policy making to give children hope for a better life. What will you do to help these children?

Summary Questions

What is an argument, and what is its role in the persuasive speech?

An argument is a stated position, with support, for or against an idea or issue. An argument consists of a claim, evidence, and warrants. In the persuasive speech, the speaker uses arguments to ask listeners to accept a conclusion about some state of affairs.

What are the various types of claims that can be posed in a persuasive speech?

A persuasive speech can focus on a claim of fact, a claim of value, or a claim of policy. Claims of fact focus on conditions that actually exist, existed, or will exist in the future; the latter are speculative claims, or claims of future fact. Claims of value address issues of judgment. For example: Is assisted suicide ethical? Should doctors be in the business of helping patients to die as well as to live? Finally, speakers use claims of policy when recommending a specific course of action to be taken by or approved of by an audience. A claim of policy speaks to an "ought" condition, proposing that certain better outcomes would be realized if the proposed condition were met.

What are the various types of evidence that can be used in a persuasive speech?

The persuasive speaker can make use of three different types of evidence in support of his or her claims. One kind is audience knowledge and opinions, or "first-order" evidence. Another is speaker expertise, or "second-order" evidence. Finally, "third-order" evidence is external evidence—examples, narratives, testimony, facts, and statistics.

What three tests of evidence can be applied to evaluate the strength of a speaker's evidence?

As you identify and apply evidence to a claim, keep in mind the three tests of evidence: Is the evidence directly relevant to the claim? Is it timely, or recent and up-to-date? Will the audience find it credible, or from a source they can trust?

What are the various types of warrants that can be used in a persuasive speech?

The motivational warrant uses the needs, desires, emotions, and values of audience members as the basis for accepting some evidence as support for a claim, and thus accepting the claim itself. Authoritative warrants rely on an audience's beliefs about the credibility or acceptability of a source of evidence. Substantive warrants operate on the basis of the audience's beliefs about the reliability of factual evidence. There are several types of substantive warrants; three that occur most commonly in speeches are causation, sign, and analogy. Warrants by cause offer a cause and effect relationship as proof for the claim. Warrants by sign infer that such a close relationship exists between two variables that the presence or absence of one may be taken as an indication of the presence or absence of the other. Warrants by analogy compare two similar cases and infer that what is true in one is true in the other.

What is the inoculation effect, and why is it important to consider in presenting arguments?

Because every argument has at least two sides, it is important to consider relevant counter-claims when presenting an argument. If you ignore such claims, you risk losing credibility with the audience and failing to persuade them to your point of view. According to the inoculation effect, by anticipating counter-arguments and then addressing or rebutting them, you can "inoculate" listeners against accepting these claims.

What are some of the fallacies that can weaken an argument?

Knowing the varieties of argument will help you avoid several fallacies that will weaken any speech in which they are identified. This text addresses the fallacies of begging the question, bandwagoning, overgeneralization, and arguing ad hominem. A fallacy is either a false or erroneous statement, or an invalid or deceptive line of reasoning. When you beg the question, you define the subject of the claim in such a way that it cannot help but support the claim, revealing a circular pattern of thought. Bandwagoning involves assigning a claim greater substance by making it appear more popular than it really is. Overgeneralization attempts to support a claim by asserting that a particular piece of evidence is true for all persons concerned. Ad hominem arguments attack an opponent instead of the opponent's arguments.

ISSUES FOR DISCUSSION

1. Explain the difference between an argument and a verbal fight.
2. Which type of claim do you think is easiest to defend? Why?
3. If evidence supports a claim, why do we need warrants?
4. In the ideal speech situation, on which order of evidence would you want to base your entire speech? Why?
5. Why avoid any of the fallacies of argument if using them can lead to your audience's acceptance of your claim?

SELF-ASSESSMENT

1. Consider an upcoming speech assignment for your class. State one or more claims that are the basis for the speech. Identify the type of claim each one is. State some evidence you have access to that will support your claim. Provide a warrant for each piece of evidence that ties it to the claim. Are these warrants implicit, or will you need to state them outright when you deliver the speech? Why?
2. When you deliver your next speech, ask a classmate to identify any fallacies in arguing that you commit. Discuss each fallacy with your classmate and determine why it was committed and how it can be avoided in the future.

TEAMWORK

1. Do the following exercise in a group of six classmates. Select a topic of mutual interest. Two people in your group will work together to state a claim. They will then present the claim to the rest of the group. Another two members of the group will work together to formulate some evidence in support of the claim, and then present the evidence to the rest of the group. The remaining two people in the group will develop a warrant that substantiates the evidence, and then present the warrant to the other four members. Once the claim, evidence, and warrant are determined for the group, develop them further until you are satisfied that a reasonably strong argument has been built. Then present the argument to the class.

2. Ask another group in class to test your argument for fallacious reasoning. Once any kind of fallacy has been pointed out, discuss with your group how to strengthen the argument to overcome the fallacy. Present your refined argument to the class.

3. Spend 30 minutes of study time this week with four or five members of your class watching a live telecast on C-Span of a speaker or political debate. Listen carefully to the presenter's message. Take note of claims and evidence. Discuss your findings with each other, assessing the impact of the arguments on your own attitudes, beliefs, or actions.

The
superior man
is modest in
his speech,
but exceeds in
his actions.
— Confucius

I am uncomfortable with meetings that do not arrive at conclusions.

— General Colin Powell

Small Group, Business, and Professional Presentations

Have you ever been assigned to a group to accomplish a project or solve a problem? If you have not been part of a group in a business setting, then recall a time when you worked in a group at school or in a club. **How did the members of the group interact with one another? Were participants able to discuss issues without becoming personal?** Were you satisfied with the results the group achieved? Were you satisfied with your contribution to the group? **When interacting in a group setting, you need to decide how active you will be in formulating ideas, making decisions, and presenting information.** Ultimately, accomplishing a group's objectives requires skills in decision making, interpersonal communication, and making presentations.

Samuel Wang works for a small business that employs several part-time workers, most of whom are college students like himself. As part of the company's community service contribution to the United Way Campaign, Samuel's boss wants to do something for the youth in the neighborhood. He has asked that Samuel and four other parttimers develop some program or activity that would be beneficial for neighborhood kids, ages 8–14. Once Samuel's group comes up with a plan, he and the others are to present it to a group of senior managers.

When Samuel meets with the other employees, none of whom he's ever had interaction with except on the most fleeting of bases, it soon becomes clear that everyone has a different idea about what type of program would be best, as well as how the group should go about developing it. There is even disagreement about who should lead the group and how the various tasks should be assigned. Samuel wonders how the group will ever come up with a viable program.

Situations like the one in which Samuel finds himself arise often in groups. Many people lack the necessary skills to work together productively. Yet along with the ability to speak in public, teamwork is one of the most valuable professional skills you can possess. In fact, today most positions demand it, since nearly all managers believe that their employees are more productive when working in groups or teams than when working individually.

Public speaking skills are relevant to the study of small groups because groups are frequently required to report on the results they've achieved. A manager might assign a committee to devise a new system for promoting employees, for example. As part of their assignment, they must orally present their findings to senior management. Additionally, many of the experiences you'll have as a speaker and audience member are likely to be related to your job, and most of those occasions will be in the context of a small group (usually between 3 and 20 persons) as opposed to a large public audience. Rather than delivering a formal public speech, you will likely be called to address a small group of fellow employees, colleagues, or customers about a business or professional issue. Such presentations are a form of **presentational speaking**—reports delivered by individuals or groups within the business or professional environment. Presentational speaking includes individual speakers addressing a group of colleagues, managers, clients, or customers; as well as multiple members of a work group addressing a similarly composed audience.

presentational speaking
reports delivered by individuals or groups within the business or professional environment.

This chapter will challenge you to develop the skills needed to become a productive member of a work group and to deliver effective reports on your activities within such a group. You will also learn how to deliver business and professional presentations to such groups. Chapter challenges include:

- Recognizing the responsibilities of an effective group participant.

- Understanding the responsibilities of the group leader.
- Developing skills for making effective decisions in groups.
- Understanding how to make group presentations.
- Recognizing the difference between speeches and business and professional presentations.
- Becoming familiar with five of the most common types of business and professional presentations.

COMMUNICATING IN GROUPS

Clear communication is vital to working cooperatively in groups and to getting to the point where you have something worthwhile to report. Unfortunately, not all interactions in groups are effective, efficient, or productive. Although groups are usually more effective working together than individuals working alone, the quality of a group's product is often determined by the competence that each person brings to a task.

Becoming an Effective Group Participant

Groups are only as good as the individuals who participate in them. Being an effective group participant requires keeping sight of the group's goals and avoiding behavior that detracts from them. Listening is key, as is critically evaluating information.

Eyes on the Prize. As a group member, your overriding responsibility is to help achieve the group's goals. Thus, ideas and information should be evaluated in light of these goals. You may frequently find it easy to go along with the majority or to become overly excited or emotional during a meeting. The more you use the group's goal as a steadying guide, the less likely you are to be diverted from your real responsibilities as a participant.

Fight the Good Fight. Whenever people come together to consider an important issue, conflict is inevitable. But conflict doesn't have to be destructive. In fact, the best decisions are usually those that emerge out of productive conflict. In **productive conflict**, questions are clarified, ideas challenged, counter-examples presented, worst-case scenarios considered, and proposals reformulated. After a process such as this, the group can be confident that its decision has been put to a good test. Because the group members have had a part in analyzing, synthesizing, and constructing the decision, it will be one that the entire group can support. Group members will have considerable ownership of the decision that is reached.

- **productive conflict** conflict in which questions are clarified, ideas challenged, counter-examples presented, worst-case scenarios considered, and proposals reformulated.

personal-based conflict

conflict in which group members argue about each other instead of with each other, wasting time and impairing motivation.

issues-based conflict

a form of productive conflict in which group members critically debate issues on their merits while steering clear of personal attacks.

groupthink

the tendency to accept information and ideas without critical analysis; results from strong feelings of loyalty and unity within a group.

Productive conflict is *issues-based* rather than *personal-based*. In **personal-based conflict**, members argue about each other instead of with each other, wasting time and impairing motivation. The group's assigned tasks remain incomplete and issues remain unresolved. Whereas personal-based conflict detracts a group from its mission, **issues-based conflict** enhances effective decision making. Issues-based conflict allows members to test and debate ideas and potential solutions. It requires each member to ask tough questions, press for clarification, and present alternative views.

Avoid Groupthink. Rather than face controversy, group participants sometimes fall into a pattern of **groupthink**—the tendency to accept information and ideas without subjecting them to critical analysis. Groupthink results from strong feelings of loyalty and unity within a group. When these feelings are more motivating than the desire to critically analyze ideas and test solutions, the quality of the group's decisions suffers.

Groups prone to groupthink typically exhibit these behaviors:

- Participants reach consensus and avoid conflict so as to not hurt others' feelings, but they do so without genuinely agreeing.
- Members who do not agree with the majority of the group are pressured to conform.
- Disagreement, tough questions, and counterproposals are discouraged.
- More effort is spent rationalizing or justifying the decision than testing it.

The best way to avoid groupthink is to engage in productive conflict, as described above, and to rigorously apply critical thinking skills.

Critical Checkpoint

Group Communication and Critical Thinking

Effective critical thinking skills lie at the heart of communicating competently in groups. The need to think critically is especially pressing when you confront problems not of your choosing and deal with people who view things differently from you. Thinking critically in a group setting requires that you remain open-minded about what you see and hear, while at the same time reviewing and evaluating information you receive. It means considering several different viewpoints before you are satisfied with the information you receive. Critical thinkers are always on the lookout for opinions, evidence, or facts that will lead them to accurate and responsible conclusions. This is an extremely important individual competency to develop as a group member.

Applying critical thinking skills in the group setting involves:

- *Watching for individual and group bias.* You and your colleagues will always come to meetings with certain preconceived notions and biases that will influence decision making. Effective group participation requires remaining alert to the possibilities of bias by objectively analyzing what is said by you and your fellow group members.

- *Considering multiple perspectives.* There is always more than one way to look at a problem or issue. Consider different perspectives and realize that your own perspective is subject to error.

- *Clarifying values.* Ideas and decisions are strongly influenced by values. Determine the values that influence the group's judgment. Understand what the group's standards are and why you use them.
- *Clarifying issues.* Much time can be wasted in groups by working on an issue that has not been clearly defined. Clarify the question the group must answer or the issue with which it must deal. To ensure that everyone keeps on task, formulate the issue in a clearly worded statement.
- *Evaluating information.* Decide what sources of information the group is basing its decisions on. Is it opinion, or data based on evidence and reasoning? Examine the credibility and the relevance of the information.
- *Probing.* Ask good, hard questions about the issues at hand. Look for underlying fallacies in reasoning. Carefully consider alternative arguments.
- *Considering the big picture.* Make plausible inferences and interpretations from valid information. Explore the implications of statements, and develop a fuller, more complete understanding of their meaning.
- *Summarizing.* Summarize relevant facts and evidence in clear, understandable statements.
- *Drawing appropriate conclusions.* Generate multiple solutions and analyze the feasibility of those solutions.

If one were to generalize about critical thinking, one might say that it involves "not taking things at face value." View the group process as an opportunity to inject a healthy dose of skepticism into discussion with your fellow group members. Encourage them to do the same.

Adopt Constructive Group Roles. Just as members of a family must coordinate various tasks to ensure that its needs are met (e.g., caretaker, breadwinner), participants in groups must fulfill certain responsibilities to help the group achieve its objectives. Group members generally assume two types of roles within the group: a task role and an interpersonal role. **Task roles** directly relate to the accomplishments of the objectives and missions of the group. "Recording Secretary" and "Moderator" are examples of task roles. Other common task roles include:

- *The Information Giver*: Offers facts, beliefs, personal experience, or other input.
- *The Information Seeker*: Asks for additional input or clarification of ideas or opinions that have been presented.
- *The Elaborator*: Offers further clarification of points, often providing information about what others have said.
- *The Initiator*: Helps the group get moving by proposing a solution, generating new ideas, providing a new organizational scheme to solve a problem, or giving new definitions to an issue.

Members also adopt various **interpersonal roles**, or styles of interacting in the group. These "relational" roles facilitate group interaction. Examples include:

- *The Harmonizer*: Seeks to smooth over tension in the group by settling differences among members.

task roles
group members' roles related directly to the accomplishments of the objectives and mission of the group.

interpersonal roles
group members' "relational" roles that facilitate group interaction.

- *The Gatekeeper:* Works to keep each member involved in the discussion by keeping communication channels open, or restricts information during periods of overload.
- *The Sensor:* Expresses group feelings, moods, or relationships in an effort to recognize the climate and capitalize on it.

Both task roles and interpersonal roles help the group maintain cohesion and achieve its mission. Sometimes, however, group members focus on individual versus group needs. These needs are usually irrelevant to the task at hand and are not oriented toward maintenance of the group as a team. Such persons can be said to display negative interpersonal roles, or **counterproductive roles**. These roles are counterproductive to the group and should be avoided.

Examples of counterproductive roles include:

- *The Blocker:* Exhibits negative and stubbornly resistant behavior, including disagreements and logic-defying opposition to ideas; frequently, blockers re-raise an issue after the group has already rejected or bypassed it.
- *The Avoider:* Displays non-involvement in the group's proceedings by such behaviors as pouting, cynicism, nonchalance, or "horseplay."
- *The Recognition Seeker:* Displays behavior that calls attention to the individual, such as boasting and focusing on personal qualifications and achievements.
- *The Distractor:* Goes off on tangents, makes pointless comments, and in general strays off-task.
- *The Dominator:* Cuts others off and uses an exorbitant amount of "floor time"; is always the first to speak on every topic.

Critical Checkpoint

· ·

Carefully Examine Ideas

True teamwork involves working toward a common goal, focusing on issues rather than personalities, and adopting positive group roles. Each of these behaviors can be enhanced by using critical thinking skills. The process of goal setting, for example, is enhanced when you consider multiple perspectives and minimize biased information. Controversy and conflict are best approached from a reasoned perspective, one in which you focus on the disagreement itself rather than on the people who are disagreeing. The most solid decisions are those reached by probing for underlying causes and reasons, clarifying issues and values, and evaluating the evidence. Finally, critical thinking is the number-one defense against groupthink. There's little danger of "following the herd" if you're committed to carefully examining ideas.

Leading a Group

Capable leadership is critical to the success of any group effort. There are many definitions of leadership, but two aspects are paramount. These are *direction* and *influence*. One of the primary functions of a leader is to provide direction. Good leaders organize, structure, guide, and facilitate a group's activities and interaction in ways that will lead to a desired outcome. Another

negative interpersonal roles within the group setting in which participants focus on individual versus group needs; these needs are usually irrelevant to the task and not oriented toward maintenance of the group as a team.

prominent feature of leadership is influence. A chief function of leadership is to influence group members to achieve a desired result.

Leaders search for opportunities to make the group process work effectively for its members and for the task or goal for which the group has formed. One of the primary responsibilities of the leader is to set goals and ensure that they are met.

Set Goals. Most negative experiences in groups result from a single underlying problem: lack of a clear goal. Each member of a group should be able to answer the following questions:

1. For what purpose(s) does the group exist?
2. Do all group members understand and accept the goals? Are they committed to them?
3. How close is the group to achieving this purpose?
4. How well are the activities or functions of the group aligned with the goals?

As a group leader, you should be a catalyst in setting group goals and ensuring that they are reached. You may either set these yourself or work with the group in establishing them. The latter option is preferable because group members are likely to be more committed and excited about goals that they have helped create. The following guidelines[1] suggest how you can do this:

1. *Identify the problem*. Specify what is to be accomplished or completed.
2. *Map out a strategy*. Determine the desired performance level and a means to evaluate whether it has been achieved.
3. *Set a performance goal*. Realize the group's capabilities and limitations, and establish a realistic target to achieve them.
4. *Identify the resources necessary to achieve the goal*. Be aware that issues of how much time, what kind of equipment, and how much money are among the important issues to consider before beginning.
5. *Recognize contingencies that may arise*. Think about the kinds of obstacles that are likely to prevent the group from achieving its goal, and consider ways to overcome those problems.
6. *Obtain feedback*. Prepare to adjust direction or methods so that the group is doing its best.

Encourage Active Participation. Group members bring with them different backgrounds, experiences, skills, and interests. To require all members of a group to participate equally on all topics would be detrimental to its effectiveness. Each member has something unique to contribute, but perhaps not at all times. Sometimes, however, a group member does not participate even if he or she does have something valuable to offer. The following are a few reasons for non-participation:

- *Apprehension*: Members may experience fear or anxiety over expressing themselves in the group.
- *Lack of self-esteem*: Members may doubt the value of their contributions.
- *Dominance*: Other group members may control the "floor."
- *Status differences*: Group members lower in the hierarchy of positions may choose not to comment on stances taken by superiors in the group.

Frank Siteman/Monkmeyer

A strong leader provides guidance, direction, and focus while helping the group achieve specific goals.

Focus on Technology

Computer Technology and Group Communication

Computer technology offers a variety of tools that enable groups to work together, from email and newsgroups to software that facilitates computerized meetings. As always, the Internet is helpful for conducting research, getting ideas, and confirming opinions. Email allows you to exchange ideas with co-members over long distances. This offers one solution to the most common complaint about group work—no time or opportunity to meet. Also available is software designed specifically to facilitate the group decision-making process. One such program, Group Decision Support Systems (GDSS), helps groups communicating via computer stay on track and steer clear of faulty decision making.

For those who want to avoid verbal interaction altogether, there is the computerized meeting. In a computerized meeting, group members gather in a large, specially equipped room that features a giant screen. Instead of speaking, participants type their comments on computers; the comments are then projected onto the screen. This sort of meeting has been found to be particularly effective for brainstorming sessions as well as for meetings that focus on sensitive evaluations. Software programs such as VisionQuest and OptionFinder help participants navigate through the process.[1]

1. William M. Bulkeley, "Computing Dull Meetings Is Touted as an Antidote to the Mouth That Bored," *Wall Street Journal*, January 28, 1992, pp. B1–B2.

Research reveals that problems arise when participation is unbalanced. A study by Hoffman and Maier,[2] for example, found that groups adopt solutions that receive the largest number of favorable comments, whether these comments emanate from one individual or many. If only one or two members participate, it will be their input that sets the agenda, whether or not their solution is optimal.

Leaders can make use of several techniques to encourage participation:

- *Directly ask members to contribute*. The leader can influence involvement by taking note of participants who are quiet and asking them to contribute ("Patrice, we haven't heard from you yet" or "Juan, what do you think about this?").
- *Redirect the discussion*. Sometimes one person, or a few, dominate the discussion. To encourage others to contribute, the leader can redirect the discussion in their direction.
- *Set a positive tone*. Some people are afraid of expressing their views because they fear ridicule or attack. A good leader minimizes such fears by setting a positive tone and stressing fairness and by encouraging a climate of politeness and active listening.

MAKING DECISIONS IN GROUPS

Effective groups do not make decisions arbitrarily or haphazardly. Rather, they engage in a deliberate process resulting in decisions that all participants understand and to which they are committed. Group decision making is best

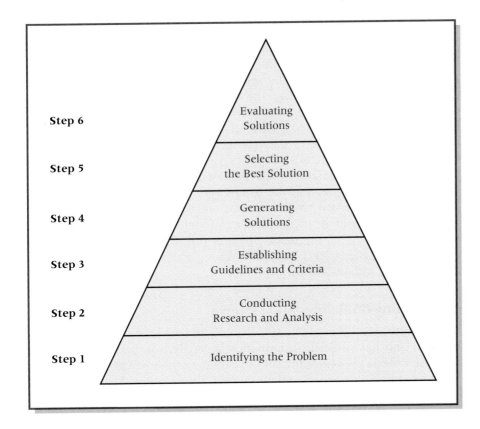

Step 6	Evaluating Solutions
Step 5	Selecting the Best Solution
Step 4	Generating Solutions
Step 3	Establishing Guidelines and Criteria
Step 2	Conducting Research and Analysis
Step 1	Identifying the Problem

FIGURE 16.1
Making Decisions in Groups

accomplished through a six-step process based on the work of the famous educator John Dewey:[3] identifying the problem, conducting research and analysis, establishing guidelines and criteria, generating solutions, selecting the best solution, and evaluating (see Figure 16.1). To illustrate each of these steps, the following discussion uses the example of a task force that has been commissioned to address a campus racial incident in which derogatory graffiti was painted on the walls of the student union building.

Identifying the Problem

The first step in making a decision is understanding what is being decided on. Before doing anything else, all members of the group must make sure that they agree on the issue or problem that has brought them together. If the group's goal is to generate a solution to a problem, then each member must understand the problem in the same way.

Identifying the problem does not mean simply announcing it and moving on, as in, "We need to find a way to reduce racial discrimination on our campus." Rather, this step involves gaining a thorough understanding of the issue at hand. Each participant should share his or her perception of the problem with the group and briefly state what he or she thinks it is about. There should be no discussion or debate until all members have had a chance to do this. At this point, ideas can be debated and positions clarified. The group leader should summarize the discussion that has occurred up to that point. If there is not agreement among the members, he or she should pinpoint the source of confusion and proceed to obtain a consensus.

Conducting Research and Analysis

Once agreement has been reached on the nature of the problem, the next step is to consider what information is needed to solve it. The group may need to research an issue for several reasons: (1) to close gaps in information necessary to analyzing the problem properly, (2) to clarify or resolve two or more inconsistent views or positions expressed by participants, or (3) to investigate past solutions to similar problems.

In the example of the racially charged incident on campus, the group will want to discover the answer to several questions: What causes people to write racially inflammatory remarks on a campus building? Is this type of discrimination widespread in the community? Are other college campuses affected in the same way? What can be done to stop this type of behavior? Did some other incident trigger this act of violence? Without research on these and other topics, the group operates out of ignorance or misperception. Better decisions are made when group members are informed with data and facts, rather than with speculation.

Establishing Guidelines and Criteria

Once the group thoroughly understands and agrees on the nature of the problem and has sufficient information to analyze it, participants should establish criteria by which any solution they propose will be judged. In the graffiti example, the criteria might be that any solution (1) receive strong Student Senate support, and (2) lie within the guidelines of the college's code of conduct.

As in identifying the problem, establishing guidelines and criteria is an interactive process that should end in consensus. Members should question each other for more information or for clarification. If there are disagreements or problems, the leader should identify the point of confusion and open the discussion for clarification. To ensure that these criteria may be used at a later point, each item should be recorded.

Generating Solutions

Once the problem has been identified and researched and criteria have been established for evaluating solutions, it's time to generate solutions. At this stage a brainstorming session is in order, with every member contributing as many desirable solutions they possibly can. To solve the problem of racially charged graffiti on campus, group members might offer proposals such as (1) installing professional security equipment in each campus building, (2) hiring more campus police, (3) developing education programs that focus on cultural diversity, and (4) creating student patrols.

It is important to note that no debate and discussion of the merits of the proposal should occur during this stage of the decision-making process. Instead, the leader should simply record each idea as it is expressed.

Steve Niedorf/The Image Bank

A brainstorming session is a great way to stimulate creativity and generate solutions to a problem. After the session, the group can select the best course of action.

Selecting the Best Solution

Once all the potential solutions have been generated, the group can begin to weigh the relative merits of each against the criteria agreed on earlier. In the example of the racially charged graffiti, the leader may say, "Okay, let's look at the first proposal—that we install professional security equipment in each campus building. Now, does that mesh well with our first criterion that we receive strong Student Senate support?"

Once the group has arrived at a short list of alternatives, they must select one alternative that can best fulfill their needs. Groups that are lucky may find the perfect solution. That is, only one proposed solution will successfully survive the evaluation. Frequently, however, one of two other things happens: Either more than one solution survives, or no solution survives. What should be done in this event? In the former case, the group should determine if two or more viable solutions are mutually exclusive. Perhaps both proposals can be adopted. If not, select the solution that has met the criteria most completely. This solution is likely to be your best. When no solution emerges, the group should return to the problem identification step to determine if the problem is adequately defined. Then each remaining step should be taken in turn until a solution is reached.

Evaluating the Chosen Solution

The final step in the decision-making process involves evaluating the group's solution. Are there any shortcomings that should be addressed before the plan is implemented? How well or poorly was the decision-making process followed? What could have been done better? What was done well?

Part of evaluating solutions involves re-evaluating the criteria and guidelines against which the solution was measured. The following questions can help determine how effective the criteria were, as well as how well or poorly the solution met the criteria:

- Were the criteria useful and appropriate for the problem?
- How strictly were the criteria used in arriving at the decision?
- Does the solution resemble the criteria that were developed?
- What other criteria would have been helpful in arriving at a better solution?
- Does the solution have any weaknesses or disadvantages?

The steps involved in the decision-making process are a proven method of producing competent group outcomes. In the words of John Dewey, the sequence of steps encourages group members to "think reflectively" about their task. In this way all the relevant facts and opinions can be discussed and evaluated, thereby ensuring a better decision.

MAKING PRESENTATIONS IN GROUPS

Once the group has achieved its goal, members face the task of reporting their results to others. They do so in the form of a written report, oral presentation, or combination of the two. Group presentations have many of the same characteristics as presentations done individually, with some important differences. As with individual reports, the group should carefully analyze its audience, use supporting material from its research phase, organize and outline the presentation according to an appropriate format, develop a suitable introduction and conclusion, and prepare effective presentational aids. But whereas in an individual presentation one person assumes all responsibilities for presenting a topic, in a group presentation some or all of the group members divide these tasks.

Assigning Tasks

In some group presentations one person may present the introduction, one or more others may deliver the body of the speech, and another may conclude the presentation. Together with the group leader, members must decide who will do what. Assignments are often linked to each member's task roles in the group. The Initiator of the group might present background information and explain the problem; the Group Statistician might explain how the data were collected; the Elaborator might present the findings and conclusions; and the Information Gatherer might offer the group's recommendations.

The Moderator's Role

symposium
a formal meeting at which several speakers deliver short speeches on related topics.

panel
a group of persons who discuss a topic in the presence of an audience.

Some group presentations, such as symposiums and panels, require the presence of a moderator. A **symposium** is a formal meeting at which several speakers deliver short speeches on related topics. In a **panel**, a group of persons discusses a topic in the presence of an audience. In such forums the moderator ensures that everyone knows their speaking responsibilities and stays within their speaking time limits. During the presentation phase, the moderator introduces the group, describes the purpose and topic of the presentation, and introduces each speaker. He or she should also be prepared to receive questions and comments for the group and direct them to the appropriate individual presenter. Finally, the moderator should be keenly aware of time, making sure the group gets started at the designated time and that each presenter stays within the allotted time for that segment of the presentation.

Ensuring Consistency of Delivery

Glaring inconsistencies between the presenters' delivery styles spell failure for the group presentation. Audiences become distracted by marked disparities in style, such as a captivating speaker followed by an extremely dull one. As in individual presentations, practice is the key to overcoming such disparities and achieving a good balance of delivery style. Together with the other members, each participant should practice his or her portion of the presentation in the same order as it will be given in final form, and do so until it proceeds smoothly. And as in individual presentations, group members should keep in focus the purpose and nature of the presentation while isolating the proper delivery style.

BUSINESS AND PROFESSIONAL PRESENTATIONS

Beyond the panel and symposium, there are many other forums in which groups deliver their findings. In the business and professional arena, architectural teams report on their progress to the firm's partners; company representatives inform employees of new policies and procedures; task forces describe their results to senior management; and so forth. Although there are countless types of business and professional organizations and related opportunities for speaking, you will likely find yourself, either individually or as part of a group, delivering one of five kinds of presentations. These include sales presentations, technical reports, progress reports, staff reports, and investigative reports. Before reviewing these, let's consider some differences between giving a business and professional presentation and delivering a formal public speech.

Public versus Presentational Speaking

Many people use the terms *speech* and *presentation* interchangeably. Yet there are clear differences between a speech delivered in public and a presentation delivered in a business and professional environment.[4] First, the audience for a presentation can be as small as three people. Second, presentational speaking is less formal than public speaking. Priscilla Rogers, a professor of business communication, suggests that on a continuum a presentation would lie midway between public speaking on one end and conversational speaking on the other.[5] Presentational speaking also usually occurs in more limited settings than does public speaking. Public speeches can be delivered just about anywhere an audience can gather—indoors or outdoors, large arena, or small park. In contrast, presentations made in the business or professional context are more likely to be delivered indoors, at a business site.[6]

Robert Reichert/Gamma Liaison

Professor Rogers offers the following examples to help distinguish presentational speaking from public speaking, as well as from conversational speech:[7]

Although business presentations and public speaking differ to some extent, you can use skills you have honed in public speaking to strengthen your professional presentations.

Presentational Speaking
    Sales presentations
    Progress reports
    Briefing sessions
    Explanations of policies, plans, and proposals

Public Speaking
    Formal introductions (e.g., of keynote speakers or award recipients)
    Press statements
    Personal tributes
    Presidential addresses

Conversational Speaking
    Recruiting luncheons
    Elevator talk
    Appraisal interviews
    Phone conversations

Communication professor Frank Dance suggests some further differences between presentational and public speaking:[8]

Topic Selection. Topics for public speeches can be assigned, but often are left to the speaker's discretion. Even when a topic is assigned, public speakers are given some leeway in developing and presenting the topic. They can even be excused for deviating from a predetermined topic if the topic they prefer to present is relevant to the audience. In contrast, topics for business presentations are either assigned by the presenter's superiors or clients or assumed as part of one's role in a work group or project. Presentational speakers generally have less leeway in terms of developing and delivering the topic; they often follow a prescribed or traditional approach depending on the kind of presentation. Presentational topics are more specific, task oriented, and management- or client-directed.

Audience Composition. Public speaking audiences may be more diverse than presentation speaking audiences. They are more likely self-selected or voluntary, and they probably expect to be attending a one-time event. In contrast, listeners who attend a business or professional presentation are more likely to be part of a "captive" audience. As a group they are also more similar, in that there is an ongoing relationship among the participants; that is, they are part of a "team." They may expect to attend the same event with the same presenter, even on the same topic, several times during the course of a project or series of meetings.

Audience Participation. In general the public speaker delivers his or her speech uninterrupted. If there is a question-and-answer period, it almost always takes place at the end of the speech. In business and professional presentations, verbal interaction between speaker and audience is generally the rule rather than the exception. Audience members ask questions and make comments during and after the talk. It isn't unusual for a presentation to be stopped midway when a discussion ensues or time runs out.

Speaker Expertise. Listeners generally assume that a public speaker has more expertise or considerably more firsthand knowledge than they do on the topic. The speaker is frequently the reason many audience members attend a speech, regardless of the topic. Presentational speakers, in contrast, are more properly thought of as "first among equals" in that they may be no more expert on the topic than are members of the audience. It just happens that the presenter has been designated to fulfill this particular task for the moment or for a time. A presentation audience attends more to gain information than to hear the presenter.

Types of Presentations

Five of the most common types of business and professional presentations are sales presentations, technical reports, progress reports, staff reports, and investigative reports.[9] As noted, any of these presentations can be delivered by individuals or by multiple presenters. Keep in mind that many industries have their own preferred styles and requirements for making presentations. The following discussion provides some basic and common features of these presentations.

Sales Presentations

PURPOSE. A **sales presentation** attempts to lead a potential buyer to purchase a service or product described by the presenter. The general purpose of sales presentations is to persuade.

AUDIENCE. A sales presentation can be directed to an audience of one or many. It depends on who has the authority to make the purchase under consideration. Some sales presentations are invited by the potential buyer. Others are "cold sales" in which the presenter/seller approaches a first-time potential buyer with a product or service. In some cases the audience might be an intermediary—for example, a community agency's office manager. He or she then recommends to the agency director whether the purchase would be worthwhile. Sales presentations are most successful when they are clearly audience-directed. That is, the product or service must be presented in such a way as to show how it meets the needs of the potential buyer.

ORGANIZATION. With its focus on audience needs, the motivated sequence developed by Alan Monroe(see Chapter 14) offers an excellent way to organize sales presentations. Sometimes referred to as the *basic sales technique*, Monroe's sequence involves (1) drawing the potential buyer's attention to the product; (2) isolating and clarifying the buyer's need for it; (3) describing how the product will satisfy the need and provide long-term benefits of other kinds; and (4) inviting the buyer to purchase the product. The extent to which each segment is developed depends on the nature of the selling situation. In cold-sale situations, the seller/presenter may have to spend more time discovering the potential buyer's needs. For invited sales presentations, the buyer's needs will most likely be known in advance. In this event, more time can be spent by the presenter detailing the characteristics of the product and showing how it will satisfy the buyer's needs.

> **sales presentation**
> a presentation that attempts to lead a potential buyer to purchase a service or product.

Technical Reports

PURPOSE. Sometimes an organization needs detailed information about a procedure or a device in order to decide whether to adopt or purchase it. Such information is routinely presented in a **technical report**. For example, a company might be interested in upgrading its telephone system. The facilities manager is given the task of learning from the original system provider the recommended equipment for making the upgrade. The manager then prepares a technical presentation that will provide the necessary information to assist the company in making its decision.

> **technical report**
> a report that gives detailed information about a procedure or device.

AUDIENCE. The audience for a technical report can vary from a single individual to a large group; the person or persons have primary or sole decision-making responsibility. In the telephone system example, the facility manager will present his or her technical report to company officers who are authorized to decide, on the basis of the report, whether or not to upgrade to the newer system.

ORGANIZATION. Depending on its subject, a technical report can be quite lengthy and formally organized, or relatively brief and loosely structured. A lengthier, more formal technical report is organized in a manner similar to an investigative report, with a full introduction, statement of problem, method of inquiry, facts learned, explanation, conclusion, and recommendation. If

Promoting Ethical Communication in the Workplace

Hostile takeovers, industrial espionage, workplace sabotage, mail tampering, petty theft, and eavesdropping are some of the more obvious instances of unethical practices permeating the workplace. The practice of unethical communication has become so widespread that business programs at most colleges and universities now require a course in business ethics. What is most disturbing about unethical communication is that it occurs at all levels of the organization and is practiced in very subtle ways—a white lie here, misleading information there. Literally thousands of instances of unethical messages are exchanged in the workplace on a daily basis. Why is this problem so widespread in the professional world? Employees in numerous surveys have listed the following as reasons for compromising their ethics standards:

- Pressure to produce results.
- Misunderstanding the difference between unethical and ethical behavior.
- The fact that everyone else is doing it.
- Profit motive.

- Personal advancement.
- Refusing to take an ethical position.
- Ease of getting away with unethical communication.

How can you ensure that your business and professional messages are ethical? Review the pillars of character that were discussed in Chapter 4. Whether you are participating in group discussions, giving reports, or making business presentations, it is critical to keep in mind the ground rules suggested by Michael Josephson from the Josephson Institute of Ethics. *Trustworthiness* is ensured when you are forthright and truthful. *Respect* is demonstrated when you treat people properly; you should focus on the issues rather than personalities when speaking. You can maintain an ethical level of *responsibility* when you communicate in ways that are accurate. You must communicate your message so that all sides of the argument are presented—not just the side that helps you the most. Finally, you can demonstrate *fairness* when you have made a genuine effort to be objective and open-minded.

the facilities manager in the telephone system example must interview several people and read several sources of information pertaining to the upgrade, the presentation might be suited to the more formal plan. On the other hand, if the technical information is relatively straightforward and limited in scope, the presenter can begin with a statement of recommendation, a brief overview of the problem, and a review of the facts on which the recommendation is based.

Staff Reports

staff report
a report that informs managers and other employees of new developments that affect them and their work.

PURPOSE. A **staff report** informs managers and other employees of new developments that affect them and their work. For example, a company's personnel division might implement a new plan for subscribers to the company's health insurance program. To explain the changes, the personnel director will present the plan at a meeting of the sales division. He or she will review the reasons for the new plan, explain how it works, and describe its ramifications. Another function of staff reports is to report on the completion of a project or task. For instance, the district manager of a restaurant chain might assign three local restaurant managers the task of devising a plan for expanding the seating capacity at each location. The managers will present their design at the next district meeting.

AUDIENCE. The audience for a staff report is usually a group but may be an individual. The chain restaurant managers will make their report in a meeting with the district manager alone, or in a meeting of managers from the whole district. The recipients of a staff report then use the information for implementation of new policy, coordination of other plans, or making other reports to other groups.

ORGANIZATION. Formal staff reports typically include a statement of the problem or question under consideration (sometimes called a "charge" to a committee or subcommittee), a description of procedures and facts used in addressing the problem, a discussion of the facts most pertinent to the problem, and then a statement of conclusions followed by recommendations (see Figure 16.2 for an example).

Progress Reports

PURPOSE. A progress report is similar to a staff report, with the exception that the audience can include persons outside the organization as well as

---

I. The Committee's Charge
   The Facilities Planning Committee was charged with the task of making recommendations for beautifying the grounds around the headquarters offices.
II. Procedures
   A. Each person who has offices or otherwise works in the headquarters building was invited to provide in writing a list of reasonable improvements they would like to see made to the grounds around the building
   B. Lists were compiled and categorized
      1. Lawn and bedding improvements
      2. Structural improvements
   C. Categories were assigned to two different subcommittees for further development
III. Facts
   A. Lawn and bedding
      1. Currently 3.2 acres of "green" grounds
      2. Frequent requests were made to plant more trees and shrubbery
      3. Current lawn and bedding can be retained with addition of trees and shrubs
   B. Structural improvements
      1. Frequent requests for benches and tables in select locations
      2. Currently 920 cubic yards of sidewalk on grounds
      3. Frequent requests to add additional sidewalk from east end of parking lot to front of building
         a. Will require 315 more cubic yards of sidewalk
         b. Will displace that much lawn and a 24-cubic-foot section of shrubbery at east end of the building
IV. Conclusions and Recommendations
   A. Too early to state definitive conclusions
   B. Committee recommends inviting bids from landscape contractors for:
      1. A variety of moderate-size fruit and hardwood trees
      2. Additional shrubbery, up to 1000 cubic feet
      3. Concrete and wood benches for four locations around the building

FIGURE 16.2
Organization of a Staff Report

within it. **A progress report** updates clients or principals on developments in an ongoing project. On long-term projects, such reports may be given at designated intervals or at the time of specific task completions throughout the duration of the project. For example, subcontractors on a housing construction project meet weekly with the project developers. On short-term projects, reports can occur daily. For example, medical personnel in the intensive care unit of a hospital meet each morning to review the treatment protocol and progress of each patient.

AUDIENCE. The audiences for progress reports vary greatly. An audience might be a group of clients or customers, developers and investors, next-line supervisors, company officers, media representatives, or same-level co-workers assigned to the same project. For example, a work team consisting of two design engineers, two marketing specialists, two production engineers, and a cost analyst may be assigned to the development of a new product. Once a week, members of the team present the rest of the team with a progress report concerning their aspect of the project, especially during the early stages of the project. Once the project is well under way and activity is focused on one particular segment, such as marketing, those representatives may be the only ones making progress reports, and the audience may extend to potential buyers, corporate officers, and other staff in the various departments. Progress reports are commonplace in staff and committee meetings where subcommittees report on the progress of their designated tasks. Audience questions are common at the end of progress reports.

ORGANIZATION. There is no set pattern of organization for a progress report. In many instances the report begins with a brief statement to review progress made up to the time of the previous report followed by a more thorough statement of new developments since the previous report. This statement may include descriptions of personnel involved and their activities, time spent on tasks, supplies used and costs incurred, problems encountered and how they were handled, and an estimate of tasks to be completed for the next reporting period.

Investigative Reports

PURPOSE. Sometimes a company or agency faces a question or problem that it can't solve on its own. To find an answer, the company conducts or commissions an **investigative report** or study of the problem. For example, a large church might want to attract a greater segment of the surrounding community to attend services but isn't certain how to go about it. The church hires a consultant group to study current members' reasons for attending the church, new members' reasons for joining the church, and local nonmembers' potential interests in visiting a church. The consulting firm then plans a study involving a survey or interview of representative persons, compiles information obtained from the survey or interview, draws conclusions from the information, and sets recommendations. The approach is similar both to that done by polling groups who conduct surveys to identify people's attitudes and preferences for some issue, and to work done by marketing specialists who study consumer reactions to a new product.

AUDIENCE. The audience for an investigative report is usually a group whose planning and decisions on a matter depend significantly on the results of the investigation. In the example of the church study, the audience might be any of a number of committees (e.g., membership committee, community relations committee), or the church's governing board. The report will be delivered by the principal investigator—the member of the consulting firm who oversees and supervises the study—or by a close collaborator on the study. The audience will probably ask questions throughout the presentation and make direct challenges to some of the conclusions and recommendations.

ORGANIZATION. Investigative reports follow a strict, systematic structure taking one of two forms. The *indirect method* of organization presents the conclusions and recommendations last, preceded in order by (1) background or history leading to the problem, (2) statement of the problem, (3) method of investigation, (4) findings, (5) conclusions relative to the problem, and (6) recommendations. The indirect method closely parallels the introduction-body-conclusion format of public speeches. The *direct method* begins with the most important conclusions and recommendations, then describes (1) the problem to which they apply, (2) the method used to investigate the problem, and (3) the chief findings related to the problem.

Although most investigative reports are organized according to the indirect method, the direct method is often preferred for many kinds of business presentations because it "gets to the point" sooner than the indirect method does. The direct method is suitable when the audience is mainly interested in and promptly needs precise information in order to make immediate decisions.

DELIVERING THE PRESENTATION

Delivery is another factor that distinguishes presentations from public speeches. "Energetic," "expressive," and "dynamic" best describe the general expectations for delivery of public speeches. The same is expected of some kinds of business presentations, such as sales presentations, but not of others. In fact, the range of delivery styles may be broader for presentations than for speeches. One group of researchers studied the characteristics that businesspeople associate with effective presentations for different general purposes (e.g., persuading, explaining, informing).[10] They found two sets of characteristics distinguishing four general purposes. One set of characteristics contrasts *relational messages* (those concerned with people, relationships, motivation, needs, and the like) with *instrumental messages* (those concerned with facts, tasks, and procedures). The other set contrasts *conventional message content* (content that follows established procedures for routine issues or problems) with *dynamic content* (content that expresses innovative ideas and creative approaches). When the two sets of characteristics are crossed, as in Figure 16.3, four presentational delivery styles emerge. Let's look at each style.

Baros & Baros/The Image Bank

Business presentations require more flexibility on the speaker's part than public speeches do. Tailor your presentation to one of the four delivery styles: informational, instructional, relational, or transformational.

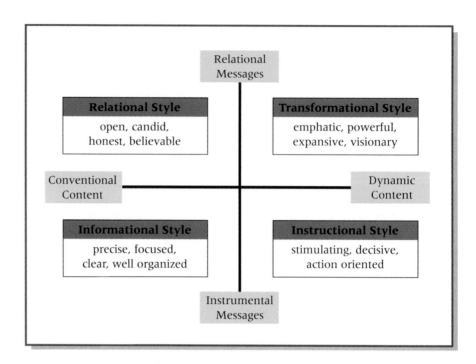

FIGURE 16.3
Presentational Delivery Styles

Informational Delivery

When your presentation is laden with facts, you will probably want to use an **informational style of delivery**; that is, one that is precise, disciplined, focused, clear, logical, and well organized. This is because the audience will be most concerned with getting the facts and will want the presentation to be predictable and easy to follow. Reliance on detailed notes and graphs and charts to present complex data will be expected. Technical reports and many investigative presentations make use of an informational style of delivery.

Instructional Delivery

As with informational delivery, the instructional style of delivery emphasizes facts and procedures. But instead of the speaker doing all the talking while the audience listens passively, the instructional style involves more audience interaction. Training or teaching involves the kind of presentation that uses instructional delivery. The **instructional style of delivery** is stimulating, engaging, consequential, decisive, and action oriented. It is best done extemporaneously, and the speaker should allow time for questions and comments during the presentation. Progress reports and staff reports are both well suited to this style.

Relational Delivery

When the success of a presentation hinges on the presenter's credibility with the audience, the best bet is a **relational style of delivery**. This style is open, candid, honest, believable, plausible, and trustworthy. Presentations delivered relationally are usually extemporaneous. Some sales presentations are suited to this style, especially those attempting to establish a lasting relationship with clients. Staff presentations and progress reports that deal with

informational style of delivery
a delivery style that is precise, disciplined, focused, clear, logical, and well organized.

instructional style of delivery
a delivery style that is stimulating, engaging, consequential, decisive, and action oriented.

relational style of delivery
a delivery style that is open, candid, honest, believable, and trustworthy.

sensitive, personnel-oriented issues should also be delivered using the relational style.

Transformational Delivery

When your aim is to motivate the audience, you should select a transformational style of delivery. The **transformational style of delivery** assumes the presentation of relational ideas in a dynamic, creative fashion. This style is emphatic, powerful, insightful, expansive, and visionary. Presentations delivered transformationally should be extemporaneous. A staff presentation encouraging a work group to become more cohesive and increase its productivity would be delivered using this style. An investigative report that recommends a major change in policy might also be delivered using this style.

transformational style of delivery
a delivery style that is emphatic, powerful, insightful, expansive, and visionary.

SUMMARY QUESTIONS

What makes an effective group participant?

Being an effective group participant requires keeping sight of the group's goals and avoiding behavior that detracts from them. Conflict should be handled productively, by focusing on issues-based rather than personal-based conflict. To avoid groupthink, participants should rigorously apply critical thinking skills to the decision-making process. Group members should also avoid counterproductive behaviors exemplified in counterproductive roles such as the Blocker, the Avoider, and the Dominator. Instead, focus on productive task and interpersonal roles that promote group cohesion and help achieve goals.

What makes an effective group leader?

Good leaders organize, structure, guide, and facilitate a group's activities and interaction in ways that will lead to a desired outcome. One of the primary responsibilities of the leader is to set goals and ensure that they are met. To help the group meet its goals, the leader can engage in a four-step process in which the group (1) identifies the problem, (2) maps out a strategy, (3) sets a performance goal, and (4) identifies the resources necessary to achieve the goal. Another important function is to encourage active participation among all members. The leader can do this in one of several ways: by directly asking members to contribute, by redirecting the discussion, or by setting a positive tone.

How can a group go about reaching a solution to a problem or issue that it has been charged with solving?

Group decision making is best accomplished though a six-step process: (1) identifying problems, (2) conducting research and analysis, (3) establishing guidelines and criteria, (4) generating solutions, (5) selecting the best solution, and (6) evaluating the solution.

How do group presentations differ from individual presentations?

Whereas in an individual presentation one person assumes all responsibilities for presenting a topic, in a group presentation some or all of the group members divide these same tasks. Certain assignments are linked to each member's task roles in the group. Some group presentations, such as panels and symposiums, require the presence of a moderator.

What is the difference between public speaking and presentational speaking?

Several factors distinguish formal public speeches from presentations. These include degree of formality (public speeches are more formal and less related to conversational speech than presentations); audience size (can be as few as three for a presentation); audience composition (audiences for public speeches tend to be more diverse than audiences for presentations); audience participation (there is little verbal interaction between speaker and audience during a public speech, whereas in a presentation such interaction is the rule); setting (presentational speaking tends to occur in more limited settings, such as business sites, than does public speaking, which can occur virtually anywhere a large crowd can gather); topic selection (topics are often left to the public speaker's discretion, whereas topics for business and professional presentations are assigned by superiors or clients); and speaker expertise (public speakers usually have greater expertise on the speech topic than do audience members; presentational speakers usually are no more knowledgeable than the listeners are).

What are five of the most common types of presentations that might be delivered in the business and professional arena?

Although there are countless types of business and professional organizations and related opportunities for speaking, you will likely find yourself, either individually or as part of a group, delivering one of five kinds of presentations. These include sales presentations, technical reports, staff reports, progress reports, and investigative reports.

What are the different styles of delivery that are appropriate to business and professional presentations?

Four styles of delivery are especially appropriate to business and professional presentations. These include the informational style, instructional style, relational style, and transformational style. When your presentation is laden with facts, you should use an informational style of delivery; that is, one that is precise, disciplined, focused, clear, logical, and well organized. When you want to show how something is done, select the instructional style of delivery, one that is stimulating, engaging, consequential, decisive, and action oriented. When the success of a presentation hinges on the presenter's credibility with the audience, the best bet is a relational style of delivery, one that is open, candid, honest, believable, plausible, and trustworthy. Finally, when your aim is to motivate the audience, select a transformational style of delivery, one that is emphatic, powerful, insightful, expansive, and visionary.

ISSUES FOR DISCUSSION

1. Explain one of your own experiences as a member of a group, such as a committee, a campus club, a dormitory government, a sorority, and so on. Describe the purpose of the group, the setting, and the other members. When making decisions, what roles did each of the members fulfill? Illustrate these roles with specific instances of behaviors or interactions.

2. What are some ways in which individuals who assume counterproductive roles in groups negatively affect the ability of the group to work together and make decisions?

3. Why is it important for a group to have a clear set of goals?

4. How is preparing and practicing a group presentation similar to and different from preparing and practicing a public speech?

5. Why do the different kinds of business presentations utilize different styles of delivery? Why can't a speaker just use his or her preferred style of delivery for any kind of presentation?

Key Terms

counterproductive roles
groupthink
informational style
   of delivery
instructional style
   of delivery
interpersonal roles
investigative report
issues-based conflict
panel
personal-based conflict
presentational speaking

productive conflict
progress report
relational style
   of delivery
sales presentation
staff report
symposium
task roles
technical report
transformational style
   of delivery

SELF-ASSESSMENT

1. Recall the elements of critical thinking from Chapter 3 (evaluating evidence; analyzing assumptions and biases; resisting false assumptions, overgeneralizations, and either-or thinking; identifying contractions; considering multiple perspectives; summarizing and judging facts). How could you be a more effective group member by using the elements of critical thinking?

2. Approximately how many times have you had the opportunity to serve as a group leader? How would you assess your leadership skills in these instances? Were you able to effectively set goals and encourage active participation among group members? If you haven't served as a group leader, do you look forward to that opportunity? Why or why not?

3. Recall a situation in which a group you were part of was guilty of groupthink. Did you go along with the group decision even if you didn't agree with it, just to avoid causing conflict? Or did you pressure others to go along with the group decision to keep them from voicing dissent? Analyzing the decision in retrospect, was it the right decision?

4. Review the interpersonal roles that facilitate group interaction (the Harmonizer, the Gatekeeper, and the Sensor) and counterproductive roles that harm group interaction (the Blocker, the Avoider, the Recognition Seeker, the Distractor, and the Dominator). Which roles have you displayed in the past? If you have assumed one of the positive roles, how did it make you feel when you helped the group interact? If you have displayed counterproductive roles, how did your behavior negatively affect the group? How might you avoid counterproductive roles in the future?

5. Consider your preferred or most likely occupation after receiving your college degree. Which kinds of presentations do you anticipate will be required in your job? Why?

6. Review the different styles of delivery appropriate to business and professional presentations. Which style is most appropriate to the kind of presentation you identified in Exercise 5? Why? Which style of delivery is most natural to you personally? Why? Do you see much discrepancy between your personal style and the style that might be required for presentations early in your career? If there is a discrepancy, what can you do to overcome it?

TEAMWORK

1. Not all tasks, projects, or activities in an organization are best performed by groups or teams, but rather by individuals working alone. Form a small group of four or five people and list three different situations in which it would be productive for individuals to work alone. For each, explain why you think greater effectiveness and efficiency would result by individuals working alone.

2. Form a group of four or five people. Imagine that you are a group of employees who work for Nike. You have been given the responsibility to select a celebrity to endorse a new line of youth turbo-light shoes. He or she will be seen in television commercials and in newspaper and magazine advertisements. Using the group decision-making process, select a celebrity. While making your decision, consider what kind of image you want the product to portray. What celebrity will best help create that image and convey the right message to your audience?

3. Now that your group has selected a celebrity to endorse a new line of Nike youth shoes, you are expected to give a formal presentation to brief your division director on your group's selection. Which kind of presentation will your group use? How will you divide the presentation among the group members? Prepare a general outline of the presentation. What style of delivery will be needed for this presentation? Why?

Kind words can be short and easy to speak, but their echoes are truly endless.

—Mother Teresa

The three most difficult things for a man to do are to climb a wall leaning towards you, to kiss a girl leaning away from you, and to make an after-dinner speech.

—Winston Churchill

17
Special Occasion Speeches

Can you recall a particularly inspiring sermon or commencement address? Perhaps you've recently attended a banquet or awards ceremony at which a speaker made a strong impression. **What was it about the speech that stayed with you?** Did humor play a role? Was the speaker particularly insightful? Was he or she inspiring?

From televised award shows like the Academy Awards to toasts at family dinners, we are surrounded by opportunities to listen to speeches that honor the special nature of a person or event. **It is very likely that you will be called upon to speak at a special occasion. As a speaker at such a time, it will be up to you to deliver a speech that captures the essence of a moment.**

Daisy died December 22, 1931, when she was hit by a Yellow Cab on University Place. At the moment of her death she was smelling the front of a florist's stoop. It was a wet day, and the cab skidded up over the curb—just the sort of excitement that would have amused her had she been at a safer distance. She is survived by her mother, Jeannie; a brother, Abner; her father, whom she never knew; and two sisters, whom she never liked. She was three years old.[1]

Daisy (1928–1931) was the beloved dog of early *New Yorker* magazine writer and children's author E. B. White. Here White eulogizes Daisy before a small gathering of family and friends. Not many dogs, or people for that matter, have the distinction of being memorialized by such an illustrious wordsmith as White. Yet we've all attended ceremonies at which a speaker spoke movingly about someone or something we cared about.

Special occasion speeches can be the most memorable, the most powerful, and the most important kinds of speeches we hear. Special occasion speeches are most often given to bring a group together and focus their attention on a shared experience. When delivered well, these speeches build a bond between audience members. Think of a time when you attended a graduation or saw a coach rallying the team for a crucial game. Consider the stirring words usually spoken by political figures on inauguration day or the solemn eulogies given at the time of a loved one's passing. Whether acknowledging an achievement, commemorating an historical event, toasting someone special, or remembering the deceased, a special occasion speech allows a speaker the opportunity to connect audience members with a powerful message that helps people put the significance of an event in perspective.

In his capacity as eulogist for his dog, Daisy, E. B. White was acting as a special occasion speaker. It is highly likely that at some point in your career or personal life you will be called on to deliver a special occasion speech. This chapter explains the nature of special occasion speaking and describes what preparing such speeches entails, including:

- The five broad functions of special occasion speeches.
- The different types of special occasion speeches you are likely to encounter.
- Techniques that will help you deliver an effective special occasion speech.

FUNCTIONS OF SPECIAL OCCASION SPEECHES

Special occasions stand out from the ordinary rhythm of life, marking passages, celebrating life's highlights, and offering solace in times of tragedy. In addition to speeches, such occasions often include the observance of important ceremonies and rituals. These rituals symbolically express the event's meaning to the community, while the speaker's words literally give voice to that meaning. Thus, for example, when Earl Spencer eulogized his sister Diana at Westminster Abbey in 1997, he articulated the emotions of millions who mourned her. When Abraham Lincoln dedicated the battlefield at Gettysburg in November 1863, his message that freedom must not perish lest the soldiers die in vain expressed his audience's deepest feelings and highest ideals.

There are many kinds of occasions that call for speeches, some serious and some lighthearted. As is evident by its name, a **special occasion speech** is one that is prepared for a specific occasion and for a purpose dictated by that occasion. A speaker might be invited to present an award, offer a toast, dedicate a building, entertain or inspire a gathering, or eulogize the deceased. In the special occasion speech, the occasion gives rise to the speech content, at least in its broad contours. Dedication ceremonies call for speeches that pay tribute. Awards ceremonies call for presentation speeches that acknowledge accomplishments and acceptance speeches that display gratitude. In each of these instances, audiences have definite expectations of the speaker. More so than in other kinds of speeches, they look to the speaker to fulfill quite specific functions dictated by the event.

Special occasion speeches can be either informative or persuasive. However, neither of these functions is the main goal; the underlying function of a special occasion speech is to entertain, celebrate, commemorate, inspire, or set a social agenda.

special occasion speech
a speech prepared for a specific occasion and for a purpose dictated by that occasion.

Entertainment

Many kinds of special occasions call for a speech that entertains. Banquets, awards dinners, and roasts, for example, frequently highlight speakers whose main purpose is to entertain those in attendance. In such cases listeners expect a lighthearted speech that amuses them. Depending on the event, they may also expect the speaker to offer a certain degree of insight into the topic at hand.

Celebration

Often the function of a special occasion speech is to celebrate a person, place, or event. Weddings, anniversaries, retirement parties, and awards banquets all call for speeches that recognize the person(s) or event being celebrated. The audience expects the speaker to praise the subject of celebration and cast him or her in a positive light. The listeners also expect a certain degree of ceremony in accordance with the norms of the occasion.

Commemoration

To commemorate is to remember by ceremony a notable person, place, or event. Commemorative events occur on important anniversaries, such as the fiftieth anniversary of the landing of Allied troops at Dunkirk or the bicentennial of the American Revolution. Additionally, speakers deliver commemorative speeches about events or persons of note at dedications of memorials to them or at gatherings otherwise called in their honor, including funerals.

Inspiration

Another function of the special occasion speech is to inspire. Inaugural addresses, keynote speeches at conventions, and commencement speeches all have inspiration as their main function. With their examples of achievement and heroism, many commemorative speeches also inspire audiences as well as pay homage to the person or event being commemorated.

Social Agenda Setting

Yet another function of the special occasion speech is social agenda setting—establishing or reinforcing the goals and values of the group sponsoring the event. Occasions that call for agenda-setting speeches include gatherings of issues- or cause-oriented organizations, fund-raisers, campaign banquets, conferences, and conventions. A speaker invited to a fund-raiser for the homeless, for example, might be asked to describe the organization's activities and outline its plans, or agenda, for the future. In their capacity as spokespersons for Habitat for Humanity, former president Jimmy Carter and former first lady Rosalynn Carter often perform this function. Similarly, speakers asked to deliver keynote addresses at conferences or conventions are charged with establishing the theme of the meeting and with offering a plan of action related to that theme.

Politically oriented organizations also routinely hold meetings at which invited speakers perform the function of agenda setting. GOPAC, for example, is a Republican organization dedicated to placing candidates who will run on its platform of "shared beliefs to renew America." It holds biannual dinner meetings at which legislators and others are asked to share their commentary and analysis of the issues of the day and offer a vision or plan for the issue in question.

TYPES OF SPECIAL OCCASION SPEECHES

With the various functions of special occasion speeches in mind, let's turn to the different types of such speeches you are likely to encounter. These include speeches of introduction, speeches of acceptance, award presentations, roasts and toasts, eulogies and other speeches of tribute, after-dinner speeches, and speeches of inspiration.

Speeches of Introduction

A **speech of introduction** is a short speech with two goals: to prepare or "warm up" the audience for the speaker, and to motivate them to listen to what he or she has to say. Many occasions call for speeches of introduction. You might be asked to introduce a guest speaker at a monthly meeting of a social organization to which you belong, introduce an award presenter at your company's annual banquet, or introduce an outside expert at a

speech of introduction
a short speech with the two goals of preparing the audience for the speaker and motivating them to listen to what he or she has to say.

quarterly sales meeting. A good speech of introduction balances four elements: the speaker's background, the subject of the speaker's message, the occasion, and the audience.

Describe the Speaker's Background. A key part of the introducer's task is to tell the audience something about the speaker's background and qualifications for speaking. The object is to heighten audience interest and build the speaker's credibility. If you don't know the speaker personally, be sure to contact him or her days or even weeks before the event. Ask the speaker to describe important achievements, offices held, and other activities that will show the audience what kind of speaker they are about to hear and why they should listen.

When describing the speaker, be selective about which of the speaker's awards and achievements to mention. Steer clear of lavish or excessive praise. Reciting too many accolades can cause your audience to glaze over. On the other hand, mentioning too few of the speaker's accomplishments can lead listeners to wonder why they should even be interested. Strive to create a positive and realistic portrait of the person you are introducing.

Identify the Speaker Correctly. Few things make an introducer look less credible than mispronouncing a name or otherwise incorrectly identifying the speaker. As you prepare your remarks, make certain that you address the speaker properly, assigning him or her the proper title, such as "vice president for public relations" or "professor emeritus." If his or her name is difficult to pronounce, ask ahead of time for the correct pronunciation and then practice it several times.

Briefly Preview the Speaker's Topic. Part of the introducer's job is to give the audience a sense of why the speaker's subject is of interest to them. Is the subject timely? What is its significance to the audience? What special connections exist between the subject and/or the speaker and the occasion? Is he or she an expert on the topic? Why was the speaker invited? Details such as these help the audience understand the speaker's role and build his or her credibility. Keep in mind, however, that it is not the introducer's job to evaluate the speech or otherwise offer critical commentary on it. The rule is: Get in and out quickly with a few well-chosen remarks. Introducers who linger on their own thoughts run the risk of stealing the speaker's thunder. Forced to cool his or her heels, the waiting speaker suffers mounting anxiety as "the moment" comes and goes and the introducer drones on.

Ask the Audience to Welcome the Speaker. A final part of the introducer's task is to cue the audience to welcome the speaker. This can be done very simply by saying something like, "Please welcome Anthony Svetlana." Hearing this, the audience will provide applause, thereby paving the way for the speaker to take his or her place at the podium.

Be Brief. At most, an introduction should last only a few minutes. One well-known speaker recommends a two-minute maximum.[2] The introducer should speak just long enough to accomplish the goals of preparation and motivation. Speaking longer will only hurt your cause, because your role is not to deliver a presentation but to introduce the person who will deliver a presentation.

Practice Good Speaking Habits. Finally, even though you are only introducing, you still should practice good speaking habits. Pay attention to language and delivery. Consider devices that will capture the audience's attention, such as quotes, short anecdotes, and startling statements (see Chapter 9). Don't burden the speaker with the added task of having to overcome the audience's boredom brought on by your introduction.

In the following excerpt from a speech by Frank D. Stella, of F. D. Stella Products Company, Mr. Stella introduces Richard A. Grasso, chairman and chief executive officer of the New York Stock Exchange, to the Economic Club of Detroit. Notice how Stella makes use of the date of the occasion—April 15, or income tax day—to involve the audience. Stella also provides a quick overview of who the speaker is and a reference to why he was a good choice for this speaking occasion.

> Happy April 15! This may be only a quirk of history, but do you realize that not only is today Tax Day, it is also the anniversary of the sinking of the Titanic! Talk about double jeopardy!
>
> It's interesting, therefore, that we have scheduled today's speaker for April 15: If your company or individual stock did well in 1995 and was listed on the New York Stock Exchange, you can, in part, thank Dick Grasso for keeping the Exchange so strong and competitive; but if your taxes went up because your stocks did so well, you can thank Dick for capital gains, the market upsurge, and profitability.
>
> It is a distinct honor for me to introduce Richard A. Grasso, chairman and chief executive officer of the New York Stock Exchange. He has enjoyed a remarkable 28-year career at the Exchange....[Mr. Stella goes on to provide a more detailed background on Mr. Grasso.][3]

Responding to Introductions. Speakers who have been introduced should respond to the introduction in some way. Acknowledging and thanking the introducer is the most common method. For example:

- I appreciate those kind words.
- Thank you for making me feel welcome today.
- This is a wonderful event, and I appreciate being part of it.

If you are comfortable ad-libbing, you might decide to respond to the introducer's remarks. Notice how the following speakers use this strategy:

- Thank you so much, Helen. I have to agree with you that this audience must really be committed to the United Way—or hungry!—to be here on a stormy day like this.
- I am honored to be with you tonight. Something that Brad said in his remarks earlier really struck me. If we are to truly make a difference, we have to be able to think out of the box. The box I would like for us to think our way out of tonight is...

Most of us are not used to being publicly honored, and accepting praise and accolades from a speaker who introduces us can be awkward. One of the ways to show your humility toward a gracious introduction is through humor. The following are some standard lines that can be used to demonstrate humility with humor.

- That introduction was so gracious, you were more than halfway through it before I realized you were talking about me.[4]
- After an introduction like that, I can hardly wait to hear what I'm going to say.[5]
- I'm really not as good as she said, but neither am I as bad as my mother-in-law thinks. So, I guess it averages out.[6]
- Thanks. You read that just as I wrote it. Except you left out the word "beautiful" [or "handsome"].
- That great introduction reminds me of what my mother said about perfume. It's okay to smell it as long as you don't swallow it.

Speeches of Acceptance

In all likelihood you will receive an award at some point in your life. You may be honored for doing exceptional work, making a unique contribution to the community, or giving many years of service to an organization. In such cases, it's good to have some knowledge of how to accept an award gracefully. Remember that your purpose in a **speech of acceptance** is to express gratitude for the honor bestowed on you. Your speech should reflect that gratitude.

speech of acceptance
a speech in which the recipient expresses gratitude for the honor bestowed on him or her and acknowledges others who have contributed to his or her success.

AP/Wide World

Jody Williams and Tun Channareth accept the 1997 Nobel Peace Prize for their work with Williams's coalition, the International Campaign to Ban Landmines. Their efforts resulted in nearly 100 nations signing a treaty to ban land mines worldwide.

Prepare. If you know you will be given an award, make sure to prepare an acceptance speech. Because the award is not a surprise, the audience will probably expect a fairly sophisticated acceptance speech. If you think it is likely that you will receive an award, prepare in advance so you will not be caught off guard. In fact, if you think there is any possibility of receiving an award, preparation is advisable. In this way, your acceptance will go smoothly and you can avoid using standard responses such as "I really just don't know what to say."

React Genuinely and with Humility. Genuineness and humility are possibly the most important parts of expressing gratitude. Offering a sincere response shows your audience how much the award means to you. If you are surprised by receiving the award, show it. If you are not surprised, don't try to feign excitement. Explain why the award is important to you and describe the value you place on it. Tell your listeners how it will affect your future and how it gives meaning to whatever you did in the past that led to its receipt. Express your gratitude with humility, acknowledging your good fortune in having received it.

Thank Those Giving the Award. Even though the attention is focused on you, don't forget to express your gratitude to the people giving you the award. If the award is given by an organization, specifically thank that organization. If it is given by a combination of organizations, remember to mention all of them. If there is a sponsor of the award, such as a donor that makes the award possible, remember to name the donor as well.

Thank Others Who Helped You. If the reason for your award represents a team effort, be sure to thank all members. If there are people who have given you inspiration that helped you achieve the award, thank them.

Notice in the following example how the speaker thanks someone from his past for inspiration.

> I am also grateful to Ben Stanford, who early in my career taught me one of my most valuable lessons—it's not what you pay for a property that's important, but how you pay for it.

It is also appropriate to thank one's family and friends. However, deciding who to thank beyond those who directly contributed to a project can be tricky. Be careful not to make the acknowledgments too long. Often it is impractical, and maybe even impossible, to thank literally everyone who has contributed to your success. Try not to take more than your share of time, especially if other recipients are waiting. Avoid the penchant for dragging out the ceremony.

Accept the Award Gracefully. Although humility is important, avoid responses such as, "I really don't deserve this" or "I can't believe I've been selected." Rather than seeing see this as a humble response, those giving the award might view such a response as leaving their judgment open to question. If you receive an award, it is because someone thinks you deserve it. Accept the award gracefully by showing that you value it and the people who gave it to you. The following are some examples of graceful acceptance:

- I am indeed humbled by this award and want to express my sincere gratitude to the committee who selected me.
- This award is something that everyone in our profession aspires to. I am honored by your show of support.
- There are few people in this world who understand how much this award means to me. I accept the award with the knowledge that it carries with it a tremendous responsibility.

End by Expressing Thanks. The overall goal of the acceptance speech is to express appreciation. Leaving with a final expression of gratitude helps reinforce that goal. Using "Thanks" or "Thank you" as final words allows you to leave the audience with the idea that you are grateful and provides a natural capstone to the speech. This also serves as a signal to the audience that your acceptance is concluded.

Speeches of Presentation

The job of presenting an award can be an honor in itself. No doubt you will be asked to present an award to a friend, colleague, or employee sometime during your life. Whether you are presenting a bowling trophy or a Nobel Prize, your goal in the **speech of presentation** is twofold: to communicate the meaning of the award, and to explain why the recipient is receiving it.

> **speech of presentation**
> a speech in which the speaker communicates the importance of the award and explains why the recipient is receiving it.

Convey the Meaning of the Award. It is the presenter's task to explain the meaning of the award to the audience. What is the award for? What kind of achievement does it celebrate? Who or what does the award represent? What is the significance of its special name or title? You might offer a brief history of the award, such as when it was founded and the names of some of its previous recipients. If the award has a unique shape or design, explain the significance of the design. If there is an inscription, read it. Because you are a presenter, it is also your job to identify the sponsors or organizations that made the award possible and to describe the link between the sponsor's goals and values and the award. All this is information the audience will be curious about, and mention of it establishes the award's credibility and increases the honor for the recipient.

The following excerpt is a common way of communicating to the audience the significance of the award:

> It is an honor and a privilege to be the one making this presentation today. This plaque is only a token of our appreciation for Hanna's achievements, but we hope that this symbol will serve as a daily reminder of our admiration for her great work. Let me read the inscription. "Hanna Rosenthal, in appreciation for the outstanding work..."

Talk about the Recipient of the Award. The second part of the presenter's task is to explain why the recipient is receiving the award. Tell the audience why the recipient has been singled out for special recognition. Describe his or her achievements, the kind of work he or she does, and special attributes that qualify him or her as deserving of the award. Explain how the recipient was selected. What kind of selection process was used? What set him or her apart from other nominees or finalists? The following example illustrates how this can be done:

> And, I might add, these were just *some* of the accomplishments of Carol Bosno. When the selection committee reviewed all the nominees (some 84 of them), it became clear that Carol would be our choice. The committee met four times to narrow the list of nominees, and at each meeting it was clear who our winner would be. The other nominees were outstanding in their own right, but Carol stood apart in many ways.

Sometimes it is appropriate to mention the finalists for an award, especially when these finalists represent strong achievements. In addition to honoring them, acknowledging finalists shows the strength of the field from which the winner was drawn. Of course, it is important to use discretion when doing this. If you do mention finalists, your words should have the effect of making them feel honored rather than left out.

Consider the Physical Presentation. Plan the actual presentation of the award. Don't set up yourself and the recipient for an awkward presentation. If you are to hand the award to the recipient, make sure you do so with your left hand so you can shake hands with your right hand.

Consider Yourself. Sometimes you yourself will have a special relationship to the award that can be profitably mentioned for the proceedings. Perhaps you have received the same award in the past, or you were on a committee that established it. If so, mention this in your presentation. This personalizes the presentation and further honors the recipient. One way to do this is with humor:

> I know that the selection committee knew that the only way I would ever get my hands on this prestigious trophy was to make me the presenter.

Interview

Special Occasion Speeches: A Real World Perspective

Vicki Moore is Director of Marketing at Northern Telecom Enterprise Networks, a multinational corporation in the telecommunications industry. Like every manager with employees reporting to her, Ms. Moore often finds herself making special occasion speeches, usually in the form of award presentations.

Do you ever find yourself making special presentations to employees at Northern?

Yes, every few months. I am called upon to present awards based on superior performance, or special recognition on behalf of an employee's peers.

Do you have a particular plan for making these types of speeches?

When I am called on to present these awards, I always like to set the scene by describing what the award is for; then I point out the special circumstances that caused this employee to receive the recognition. I then like to extend congratulations on behalf of the organization and the winner's fellow workers to point out how proud everyone is of them.

What are some of the more important elements of these types of speeches?

I like to keep the presentation brief, yet sincere. I often like to use some humor in my presentations. Humor can transmit warm appreciation for the

employee's work. I try not to interject anything overly personal or embarrassing that may detract from the particular presentation. After the awarded employee has an opportunity to receive his or her recognition, when appropriate I like to mention other employees' contributions in similar areas.

In summary, I describe the award, describe the reason the employee is receiving it, offer personal remarks as they relate to the circumstances, and then conclude with a warm and lighthearted anecdote about the person receiving the award. This formula seems to be quite effective for me.

Do you ever feel nervous about making these speeches?

At first I did. You know you are on stage, but at the same time you want to do a good job because you are usually honoring someone for their special work. I try to think more about the person or the reason I am speaking rather than myself. This seems to help any nervousness I might experience.

Do you enjoy giving these speeches?

You know, at first I saw the assignment as a chore. Now that I have some experience and know that I can do a good job, I really have a good time at these events. I think I would feel left out if I didn't get to speak.

Roasts and Toasts

Just as you may be called on to present awards, you may be called on to speak at a roast or make a toast at an important event such as a wedding or another celebration. A **roast** is a humorous tribute to a person, one in which a series of speakers jokingly poke fun at him or her. A **toast** is a brief tribute to a person or event being celebrated. Both roasts and toasts call for short speeches whose goal is to celebrate a person and his or her achievements. Should you be asked to speak at such events, it will be helpful to follow these guidelines.

roast
a humorous tribute to a person, one in which a series of speakers will jokingly poke fun at him or her.

toast
a brief tribute to a person or event being celebrated.

Prepare. Remember that the audience is looking to you to set the tone and express the purpose of the gathering. Being caught off guard and stammering for something to say can really let the air out of your speech and make it less than meaningful. Also remember that others who speak before you may use material you had planned on using. Don't be alarmed. Make reference to this fact and put a different spin on it.

Before delivering a roast or toast, many speakers rehearse in front of a trusted friend or friends. This is especially helpful if you are considering telling a joke you are unsure about. Practicing with friends also allows them to time your speech. People often speak for a lot longer than they think. Have someone listen to your presentation and time you. In that way you can see if your speech fits into the time limitations set for your presentation.

Highlight Remarkable Traits of the Person Being Honored. Because these speeches are usually short, try to restrict your remarks to one or two of the most unique or recognizable attributes of the person. Convey what sets him or her apart—the qualities that have made him or her worthy of celebrating. In other words, what would you want said about you if you were being honored?

Focus on Ethics

A Roast That Smoldered and Burned

In 1993 the actor Ted Danson was invited to speak at a Friars Club luncheon roast in honor of actress Whoopi Goldberg. Romantically linked with Goldberg at the time, Danson appeared at the event in blackface and delivered a routine about the actress that was laced with racial stereotypes, racial epithets, and crude references to interracial sexuality. Another speaker in attendance, the television host Montel Williams, was so offended by Danson's remarks that he walked off the dais as Danson was speaking. New York mayor David Dinkins, who stayed, later described Danson's remarks as "way, way over the line."[1] Others said that Danson had crossed the bounds of civility and fanned the flames of racial hatred.

Both Danson and Goldberg defiantly rejected the criticism that Danson's humor went beyond the bounds of acceptable speech. Claiming that Danson was merely poking fun at political correctness, Goldberg noted that, "If they (the critics) knew me, they would know that Whoopi has never been about political correctness. I built my whole career on destigmatizing words like 'nigger.'"[2]

In support of the couple, theater critic Frank Rich wrote that what Danson had done was to

> blast open the excessively polite verbal and social codes that often mask the truth about what people are really feeling and thinking. In this case, the codes they cracked are those that obscure or distort any public discussion of racial animosities and fears.[3]

Given what you know about the situation, would you agree with Rich or with the critics of Danson and Goldberg? How far do you think a speaker should go in an occasion such as a roast? Considering the standards for ethical speech described in Chapter 4 (trustworthiness, respect, responsibility, and fairness), do you think Danson's act was ethical? Why or why not?

1. Lena Williams, "After the Roast, Fire and Smoke," *New York Times*, October 14, 1993, p. C1.

2. Ibid.

3. Frank Rich, "Public Stages," *New York Times*, November 7, 1993, p. C1.

Be Positive. Even if the speech is poking fun at someone, such as in a roast, keep the tone good-natured and positive. Remember, the overall purpose of your speech is to pay tribute to the honoree. It's great to have fun, but avoid saying anything that might embarrass the person being honored. This could turn what should be festive atmosphere into an uncomfortable situation. As described in Chapter 6, well-known radio personality Don Imus crossed the line at a 1996 annual White House roast of the president. Although listeners at certain roasts expect biting wit, Imus' "jokes" humiliated the president and embarrassed and angered the audience. Although unrepentant at the time, Imus later acknowledged the inappropriateness of his remarks and admitted that he had yet to be invited back to another such event.

Be Brief. Usually several speakers are involved in roasts and toasts. Be considerate of the other speakers by refraining from taking up too much time. This is particularly important for toasts, which are expected to be very short. Violating these expectations can make the toast awkward, especially if everyone is holding a glass in anticipation of the toast ending.

Eulogies and Other Tributes

The word **eulogy** derives from the Greek word meaning "to praise." Those delivering eulogies, usually close friends or family members of the deceased, are charged with celebrating and commemorating the life of someone while consoling those left behind. Given these goals, the eulogy can be one of the most difficult and challenging special occasion speeches. At the same time, probably more people with little or no experience in public speaking at one time or another deliver a eulogy than nearly all other types of special occasion speeches.

eulogy
a tribute to a deceased person.

Should you be called on to give a eulogy, the following guidelines will help ensure an effective speech:

Balance Delivery and Emotions. Many speakers fight the tendency to become overly emotional in a eulogy. Despite the sense of grief the speaker may feel, his or her job is to help others feel better. The audience looks to the speaker for guidance in dealing with the loss and for a sense of closure. Therefore, it is essential to stay in control. Showing intense grief will probably make the audience feel worse. If you do feel that you are about to break down, pause, take a breath, and focus on your next thought.

Refer to the Family of the Deceased. Families suffer the greatest loss, and a funeral is primarily for their benefit. Make sure your presentation shows respect to the family; mention each family member by name. Make it clear that the deceased was an important part of a family by humanizing that family.

Commemorate Life—Not Death. Make sure you focus on the life of the person rather than the circumstances of the death. A eulogy should pay tribute to the deceased person as an individual and remind the audience that he or she is still alive, in a sense, in our memories. Talk about the contributions that he or she made and achievements accomplished. Focus on demonstrating the kind of character that the person had. You might want to tell a story or anecdote that illustrates the type of person you are eulogizing. Even humorous stories and anecdotes may be appropriate if they effectively humanize the deceased.

AP/Wide World

Charles, Earl Spencer, eulogizes his sister Diana, Princess of Wales, at Westminster Abbey. His powerful speech was praised by some, questioned by others, but remembered by all.

Be Positive But Realistic. Emphasize the deceased's positive qualities. This seems obvious, but care must be taken in selecting stories and anecdotes, as well as in planning descriptions of the person, to ensure that none of the speech is interpreted as casting the deceased in a negative light. It is also important, however, to avoid excessive praise. This may ultimately sound insincere and provide a distorted picture of the person.

When the Princess of Wales, Diana Spencer, died in a car crash in 1997, her brother, Earl Spencer, eulogized her in a speech broadcast to billions. In his speech, he praised his sister as loving and beautiful but also acknowledged that she was at heart an extremely vulnerable young woman with "deep feelings of unworthiness of which her eating disorders were merely a symptom."[7] This realistic assessment of the princess's vulnerabilities deeply touched many in the audience, who later took the unprecedented step of applauding the speech once it was over.

Critical Checkpoint

Earl Spencer's Controversial Eulogy

The reaction by the billions of strangers who listened to Earl Spencer's eulogy of his sister Diana, the Princess of Wales, was largely positive. But a certain portion of the audience did feel that the speech was unnecessarily critical of the English monarchy, Princess Diana's former in-laws, especially given the presence of the royal family at the ceremony and their central role in the funeral. Reporter Sarah Lyall wrote in the *New York Times*:

> His tone was respectful and his demeanor composed. But Lord Spencer's searing address at Westminster Abbey represented an enormous break with tradition and a stunning indictment of the way his sister had been treated by the two forces that had most influenced the way she lived her final years: the royal family and the news media.[1]

Specifically, critics charged that Earl Spencer should not have mentioned that the queen had taken away the title of "Her Royal Highness" as a condition of Diana's divorce from Charles, Prince of Wales. Here is how Earl Spencer put it:

> All over the world she was a symbol of selfless humanity, a standard-bearer for the rights of the truly downtrodden, a truly British girl who transcended nationality, someone with a natural nobility who was classless, who proved in the last year that *she needed no royal title to continue to generate her particular brand of magic.* [emphasis added]

Some people also objected to the criticism of the monarchy implied in the way they would bring up Diana's sons, Princes William and Harry:

> On behalf of your mother and sisters, I pledge that we, your blood family, will do all we can to continue the imaginative and loving way in which you were steering these two exceptional young men, *so that their souls are not simply immersed by duty and tradition* but can sing openly as you planned. [emphasis added]

How do you react to these criticisms? Given the circumstances, do you feel Earl Spencer's remarks were appropriate? If you saw the speech on television, how did it strike you? Did you find it memorable? Did it move you? (See end of chapter for the full text of the speech.)

1. Sarah Lyall, "For Media and the Royals, Earl Takes Off His Gloves," *New York Times*, September 7, 1997, p. A11 (http://search.nytimes.com/).

After-Dinner Speeches

In the course of his career, nineteenth-century humorist and writer Mark Twain was said to have given over 150 after-dinner speeches. Extremely popular at the time, lavish dinner affairs were attended by a host of male notables who spent several hours eating and drinking, after which they spent several more hours listening to humorous toasts and speeches.[8] Twain's speeches were so well received that many of them were reprinted in the next day's newspaper.

Today, after-dinner speaking continues to takes place around the time of a meal, although not necessarily a dinner. The contemporary after-dinner speech is just as likely to occur before, after, or during a breakfast or lunch seminar or other type of business, professional, or civic meeting as it is to follow a formal dinner. In general, an **after-dinner speech** is expected to be lighthearted and entertaining (see exceptions below). At the same time, listeners expect the speaker to provide some insight into the topic at hand. Balancing these two goals can make the after-dinner speech one of the most challenging but enjoyable kind of speeches you can deliver.

> **after-dinner speech**
> a lighthearted and entertaining speech delivered before, during, or after a meal.

Choose the Right Topic. Finding a topic that allows a speaker to fulfill the goals of an after-dinner speech can be a challenge. The topic must be serious enough to merit discussion and allow the speaker to make an important point. At the same time, it must be light enough to provide material that the

Public Speaking in Cultural Perspective

Culture and Ceremonial Toasts

Making toasts at dinner, at ceremonies, and at special occasions is a universal experience. The lifting of a glass and a salute to individuals or parties convey a sense of respect, honor, and courtesy. Some toasts are made spontaneously, while others are carefully crafted and developed. Many cultures view toasts as ceremony and ritual, and the timing of the toast during an occasion varies from culture to culture. For instance, Finnish culture encourages toasts at the beginning of the meal. In Denmark and Sweden, guests do not toast the host or elder guests until the host or elders have toasted them. In China, it is not customary to drink anything at dinner until a toast is made. In Russia, toasts are made before each course is served.

When dining or celebrating in a culture other than your own, and you are unfamiliar with its toasting rituals, it is best to follow the lead of those around you. If you are planning to make a toast at a special occasion, ask the host beforehand about the toast customs for that culture and how long the toast should be. In most cases, the shorter the toast the better. Making the effort to learn a short toast in the language of those you are celebrating with will make a positive impression and display your interest in, and respect for, the culture you are interacting with. A few examples of toasts are listed below, each roughly translated as "your health."

Culture	Pronunciation
Cantonese	Yum-*sing*
French	Ah-votre-sahn-*tay*
German	*Pro*-zit
Italian	Sah-*loo*-tay
Mandarin	Kam-*pay*
Portugese	Sah-*ude*
Russian	Nah-zda-*roe*-vee-ah
Spanish	Sah-*lood*

SOURCE: Adapted from material in Roger E. Axtell, ed., *Do's and Taboos Around the World*, 3rd ed. (New York: John Wiley & Sons, 1993).

speaker can use to build jokes and entertain the audience. Genocide and world hunger probably wouldn't fit the bill. Balancing the two is very important to setting a tone for the speech that fits with the occasion and the audience.

Avoid Stand-Up Comedy. Many speakers are tempted to treat the after-dinner speech as an opportunity to engage in stand-up comedy, stringing together a series of jokes only loosely centered on a theme. There are two problems to this approach. First, the after-dinner speech is still a speech. A comedy routine does not have a recognizable introduction, body, or conclusion. This absence of a structure makes it difficult to deliver the serious point that the after-dinner speaker seeks to make, because there will be no place where such points naturally fit. Second, most people are not comedians. To keep an audience laughing for any length of time requires a great deal of practice and skill as well as a major investment in speechwriting. For non-comedians, this can be a challenge too difficult to overcome.

Rather than trying to be a comedian, work within your natural style. The most convincing speakers are the most naturally believable. Trying to become funnier—or more serious—than you normally are will likely set you up to fail because it will make your job harder. The speech becomes an acting challenge. If you are naturally very funny, use that. If you have more of a dry sense of humor, plan jokes that are within that kind of humor. Do not be fooled into thinking that a goal of humor means that you have to become a Chris Rock or a Dennis Miller.

Recognize the Occasion. Make sure to connect the speech you are giving with the occasion. Delivering a speech unrelated to the event that gives rise to it may leave the impression that the speech is canned, that is, one that the speaker uses again and again in different settings. Canned speeches can be an immediate turn-off for many audiences. Further, audiences want to be recognized for who they are and for the event they have come to participate in.

The After-Dinner Speech and Social Agenda Setting. Rather than entertain, the purpose of certain after-dinner speeches is social agenda setting. In such situations the speaker is invited to a dinner featuring serious events and causes. For example, each year the members and supporters of the Holocaust Memorial Center gather to celebrate the date that America's first Holocaust museum was opened to the public. At every dinner event, a person prominent in Holocaust studies or related fields addresses the group.[9] Clearly, when the purpose of the after-dinner speech is agenda setting, the speaker must focus more closely on the serious side of the equation than on that of entertainment. Nevertheless, even when charged with this goal, the after-dinner speaker should make an effort to keep his or her remarks low-key enough to accompany the digestion of a meal.

Speeches of Inspiration

Many of the types of special occasion speeches discussed thus far may well be inspiring. For example, presentation and acceptance speeches might inspire by highlighting the receiver as a model of the values embodied in the award. Certain occasions, however, call for a speech that is meant to inspire as its main goal. A **speech of inspiration** seeks to uplift the audience and help them see things in a positive light. John F. Kennedy's inaugural address, in which he challenged Americans to "Ask not what your country can do for you, but what you can do for your country" is one such example. Every week, ministers, rabbis, priests, and mullahs deliver inspirational speeches in the form of sermons. Commencement addresses, "pep talks" at sales meetings, and nomination speeches at rallies and conventions are all inspirational in nature.

speech of inspiration
a speech that seeks to uplift the audience and help them see things in a positive light.

In the business world, occasions for inspirational speeches are so frequent that some people earn their living as inspirational speakers. Even though fate may have another career plan in store for you, it's quite likely that you may be asked to give a speech to inspire members of a peer group to support each other, urge a social organization to remain true to its mission, or motivate your child's basketball team before a big game. Regardless of the occasion, the goal in speaking to inspire is to motivate the audience to positively consider, reflect on, and sometimes even act on the speaker's words.

Effective speeches of inspiration touch on deep feelings in the audience. Their emotional force is such that our better instincts are aroused. They urge us toward purer motives and harder effort and remind us of a common good. To arouse such feelings and accept such messages, positive speaker ethos is critical. The audience must respect the speaker and be positively disposed toward his or her character. Thus, as in a persuasive speech, to create an effective inspirational speech you'll need to appeal to the audience's emotions (pathos) and display positive ethos.

Appeal to the Audience's Emotions. As described in Chapter 14, two means of invoking emotion, or pathos, are *vivid description* and *emotionally charged words*. This and other techniques of language, such as repetition, alliteration, and parallelism, can help transport the audience from the mundane to a loftier level (see Chapter 10).

President Franklin Delano Roosevelt, who led our country through a devastating economic depression and a shattering world war, brought the nation together through his many inspirational speeches. Roosevelt frequently delivered "fireside chats": speeches broadcast on the radio whose purpose was to inspire Americans during the war effort and build their support for it. In one of the earliest of these speeches, Roosevelt sought to arouse support for giving arms to Britain:

> The experience of the past two years has proven beyond doubt that no nation can appease the Nazis. No man can tame a tiger into a kitten by stroking it. There can be no appeasement with ruthlessness. There can be no reasoning with an incendiary bomb.[10]

Deeply inspired by Roosevelt's words, including his artful use of vivid description ("tame a tiger into a kitten by stroking it") and emotional words ("appeasement," "ruthlessness," "incendiary"), Americans rallied to Roosevelt's call time and time again.

Use Real-Life Stories. Another way to inspire listeners is through real-life examples and stories. Few things move us as much as the example of the ordinary person who achieves the extraordinary, whose struggles result in triumph over adversity and the realization of a dream. Recognizing this, in their State of the Union addresses several recent U.S. presidents have taken to weaving stories about "ordinary American heroes" into their remarks. Ever cognizant of the power of the televised sound bite, the politicians usually invite these people to attend the speech and then strategically seat them to permit the best camera angles.

Be Dynamic. If it fits your personality, use a dynamic speaking style to inspire not only through content but through delivery as well. An energetic style can do a great deal to motivate the audience. When combined with a powerful message, this can be one of the most successful strategies for inspirational speaking.

Make Your Goal Clear. Inspirational speeches run the risk of being vague, leaving the audience unsure what the message was. Make sure that the audience cannot mistake your message for something else. Whatever you are trying to motivate the audience to do, let them know. If you are speaking about a general goal, such as remaining positive in life, let your audience know that. Make it clear that you are speaking on a general level and you are trying to motivate them in a way that will affect their lives in a broad way. If you are trying to motivate an audience to a specific action, such as donating money to a particular charity, clearly tell them so.

Use a Distinctive Organizing Device. Many successful inspirational speakers, especially those in the business world, use devices such as acronyms or steps to organize their speeches. This clarifies the organizational pattern of the speech and helps the audience remember the message. For example, a football coach speaking at a practice session might organize a short inspirational speech around the word WIN. His main points might be Work, Intensity, and No excuses, forming the acronym WIN. This device emphasizes the goal of the constituent elements of the speech. All three are aimed at winning games.

Here is an example of using steps. Giving an inspirational speech entitled "Give Your Life a Dream with Design" to a graduating high school class, David Magill organized his presentation around three steps: "1. Design Your Vision," "2. Just Do It," and "3. Dig Deeper." Magill introduced his main points by saying,

> My advice is simple, has three steps, and is easy to remember because the operative word in each step begins with the same letter with which *dream* begins—the letter D.[11]

Close with a Dramatic Ending. Using a dramatic ending is one of the best means for inspiring your audience to feel or act in the ways suggested by the theme of your speech. Recall from Chapter 9 the various methods of concluding a speech, including quotations, stories, rhetorical questions, and the call to action:

- I would challenge you today to...
- I want you to join with me tonight in pursuing excellence in...

- I think this can easily be summed up by the famous quote from Will Rogers, who quipped, "I never met a person (man) that I didn't like."

- What I am trying to say tonight can be boiled down to what Robert Kennedy said many times during his 1968 campaign for president, "Some men see things as they are, and say Why? I dream things that never were, and say Why not?"

One of the most famous speeches in recent time was an inspirational message delivered by Dr. Martin Luther King at the steps of the Lincoln Memorial to a crowd in excess of 200,000. The theme was equal rights. King's closing words evoke great poetic drama:

> Let freedom ring from Lookout Mountain of Tennessee.
> Let freedom ring from every hill and molehill of Mississippi. From every mountainside, let freedom ring.
> And when this happens, when we allow freedom to ring—when we let it ring from every village and every hamlet, from every state and every city—we will be able to speed up that day when all of God's children, black men and white men, Jews and Gentiles, Protestants and Catholics, will be able to join hands and sing in the words of the old Negro spiritual, "Free at last! Free at last! Thank God almighty, we are free at last!"[12]

DELIVERING THE SPECIAL OCCASION SPEECH

Because audiences bring such specific expectations to special occasions, delivery is especially critical in this type of speech. Listeners expect the speaker to exhibit a certain degree of formality and speak in a certain tone. They anticipate that the speaker will make them chuckle or soothe their grief, infuse them with purpose or warm them with good will. Additionally, because multiple speakers are often involved in such events, listeners count on the speaker to smoothly coordinate his or her remarks to accommodate those of others. The more a speaker can fulfill these expectations, the more successful his or her speech will be.

Charles Archambault, U.S. NEWS & WORLD REPORT

A dynamic and effective special occasion speech will also be a memorable one. Present a speech that will have a lasting positive impact on your audience.

Thus, when delivering your special occasion speech, always remember to consider the appropriate level of formality for the occasion and adapt your communication style to it. Off-the-cuff remarks may work well in an after-dinner speech but strike a discordant note at a dedication ceremony. An energetic style of delivery might be just what's needed for an inspirational speech before a big game, but slightly off key in a speech to strengthen the resolve of hospice workers.

The audience will count on you to act, deliver, and time your speech in different ways to satisfy their expectations. Paying attention to these expectations will help you deliver a memorable and meaningful special occasion speech.

Critical Checkpoint

Managing Audience Expectations for the Special Occasion Speech

If you consider the types of special occasion speeches discussed in this chapter, you can probably tell that most of them involve the use of *emotional appeal*. For example, speeches of introduction use humor, ego-support, and compliments to create a positive feeling toward the featured speaker. Speeches of acceptance include modesty and politeness in order for the speaker to convey that he or she feels humble, unpretentious, and honored by the award. People attending roasts and toasts usually expect a great deal of humor, interest, and surprise. This is often the case with after-dinner speeches as well. On the other hand, eulogies are more solemn events, with audience mood including anger, sadness, or even depression.

What happens when audience expectations are violated in special occasion speeches? For example, at a recent funeral service a eulogy made use of humorous stories about the deceased that created a lighter tone for the funeral service. Several audience members commented that this was unusual, but appreciated. Others commented that such humor was inappropriate. Recall the comments made by Ted Danson in a roast of Whoopi Goldberg (see the Focus on Ethics box on page 430) and how such violations of expectations were viewed negatively by many in attendance. You can probably remember speeches of inspiration that fell flat because of an insufficient emotional appeal.

- What is the best method for determining where emotional appeal and audience expectations should meet?

- How might you determine whether it is appropriate to violate audience members' expectations about the tone and emotional appeal of a particular special occasion speech (e.g., using humor in a eulogy)?

- How do the challenges of using an emotional appeal in a special occasion speech differ from those of using an emotional appeal in informative and persuasive speeches?

Sample Eulogy

In the summer of 1997, Princess Diana's sudden and tragic death in a Paris automobile accident shocked the world and inspired a tremendous outpouring of grief. Considering how difficult it is to deliver any eulogy, imagine the added complexity the Earl Spencer—Diana's brother—faced addressing a worldwide audience about a well-loved international celebrity. Review the suggestions in this chapter for delivering a eulogy, as well as the Critical Checkpoint on p. 432, and read the full text of his tribute below.

I stand before you today the representative of a family in grief, in a country in mourning before a world in shock.

> *Spencer begins with a simple yet powerful expression of grief that extends from the personal level to the global level.*

We are all united not only in our desire to pay our respects to Diana but rather in our need to do so.

For such was her extraordinary appeal that the tens of millions of people taking part in this service all over the world via television and radio who never actually met her, feel that they, too, lost someone close to them in the early hours of Sunday morning. It is a more remarkable tribute to Diana than I can ever hope to offer her today.

Diana was the very essence of compassion, of duty, of style, of beauty. All over the world she was a symbol of selfless humanity, a standard-bearer for the rights of the truly downtrodden, a truly British girl who transcended nationality, someone with a natural nobility who was classless, who proved in the last year that she needed no royal title to continue to generate her particular brand of magic.

> *Note Spencer's use of clear, descriptive language and parallel structure to describe Diana.*

Today is our chance to say "thank you" for the way you brightened our lives, even though God granted you but half a life. We will all feel cheated that you were taken from us so young and yet we must learn to be grateful that you came along at all.

Only now you are gone do we truly appreciate what we are now without and we want you to know that life without you is very, very difficult.

We have all despaired at our loss over the past week and only the strength of the message you gave us through your years of giving has afforded us the strength to move forward.

> *With this transition the speech's point of view changes. Spencer directly addresses Diana as "you," speaking on behalf of himself, as well as all mourners. This is an effective way to make the audience feel as though Spencer is expressing everyone's feelings, not just his own.*

There is a temptation to rush to canonize your memory. There is no need to do so. You stand tall enough as a human being of unique qualities not to need to be seen as a saint. Indeed to sanctify your memory would be to miss out on the very core of your being, your wonderfully mischievous sense of humor with the laugh that bent you double, your joy for life transmitted wherever you took your smile, and the sparkle in those unforgettable eyes, your boundless energy which you could barely contain.

> *Spencer focuses on the humanity of Diana and reminds mourners to remember her life as a complex human being rather than to think of her as a saint.*

But your greatest gift was your intuition, and it was a gift you used wisely. This is what underpinned all your wonderful attributes. And if we look to analyze what it was about you that had such a wide appeal, we find it in your instinctive feel for what was really important in all our lives.

Without your God-given sensitivity, we would be immersed in greater ignorance at the anguish of AIDS and HIV sufferers, the plight of the homeless, the isolation of lepers, the random destruction of land mines. Diana explained to me once that it was her innermost

> *Once again switching point of view, the speech focuses on Diana's achievements and highlights her legacy.*

feelings of suffering that made it possible for her to connect with her constituency of the rejected.

And here we come to another truth about her. For all the status, the glamour, the applause, Diana remained throughout a very insecure person at heart, almost childlike in her desire to do good for others so she could release herself from deep feelings of unworthiness of which her eating disorders were merely a symptom.

By directly referring to Diana's insecurities and eating disorders, Spencer acknowledges her vulnerabilities, deeply touching the audience and further emphasizing Diana's humanity rather than her celebrity.

The world sensed this part of her character and cherished her for her vulnerability, whilst admiring her for her honesty. The last time I saw Diana was on July the first, her birthday, in London, when typically she was not taking time to celebrate her special day with friends but was guest of honor at a charity fund-raising evening.

She sparkled of course, but I would rather cherish the days I spent with her in March when she came to visit me and my children in our home in South Africa. I am proud of the fact that apart from when she was on public display meeting President Mandela, we managed to contrive to stop the ever-present paparazzi from getting a single picture of her.

That meant a lot to her.

These are days I will always treasure. It was as if we'd been transported back to our childhood, when we spent such an enormous amount of time together, the two youngest in the family.

Spencer offers private memories of his sister to personalize Diana and to show a side of her that the audience would not ordinarily know about.

Fundamentally she hadn't changed at all from the big sister who mothered me as a baby, fought with me at school and endured those long train journeys between our parents' homes with me at weekends. It is a tribute to her level-headedness and strength that despite the most bizarre life imaginable after her childhood, she remained intact, true to herself.

There is no doubt that she was looking for a new direction in her life at this time. She talked endlessly of getting away from England, mainly because of the treatment she received at the hands of the newspapers.

I don't think she ever understood why her genuinely good intentions were sneered at by the media, why there appeared to be a permanent quest on their behalf to bring her down. It is baffling. My own, and only, explanation is that genuine goodness is threatening to those at the opposite end of the moral spectrum.

Spencer's condemnation of the media that constantly pursued Diana for photographs and news stories sparked controversy: Is a eulogy an appropriate way to express such comments?

It is a point to remember that of all the ironies about Diana, perhaps the greatest is this; that a girl given the name of the ancient goddess of hunting was, in the end, the most hunted person of the modern age.

She would want us today to pledge ourselves to protecting her beloved boys, William and Harry, from a similar fate. And I do this here, Diana, on your behalf. We will not allow them to suffer the anguish that used regularly to drive you to tearful despair.

Addressing Diana's sons directly, Spencer focuses audience attention on the suffering of her family members.

Beyond that, on behalf of your mother and sisters, I pledge that we, your blood family, will do all we can to continue the imaginative and loving way in which you were steering these two exceptional young men, so that their souls are not simply immersed by duty and tradition but can sing openly as you planned.

Spencer's critical comments about the "duty and tradition" of the royal family also caused controversy: Is a eulogy an appropriate way for Spencer to send a message to the royal family about how to raise Princes William and Harry?

We fully respect the heritage into which they have both been born, and will always respect and encourage them in their royal role. But we, like you, recognize the need for them to experience as many different aspects of life as possible, to arm them spiritually and emotionally for the years ahead. I know you would have expected nothing less from us.

William and Harry, we all care desperately for you today. We are all chewed up with sadness at the loss of a woman who wasn't even our mother. How great your suffering is we cannot even imagine.

I would like to end by thanking God for the small mercies he has shown us at this dreadful time; for taking Diana at her most beautiful and radiant and when she had so much joy in her private life.

Above all, we give thanks for the life of a woman I am so proud to be able to call my sister: the unique, the complex, the extraordinary and irreplaceable Diana, whose beauty, both internal and external, will never be extinguished from our minds.

Spencer's conclusion, encompassing Diana's complexity and humanity, prompts audience members to contemplate her lasting significance.

SUMMARY QUESTIONS

What is a special occasion speech, and what are its five broad functions?

A special occasion speech is one that is prepared for a specific occasion and for a purpose dictated by that occasion. Depending on the nature of the occasion, the function of a special occasion speech is to entertain, celebrate, commemorate, inspire, or set a social agenda.

What are the different types of special occasion speeches?

Special occasion speeches include: speeches of introduction; speeches of acceptance; award presentations; roasts and toasts; eulogies and other speeches of tribute; after-dinner speeches; and speeches of inspiration. A speech of introduction is a short speech with the two goals of preparing the audience for the speaker and motivating them to listen to what he or she has to say. In the speech of acceptance, a recipient expresses gratitude for the honor bestowed on him or her and acknowledges others who have contributed to his or her success. Speeches of presentation communicate the importance of the award and explain why the recipient is receiving it. A roast is a humorous tribute to a particular person. A toast is a brief tribute to a person or event being celebrated. Eulogies pay tribute to the deceased. An after-dinner speech is a lighthearted and entertaining speech delivered before, during, or after a meal. Speeches of inspiration explicitly seek to uplift audiences and help them see things in a positive light.

ISSUES FOR DISCUSSION

1. What role do special occasion speeches play in personal, social, and professional settings? Why do people find these types of speeches so important? What would society be like if such speeches were not part of our lives?

2. What are some of the most noteworthy aspects of special occasion speeches that you have heard? Do poorly constructed and delivered special occasion speeches do more harm than good?

3. If you were asked to develop and deliver one of the special occasion speeches discussed in this chapter, which one would you choose? Which one would you find less appealing than others? Why?

SELF-ASSESSMENT

1. Research three eulogies delivered by well-known persons (see, for instance, Phyllis Theroux, ed. *The Book of Eulogies*, New York: Scribner, 1997). Do you see any commonality in their structures? What gives the eulogies power? Language usage? Personal stories?

2. Visit a guest speaker on your campus. How does the introducer capture your attention and add to the credibility of the speaker? What are the strengths/weaknesses of the introducer's presentation?

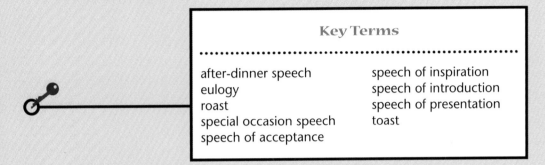

Key Terms

after-dinner speech
eulogy
roast
special occasion speech
speech of acceptance

speech of inspiration
speech of introduction
speech of presentation
toast

TEAMWORK

1. Choose members of your class to hold an "in-class" awards banquet. Select a Master of Ceremonies, an introducer of the Main Speaker, a Main Speaker, an Awards Presenter, and an Awards Recipient. Give each person a strict time frame. Each should prepare his or her speech and coordinate with the other speakers.

2. Prepare a "roast" of your instructor. Allow everyone three minutes to pay tribute to his or her fine teaching. Practice your roast, coordinate with other speakers, and consider the other audience members. Is "roasting" a friend different from "roasting" an instructor? If so, how?

Appendix: Speeches for Analysis

Kristina Wong
Answering America's Call

Wendy Kopp
Commencement Address at Drew University

Reverend Tom Grey
Testimony against Legalized Gambling
before the U.S. House Judiciary Committee

Renzi Stone
Live Longer and Healthier: Stop Eating Meat!

Amber Mixon
Making Dreams Reality

William Jefferson Clinton
Address at the *Time* Magazine 75th Anniversary
Celebration

Nancy S. Dye
Late Night Reflections of a College President:
A Virtual University

Answering America's Call

Kristina Wong

The speech that follows won first place in California at the state-level competition of the 1996 Veterans of Foreign Wars Voice of Democracy Scholarship Program. Today its author, Kristina Wong, is an undergraduate at UCLA. Her speech is both informative and inspirational, and her use of lively language helps create a compelling message. Note the effectiveness of her introduction in which she pretends to have a telephone conversation with a personified America. In the conclusion she returns to this image, leaving the audience with a call to action and an admonishment not to "hang up" the next time America calls. Part of this speech was excerpted in the Making a Difference profile on p. 24.

1   "Hello?...Oh, America! How are you!...Great. I'm sure you're still as generous as always....What's that?...Sure...Of course I will. Of course! If you are kind enough to create such opportunities, I should be gracious enough to offer you what I can in return....No, no, no...Don't be silly, we depend on each other. Without you I couldn't be here...And you couldn't be where you are...Alright, thanks for calling. Bye."

2   That was America calling. She calls on me as she does all of us to take advantage of her innumerable opportunities. Now, more than ever, the chance for Americans to answer her call is marvelous. These opportunities are practically flung at Americans, so how could anyone resist answering America's call?

3   America was founded over 200 years ago on the principles of life, liberty, and freedom, and she calls on us to take advantage of these principles. In regards to life, the chance is ours to live where we want, how we like, and with as much education as we would like to receive. Of course in doing this we must also respect other Americans' rights to live as they choose. We are offered excellent free public education. We are offered financial assistance when we stumble. The life America offers is unique from that of all other countries. Nowhere else in the world is there such a diversity of talent, culture, and experience.

4   We are granted liberty—the opportunity for us to live with rights not granted by other countries. We may speak freely as long as we do not take license which injures others in doing so. America welcomes refugees whether they are political prisoners, prisoners of war, or those who are oppressed by the economic shackles that have bound them in their native lands. In America, we can speak out to government about issues that concern us.

5   Along with liberty we are granted Freedom—freedom to exercise our rights to pursue the religion of our choice, to elect the candidate we support, and assemble at will. We have the right to publish our ideas and share them with other Americans no matter how orthodox or unorthodox they may be. We can also create groups to reform government or educate the community on issues of concern.

6   It can clearly be seen that America's opportunities are hard to turn down! But America doesn't just call on us to take advantage of her bounty, she also asks us to help sustain her services by giving back to her something in return. By doing this we keep America in balance. Without contributions from Americans, she is incapable of fulfilling the promises of life, liberty, and freedom. She needs our help.

7   One way we help is through the financial contributions we make each April—those infamous taxes which fund the services America offers.

Another way we contribute is in the form of direct service. Some of us are called to serve in the military to fight and defend America, while others of us are asked to serve in the community by volunteering our time and skills to assist those in need. **8**

And America, most of all, requests the moral support of her citizens. We sing the National Anthem before sporting events to remember the efforts of those who defended our country. We also build national spirit by observing holidays such as Veterans Day, Independence Day, and Presidents Day. We display our national pride by hanging our American Flag as a symbol of unity and spirit. **9**

I, too, have answered America's call. I have taken a citizen's role in government through my work canvassing for the Sierra Club on environmental protection issues. I have also served America by giving my time at a convalescent home where I assisted the elderly with their art activities. I have donated time at a local soup kitchen, serving meals to the homeless. I have further involved myself in working for the environment by being on my school's Green Team, which collects recyclables in the school. My team's efforts enabled us to earn a can crusher this year to further our recycling activities. This work led me to volunteer at a local recycling center, where I have spoken to the community about keeping open recycling centers which were scheduled to close. **10**

America has kept her promise of life, liberty, and freedom. She gives us the right to voice our opinions on our government. She gives us the freedom to pursue our goals and to reach for excellence. She gives us the opportunities for education and success. She only asks that we answer her call by giving her our time, service, and talents in return. So, the next time America calls, don't hang up. **11**

Commencement Address at Drew University

Wendy Kopp

Wendy Kopp came up with the idea of Teach for America while writing her senior thesis at Princeton University. As you read in the Making a Difference profile on pp. 108–109, once Kopp graduated she made her dream into reality, creating a successful organization through which several thousand college graduates already have been sent to teach in needy public schools across the country. In the commencement address reprinted here, delivered at Drew University on May 20, 1995, Kopp explains that she and others were able to make Teach for America a success because they all believed that the organization's goals justified a great investment of work, time, and sacrifice. Ultimately her message is meant to inspire the audience members to dedicate themselves to pursue their own convictions and to find a way to make a difference.

I'm honored to have the chance to talk with you all on this important occasion, and I'm truly excited to have a few minutes to share what I have learned since graduating from college six years ago. **1**

At that time, back in May of 1989, I was still a college senior just two weeks away from my own graduation. I remember very clearly what I was thinking and doing. **2**

I was obsessed with the idea of a national teacher corps—a corps of recent college graduates who would commit two years to teach in urban and rural public schools suffering from persistent teacher shortages. I imagined thousands of the nation's most talented graduating seniors from all different academic majors clamoring to be a part of a movement to build our nation's future. I imagined **3** hundreds of them working in schools across the country going above and beyond to motivate their students to fulfill their true potential. I imagined an ever-expanding force of leaders who would advocate throughout their lives for educational excellence and equity. I envisioned this national teacher corps changing lives and deepening the conscience of our nation.

4   I was determined to make Teach For America a reality, and luckily I was uncommonly naive—so naive that I believed that this could happen. The plan was to recruit 500 people in the first year, train them together during a summer, place them in five or six sites across the country, and support the entire effort on grants from corporations and foundations.

5   I began by writing letters to 30 CEOs at randomly selected corporations, hoping that one of them would give me a seed grant. Miraculously, one of the letters reached an executive at Mobil who took the time to read my proposal, thought it was a great idea, and decided to give me the $26,000 necessary to spend my summer working to get Teach For America off the ground.

6   I knew I could not create Teach For America alone, and so I began searching for a group of other recent college graduates who would dedicate themselves full-time to this mission. Within a few months, some phenomenal individuals had come together. Many of them would devote 16 or more hours a day, for two or three or four or five years even, to see through the creation of Teach For America.

7   Our first step was to find a student on each of 100 college campuses to spread the word about Teach For America. One hundred students across the country determined that this had to happen and took the personal initiative to distribute fliers, to hold events, to encourage their peers to commit two years to teach in the nation's most under-resourced public schools.

8   In response to this call to action, 2,500 individuals applied to Teach For America in a four-month period. Of these, 500 charter corps members committed to Teach For America. We organized an eight-week summer training program for them, and then they traveled to school districts in five different places across the country. They assumed teaching positions in school districts where someone—a superintendent or a personnel director—had understood our vision, believed in it, and decided to help us make it a reality. By the end of the year, corporations and foundations had committed more than $2 million to us to pay all the expenses we incurred.

9   Over the past six years, we have inspired 18,000 individuals to compete to enter Teach For America. As of this coming fall, we will have trained and placed more than 3,000 of them in 15 communities across the country. At any given time, 1,000 Teach For America corps members everywhere from South Central Los Angeles to the rural South to the South Bronx are going above and beyond to help their students excel. And each year, the force of alumni who have been fundamentally shaped by this experience and who are acting on this experience expands by 500.

10   I tell this story in such great detail because I want to convey how and why Teach For America actually came to be. Teach For America came to be because people with strong convictions—convictions fundamentally based on compassion for others and on an ambitious sense of the possible—were willing to take difficult steps to act on those convictions. Teach For America is here today because of the executive at Mobil, because of the recent college graduates who devoted themselves to our staff, because of the 100 college students who committed to inspire their peers to apply, because of the 500 charter corps members, because of the district superintendents, because of the people who committed funds. It would have been easier for the executive at Mobil to have not made that grant. It would have

been easier for the people who joined our staff to remain in their other jobs. It would have been easier for those 500 recent college graduates to take positions with organizations that had proven records and offered more security. But for all these people, it wasn't an option to do what was easier.

I know I'm speaking here today because I'm a young person who has started 11 an organization, but I didn't want you all to come away from this thinking that the way to make a difference is to go start your own organization. That might be the right thing for some people, but it won't be for everyone. I do believe, however, that all of us owe it to ourselves and to the world to spend our lives searching for what we believe, searching constantly for what's "right." We owe it to ourselves and to the world to base our convictions on compassion for others—whether that means to us compassion for members of our families or communities or nation. We owe it to ourselves and to the world to operate on the assumption that positive change can happen. We owe it to ourselves and to the world to make the daily choices—always—to act on our beliefs.

There's no excuse for living life any other way, but there are many people 12 who do. There are people whose reason for being is to shoot down what other people believe. There are people whose sole purpose in life is to be well liked. There are others who are guided by cynicism and doubt, some who live simply to get by, and still others who simply don't have the personal confidence to act on their beliefs. It's easier for people to live this way, but ultimately it's less fulfilling and less meaningful.

The coming years have the potential to be the most broadening, expanding, 13 enlightening years of your lives. I hope you will use them to engage yourself in a constant search for what is right. Put yourselves in foreign situations, in challenging situations, in situations which will deepen your empathy for others, your understanding of others, your concern for others. I hope that as we learn, we'll hold on to our sense of possibility. We'll certainly learn about lots of obstacles to change, but in spite of those obstacles we must hold on to the belief that positive change can happen—because it is that belief that will give us the purpose and the strength to act on what we believe is right. Then it's simply a matter of refusing to compromise the convictions we form.

I want to leave you with a short story that illustrates the power of this 14 approach to life. Two Teach For America corps members in the Rio Grande Valley in Texas wrote me last week to tell me about a student of theirs. Juan is, they wrote, "at once, the callous-handed field worker who helps his family pay for a small, two-room house by picking citrus fruit or pulling onions, and the wide-eyed, book-toting genius who insatiably absorbs knowledge and ideas before throwing that knowledge back to a teacher with questions—questions that demonstrate not only a comprehensive understanding of the material but also a profound desire and ability to challenge it and make it his own." Our corps members described their dream that Juan would attend summer school at Oxford University, where he would learn from Rhodes Scholars and university professors, and where he would continue his unbelievably rapid intellectual growth. Now Juan has been accepted to a highly competitive program there, and his two teachers are working furiously to raise [the] $5,500 necessary to enable him to go. These teachers didn't have to notice Juan's potential, they wouldn't have had to encourage him to apply to the Oxford program, and now they wouldn't have to go to extraordinary effort to raise the necessary funding. But their conviction, compassion, their sense of possibility, and their determination to do what is right has led them down this path. Juan's life may very well be different because of it.

I wish you all the best. Thank you very much. 15

Testimony against Legalized Gambling before the U.S. House Judiciary Committee

Reverend Tom Grey

As you learned in the Making a Difference profile on pp. 360–361, Reverend Tom Grey is the executive director of the National Coalition against Legalized Gambling (NCALG). By speaking with passion and eloquence and supporting his arguments with convincing hard data, Grey has helped many communities defeat efforts to expand legalized gambling. On September 29, 1995, Grey delivered this persuasive speech while testifying before the U.S. House Judiciary Committee in support of a bill to fund a national study on the effects of gambling. As you read his words, note how he frames the issue of gambling expansion as a battle between (1) well-funded gambling promoters with hidden political connections, and (2) ordinary citizens trying to protect their communities. He supports his claims by citing a combination of independent studies, statistics, and specific examples. Which arguments do you find most convincing? Are Grey's arguments based on public policy or personal morality? Which kind of argument do you think would be most effective?

1   Chairman Hyde and distinguished Members of the Committee:

A battle is raging across our country. Ambitious gambling promoters have been invited into our communities by some state and local officials under the guise of prosperity, economic development, jobs, and a painless new source of government revenue.

2   Armed with unlimited capital and hidden political connections, these gambling promoters insist that gambling is productive, that it meets the desires of the public, and that the growth of gambling throughout America is inevitable. They pledge that by the year 2000, every American will live within a two-hour drive of a gambling casino.

3   Ladies and gentlemen, these gambling interests are wrong.

4   The recent, rapid spread of gambling was never the result of a popular movement. Rather, it was driven by self-interested gambling pitchmen with money, high-priced lobbyists, and pie-in-the-sky promises. Cash-starved municipalities and legislatures, eager for a way to increase revenue while avoiding voter backlash, were vulnerable to the prospect of something-for-nothing.

5   Individual citizens questioned whether this "free lunch" program could rationally achieve its promise. And as the guarantees of economic prosperity evaporated, state and local groups spontaneously sprang up across the nation to oppose the further spread of gambling. In 1994, these varied citizen groups created the National Coalition Against Legalized Gambling (NCALG).

6   What is the National Coalition Against Legalized Gambling? NCALG is a grassroots movement. Our members span the entire political spectrum from conservative to liberal. Our coalition encompasses both business and labor, both religious and secular, with concerned citizens in every state.

7   Our arguments against the expansion of legalized gambling are based on public policy, sound economics, and quality of life within our communities, not on personal morality.

8   I have attached to my written testimony references to objective, academic studies showing that the expansion of gambling is bad for families and businesses. These studies show that:

- gambling enterprises cost more jobs than they create;
- gambling misdirects prudent government investment away from sound economic development strategies;

- gambling sucks revenues from local economies;
- gambling establishments tend to attract crime; and
- gambling addiction destroys individuals, undermines families, and weakens our business community.

If the members of NCALG were to base our opposition to gambling on personal morality, we would lose in the political arena. After all, a majority of Americans gamble. But because our arguments are based on cold, hard facts, our organization and its affiliates have consistently beaten the gambling interests on ballot questions and in state legislatures over the past year—winning fifteen major battles and only narrowly losing the remaining two.   *9*

Turning the political tide.   *10*

In November 1994, the issue of gambling was on more state ballots than any other issue. Of ten statewide referenda, NCALG won six at the ballot box (Colorado, Florida, Minnesota, Oklahoma, Rhode Island, and Wyoming) and two in the courts (Arkansas and New Mexico). Most of our victories were by landslide margins.   *11*

After their November debacle, the casino companies targeted legislatures in seven states. But this year we completely shut them out. The casinos lost major battles in Alabama, Illinois, Maryland, Pennsylvania, Texas, Virginia, and West Virginia.   *12*

Virginia illustrates the dynamics of the current gambling debate. In Richmond this year, over a dozen casino companies pushed to legalize riverboat gambling. They hired more than 50 lobbyists, bought newspaper ads, and even aired television commercials. While the casinos spent over $800,000 on direct lobbying in Richmond and millions more on indirect lobbying across the state, thousands of citizens, armed with the facts, mobilized at the grassroots level against the casinos. When the smoke cleared, the gambling bill was crushed in committee.   *13*

The political tide has turned. What had been forecast as inevitable has now become undesirable. But why?   *14*

The tide turned not simply because all of the major conservative Christian groups oppose the expansion of gambling, although they do. It is not simply because mainline churches—liberal, conservative, and moderate—are almost universally opposed to more gambling, although they are. Resistance to government-sponsored gambling is growing because voters from every walk of life recognize that legalized gambling is, based on the facts, poor public policy.   *15*

Gambling feeds voter cynicism.   *16*

For the past three years, I have traveled across the nation and talked to countless thousands of Americans about this issue. You know that voters are angry and cynical about government. Let me tell you, the expansion of legalized gambling has fed that anger and cynicism.   *17*

To many Americans, government's promotion of gambling is a cop-out and a double-cross. We see public officials sacrificing our communities to a predatory enterprise—for money. Citizens see government living off gambling profits, taken from the poorest and weakest of our citizens, instead of facing up to rational choices regarding budgets and taxes.   *18*

We see massive amounts of money pumped into pro-gambling lobbying efforts. Public officials have been answering to these outside monied interests while ignoring the voices of their own constituents. This leaves citizens to wonder who government really represents.   *19*

Worse, people see scandals like the one unfolding in Louisiana, where lawmakers are being investigated for taking bribes from gambling promoters. The   *20* payoff was made not merely to usher in gambling, but to prevent a voters' referendum to keep gambling out.

21   When the right of the people to be heard is bought and sold, we become convinced that the bedrock foundation of democracy—a government of the people—is under attack.

22   Now, I believe strongly in democracy. I fought for it as an infantry captain in Vietnam, and I continue to protect it as an active member of the Army Reserve. But in order for democracy to work, you as elected officials have to win back the trust of average citizens. And you can start here.

23   Enact H.R. 497.

24   H.R. 497 is a very modest measure. Twenty years ago—when the contagion of casino gambling was quarantined to two geographic areas—a federal commission conducted a study of legalized gambling. An enormous amount has changed since then—the contagion has spread. It's time for a fresh inquiry.

25   The National Coalition Against Legalized Gambling supports H.R. 497, as well as S. 704, because we believe that a national study will allow citizens to make an informed decision about the expansion of gambling in America.

26   And frankly, we are astonished by the opposition to this bill by the American Gaming Association. If they believe that the spread of gambling enhances our national economy, then what is it about an objective study that makes them afraid?

27   When everyone is fully informed, we're glad to let this issue be decided the good, old-fashioned American way, at the ballot box.

28   Mr. Chairman, thank you.

Live Longer and Healthier: Stop Eating Meat!

Renzi Stone

While he was a student at the University of Oklahoma, Renzi Stone delivered this persuasive speech to his public speaking class. The speech is noteworthy because of its strong, attention-grabbing introduction. To persuade his audience to listen to his claims about the benefits of vegetarianism, Stone first refutes several stereotypes about vegetarians. Why do you think he starts the speech this way? How convincing are his arguments in support of vegetarianism?

1   What do Steve Martin, Dustin Hoffman, Albert Einstein, Jerry Garcia, Michael Stipe, Eddie Vedder, Martina Navratilova, Carl Lewis, and 12 million other Americans all have in common? All of these well-known people were or are vegetarians. What do they know that we don't? Consuming a regimen of high-fat, high-protein flesh foods is a sure-fire prescription for disaster, like running diesel fuel through your car's gasoline engine. In the book *Why Do Vegetarians Eat Like That?* David Gabbe asserts that millions of people today are afflicted with chronic diseases that can be directly linked to the consumption of meat. Eating a vegetarian diet can help prevent many of those diseases.

2   In 1996, 12 million Americans identified themselves as vegetarians. That number is twice as many as in the decade before. According to a recent National Restaurant Association poll found in *Health* magazine, one in five diners say they now go out of their way to choose restaurants that serve at least a few meatless entrees. Obviously, the traditionally American trait of a meat-dominated society has subsided in recent years.

In discussing vegetarianism today, first I will tell how vegetarians are per-   *3*
ceived in society. Next, I will introduce several studies validating my claim that a
meatless diet is extraordinarily healthy. I will then show how a veggie diet can
strengthen the immune system and make the meatless body a shield from
unwanted diseases such as cancer and heart disease. Maintaining a strict vegetarian diet can also lead to a longer life. Finally, I will put an image into the audience's mind of a meatless society that relies on vegetables for the main course at
breakfast, lunch, and dinner.

Moving to my first point, society generally holds two major misperceptions   *4*
about vegetarians. First of all, society often perceives vegetarians as a radical
group of people with extreme principles. In this view, vegetarians are seen as a
monolithic group of people who choose to eat vegetables because they are
opposed to the killing of animals for food. The second major misconception is
that because vegetarians do not eat meat, they do not get the proper amounts of
essential vitamins and minerals often found in meat.

Here is my response to these misconceived notions. First of all, vegetarians   *5*
are not a homogeneous group of radicals. Whereas many vegetarians in the past
did join the movement on the principle that killing animals is wrong, many join
the movement today mainly for its health benefits. In addition, there are many
different levels of vegetarianism. Some vegetarians eat nothing but vegetables.
Others don't eat red meat, but do occasionally eat chicken and fish.

Secondly, contrary to popular opinion, vegetarians get more than enough vit-   *6*
amins and minerals in their diet and generally receive healthier nourishment
than meat eaters. In fact, in an article for *Health* magazine, Peter Jaret states that
vegetarians actually get larger amounts of amino acids due to the elimination of
saturated fats which are often found in meat products. Studies show that the
health benefits of a veggie lifestyle contribute to increased life expectancy and
overall productivity.

Hopefully you now see that society's perceptions of vegetarians are outdated   *7*
and just plain wrong. You are familiar with many of the problems associated
with a meat-based diet, and you have heard many of the benefits of a vegetarian
diet. Now try to imagine how you personally can improve your life by becoming
a vegetarian.

Can you imagine a world where people retire at age 80 and lead productive   *8*
lives into their early 100s? Close your eyes and think about celebrating your sev-
entieth wedding anniversary, seeing your great-grandchildren get married, and
witnessing 100 years of world events and technological innovations. David
Gabbe's book refers to studies that have shown a vegetarian diet can increase
your life expectancy up to 15 years. A longer life is within your reach, and the
diet you eat has a direct impact on your health and how you age.

In conclusion, vegetarianism is a healthy life choice, not a radical cult. By   *9*
eliminating meat from their diet, vegetarians reap the benefits of a vegetable-
based diet that helps prevent disease and increase life expectancy. People, take
heed of my advice. There are many more sources of information available for
those who want to take a few hours to research the benefits of the veggie lifestyle.
If you don't believe my comments, discover the whole truth for yourself.

Twelve million Americans know the health benefits that come with being a   *10*
vegetarian. Changing your eating habits can be just as easy as making your bed
in the morning. Sure, it takes a few extra minutes and some thought, but your
body will thank you in the long run.

You only live once. Why not make it a long stay?   *11*

Making Dreams Reality

Amber Mixon

Amber Mixon delivered this informative speech to her public speaking class at the University of Oklahoma. Note how Mixon effectively introduces her speech topic by asking her classmates to think about world hunger in terms of how much money a typical college student spends on food each day. She goes on to clearly explain how an organization called Feed the Children is addressing world hunger and related problems, and how students can volunteer their time and energy to support the cause.

1   Did you know that 20 percent of children in the United States under 18 years of age are hungry? Consider for a moment the amount of money that you as a college student spend in a single day on food alone. Did you know that 1.3 billion people worldwide live on less than one dollar a day? Have you ever volunteered your time to help the hungry? When some students think of volunteering, they focus on the benefits that it brings to their standing in a school organization or the status it earns them on their resumé rather than thinking about how important it is to help those less fortunate than they are.

2   However, even if people choose to ignore the hunger problem in our world, one organization has dared to bridge the gap between the impoverished and those unaware of these circumstances. That organization is Feed the Children. Though I don't volunteer often, I have been lucky enough to experience the fulfillment FTC workers experience every day when I volunteered once during Christmas for our church's annual Feed the Children stocking-stuffing event.

3   Today, I would like to tell you about how FTC began, then discuss different outreach divisions that FTC has created, and finally inform you about ways you can contribute your time or money to make a difference. I will begin by sharing with you a quick overview of how Feed the Children began. I gathered most of the information about this organization from the Web site they have established, as well as by talking with several volunteers.

4   Feed the Children began with a simple "down-home feeling" that has continued to thrive in the hearts of its workers throughout its nearly twenty-year history. The founder, Larry Jones, first realized this global hunger problem when he took a trip to Haiti in 1979. After witnessing the devastating effects of poverty, hunger, and poor medical care, he decided to start an organization to address the needs of victims, particularly helpless children. The driving statement behind FTC was quickly put into motion: "Feed the Children is an international, non-profit, Christian organization providing food, clothing, medical equipment and other necessities to people who lack these essentials because of famine, drought, flood, war, or other calamities."

5   Today FTC has grown to an incredible size. The organization now ministers to the needs of 74 countries, including the United States. FTC has also acquired its own fleet of semi trucks in order to increase the efficiency and timeliness of each delivery. They are also the head of a vast network of volunteer associations throughout the world.

6   It is clear that through the perseverance and dedication of many individuals, this organization has met with success. To aid as many people as possible, Feed the Children has four separate divisions that respond to specific problems: feeding the impoverished, providing relief during emergencies, offering personal assistance, and providing medical assistance. By specializing how each division

responds to problems, FTC is particularly effective in delivering the critical necessities people need at the time they most need them.

Of Feed the Children's four goals, the most well-known aspect of FTC is its overwhelming adeptness at distributing food and necessity items. In 1996, sixty million pounds of food and supplies were delivered by FTC. Feed the Children has also proven its helpfulness in delivering emergency aid. In the United States, FTC responded quickly and provided assistance to victims of the 1998 Florida tornadoes as well as to the bombing of the Murrah Federal Building in Oklahoma. *7*

Beyond providing emergency supplies and relief in times of need, Feed the Children also attempts to solve long-term problems. Feed the Children stands strong behind its belief that education helps reduce poverty rates. Therefore, FTC created a program, called Hope for Kids, that provides essential learning tools for America's poorest school systems, thus giving kids a chance to succeed. *8*

Ultimately, Feed the Children meets needy people at the source of their needs, be it hunger, emergency assistance, personal help, or medical assistance. Running a large, global relief organization requires tremendous effort from a lot of dedicated staff as well as volunteers. Feed the Children encourages assistance from volunteers because it helps the organization reach more needy people. On a financial level, Feed the Children accepts tax-deductible donations, consisting of cash, new toys, new household items, and so on. FTC also encourages community fund-raising projects such as recycling, bake sales, and garage sales that generate funds for FTC programs. People can also help out by donating time at their Oklahoma City headquarters. Volunteers can help in many ways, from working in public relations to cleaning to stuffing food boxes. Aiding FTC can even be as easy as attending a Garth Brooks concert and donating a few cans of food. *9*

As you can see, helping out this organization is not difficult at all. It could be as in-depth as spending a Saturday sorting food boxes, or as easy as putting a check in the mail. Now that we have taken an overall look at Feed the Children, I will conclude with a few final ideas. *10*

Today, I began by presenting to you the history of the Feed the Children organization and how it is divided into four functional divisions—medical, personal self-help, food provision, and emergency relief. I also shared several ways in which people, even busy college students, can get involved in this organization. Reflecting back on what I said in my introduction, it's easy to see what a big difference even one dollar used by FTC can make to someone who lives on only one dollar a day. As FTC stated in a press release: "Feed the Children isn't just an organization—it's people helping people." *11*

Address at the *Time* Magazine 75th Anniversary Celebration

William Jefferson Clinton

On March 3, 1998, Time *magazine hosted a celebration at New York's Radio City Music Hall to commemorate 75 years of reporting on world events. From President Clinton and Mikhail Gorbachev to Toni Morrison and Steven Spielberg, newsmakers from all walks of life gathered to honor the magazine and the people and events it covered for nearly eight decades. In the speech reprinted here, President Clinton pays tribute to former president Franklin Delano Roosevelt. Political analysts often note Clinton's effectiveness as a public speaker, referring especially to his*

1   Thank you very much. Thank you Walter, Gerry Levin, and all the people at *Time*. Tonight, *Time* has paid tribute to the time it not only observed but helped to create—the stunning years your founder, Henry Luce, so unforgettably called the American Century.

2   To me, one man above all others is the personification of our American century: Franklin Delano Roosevelt. Now, that choice might have pained Henry Luce, but surely he would not be surprised. The story of this century we're about to leave is really many stories—of the ascendance of science and technology; the rise of big government and mass media; the movements for equality for women and racial minorities; the dynamic growth and disruptive force of the Industrial Age.

3   But when our children's children look back, they will see that above all else, the story of the twentieth century is the story of the triumph of freedom. Freedom, the victory of democracy over totalitarianism, of free enterprise over state socialism, of tolerance over bigotry and ignorance. The advance of freedom has made this the American Century; for in this century, America has made freedom ring. The embodiment of the triumph, the driving force behind it, was Franklin Delano Roosevelt.

4   Today, with the happy outcome known to all, it is tempting to look back and say the victory was assured, inevitable—but it wasn't. In the face of the twentieth century's greatest crisis, decisively, irrevocably, President Roosevelt committed America to freedom's fight. Because of that commitment and its embrace by every American leader since, today we can say, for the very first time in all of human history, a majority of the world's people live under governments of their own choosing in freedom.

5   Winston Churchill said that Franklin Roosevelt's life was "one of the commanding events in human history." He was born to privilege, but he understood the aspirations of farmers and factory workers and forgotten Americans. My grandfather came from a little town of about 50 people. He had a fourth-grade education. He believed Franklin Roosevelt was his friend, a man who cared about him and his family and his child's future. Polio put him in a wheelchair, but he lifted our troubled nation to its feet and he got us moving again.

6   He was a patrician who happily addressed the Daughters of the American Revolution as "my fellow immigrants." He was a master politician, a magnificent commander-in-chief. Yes, his life had its fair share of disappointments and failures, but they never broke his spirit or his faith in God or his people. Because he always rose to the occasion, so did we. FDR was guided not by the iron dictates of ideology, but by the pragmatism by what he called bold, persistent experimentation. If one thing doesn't work, he said, try another thing; but above all, try something. It drove his critics crazy, but it worked.

7   He brought joy and nobility to public service as he completed the mission of his kinsman, Theodore Roosevelt, forging a progressive government for the Industrial Age, taming the savage cycle of boom and bust, giving our citizens the economic security and the skills they needed to build the great American middle class.

8   In our century's struggle for freedom, President Roosevelt won two great victories.

By confronting the gravest threat capitalism had ever faced—the Great 9
Depression—he strengthened economic liberty for all time, teaching us that free markets require effective government, one in which individual initiative and the call of community are not at odds, but instead are woven together in one seamless social fabric.

By confronting and defeating the gravest threat to personal and political liberty the world has ever faced, he forever committed America to the front lines of the struggle for freedom. He taught us that even the expanses of two great oceans could not shield America from danger or absolve America from responsibility. He taught us that our destiny, forever, is linked to the destiny of the world, that our freedom requires us to support freedom for all others, that humanity's cause must be America's cause. 10

Now we know what came of Roosevelt and his generation's "rendezvous 11 with destiny." What will come of ours? To this generation of the millennium, in President Roosevelt's words, "much has been given" and "much is asked."

When Roosevelt ran for president in 1932, he said, "new times demand new 12 responses from government." He saved capitalism from its own excesses, so it could again be a force for progress and freedom. Now we work to modernize government, saving it from its excess of debt, so that again it is a force for progress and freedom in a new era.

As Roosevelt gave Americans security in the Industrial Age, now we work to 13 give Americans opportunity in the Information Age. As Roosevelt asked us to meet the crushing burden of the Depression with bold, persistent experimentation, now we must bring the same attitude to the challenges and unrivaled opportunities of this era to our schools, our streets, our poorest neighborhoods, to the fight against disease, the exploration of space, the preservation of the environment.

As Roosevelt established that security and opportunity for ordinary Americans 14 required our leadership and cooperation with like-minded people throughout the world, now we must commit ourselves to the common struggle against new threats to the security and prosperity of ordinary people everywhere. For even more than in President Roosevelt's time, our prospects are bound to the world's progress.

Like FDR, we look around us and see a world that is not yet fully free. The 15 advance of democracy has been steady, but it isn't irreversible.

For our generation, what does "freedom" mean? Well, at least the long, 16 delayed achievement of President Roosevelt's dream of a Europe undivided, democratic and at peace for the first time in history. What does "freedom from fear" mean? Well, at least, freedom for our children from the worry of nuclear, chemical, or biological weapons. What does "freedom from fear" or "freedom from want" mean? Well, at least, for the world, a fair chance for people in every land to develop their minds, find reward in honest labor, and raise their children in peace according to the dictates of their conscience.

America must work to secure this kind of freedom with our allies and friends 17 whenever possible, alone if absolutely necessary. We work today through the United Nations, which FDR helped to create and which he named. I salute Secretary General Kofi Annan tonight for what he has done. Bearing an unequivocal message from the international community, backed by the credible threat of force, the Secretary General obtained Iraq's commitment to honor United Nations resolutions on weapons inspection. Now the Security Council clearly and unanimously has supported the agreement. Iraq must match its words and its deeds, its commitment with compliance.

18   In the tradition of FDR, America and its partners must make sure that happens. And in the tradition of FDR, America must support the United Nations and other institutions for global security and prosperity, and that means we ought to pay our fair share.

19   In the darkest hours of the Second World War, Franklin Roosevelt proclaimed, "We have faith that future generations will know that here in the middle of the twentieth century, there came a time when men of good will found a way to unite and produce and fight to destroy the forces of ignorance and intolerance and slavery and war."

20   More than any other twentieth-century American, Franklin Roosevelt fulfilled the mandate of America's founders. When everything was on the line, he pledged our lives, our fortunes, our sacred honor to the preservation of liberty, the pursuit of happiness, the creation of a more perfect union.

21   The next century is now barely 700 days away. It will be many things new: a time of stunning leaps of science; a century of dizzying technology; a digital century; an era in which the very face of our nation will change.

22   Yet in all the newness, what is required of us still is to follow President Roosevelt's lead, to strengthen the bonds of our union, widen the circle of opportunity, and deepen the reach of freedom. That is the tribute we ought to pay to him. God willing, we will. And if we do, we will make the twenty-first-century the next American Century—and the happy warrior will be smiling down on us.

23   Thank you and God bless you.

Late Night Reflections of a College President: A Virtual University

Nancy S. Dye

As the president of Oberlin College, Nancy Dye is committed to addressing the formidable challenges of delivering a top-notch education to students. In the persuasive speech reprinted here, which was delivered to the Cleveland City Club on July 11, 1997, Dye ruminates about the current trend in American higher education to proclaim the virtues of the virtual university—a campus that exists only in cyberspace. Her speech is well organized and easy to follow, and she uses the phrase "late at night" as an effective refrain to maintain continuity throughout the various parts of the speech. As you read Dye's words, pay close attention to how she frames her argument against the virtual university by focusing on how actual *colleges and universities provide the best learning environment for students—through human interaction. Do you find her claims convincing?*

1   A few months ago, I was leafing through an issue of *Forbes Magazine*, when words seemed to leap off the page. The words were Peter Drucker's, and this is what he had to say: "Thirty years from now, the big university campuses will be relics. Universities won't survive....Higher education is in deep crisis. The college won't survive as a residential institution. Today's buildings are hopelessly unsuited and totally unneeded."

2   What Peter Drucker and many others are talking about is the so-called "virtual university." Education, they believe, can, should, and will take place completely off-campus and online. Students can go to college on the Internet. They

will be served by institutions like the University of Phoenix, which already enrolls thousands of individuals who complete course work and degrees via computer.

Over the past year or so, I don't think that a day has passed that I have not read about the coming of the "virtual university," or heard the prediction that distance learning will completely re-invent colleges and universities as we know them. I am exhorted to get on the bandwagon. Listen, for example, to the advice to college presidents from Lewis Perelman, author of the new book, *School's Out.* "If I were a college president," he tells me, "I would get rid of all the old buildings and bricks and mortar and grounds, and go virtual." **3**

If you haven't heard yet about the virtual university, you will very soon. It's hot. **4**

Now distance learning is not new: It has been central to the efforts of universities' extension divisions over most of the twentieth century. And picking up a magazine and reading that higher education is in crisis is not a new experience for me. It happens all the time. But Peter Drucker's assertion that the demise of colleges' physicality is inevitable still comes as a shock. So does his and others' belief that the vast and richly varied enterprise of American higher education, so envied throughout the world, can be replaced easily by an electronic substitute. **5**

So, late at night, I find myself thinking about the virtual university. The idea is not very surprising, really. We have virtually everything else available virtually. We have virtual salons, known as "chat rooms." **6**

We have the promise of the virtual library and the virtual workplace. There are virtual law firms on the Internet. And those of us saddled with the old-fashioned actuality of bricks and mortar have been busy bringing virtuality to our students and faculty by wiring our residence halls and classrooms, and by investing a lot of capital in campus computer networks that connect us all to each other and the world at large. **7**

Late at night, I begin to understand the romance of the virtual university. It promises to be affordable, at a time when tuition continues to rise faster than inflation and wages. It promises universal access to higher education. It promises to transform professors into individual entrepreneurs, whose success will depend entirely upon their ability to appeal to their electronic customers. In the virtual university, there will be no need to deal with the issues surrounding the developing and tenuring of faculty, and the housing, feeding, and follies of students. In one fell swoop, we could wipe out deferred maintenance—the plague of aging college campuses. The economic ills that now ail higher education would be remedied, thanks to the kind of quick technological fix Americans have always found deeply appealing. **8**

If so many people find the virtual university so promising, I find myself wondering, why fight it? Why am I troubled by it? I find myself thinking, too, about its implications for what we, as educators, are doing. The threat or promise of the virtual university—depending upon one's point of view—compels us to reflect on what it is that actual colleges are trying to accomplish, and to ask whether virtual colleges could do things better. I will return in a few minutes to the virtual university, but now I want to turn to this second question of what it is that actual colleges, especially liberal arts colleges, like Oberlin, are trying to accomplish. **9**

Individuals enter college—including that uniquely American institution, the liberal arts college—for many reasons. Above all, students and their parents tell us that they come to college to learn the arts that will serve them well in making a living. Throughout the history of the Western university, this has always been **10** the main reason for seeking an education, and a very good reason it is. Liberal arts colleges today believe that the best preparation for making a living comes through learning the arts of writing clearly and persuasively, reading carefully, evaluating evidence effectively, reasoning quantitatively and analytically, doing research, and thinking critically. A liberal education also involves acquiring familiarity with basic concepts of science, and gaining a sense of history—a particularity of time and place, and an ability to see oneself and one's life in time. All of these skills and competencies have long been central to a liberal education. They seem even more important today, as we educate a generation of students who are coming of age at a time when knowledge is expanding at a rate faster than ever before, and who can expect to change careers four or five times during their lives. Colleges like Oberlin take pride in the success they enjoy in enabling generation after generation of students to master these arts and to go on to great achievement in graduate and professional schools and in their professional lives.

11   Another essential goal of liberal education is to nurture individual students' intellectual and artistic creativity. Science education provides an excellent example. Liberal arts colleges have long been very successful in producing scientists. Oberlin, for example, has consistently produced more graduates who have gone on to complete doctorates in the natural sciences than any other undergraduate institution. We think that this success has a lot to do with the interaction between individual students and their teachers. Leading liberal arts colleges have long understood the value of the old institution of apprenticeship. This summer at Oberlin, scores of science students are working in research labs alongside their professor-mentors. Many of these students will present papers at conferences and co-author articles for scientific journals based on their laboratory research. My point here is not that these achievements look good on student resumés—although they do—but rather that we believe that by doing collaborative research and by learning science by actually doing science within a close, ongoing relationship with a mentor, our students develop their creative gifts, and gain confidence in their abilities to complete hard intellectual tasks. This does much to convince us that excellence in education happens in relationship.

12   An excellent education is not only about building a strong foundation for entering a profession. Our students also come to us full of idealism. They look to college to help them learn arts by which they can make the world a better place. This is tricky. Educating our students for the adult lives they will lead ten, twenty, forty years down the road forces us to think about the needs of future generations, even while the primary function of the academy has always been to preserve and transmit knowledge accumulated by generations past. Certainly it is vital to educational excellence that students read and study the texts that have stood the test of time, and that we regard as the best of what has been thought and written. But we also need to ground education in our best assessments of what our current students will need as they live their lives, and the needs of the society they will inherit.

13   We know, for example, that a growing number of students are coming to college already realizing that we desperately need to reduce the size of the human footprint. Many are deeply committed to conserving the earth's resources, and to creating a future that is ecologically and economically sustainable. Environmental studies is the fastest growing major at many colleges, including Oberlin. What are the arts that our students will need for this endeavor? Here, frankly, the Western intellectual tradition is not up to the task that confronts us, for that tradition is grounded in the belief that human beings can and should assert mastery over

nature. Our students will inherit a world in which human survival will depend upon finding ways to live in harmony with nature.

We provide strong degree programs in geology and chemistry, physics and biology, and courses in environmental economics, politics, and law so that students can gain some of the knowledge and competencies they will need to help save the environment. But we have to do more than this: We also need to help students develop the imagination to be concerned about future generations, about posterity. And we need to enable students to make connections among discrete academic fields of knowledge and apply their knowledge to real world environmental problems.   *14*

One way Oberlin is trying to realize these goals is by building the Adam   *15* Joseph Lewis Environmental Studies Center. This new structure will be a model and a laboratory for sustainable design in the areas of energy, water, waste, materials, landscape, and aesthetics. And it will serve as a campus center for interdisciplinary exchange about sustainability among faculty and students in the natural and social sciences and the humanities. Planning and building this center are themselves educational experiences. As David Orr, Oberlin's professor of environmental studies, has written, "the design, the construction, and the operation of academic buildings can be a liberal education in a microcosm that includes virtually every discipline in the catalog." Students and faculty, architects and engineers, have worked together through the myriad of economic, ecological, material, and ethical issues involved in planning this building. They have designed and are now preparing to build a structure that discharges no waste water; generates more electricity than it uses; employs no materials known to be carcinogenic, mutagenic, or endocrine disrupters, and uses products and materials grown or manufactured sustainably; and is landscaped to promote biological diversity. You are all invited to come out and see it in about a year and a half.

All too often, students engage with environmental issues only as problems.   *16* Giving students opportunities to participate in the planning and programming of this building has given them a chance to work to solve real problems. This kind of effort builds confidence and hope. Our experiences with projects like this one help convince us that an excellent education must be one that embodies tangible, tactile, experiential elements that can't be mediated by computer.

Most of all, students come to college today wanting to learn how to live   *17* together in a richly diverse America. They want to build bridges across the lines of race and class and ethnicity. They want to respect and celebrate our differences and at the same time establish some cultural common ground. They want answers to the question of how we can create a genuinely diverse community. They want to learn how to make diversity work. In voicing these concerns, they are reflecting the most important issues we face as a democratic society.

Diversity is not a new issue for America. Racial, ethnic, political, and religious   *18* diversity have always been part of our national fabric. At times, such as during the decades around the turn of the twentieth century, the social debate over issues of inclusion and pluralism was every bit as wide-ranging and intense as it is today. But diversity is a relatively new phenomenon for American colleges and universities. Until recently, higher education did not come close to reflecting the demographics of our society. Even Oberlin—the first college in the United States to make access central to its mission; to admit and educate students without regard to gender, race, or socioeconomic circumstance; and to stress the importance of interracial education—is far more diverse now than it has been at any time during its 163-year history.

19   Consider, for example, the cosmopolitan makeup of Oberlin's student body. We count among our students individuals from each of the fifty states, and more than forty nations around the world. Our students reflect the entire socioeconomic spectrum. About twelve percent of them are the first individuals in their families to attend college. Our students are African American and white, Latino, Native American, and Asian American. A good number of them come from families new to the United States, from the Caribbean, the Middle East, and from Korea, Vietnam, India, and Pakistan. They are Catholic and Muslim, Jewish and Buddhist, and Hindu and Protestant. A significant number are evangelical Christians. Our students hold and express a wide range of political and social opinions, many of which cannot be neatly pidgeonholed as liberal or conservative. In short, Oberlin—like our colleges and universities generally—looks like America. Issues of diversity that are playing themselves out in American society are also playing themselves [out] on our campuses. Dealing with these issues brings to the fore the old-fashioned and long-neglected subject of civic virtue: How do we educate students to be engaged and responsible participants in the lives of their communities?

20   Critics of higher education tell us that colleges often make a hash of educating students for engaged citizenship in a diverse society. They say we make too big a deal about difference and too little a deal about common values. There is truth to this. We need to do more on our campuses to help students learn that each of us has more than one identity, and that American identity is a matter of common belief in the political principles underlying the Republic, not a matter of race or ethnicity. We need to work harder to provide continuous encouragement to students to interact with and come to know and like one another across the lines of race and ethnicity. And we need to help students develop their imaginations and heighten their capacity for empathy for people different from themselves.

21   Our critics also tell us that colleges and universities have transformed themselves into cultural battlegrounds, rather than sticking with their legitimate jobs of transmitting and creating knowledge. This, in a nutshell, was Allan Bloom's argument about higher education in his bestseller of a few years ago, *The Closing of the American Mind*. He thought that if professors would just teach the great texts of Western civilization, students would come to think alike about what constitutes a good life and a just society. I think that Bloom's criticism, and his proposed solution, are off the mark. College students should read the "great books," but contemporary campuses will remain full of disagreement and contentiousness. Conflict is inevitable and sometimes desirable on a college campus that brings together students with widely differing experiences, perspectives, ideas, and values, just as conflict is inevitable in a democratic society. We don't need an end to fractious discussion. We do need, on and off campus, better and more civil ways to disagree with one another about the many social, political, cultural, and moral issues that divide us. Students need to learn how to disagree, and also to realize that people can disagree strenuously without severing their relationships with one another. As political philosopher Amy Guttman tells us, our schools and colleges must "aim to develop their students' capacities to understand different perspectives, communicate their understandings to other people, and engage in the give-and-take of moral argument with a view to making mutually acceptable decisions." These are goals, she goes on, "which entail cultivating moral character and intellectual skills at the same time, [and] are likely to require some significant changes in traditional civics education, which has neglected teaching this kind of moral reasoning about politics."

Late at night, I do not find myself troubled by conflict and disagreement on **22** campus or in America. What does trouble me is what seems to be an increasing willingness of Americans to abandon civic enterprise, democratic discourse, and political participation altogether.

This brings me back to the virtual university. Instead of cultivating the arts of **23** actual face-to-face human relationship, the virtual university encourages us to be on our own in the virtual marketplace, free to make our individual learning contracts in cyberspace. Late at night I think especially about this. All of us will be on our own. In this cool electronic universe, we will not need to recognize that real education is always a social process. We will be free to contract exactly as we wish, meeting our individual needs with professors and courses and virtual colleges as we see fit. We will be free to expand or limit our access to information and ideas and opinions as we feel comfortable. There will be no conflict on the virtual campus, for we need never come into contact with one another. We can come to the table or leave the table, as we please. All of us will be on our own. Could this be the most fundamental appeal of the virtual university in this time of social and cultural uncertainty? This is what troubles me most of all about the prospect of virtual education.

Late at night, after worrying a while about the virtual university, I find it **24** comforting to turn my thoughts to our earliest ideas about colleges in the first years of the American republic. From the end of the American Revolution through the first half of the nineteenth century, Americans looked to their colleges, in the words of the Northwest Ordinance, to further "religion, morality, and knowledge, [these] being necessary to good government and the happiness of mankind." Americans embodied their hopes for the new republic in the colleges they created, many of them here in Ohio, their hopes for an educated citizenry, capable of self-governance in an independent republic; their hopes for building a society in which individuals could have access to education and could better themselves economically and socially by dint of their own efforts; and their hopes for creating a genuinely American democratic culture. Many colleges and universities have long since ended their formal relationship with religion. And most of us don't put morality in the forefront of our mission in ways that would be recognizable to our nineteenth-century counterparts. The phrase happiness of mankind" does not trip easily off our tongues. But when we look closely at the mission of American colleges, it is not really so different from the one that the drafters of the Northwest Ordinance had in mind. We are very much in the business of educating citizens. We are very much in the business of furthering knowledge, and we know that the best teaching and learning happens in relationship, face to face. And, like our early American predecessors, we are concerned about furthering the "happiness of mankind." For us today, this translates most clearly into realizing our need to learn to live together, across the lines of race and class and ethnicity, and to helping our students identify and master those arts that will best serve them in going about those most essential human tasks of love and work. Learning these arts seems to me to be inextricably tied to the sometimes messy, often ambiguous, always inexact, and usually contentious relationships in the actual rather than the virtual university.

Notes

Chapter 1

1. Quoted in Leslie Wayne, "Leaping to the Lectern," *New York Times,* September 8, 1995, pp. D1–2.

2. For a discussion of public discourse in the eighteenth and nineteenth centuries, see Neil Postman, *Amusing Ourselves to Death: Public Discourse in the Age of Show Business* (New York: Penguin, 1985), pp. 44–45.

3. "Public Speaking," *Compton's Online Encyclopedia.* http://www.comptons.com.

4. Donna Uchida, Marvin J. Cetron, and Floretta McKenzie, "What Students Must Know to Succeed in the 21st Century," special report (World Future Society) based on *Preparing Students for the 21st Century,* a report on a project by the American Association of School Administrators, 1996.

5. Quoted in William Safire, *Lend Me Your Ears: Great Speeches in History,* rev. ed. (New York: Norton, 1997), pp. 461–463.

6. Deborah Gillan Straub, ed., *Voices of Multicultural America: Notable Speeches Delivered by African, Asian, Hispanic, and Native Americans* (New York: Gale Research, 1996).

7. National Opinion Research Center, *General Social Survey, Cumulative Codebook* (Chicago: University of Chicago Press, various years).

8. Frances Moore Lappe and Paul Martin Du Bois, *The Quickening of America: Rebuilding Our Nation, Remaking Our Lives* (San Francisco: Jossey-Bass, 1994), p. 15.

9. Andrew D. Wolvin and Carolyn Gwynn Coakley, *Listening* (Dubuque, IA: W. C. Brown, 1982), p. 125.

10. Richard Carelli, "Abortion Foes May Confront Patients. High Court Says It's Free Speech," *New Orleans Times-Picayune,* February 20, 1997, p. A1.

11. David G. Savage, "Ruling Is Victory for In-Your-Face Free Speech. Right to Be Alone Is Considered Secondary," *Sun-Sentinel* (Fort Lauderdale), February 23, 1997, p. 11A.

Chapter 2

1. J. B. Donovan, "Power to the Podium: The Place to Stand for Those Who Move the World," *Vital Speeches of the Day* 58 (1991): 149–150.

2. Cited in Roger E. Axtell, *Do's and Taboos of Public Speaking: How to Get Those Butterflies Flying in Formation* (New York: Wiley, 1992), p. 10.

3. See, for example, M. J. Beatty, "Situational and Predispositional Correlates of Public Speaking Anxiety," *Communication Education* 37 (1988): 28–39. Adapted from S. Tobias, "Anxiety and Cognitive Processes of Instruction," in R. Schwarzer, ed., *Self-Related Cognitions in Anxiety and Motivation* (Hillsdale, NJ: Lawrence Erlbaum Associates, 1986), pp. 35–54.

4. Adapted from J. C. McCroskey, "Oral Communication Apprehension: A Summary of Recent Theory and Research," *Human Communication Research* 4 (1977): 79–96.

5. Ibid.

6. For example, see J. J. Seta, M. A. Wang, J. E. Crisson, and C. E. Seta, "Audience Composition and Felt Anxiety: Impact Averaging and Summation," *Basic and Applied Social Psychology* 10 (1989): 57–72.

7. M. T. Motley, "Public Speaking Anxiety qua Performance Anxiety: A Revised Model and an Alternative Therapy," *Journal of Social Behavior and Personality* 5 (1990): 85–104.

8. J. Ayers and T. S. Hopf, "Visualization: Is It More Than Extra-Attention?" *Communication Education* 38 (1989): 1–5; J. Ayers and T. S. Hopf, *Coping with Speech Anxiety* (Norwood, NJ: Ablex, 1993).

9. Ayers and Hopf, "Visualization," pp. 2–3.

10. Laurie Schloff and Marcia Yudkin, *Smart Speaking* (New York: Plume, 1991), pp. 92–93.

11. Cited in ibid., p. 148.

12. William Safire, ed., *Lend Me Your Ears: Great Speeches in History* (New York: Norton, 1992), p. 484.

Chapter 3

1. L. K. Steel, J. Summerfield, and G. de Mare, *Listening: It Can Change Your Life* (New York: Wiley, 1983).

2. George Lazarus, "Listen to Win, and Keep, Ad Clients," *Chicago Tribune*, April 14, 1997, p. 4.

3. Quoted in Cynthia Crossen, "Blah, Blah, Blah: The Crucial Question for These Noisy Times May Just be: 'Huh?'" *Wall Street Journal*, July 10, 1997, p. A1.

4. Andrew Wolvin and Carolyn Coakley, *Listening*, 4th ed. (Dubuque, IA: W. C. Brown, 1992).

5. Ibid., p. 28

6. Thomas E. Anastasi Jr., *Listen! Techniques for Improving Communication Skills*, CBI Series in Management Communication (Boston: CBI Publishing, 1982), p. 35.

7. S. Golen, "A Factor Analysis of Barriers to Effective Listening," *Journal of Business Communication* 27 (1990): 25–36.

8. With thanks to Anastasi, *Listen!*, p. 30.

9. Ibid.

10. Quoted in Alison Mitchell, "State of the Speech: Reading between the Lines," *New York Times*, February 2, 1997, p. E5.

11. C. Wade and C. Tavris, *Psychology*, 4th ed. (New York: HarperCollins, 1996), pp. 31–35.

12. *Bartlett's Familiar Quotations*, 1901 version; found through Alta Vista on the Internet. URL:www.columbia.edu/acis/bartleby/bartlett/

13. Based on Anastasi, *Listen!*, pp. 32–33.

14. Ron Hoff, *I Can See You Naked*, rev. ed. (Kansas City, MO: Andrews and McMeel, 1992), pp. 300–311.

Chapter 4

1. Simon Wiesenthal Center Press Release, http://www.wiesenthal.com/resource/index.html. Simon Wiesenthal home page, 1997.

2. *Merriam-Webster's Collegiate Dictionary*, 10th ed. (Springfield, MA: Merriam-Webster, 1993).

3. For an excellent discussion of the tension between these two rights, see Douglas M. Fraleigh and Joseph S. Tuman, *Freedom of Speech in the Marketplace of Ideas* (New York: St. Martin's Press, 1997).

4. W. A. Haskins, "Freedom of Speech: Construct for Creating a Culture Which Empowers Organizational Members," *Journal of Business Communication*, 33 (1996): 85–97.

5. Andrew D. Wolvin and Carolyn Gwynn Coakley, *Listening* (Dubuque: IA: W. C. Brown, 1982), p. 125.

6. *Concise Columbia Electronic Encyclopedia* (New York: Columbia University Press, 1994). Located on AOL.

7. Louis A. Day, *Ethics in Media Communications: Cases and Controversies*, 2nd ed. (Belmont, CA: Wadsworth Publishing, 1997), p. 3.

8. Ibid.

9. Cited in E. P. J. Corbett, *Classical Rhetoric for the Modern Student* (New York: Oxford University Press, 1990), p. 80.

10. Ibid., p. 81.

11. D. A. Infante, A. S. Rancer, and D. F. Womack, *Building Communication Theory*, 3rd ed. (Prospect Heights, IL: Waveland Press, 1997), p. 158.

12. Edward D. Steele and W. Charles Redding, "The American Value System: Premises for Persuasion," *Western Speech* 26 (1962): 83–91; Robin M. Williams Jr., *American Society: A Sociological Interpretation*, 3rd ed. (New York: Alfred A. Knopf, 1970).

13. World Values Survey, 1989–1992, as cited in Rodney Stark, *Sociology*, 6th ed. (Belmont, CA: Wadsworth Publishing, 1996), p. xvii.

14. Williams, *American Society*.

15. D. Moore, "Most Americans Say Religion Is Important to Them," *Gallup Poll Monthly* (February 1995): 16–21.

16. D. Moore, "Public Polarized on Gay Issue," *Gallup Poll Monthly* (April 1993): 30–34.

17. *World Values Survey*, 1989–1992.

18. W. Gudykunst, S. Ting-Toomey, S. Suweeks, and L. Stewart, *Building Bridges: Interpersonal Skills for a Changing World* (Boston: Houghton Mifflin, 1995), p. 92.

19. Ibid.

20. Day, *Ethics in Media Communications*, p. 75.

21. Judy Hunter, "Lecture on Academic Honesty," as presented to entering students at Grinnell College, Fall 1995. Grinnell College Writing Lab Page, http://ac.grin.edu/~hunterj/achon/lecture97.html, found on December 10, 1996.

Chapter 5

1. National Opinion Research Center, *General Social Survey, Cumulative Codebook* (Chicago: University of Chicago Press).

2. *World Almanac and Book of Facts* (Mahwah, NJ: World Almanac Books, 1996).

3. J. C. McCroskey, V. P. Richmond, and , R. A. Stewart, *One-on-One: The Foundations of Interpersonal Communication* (Englewood Cliffs, NJ: Prentice-Hall, 1986).

4. Ibid.

5. For an excellent review of communication traits, see D. A. Infante, A. S. Rancer, and D. Womack, *Building Communication Theory*, 3rd ed. (Prospect Heights, IL: Waveland Press, 1997).

6. L. R. Wheeless, "An Investigation of Receiver Apprehension and Social Context Dimensions of Communication Apprehension," *Speech Teacher* 24 (1975): 261–265.

7. D. A. Infante and A. S. Rancer, "A Conceptualization and Measure of Argumentativeness," *Journal of Personality Assessment* 46 (1982): 72–80.

8. Ibid.; Wheeless, "An Investigation."

9. R. Berko, A. Wolvin, and R. Ray, *Business Communication in a Changing World* (New York: St. Martin's Press, 1997).

10. Women in Communications home page. http://mars.utm.edu/angibone/women.html. Accessed on AOL.

Chapter 7

1. www.columbia.edu/acis/bartleby/bartlett/.

2. Robert E. McAfee, "The Road Less Traveled: A Conversation with My Son," speech delivered to the American Medical Association. Cited in *American Speaker* (1995): INA/S (Washington, DC: Georgetown Publishing Co).

3. David K. Scott, "Truth and Hyperventilation," speech delivered to the National Society of Fundraising Executives, Springfield, Massachusetts, November 14, 1996. From *Executive Speaker* 18 (February 1997): 5.

4. Katharine Q. Seelye, "Congressman Offers Bill to Ban Cloning of Humans," *New York Times*, March 6, 1997, p. A3.

5. Reprinted in *Des Moines Register*, Op Ed section, July 2, 1995, and found on the World Wide Web at http://www.usdoj.gov/wawo/bonoped.htm, "Breaking the Silence on Domestic Violence," by Bonnie Campbell, Director, Violence Against Women Office, U.S. Department of Justice.

6. James O. Freedman, "Idealism for Your Sake and That of Society," *Vital Speeches of the Day*, 62 (November 15, 1995): 93–96.

7. Helen Zia, speech delivered to the annual convention of the Asian American Journalists Association , August 27, 1992. Reprinted in Deborah Gillan Straub, ed., *Voices of Multicultural America: Notable Speeches Delivered by African, Asian, Hispanic, and Native Americans, 1790–1995* (New York: Gale Research, 1996), p. 1334.

8. Ron Glover, "Establishing a Presence around the Globe," speech delivered at Corporate Image Conference, New York City, January 21, 1993. From "IRAs and the IRA," *Executive Speaker* (February 1993): 10.

9. Cited in "Speechwriters," *Executive Speaker* (December 1993): 6.

10. John C. Reinard, *Foundations of Argument* (Dubuque, IA: W. C. Brown, 1991).

11. John Ruff, "Globalization of a Food Processor," speech delivered to Food Update 96, Point Vedra Beach, Florida, April 22, 1996. From *Executive Speaker* 18 (March 1997): 10.

12. Alex Trotman, "The Climate for Change," speech delivered to the Economic Club of Detroit, Detroit, Michigan, September 16, 1996. From *Executive Speaker* 18 (March 1997): 11.

13. H. L. Fuller, "Global Competition and the New World of Work," speech delivered to the Chicago section of the American Institute of Chemical Engineers. Cited in *American Speaker* (September/October 1995): 5–19 (Speech Analysis Section).

14. Peter G. Peterson, "Gutsier Leadership and Enlightened Followership," speech delivered to Business Executives for National Security, New York City, April 22, 1992. Cited in *Executive Speaker* (January 1993): 6.

15. Peter Frances, "Lies, Damned Lies . . ." *American Demographics* 16(1994): 2.

16. Robert Balay (ed.), *Guide to Reference Books*, 11th ed. (Chicago: American Library Association, 1996).

17. Mark Henricsk, "Encyclopedias On CD-ROM." *Kiplinger's Personal Finance Magazine* (January 1997): 157–160.

Chapter 8

1. E. Thompson, "An Experimental Investigation of the Relative Effectiveness of Organization Structure in Oral Communication," *Southern Speech Journal* 26 (1960): 59–69.

2. R. G. Smith, "Effects of Speech Organization upon Attitudes of College Students," *Speech Monographs* 18 (1951): 292–301.

3. H. Sharp Jr. and T. McClung, "Effects of Organization on the Speaker's Ethos," *Speech Monographs* 33 (1966): 182ff.

4. G. H. Bower, "Organizational Factors in Memory," *Cognitive Psychology* 1 (1970): 18–46.

5. From "Implementing Sales Contests to Motivate Our Salespeople," speech by Kally Arlington, a student at Texas Tech University, February 1996.

6. Leonard J. Rosen and Laurence Behrens, *The Allyn & Bacon Handbook* (Needham, MA: Allyn & Bacon, 1992), p. 103.

7. T. J. Donahue, "Trucking's Agenda for Highway Safety," *Vital Speeches of the Day* 61, no. 15 (May 15, 1995): 477–480.

Chapter 9

1. Ron Hoff, *I Can See You Naked*, rev. ed. (Kansas City, MO: Andrews and McMeel, 1992), p. 41.

2. Joseph Hankin, "In Today, Already Walks Tomorrow: The Future of Higher Education," speech delivered to the Freshman Year Experience Tenth International Conference, Warwick, England, July 25, 1997. From *Executive Speaker* 18 (September 1997): 1.

3. Marian Wright Edelman, "Educating the Black Child," speech delivered to the Congressional Black Caucus, September 26, 1987. Reprinted in Deborah Gillan Straub, ed., *Voices of Multicultural America: Notable Speeches Delivered by African, Asian, Hispanic, and Native Americans, 1790–1995* (New York: Gale Research, 1996): 341–343.

4. "Evangelist Billy Sunday Preaches a Revival Sermon," in William Safire, ed., *Lend Me Your Ears: Great Speeches in History* (New York: Norton, 1992): 676.

5. Henry C. Cisneros, speech delivered to the National Press Club, Washington, DC, on April 13, 1993. Reprinted in Straub, ed., *Voices of Multicultural America*, p. 246.

6. http://sunsite.unc.edu/icky/speech2.html.

7. William Safire, *Lend Me Your Ears: Great Speeches in History* (New York: Norton, 1992) p. 676.

8. A. M. Rosenthal, Convocation address at Colby College, Waterville, Maine, November 18, 1981. Reprinted in William Safire, *Lend Me Your Ears: Great Speeches in History* (New York: Norton, 1992), p. 676.

9. Nido R. Qubein, *How to Be a Great Communicator* (New York: Wiley, 1997), p. 211.

10. http:// www.feminist.com/hill.htm.

11. James A. Unruh, "Mining the Gold in Your Organization," speech delivered to the Chief Executives Club of Boston, Boston, Massachusetts, January 16, 1997. Reprinted in *Vital Speeches of the Day* 63, no. 11 (March 15, 1997): 336.

12. Nelson Mandela, "Our March to Freedom Is Irreversible," speech delivered in Cape Town, South Africa, February 11, 1990. Reprinted in Brian MacArthur, ed., *The Penguin Book of Twentieth-Century Speeches* (New York: Penguin, 1992), p. 468.

13. Excerpted from *Executive Speaker* (June 1993): 5.

14. M. Runyon, "No One Moves the Mail Like the U.S. Postal Service," *Vital Speeches of the Day* (1994).

15. Unruh, "Mining the Gold in Your Organization," p. 336.

16. Robert L. Darbelnet, "U.S. Roads and Bridges," *Vital Speeches of the Day* 63, no. 12 (April 1, 1997): 379.

17. Holger Kluge, "Reflections on Diversity," speech delivered to the Diversity Network, Calgary, Alberta, Canada, October 29, 1996. Reprinted in *Vital Speeches of the Day* 63, no. 6 (January 1, 1997): 171–172.

18. Excerpted from *Executive Speaker* (October 1993): 7.

19. http://www.feminist.com/hill.htm.

20. http://www.dtic.dla.mil/defenselink/pubs/di96/di1104.html.

21. Excerpted from *Executive Speaker* (August 1996): 8.

22. Excerpted from *Closings and Summaries* (Dayton, OH: Executive Speaker, 1994) p. 6.

23. Excerpted from *Executive Speaker* (September 1993): 8.

Chapter 10

1. Rumer Godden, *Black Narcissus*, cited in David Grambs, *The Describer's Dictionary* (New York: Norton, 1993), p. 144.

2. William Safire, *Lend Me Your Ears: Great Speeches in History* (New York: Norton, 1992), p. 26.

3. Thomas R. Horton, American Management Association, "That Old Management Magic," speech delivered to the Commonwealth Club of California, San Francisco, October 5, 1987. From *Executive Speaker Newsletter* 9 (March 1988): 1.

4. Frederick W. Hill, McDonnel Douglas Corporation, "Learning to Lead: In an Increasingly Diverse World," speech delivered to the African-American Leadership Program, Greensboro, North

Carolina, July 30, 1996. From *Executive Speaker* 17 (November 1996): 1.

5. Catherine H. Zizik, "Powerspeak: Avoiding Ambiguous Language," *Speech Communication Teacher* (Summer 1995): 8–9.

6. Andrea Lunsford and Robert Connors, *The St. Martin's Handbook*, 3rd ed. (New York: St. Martin's Press, 1995), p. 101.

7. Safire, *Lend Me Your Ears*, pp. 496–497.

8. Alan Born, "800 Days: Trauma, Decision, Action," speech delivered to the Harvard Business School, Greenwich, September 21, 1987.

9. *Speaker's Idea File* (Chicago, IL: Ragan Communication).

10. Gloria Anzaldúa, "Entering into the Serpent," reprinted in Lunsford and Connors, *St. Martin's Handbook*, p. 25.

11. Howard K. Battles and Charles Packard, *Words and Sentences,* Book Six (Lexington, MA: Ginn and Company, 1984), p. 110.

12. Jesse Jackson, speech delivered in Atlanta, Georgia, June 19, 1978. Reprinted in Deborah Gillan Straub, ed., *Voices of Multicultural America: Notable Speeches Delivered by African, Asian, Hispanic, and Native Americans, 1790–1995* (New York: Gale Research, 1996), pp. 594–599.

13. Lunsford and Connors, *St. Martin's Handbook*, p. 347.

14. *Speaker's Idea File*, p. 16.

15. Lloyd E. Reuss, speech delivered to the Grand Rapids Chamber of Commerce, Grand Rapids, Michigan, January 28, 1987. From *Executive Speaker* 8 (July 1987): 3.

16. Robert Kilpatrick, speech delivered to the American Chamber of Commerce Executives Management Conference, in Hartford, Connecticut, October 13, 1981. From *Executive Speaker* 3 (April 1982): 4.

Chapter 11

1. J. A. Winans, *Public Speaking* (New York: Century, 1925). Professor Winans was among the first Americans to contribute significantly to the study of rhetoric. His explanation of delivery is considered by many to be the best coverage of the topic in the English language. His perspective infuses this chapter.

2. Ibid., p. 17.

3. T. M. Conley, *Rhetoric in the European Tradition* (New York: Longman, 1990).

4. J. C. McCroskey, *An Introduction to Rhetorical Communication*, 6th ed. (Englewood Cliffs, NJ: Prentice-Hall, 1993), p. 254.

5. A. Mulac and A. R. Sherman, "Behavioral Assessment of Speech Anxiety," *Quarterly Journal of Speech* 60 (1974): 134–143.

6. J. K. Burgoon, D. B. Buller, and W. G. Woodall, *Nonverbal Communication*, 2nd ed. (New York: McGraw-Hill, 1996).

7. Ibid.

8. Ibid.

9. Roger E. Axtell, *Do's and Taboos of Public Speaking: How to Get Those Butterflies Flying in Formation* (New York: Wiley, 1992), p. 67.

10. Laurie Shloff and Marcia Yudkin, *Smart Speaking* (New York: Plume, 1992), p. 108.

11. Winans, *Public Speaking*, p. 385.

12. McCroskey, *Introduction to Rhetorical Communication*.

13. L. Cooper, *The Rhetoric of Aristotle* (Englewood Cliffs, NJ: Prentice-Hall, 1932).

14. Much of the extant research on the effects of speaker delivery is dated. For a good review of studies in this area, see McCroskey, *Introduction to Rhetorical Communication*, pp. 249–252.

Chapter 12

1. R. Heinich, M. Molenda, and J. D. Russell, *Instructional Media and the New Technologies of Instruction*, 4th ed. (New York: Macmillan, 1993), p. 66.

2. Cheryl Currid, *Make Your Point: The Complete Guide to Successful Business Presentations Using Today's Technology* (Rocklin, CA: Prima Publishing, 1995), p. 117.

3. *Merriam-Webster's Collegiate Dictionary*, 10th ed. (Springfield, MA: Merriam-Webster, 1993).

4. Currid, *Make Your Point*, p. 117.

5. Ibid., p. 113.

6. Ibid., p. 73.

7. Ibid., p. 65.

Chapter 13

1. John R. Johnson and Nancy Szczupakiewicz, "The Public Speaking Course: Is It Preparing Students with Work-Related Public Speaking Skills?" *Communication Education* 36 (April 1987): 131–137.

2. Kenneth D. Frandsen and Donald A. Clement, "The Functions of Human Communication in Informing: Communicating and Processing Information," in Carroll C. Arnold and John Waite Bowers, eds., *Handbook of Rhetorical and Communication Theory* (Needham, MA: Allyn & Bacon, 1984), p. 338.

3. Katherine E. Rowan, "A New Pedagogy for Explanatory Public Speaking: Why Arrangement Should Not Substitute for Invention,"*Communication Education* 44 (July 1995): 236–250.

4. E. Thompson, "An Experimental Investigation of the Relative Effectiveness of Organization Structure in Oral Communication," *Southern Speech Journal* 26 (1960): 59–69.

5. A. C. Nichols, "Effects of Three Aspects of Sentence Structure on Immediate Recall," *Speech Monographs* 32 (1965): 164–168.

6. Frandsen and Clement, "Functions of Human Communication," p. 340.

7. Howard K. Battles and Charles Packard, *Words and Sentences,* Book 6 (Lexington, MA: Ginn and Co., 1984), p. 459.

8. John B. Donovan, "Children: Crisis and Culture," speech delivered to the International Cultures Festival, New York, June 15, 1997. Reprinted in *Vital Speeches of the Day* 63, no. 22 (September 1, 1977): 701.

9. Prince Charles, "A Monstrous Carbuncle," speech delivered in London, May 30, 1984. Reprinted in Brian MacArthur, ed., *The Penguin Book of Twentieth-Century Speeches* (New York: Penguin, 1992), p. 437.

Chapter 14

1. Reprinted from G. R. Suriano, *Great American Speeches* (New York: Gramercy Books, 1993).

2. E. P. J. Corbett, *Classical Rhetoric for the Modern Student*, 3rd ed. (New York: Oxford University Press, 1990).

3. Communications scholars Winston Brembeck and William Howell define the goal in this way: "Persuasion is communication intended to Influence choice." See Winston L. Brembeck and William S. Howell, *Persuasion: A Means of Social Influence*, 2nd ed. (Englewood Cliffs, NJ: Prentice-Hall, 1976).

4. Otis M. Walter and Robert L. Scott, *Thinking and Speaking: A Guide to Intelligent Oral Communication*, 3rd ed. (New York: Macmillan, 1973), p. 24.

5. J. C. McCroskey, V. P. Richmond, and R. A. Stewart, *One-on-One: The Foundations of Interpersonal Communication* (Englewood Cliffs, NJ: Prentice-Hall, 1986).

6. Ibid.

7. Kathleen Kelley Reardon, *Persuasion in Practice* (Newbury Park, CA: Sage Publications, 1991), p. 210.

8. Ibid.

9. R. H. Fazio, "How Do Attitudes Guide Behavior?" in R. M. Sorrentino and E. T. Higgins, eds., *The Handbook of Motivation and Cognition: Foundations of Social Behavior* (New York: Guilford, 1986), pp. 204–243.

10. Reardon, *Persuasion in Practice*, p. 33.

11. Ibid., p. 11.

12. Corbett, *Classical Rhetoric for the Modern Student*, pp. 1356a, 1377b.

13. Corbett, *Classical Rhetoric for the Modern Student*.

14. Reprinted from Suriano, *Great American Speeches*, pp. 298–303.

15. Reprinted from ibid., pp. 244–248.

16. Corbett, *Classical Rhetoric for the Modern Student*.

17. Ibid., p. 80.

18. R. A. Stewart, "Perceptions of a Speaker's Initial Credibility as a Function of Religious Involvement and Religious Disclosiveness," *Communication Research Reports* 11 (1994): 169–176.

19. For an extensive review of the history of the field of communication from the classical period to the present era, see D. Infante, A. Rancer, and D. Womack, *Building Communication Theory*, 3rd ed. (Prospect Heights, IL: Waveland Press, 1997).

20. A. Maslow, *Motivation and Personality* (New York: Harper & Row, 1954).

21. For an assessment of the McGruff campaign's persuasive strategies, see R. M. Perloff, *The Dynamics of Persuasion* (Hillsdale, NJ: Lawrence Erlbaum Associates, 1993).

22. I. Ajzen and M. Fishbein, *Understanding Attitudes and Predicting Social Behavior* (Englewood Cliffs, NJ: Prentice-Hall, 1980).

23. J. C. McCroskey, *Introduction to Rhetorical Communication*, 6th ed. (Englewood Cliffs, NJ: Prentice-Hall, 1993).

24. For good reviews of the literature on source credibility in general, see Perloff, *The Dynamics of Persuasion*; and Infante et al., *Building Communication Theory*.

25. K. K. Sereno and G. J. Hawkins, "The Effects of Variations in Speakers' Nonfluency upon Audience Ratings of Attitude toward the Speech Topic and Speakers' Credibility," *Speech Monographs* 34 (1967): 58–64.

26. Alan H. Monroe, *Principles and Types of Speeches* (Chicago, IL: Scott Foresman, 1935).

27. Lee P. Brown (director, Office of National Drug Control Policy), speech delivered to the First Latin American Drug Experts Conference, Caracas, Venezuela, March 21, 1994. Reprinted as "The International Drug Problem: Law Enforcement, Education, Treatment and Economic Development," *Vital Speeches of the Day* 60 (1994): 489–492.

28. Robert E. Allen (chairman and CEO, American Telephone & Telegraph Company), speech delivered to the Economic Club of Detroit, Detroit, Michigan, November 8, 1993. Reprinted as "The Information Superhighway: Moving into the Fast Lane," *Vital Speeches of the Day* 60 (1994): 214–217.

29. Roy Romer (governor of Colorado), speech delivered to the First Extraordinary Session of the Fifty-Ninth General Assembly, Denver, Colorado, September 7, 1993. Reprinted as "Guns in the Hands of Kids: Taking Responsibility for Each Other," *Vital Speeches of the Day* 60 (1993), 58–62.

30. Ibid.

31. Ibid.

32. Bill Bradley (U.S. senator from New Jersey), speech delivered to the Town Hall Los Angeles, Los Angeles, California, January 11, 1996. Reprinted as "Race Relations: The Best and Worst of Times," *Vital Speeches of the Day* 63 (1996), 241–245.

33. Allen, "The Information Superhighway."

34. Romer, "Guns in the Hands of Kids."

35. Bradley, "Race Relations."

Chapter 15

1. Annette T. Rottenberg, *Elements of Argument*, 4th ed. (Boston: Bedford Books of St. Martin's Press, 1994), p. 6, quoting from Wayne C. Booth, "Boring from Within: The Art of the Freshman Essay," adapted from a speech delivered at the Illinois Council of College Teachers of English, May 1963.

2. *Merriam-Webster's Collegiate Dictionary*, 10th ed. (Springfield, MA: Merriam-Webster, 1993).

3. Austin J. Freeley, *Argumentation and Debate*, 8th ed. (Belmont, CA: Wadsworth Publishing, 1993), p. 158.

4. Thomas A. Hollihan and Kevin T. Baaske, *Arguments and Arguing* (New York: St. Martin's Press, 1994), p. 27.

5. The model of argument presented here follows S. Toulmin, *The Uses of Argument* (New York: Cambridge University Press, 1958), as described in J. C. McCroskey, *An Introduction to Rhetorical Communication*, 6th ed. (Englewood Cliffs, NJ: Prentice-Hall, 1993).

6. Rottenberg, *Elements of Argument*, p. 10.

7. Citation: Bill Clinton, "Remarks by the President at University of California at San Diego Commencement." Whitehouse home page. June 16, 1997. December 17, 1997. http://www.whitehouse.gov/Initiatives.OneAmerica/speech.html.

8. William Safire, excerpted from a speech reprinted in W. Safire, *Lend Me Your Ears: Great Speeches in History* (New York: Norton, 1992), p. 922.

9. Jacob Neusner, excerpted from a speech reprinted in Safire, *Lend Me Your Ears*, p. 944.

10. Rottenberg, *Elements of Argument*, p. 23.

11. Dennis S. Gouran, "Attitude Change and Listeners' Understanding of a Persuasive Communication," *Speech Teacher* 15 (1966): 289–294. James P. Dillard, "Persuasion Past and Present: Attitudes Aren't What They Used to Be," *Communication Monographs* 60 (1993): 94.

12. Freeley, *Argumentation and Debate*, p. 175.

13. Adapted from McCroskey, *Introduction to Rhetorical Communication*.

14. Ibid.

15. E. P. J. Corbett, *Classical Rhetoric for the Modern Student* (New York: Oxford University Press, 1990).

16. For a fuller description of the whole range of fallacies, see Corbett, *Classical Rhetorical for the Modern Student*.

Chapter 16

1. D. O'Hair, G. Friedrich, and L. Shaver, *Strategic Communication in Business and the Professions*, 3rd ed. (Boston: Houghton Mifflin, 1998).

2. L. R. Hoffman and N. R. F. Maier, "Valence in the Adoption of Solutions by Problem-Solving Groups: Concept, Method, and Results," *Journal of Abnormal and Social Psychology* 69 (1964): 264–271.

3. John Dewey, *How We Think* (Boston: D. C. Heath Co., 1950).

4. For a review, see P. S. Rogers, "Distinguishing Public and Presentational Speaking," *Management Communication Quarterly* 2 (1988): 102–115.

5. Ibid.

6. F. E. X. Dance, "What Do You Mean Presentational Speaking?" *Management Communication Quarterly* 1 (1987): 260–271.

7. Rogers, "Distinguishing Public and Presentational Speaking."

8. Dance, "What Do You Mean Presentational Speaking?"

9. Part of this classification of business presentations is adapted from R. V. Lesikar, J. D. Pettit Jr., and M. E. Flatley, *Basic Business Communication*, 6th ed. (Boston: Irwin, 1993).

10. Robert E. Quinn, Herbert W. Hildebrandt, Priscilla S. Rogers, and Michael P. Thompson, "A Competing Values Framework for Analyzing Presentational Communication in Management Contexts." *Journal of Business Communication* 28(3) (1991): 213–232.

Chapter 17

1. E. B. White, "Daisy," reprinted in Phyllis Theroux, ed., *The Book of Eulogies* (New York: Scribner, 1997), p. 315.

2. Roger E. Axtell, *Do's and Taboos of Public Speaking: How to Get Those Butterflies Flying in Formation* (New York: Wiley, 1992), p. 150.

3. Frank D. Stella, introductory remarks delivered to the Economic Club of Detroit, Detroit, Michigan, April 15, 1996. From *Executive Speaker* 17 (November 1996): 3.

4. Gene Parret, *I Love My Boss and 969 Other Business Jokes* (New York: Sterling Publishing, 1993).

5. From David Roper, *The Toastmaster*, June 1993.

6. Ibid.

7. Quoted in Sarah Lyall, "For Media and the Royals, Earl Takes Off His Gloves," *New York Times*, September 7, 1997, p. A11.

8. Paul Fatout, ed., *Mark Twain Speaks for Himself* (Purdue University Press, 1978).

9. Holocaust Memorial Center Museum notes.

10. Franklin Delano Roosevelt, "The Arsenal of Democracy," speech broadcast from Washington, DC, December 29, 1940. Reprinted in Brian MacArthur, ed., *The Penguin Book of Twentieth-Century Speeches* (New York: Penguin Books, 1992), pp. 194–197.

11. D. Magill, "Give Your Life a Dream with Design," *Vital Speeches of the Day* 62, no. 21 (1996): 671–672.

12. Martin Luther King, excerpted from a speech reprinted in Deborah Gillan Straub, ed., *Voices of Multicultural America: Notable Speeches Delivered by African, Asian, Hispanic, and Native Americans* (New York: Gale Research, 1996), p. 210.

Credits

Text, Tables, Figures, and Boxes

36 S. Tobias. Adapted from a model, "Anxiety and Cognitive Processing of Instruction" in *Self-Related Cognitions in Anxiety and Motivation*, edited by R. Schwarzer, pp. 34–54. Copyright © 1986 Lawrence Erlbaum Associates. Reprinted by permission of the publisher. **80** *Compton's Living Encyclopedia.* "A Crosscultural View of Ethics," courtesy of Compton's Learning Company, Chicago, Illinois 60106. **118** *Reforma* web site. Home page of The National Association to Promote Library Services to the Spanish Speaking. By permission of Romelia Salinas, salinas@clnet.vcr.edu. **237** Andrea Lunsford and Robert Connors. "Figures of Speech" table from *The St. Martin's Handbook*, 3rd ed. (New York: St. Martin's Press), pp. 428–429. Copyright ©1995 Andrea Lunsford and Robert Connors. By permission of the publisher. **432** Sara Lyall. Excerpt from "For Media and the Royals, Earl Takes Off His Gloves" from the *New York Times*, September 7, 1997, p. A11. Copyright © 1997 by The New York Times Company. Reprinted by permission. **437** Martin Luther King Jr. Excerpt from "I Have a Dream" speech. Reprinted by arrangement with The Heirs to the Estate of Martin Luther King Jr., c/o Writers House, Inc., as agent for the proprietor. Copyright © 1963 by Martin Luther King Jr., copyright renewed 1991 by Coretta Scott King. **439** Charles Spencer. Eulogy by the 9th Earl Spencer at the funeral of his sister, Princess Diana, in London, Saturday, September 6, 1997. The *New York Times*, September 6, 1997. Copyright © 1997 by The New York Times Company. Reprinted by permission.

Chapter Openers

The following courtesy of Gerald & Cullen Rapp, Inc., Applied Graphics Technologies, Inc., and the i spot: **2** James Steinberg; **52** Celia Johnson; **96** Robert Neubecker; **148** Celia Johnson.

The following courtesy of The Stock Illustration Source, Inc.: **28** Normand Cousineau; **74** Robert Neubecker; **126** Michael Sheehy; **178** Robert Neubecker; **202** Jose Ortega; **226** Dennis Balogh; **250** James Yang; **278** Michael Sheehy; **308** Celia Johnson; **334** Jose Ortega; **366** Michael Sheehy; **392** Robert Neubecker; **418** Jose Ortega.

"Making a Difference" Box Photos

24 Kristina Wong; **36** Charlton McIlwain; **108** Stan Godlewski; **134** Steve Somerville Photography; **272** Beverly DeSmith; **323** Associated Press/Wide World Photos; **360** National Coalition Against Legalized Gambling.

Interview Photos

14 Olin Mills, Dallas; **60** Scott Welch; **160** Jon Thompson, JQT Photo-Graphics, Lubbock, Texas; **313** Richard Mason; **429** Stringfellow Photographers, Dallas, Texas.

Index